A Cruising Guide to the Windward Islands

Including
Martinique, St. Lucia, St. Vincent and the Grenadines, the Tobago Cays, Carriacou, Grenada, Barbados, Trinidad and Tobago

SECOND EDITION

by
Stephen J. Pavlidis

Cocoa Beach, Florida

A Cruising Guide to the Windward Islands
Second Edition
by
Stephen J. Pavlidis

Copyright © 2013 by Stephen J. Pavlidis
ISBN 978-1-892399-37-3
Ver. 4.1.13

Published in the USA by:
Seaworthy Publications, Inc.
2023 N. Atlantic Ave., #226
Cocoa Beach, Florida 32931
Phone 310-610-3634
Fax 321-400-1006
email orders@seaworthy.com
www.seaworthy.com - Your Bahamas and Caribbean Cruising Advisory

__CAUTION:__ Sketch charts are not to scale and are not to be used for navigational purposes. They are intended as supplements for NOAA, DMA, or British Admiralty charts and no warranties are either expressed or implied as to the usability of the information contained herein. The Author and Publisher take no responsibility for their misuse.

A publication like this is actually the result of a blending of many people's talents, knowledge, and experiences. I would like to take this opportunity to thank the following for their help in this effort: John & Katy Stickland of *Store Bay Marine Services*; Gil, Skyler, Kaia, Anspacher and Sandra Romano of the S/V *Kauhalekai*; Capt. Lee Bakewell of the S/V *Winterlude* for his help with programming; Billy Bones; Eduardo Calcano of the S/V *Cisne;* Annette and Arnold Callender, and Leslie of *Trump Tours* in Trinidad; Danielle Courteau; Jack Dausend; Ken and Vesta Douglas of the S/V *Great White Wonder,* Ashley and Carol Erwin of the S/V *Blind Date;* Ralph Gibson; Kathy and Jerry of the S/V *Po'oino Roa*; Jesse James' *Members Only Maxi-Taxi*; John and Vivian and the staff at *Bluewater Books and Charts* in Ft. Lauderdale; Cous and Martha of the S/V *Orca*; Rick Harrison of the S/V *Nosirrah;* Kenroy; Gaylord Kelshaw; Sandy and Ron Levonson of the S/V *Slow Dance;* Trevor and Ley Liverson of the S/V *Boon;* Malcolm Moritz; Mike of the S/V *Akka*; Patty and Mike of the S/V *Galadriel*; Melodye and John Pompa of the S/V *Second Millenium*; Joseph Ramnath; Norman Sabeney; Jean A. Stampfli; Jerry Stewart of *Tyrrel Bay Yacht Haulout;* Pat Turpin; Jack and Pat Tyler of S/V *Whoosh*. If there is anybody that I have neglected to mention here, rest assured that it is an oversight and I sincerely apologize. All photos are courtesy of the author except where noted.

Library of Congress Cataloging-in-Publication Data

Pavlidis, Stephen J.
 A cruising guide to the Windward Islands : including Martinique, St. Lucia, St. Vincent and the Grenadines, the Tobago Cays, Carriacou, Grenada, Barbados, Trinidad and Tobago / by Stephen J. Pavlidis. -- Second edition.
    p. cm.
 Includes bibliographical references and index.
 ISBN 978-1-892399-37-3 (pbk. : alk. paper) -- ISBN 1-892399-37-7 (pbk. : alk. paper) 1. Boats and boating--Windward Islands (West Indies)--Guidebooks. 2. Nautical charts--Windward Islands (West Indies) 3. Windward Islands (West Indies)--Guidebooks. I. Title.
 GV776.29.W56P38 2013
 797.10972984--dc23
                    2013009107

Introduction

The Windward Islands

The Windward Islands are some of the finest cruising grounds in the world. This is not hype nor is this some jaded line from a local travel magazine. This is a fact, and when you drop anchor here, you will do nothing less than agree. I cannot imagine how anybody could not find something to love in these islands. From cosmopolitan Martinique to the Bahamian-like Tobago Cays, from the popular anchorages along the southern shore of Grenada to the rainforests found on the larger islands in this chain, this string of volcanic islands has something to attract the most discerning visitors.

The Windward Islands lie just south of the Leeward Islands and north of the dual-island nation of Trinidad/Tobago and the northern coast of South America (but for purposes of this guide we are including Trinidad/Tobago and Barbados in this publication). Many people find that they are confused by the nomenclature used in describing the island groups of the Eastern Caribbean, the Windwards, the Leewards, you've heard those names for years, but you're not quite sure where they are, and why they're named as they are. This is not unusual, it can be confusing so let's see if we can straighten this out.

Although you'll hear different definitions, the generally accepted description is that the islands are divided into two main groups, the *Greater Antilles* and the *Lesser Antilles*. The term *Antilles* comes from *Antilia*, a mythical island that Old World Europeans believed existed somewhere in the mid-Atlantic.

The *Great Antilles* consists of Cuba, Jamaica, Hispaniola, Puerto Rico and the islands surrounding those larger islands. The *Lesser Antilles* begin with the Virgin Islands in the north and follows the chain of islands of the eastern Caribbean as they arc southward to Trinidad and Tobago, just off the Venezuelan coast. This definition often includes the ABC's, Aruba, Bonaire, and Curacao.

The terms *Windward* refers to the fact that some of the islands lie more upwind than the *Leeward* Islands, both of which lie in the Lesser Antilles. The *Windward Islands* jut out a bit farther into the Atlantic and are more exposed to the northeast trade winds. The *Windward Islands*, which are south of the *Leeward Islands*, consist of Dominica, Martinique, St. Lucia, St. Vincent, The Grenadines, and Grenada. Barbados is the most exposed to windward of these islands being a bit over 80 nautical miles southeast of its nearest neighbor, St. Lucia.

So what will you find here? What is the draw? Even with the help of a Thesaurus, I cannot paint a picture with enough detail that could ever cover all that is available for you in the Windward Islands. Here you'll find some of the most breathtaking scenery in the entire Caribbean, a plethora of anchorages, several good hurricane holes, marine services and yards to repair or assist you in repairing whatever is wrong with your vessel, Internet access that is never very far away, enough rain-forests to pique your interest for a long time to come, friendly open people, and history galore on every island you visit. If you've arrived from the Leeward Islands you're probably accustomed to sailing from one mountainous island to the other, but if you're chartering here for the first time, you'll discover the thrill of sailing where when one island drops astern, a new one lies just off your bow. And then there's the Tobago Cays, arguably one of the most beautiful anchorages in the Caribbean! I just can't list it all here, it's all in the following pages, read on and enjoy the Windward Islands.

Stephen J. Pavlidis

Table of Contents

The Basics

Those of you familiar with my work know that I always include sections here on *Currency*, *Customs* and *Immigration*, and even pieces on getting around on land. Due to the fact that each island in the Windwards is a separate nation, these topics will be discussed in the appropriate chapter on each island or island group.

Upon arrival in Chaguaramas, Trinidad, you should pick up a free copy of the *Trinidad/Tobago Boater's Directory*. This helpful publication is available at all marinas, *YSATT*, and most of the marine chandlers. There is a wealth of information here including daily tide tables as well as an up-to-date listing of marine services available.

Anchoring

Three words...you will roll! You've come all this way and almost every anchorage, save a precious few, will roll you, at times gently, at times almost violently, you will have to get used to it. You will learn to utilize a bridle or stern anchor, or you will lose sleep and curse every swell that works its way into your anchorage. At the very least it will make you appreciate the really calm anchorages such as Marigot Bay in St. Lucia, the Tobago Cays, or Hog Island in Grenada. At times it will seem like being underway is much calmer and the motion easier!

If this is your first visit to the Caribbean, and say perhaps that you are used to anchoring in areas such as the Bahamas where 15'-20' of water is considered a deep anchorage, well I have news for you. In the Caribbean, 15'-20' is considered a shallow anchorage, 30'-40' and more being the norm in a lot of places. Quite often you will find yourself anchored next to any one of the numerous charter boats you'll see in almost every anchorage.

You'll learn to keep an eye on charter boats as they anchor nearby with too little or too much scope at times. This is not an indictment of all charterers, only the few that give all a bad name.

Don't let me scare you off, the Caribbean is well worth a bit of roll, and you will get used to it, tis a small price to pay for paradise!

Caribbean Etiquette

Proper etiquette is important when visiting foreign lands; lack of it can be embarrassing at the least and can create serious misunderstandings. For instance, when greeting people as you board a bus, give a hearty "Good morning" (if indeed it is morning) all around and it will be returned. The rule is greetings first, business later. Not offering a greeting first may be received as rude.

If you approach a home that has a fence, stop at the front gate and say loudly "inside." If you receive no answer, try again. If there is still no answer, the folks are either not at home or don't wish to be disturbed. And by the way, when two people are speaking, as with good manners everywhere, it is extremely rude to interrupt. West Indians don't do it, neither should you.

Many Americans judge a man by the grip of his handshake, this does not work in the Caribbean where a soft, gentle hand "embrace" is more the norm.

I have head some folks (Canadians and Americans, never the British) say that they are surprised that West Indians do not smile. This can create the misconception that the person does not like the cruiser. This is, to say the least, ridiculous. West Indian manners call for a reserved face to be shown, saving the smile for something funny or someone they are familiar with. The lack of a smiley-face should not imply a negative attitude to the visitor unaccustomed to the lifestyle here in the Caribbean.

Let's discuss a very important subject, it will be a part of a lot that you do here in the Caribbean. Let's take a moment and touch briefly upon the Caribbean pastime of liming. If you're invited to join a group for a drink or a bite to eat, by all means, do! Hang out! You'll be liming! People in the Caribbean can be found liming everywhere, in the streets, in restaurants and bars, at home, or even on your boat. Liming is just chilling, hanging out...get the picture?

I cannot end this section on etiquette without mentioning dress. What we cruisers take for granted in the way we dress while aboard is quite different from what is expected of us in public in the Caribbean. In town, a bathing suit is not acceptable and men should wear shirts as well as shoes. We should all dress as we would in going to our local mall when we go into any town in the Caribbean. Shorts and shirts are fine, bathing gear is not and is considered inappropriate. On some of the islands, particularly the French islands, it is not unusual for women to go topless on the beaches and even aboard their own boats, and yes gentlemen, it is rude to stare!

Chartering

Chartering in the Windward Islands (especially in the Grenadines but not in Trinidad/Tobago) is big business, and not very difficult to arrange. Winter is the season for chartering and prices are higher then and reservations should be made well in advance for November through May. Prices from May to November may be as much as 40% lower, but don't fret, the winds will still be steady.

You can charter just a boat, called a bareboat, or a captained vessel where you do as little or as much work on board as you desire. If you choose to go bareboat, you will likely have to prove to the charter company your skill level. This is usually done by a check-out sail before they let you take their expensive toys out on the water all by yourself.

Captains can be hired for somewhere between US$100-$150 a day and it is customary to tip them. Some charters are there and back again, while others will allow you to take the vessel downwind where a charter company captain will return it to the base after you fly out.

You usually provision these boats yourself or have the charter company do it for you, the choice is yours. Some folks opt for the convenience of a completely stocked larder courtesy of the charter company, while others prefer the island shopping experience. A good idea is not to plan on having all your meals aboard as there is an abundance of good restaurants ashore that cater to mariners.

Currency

With the exception of the French island of Martinique, the currency in use is the *EC*, or Eastern Caribbean dollar, which is set at a fixed rate of EC$2.67 per US$1.00. Throughout the islands you'll find people that will gladly accept U.S dollars for payment, in fact, I don't recall meeting a merchant that wouldn't take my dollars. Dealing with independent businesses you often don't get quite such a good rate

while some will give you a discount if you make your purchase with *Traveler's Checks*.

As you head down-island you'll find money changing kiosks in many places such as St. Martin, and I would suggest that you stock up with a good supply of *Euro's* and *EC's* so you'll be all set when you arrive at your next destination.

If you head south to Trinidad and Tobago you'll need Trinidad/Tobago dollars or *TT*s as they're commonly called. Paper currency comes in denominations of $1, $5, $10, $20, and $100 (a "blue one"), while coins come in 1¢, 5¢, 10¢, 25¢, and 50¢ pieces.

In Trinidad and Tobago, *ATM*'s are happy to spew out *TT's* for you. Although the *TT* is the official currency in Trinidad and Tobago, many businesses will accept U.S. dollars for payment...check first however. Also, if you're ever unsure as to whether or not you've been quoted a price in *TT*$ or US$, ask!

At the end of your cruise, as you head home, be sure to trade in all your Euros, ECs, and TTs, perhaps to other cruisers who will need them. It will be virtually impossible to change them once you get home.

Trinidad/Tobago adds on a *VAT* (*Value Added Tax*) of 15% on all goods and services except those marine services (and materials) relating to yachts in transit. Materials purchased not in relation to a service will not be *VAT* free. For instance, if you contract *Power Boats* to paint your bottom, there will be no *VAT* on the paint or the labor. However, if you enter *Budget Marine* and purchase a gallon of bottom paint, you will have to pay the *VAT*, but if *Power Boats* then applies the paint, there will still be no *VAT* on the service. Although you may not notice it on a receipt, rest assured that the *VAT* has been collected. If a merchant offers a "*VAT* free" item, it simply means that the merchant is giving you a 15% discount on the goods and that the item is NOT "*VAT* free."

Hotels always include a 10% service charge as well as a 10% *Hotel Room Tax*. If leaving by plane a *Departure Tax* of *TT*$100 (must be paid in *TT*'s) will be assessed.

A final note on tipping. Unlike the United States, tipping is not always expected in the islands. In some places you will find a service charge added to the bill for your meal; no tip is expected here but it would certainly be welcome. Generally, a 10% tip is the norm. Contrary to what you expect, taxi drivers do not expect a tip (but I find this to be changing with those drivers who consistently work with tourists). But you will find a lot of drivers that go out of their way to help you and are certainly deserving of a tip. And don't forget the children that offer to watch your dinghy or carry your bags for you, a little coinage goes a long way.

Customs and Immigration

Since the Windward Islands (as shown in this guide) are made up of six different nations, Martinique, St. Lucia, Barbados, St. Vincent and the Grenadines, Grenada, and Trinidad/Tobago, each country's particular customs regulations will be discussed in detail in the appropriate chapter.

It is now possible to download *Customs* forms for some of the Windward Islands before you arrive in their waters. For the links that are available visit Seaworthy.com and click on the *Customs and Immigration* link on the left side of the screen, then click on the island that you plan to visit, if forms are available you will be directed to the download site. All of these islands now require simple one-page forms.

eSeaClear is a service that provides vessel operators the ability to submit electronic notifications of arrival to participating *Customs* offices in the Caribbean. Registered users can access the system via the Internet to enter and maintain information about their vessel and crew. Prior to arrival at a new country the vessel operator simply insures that the information is accurate and submits a new notification. Upon arrival, *Customs* can access the notification information to process your clearance more efficiently and without the need for the Ship's Master to fill out the declaration forms.

The problem with *eSeaClear* is that although the web site is up and running, *Customs* officers are no longer using it. There are rumors that there will be a new system to take its place but how long before it comes online is anybody's guess.

One thing that I must mention here is that it is absolutely imperative to get a clearance out from your last port of call. You will need it when you clear in at your next destination and you may be forced to return to your last port to obtain one if you arrive sans departure clearance. Also dress accordingly,

shirts and shoes are required gentlemen! Dogs are not permitted ashore in St. Lucia, Barbados, St. Vincent, Trinidad, and Tobago, and all dogs must have current rabies vaccination certificates. Once you've presented your rabies certificate and cleared in, you may take your dogs ashore on Martinique and Grenada.

Ports of Entry
Martinique - St. Pierre, Fort de France, Le Marin, LaTrinité, Anse Mitan, Trois Ilets
St. Lucia - Rodney Bay (*Rodney Bay Marina*), Castrios, Marigot Bay, Soufrière, and Vieux Fort
Barbados - Bridgetown, Port St. Charles
St. Vincent - Blue Lagoon, Wallilabou, Kingstown, *Ottley Hall Mar.*, Young Island Cut
The Grenadines - Port Elizabeth (Bequia), Clifton (Union Island), Grand Bay (Mustique), Charlestown (Canouan)
Carriacou - Hillsborough
Grenada - St. George's (*Grenada Yacht Services*), Prickly Bay (*Spice Island Marina*), St. David's Bay (*Grenada Marine*), Petite Calivigny Bay (*Le Phare Bleu Marina*), Grenville
Trinidad - Chaguaramas, Port of Spain, Point-a-Pierre (currently not available)
Tobago - Scarborough, Charlotteville

Electricity

The islands of the Eastern Caribbean use 220 volt, 50-cycle AC power ashore. Most boats will require a step-down transformer to obtain 110 volt, 50-cycle shore power unless you have 220 aboard your vessel. Ashore, in hotels and private homes, you'll need an adaptor to plug in a 110 volt, 60-cycle gadget. Most hotels will have adaptors, but few have transformers while some marinas will rent you a transformer.

Emergency and Medical Numbers

The following is an incomplete list of emergency and medical service phone numbers available in the Windward Islands.

Martinique (0596)
Ambulance: 75 15 75
Customs (Marin): 74 91 64
Clinic: 71 82 85
COSMA (LIfeboat): 70 92 92

Fire (Pompiers): 18
Hospital: 55 20 00
Medical Emergency: 63 33 33/60 60 44
Police: 17

St. Lucia (758)
Customs (Castries): 458-4846
Customs (Marigot): 458-3318
Customs (Rodney Bay): 452-0235
Customs (Soufriere): 459-5656
Customs (Vieux Fort): 468-4933
Marine Emergency: HELP 4357 (VHF ch. 16)
Police (Marine): 452-2595
Rodney Bay Medical Center: 452-8621
Hospital (also a hyperbaric chamber): 459-2000

Barbados (246)
Ambulance: 511
Brigade House Medical Centre: 436-6215.
Coast Guard: 436-6185
Customs: 430-2300
Fire: 311
Health offices: 426-5080
Immigration: 426-1011
Port Authority: 430-4700
Police: 211

St. Vincent (784)
Botanic Clinic (private hospital): 457-9781
Customs (Chateaubelair): 458-7907
Customs (Kingstown): 456-1083
Customs (Chateaubelair): 485-7902
Emergency: 999 (for a marine emergency,
    contact *St. Vincent Signal Station* on VHF 16)
Kingstown General Hospital: 456-1185
Kingstown Medical College: 458-4832
Maryfield Hospital: 457-8991
Medical Associates Clinic: 457-2598
Police: 911/999
Police (Chateaubelair): 458-2229

The Grenadines (784)
Bequia (784)
Bequia Hospital: 458-3294
Dental (Saturday AM only): 459-0745
Police: 458-3211
Customs: 457-3044
Mustique (784)
Clinic: 458-4621
Doctor: 488-8353
Union Island (784)
Customs: 458-8360
Hospital/Health Center: 458-8339
Carriacou (473)
Customs: 443-7659
Emergency: 774

Grenada (473)
Ambulance:
Coast Guard: 399
Customs (Prickly Bay): 444-4509
Customs (St. Georges): 440-2239
Emergency (Police, Coast Guard): 911
Hospital: 440-2051
Island Dental Care: 437-4000
Medical School: 444-4271
Police: 911
Port Authority: 444-7447
St. Augustin Medical Clinic: 440-6173
Sunsmile Dental Clinic: 444-2273

Trinidad (868)
Ambulance: 990
Coast Guard: 800-8824
Customs: 634-4341
Emergency: 990
Immigration: 634-4050
Mt. Hope Medical Center: 645-4673
Port of Spain General Hospital: 623-2951/2952
Police (Carenage): 637-3123
Police (Chaguaramas): 634-4304
Rapid Response: 999
San Fernando General Hospital: 652-3581
St. Clair Medical Center: 628-1451
West Shore Medical (Cocorite): 622-9878

Tobago (868)
Ambulance: 639-2108
Customs (Scarborough): 639-2415
Customs (Charlotteville): 660-6137
Fire/Ambulance: 990
General Hospital: 639-2551
Immigration: 639-2681
Police (Scarborough): 639-1200
Police (Charlotteville): 660-4388

Getting Around

Cruisers must find a way to get around on the islands they visit. Some love to walk everywhere locally, but eventually a taxi or bus is required for one reason or another. We won't discuss rental cars here, they're available almost everywhere, check the *Appendices* in the back of this guide for more information.

First, if you take a taxi, ALWAYS negotiate the fare before entering the cab and getting underway (and make sure the price quoted is in Euros, ECs, TTs, or US$). It's a sinking feeling when you and the driver cannot come to terms on the fare and the taxi has entered some area where you are not familiar with the streets and have no idea where you are or where you can catch another taxi. You find yourself forced to pay his price to get to where you need to go. Don't laugh, this happens and you don't want to learn this first hand. Agree first, then get in the cab.

Don't think that all taxi drivers are the descendents of pirates, they're not, only an unscrupulous few. Most are dedicated to their jobs and do not hesitate to go out of their way for their passengers. Nearly all are fonts of local knowledge such as the best places to eat (even if they may direct you to their cousin's restaurant) and where is the best grocery store. Once you find a good driver that you trust, you can use him like an agent to tend to your matters ashore.

Buses are the primary means of public transportation in the islands and for the most part, cover the major roads and communities. These buses are a sight to see! Loud (usually with a radio, music or talk, or CD on high volume) and colorful, with fanciful names that describe something personal for the driver (such as *Da Boss*) or something to inspire others (*God is My Co -Pilot*).

Travel by bus is the best way to get a feel for the local culture. Some are old school buses, but today the drivers are turning more and more to mini-buses and vans. Always come aboard with a cheerful "Good Morning" all around, remember, pleasure before business. In general, follow what the locals do, but in most cases, when you are ready to disembark, shout out "Bus Stop" as you approach your destination. And don't be in a hurry, especially if the driver stops to chat up a pretty woman, it's his route and he will run it the way he pleases. Just sit back and enjoy the ride.

Some buses cannot run without the driver's helper, usually a young man who may spend the bulk of his time hanging out the side of the bus helping folks aboard and encouraging others to board his bus.

Although the driver normally runs a set route, they are not adverse to going off the beaten path, especially if you need help in dropping your bags of groceries at your dock instead of having to walk a quarter of a mile to the marina from the bus stop. Just ask the driver to drop you off as close as possible to your boat and be sure to tip him for the convenience. And don't forget to thank the other riders even though they're probably used to such side trips. And don't forget most buses stop running after dark. If you're going to the other side of the island, make sure that you can catch a bus back when you are set to return.

Holidays

All of the Windward Islands celebrate the usual holidays such as Christmas, New Year's, and Easter. Holidays particular to each island nation are listed below.

Martinique: *Recovery Day*, Jan. 2; *Carnival,* approximately 40 days before *Easter; Labor Day,* May 1; *Victory (Armistace) Day*, May 8; *Abolition of Slavery*, May 22; *Ascension Day*, varies in May; *Bastille Day*, July 14; *Virgin Mary Day*, Aug. 15; *All Saints Day*, Nov. 1; *Victory Day*, Nov. 11.

St. Lucia: *Carnival,* approximately 40 days before *Easter; Independence Day*, Feb. 22; *Labor Day*, May 1; *Whit Monday*, changes every year in May or June; *Corpus Christi*, changes every year in May or June; *Emancipation Day*, the first Friday in August; *Thanksgiving*, varies in October; *All Saints Day*, Nov. 1-2; *St. Cecilia Day,* Nov. 22; *National Day*, Dec. 13; *Boxing Day*, Dec. 26.

Barbados: Errol Barrow Day, Jan. 21; *Heroes Day*, April 28; *Labor Day*, May 1; *Whit Monday*, varies in May or June; *Emancipation Day*, Aug. 1; *Kadooment Day*, first Monday in August; *Independence Day*, Nov. 30.

St. Vincent and the Grenadines: *Recovery Day*, Jan. 2; *Discovery Day*, Jan. 22; *Labor Day*, first Monday in May; *Whit Monday*, varies in May and June; *Carnival*, second Monday and Tuesday in July; *August Bank Holiday*, first Monday in August; *Independence Day*, Oct. 27; *Boxing Day*, Dec. 26.

Grenada: *Recovery Day*, Jan. 2; *Independence Day*, Feb. 7; *Labor Day*, first Monday in May; *Whit Monday*, varies in May and June; *Corpus Christi*, varies in May and June; *Carriacou Regatta and Carnival*, first Monday and Tuesday in August; *Thanksgiving*, Oct. 25; *Boxing Day*, Dec. 26.

Trinidad and Tobago: Carnival, Feb., date varies; Eid-Ul-Fitr, the beginning of the Islamic New Year. The date is determined by the position of the moon and marks the end of Ramadan and a month of fasting for Moslems; March/April, date varies, Spiritual Baptist Liberation Shouter Day, this holiday is in recognition of the African based religion that suffered persecution in colonial Trinidad; May/June, date varies, Corpus Christi; June 19, Labour Day; August 1, Emancipation Day; August 31, Independence Day; September 24, Republic Day; October, date varies, the Hindu fete Diwali; December 26, Boxing Day.

Hurricane Holes

Cruising the Windward Islands during hurricane season, the prudent skipper will keep one ear on the SSB and ham weather nets, take notes, and read every cruising guide he can get his hands on to find where the best hurricane holes lie. From June until December, it is not advisable to sail anywhere in the Caribbean without knowing the closest holes to your location and exactly how far away they lie. There's only one problem with this. **THERE IS NO SUCH THING AS A HURRICANE HOLE!** There is no anchorage so secure that it cannot be decimated by a strong hurricane and a high storm surge. There are no guarantees; there is no Fort Knox to hide in when a named windstorm threatens. Now, with that out of the way we can discuss how to protect yourself in those special places that offer the best hurricane protection. Let's begin by passing along a few hints as to how to secure your vessel while getting along with your neighbors, and then learn where to find the best protection.

First, make sure your fuel is topped off and that you have enough food and water for an extended period. Also, make sure that you have enough cash to see you through as phone lines may be down for a while after the storm passes which would prohibit credit card usage. Once your tanks, lockers, and wallet are topped off, you can head for protection. Some skippers prefer to head to sea when a hurricane threatens. Some will take off at a ninety-degree angle from the hurricane's forecast path, those in the lower Caribbean usually head toward Venezuela. I cannot advise you as to what course of action to take, that is up to each individual cruising boat and their own particular circumstances, but I for one, unless absolutely necessary, will not gamble with racing a storm that is unpredictable (no matter what the forecasters claim). Whatever course you choose to take, the prudent skipper will make his or her move EARLY.

For protection, most of us would prefer a narrow creek that winds deep into the mangroves where we will be as snug as the proverbial bug-in-a-rug. But these creeks are rare, and to be assured of space you must get there early. When a storm threatens, you can bet that everybody will soon be aware of it and the early birds will settle in the best places. Yes, those early birds might have to spend a night or two in the hot, buggy mangroves, but isn't that better than coming in too late and finding the best spots taken and

your choices for protection down to anchoring in the middle of a pond with a bit of fetch and no mangroves to surround you like a security blanket? Hint number one...get to safety early and secure your vessel.

So how do you secure your vessel? Easy! First, find a likely looking spot where you'll be safest from the oncoming winds, a spot with a short fetch and good holding. Try to deduce by the forecast path of the storm where the wind will be coming from as the storm passes and plan accordingly (remember that the winds blow counterclockwise around the center in the northern hemisphere).

If your chosen spot is in a creek that is fine. Set out bow and stern anchors and tie off your vessel to the mangroves on each side with as many lines as you can, including lines off the bow and stern to assist the anchors. Use plenty of chafe protection as the lines lead off your boat and rig your lines so that they don't work back and forth on the mangroves as well. For chafe protection I like old fire-hose, leather, and if nothing better is available, towels secured with duct tape. If chain can be used to surround the mangroves, that will help (not the mangroves of course). If other boats wish to proceed further up the creek past your position, remove the lines from one side of your boat to allow them to pass. Courtesy amongst endangered vessels will add to the safety factor of all involved, especially if somebody needs to come to somebody else's aid.

If your only choice is to head into the mangroves bow or stern first, always go in bow first; it stands to reason that if you place your stern into the mangroves serious rudder damage could result. I prefer to go bow-in as far as I can, until my boat settles her keel in the mud (trying to keep the bow just out of contact with the mangroves), tie off well, and set out at least two stern anchors (the largest ones you have) with as much scope as possible. If other boats will be tying off into the mangroves in the same manner on each side of you, courtesy dictates that each skipper assist the other in the setting of anchors (so that they don't trip each other) and the securing of lines in the mangroves (and don't forget to put out fenders). Work with other skippers to assure that everybody will have swinging room in the event of a wind shift.

If you must anchor in the open, away from the mangroves, place your anchors to give you 360° protection. The greatest danger to your vessel will likely be the other boats around you, and in the Caribbean there's going to be a better than average chance that you'll be sharing your hole with several unattended boats, often times charter boats that are not secured as well as you would like them to be. A good lookout is necessary for these added dangers. I've seen some folks that put out three anchors 120° apart, whose rodes lead to a swivel. From the swivel, a chain leads over the bow roller to fasten strongly to the deck. This eliminates chafe at the bow roller.

There are differing opinions on whether to haul-out for a hurricane, or to tie off in a marina. A lot of cruisers will tell you they've had success at both, but there's an equal number that will advise against it. On the hard, a domino effect can topple one boat after another, and slips in marinas, if the owners will let you stay for a blow, are often narrow and care must be taken to avoid contact with your neighbor, the dock, and the pilings. Here again, I cannot recommend which way you should go. I believe such protection is a crapshoot, so I'll take my chances at anchor thank you very much.

Once secure, your next step is to strip everything off your boat and stow it below. Sails, bimini, awnings, rail-mounted grill, solar panels, jerry cans, and anything small and loose that can become a dangerous object should it fly away at a hundred miles an hour. Make sure that your neighbors do the same, their loose objects could be hazardous to your health. If you cannot move your wind generator below deck, try to remove the blades or at least secure their movement with several lines. In addition, don't forget to secure your dinghy!

The decision to stay aboard is a highly personal one. Some of us that have insurance will head for a hotel or some other shelter ashore (especially those skippers with children aboard), while others, whose only insurance is their seaman's skills, will ride the storm out aboard. If you decide to stay aboard, pack all your important papers in a handy waterproof container, and in the most severe of circumstances, use duct tape to secure your passport, wallet, and/or purse to your body. Plan ahead as you secure your vessel so that you will not have to go on deck if you don't absolutely have to, it is most difficult to move about in hundred-knot winds. Keep a mask and snorkel handy in the cockpit, you might need it to stand watch. Also, keep a flashlight and a sharp knife close at hand; you never know when you might need them.

Okay, now let's talk about where you can find some protection in the Windward Islands in the event of a named windstorm. Let's start with Martinique and work our way south.

Heading south from the Leeward Islands, the first protection that you will find along the western shore of Martinique is in Baie de Fort du France. The best protection in Fort du France is without a doubt in the small cove lying just north of the runway at the airport in Fort du France at Cohé de Lamentin. For those with shallow draft vessels, there are several small rivers and streams leading into Baie de Fort du France where one could find shelter. South of Fort du France one can find a bit of shelter in the lee of the small cays at Trois Ilets.

At the southern end of Martinique there are several small coves that are open to the south, but Le Marin (Cul-de-Sac du Marin) offers the only true hurricane protection. Although the primary anchorage here is usually crowded, there are two small mangrove-surrounded coves that are deep and well protected. The first cove is called *Baie des Cyclones* and lies SSE of the marina docks just under Pte. Malé. The second cove, that is a bit more exposed, lies a bit southwest, just inside Pte. Marin and south of Îlet Baude.

The eastern coast of Martinique is seldom cruised, but it offers many nice anchorages and a couple of places to duck into in the event of an oncoming storm. Cul-de-Sac Petite Grenade offers good protection in the lee of the mainland and a small cay (Îlet Petite Grenade) and is further protected by offshore reefs. I've heard Le Francois is a good hurricane hole, but only if you are able to secure your vessel in Rivière du Francois at the southern end of the bay. Baie au Trésor is often regarded as a hurricane hole due to the protection offered by the mainland and the reefs in the bay; however I find it a bit too open for my needs.

In St. Lucia, my choice would be in *Marigot Bay*, tucked up nice and snug into the mangroves, far away from the entrance channel. *Marigot Bay* offers high hills all around, except to the west, to seaward, and good protection from seas. The only problems here would, as usual, come from unattended boats that would lie here. *Rodney Bay Lagoon* at the northwestern end of St. Lucia is another alternative. Enter the bay and head past the marina to anchor in the small lagoon to the southwest. Protected from seas here, your primary concerns would be the holding in the dredged lagoon, and flying debris from nearby condos. Given the choice I would rather be in *Marigot Bay*, but then again, I just like mangroves for protection.

Barbados...there is NO hurricane protection that I would even consider in Barbados. However, the Carenage in Bridgetown, and inside the lagoon at the Port St. Charles complex offer the only real protection and should be used only if you do not have time to get to better protection at St. Lucia or Martinique.

There is no place in St. Vincent and the Grenadines that I would feel comfortable in hiding from an approaching storm, but Carriacou and Grenada offer very good hurricane protection. As cruisers (and some insurance companies know), few hurricanes pass this far south, a near miss is more likely in these waters, but don't bet on it. In Carriacou, *Tyrrell Bay* has a wonderful mangrove-lined creek and pond on the north side of the bay that offers good protection. The creek will carry almost 5' at low water if you stay close to the northern shore as you follow the creek to the inner lagoon.

In Grenada, some cruisers tout St. George's on the western shore as a viable hurricane hole. I've never thought about riding out a storm in St. George's, it's a bit too crowded for my tastes, as well as not having any mangroves around, I much prefer the southern shore of Grenada if I'm in search of protection. Here you'll find two great spots to ride out a storm at Port Egmont and *Calivgny Harbour*. Both are mangrove-lined harbors that offer deep water right up to the mangroves in many places. Entrance is not difficult, but should not be attempted at night. Port Egmont is the larger of the two and has a small bridge at its northwestern corner that is far enough out of the way as not to be a problem. Cruisers can also find a bit of protection tucked into the mangroves in *Mt. Hartman Bay* and behind Hog Island although these two anchorages are open to southerly winds.

Further south Trinidad and Tobago are generally considered to be outside of the normal hurricane zone, but if the truth be known, hurricanes, though extremely rare, are not unknown here. Between 1850 and 2000, two hurricanes and five tropical storms hit Trinidad/Tobago. Since 1990, four tropical storms have hit the Trinidad and Tobago area while the last hurricane to visit was *Flora* in 1963. In 1995, *Hurricane Iris* passed 180 miles north of Trinidad, but brought heavy southerly winds that did a lot of damage along the *Gulf of Paria*. *Hurricane Lenny*, although far to the north of Trinidad, brought huge seas to the northern and western coasts of Trinidad and Tobago in November of 1999.

Although your chances of getting hit by a hurricane in Trinidad or Tobago are small, don't get complacent. There is little hurricane protection on these islands, save one tiny spot on the island of Tobago, *Bon Accord Lagoon,* and a small cove at Port of Spain, Trinidad. *Bon Accord Lagoon* is off-limits to boaters during the year, but it is available in case of a hurricane. The entrance is tricky, a winding path over a shallow reef before reaching the safety of the small, protected cove.

Just south of *Grier Channel*, the entrance to the commercial docks in Port of Spain, Trinidad, is the *Sea Lots Channel*, which leads to a small cove that offers fair protection in the event of a major windstorm. The cove is used primarily by commercial fishing vessels, and there are some large wrecks ashore, but a cruising boat could find some shelter in the southern end of the cove between the wrecks and the mangroves. You'll have to get here early though as the commercial boats will certainly be heading here the minute they realize a storm is on its way. Please note that the primary danger here would be from other boats.

If you're not happy with the protection in the Windwards, and if there is time, you can head southwestward to Venezuela for better protection. Hurricanes are usually not a problem for boaters in the waters of Venezuela which is why so many cruisers flee the Leeward and Windward Islands, as well as Trinidad and Tobago if a storm threatens. Those heading south from the Leewards or Windwards usually head to Isla Margarita as most storms stay north of there. But for those wanting a bit more protection, the waters of the *Rio Macareo* or the *Rio Orinoco* will give shelter to Trinidadian cruisers who don't wish to travel a long distance for shelter.

Those heading south from the more northerly islands can find shelter at Puerto La Cruz and in one of my favorite places, *Laguna Grande*.

Internet in The Windwards

Internet facilities are not hard to find in the Windward Islands, most marinas have access available to guests. Below I have some sites listed that may give you some added information on the various Windward Islands.

Caribbean

www.caribbeansupersite.com
www.caribbeanweather.com
www.caribcruiser.com
www.caribshop.com
www.rotishops.com

Martinique

www.caribbizz.com
www.cieux.com
www.frenchcaribbean.com
www.fwinet.com
www.martinique.org
www.sasi.fr/guidemartinique

St. Lucia

www.paradisestlucia.com
www.stlucia.org
www.sluonestop.com
www.smma.org.lc.

Barbados

www.barbados.org.bta
www.barbadosyachtclub.com
www.funbarbados.com
www.insandouts-barbados.com
www.nationnews.com/ bajannewspaper

St. Vincent and the Grenadines

www.bequiasweet.com
www.grenadagrenadines.com
www.grenadines.net
www.islandtimeholidays.com
www.svgtourism.com
www.vincy.com

Grenada

www.grenada.org
www.grenadagrenadines.com
www.grenadamarine.com
www.grenadayachtclub.com
www.spiceisle.com
www.truebluebay.com

Trinidad and Tobago

www.anansi.mit.edu/tnt
www.backtobasic.com
www.boatersenterprise.com
www.callaloo.co.tt
www.carib-link.net/discover
www.carnival.ncc.com
www.davidrudder.co.tt/homepage.htm
www.gov.tt
www.hartsCarnvial.com
www.ladycharli.com

www.tidco.tt
www.trinibase.com
www.trinidadexpress.com
www.tv6tnt.com
www.visittnt.com

Language

In the Windward Islands, with the exception of Martinique, the official language is English. Martinique, of course, is a French speaking island so I have included a few useful French phrases in *Appendix F* on page 360.

Most of the locals that you meet will likely (among themselves) speak a *patois* that you might not understand, especially at first when the speed of their speech overwhelms your untrained ears. The term patois come from the French language and can mean anything from "rude, incomprehensible speech" to any form of non-Parisian French. In our usage it means simply, and in a non-derogatory way, the language of the local population.

This *patois* is sometimes called *Creole* and is a mixture of English, French, and African. Once you listen to it you'll begin to make out certain words and phrases and before long you will start understanding at least the basics of conversation.

Phoning Home

All over the Windward Islands you'll find card phones. You'll have to purchase cards to use them, but they're easy enough to find. You can pick them up at *Post Offices* and shops throughout the islands. In Martinique you can pick them up at change bureaus.

The phone system in Trinidad and Tobago is very good and quite easy to use. Most public phones use a card though some still take coins. *TSTT* (*Telecommunication Service of Trinidad and Tobago*) phone cards are sold in most stores and marinas. The area code for Trinidad and Tobago is 868 and the emergency number in both islands is 999.

It's really very easy to have phone communications in the islands aboard your boat or in your pocket wherever you travel inland. *GSM* phones are the way to go. You can pick one up in the islands or bring your own and simply replace the SIM card for your local area (approximately EC$30-EC$50).

Digicell and *Lime* (*Cable and Wireless*) work well in the islands, including Barbados. Roaming rates, whether inter-island or overseas from any island other than the island where you purchased your SIM card can cost from 3-10 times as much as if you were not roaming. Many cruisers get around this by having one phone for incoming calls and one for outgoing calls (buying a new SIM card for each island as they cruise).

Digicell works well in Martinique but you will be better off getting a local SIM card (without the local SIM card you will have to add a "+" before every number you dial).

Provisioning and Shopping

Provisioning in the Windward Islands offers no real problems, each major island has a number of large supermarkets and several have outlets that specialize in wholesale goods and frozen items. I'll deal with where to shop in each particular chapter and share with you what I know of shopping here and where my favorite stores are located.

Each island has food items particular to that island. Hot sauces, rums, certain spices, packaged goods, all may be specific to a particular locale and worth investigating and if you like them, lay in a supply of the best. A hint: stock up on your favorite French goodies in Martinique because you won't find them farther south. And speaking of Martinique, don't forget that the largest and best stocked stores will be found there.

Fresh water is usually not a problem, most fuel docks and marinas can supply you with potable water and bottled water is easily available at most stores throughout the islands.

Trinidad is a great place to provision, especially if heading back up-island or to Venezuela. Although some things in Venezuela will be cheaper, your selection of items in Trinidad, at least for Americans and Canadians, will be brands that you will recognize and with which you are familiar. In Venezuela you'll find a lot of brands that you've never seen before, a lot of items manufactured in Venezuela with Spanish labels, so brush up on *su Espanol* before shopping in Margarita.

Rastafarians

Everywhere you look in the Caribbean, you will see and meet Rastafarians. The man that sells you fruit and veggies, the boat boy that takes your line, or perhaps the guy that is working on your boat in the yard (such as Kenroy who helped me paint *IV Play* in Carriacou), Rastafarians, Rastas for short, are as much a part of the Caribbean as the trade winds. A goodly number of cruisers on their first voyage to the Caribbean bring preconceived notions with them about these highly religious folks and I strongly urge visitors to these islands to come here with an open mind.

Mention the word Rasta and a vision of dreadlocks, ganja, and reggae music comes to mind, but there is a lot more to these people than that, remember, don't judge a book by its cover. True Rastas maintain certain dietary practices and other religious beliefs that is the hallmark of this particular Christian religion. Sure, there are many folks who you'll meet that sport the dreadlocked look of the Rastafarian, and who will claim to be a follower of Rastafari, but who are not what they seem. This book's cover is a false one. Sometimes it is difficult to tell the difference, but if you observe them, the speech, their diet, you will soon learn the difference. This is not to say that there is a clear line between true Rastas and false Rastas, there are all kinds of Rastafarians the same as there are all manner of Catholics, Protestants, or Jews. Some live a life with a strict adherence to their beliefs, while others live a life a bit more relaxed. Some fear Rastafarians feeling that they are involved with drug smuggling and other assorted crimes. Not all are involved with illegal activities, one cannot indict an entire religion for the indiscretions of a few.

Where lie the roots of the *Rastafari*? It is generally accepted that the movement began in Jamaica in the 1930s when Marcus Garvey sought to bring the black race to a higher prominence. Garvey wanted an exodus of blacks from the Americas back to Africa and the establishment of a black nationality. Garvey preached that Africans would someday rise again to their true stature and that a black King would be crowned and he would lead all blacks to freedom. The crowning of Haile Selassie I as Emperor of Ethiopia became Garvey's prophecy fulfilled. Selassie, whose real name was Ras (Prince) Tafari Makonnen, is believed to be the 225th direct descendent of King Solomon and Queen Sheba and is said to be the second Messiah, Jesus in all his Kingly glory.

Rastafari is a religion full of ideals of purity, strength, and freedom from corruption and oppression that plagued black people for centuries. Rastas celebrate their Sabbath on Saturdays and view our modern society as "Babylon," an evil institution that is responsible for that same corruption and oppression. Most Rastas tend to distance themselves from Babylon as much as possible, seeking independence from the evils associated with it. That is why so many Rastas that you meet are self-sufficient, many of them farming, or earning a living from their own talents, such as wood-carving and crafts, preferring to live peaceful, simple, healthy lives. These people are very proud of who they are and are eager to educate others about their beliefs and way of life. During his reign, Haile Selassie stressed education as the way forward for his people, and as a result, Rastas seek knowledge from the Bible as well as academically. Many are well educated and hold excellent positions. However, because of a lack of understanding, many Rastas are prevented from achieving levels of success they deserve.

Without a doubt, a better understanding of the Rastafarian culture will assist in removing the barriers that prejudice has placed in their paths. One of those prejudices stems from the Rasta's use of ganga, marijuana, for religious, meditational, medicinal, and culinary purposes and justified by several quotations from the Bible. The most obvious icon of the Rasta is the dreadlocks, the long locks that are seen as a symbol of strength that also has a basis in the Bible, in the story of Samson. And what discussion of Rastafari would be complete without the mention of Reggae music and especially the music of Bob Marley, who helped bring the message of Rastafari, of Jah, of Haile Selassie, to the world.

Rum

For some reason, cruising the Caribbean and drinking rum go hand in hand, in fact, when I'm cruising in the Caribbean, I often have a rum drink in my hand. Most of the islands in the eastern Caribbean will have a rum distillery somewhere on their shores. Some islands such as Martinique, Guadeloupe, or Barbados will have many distilleries, and no visit to these islands is complete without a tour and sampling, one could make a whole day of it, others of us could make a whole week of it, while a few of us choose to make it a lifestyle.

The term *rum* originated in the West Indies, some say in the taverns along the waterfront in Bridgetown, Barbados, but nobody truly knows for sure. *Rumbullion* is an old English word used in the 1600s to describe an intoxicated individual. When sailors in the West Indies distilled a liquor from sugarcane they called it *rum*. Although popular amongst the sailing crowd, rum as a popular drink really didn't catch on until World War II when French soldiers stationed on Martinique discovered its powers and brought it home with them. I'm sure that Ernest Hemingway and the *Cuba Libre* also had a part to play in the emergence of rum as a popular libation.

Most brands of rum that you find in these islands are available in liquor stores at home, but some rums are truly exotic and cannot be purchased anywhere but the island on which they are distilled. Rum is a natural product of Martinique, Guadeloupe, and Barbados as it's made from genuine sugarcane, the cash crop for so many years on the island's plantations. Some rums, such as those produced in Puerto Rico, Haiti, and some other Caribbean islands are made from molasses or other sugar by-product and some rum connoisseurs consider them inferior. On Martinique in particular, rum has been elevated to a special status. In 1996, Martinician rum was granted an *AOC*, *Appelation d'Origine Contrôlée*, not an easy award to win and one which guarantees that rum production is as strictly controlled as the production of the great wines of France.

Many of these rums begin their life as sugar cane, which after harvesting is brought to a crushing station where a large water-powered wheel squishes the juice from the cane and sends it to the next stage of the process, the boiling room. Here the cane juice is boiled at different temperatures in different tanks after which it is sloughed off to the fermentation and storage areas. After aging the product is distilled and the final product is ready...rum. This is the process in a nutshell, different distillers use different methods, this is only meant to give you an idea of the processes involved.

Now let's discuss the different kinds of rum you'll find and what the labels mean, you may want to look for these classifications on the bottles when you shop, and believe me, you'll find lots and lots of different bottles and brands of rum. Rum that is made from sugarcane is given the name *Rhum Agricole* while rum distilled from molasses is referred to as *Rhum*

Industrial. White rum from sugar cane juice (*vésou*) is called *Rhum Blanc Agricole*, it is not aged, and has a strong, some say rough taste and is best mixed into a punch such as *Ti-punch* popular on the French islands of Guadeloupe and Martinique. Another favorite is *Planter's Punch*, or *Punch Planteur*.

What many consider the top of the line rum is *Rum Vieux*, aged rum that ripens in oak barrels from 3-15 years or more which gives it its rich, distinctive amber color. Rum that is aged 18 months is called *Rhum Paile*, while *Rhum Ambré* is aged three years. Rum aged from 5-7 years is called *Rhum Vieux Traditionnel*, rum aged 8-12 years is called *Rhum Vieux Hor d'Âge*, and rum aged 15 years or more is called *Rhum Vieux Milléslimeé*.

Safety and Security

One of the greatest concerns of cruisers in the Caribbean is crime. I would love to paint a picture of a tropical Eden, but that would be a lie. Crime does exist here, crimes upon cruisers exists here, but it is a fact of life that we deal with here and simple precautions will usually keep you out of harm's way.

First and foremost, avoid high-risk anchorages, and buddy-boat for safety's sake, currently this is a special concern for vessels transiting the waters off the northern shore of Venezuela between Trinidad and Margarita but rarely a concern in the Windward Islands. However, today there is some activity along the northern shore of Trinidad as you will learn when you read that chapter.

You'll learn of these trouble spots by talking to other cruisers or by listening to the *Safety and Security Net*, which we'll learn about in a moment.

When leaving your vessel, lock it, hatches and large ports, don't leave an opening for a skinny child to enter (don't laugh!) and don't leave items on deck that you do not want stolen. At night, you might also wish to lock yourself inside your boat so you don't wake up with an intruder hovering above you.

The choice of carrying weapons aboard is strictly a personal one, I prefer to have one and not need it than need one and not have it, but that's just me. Some folks like to keep a flare gun handy as well as a spotlight for blinding intruders in the night. Don't laugh at a flare gun, it can be a very effective weapon.

One of the greatest temptations for a thief is your dinghy, *lock it or lose it* as is the motto of the *Safety and Security Net*. You can usually tell someone who has cruised in the Caribbean, they often have their dinghy hoisted in the air at night. Some of us don't do that, preferring instead to use a wire cable and lock, but either way, a good thief can still get away with your dinghy despite your best efforts it seems.

A lot of cruisers try to make their dinghy look as unappealing as possible by joining in a competition to see who can have the ugliest outboard motor. Thieves tend to concentrate on those nice, new looking outboards, ones that look like they have a long life ahead of them. Here again, *lock it or lose it*. Don't keep anything in your dinghy that you don't want stolen, not that these items will be stolen, just don't take that chance. Another idea is not painting the name of your boat on it such as "Tender To My Boat." This only informs people when you are NOT on your boat.

If you plan to travel about on land in questionable areas, and you will learn where they are by talking to other cruisers or listening to the *Safety and Security Net*, do not advertise by wearing a lot of jewelry. Keep your money safe in your pocket or other location. Women, this means that you should keep your cash on your person instead of in a purse or fanny pack as people have been known to sneak up from behind and slice the strap on a purse or fanny pack and make off with it. If you're attending a major event such as *Jump Up* or *Carnival*, keep your money in your shoe as there may well be pickpockets working the crowd with surgical precision. If you're walking about at night, do so in a group, there is strength in numbers, and ladies, please, never walk around unescorted!

Vessels equipped with SSB receivers can tune in to the *Caribbean Safety and Security Net* on 8104 at 0815 daily. Although the *Safety and Security Net* is sometimes jokingly referred to as the *Moan and Complain Net* by its detractors, it offers cruisers the latest scoop on what's going on where. If a dinghy has been stolen in St. Vincent, if the Montserrat Volcano is acting up, or if somebody was robbed while walking down the streets of some Caribbean town at night, you'll learn about those happenings on the net. What's to gain from this information? Well, you'll learn where to take special security measures and what areas you might wish to avoid. Besides accessing the net on SSB, you can visit their website at http://www.safetyandsecuritynet.com/.

Boat Boys and Land Sharks

A favorite question of new cruisers to the Caribbean is how to handle the boat boys. This problem has lessened in recent years as the boat boys have become more organized; however there are still a few places where they may still seem a bit intimidating. I've found that when heading south it's a good idea to pick the brain of a northbound cruiser and ask them who they choose in a particular location. Boat boys understand repeat business and if they greet you as you approach and you let them know that you want Rupert and only Rupert, there should not be a problem. If you don't have the name of a local boat boy to use, it's best to choose the first one to greet you and treat him well as long as he does the same in his dealings with you. And if your boat boy greets you two miles out and wants a tow in, politely refuse him and blame it on your insurance regulations. When you are near your chosen anchorage area or mooring, negotiate a fee before handing a line over, always set a price first! Never allow somebody to take over your helm offering to bring you in safe and sound, trust only yourself at the helm of your own boat.

In most Caribbean anchorages you will be approached by local vendors in small boats (it's a good idea to keep fenders out on both sides of your vessel for just such an event) asking to do your laundry or sell you fruits and veggies, handmade crafts, or offering to get you anything you need from town. If you've already got a boat boy, tell them so and there should be no problem. If you're in some anchorage where there is no boat boy per se, the lady that wants to do your laundry might actually be a good deal if you're tired of washing your clothes in a bucket. It's all a learning experience and you will soon learn to trust your gut instinct about people. Most of these vendors know the difference in charter boats and cruising boats and generally know that the charter boats are the best customers, so if you're chartering, either put out a sign saying that you're not buying anything, or relax and enjoy, it's all a part of the show and certainly gives you something to talk about.

I've found a lot of what I call "land sharks" that abound in the Caribbean, hanging around marinas and scenic overviews wanting to work on your boat or guide you to a certain waterfall or other tourist haunt. Use caution with the guys that want to work on your boat; I've found several, such as Kenroy in Tyrell Bay, Carriacou, that are extremely diligent, hardworking, conscientious laborers who give you a fair day's work for a fair day's pay and who are worth the largest tip you can afford to give them. On the other hand, there are those that have no idea of what they're doing and who then want to borrow every tool you have so they can do the work they've contracted to do. If in doubt, ask around, check with other boaters, check with the local yard or marina office, or question the man to see if he does indeed know what he is talking about.

Sailing in the Windward Islands

The first time cruiser to the Windward Islands will him or herself on a nearly vertical learning curve when it comes to sailing in these waters. Not that sailing here is so different than anywhere else, rather there are certain things that one must learn when sailing these islands that can be expensive to learn the hard way. For instance, the trade winds may not be exceptionally strong, but they are steady. I suggest that you do a complete sail and rigging check on your boat before leaving for the Caribbean where the winds and seas will do their best to find the tiniest flaw in your rig and create havoc.

If you are not used to sailing among mountainous islands, say you're used to the flatter landmasses in The Bahamas, you will learn a new way of dealing with the wind when sailing in the lee of these islands. Let's pretend that we're heading southbound, leaving the leeward shore (western shore) of one island and heading for the leeward shore (western shore) of the next island that lies to the south. While we're pretending, let's just say that the winds are easterly, about 15 knots, and seas are running about 6', pretty normal stuff as you'll later learn. As you leave the southern tip of one island to cross a channel to another, you may find the wind and seas "bending" around the tip and coming at you a bit more on the nose than expected. Don't panic. As you head out into the channel, you'll notice the seas coming more on your beam (depending of course on wind and sea direction, we're talking in general terms here). Conversely, as you approach the northern tip of the next island, you may find that the wind and seas are now a bit more aft of the beam, on your quarter perhaps as you pass the tip of your destination island. The winds may even pick up in velocity as you approach the tip or leave the tip of an island, but generally, in normal trade wind conditions, you can expect anywhere from 10-20 knots of wind and seas in the range of 4'-8' between the islands.

Once in the lee of your destination island you will first wonder where the wind went. Well, that's why it's called the *leeward* side of the island. If you are very close in to shore, you might pick up a bit of a breeze, then again, if you are five or more miles out, you too may pick up a breeze out there. You may also find the wind has been affected by the island and is now coming at you from your starboard bow (remember, we're talking about heading south), from the south through the west.

Confusing? Yes, of course, but that's what makes sailing here so much fun. But, since we're speaking in general terms here, most of us crank up the diesel and motorsail south to our destination anyway; however there's still wind to deal with so let's see what we may find.

Well, you may find that you are now motorsailing south with little or no wind, your sails flogging in the few zephyrs that make their way to your boat. Sometimes you'll be on starboard tack, and sometimes you may find yourself on port tack with your iron genny really doing all the work. But what's that up ahead? Looks like choppy water and white caps? What is this? If you see this in a normally calm area, look to shore and you'll probably notice that you are sailing into a funnel of easterly wind caused by a valley or some other land formation. If you're not diligent, these areas of gusty winds can lay you on your beam and then you'll come to realize why so many Caribbean boatyards have damaged and broken masts and booms scattered about. Use your eyes to scan the water in front of you and prepare for gusty winds when you see the choppy water ahead. You'll get used to playing the gusts in the lee, and if your boat is fast, you'll enjoy sailing close in and getting what breeze you can off the land. There's usually always some sort of wind to catch in the lee of the islands if you're a patient sailor, and you wouldn't be a sailor if you didn't have some tiny bit of patience in you.

The Windward Islands employ *IALA B* buoyage system, that's *Red-Right-Returning*.

Tides and Currents

Currents in the Windward Islands generally set west-northwest at an average drift of 0.5-1 knot. There are places among the islands, particularly in small passes where the tide can run quite strong at times, often as much as 2-3 knots. The current is affected by tide close to the land masses of the islands, usually within a couple of miles from shore. About an hour or so before low water, a counter-current may begin flowing east at about 1 knot or less. It can be used to your benefit if you're a sailboat, but be aware that it can also create rougher seas depending on the strength of the current, tide, and wind.

Tides are generally about 2', although at times they can be between 10" - 3' in some places, particularly on the windward side of some islands.

Bear in mind that there is a westward setting current along the southern coast of St. Vincent that can be as strong as two knots. This current may reverse during the early stages of a flood tide and can create rough seas depending on wind speed and direction.

Time

Time in the Windward Islands is *Atlantic Standard Time (AST)* and there is no such thing as *Daylight Savings Time*.

Weather

The outstanding feature for mariners in the Windward Islands is the steadiness of the easterly trade winds that blow about 80% of the time year-round. Winds from the east and southeast are particularly dominant in summer when the Bermuda High has shifted north while northeasterlies are more prominent from around November through April and give way to easterly and southeasterly winds in the spring. During the summer months the easterly wave occurs and is characterized by winds out of the east/northeast ahead of the wave and followed by an east/southeast wind. In summer the trades tend to lessen at night and strengthen during the day. Gale-force winds are rare, but they can occur within a severe thunderstorm, or as an effect of a passing tropical storm or hurricane.

Herb Hilgenberg

Weather coverage is usually quite good in the islands especially if you have an SSB or HF receiving capabilities. A cruisers favorite is the guru of weather forecasters, Herb Hilgenberg, *Southbound II*, from Canada. Herb operates from his home in Canada and you can tune in to Herb on 12.359 MHz, upper sideband, at 2000 Zulu.

Chris Parker

All cruisers suffered a loss when David Jones passed away in November of 2003. But the *Caribbean Weather Center* continues to provide all the same services that David provided with Chris Parker at the microphone from his sailboat *Bel Ami*. Chris' weather nets are conducted 6 days a week, Monday through Saturday, but also Sundays when Tropical or other severe weather threatens. Chris' summer schedule, April to October, begins on 4.045 MHz at 0630 AST/EDT; then Chris moves to 8.137 MHz at 0700 AST/EDT; Chris is back on 4.045 MHz at 0800 AST/EDT; then Chris moves to 8.104 MHz at 0830 AST/EDT; Chris moves up to 12.350 MHz at 0915 AST/EDT; and finishes up at 6.221 MHz at 0930 AST/EDT. When severe weather or tropical weather systems threaten Chris will also transmit in the evenings, usually on 8.104 MHz at 2000 AST/EDT and Chris will usually announce this on the morning net.

Chris' winter schedule, November to March, begins at 0700 AST/0600 EST on 8.137 MHz; Chris then moves to 4.045 MHz at 0730 AST/0630 EST; Chris can then be found on 8.104 MHz at 0830 AST/0730 EST; Chris them moves up to 12.350 MHz at 0930 AST/0830 EST; Chris then finishes on 6.221 MHz at 1000 AST/0900 EST. Quite often during the winter months Chris may be late in getting to the 12 meg frequency. When severe weather or tropical weather systems threaten Chris will also transmit in the evenings, usually on 8.104 MHz at 1900 AST/1800 EST and Chris will usually announce this on the morning net. Chris begins the net with a 24-48 hour wind and sea summary followed by a synoptic analysis and tropical conditions during hurricane season. After this, Chris repeats the weather for those needing fills and finally he takes check-ins reporting local conditions from sponsoring vessels (vessels that have paid an annual fee for this service). Those who seek more information about weather, weather patterns, and the forecasting of weather, should pick up a copy of Chris Parker's excellent publication: *Coastal And Offshore Weather, The Essential Handbook*. You can pick up a copy of Chris Parker's book at his web site: http://www.mwxc.com.

George Cline

Another well-respected forecaster is a ham operator named George Cline, KP2G. George can be found on the *Caribbean Maritime Mobile Net* located at 7.250 MHz, lower sideband at 0715 AST, 15 minutes into the net. Daily, except Sunday, George gives an overview of the current Caribbean weather from the Turks and Caicos to Trinidad as well as the western Caribbean basin. During hurricane season George provides weather updates at 7086.0 LSB at 1630 if weather is threatening the islands. During the high season George may return to the airwaves at 1630 AST, on the afternoon cocktail net at 7.086 lower sideband if there are enough listeners.

NMN Broadcasts

On 4.426, 6.501, 8.764, 13.089, and 17.314 MHz, you can pick up the voice weather broadcasts from NMN four times a day at 0530, 1130, 1730, and 2330 EST.

Ham and SSB Nets

You can pick up the Caribbean Weather Net on 8137 USB at 0700, ad on 7086 LSB at 0710.

In the afternoons you can join in on the *Cocktail and Weather Net* at 7086 LSB daily except Sunday at 1630.

VHF

In southern St. Vincent, *Sam's Taxi* gives weather forecasts at 0900 and 1730 daily on VHF ch. 06, and in Martinique, *COSMA* gives weather forecasts in French at 0730 and 1830 on VHF ch. 11. In Rodney Bay, St. Lucia, there is a daily VHF net on ch. 68 at 0750, Monday through Friday, where you can pick up on the latest weather forecasts. There is a cruiser's net in *Prickly Bay*, Grenada, with a daily weather forecast at 0730 on VHF ch. 68. In Trinidad, *North Post Radio* gives weather reports at 0940 and 1640 daily on VHF ch. 27. In Chaguaramas tune in to the daily Cruiser's Net on VHF ch. 68, every morning at 0800.

AM and FM

In Martinique you can pick up *Radio Caraibes* at 89.5 on the FM band, but be forewarned that it is in French. In St. Lucia, you can pick up weather forecasts on the FM bands thanks to *WAVES* at 93.5 and 93.7 at 0730 and 1630. St. Vincent boasts *St. Vincent Radio* at 705 on the AM band and 100.5 on the FM band, (weather at 0745) and *Sound of the Nation* (weather after the 0700 news) at 89.7/90.7/107.5 on the FM band.

In Barbados you can listen to the *Barbados Broadcasting Company* on 900 AM for weather after the 0715 news show. In Carriacou you can pick up the weather on *Radio Kayak* at 106 FM at 0725 and 0915, while in Grenada, *Radio Grenada* gives weather forecasts after the 0700 news on 535/540 AM and *Sun Radio* will give you weather at 0700, 1200, and 1800 at 87.9/98.5/105.5 on the FM band.

Trinidad and Tobago has a wealth of AM and FM stations where you can receive weather periodically during the day. On the AM band you can tune in to *NBS Radio* at 610, and *Radio Trinidad* at 730 on your dial. On the FM band, the popular *Hott 93* (93.5) has a local forecast every morning at 0730. Other FM stations with periodic weather broadcasts are *Central Radio* (90.5), *Radio ICN* (91.1), *Love* (94.1), The Rock (95.1), WEFM (96), *Music Radio 97* (97.1), *YesFM* (98.9), *NBS Radio* (100), *Power 102* (102.5), *WABC* (103), *Radio 104* (104), *Radio Tempo* (105), *Classic Radio* (106).

Using the Charts

For the soundings on the charts I use my dinghy (*Afterglow*) with a computer-based hydrographic system consisting of an off-the-shelf GPS and sonar combination that gives a GPS waypoint and depth every two seconds including the time of each observation. The software used records and stores this information in an onboard computer. When I begin to chart an area, I first put *Afterglow's* bow on a well-marked, prominent point of land and take GPS lat/longs for a period of at least ten minutes. I use the average of all these positions to check against the lat/long shown on the topos that I use to create the charts. I also use cross bearings to help set up control points for my own reference. At this point I begin to take soundings.

My first objective is to chart the inshore reefs. Then I'll plot all visible hazards to navigation. These positions are recorded by hand on my field notes as well as being recorded electronically. I rely primarily on my on-site notes for the actual construction of the charts. The soundings taken by the system are later entered by hand but it is the field notes that help me create the basis for the chart graphics. Next I will run the one-fathom line as well as the ten-fathom line and chart these. Here is where the system does most of the work. Finally, I will crisscross the entire area in a grid pattern and hopefully catch hazards that are at first glance unseen. It is not unusual to spend days sounding an area of only a couple of square miles.

Due to the speed of *Afterglow*, each identical lat/long may have as many as ten or twenty separate soundings. Then, with the help of *NOAA* tide tables, the computer gives me accurate depths to one decimal place for each separate lat/long pair acquired on the data run. A macro purges all but the lowest depths for each lat/long position (to two decimal places). At this point the actual plotting is begun including one fathom and ten fathom lines. The charts themselves are still constructed from outline tracings of topographic maps and the lat/long lines are placed in accordance with these maps. The soundings taken are shown in feet at MLW, *Mean Low Water*, the average low tide. Since MLW is an average, cruisers must be aware that there are times when there will be less water than shown, particularly on spring low tides, during the full moon and new moon.

These charts are as accurate as I can make them and I believe them to be superior to any others. However, it is not possible to plot every individual rock or coral head so piloting by eye is still essential. On many of the routes in my guides you must be able to pick out the blue, deeper water as it snakes among sandbanks, rocky bars, and coral heads. Learn to trust your eyes. Never approach a cut or sandbar with the sun in your eyes, it should be above and behind you. Sunglasses with polarized lenses can be a big help in combating the glare of the sun on the water. With good visibility the sandbars and heads stand out and are clearly defined. As you gain experience you may even learn to read the subtle differences in the water surface as it flows over underwater obstructions.

All courses shown are magnetic. All waypoints for entrances to cuts and for detouring around shoal areas are only to be used in a general sense. They are meant to get you into the general area, you must pilot your way through the cut or around the shoal yourself. You will have to keep a good lookout, GPS will not do that for you. The best aids to navigation when near these shoals and cuts are sharp eyesight and good light.

Not being a perfect world, I expect errors to occur. I would deeply appreciate any input and corrections that you may notice as you travel these waters. Please send your suggestions to Stephen J. Pavlidis, C/O Seaworthy Publications, 2023 N. Atlantic Ave. #226, Cocoa Beach, Florida, 32931, or email me at steve@seaworthy.com

Legend		
▨ water depth less than 1 fathom		☐ water depth over 10 fathoms
☐ water depth between 1 fathom and 10 fathoms		
– – – large vessel route–6' draft		⟀ light
– · – · shallow vessel route		⚓ anchorage
+ rock or coral head		⊕ GPS waypoint
++++ reef		⬤ tower
═══ road		⊥ wreck–above hw
m mooring		⬭ wreck–submerged
dm dinghy mooring		☐ building

List of Charts

Those of you who are familiar with my work know that I always have an index of charts for the region covered by any particular guide. With this Windward Islands Guide and the following Leeward Islands Guide I will stray from that format a bit. Each island or island group in the Windwards and Leewards is basically a different nation, so the first chart in each group will serve as the index chart for that island or island group. For instance, MAR-1, the overall chart of Martinique, will also show you the locations of all the other charts pertaining to Martinique.

The prudent navigator will not rely solely on any single aid to navigation, particularly on floating aids.

CAUTION:

The Index charts are designed strictly for orientation, they are NOT to be used for navigational purposes. All charts are to be used in conjunction with the text. All soundings are in feet at Mean Low Water. All courses are magnetic. Projection is Transverse Mercator. Datum is WGS84. North is always "up" on these charts.

Differences in latitude and longitude may exist between these charts and other charts of the area; therefore the transfer of positions from one chart to another should be done by bearings and distances from common features.

The author and publisher take no responsibility for errors, omissions, or the misuse of these charts. No warranties are either expressed or implied as to the usability of the information contained herein. Always keep a good lookout when piloting in these waters.

Chart #	Description	Page #
Martinique		
MAR-1	Martinique	29
MAR-2	St. Pierre	34
MAR-3	Case Pilote	38
MAR-4	Schoelcher	38
MAR-5	Baie de Fort-de-France	42
MAR-6	Baie des Flamands, Fort-de-France	42
MAR-7	Marina de Port Cohé	45
MAR-8	Trou Etienne to Pointe des Pères, Trois Îlets	46
MAR-9	Pointe d'Alet to Trou Etienne, Anse Mitan	48
MAR-10	Îlet à Ramiers to Pointe d' Alet, Anse à l'Âne	50
MAR-11	Anse Noire	52
MAR-12	Grande Anse d'Arlet	52
MAR-13	Petite Anse d'Arlet, Anse Chaudière	54
MAR-14	Caye d'Obian to Grande Pointe, Baie du Marigot	55
MAR-15	Anse du Céron, Trois Rivières	57
MAR-16	Ste. Luce to Passe du Marin, Ste. Luce, Rivière Pilote	58
MAR-17	Pointe Borgnesse to Ste. Anne, Cul-de-Sac du Marin	62
MAR-18	Le Marin	62

Chart #	Description	Page #
GND-2	Bequia	160
GND-3	Bequia, Admiralty Bay	161
GND-4	Bequia, Friendship Bay	166
GND-5	Mustique	170
GND-6	Mustique, Britannia Bay	171
GND-7	Canouan	173
GND-8	The Southern Grenadines - Canouan to Carriacou	176
GND-9	Mayreau to the Tobago Cays	177
GND-10	Mayreau, Saltwhistle Bay	177
GND-11	The Tobago Cays	180
GND-12	Union Island, Palm Island	183
GND-13	Union Island, Clifton Harbour	183
GND-14	Petit St. Vincent and Petite Martinique	190
Carriacou		
CAR-1	Carriacou	194
CAR-2	Hillsborough Bay to Tyrrel Bay	197
CAR-3	Tyrrel Bay	197
CAR-4	Île de Ronde, Kick Em Jenny	202
Grenada		
GRE-1	Grenada	206
GRE-2	Grenada Bay	207
GRE-3	Halifax Harbour	207
GRE-4	Happy Hill to Grand Mal Bay	209
GRE-5	St. George's Harbour	209
GRE-6	Long Point to Prickly Point	216
GRE-7	True Blue Bay	218
GRE-8	Prickly Bay	218
GRE-9	Mt. Hartman Bay, Hog Island	222
GRE-10	Hog Island to Petite Bacaye	225
GRE-11	Petite Bacaye to St. David's Point	228
GRE-12	Grenville	230
Trinidad - Index Chart		252
Chaguaramas Bay Facilities Directory		264
TRI-1	Trinidad and Approaches	253
TRI-2	Bocas del Dragon	257
TRI-3	Monos Island, Morris Bay, Grand Fond Bay	258
TRI-4	Scotland Bay	258
TRI-5	Chacachacare	260
TRI-6	Chaguaramas Bay	264
TRI-7	Gaspar Grande Island, Bombshell Bay to Bayview Marina	273

Martinique

Port of Entry: Anse Mitan, Fort-de-France, LaTrinité, Le Marin, St. Pierre, Trois Ilets
Fuel: Baie Tourelles, Le François Le Marin, Le Robert, Pointe du Bout
Haul-Out: Fort-de-France, Le Marin
Diesel Repairs: Anse Mitan, Baie des Tourelles, Case Pilote, Dillon, Fort-de-France, Le Marin, Trois Îlets
Outboard Repairs: Baie des Tourelles, Fort de France, Le Marin
Propane: Fort-de-France
Provisions: Anse Mitan, Fort-de-France, LaTrinité, Le Marin, St. Pierre, Trois Ilets
Important Lights: See *Appendix A*

Few words that I have found have that certain magic that conjures images of the Caribbean as easily as *Martinique*. The Caribs called the island lying between Dominica to the north and St. Lucia to the south *Madinina*, the *Island of Flowers,* while Columbus was told by the *Ciguayo* Indians in Hispaniola that the island was called *Matinino*, the *Island of Women*. It is the Spaniards though, who are credited with naming the island, they called her *Martinica*, after Saint Martin. Along with Barbados, Martinique has one of the highest standards of living in the Caribbean. Martinique also earned fame when she played a minor part in the remake of the movie *The Thomas Crown Affair*.

Covering more than 680 square miles, this 30 mile long, 18 mile wide island, the northernmost of the Windward Islands group, has a population of almost 400,000 people, of which over 130,000 live in the capital, Fort-de-France. The topography of Martinique is dominated by *Mt. Pelée,* which towers over the northern part of the island at over 4,582', overshadowing the nearby *Pitons de Carbet*, a series of peaks south of the volcano which include *Piton Lacroix* (*Morne Pavillon*) at 3,922', *Morne Piquet* at 3,804', *Piton Dumauzé* at 3,637', *Piton de l'Alma* at 3,624', and *Piton Boucher* at 3,509'.

Inland, the northern part of Martinique is primarily rainforest, not like Guadeloupe or Dominica which tend to be drier, but more akin to a rainforest particular to Central America rather than the Antilles. The *Plaine du Lamentin* covers the central part of the island and is home to a third of the island's population. The southern part of the island is covered with rolling hills called *mornes* with none higher than *Montagne du Vauclin* at 1653'.

For those needing a bit of help with the French language, see *Appendix F* in the back of this book.

A Brief History of Martinique

In 1493, on his second voyage to the New World, Christopher Columbus stopped at the island of Hispaniola where the indigenous Arawak and Ciguayo Indians warned the *Admiral of All Oceans* that there were ferocious cannibalistic tribes on the islands to the south. This did not deter Columbus as he set forth for Dominica, Marie Galante (which he named after his ship), and Guadeloupe where his crew was able to take on fresh water. From here Columbus sailed to *Matinino*, the *Island of Women*, which was said to be inhabited by a tribe of fierce Amazons, reason enough for the Great Discover not to land on what is today known as Martinique. Finally, in June of 1502, Columbus actually set foot on Martinique at what is today Le Carbet on the western coast of Martinique, just south of St. Pierre. Instead of a fierce tribe of Amazons, Columbus found the cannibalistic Kalinargo, sometimes called the Kalina (Columbus renamed them *Caribs*), who sprang from the *Rio Orinoco* region of Venezuela, descendants of the Galibi who lived between the *Rio Orinoco* and the *Amazon*.

The Spanish never took an interest in Martinique, most likely because the island had no mineral resources (spelled G-O-L-D!). The French however, WERE interested in the island and on June 25, 1635, two settlers, de l'Olive and du Plessis arrived in Martinique from Dieppe and landed near Le Carbet. The land on this part of Martinique is mountainous and the two gentlemen soon declared the island unfit for farming claiming that the topography, as well as snakes, made the island less than ideal for their desires so they quickly abandoned Martinique for Guadeloupe.

A few months later, on September 15, 1635, Pierre Belain d'Esnambuc landed a few miles north of Le Carbet at what is now St. Pierre and claimed Martinique for France. D'Esnambuc built a small fort and a chapel at the mouth of *Rivière Roxelane*, founded the *Trading Company of St. Christopher*, and named the settlement after the saint for whom he was named. D'Esnambuc passed away two years later and his nephew, Jacques du Parquet, became Lieutenant General of Martinique and the colony truly began to grow. Du Parquet improved relations with the Caribs (hoping to avoid bloodshed), introduced sugar cane to the island, and set up a militia unit at Fort Royal, which today is known as Fort-de-France. In 1642, Louis XIII authorized the use of African slaves in the

French Antilles and the planters in Martinique found themselves with a new, and cheap, work force.

In 1650, Jacques du Parquet purchased Martinique and became governor, a position he held until his death in 1658 when his wife took over control of the island. She had her hands full trying to keep the

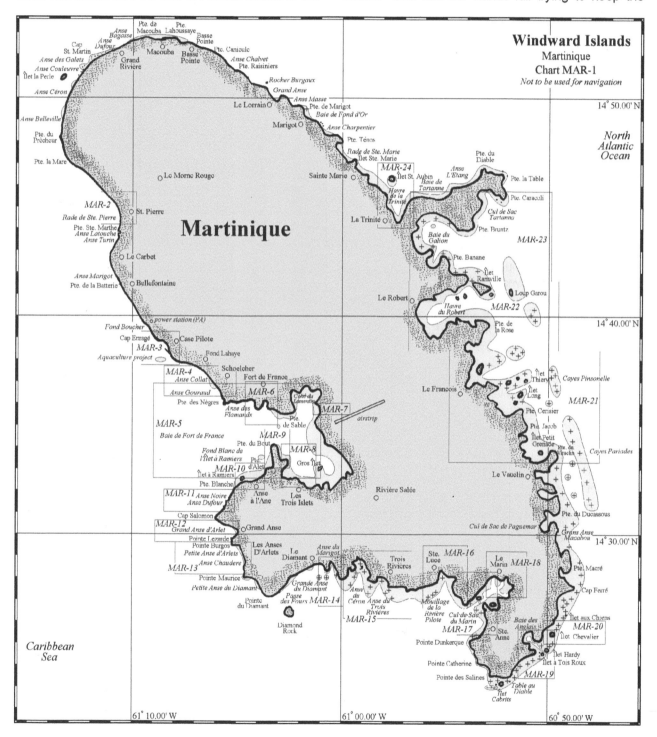

planters happy and soon found herself failing in her efforts to keep the colonists from waging war against the Caribs. A very fertile area of Martinique known as *Cabesterre* was at the center of the conflict and the Martinician militia began attacking the Carib tribes that were living along the northeastern coast and the Caravalle Peninsula. The Catholic Church even joined in the conflict as the Jesuits joined with the colonists to attack from the sea while the Dominicans launched an inland invasion. The two groups agreed that whichever order arrived first would be in charge of all future parishes on this part of the island, an agreement in which the Dominicans prevailed. In 1660, a peace treaty was signed with the few remaining Caribs, most of whom had been killed, expelled, or simply fled to Dominica or St. Vincent, the Carib's last places of refuge which the French agreed to leave alone.

In 1664, Louis XIV restructured Martinique, Guadeloupe, Marie-Galante, Grenada, and the Grenadines when he ordered that the islands be purchased by the *Compagnie des Indes Occidentales* (which controlled foreign commerce) and favorably compensated du Parquet's heirs for their interests in the islands. Five years later Martinique became the capital of the French islands when the Marquis de Baas became Governor General of the French islands in the Caribbean. One of de Baas' first moves was to reinforce Fort Royal, a timely decision as was shown in 1674 when Dutch troops attacked the fort and were defeated. A year later, in 1675, all of the French Caribbean colonies were ceded back to the Crown and the control of commerce was removed from the *Compagnie des Indes Occidentales*. In 1692, the capital of Martinique was moved from St. Pierre to Fort Royal.

In 1717, France tried to ensure exclusive trade regulations with its colonies in the Caribbean and tried to stop illegal sugar trading among the French islands and their neighbors. Representatives of the French Government, Governor General Antoine d'Arcy and his steward, Louis-Balthazar de Rincouart d'Hérouville, arrived in Martinique and were invited to a banquet at the *Bourgeot* estate near Le Diamant. The unsuspecting dinner guests were taken captive by a hundred furious colonists and expelled from the island. France soon relaxed the commerce regulations enough to satisfy Martinique's irate planters and put an end to their rebellion which became known as the *Gaoulé*, said to be a Carib word for *revolt*.

Realizing the sugar wealth of Martinique, the English entered the scene in 1762 when they attacked Fort Royal from inland and took control of the island for the first of several periods of British rule. The British occupation only lasted 9 months as the *Treaty of Paris* returned Martinique to France while ceding Canada to the British. Island defenses were strengthened and Fort Bourbon (now Fort Dessaix) was built on the hills overlooking Fort Royal to protect the fort from another inland invasion.

During the French Revolution, England again took control of Martinique when the rural planters, the Royalists, joined forces with the British to recapture the island in 1794 from the Republicans who controlled Fort Royal and St. Pierre. The British held the island until 1802 when Napoléon Bonaparte took control of Martinique with the *Treaty of Amiens*. Of course Napoléon may be said to have a particular interest in Martinique, his wife, the Empress Joséphine, was born there as Marie-Josèphe Rose Tascher de la Pagerie.

Legend has it that when the future Empress Joséphine was born in 1763, a witch named Euphrèmie David predicted that the baby would one day be more than a queen. When Joséphine came of age at 16 she wed the Viscomte Alexandre de Beauharnais in an arranged marriage. De Beauharnais was a wealthy French Army officer, and Joséphine soon gave birth to two children, Eugène, the future Viceroy of Italy, and Hortense, the future Queen of Holland.

The French Revolution found Joséphine and her husband incarcerated, Joséphine was released, but her husband was guillotined, which may have been just fine with Joséphine as there was said to be no love lost between the couple, it seems that Alexandre had originally wanted to marry one of Joséphine's more attractive sisters. Joséphine found herself single at the age of 31 and soon met, fell in love with, and married an unknown officer named Napoléon Bonaparte.

On December 1, 1804, Joséphine became Empress Joséphine when Napoléon became Emperor by placing a crown on his own head. Napoléon had their marriage annulled in 1809 because Joséphine was unable to bear him an heir. Joséphine was over 40 at this time (it is said that Joséphine pretended that she lost her birth certificate so Napoléon would not find out her true age), six years older than her husband who then had a son with his new wife Marie Louise, the daughter of the Emperor of Austria. After her life with Napoléon, Joséphine lived quietly outside Paris at *Château de Malmaison* where Napoléon would often visit her until her death of pneumonia in 1814. Joséphine's daughter married Napoléon's brother Louis who was installed as the King of Holland when Napoléon created that position. Their son, also named Louis, became the Emperor of France, Napoléon III in 1852.

It is said that Napoléon reintroduced slavery to the island by repealing a law that the Republicans had passed in 1794 to repeal previous slavery legislation. This slavery repeal never actually came into effect as the British, who favored slavery, almost immediately took control of Martinique. In 1809, the British returned to Martinique as conquerors and controlled the island until 1814 when a treaty was signed in Paris in which France lost St. Lucia and Tobago but regained Martinique and Guadeloupe.

In 1834, England abolished slavery, but France did not do so until May 22, 1848, and the intervening years were filled with unrest and slave riots on Martinique. During this period many Martinician slaves fled to the English islands and white French planters found themselves suppressing more and more slave uprisings such as those that plagued St. Pierre in 1831 and Grande Anse in 1833.

It became clear to the government of France that slavery was quickly becoming a thing of the past and despite heavy opposition from the planter's, and thanks in no small part to the lobbying of Victor Schoelcher, the undersecretary to the *Naval Minister* in charge of the islands, slavery was abolished on March 4, 1848. The official decree was signed by Schoelcher, the namesake for a small coastal community northwest of Fort-de-France, on April 27, 1848. The decree, besides granting slave owners compensation for their losses, stipulated that the abolition law would not be instituted in the French colonies for two months. Upon learning of the delay, slaves revolted in St. Pierre and the Governor of Martinique found himself with no choice but to emancipate the slaves early, on May 22, 1848.

Plantation owners on Martinique found, as their British counterparts had a decade earlier, that they needed a new source of labor to work their fields. Between 1852 and 1884, over 25,000 indentured

servants brought over from India became the primary source of Martinique's manpower. The compensation awarded to the former slave owners allowed them to reorganize production and 25 large sugar factories were constructed by the end of the 1800s. Due to the decline of the Caribbean sugar industry, by World War II only 15 of these production facilities remained and today only one functioning sugar factory still stands on Martinique.

By far, the biggest event of the 20th century, as far as Martinique is concerned, was the eruption of *Mt. Pelée*. On May 8, 1902, an estimated 29,933 people died and the city of St. Pierre, the *Paris of the Caribbean*, was completely destroyed by a huge eruption that decimated the landscape without a major lava flow.

A few years after the catastrophe at St. Pierre, World War I broke out and over 52,000 French West Indians were called up for service. World War II again threw the world into turmoil and the French Islands found themselves isolated under the Vichy government. Gold from France was stored in Martinique and the Allies blockaded the island resulting in a shortage of basic supplies for the islanders. Many Martinicians fled to other islands to join the Free French movement and on June 30, 1943, Martinique joined de Gaulle's Free France.

On March 19, 1946, Martinique, Guadeloupe, French Guiana, and Reunion Island had their status as a colony changed to that of a *French Overseas Department*, *département d'outre-mer* (DOM), meaning that the island is the same as France, the mother country, and all Martinicians enjoy the benefits of being French citizens. The political left pushed this assimilation as a means to insure greater social justice, yet today some of the same voices criticize the failure of the departmentalization claiming that it was only an attempt to keep the former colonies more dependent on France.

Martinique later became a French *région* with the representation of four deputies in the French *National Assembly* and two Senators in the *Sénat*. The island has two local assemblies as well, the *Conseil Régional*, which deals with economic, labor, and territorial matters, and the *Conseil Général*, which handles social concerns. Martinique is divided up into 34 communities, each with its own mayor and administrators.

Customs and Immigration

Ports of Entry: St. Pierre, Fort-de-France, Le Marin, LaTrinité, Anse Mitan, Trois Ilets, Grand Anse D'Arlet

Customs officers can also act as Immigration officers and take care of those formalities. Only skippers can come ashore to clear; all crew must remain on the vessel until pratique is granted. As of this writing, there are no entry fees for United States and British flag vessels, but some nationalities are charged on a per ton/per day basis.

French citizens only need to present their national identification card to enter Martinique; all other visitors will need a valid passport. Americans, Canadians, and members of the EEC are admitted without a visa for stays of up to three months. If arriving by plane, all travelers, except French citizens, need an ongoing or return ticket.

Fees

There are no overtime charges involved with clearing in or out of Martinique. If you arrive after hours on the weekend, depending on your location, you can wait until Monday morning to clear.

Firearms and Pets

Firearms must be declared upon arrival. Pets over three months old are admitted with valid health certificate and rabies inoculation. For more information contact Capitainerie of Le Marin at 596-74-83-83 (Fax: 596-74-92-02).

Speed Limit

Martinique maintains a 5-knot speed limit within 300 meters of shore.

US Documentation or State Registration?

Martinique is French in flavor and in government, make no mistake about that, and one of the most frequently asked questions concerning the French islands is about their failure to recognize U.S. vessels that are only state registered and not federally documented. To make this clear, foreign yachts traveling in French waters need NATIONAL registration with the original documents aboard. Although some Customs officers have allowed U.S. state registered vessels to stay in French waters, these cases are frowned upon and you will find Customs officers to be efficient, friendly, and easy to get along with except in

this one regard. It is not recommend that you visit a French Island without U.S. documentation.

VAT

Foreign boats staying over six months are subject to a VAT and import tax the same as if you were visiting France unless the boat is declared to be out of commission and its registration papers left with Customs.

Visas

Citizens of the U.S. or EU do not need a Visa to visit Martinique. Citizens of the following countries need to obtain a visa prior to arrival: Afghanistan, Albania, Algeria, Angola, Antigua and Barbuda, Armenia, Azerbaijan, Bahamas, Bahrain, Bangladesh, Barbados, Belize, Benin, Bhutan, Belorussia, Bosnia, Botswana, Brazil, Burkina Faso, Burma, Burundi, Cambodia, Cameroon, Cape Verde, Central Africa, Chad, China, Colombia, Comoros, Congo, D.R. Congo (ex-Zaïre), Cuba, Djibouti, Dominica, Dominican Republic, Ecuador, Egypt, Equatorial Guinea, Eritrea, Ethiopia, Fiji, Gabon, Gambia, Georgia, Ghana, Grenada, Guinea, Guinea Bissau, Guyana, Haiti, Hong Kong (except S.A.R.), India, Indonesia, Iran, Iraq, Israel, Ivory Coast, Jamaica, Jordan, Kazakhstan, Kenya, Kirghizstan, Kiribati, Kuwait, Laos, Lebanon, Lesotho, Liberia, Libya, Macao (except S.A.R.), Macedonia, Madagascar, Malawi, Maldives, Mali, Marshall Islands, Mauritania, Mauritius (exception: no visa required for Reunion and less than 15-days stay), Micronesia, Moldavia, Mongolia, Morocco, Mozambique, Namibia, Nauru, Nepal, Niger, Nigeria, North Korea, Oman, Pakistan, Palau, Palestinia, Papua, Peru, Philippines, Qatar, Refugees, Russia, Rwanda, Solomon, Samoa, Saudi Arabia, Senegal, Serbia, Seychelles (exception: no visa required for Reunion and less than 15-days stay), Sierra Leone, Somalia, South Africa, Sri Lanka, St Kitts, St Lucia (exception : no visa required for French West Indies and less than 15-days stay), St Thomas, St Vincent, Sudan, Suriname, Swaziland, Syria, Tadjikistan, Taiwan, Tanzania, Thailand, Togo, Tonga, Trinidad & Tobago, Tunisia, Turkey, Turkmenistan, Tuvalu, Uganda, Ukraine, United Arab Emirates, Uzbekistan, Vanuatu, Vietnam, Yemen, former Yugoslavia, Zambia, and Zimbabwe.

Pilotage of Large Vessels (over 50m)

For all vessels with LOA of 50m or more, Martinique's official ports require pilots to be on board or the ship's Captains be appropriately authorized by them. The port areas include St. Pierre, Fort de France,

Le Marin, Le Vauclin, Le François and Le Robert. The pilots are welcoming and flexible and make every effort to meet the demands of the industry. Please contact *Douglas Yacht Services* by phone (0596-45 89 75), or email them (douglas@yachtservices.fr) should you require assistance.

Getting Around on Martinique

Martinique can boast of a very efficient bus system and taxis (TC), all of which run on fixed routes. Private taxis will take you anywhere you need to go. If you rent a car you will drive on the right.

The Western Coast of Martinique

The western coast of Martinique is home to several very nice, and secluded, anchorages, as well as the huge *Baie de Fort-de-France* and the service facilities in this cosmopolitan city. Generally the settlements in the areas where you anchor on Martinique will be more modern and with more facilities than those on Martinique's neighbors in the Windward Islands. When approaching the leeward coast of Martinique be advised that if approaching at night, the light at Pointe Prêcheur (Fl R 5s, 72', 18 M) is not visible when east of the rhumb line from Scott's Head, Dominica to Pointe Prêcheur, and that Îlet la Perle, although over 88' above sea level, blends into the mainland of Martinique and is difficult to discern (Chart MAR-1).

As you sail southward along the leeward coast of Martinique, see Chart MAR-1, you will find several small harbors that offer anchoring possibilities long before you arrive at St. Pierre. *Anse des Galets*, just south of Cap St. Martin, *Anse Couleuvre* near Îlet la Perle, and *Anse Céron* (not to be confused with *Anse du Céron* on the southern coast of Martinique) offer lee anchorages that are good in settled weather and like most of the leeward anchorages in the Windward Islands, are not tenable in northerly swells. At *Anse Céron* you can visit *Habitation Céron*, a large plantation that was a sugar factory run by a huge waterwheel. The restaurant near the river, *La Mélodie*, is also worth a visit as all the food served originates from the plantation's grounds, including the freshwater crayfish. Nearby are several hot springs of volcanic origin.

The anchorages mentioned are the last ones you will see along this coast that offer a great deal of solitude away from the hustle and bustle of towns. Just north of St. Pierre, Le Prêcheur offers a small

market and a very nice restaurant. Le Prêcheur is named for a lava formation that resembles a preacher and is known as the home of Françoise d'Aubigné, who later became the *Marquise de Maintenon*, the second wife of King Louis XIV of France.

The town of Le Prêcheur sits on a point and you can anchor in the small coves either north or south of the point. The northern cove has a dock where you can land your dinghy. Just south of Le Prêcheur you can dine on fresh seafood high above the Caribbean at *La Factorie*. About three miles north of St. Pierre (on highway *D10*) are the cliffs known as *Tonbeu des Caraibes*, sometimes called *Le Coffre à Morts*. Legend has it that Carib Indians threw themselves to their deaths off these cliffs rather than fall into the hands of their French pursuers.

St. Pierre

Waypoints:
St. Pierre- ¼ nm W of anchorage
14° 44.50' N, 61° 11.00' W

St. Pierre is best known for being the victim, along with almost 30,000 residents and a dozen ships in the harbor, of the 1902 eruption of *Mt. Pelée,* the dominant feature of the topography of northern Martinique.

You can use the town dock for a dinghy landing. You may also ask the officials at the town hall if you may approach the dock to take on water.

Navigational Information

As shown on Chart MAR-2, a waypoint at 14° 44.50' N, 61° 11.00' W, will place you approximately ¼ mile west of the anchorage at St. Pierre. From the waypoint head east and anchor wherever your draft allows, this is a very pleasant anchorage as you will come to learn (but not when northerly swells are running). Some cruisers like to anchor close to the town dock, others prefer to anchor south of the dock near Pointe Ste. Marthe where there is a bit less roll; I sometimes like to anchor a bit northward directly opposite the conspicuous ruins ashore and near the local fishing boats if for no other reason than shore access. Be advised that in periods of strong winds, the gusts coming down *Mt. Pelée* can be quite strong.

By the time this guide is published, expect to see a new group of buoys designating a no-anchor

St. Pierre and *Mt. Pelée*

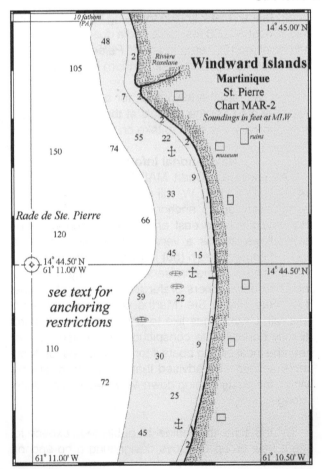

Ruins at St. Pierre

zone set in place to protect the wrecks lying on the bottom of the harbor. There will be a series of three buoys and the head of the jetty, and no anchoring will be permitted between the buoys and jetty

What You Will Find Ashore
Customs and *Immigration*

If you need to clear *Customs* (*Douanes*) the office (computer check-ins) is located just south of the museum on *Rue Victor Hugo* and the best time to clear is in the mornings. The office is open Tuesday-Friday from 0900-1500, and on Saturdays from 0900-1200. As stated previously, if you arrive after hours on the weekend you can wait until Tuesday morning to clear.

Internet

On the southern side of town is *L'Escapade*, a restaurant with both Wi-fi and computer stations. A good spot to enjoy a meal and surf the net. Located on the waterfront, *Fish Bo Kai* also has free Wi-fi.

Laundry

You can do your laundry at the Laundromat by the waterfront. *L'auxilaire* near the river, will do your laundry for you.

Marine Facilities
Fuel

There is a small gas station right on the water if you need to jerry jug fuel to your vessel or just pick up some ice.

Marine Services

PBS can repair, rebuild, and balance your propeller as well as perform repairs, modifications, and new installations on any part of your stern gear including your shaft, stern glands, and cutlass bearings. *PBS* can also handle welding and some fabrication and can be reached by phone at 0596-78 17 00. *PBS* will also pick and deliver to other marine locations around Martinique.

Another stop for metal fabrication and welding is *Proto Meca*, near *PBS*, you can phone them at 0596-78 34 49. *Proto Meca* also handles some engine work including machining, and carpentry.

Provisioning

For provisioning try *8 à Huit*, *Nord Cash* near the church, and *Ecomax* on the north side of town just across the bridge over *Rivière Roxelane*.

Dining

St. Pierre has no shortage of good places to eat, and that is typical of every town in Martinique, dining is important here, and fine dining is a necessity.

L'Escapade offers Wi-fi and Internet access computers. *La Tamaya* is a quaint eatery with a lot of ambiance and excellent fare. *La Caraibes* is a local hangout offering 30 different kinds of beer as well as live music. Next door is a good spot for some Chinese take out, *Tai Loong*. *Le Fromager*, with a great view of the harbor and good food to match, is located in the hills on the road to Fond St. Denis and is worth the trip. A new spot, located on the beach is *Fish Bo Kai*, with free Wi-fi and showers!

Historic St. Pierre

Prior to 1902, St. Pierre was a thriving port town of 28,000 people, and was called the *Paris of the Caribbean*. The town had a magnificent theater that seated over 800 next to the jail overlooking the harbor. The occasional earthquake would shake the buildings, or a deep rumble would emanate from 400,000-year-old *Mt. Pelée*, but nothing seemed serious enough to warrant concern for the citizens of St. Pierre. Early in 1902, a sulfurous odor was noticed in the area and a few residents commented on the boiling water that was filling a crater lake on the mountain, but still this was not enough to be concerned about. When, during the early spring of 1902, boiling water and mud streamed down the side of *Mt. Pelée* and buried a plantation, some families sent their children to live with family and friends in other parts of Martinique.

On April 25, 1902, during an intense election campaign when votes were needed in town, *Mt. Pelée* belched hot ashes down onto St. Pierre and as May began, a series of lava flows affected some nearby towns and businesses, but still the good people of St. Pierre were not concerned. On May 2, 1902, the mountain spewed out a river of lava engulfing part of the Lavenière estate killing 25 workers. A few days later, on May 5, a tidal wave hit St. Pierre throwing ships onto the shore and knocking down buildings, and still the population remained unmoved.

So, while the people of the town were deeply immersed in life in St. Pierre, just a few miles away a stone spire was pushed upwards from deep within *Mt. Pelée*. Standing a hundred feet high, the spire caused concern among residents and merchants alike. The merchants were worried about the loss of sales if the residents fled so they asked Governor Mouttet for assistance. The young governor and his family arrived in St. Pierre from Fort-de-France and assured the residents that *Mt. Pelée* would not erupt, and if it did it would blow upwards, with only a minor lava flow down its sides. This calmed the local's fears and most remained making the merchants happier. A day before the eruption, May 7, 1902, the local paper announced that "...*Montagne Pelée does not present any more risk to the population than Vesuvius does to the Neapolitans.*"

Well, as we all know, *Mt. Pelée* did erupt, at approximately 0800 on May 8, 1902, and the eruption was unusual in that there was little if any lava flow. Instead, a whole section of the southern side of the mountain blew out from the enormous pressure of super-heated gasses estimated to have been in the range of 1800°-3600° F vaporizing anything in its path. Many ships sank in the harbor and Governor Mouttet died along with 22,000 other people in St. Pierre within a few minutes of the eruption, except one man who was locked in the jail.

Auguste Cyparis had been incarcerated for drunkenness (some say murder) and that saved his life as only minute traces of gas and steam could enter his thick-walled cell. Cyparis remained in the cell for four days and three nights after the eruption, living off a trickle of water that found its way into his cell until he was found by people from a nearby parish who had come to St. Pierre to search for anything that had not been destroyed. Cyparis was later featured in *Barnum & Bailey's Circus* where he exhibited his wounds.

As to the stories told of other survivors, their numbers range from one to six depending on to whom you speak, but it is generally believed the only other survivor was an old cobbler named Léon Léandre who lived on the outskirts of St. Pierre who happened to have been in his cellar when the eruption occurred. To get a first hand view of what life was like in St. Pierre before the eruption, I suggest you read Lafcadio Hearn's *Two Years in the West Indies*. Hearn was a writer for *Harper's* magazine who arrived on the island in 1887, the same year as Gauguin.

Mt. Pelée is now considered dormant, the last two eruptions were in 1929 and 1932, but if you talk to somebody that lives in St. Pierre, especially the old timers, they are not so sure that the term *dormant* means much at all. Every May, the residents of St. Pierre commemorate the eruption of *Mt. Pelée* in the *Saint Pierre Festival*.

In the early 1990s, some officials in St. Pierre came up with the brilliant idea of acquiring a submarine to take tourists to view the wrecks that littered the harbor from the 1902 eruption. In 1993, a German built submarine was put in use, but it was quickly discovered that the construction was far below French standards and the repairs and renovation put off the launch date until 1995. The submarine, the *Mobilis*, actually did begin taking passengers down to the wrecks, but after a few years this was removed as the costs involved were staggering and the owners were losing money; so today you can only view the wrecks by diving on them.

Twelve of the wrecks of the ships that were in the harbor the day St. Pierre died have been found, several with human bones aboard which prompted this area to be considered a memorial grave and to be kept intact. The team that discovered the wrecks was headed by the great Jacques Yves Cousteau who also filmed the expedition. Three of the most popular wrecks are the *Tamaya*, a three-masted ship lying in 278' of water, the liner *Roraima* which lies in only 164' of water, and the *Raisinier* lying in only about 50' of water; all three ships have lain there for over a century.

Discovering St. Pierre

Today, you can take a one-hour tour of St. Pierre on the mini-train called the *Cyparis Express*. The tour runs Monday-Friday from 100-1300 and from 1430-1700. Tickets can be purchased at the *Place des Ruines du Figuier* near the conspicuous ruins that once were stores and warehouses, and of course Cyparis' old jail cell with its thick walls that were built in 1660. Another interesting stop is the *Musée Vulcanologique*, the volcano museum. Here you can get a glimpse of what life was like in St. Pierre prior to May 8, 1902. Displays include petrified food, melted glass and other deformed items, and of course photos of the *Paris of the Caribbean*.

Across from the museum is the *Ancien Théâtre*, or *Old Theater*, much of which survived the eruption. The original theater seated 800 on three levels and was built in 1786 as a smaller scale version of its sister theater in Bordeaux. If you follow *Rue Schoelcher* until it becomes *Allée Pécoul* it will end at the *Château Depaz* on the *Pécoul* plantation. This is one of the oldest homes on Martinique and was rebuilt after the eruption by Victor Depaz who was studying in France at the time of the eruption and was the only surviving member of his family. My favorite stop here is the rum distillery, *Habitation Depaz*, offering free tours and rum sampling (I ask you, how can one refuse an offer like that?). Rum connoisseurs highly favor the *Depaz Special Reserve*.

South of St. Pierre, up in the mountains, you'll find *Canal de Beauregard*, an awesome trek for those with no fear of heights. Slaves built the canal in the mid-1700s to bring water around a steep mountain to supply the rum distilleries in St. Pierre. For the most part the walk is shady and level, but there are sections where no guardrails protect you from a long, long fall.

Le Carbet and Bellefontaine

Navigational Information

South of St. Pierre is *Le Carbet,* a pleasantly calm anchorage with a nice little town to explore. Just south of Pointe Ste. Marthe are two small coves where you can drop the hook, *Anse Latouche* is tiny and shallow, and the next one southward is *Anse Turin* which is larger and more open. You can anchor in front of the church or south of the river mouth near the dock, and the best spot, in front of the *Hotel Marouba* at the south end of the beach just north of a rock outcropping.

What You Will Find Ashore

The term *carbet* is a Carib word that was used to designate the biggest hut in the village, the place where the village meetings were held. As I said, there is a lot worth seeing here; the *Musée Paul Gauguin* lies across from *Anse Turin* and displays memorabilia of the artist's life here on Martinique. Gauguin arrived on Martinique from Panama in 1887 with his friend and fellow artist Charles Laval. The artist pawned his watch to build a studio in a rented wooden shack in Le Carbet where he created many paintings that are now described as his *Antilles* or *Martinique Period.* Some say that Gauguin's stay on Martinique, though brief at only 4 months, played a decisive role in his career, even the artist himself said that to understand him and his art, one had to understand his Martinique period. Here he created his first tropical frescoes, before his better-known *Tahiti* period. Although there are no original paintings here, there are several reproductions, many works by local artists, and are some unique faïence mosaics made of once-white pieces that turned pink, maroon, blue, and black due to the eruption in 1902.

Just north of the museum is the valley of the butterflies, *La Vallée des Papillons.* Two thousand butterflies are bred here in a farm built among the 17th century stone ruins and waterwheel of one of Martinique's oldest plantations. It's best to arrive early in the morning when the short-lived butterflies first emerge to fly. Another place of interest for cruisers are the rum distilleries, *Habitation Lajus* with tours from Monday through Saturday, and *Distillerie Neisson*, with free tours and sampling of their international award winning rums.

A great restaurant right on the beach in Le Carbet is *Le Trou Crabe,* where you will be dining under a palm tree just off the beach in an elegantly casual atmosphere. An interesting feature, as if the view of the harbor is not enough, is the restaurant's 2,000-gallon aquarium. Saturday night a live band entertains and the French chef prepares a special lobster feast.

The best Creole dining in Le Carbet is without a doubt *Le Poids du Roy*; if you want economy, try *La Paillotte*, for seafood and live music on Saturday nights try *La Datcha*, and if it's wine or ambiance you crave, try *Le Trou Crabe*. The *Centre de Thalassothérapie du Carbet* specializes in saltwater therapy.

Another worthwhile detour is the town of Morne Vent, or as it is better known, *La Petite Suisse*, or *Little Switzerland*. Take *D20* off *N2* just before Le Carbet and you'll find yourselves on a road to this picturesque little village located 1400' up on the way to the Pitons du Carbet.

Bellefontaine can be easily recognized by the huge stacks just south of town at the *Électricité de France* power station. You can anchor off the town dock but be prepared for a little roll. A calmer anchorage can be found south of the power station in *Fond Boucher*, just north of Cap Enragé (see Chart MAR-1). Do not attempt to anchor near the power station docks as they must be kept open for commercial vessels.

In Bellefontaine you'll find a boat-shaped house called *Le Torgileo* on a hill above the town. Built in 1948 as a hotel, it is now a very nice restaurant. Also above the town is the *Panorama Verrier*, a great view and photo op of the Caribbean and *Mt. Pelée* that's not to be missed. It's hard to find, but worth the effort. There is a steep road leading up from the center of town just before the *D20* turnoff, the spot is ahead three miles on your left. Another route is to take *D63* outside Bellefontaine, then take an almost immediate right on *D63*, a little further on you'll take a left at the partially hidden old sign that points to Verrier.

Case Pilote

Waypoints:
Case Pilote- ¼ nm W of anchorage
14° 38.50' N, 61° 08.70' W

Case Pilote is one of the oldest villages on Martinique and was named after a Carib chief, *Pilote*, who had a hut, called a *case*, in the area. In 1635, Pilote agreed to give the French government of Martinique all the property he owned in exchange for some land in the southern end of Martinique to which he later retired at *Rivière Pilote*.

Navigational Information

As shown on Chart MAR-3, a waypoint at 14° 38.50' N, 61° 08.70' W, will place you approximately ¼ mile west of the anchorage. From the waypoint head east to anchor off the northern of town north of the river mouth (keep an eye out for the shoal off the mouth of the small river that is shown on the chart), or in the small cove just north of Case Pilote proper. Please don't anchor so as to block passage to and from the fishing harbor. This is a working fishing harbor and it is not unusual for the fishermen to ask you to move if you're in their way.

Heading south from Case Pilote to Schoelcher or *Baie de Fort-de-France* you must clear the well-

marked floating aquaculture project just south of Case Pilote as shown on Chart MAR-1 (PA). The entire project, which sits about ¼ mile offshore and extends perhaps another ½ mile westward, is well marked by buoys and floats. You have plenty of water to pass between the aquaculture project and the mainland of Martinique, but never try to pass between the buoys!

A bit further south you can anchor in settled weather at *Fond Lahaye*, a small fishing village that was originally built for the refugees from the 1902 eruption of *Mt. Pelée*.

What You Will Find Ashore

The small fishing harbor is usually full so berthing for cruisers is rare here. Do not labor under the misconception that the fishing harbor offers any protection from a hurricane. It was destroyed by

Case Pilote

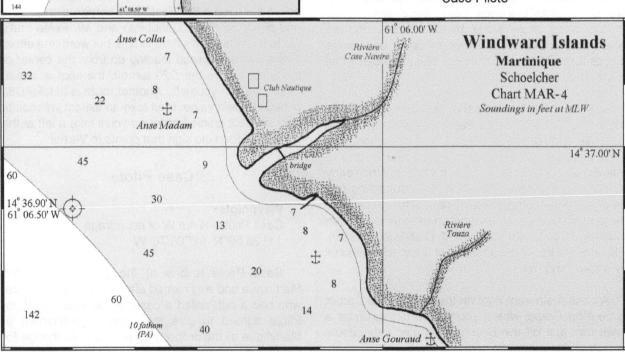

Hurricane David in 1979 and damaged by *Hurricane Lenny* in 1999.

A landmark in Case Pilote is the *Notre Dame de l'Assomption*, one of the oldest churches on Martinique (built in 1776) and an important historical monument. In town there's a gas station if you need to jerry jug fuel to your boat, and an *8 à Huit* near the main square for groceries. Also on the square is the charming *Céleste's Village* serving very good French and Creole meals at attractive prices, and *Snack le Pilote* serving pizza at night.

Overlooking the harbor is *Le Deux Gros* serving very good seafood and steaks. Right on the water is *Snack Bar de la Plage* and offers a good variety of food in an informal atmosphere. Just a bit away from town, and hidden in the *Maniba* residential complex, is one of the best restaurants in Case Pilote, *La Maniba*, never mind the furnishings, concentrate on the gastronomical delights offered here, oh, and don't come looking like you just stepped off the boat.

Marine Services

Located just to the east of the entrance to the harbor is *Inboard Diesel*, a *Volvo-Penta* dealer and repair shop. The owner, Frank Ågren, is the primary *Volvo-Penta* dealer for the Windward Islands and often has a couple of slips inside for his customers. *Inboard Diesel* can repair your old diesel, install a new diesel, or fix any electrical problems that you may be experiencing. *Inboard Diesel* is also a dealer for *Northern Lights* and *MTU*. Frank can be reached at 0596-78 71 96 or you can email *Inboard Diesel* at Beatrice.ids@wanadoo.fr.

Nearby, *Renovboats* can handle your fiberglass repairs or painting. Their main office has moved to Schoelcher, but there is still a small office here in Case Pilote. *Renovboats* can be reached at 0596-25 01 92 in Case Pilote.

Schoelcher

Waypoints:
Schoelcher- ¼ nm W of anchorage
14° 36.90' N, 61° 06.50' W

Schoelcher, pronounced *shell-share*, is actually a suburb of Fort-de-France, so much so that you'll probably never realize when you pass from *Baie de Fort-de-France* into Schoelcher or vice versa.

Schoelcher, with a population of over 20,000, is one of the more heavily populated areas in Martinique and is home to the *University of the French West Indies and Guyana*. In 1888, the town was named after Victor Schoelcher, the undersecretary to the *Naval Minister* in charge of the islands who fought so defiantly against slavery in the islands.

Prior to 1888 the town was known as *Case Navire* and was actually more a part of Case Pilote, when, due to the presence of two rivers here, *Rivière Touza* and *Rivière Case Navire*, Case Navire/Schoelcher was an important stop for sailing vessels in need of fresh water.

Navigational Information

As shown on Chart MAR-4, a waypoint at 14° 36.90' N, 61° 06.50' W, will place you approximately ¼ mile west of the anchorage. You can anchor north of *Rivière Case Navire* in Anse Madam (check out the sailing school), or south of the river and off the town dock as shown on the chart. You can land your dinghy at the dock by the park to visit ashore.

What You Will Find Ashore

In town there is a dramatic stature of the community's namesake, Victor Schoelcher, on the square in front of the *Palace of Justice*. It shows the Frenchman breaking a slave's chains and declaring that slavery will never again be permitted on French soil. If you need to provision there is an *8 à Huit* located a short walk from the dock. In town itself you'll find everything you'll need; a pharmacy, photo shop, bicycle shop, a cinema, pizza parlor, and numerous places to shop and dine scattered all about the town. If you can't find the provisions you need, you can take a taxi to the larger malls in Fort-de-France or the *Leader Price* store at Terreville (on the road to L'Enclos).

A very good restaurant, *Le Sunset*, sits off *N2* in a small hotel of the same name. The *Pomme Cannelle* is located in the *Hotel Anse Colas* on *Route Petite Tamarin* and serves good Creole cooking but sadly the view is only of the pool. *Bleu Marine* in the *La Batelière* hotel is one of the nicest places to dine in Schoelcher. The view here is also of the pool, but with the sea in the background. *Le Foulard* is a seaside restaurant next to the market that is extremely popular and definitely worth a stop. A favorite restaurant of mine is *La Vague du Sud*, right on the water's edge where the owners keep their boat. Another excellent choice is *Arc en Ciel* right on the beach where you can choose from seafood, pizza, or West Indian fare while *Jardin de Jade* serves Chinese food.

Go south a bit to Anse Gouraud (you can anchor here) and you'll find the *Batelière Casino* next to the huge *Batelière Mall* that is definitely worth a day's visit, especially if you haven't been to a mall in some time. The *Madiana Conference Center* is home to several restaurants where you can quaff a mug of *brasserie*, beer that is brewed on the spot, and then catch the latest release at the cinema. A bit further south you can anchor in the lee of Pointe des Nègres along with some of the boats that belong to members of the private military club located in the fort on the point.

Baie de Fort-de-France

Waypoints:
Baie de Fort-de-France- ¾ nm WNW of channel
14° 35.00' N, 61° 05.40' W

The first thing you'll notice when you enter the Fort-de-France area, the *Baie de Fort-de-France*, is that the harbor seems to go on forever. With your bow pointing eastward your eyes will scan the hillsides around you and see nothing but structure after structure, this is because cosmopolitan Fort-de-France, the capital of Martinique and the most important city on the island, is the center of shipping activity, manufacturing, administration, regional banks, foreign consulates, as well as the home to over 130,000 people. The city of Fort-de-France is spread about the hills on the northern side of *Baie de Fort-de-France* and it is difficult to discern where Fort-de-France ends and its suburbs, such as Schoelcher or Le Lamentin begin.

Fort-de-France is very busy as anyone who has driven through the area and fought the traffic jams can tell you. But it wasn't always this way. Until the eruption of *Mt. Pelée* in 1902, St. Pierre gave Fort-de-France some serious competition. At the turn of the 20th century there were over 30,000 people living in St. Pierre and only half that many residing in Fort-de-France. After the destruction of St. Pierre, Fort-de-France's population grew dramatically over the first few decades of the 1900s. But like St. Pierre, Fort-de-France has had it own share of hard times surviving several natural disasters and military attacks. In 1674 the Dutch attempted to take Fort

Royal and were as unsuccessful as the British who attacked the city in 1759, and who again attacked, a bit more successfully in 1762, and 1794. The British were finally successful in taking the city, as well as the rest of the island, in 1809. In 1839, an earthquake killed over 500 residents of Fort-de-France, and the entire city was destroyed by fire in 1890 and destroyed again by a hurricane a year later.

If you remember from the history section at the beginning of this chapter, Du Parquet built *Fort Royal*, now *Fort St. Louis*, in 1639 and a small community sprang up around the fort. However the true founder of Fort-de-France is said to be Charles du Courbon, Conte de Blenac, the Governor General of the Windward Islands from 1677-1696, the man responsible for laying out the city we know today. In 1681 the capital was moved to Fort-de-France from St. Pierre and the city retained the name of *Fort Royal* until 1802 when Napoléon ordered the town's name changed to Fort-de-France though *Fort Royal* did not become *Fort Saint Louis* until 1814 (and was called *Fort Edward* during the brief British occupations of 1762, 1794, and 1809). At the beginning of the 20th century, the fort was a zoo for a brief period of time and after World War II it became the staff headquarters of the Antilles-Guiana division of the French Navy. Nearby, on the hills overlooking the harbor, stand *Fort Tartenson* and *Fort Desaix*, to offer more protection from the invading British.

Navigational Information
There are several areas where you can anchor or secure a slip along the shoreline of *Baie de Fort-de-France*, we will discuss each on in turn taking a clockwise tour of the bay. As shown on Chart MAR-5, a waypoint at 14° 35.00' N, 61° 05.40' W, will place you approximately ¾ mile west/northwest of the marked entrance channel into Baie de Fort-de-France. From this waypoint you have your choice of destinations. You can opt for the northern side of the bay to anchor off the Fort-de-France proper in *Baie des Flamands* as shown on Chart MAR-6, or you may choose to head eastward to anchor in Cohe de Lamentin or get a slip in the *Marina de Port Cohe* as shown on Chart MAR-7. Others still may decide that they like the southern part of *Baie de Fort-de-France* better and anchor off Trois Îlets as shown on Chart MAR-8, or perhaps at *Anse Mitan* and Pointe du Bout as shown on Chart MAR-9, or at Anse à l'Ane as shown on Chart MAR-10. Whichever place you choose to begin your exploration of *Baie de Fort-de-*

France, you'll find good shopping, even better dining, pleasant anchorages, comfortable marinas, and easy access to shoreside facilities. Let us begin our discussion with the area just off downtown Fort-de-France, the *Baie des Flamands*.

Fort-de-France, *Baie des Flamands*, and *Baie des Tourelles*

Waypoints:
Baie des Flamands, - ½ nm SSW of anchorage
14° 35.50' N, 61° 04.50' W

Baie de Fort-de-France- ¾ nm WNW of channel
14° 35.00' N, 61° 05.40' W

Navigational Information
From the waypoint at the western end of *Baie de Fort-de-France*, head approximately northeast (see Chart MAR-5) to a waypoint at 14° 35.50' N, 61° 04.50' W, which will place you approximately ½ mile south/southwest of the anchorage in *Baie des Flamands* as shown on Chart MAR-6. From this position continue north/northeastward keeping the large cruise ship dock to port as your round up into the head of the bay to anchor right off the center of Fort-de-France. Keep a sharp eye out for the well-marked shoal to starboard, *Banc du Ft. St. Louis*. If you are approaching at night (not advisable), bear in mind that the lights of anchored vessels may be hard to distinguish from the background lights of Fort-de-France.

Anchor only in the designated anchorage area as shown on the chart, anchoring outside this area is prohibited, especially in the vicinity of the cruise ship docks; however when cruise ships are not at the dock or not expected, cruisers will often anchor in a wider area infringing on the waters off the cruise ship dock. The bottom here is mud and the holding ranges from poor to almost good, make sure your anchor is set before you venture ashore. Also, when the wind dies, the fluky current will spin the anchored boats in every direction.

What You Will Find Ashore
As we begin our discussion of what you'll find in and around Fort-de-France, let me warn you that this section will be incomplete. Yes, that's right, incomplete. I could write an entire book on what is available here, all the places to dine, all the sights, so all I can do here is highlight the best, the most notable,

and of course the ones that I've seen, the rest of the exploration is up to you. Trying to write a complete section on Fort-de-France is as daunting a challenge as tackling the same topic in any major cosmopolitan city, so I do the best I can and leave the rest to you. If you feel that something should be added, please contact me through my website at www.seaworthy.com and I'll check it out. If I use your suggestion (any suggestion concerning any of my guides) I'll send you a free copy of that guide when it is reprinted with your addition inside.

Customs and *Immigration*
You can clear *Customs* at the *Sea Services* chandlery (109 *Rue Ernest Deproge*) where you'll find a computer for this purpose located in the hallway.

Dinghy Landing and Garbage Bins
You can land your dinghy anywhere along *La Savanne* and small trash receptacles can be found along the dock with larger bins located near the road.

Internet
A note to those who have never used a French keyboard...they will drive you nuts. Some of the letters and punctuation marks are not located where you expect them to be, so even the fastest typist is sometimes reduced to the level of a hunt-and-peck typist that uses two fingers.

Cyber Deliss, located near *Sea Services*, is a top notch restaurant that offers Internet access. If you bring your laptop the Wi-fi is free while you dine.

Not far from the *Place de la Savane* you can access the Internet at *Difinitel Micro* on *Boulevard Allègre*, and at *The Web Café* on *Rue Blenac* behind the *Post Office*. The *Cybercafé Pizzeria Panet* (0800-1700) is a good spot to enjoy one of their fine pizzas and surf the net.

Ferries
There is a regular ferry service between the ferry docks near *Place de la Savane* and the resort areas around Baie de Fort-de-France. The ferries, called *vedettes*, make frequent short trips, usually about 20 minutes, between Fort-de-France and Point du Bout, l'*Anse Mitan*, and l'Anse à l'Âne. For information on the ferry from Fort-de-France to Pointe du Bout, phone *Société Somatour* at 0596-75 05 53. For information on the ferry service between Fort-de-France and l'*Anse Mitan* and l'Anse à l'Âne, phone *Société Madinina* at

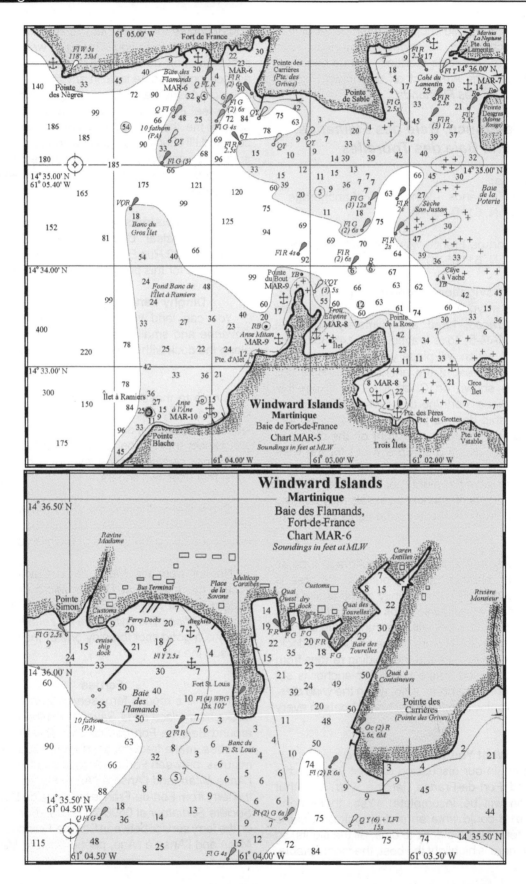

0596-63 06 46. For those wishing to venture further, *L'Express des Îlets* runs between Fort-de-France and Guadeloupe, Dominica, Les Saintes, and St. Lucia, for more information call 0596-63-12-11. *Brudey Frères* runs a 350-seat catamaran between Fort-de-France and Guadeloupe with a stop in Dominica, for more information phone 0596-70-08-50.

Marine Facilities
Just to the east of *Baie des Flamands* is the major marine services area located at *Quai Quest* and *Baie des Tourelles* as shown on Chart MAR-6. Although primarily for commercial vessels, private yachts have several services from which to choose.

Boatyards
Caren Antilles, who also have a location in Le Marin, has a hual-out yard in *Baie des Tourelles*. The yard has a 35-ton lift and can accommodate vessels with drafts to 7'. The nearby *Martinique Dry Dock* can handle vessels up to the size of some ships.

As nice as *Caren Antilles* is, the largest boatyard in the Windward Islands is probably *Multicap Caraibes* at the northern end of *Quai Quest* as shown on Chart MAR-6. Besides constructing some of the commercial charter boats and ferries that you will see up an down the island chain, the *Multicap Caraibes* yard can handle ANY problem you might have from your keel to your masthead, monohull or multihull, power or sail, glass, wood, steel, or composite. Here too you can purchase almost any marine product on the market, and have it repaired as well.

Electrical and Electronics
For electronic sales and repairs, visit *Carib Electronic Engineering* where the owner Alain Belat maintains a supply of *autopilot* spares. *Cadet-Petit* are electrical specialists and are the place to go for alternator, generator, and starter motor repairs and rewinding.

Fuel
Located in *Baie des Tourelles*, DCML has a fuel dock with water, beer, coffee, ice, and sandwiches. The dock is open from 0800-1900 daily except Sundays and holidays when they are open from 0800-1200.

Marine Supplies
Sea Services is a large chandlery (109 *Rue Ernest Deproge*) with several employees that speak fluent English. They are open weekdays from 0815-1715 and on Saturdays from 0830-1230. The store also has a nautical boutique with the same name next door. *Coopemar* is the on-site chandler at *Caren Antilles*.

Plus Nautique is another chandler in Fort-de-France and they handle inflatables and life rafts, electronics and electrical supplies, and have an excellent supply of used gear where you'll likely spend hours (as I do every chance I get) rummaging. *La Survy* also handles inflatables; they are *Zodiac* and *Bombard* dealers.

SCIM is also located in Dillon across form the *Euromarché* supermarket and is a chandler as well as an *OMC* outboard dealer.

Mechanical
For diesel repairs my first recommendation would be *Martinique Diesel* near the airport in Le Lamentin. *Multicap Caraibes* (also fabrication, welding, fiberglass repairs, and painting), *Croquet* in Dillon, and the *Volvo-Penta* dealer in Fort-de-France may also be of service to you.

SCIM is also located in Dillon across form the *Euromarché* supermarket and is a chandler as well as an *OMC* outboard dealer. Just outside the *Caren Antilles* yard is *S.A.V. des Moteurs*, an *OMC* dealer.

Global Impex are dealers for *Mercury* outboards and can handle outboard repairs, *Polymar* are the folks to contact for fiberglass repair and painting, for carpentry and custom woodworking try *Nautic-Bois*, while *Speedy Jet Services,* and *Yave Marine* can handle your engine repairs. *Yave* is also a *Mercury* dealer and can attend to your ailing outboard.

Propane
If you need propane you'll have to take a taxi to *Antilles Gas*, their phone number is 0596-50 33 30 (mornings only for tank refills) and they are located just north of *Cohé du Lamentin*.

Sails and Rigging
For sail and canvas repairs, try *Helenon* next to *Littoral*, a nice chandlery. To access the shop, take your dingy up the canal (to the west of the cruise ship docks) to *Helenon* and climb the ladder up the wall. For just canvas repairs you can also try *Captio-Land* or *Madinina Confection*. For rigging repairs try *Multicap Caraibes* or *Sea Services*.

Manu Voile is a sail loft with over 20 years of experience and they can handle repairs as well as new construction.

Welding and Fabrication

Mécanique Plaisance can handle all your fabrication and welding needs as well as your refrigeration repairs. Also available for fabrication and welding you can try *Polymar, Chalmessin,* or Jean-Michel Rolland who can work in aluminum and stainless steel (MIG and TIG). *Polymar* also fills SCUBA tanks.

Provisions

East of the area, where *Rue Victor Severe* reaches the *Rivière Madame,* you'll find the public fish market, *Marché aux Poissons,* standing in front of *Parc Floral Sermac.* Here a large complex of buildings and gardens offers you the opportunity to stroll through displays of indigenous flora as well as geographical structures, all surrounded by the hustle and bustle of nearby markets and vendors. In fact, the *Marché aux Légumes* is a huge produce market right next to the *Parc Floral.* Back toward the waterfront between *Rue Blenac* and *Rue Saint-Louis* is a huge covered market, *Marché Couvert,* where you can shop for crafts, food, flowers, as well as herbs and spices.

Other stops for provisions can be *Match* on *Rue de la République, Super H,* and the large *Euromarché* store in Dillon across from *SCIM* (northwest of *Cohé du Lamentin).* Just across the street from *Sea Services* is the *Leader Price* supermarket. Near the *Caren Antilles* yard is *The Caribbean Supplier,* the place to stock up on duty-free wines and spirits.

Dining

For dining, well, where do I begin? *Coco Loco, La Croisiere, Le Foyal, Lina's, La Cave a Vin, Aux Vieux Foyal, El Raco, La Cave à Vin, Le Terminal, Marie Saintes, Le Pub,* the *Soup Bar,* and the list is endless. Part of the fun of cruising is making the difficult decision of where to dine...enjoy yourselves, somewhere in Fort-de-France there is a restaurant that will satisfy your oddest cravings. At *Caren Antilles, Le Grand Voile* is open for lunch.

Discovering Fort-de-France

At the center of Fort-de-France lies *Place de la Savane,* the 12½-acre flower-filled waterfront park across *Boulevard Alfassa* (where the *Tourist Office* is) from the ferry docks at the end of *Baie des Flamands* as shown on Chart MAR-6. Surrounded by busy roadways and even busier vendors, the park offers a haven of quiet in bustling downtown Fort-de-France and is THE place to see and be seen, to relax, or just to sit and watch other people relaxing.

On the northern side of the park is a statue of Empress Joséphine bearing a locket containing the likeness of Napoléon. The one thing that you will notice about this 1859 statue is that it has no head. The figure was beheaded in September of 1991 during a period when islanders were protesting either Martinique's independence from France, or the Empress herself who is said to have influenced Napoléon to prolong slavery in France and her colonies to benefit her family's plantation. The statue was a gift from Napoléon III and is said to stand in the very spot where a cannon ball landed at the foot of the future Empress in 1790.

A bit to the west of the statue is a large open-air market where you can buy T-shirts, handicrafts, and all sorts of clothing. Here too is a statue commemorating Pierre Bélain d'Esnambuc, considered by some to be the founder of Martinique. A bit further on sits the *Monument aux Morts* that honors those Martinicians who fought for France in two World Wars. I think I'd better mention here that *Place de la Savane* is quite safe during the day, but your safety may be a concern after dark, use caution.

At the northeastern end of the park is the ornate, domed *Bibiothèque Schoelcher.* Built in Paris at the same time as the *Eiffel Tower,* it was dismantled and shipped to Martinique in 1893. Today the library houses some 20,000 books, 10,000 of which were donated to Martinique by French politician Victor Schoelcher in 1883, along with a request that a public library be founded. If you walk down *Rue de la Liberté* towards the waterfront you'll come to *Le Musée d'Archéologie* where you can view Carib and Arawakan artifacts in fine displays of Martinique's pre-Columbian history.

Just south of *Place de la Savane,* across *Boulevard Chevalier, Fort Saint-Louis* sits overlooking the waterfront on the point of land at the eastern end of *Baie des Flamands.* The site is the original location of *Fort Royal* built in 1638. The fort is still used by the military but you can take a guided tour (in French) from Tuesday through Saturday. Watch your head when walking through the fort, many doorways were lowered to frustrate British invaders.

Cohé du Lamentin

Waypoints:
Marina de Port Cohé- ¼ nm WNW of entrance
14º 35.75' N, 61º 01.30' W

Navigational Information

At the northeastern tip of *Baie de Fort-de-France* lies the anchorages of *Cohé du Lamentin* and the *Marina de Port Cohe* as shown on Chart MAR-5, with the entrance to the marina shown in detail on Chart MAR-7. The bay is sometimes used for hurricane protection, I would prefer the creeks off the bay instead. Entrance to the anchorage in *Cohé du Lamentin* is fairly easy as shown on Chart MAR-5. From the waypoint at the western end of *Baie de Fort-de-France* head a bit south of east until you can pick up the entrance channel buoys northeast of Pointe du Bout. Follow the channel into the bay keeping the red buoys to starboard and the green ones to port (but of course I didn't have to remind you of that now did I?).

If you are approaching from *Baie des Flamands* or *Baie des Tourelles*, give *Banc du Ft. St. Louis* a wide berth and keep well off the shoreline between Pointe des Carrières (Pte. des Grives) and Pointe des Sables. There is talk of a new, large marina being planned for the area between Pointe des Carrières (Pte. des Grives) and Pointe des Sables so keep an eye out for it. Once in *Cohé du Lamentin*, anchor wherever your draft allows, the water is not very clear here (with garbage often floating by) and the bottom muddy with holding that varies from poor to almost good. Keep a sharp eye our for the shoal shown as *Sèche San Justan* and the unmarked shoal just

north of it as well as any unmarked wrecks in the surrounding waters.

The best hurricane protection here is at *Marina de Port Cohé* and the channel next to it. To enter the channel leading to *Marina de Port Cohé* make for a waypoint at 14º 35.75' N, 61º 01.30' W, which will place you ¼ mile west/northwest of the entrance channel as shown on Chart MAR-7. As you approach the narrow and difficult to discern entrance, make sure that you keep the red buoy off Pointe Desgras (sometimes shown as Morne Rouge) to starboard and the conspicuous wrecked barge north of the entrance channel to port.

When entering favor the northern shore (keeping the red marker to starboard) and then, keeping mid-channel, you should not have a problem. The controlling depth here is a bit over 5½' at MLW. Fresh water is available at the marina (and sometimes slips) and the airport is less than 1½ miles away. The *Marina de Port Cohé* usually charges boats a fee to enter their channel during a hurricane and the waters there are always full.

There is another small marina in the extreme northern part of *Cohé du Lamentin*, *Marina La Neptune*. Primarily a sailing school, the marina offers absentee yacht owners a safe haven and somebody to tend their vessel while they are away; however the marina is usually filled with local vessels. As shown on Chart MAR-5, the marina lies just north of Pointe du Lamentin with a controlling depth of a bit less than 6'.

What You Will Find Ashore

On the main highway from Fort-de-France to Le Lamentin, *N1*, you will find the *Euromarché* supermarket in Dillon. *SCIM* is also located in Dillon across form the *Euromarché* supermarket and is a chandler as well as an *OMC* outboard dealer. Just south of *N1*, and north of *Cohé du Lamentin*, is *Antilles Gas* where you can get your propane tanks filled. If you need a mall fix, you'll certainly get one at *La Galleria*, just off *N1* north of *Cohé du Lamentin*. Located near the airport in Le Lamentin, *Martinique Diesel* is the place to go for diesel repairs. Nearby, *Atelier Sylvestre* (0596-50 23 63) makes hydraulic hoses while you wait.

In nearby *Rivière Salée* you can visit the huge chandler, *WIND*, *West Indies Nautic Distribution*. Specializing in boat building and repairing materials,

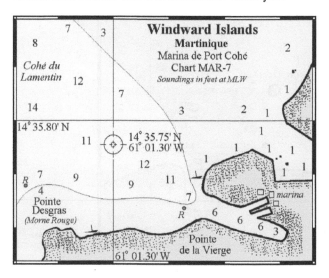

they will even deliver to your boat. Most chandlers in Fort-de-France will have a copy of their catalog available for you to look through. Upstairs from *WIND* is *Tech Sails*, a branch of *North Sails* of Point à Pitre, Guadeloupe.

Also in *Rivière Salée*, *ETPI* can handle your fabrication and welding needs as well as metal finishing such as galvanizing (anchors and chains), chrome plating, or polishing. *IBB, Industry Batiments and Bateau*, offers electronic and electrical repairs and they're mobile, owner Gottfried Strasser will drive to your boat to fix your problem.

Trois Îlets and Trou Etienne

Waypoints:
Trou Etienne- ¼ mile NNE of the entrance
14° 33.65' N, 61° 02.80' W

Trois Îlets- 1 nm NNW of
14° 33.60' N, 61° 01.95' W

Charming *Trois Îlets* takes its name from the *les Trois Îlets*, the three islands (Tébloux, Charles, and Sixtain, sometimes shown as Sistain) lying just offshore as shown on Chart MAR-8. This area was

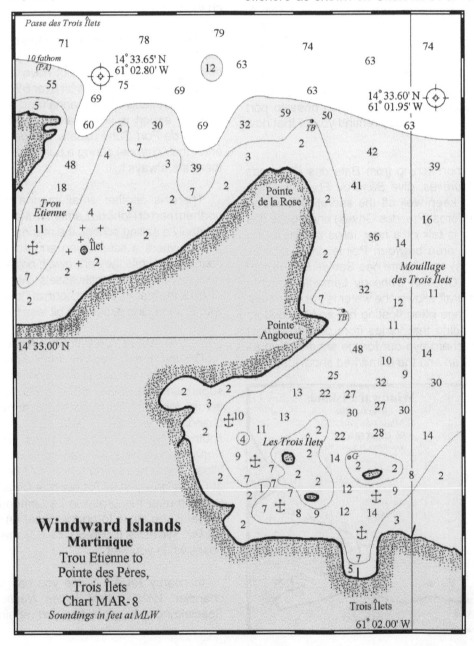

originally named *Cul-de-Sac-à-Vaches*, meaning *a barricade for cows*, when it was settled back in the late 1600s. Nearby Gros Îlet was once called *l'Îlet-à-Vaches*, or Cow Island.

Although *Trois Îlets* is known far and wide as a tourist haven famed for its stunning beach, the town has a surprisingly rural quality about it that is embodied by the quaint open-air market on the central square. Also on the square is the *Eglise Notre-Dame-de-la-Délivrance*, the *Church of Our Lady of Deliverance*, the site of the marriage of the parents of the Empress Joséphine as well as where the Empress herself was baptized on July 27, 1763. Inside the church is the original baptismal font as well as a painting, *The Assumption*, donated by Joséphine's grandson, Louis. Also in town is the pottery village and the sugarcane museum, *Maison de la Canne*, just east of town on road *D7*. This old rum factory has been restored and the displays are both in French and English.

One of the more interesting displays is the *Code Noir*, or *Black Code*, which dictated proper conduct between slaves and whites in the plantation era. *The Pottery Village*, *Le Village de la Poterie*, sits about ½ mile past the museum and has been producing bricks for homes and buildings on Martinique since the 1700s.

West of *Trois Îlets*, off highway *D7*, lies the small town of *Domaine de la Pagerie*, the birthplace of Empress Joséphine. You can visit the small stone house that once was the kitchen for the Tascher de la Pagerie estate and which today holds many of Empress Joséphine's possessions including furniture and pictures and letters from her husband, Napoléon. Another worthwhile visit here is the botanical gardens, *Le Parc Naturel des Floralies*. Here you can view over 100 types of flowers set about in small gardens with a lake, an aquarium, an open-air theater, and an aviary to keep your interest from waning.

Navigational Information
From the waypoint at the western end of *Baie de Fort-de-France* as shown on Chart MAR-5, you can head for a position north of Pointe du Bout from which you can make your way eastward passing north of Pointe du Bout, *Trou Etienne*, and Pointe de la Rose keeping the black and yellow buoys to starboard. A waypoint at 14° 33.65' N, 61° 02.80' W, will place you approximately ¼ mile north/northeast of the entrance to *Trou Etienne* where you can anchor in deep water

west of the tiny island called Îlet as shown on Chart MAR-8. This is a wonderfully protected anchorage in nearly all conditions except when the wind is strong out of the north through east when the anchorage gets very choppy due to the fetch.

Both the anchorage at *Trou Etienne* and the one at *Trois Îlets* are perfect for those times when northerly swells make other anchorages such as *Anse Mitan* untenable. The moorings you see near shore are private and you'll need to anchor so as to clear these should their owners come home to roost.

Heading to *Trois Îlets* from Point du Bout, head north of Point du Bout and Pointe de la Rose (give this point a wide berth) as shown on Chart MAR-8, to a waypoint at 14° 33.60' N, 61° 01.95' W, which will place you approximately 1 mile north/northwest of the anchorage areas at *Trois Îlets*.

From this waypoint, head south until you can pass between the easternmost of *les Trois Îlets* and the other two (keeping the green marker to port as you head south) where the deeper water lies. Anchor wherever your draft allows, west of the two islands, or even in the small cove off town. Another option is to parallel the shoreline from Pointe Angbœuf southwestward to anchor off the westernmost of *les Trois Îlets*. On the point to the west is a Trent Jones designed golf course situated southwest of Pointe Angbœuf.

What You Will Find Ashore
Internet
Alphatext (located at *2 Rue Papin Dupont*) has internet access and they're open from 0800-1230 and 1400-1700 weekdays, and 0830-1230 on Saturdays. *Alphatext* is closed on Sundays and Wednesday afternoons.

Provisions
In Trois Îlets there is an open-air market in the square and to the left of the church is a grocery store, *Chez Zozime*. Next to the church is a bakery, and, if you head out of town on the road to *Rivière Salée*, you'll find a nice little butcher shop.

Dining
You can dine at *Le Boucaut* in a large airy pavilion where you must walk past a waterfall and over a small bridge to be seated. The restaurant offers theme night buffets or an *à la carte* menu. Another good spot for dining out is *Les Passages du Vent* with its

ever-changing art exhibits. For pizza try *Aux Trois* which sits just across the road from *Les Passages du Vent*. Nearer the water, *Bomaki* offers good local dishes and live music several nights a week.

The *Fleur de Sel* is open for dinner Monday-Saturday from 1930-2230. Their fare is very good and the ambiance equal to their cuisine. For Creole fare try *Dadou et Andrea* (closed Sundays).

Garbage
There are trash bins at both ends of the Trois Ilets waterfront.

Marine Facilities
Sail Repair
Those in need of sail work can visit *Voilerie Caraibes Martinique* in Trou Etienne at the *Somatras Marina* complex. They monitor VHF ch. 16 and can construct or repair any sail or bimini. You can access the sail loft by dinghy, their dock is in Trou Etienne.

Anse Mitan and Pointe du Bout

Waypoints:
Anse Mitan- ½ nm NNW of
14° 33.80' N, 61° 03.50' W

Jutting out into Baie de Fort-de-France, the peninsula called Pointe du Bout is the tourist capital of Martinique, and it may well be the cruiser's capital as well, *Anse Mitan* is an extremely popular anchorage. Let's begin with Pointe du Bout and then explore *Anse Mitan*.

Navigational Information
As shown on Chart MAR-9, a waypoint at 14° 33.80' N, 61° 03.50' W, will place you approximately ½ mile north/northwest of *Anse Mitan* and just west of the tip of Pointe du Bout. From the waypoint you can head generally east to anchor off Pointe du Bout in the lee of the land and the shoal that works northward from the point. This anchorage can be a bit rolly at times. If you're not comfortable here you can head north around Pointe du Bout to enter the marina from the north, or head south passing between the marina dock and *Caye de l'Anse Mitan* to anchor off *Anse Mitan* proper taking care not to anchor in the ferry lanes or in the swimming area directly off the beach.

To enter *Somatras Marina* at Pointe du Bout, sometime shown as *Marina Pointe du Bout,* give them a shout first on VHF ch. 09 to check on the

availability of berthing. The entrance, as shown on Chart MAR-9, is from the north. From the waypoint west of Pointe du Bout, head eastward around the northern tip of Pointe du Bout giving the shoal that lies off the point a wide berth. Here you'll see a yellow and black buoy, *GBB*, you can pass inside the buoy, but not too far inside, but it's better to go north of the buoy for safety's sake. Once past the buoy you'll see the marina entrance open up to starboard. When

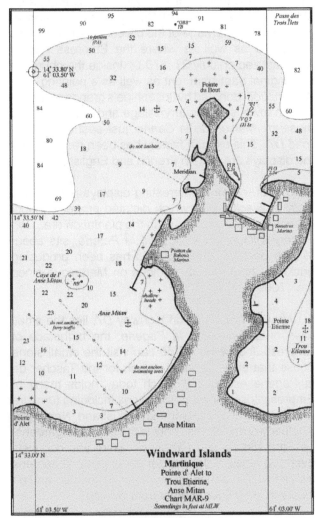

The anchorage at *Anse Mitan*

you can clear the other yellow and black buoy, *B1*, that sits just east of Pointe du Bout to starboard, turn southward to enter the marina between the red and green marks.

The marina is small and there's not a lot of room to maneuver so it's best to know where you're going before entering; entering the marina the first dock to starboard is reserved for ferries.

West of the peninsula, and on the route to *Anse Mitan*, lies a large reef marked by a red and black buoy. The reef is shown on Chart MAR-9 as *Caye de l'Anse Mitan*, but it is shown on some charts as *Caye des Couillons*, or *Idiot's Reef*. This reef is easily seen in good light and just as easily avoided. If you are planning to anchor in *Anse Mitan* you can pass between the reef and *Ponton du Bakoua* marina or pass west of the reef heading down the marked ferry lanes towards the dock. Anchor north of the dock and designated swimming area that is sometimes marked, sometimes not. Holding is good here in sand, but there are a few isolated coral patches that you'll have to avoid dropping the hook atop.

What You Will Find Ashore
Now let's discuss what facilities we'll find in this area starting with the area around *Somatras Marina* and working our way southward to *Anse Mitan*.

Customs and *Immigration*
Cruisers are able to clear using the computer at the *Customs* office at the *Somatras Marina* office (open from 0900-1230 and 1500-1800 on weekdays, and from 0900-1200 on Saturdays).

Internet
The Laundromat at *Village Creole*, *Laverie Prolavnet*, has an internet access computer. Two eateries, *Pizza Place* (behind the beach) and *Le Marine* offer Internet access.

Marine Facilities
Marinas
Somatras Marina (*Marina Pte. du Bout*; VHF ch. 09) is a small marina that offers stern-to berthing with full electric, water, garbage bins, shower facilities, mail service, weather forecasts, laundry service, phone and fax service, a car rental, a sail loft, a small market, and numerous shops and restaurants. The complex surrounding the *Somatras Marina* houses most of the marine services in the area.

Sail Repair
Those in need of sail work can visit *Voilerie Caraibes Martinique* at the *Somatras Marina* complex. They monitor VHF ch. 16 and can construct or repair any sail or bimini.

Mechanical Repairs
For diesel engine or generator sales or repairs, visit *Mécanique Plaisance* on the western side of the *Somatras Marina* complex. *Mécanique Plaisance* is a dealer for *Yanmar*, *Volvo-Penta*, *Perkins*, and *Westerbeke* generators, as well as a chandlery and a fully equipped machine shop.

Electric and Electronic Repairs
Croiseres & Assistance monitors VHF ch. 16 and they're located on the eastern side of the marina complex. This is the place to go for electronic and electrical repairs as well as engines.

Provisions
For groceries while at the marina, try *Bora Bora*, a nice little grocery and deli with an in-house butcher shop, they'll deliver to your dock. For fresh produce, visit *Jardin Créole* near the beach. For delivery to your dock, contact the local *8 à Huit*, the best supermarket in the area. Nearby, *La Baguette* offers freshly baked goods.

Dining
In Pointe du Bout try *L'Embarcadère* for light snacks, they're at the ferry docks or *Delifrance* on the main road into Pointe du Bout for pastries, breads, and sandwiches. You can get ice cream (and breakfast) at *Boule de Neige* located near *Délifrance*. In the marina area try *La Marine* for good steaks and seafood. If your appetite is hearty enough, you can also try *Davidiana* and *Chez Gilles* also near the marina. For a more upscale experience visit *La Manureva*.

Near the entrance to the *Boukoua Hotel* is *The Cotton Club*, both a restaurant and a nightclub for those inclined for a full night out. If you have a more elegant, and expensive evening in mind, try the more cosmopolitan *Châteaubriand Restaurant* which is only open for dinner. Tuesdays there is a steel band performing and Saturday is *Salsa Night*. The *Casino du Méridien* features the *La Braka* discotheque for those cruisers with happy feet that need to dance. The *Corossol* on the road just outside Pointe du Bout, specializes in crepes and salads.

Between *Somatras Marina* and *Anse Mitan* are several nice restaurants. *Au Poisson d'Or*, extremely popular with locals as well as tourists, showcases waitresses in traditional dress serving up excellent grilled meats and more at reasonable prices. Just down the road from *La Poisson d'Or* is *Chez Fanny* where owner Fanny will welcome you into her casual restaurant.

Right on the beach near the ferry landing at *Anse Mitan* is *La Langouste*, the place for langouste (lobster). Just across from La Langouste is *Le Régal de la Mer*, THE place for prime rib in *Anse Mitan*. In the *Eden Hotel* is *L'Éden* with terrace dining right on the beach. One of *Anse Mitan*'s nicest restaurants is *La Bonne Auberge* with its long bar and wooden furniture, it definitely has atmosphere.

Hemingway's is a pub-style restaurant owned by a Texan named Hemingway who is known by his nickname, Ernest. It sits right on the water and features a hot and cold buffet. *La Villa Creole* offers

candlelit tables that provide the ambiance while owner Guy Dawson provides the entertainment with his guitar. Also, right on the beach is *Barracuda* with loud music every night. The *Caryou Hotel* has a wonderful breakfast buffet in their restaurant. Somewhat off the beach is *Restaurant Cannelle* located in the *Alamandas Hotel*. At the *Bambou,* a hotel that will remind you of a campground, there is live music every night for dinner at the hotel's restaurant.

Near the *Bokoua* complex, is *Le Village Créole*, a made-to-order small French hamlet just over a decade old. This tiny fantasy town is full of Parisian type sidewalk cafés and ultra-chic boutiques.

Anse à l'Âne

Waypoints:
Anse à l'Âne- ½ nm NW of anchorage
14° 33.20' N, 61° 04.50' W

Anse à l'Âne is a wonderful anchorage not far

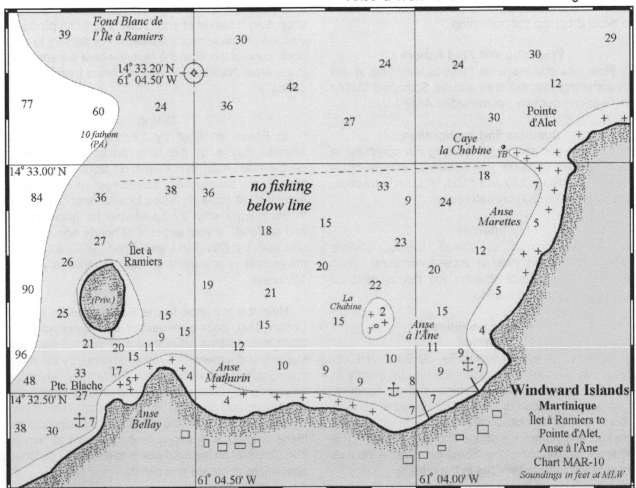

from *Anse Mitan*. Hurry and visit this place while it is still somewhat unspoiled, the area is quickly being developed and losing its wild charm as is evidenced by the large hotels now located here. The lovely beach is not busy during the week, but on the weekend it's another story.

Navigational Information

As shown on Chart MAR-5, it is located at the southwestern end of *Baie de Fort-de-France*. A waypoint at 14° 33.20' N, 61° 04.50' W, will place you approximately ½ mile northwest of the anchorage as shown in detail on Chart MAR-10. The only danger here is the large reef, *La Chabine*, that lies in the middle of the entrance to the bay. The reef is easily seen and avoided and is evident by a yellow marker; the reef can be passed on either side. Anchor north or south of the town docks, but leave the docks open for the ferries.

If you are approaching *Anse à l'Âne* from south of *Baie de Fort-de-France*, you can pass either north of Îlet à Ramiers or between the island and the mainland at *Anse Bellay* in 9'-15' of water. As shown on Chart MAR-10, you can anchor in a small cove west of *Anse Bellay* and Pointe Blanche in settled conditions. It is also possible to anchor in the lee of Îlet à Ramiers in an emergency, but fishing and landing ashore is prohibited. Ashore are the ruins of an old fort and the entire island belongs to the French navy.

What You Will Find Ashore

Please note that fishing is not permitted south of the line shown on Chart MAR-10. To venture into town you can tie your dinghy to the town's dinghy dock or at the inner end of the ferry dock (please do not block the ferries).

Garbage

Trash receptacles are located at the car park in town.

Fuel

There is a gas station on the main road in town, you'll have to jerry jug your fuel.

Provisions

There is a branch of *8 à Huit* in town for all your provisioning needs. They're open from 0800-2000 daily except Sundays when they are open from 0800-1300. Nearby is *Pomme Canelle*, a produce market that also sells smoked meats and flowers.

Dining

Chez JoJo run by Mama Joséphine, is a popular beach restaurant that is known for its festive Friday night feasts with a *zouk* band. Saturday is barbeque night and Sunday is the day for grilled lobster. Next door is *Pignon sur Mer,* a bit quieter than *JoJo's* with moderately priced Creole meals. Right on the beach is *Épi Soleil* for burgers and casual fare, and *Le Nid Tropical* for your typical beach-shack fare with your not-so-typical pastries. A bit off the beach sits *Reflet du Mer*, *Ti Calebasse* for seafood, and a pair of *Chez Ginettes'*.

Anse Noire and Anse Dufour

Waypoints:
Anse Noire- ¼ nm NW of anchorage
14° 31.80' N, 61° 05.50' W

Navigational Information

Leaving *Baie de Fort-de-France* behind and heading southward along the western shore of Martinique once again, the first anchorage of note that you will come to is *Anse Noire*. As shown on Chart MAR-11, a waypoint at 14° 31.80' N, 61° 05.50' W, will place you approximately ¼ mile northwest of the anchorage in the small cove at *Anse Noire* with the small black sand beach line with coconut palms and set among the surrounding hills.

Just south, around the corner you might say and not shown on the chart, is the lovely anchorage at *Anse Dufour*, sometimes shown as *Anse Blanche*. This is a pleasant enough anchorage, but it can be rolly and you'll have to deal with the fishing boats (for that reason most cruisers will anchor in *Anse Noire* and dinghy over for exploration.

What You Will Find Ashore

The anchorage at *Anse Noire* is often busy during the day and weekends, but at night it will be much quieter. Highway access is not difficult, there is a trail that leads up to the main road. On the beach you can dine at *L'Anse Noire* where you'll sit at long wooden tables eating fresh fish under the trees, one of the most unusual settings on the island.

Anse Dufour has a unique golden sand beach scattered with fisherman's huts. For dining in *Anse Dufour*, try the *Sable d'Or* restaurant, an inexpensive place to get good food, or the more moderately priced *Snack Chez Nini* right on the beach. To find *Sable*

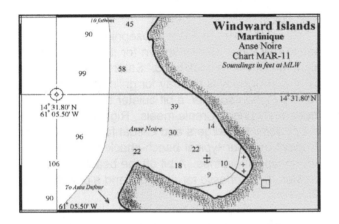

Windward Islands
Martinique
Anse Noire
Chart MAR-11
Soundings in feet at MLW

Anse Noir

Grande Anse d'Arlet

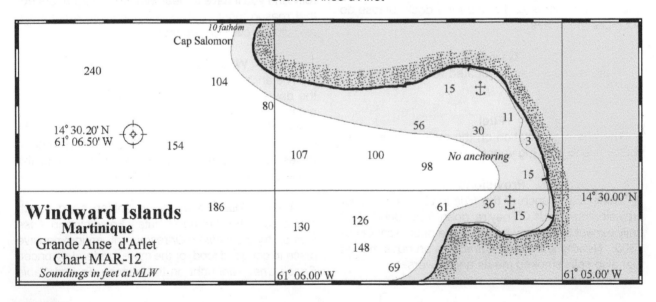

Windward Islands
Martinique
Grande Anse d'Arlet
Chart MAR-12
Soundings in feet at MLW

d'Or, climb the steps up the cliff, walk about a hundred yards or so down the road, and they'll be on your left. Another fine option is *Chez Marie Jo* (closed Sundays).

Grande Anse d'Arlet

Waypoints:
Grande Anse d'Arlet- 1 nm W of anchorage
14° 30.02' N, 61° 06.50' W

Navigational Information
When heading southward along this section of Martinique's leeward coast, you must beware of the strong currents (2-3 knots) that run off Cap Solomon (named after a Carib Indian chief), just north of *Grande Anse d'Arlet*. Just south of Cap Solomon you will find a trio of delightful anchorages, *Grande Anse d'Arlet* and *Petite Anse d'Arlet*, and the small anchorage at the southern end of *Petite Anse d'Arlet* called *Anse Chaudière,* all of whom share access to the town called Anses d'Arlet that sits inland between Grande and *Petite Anse d'Arlet*. The area was named after a Carib Indian chief named Arlet who negotiated a pact with Governor du Parquet in 1637 in which he ceded all land north of here for settlement.

As shown on Chart MAR-12, a waypoint at 14° 30.02' N, 61° 06.50' W, will place you approximately 1 mile west of the anchorage at *Grande Anse d'Arlet*. From the waypoint head into the bay and anchor in the southeastern end avoiding the small but shallow shoal that is shown on the chart. You may also anchor in the northern end of the bay, but you must keep the center open for the ferry and the local fishermen who always seem at odds with the cruisers.

What You Will Find Ashore
Quiet during the week, *Grand Anse d'Arlet* is full of families on the weekend enjoying the beach that is dotted with snack vendors and small homes. Vacation homes are springing up everywhere and the area is fast becoming one of the most popular resort areas on Martinique. Snorkelers will enjoy the diving on the southern edge of *Grand Anse d'Arlet* and along the shore between *Grande Anse d'Arlet* and *Petite Anse d'Arlet*.

Customs and Immigration
At the head of the town dock is *Le P'ti Bateau*, a restaurant that is home to a *Customs* computer so that cruisers can clear in and out from 0930-1800 daily. The restaurant also has a water hose that will reach down the dock if you require a tank fill.

Internet
Once again, *Le P'ti Bateau* is the place to go for Internet access. *Kay Zaza* yacht service center has Internet, Wi-fi, fax, laundry, and telephones.

Marine Facilities
Marine Services
For refrigeration work visit *Fraicheur Service* (0696-82 24 04). For outboard repairs, ask for Roby Mechanic or phone him at 0696-98 59 37.

My first stop when here is always *Tursiops Caraibes*. This wonderful little shop offers a book swap and a laundry service. But more than that, *Tursiops Caraibes* is an art gallery of sorts showcasing works of the owner, Daniel, and other local artists and craftspeople.

Provisions
In town there are several small grocery stores such as *Épicerie Deloy*.

Dining
Dining in *Grande Anse d'Arlet*, like anywhere in Martinique, presents no problems. A good rule of thumb here, as well as in *Petite Anse d'Arlet,* is to follow the main road along the beach to the eateries.

Again, right at the dock is *Le P'ti Bateau*, a great place to enjoy a meal and certainly easy to find. The *Ti-Sable* restaurant is located at the north end of the beach at *Grande Anse d'Arlet* and is considered the best restaurant in the area; don't miss their Sunday night Creole buffet. Also at the northern end of the beach is *Quai Sud* with its unique *Coco Bar* that is shaped like a fishing boat. For those on a budget, try *Les Délices des Anses*, *Bidjoul* (for good salads and fresh fish), *À l'Ombre des Cocotiers*, *l'Abrepain*, or the *Tamarin Plage* restaurant whose house special you will discover the moment you view the huge lobster tank in the middle of the room.

Petite Anse d'Arlet, and Anse Chaudière

Waypoints:
Petite Anse d'Arlet- ½ nm W of anchorage
14° 29.30' N, 61° 05.50' W

Anse Chaudière- ½ nm W of anchorage
14° 28.85' N, 61° 05.50' W

Navigational Information

Petite Anse d'Arlet lies just south of *Grande Anse d'Arlet* and a waypoint at 14° 29.30' N, 61° 05.50' W, will place you approximately ½ mile west of the anchorage as shown on Chart MAR-13. From the waypoint head east to anchor off the town in the northern part of the bay. The southern part of the bay is called *Anse Chaudière* and a waypoint at 14° 28.85' N, 61° 05.50' W, will place you approximately ½ mile west of the anchorage as shown the chart. From this waypoint, head east to anchor at the southern end of the bay. The anchorages here can be a bit rolly at times.

What You Will Find Ashore

Petite Anse d'Arlet, sometimes shown as Anse d'Arlet, is a lovely little town and you may tie off to the town dock to access the shoreside facilities such as the *Post Office*, restaurants, boutiques, and a pharmacy.

For dining try *Snack Mac Roger* on the beach, or *Chez Laura* at the eastern end of the beach. Lying between *Grande Anse d'Arlet* and *Petite Anse d'Arlet*, and actually closer to *Petite Anse d'Arlet*, is *Le Fatzo*. Located in a large blue-shuttered white house, here you can feast on entrees ranging from the plain to the exotic.

Anses d'Arlet lies just inland from *Petite Anse d'Arlet*, and here you can visit *Flamboyant des Isles* where you will dine on the terrace under the Poinciana trees with scenic views of the Caribbean; don't miss their Sunday Creole lunch buffet. *L'Hippocampe* features a fun Saturday night with live music and seafood.

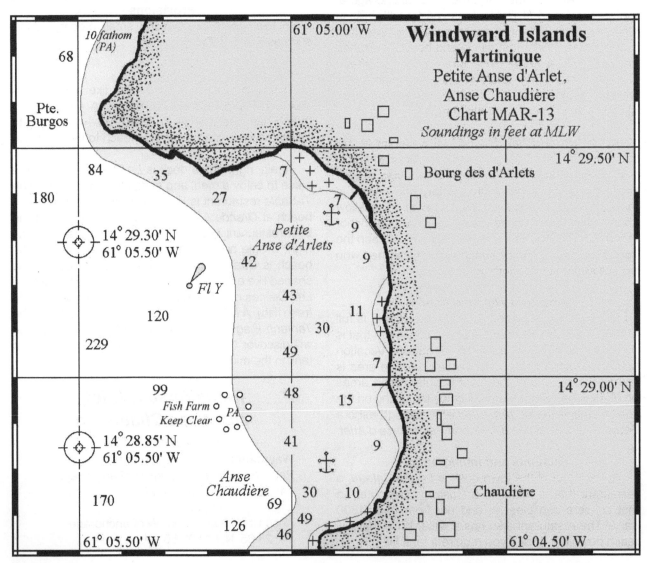

The Southern Coast of Martinique

Heading southward along the leeward coast of Martinique cruisers have the option of continuing across the *St. Lucia Channel* to *Rodney Bay,* Castries, or *Marigot Bay* in St. Lucia, or turning eastward after rounding Pointe du Diamant as shown on Chart MAR-1 to visit the anchorages along the southern shore of Martinique, particularly Ste. Anne and Le Marin, the cruising capital of Martinique. With the exception of Ste. Anne and Le Marin, the anchorages mentioned here will require a good eye, even better visibility, and an experienced skipper who is careful around reefs and knows not to try to shoot a tricky entrance with large following seas.

Navigational Information

Once you have cleared Point du Diamant you can head eastward, against the wind and the usually strong current, between the mainland of Martinique and Diamond Rock in *Passe des Fours.* It is best to do this leg in the early morning hours before the trade winds build.

Le Rocher du Diamant, Diamond Rock, is an unmistakable, huge 573' high chunk of limestone with an interesting history. During the Napoléonic wars, the British navy, led by Admiral Samuel Hood, landed 100 sailors on the rock in 1804. Diamond Rock was fortified with cannons and registered as a warship, the *HMS Diamond Rock,* a truly unsinkable vessel. The British had constructed a munitions depot, a dock, a

cistern, and even a hospital on the rock, and from here the crew of 107 men were able to control all traffic in the area and even managed to enforce a blockade of Martinique for almost 18 months. Frustrated, the French decided to attack Diamond Rock and began by floating several barrels of rum over to their foes.

To make a long story short, the British sailors, as any sailor probably would, imbibed heavily to the point that the invading French forces, along with a Spanish fleet, were able to oust them from their fortifications and take Diamond Rock on June 1, 1805. The hung over British sailors fled to Barbados and were summarily court-martialed for deserting their ship. And today, whenever a British vessel passes Diamond Rock, the crew stands at attention and salutes the rock. Diamond Rock is popular with divers because of the submerged caves and tunnels at its base.

Baie du Marigot

Waypoints:
Baie du Marigot- ¾ nm S of entrance
14° 27.40' N, 61° 00.25' W

As you head eastward along the southern shore of Martinique, the first cove to offer an anchorage, albeit a rolly one, is *Baie du Marigot* as shown on Chart MAR-13 and sometimes shown as Marigot du Diamant. Do not confuse *Baie du Marigot* with *Marigot Bay,* which lies much farther to the south on the western shore of St. Lucia.

Navigational Information
As shown on the chart, a waypoint at 14° 27.40' N, 61° 00.25' W, will place you approximately ¾ mile south

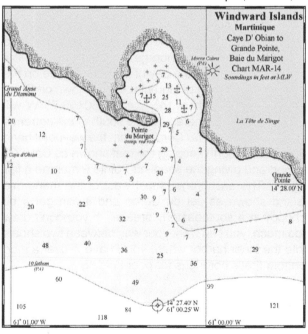

Le Rocher du Diamant (Diamond Rock)

of the tricky entrance into the bay. As you approach this waypoint you'll need to keep on its latitude or south of it to avoid *Caye d'Obian*, a large reef, lying well to the northwest of the waypoint (see Chart MAR-1 and MAR-14). From the waypoint the entrance will take careful piloting as you head northward in a narrow channel with shoals close aboard both sides and stretching up to ½ mile offshore.

As you approach the entrance avoid the large shoal to starboard as you try to keep in about 5 fathoms as the deeper water doglegs to the northeast and then to the north between the shoals. Jerôme Nouel, in his excellent *Cruising Guide To Martinique* (in French and English), suggests that incoming vessels steer 25° True on the conspicuous summit of *Morne Cabrit* to pass between the reefs until past Pointe du Marigot. I prefer to be able to see the reefs and pilot accordingly, the choice is yours.

Once inside anchor wherever your draft allows though most boats tend to anchor on the western side of the bay off the resort. I must remind you that this can be a very rolly anchorage so you might have to set a stern anchor or a bridle.

What You Will Find Ashore
On the western shore is the hotel *Novotel le Diamant* where you'll find several nice shops and places to eat, *Le Famboyant*, *La Cabana du Pécheur*, *Les Alizés*, and the hotel's poolside café. You can tie up at the resort dock and fill up a jerry jug with water.

The town of Le Diamant lies less than two miles to the west along the coast road and here you can pick up groceries at *8 à Huit* at the eastern edge of town by the *Esso* station or dine at the award-winning *Diamant Les Bains* restaurant or at *Le Diam's* where reservations are required well in advance.

Pointe Giroud

Waypoints:
Pointe Giroud anchorage- ½ nm S of entrance
14° 27.45' N, 60° 59.25' W

Navigational Information
Heading eastward from *Baie du Marigot* you will have your choice of four anchorages between Grande Pointe and *Anse Mabouyas* as shown on Chart MAR-15. All these anchorages will require good piloting skills, good light and visibility, and they

are not recommended for novices or those not used to working their way around reefs.

The first anchorage to the east of *Baie du Marigot* lies just west of Pointe Giroud as shown on Chart MAR-15. A waypoint at 14° 27.45' N, 60° 59.25' W, will place you approximately ½ mile south of the entrance channel into the Pointe Giroud anchorage. From the waypoint head generally northward into the cut that leads to the small bay; stay mid-channel and keep the reef shown as *Caye Oli* to starboard and stay.

As Pointe Giroud approaches your beam to starboard, you'll need to slow down and keep your eyes open to pilot through the gap between two shoals and into the harbor. You won't be able to take the big boat too far into the bay as the water shoals rapidly, but you'll find shelter in the lee of Pointe Giroud. This anchorage will be choppy in a southeast breeze, but in a northeasterly wind it is very comfortable.

What You Will Find Ashore
The shore surrounding the anchorage is all privately owned and landing is not permitted without invitation. You can however, take your dinghy up the river to the small town of Taupinière.

Anse du Céron

Waypoints:
Anse du Céron- ½ nm S of entrance channel
14° 27.45' N, 60° 58.75' W

Navigational Information
Just around the corner from the Pointe Giroud anchorage sits the anchorage at *Anse du Céron*, not to be confused with the bay of the same name on the northwestern coast of Martinique. As shown on Chart MAR-14, a waypoint at 14° 27.45' N, 60° 58.75' W, will place you approximately ½ mile south of the entrance channel into *Anse du Céron*. From the waypoint head a bit west of north keeping the reef shown as *Caye Oli* to port and giving the shoal off Pointe Pimentée a fair berth. The anchorage is just west of the mangrove island shown as Îlet du Céron and it can get a bit choppy in a southeasterly breeze. If you don't draw too much, you can work your way between two shoals into the inner harbor where you'll have 7' over a mud bottom that's notorious for poor holding.

Trois Rivières

Waypoints:
Anse de Trois Rivières- ¼ nm S of entrance
14° 27.45' N, 60° 58.30' W

Navigational Information

Still heading eastward along the southern shore, the next anchorage is off *Trois Rivières* as shown on Chart MAR-15. A waypoint at 14° 27.45' N, 60° 58.30' W, will place you approximately ¼ mile south of the entrance channel leading into the anchorage off the town of *Trois Rivières*, and gaining entry to the anchorage is a tricky piloting job in anybody's book. From the waypoint head east of north keeping the shoals of *Caye Mocos* to port, and the reef shown as *Caye du Gros Raisin* to starboard. As Pointe Pimentée approaches your port beam you'll be steering more towards the northeast and then east avoiding the shoals off the Pointe (and the northern part of the harbor) and the large reef to starboard, passing between the two to anchor north of the reef just off the town.

There is a small rock jetty at the northeastern end of the harbor and you can tie up the dinghy here to explore. About ½ mile north of the anchorage is a small rum distillery, *Trois Rivières*, and visitors are welcome to take a tour, indulge in some free samples (white rums with a unique vanilla flavor), and get a chance to learn about the history of this particular *rhumerie*. It was here that King Louis XIV's *Minister of Finance* built a superb château using funds he had embezzled. When the King found out what had occurred he had the Minister's villa destroyed. On the road to the distillery is the *Art et Nature* studio, where a couple of local artists explain how their particular style of painting is created exclusively from over 130 types of sand from the beaches of Martinique from which 230 earth-tone colors are derived. From *Trois Rivières* take the road to Monésie to a gourmet restaurant, *La Corniche,* in the hotel of the same name. Here you can dine on exquisite entrees with scenic views of the surrounding hills and Diamond Rock in the distance.

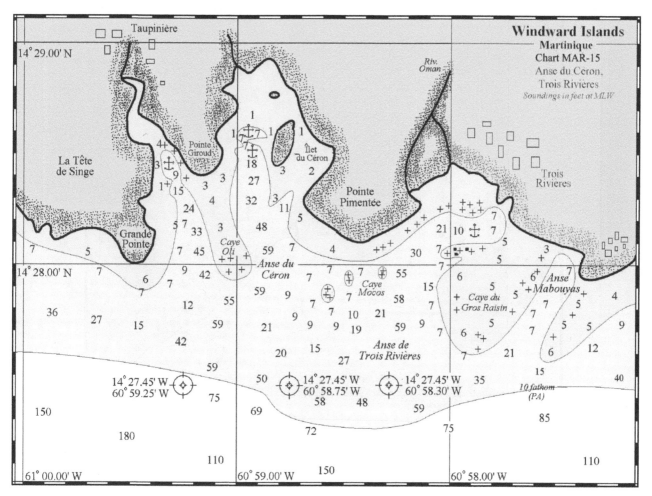

The next bay to the east, *Anse Mabouyas*, is sometimes occupied by a cruising boat seeking a lee behind the point. However the entrance can be tricky as you thread the needle between two reefs and I don't recommend the passage.

Ste. Luce

Waypoints:
Ste. Luce- ¾ nm S of anchorage
14º 27.00' N, 60º 55.00' W

Ste. Luce has had a difficult past. In 1693, British troops invaded the hamlet setting fire to it and causing most of the residents to flee into the surrounding hills. In 1817, a hurricane devastated the town and recovery took a long time. Ste. Luce is dependent on her fishing and tourism industry, and today Ste. Luce is rapidly developing into a major tourist haven and so popular a destination that the normal population of 5,000 doubles during summer holiday.

Navigational Information
Before I begin the section on Ste. Luce, let me explain that fishing in the area from the green buoy MA2 south of Pointe Borgnesse, to the yellow buoy lying southwest of Grande Caye de Ste. Luce to the southern shore of Martinique is prohibited.

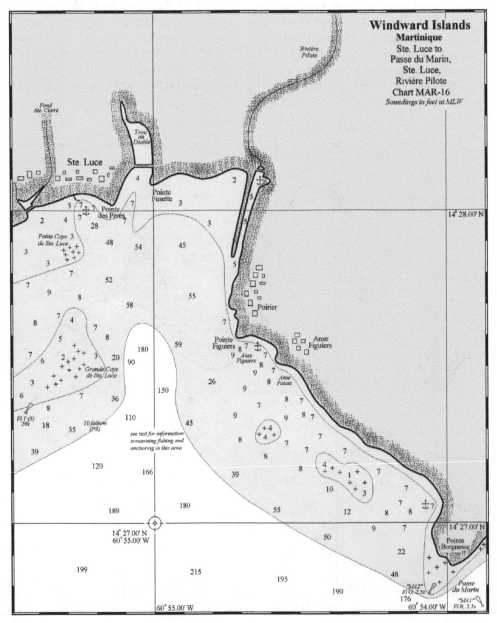

As shown on Chart MAR-16, a waypoint at 14° 27.00' N, 60° 55.00' W, will place you approximately ¾ mile south of the anchorage off Ste. Luce as shown on Chart MAR-16. From the waypoint head northward keeping the large reef, *Grande Caye de Ste. Luce* to port staying mid-channel between the reef and Pointe Figuiers to the east. Once abeam of Pointe Figuiers you can turn towards the northwest a bit, toward town, keeping the reef shown as *Petite Caye de Ste. Luce* to port as you anchor just off the town dock. This anchorage is not the place to be in a southeasterly breeze, but it can be quite comfortable in anything from west through north to northeast.

Small, shallow draft sailboats can proceed up the *Rivière Pilote* to anchor in the small basin just south of the bridge as shown on Chart MAR-16. The basin is usually full of local boats and the depths in the river range from almost 5' at the mouth of the river to a bit over 6' at the basin. Vessels can also anchor in Anse Figuiers just off the lovely beach, but here again, this is not the place to be in a southeasterly breeze (the snorkeling is very good off Pointe Figuiers). Another option is to anchor in the lee of Pointe Bornesse as shown on the chart although this anchorage gets a bit rolly in a southeasterly breeze as well; it's best to anchor here in northeast through east winds.

What You Will Find Ashore
You can tie your dinghy to the town dock to explore or avail yourself of the facilities ashore. Here you'll find two pharmacies, a laundry, several markets, a free health center, and even a shop that rents windsurfing gear, this area is very popular with the windsurfing crowd.

In Ste. Luce you can grab a bite to eat at *Palmier Chez Suzette*, the tiny kiosk near the health center that serves up the best fritters. For the heartier appetite, try *Épi Soleil* located along the waterfront where you can eat under a huge awning near the fishing fleet; check out their Friday and Saturday night barbecues. If you're in the mood for pizza you're in luck; *Pizzeria Slaac*, which is really more of a take-out than an eat-in, is the place to stop and pick from over a dozen different types of pizza. *La Casa Pepe* is actually two experiences in one; the front room is a nice restaurant, while the back room is a laid-back bar with a younger clientele. Here you can choose from three different buffets, a cold buffet, a hot buffet, and a dessert buffet, the choice is yours.

In the center of town is *La Terrasse Chez Aglaé*, an unpretentious place with plain old good food. For seafood on the shore, try *La Vague du Sud*, an upstairs restaurant with a great view of the harbor and very good seafood, or the intimate *Kai Armande*, which also doubles as an art gallery.

A very interesting eatery lies west of town on the road to Gros Raisins, where you'll see a huge transparent tent, this is the restaurant *Le Coup de Canon*. Once you've visited this place, you'll want to return for the food, the friendly service, and the unique ambiance.

A good place to stop while in the area is the *Forêt de Montravail*, just north of town on *D17*. The forest here is home to a collection of stones engraved with Arawak petroglyphs, the only petroglyphs on this side of Martinique. The site is on private property and permission must be granted before you can visit these unique stones. Organized walks through the forest begin every day except Sunday at 0930 originating from Ste. Luce.

The lovely beach at *Anse Figuiers* is a family oriented beach as the signs prohibiting nudity will attest. Here too is a small museum, the *Écomusée de la Martinique*. Located in an old rhumerie, this two story museum houses artifacts and displays depicting periods of Martinician history from Arawakan times through the plantation period and the small gift shop sells locally made crafts.

Ste. Anne

Waypoints:
Ste. Anne- 1 nm SW of
14° 26.00' N, 60° 54.10' W

Cul-de-Sac du Marin and the anchorage off the town of Ste. Anne are the most popular anchorages along any of Martinique's coasts with the inner harbor off the town of Le Marin being THE most popular. The harbor, though beset with shoals, is well marked for day or night usage though I don't recommend transiting the channel at night.

The long beach at Ste. Anne is marvelous; white sand, clear water, palm trees, the perfect recipe for Caribbean paradise, and you have your choice of three anchorages here, off the town, off the beach, or off Anse Caritan near the *Anchorage Hotel* (halfway between Ste. Anne and Pointe Dunkerque). It will seem like the entire Mouillage de Ste. Anne is just one big cruiser's anchorage.

If you take the walled trail up the hill behind the church, you'll be rewarded with a great view of the anchorage and your boat. In town you must visit the old graveyard atop the hill overlooking the water with its colorful pastel monuments and tombs. Ste. Anne is also a nice place to just stroll and window shop,

South of Ste. Anne is Salines, home of Martinique's only gay beach. Let me take a moment here to comment about beach attire on Martinique. Although many Martinicians and tourists often go nude on the beaches, there are no legal nude beaches on the island so it is possible to be arrested for going nude, but the attitude is such that most people will not say

anything and the authorities don't seem to enforce the statutes. However, throughout the island, on the beaches and at the swimming pools, the European custom of topless bathing is not uncommon.

Near Salines is the *Petrified Savanna Forest*, the *Savane des Petrifications*. Here you can stroll through an eerie desertlike area studded with cacti and volcanic boulders resembling petrified logs.

Navigational Information

As shown on Chart MAR-17, a waypoint at 14° 26.00' N, 60° 54.10' W, will place you approximately ¾ mile south/southwest of the entrance into the harbor at Marin and a mile west/southwest of the anchorage off the long beach at Ste. Anne. Exercise extreme caution if you approach this waypoint from the south or southeast as your course may bring you over land, your course will not be interrupted by unwanted landmasses if you approach the waypoint

Port de Plaisance du Marin Marina

Colorful cemetery in Ste. Anne

The anchorage at Ste. Anne

from the southwest however. In a moment we'll discuss entering the channel leading to Le Marin, for now, let's discuss Ste. Anne.

From the waypoint shown, you can head east to anchor off Ste. Anne. Please note that yellow buoys now mark a no-anchor zone directly off the beach, but don't fret, there is plenty of room to anchor with good holding. There is a dinghy dock located near the center of town but you might need a stern anchor when tied up here. Trash receptacles are located in the large parking lot just before you arrive at the market (with recycle bins).

What You Will Find Ashore
Internet
In the tourist office is a small Internet access center, *Cyber Base*, located upstairs in the back. *Snack Boubou* is a wonderful little Internet café with both computers and Wi-fi. They are open from 0730-2000 daily except Wednesdays and serve excellent food. *Croque Pain*, a bakery (boulangerie) and snack bar, has delicious baked goods, imported ice cream, and Internet access daily from 0800-1800.

Provisions
If you take a right from the dock you'll find an *8 à Huit* supermarket. There's a small town market where vendors showcase their wares, a grocery store on main street, *Salines Service*, just down from the market, and a quality bakery, *L'Epi Soleil,* a good spot to treat yourself to fresh baguettes, croissants, sandwiches, and other baked goodies along with a great view of the anchorage.

Dining
You will not lack for quality dining in Ste. Anne. *Le Hameau de Beauregard*, not to be confused with the luxury hotel *Manoir Beauregard*, is set in an 18th century coral-stone mansion this is an historical landmark as well as a Creole dining experience with a very popular Sunday afternoon buffet lunch. *Althanor*, right by the town hall is another fine place to dine as is *La Dunette* for unbeatable Tahitian fish. *Les Tamariniers* is right next to the church and serves good food at reasonable prices. Other popular restaurants are *Restaurant Anthor, Le Sud, Restaurant Frederic* and at Anse Caritan visit the *Anchorage Hotel* to dine in their open-air restaurant.

One of the best restaurants in Ste. Anne, and Martinique, is located on the beach, *Poi et Virginie.*

Charming is the keyword here with ceiling fans, tile floors, and wicker furniture, it's what someone who has never been to the Caribbean expects a Caribbean restaurant to look like, and it has a great view as well, you can see St. Lucia on a clear day. Twenty-four hour notice is required if you wish to order the highly recommended seafood platter for two (an attraction in itself) and on Friday nights a live band entertains.

Cul-de-Sac du Marin and Le Marin

Waypoints:
Cul de Sac du Marin- ¾ nm SSW of entrance
14° 26.00' N, 60° 54.10' W

The anchorages of *Cul-de-Sac du Marin* are some of the most protected, popular, and busy anchorages in the waters of Martinique. Le Marin has been an important port since the earliest years of colonization and remains so today, at least as far as cruisers are concerned. Le Marin has endured repeated attacks in 1672 (and was destroyed in 1673 by the British), 1693, 1759, 1792, 1808, and 1884; a few years later the town was devastated by a hurricane in 1891 and then again in 1903.

East of the marina is the town of Le Marin, a nice community with narrow one-way streets and a veterinary clinic on the main road. Here, in mid-May, residents celebrate the annual *Fête du Nautisme* with a nautical flea market, artist's booths, and vendors galore. In town you can visit *Église Saint-Étienne* which dates back to the 1700s and whose ornamentation and statues are not to be missed. The marble statues were originally intended for the Cathedral in Lima, Peru, but the ship transporting them got caught in a terrible storm off Martinique. The Captain, in fear for the safety of his ship and crew, swore that he would give away his precious cargo if he and his crew were somehow saved. The boat came ashore near Ste. Anne with all the passengers and crew safe and sound, and the rest is history.

Navigational Information
As shown on Chart MAR-17, a waypoint at 14° 26.00' N, 60° 54.10' W, will place you approximately ¾ mile south/southwest of the entrance channel, *Passe du Marin*, to the anchorages of *Cul-de-Sac du Marin*. Exercise extreme caution if you approach this waypoint from the south or southeast as your course may bring you over land. However, if you approach this waypoint from the southwest your course will

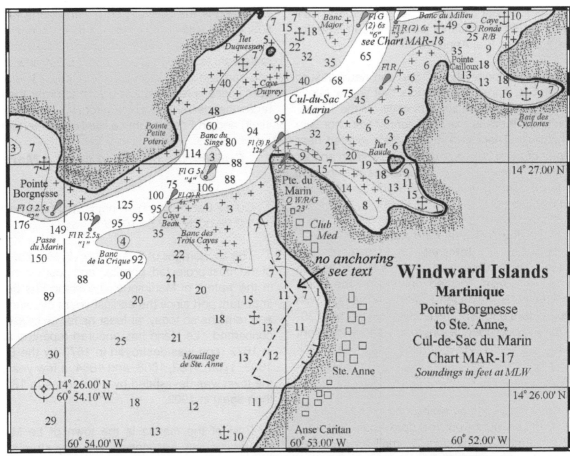

Windward Islands

Martinique

Pointe Borgnesse
to Ste. Anne,
Cul-de-Sac du Marin

Chart MAR-17

Soundings in feet at MLW

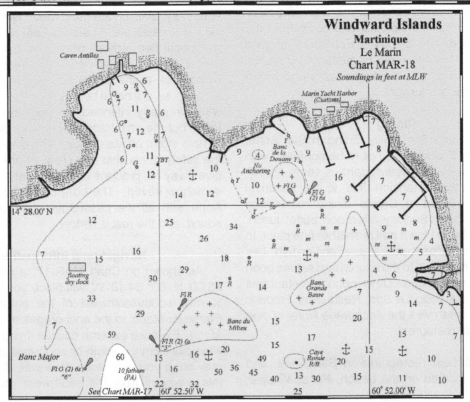

Windward Islands

Martinique

Le Marin

Chart MAR-18

Soundings in feet at MLW

not be interrupted by unwanted landmasses if you approach the waypoint from the southwest however. From the waypoint head east of north to enter the channel between markers "1," which marks the tip of *Banc de la Crique*, and "2." From the anchorages at Ste. Anne you may enter the channel east of *Banc de la Crique*, between *Banc de la Crique* and *Banc de Trois Cayes* just off *Club Med* and Pointe du Marin by keeping the red light "3" at *Caye Beau* to starboard.

The channel leading into *Cul-de-Sac du Marin* is deep for most of the way and there are several anchorages that you can enjoy before you reach the crowded anchorage off *Port de Plaisance du Marin Marina*. From the waypoint pass between "1" and "2" keeping "3" to starboard and passing on either side of *Banc du Singe* (marked by a green light) though the proper channel keeps the shoal to your port side and the red light off Pointe du Marin to starboard. If you pass north of *Banc du Singe* you can proceed north/northeast into the anchorage in the lee of Îlet Duquesney and *Caye Duprey* as shown on Chart MAR-17. If you take *Banc du Singe* to port and then clear Pointe du Marin, you can turn to starboard to work your way into the small bay south and southeast of Îlet Baude. This is a good spot to ride out just about any weather, perhaps even a minimal hurricane.

Continuing into the harbor toward the marina and Le Marin, with the passage to Îlet Baude on your starboard beam, you will take the flashing red light that sits southwest of Pointe Cailloux to starboard. Once clear of Pointe Cailloux you can turn to starboard to anchor north of Pointe Cailloux with all the other boats anchored off the marina just south of *Banc du Milieu* (see Chart MAR-18), or to proceed into the *Baie des Cyclones* for excellent protection, even in the event of a hurricane. Northwest of the red light off Pointe Cailloux is a small anchorage in the lee of *Banc Major*, good in a northeasterly, but not comfortable in a southeasterly.

Okay, now let's look at Chart MAR-18 and work our way into the marina at Le Marin. From Pointe Cailloux head northward to pass between the green light that marks the southeastern tip of *Banc Major*, and the red light that marks the southwestern tip of *Banc du Milieu*. As you pass *Banc du Milieu* you will pass another red light to starboard before the channel leading to the marina opens up to starboard. Here you will see a long line of red buoys leading northeastward while to port you will see a string of

yellow buoys that mark a no-anchoring zone and a shoal, the *Banc de la Douane*.

To starboard, south of the red buoys, is a large area of anchored and moored vessels lying between the red buoys and *Banc Grande Basse*. You can pick a spot here, anchor south of *Banc du Milieu* and eastward past Caye Ronde just off the eastern shore, or proceed northeastward following the line of buoys to get a slip in the marina, or to anchor northeast of *Banc Grande Basse*.

East of *Banc Grande Basse* is a narrow, mangrove-lined creek that would be a good spot to hide from a hurricane, but you'll have to sound your way in by dinghy first. At the northwestern tip of Cul-de-Sac du Marin is a small anchorage area west of the yellow-buoyed no-anchor zone. Here is the marked channel leading to the *Caren Antilles* yard and fuel dock.

What You Will Find Ashore
Customs and *Immigration*
Le Marin is a Port of Entry and *Customs* maintains a very nice office on the lower level by the dinghy dock at the marina. Hours are usually 0700-1230 and the officers have a computer for you to use to clear.

Internet
The marina has Wi-fi that reaches most parts of the bay. You'll need to go to the marina office to purchase a card that allows you hours of usage depending on the price of the card (EU$12 for 10 hours, EU$20 for 20 hours, and EU$26 for 30 hours). Ashore, *Mango Bay* and *Quai 13* both offer free Wi-fi so bring in your laptop when you come ashore to dine. *Cyber Marine* has several good Internet computer stations as well as ice cream and baked goods. Located in the main office of *Caren Antilles*, *Cyber Carene* offers Internet access.

Marine Facilities
The marine services in Le Marin center around two locations, the marina, and *Caren Antilles* to the west, both locations have dinghy docks for your convenience. For garbage, both locations have trash receptacles, water, and fuel. *Caren Antilles* also has recycling for batteries and oil as well as a Laundromat.

Marinas
Port de Plaisance du Marin Marina, sometimes just called *Marin Yacht Harbor* or *SAEPP*, is the focus

of boating activity in Le Marin. The marina monitors VHF ch. 16/09 and offers 600 slips with 220-volt 50-cycle electric (110-volt transformers are available at the office), 70 moorings, 30 garbage bins, a fuel dock with diesel and gasoline, telephone and fax services, showers, a *Customs* office, Wi-fi, and a compound with numerous marine related stores, shops, boutiques, and restaurants. The office is pleased to change your US Dollars into Euros and your Euros into US Dollars. The marina can handle up to 4 mega yachts with drafts to 13'.

Boatyard

At the northwestern end of *Cul-de-Sac du Marin* is the *Caren Antilles* haul-out yard that can accommodate vessels with beams to 23' on their 65-ton Travel Lift and cats up to 60' LOA with any beam on their hydraulic trailer. At the end of the bay by the haul-out is the fuel dock and small store. At the fuel dock you can get diesel, gas, water, ice, and a variety of snacks in the small store. The yard has a drop-off laundry service available.

Dock Cleaner Ecologique (*Switch Charters*) runs the dry dock and they can handle vessels up to 70 tons, 40' in width, with a draft of up to 6'.

Marine Supplies

Chandlers can be found at both the marina and at *Caren Antilles*. At *Caren Antilles*, the *Carene Shop* is the on-site chandlery with everything you need for your haul-out, they even rent tools and match paint. Upstairs is another chandlery, *Plus Nautique*, with new and used gear. At the marina *Le Ship* is a large chandler with a great selection of gear including Plastimo inflatables.

Marine Services
Electrics and Electronics

Located at the marina is *Diginav*, the electronic specialists (*Simrad, Raytheon, Diginav, Brookes and Gatehouse,* and *Furuno*) with a good supply of stock and spares. *Sud Marine Electronique* are also the people to see for electronic repairs as well as starter and alternator rebuilds. In Artimer visit *Yachting Engineering Services* (*YES*-they may move to the marina by the time this guide is published) where owner Thierry speaks excellent English and can work on any electrical, electronic, or watermaker problem that you might have. For starter and alternator rebuilds and repairs visit *Multi International* near *Sparkle Charter*.

Hull Repair and Painting

Visit *Martinique Sud Sablage,* also called *Nautic Services,* if you need your hull painted, prepped, sandblasted, or polished, as well as underwater repairs and cradle building (they'll also ship your boat). *Plastik Services* can handle the pre-painting fiberglass repairs as well as above the waterline painting while *Latitude 14°28'* can also ably assist you with your fiberglass repairs and many other typical boat jobs. *Chantier Naval PSN* specializes in hauling out and repairing small boats and dinghies.

Mechanical Repairs

Mécanique Assistance is a *Yanmar* dealer and can repair all makes of diesels as well as fixing your electrical problems. Another good diesel service is *Antilles Marine Services* carrying *Nani Diesel, Man,* and *Iveco* engines as well as drives and watermakers.

On the upper level, by the marina office is *Mécanique Plaisance* where you'll marvel at their display of engines, transmissions, and generators that surround their showroom. They are dealers for *Perkins, Yanmar, Volvo-Penta,* and *Westerbeke* and repair most models.

For outboard repairs try *Roby Mechanic*, an agent for *Mercury, Tohatsu,* and *Yamaha.* Roby has a shop by the haul-out but rarely works on outboards over 25hp.

Refrigeration

Located near *Sparkle Charter, Tilikum* also works on refrigeration and air conditioning and is your best bet for a quick and correct repair or installation. *CS Services* can also repair your refrigeration, generator, wind generator, or watermaker as well as sell you a new one and repair any of your electrical problems.

Sail Repair and Rigging

For sail repair try *Voile Assistance* located at *Caren Antilles* who can also repair or construct cushions and boat canvas. For sail repair or construction in Artimer, visit *Voilerie Caraibe Martinique* who can also build you a new set of cockpit cushions.

Located at the marina, *Caraibes Greemont* is a complete rigging shop and are *Profurl, Navtec, Lewmar,* and *Harken* dealers as well as being a general chandlery. Across from the marina is *Voilerie du Marin*; they handle warranty work for *North Sails.*

Speaking of *North Sails*, they have an office in the marina.

Welding and Fabrication

Located in the marina, *Mécanique Plaisance* can handle any welding and fabrication needs that you might have.

Laundry

If you are at the marina and need a laundry service try *Blatman and Laverie*, *Lavomatic*, or *Pressing du Port* where you can do your own laundry or they'll do it for you. You can also avail yourself of the laundry services at *Caren Antilles*.

Medical

In the yellow building on the square in town across from the church is the office of Dr. Delores (0596-74 98 24), and if you need an osteopath call Dr. Eric Alluson at 0596-55 95 28.

Provisions

There's a unique grocery store at the marina, *Caribiz*, the first on-line supermarket in the French West Indies that specializes in yacht provisioning. *Caribiz* will help you with all your provisioning needs, saving you the time of locating all your groceries. You can let them do the work for you, pack your order, and then deliver it free to your slip in the marina.

You can also try *Champion Supermarket* just outside the *Caren Antilles* compound in a small strip mall with several stores including a photo shop and a bakery. *Leader Price* has their own dinghy dock (just to the east of the *Caren Antilles* fuel dock) and an excellent location in the harbor. *Annette's Nature A* is a health food store located nearby that carries gluten free foods and other goodies for that special diet.

On the road out of town you'll find *Carefour*, as large and as nice a supermarket that you can find on the island.

Aux P'tis Delices is a wonderful bakery between the marina complex and town. Besides baked goodies you can relax here and enjoy a sandwich.

If you need the services of professional yacht provisioners try *Douglas Yacht Services* or *Appro Zagaya*.

Dining

As you have probably guessed by now, there is no shortage of quality dining in Le Marin. One of my personal favorites is located just west of the marina, a wonderful little sidewalk restaurant, *le Brochete*. Although the menu is small with only a few choices that change from day to day, the food is very good and reasonably priced, don't miss this stop.

In the marina are several good restaurants with *Mango Bay* being the favorite. Next to *Mango Bay* is *Délifrance*, a good spot for a sandwich, fresh baguettes, croissants, and daily specials. *Marin Mouillage* sits across the street while *Lagoon Bleu* is a great spot for seafood served on a large terrace with only the sea and boats for a backdrop.

Located at *Caren Antilles* is *Quai 13* (they're closed Sundays and Mondays) with a good view of the bay and the boatyard. Look for live music here in the evenings.

On the beach below the church is *La Paillotte*, also known as *Le Cayali*, a comfortable restaurant that boasts a fine menu at good prices.

The Eastern Coast of Martinique

The eastern coast of Martinique, the Windward Coast, offers a real challenge to skippers and navigators, but the rewards are a wealth of exquisite, and often empty, anchorages. Some of these anchorages will not be tenable in strong easterly winds or during periods of northerly swells, so choose your spot accordingly. Try to enter the anchorages before 1400 so that the setting sun will not be too low and in your eyes, and conversely, don't leave these anchorages until after 0900-1100 so that the rising sun will not be in your eyes. Always wear Polarized sunglasses when necessary for navigation.

Bear in mind that you'll probably wish to traverse these areas on relatively calm days, or in the morning before the trades pick up, and that once tucked into a nice snug anchorage, you might not be able to leave for several days until conditions lessen. In this section I will remind you more than once that the entrances to some of these anchorages are never to be attempted in heavy following winds and seas, and none are to be attempted at night!

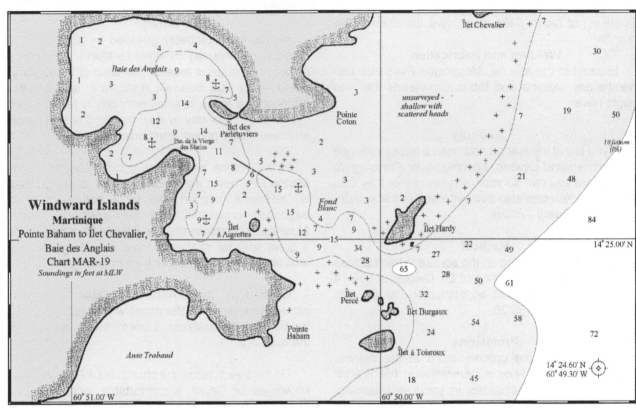

Baie des Anglais

Pointe Coton

unsurveyed -
shallow with
scattered heads

Îlet Chevalier

19 fathom
(PA)

Îlet des
Parletuviers

Pte. de la Vierge
des Marins

Fond
Blanc

Îlet Hardy

Windward Islands
Martinique
Pointe Baham to Îlet Chevalier,
Baie des Anglais
Chart MAR-19
Soundings in feet at MLW

Îlet
à Aigrettes

14° 25.00' N

65

Îlet
Percé

Îlet Burgaux

Pointe
Baham

Îlet à Toisroux

14° 24.60' N
60° 49.30' W

Anse Trabaud

60° 51.00' W   60° 50.00' W

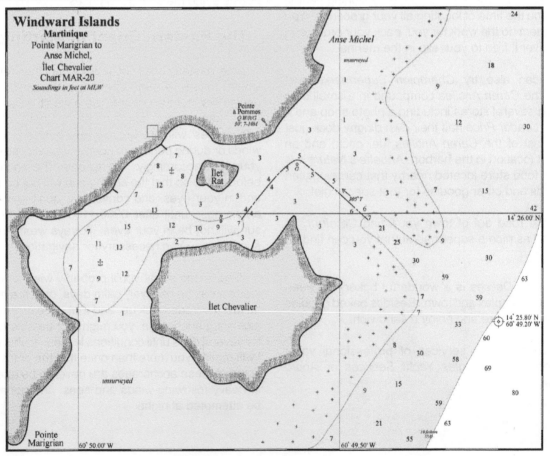

Windward Islands
Martinique
Pointe Marigrian to
Anse Michel,
Îlet Chevalier
Chart MAR-20
Soundings in feet at MLW

Anse Michel

unsurveyed

Pointe
à Pommes
Q W/R/G
30'; 7-10M

Îlet
Rat

305° T

14° 26.00' N

Îlet Chevalier

14° 25.80' N
60° 49.20' W

unsurveyed

10 fathom
(PA)

Pointe
Marigrian

60° 50.00' W   60° 49.50' W

Baie des Anglais

Waypoints:
Baie des Anglais- ½ nm SE of entrance
14° 24.60' N, 60° 49.30' W

The first anchorage you will discover as you head north along the eastern coast is *Baie des Anglais*, usually the only foray that most cruisers will make on Martinique's eastern coast, but it is a good one. The bay is isolated and secure though there are no facilities, not even a house on the shore, the holding is good, and the anchorage is open to the trade wind breezes while the shoals block the incoming swell. The entrance channel is a bit tricky, and shallow, only about 6' at MLW in one spot.

Navigational Information

From Ste. Anne first head southwest to clear Pointe Dunkerque before turning more to the south and then southeast to clear in turn Pointe Catherine and Pointe des Salines as shown on Chart MAR-1. Daytime anchorages are available in northeasterly winds in the three small coves south of Pointe Dunkerque, Anse Meunier, Petite Anse des Salines, and Grand Anse des Salines, between Pointe Dunkerque and Pointe des Salines. Keep well south of Îlet Cabrits and Table au Diable, only small shallow drafts boats can pass between these islands and the shore. Just to the southwest of Îlet Cabrits lies the wreck of the *Eden* in about 3' of water. As you proceed northeastward from Table au Diable keep Îlet à Toisroux well to port to avoid the reef system that parallels the shoreline between Table au Diable and Îlet à Toisroux. Never attempt the entrance to *Baie des Anglais* in anything but light conditions; heavy winds and seas could be disastrous. Also bear in mind that once inside the bay, outside sea conditions may make it impossible to leave for a while.

The entrance to *Baie des Anglais* lies between Îlet à Toisroux and Îlet Hardy as shown on Chart MAR-19. A waypoint at 14° 24.60' N, 60° 49.30' W, will place you approximately ½ mile southeast of the entrance channel that winds its way into the bay. From the waypoint steer approximately mid-channel between Îlet Hardy to starboard, and Îlet à Toisroux, Îlet Burgaux, and Îlet Percé to port. As you pass between Îlet Hardy and Îlet Percé you will see the reefs west of Îlet Percé to port and you should make out the shallow *Fond Blanc* to starboard as you dogleg between them and then again between *Fond*

Blanc and Îlet à Aigrettes to port where the controlling depth becomes 6' as shown on the chart. Deeper draft boats will have to anchor in the small cove best employed as a daytime anchorage that lies east of Îlet à Aigrettes and northwest of *Fond Blanc*.

Vessels venturing further into the bay may be able to utilize an old stone tower on the shore (behind and to the left of Îlet des Parletuviers) as a beacon and steer 320°T with the tower on your bow (if you put the tower on your bow and the northern shore of Îlet Burgaux on your stern you will be close). If you cannot make out the tower, you will have to eyeball your way over the soft mud shoal with 6' over it at MLW lying north of Îlet à Aigrettes. Never try this in strong following winds or seas, though the seas will have lessened tremendously by the time you are this far into the bay. Once over the bar you'll be in the deeper anchorage area of *Baie des Anglais* proper and you can choose to anchor wherever your draft allows. A good spot is on the western side of the bay northwest of Pointe de la Vierge des Marins, or in what I consider the best spot, on the eastern side of the bay in the lee of Îlet des Parletuviers and the mainland shore.

What You Will Find Ashore

Although there is very little ashore, a small trail begins south of Îlet à Aigrettes, which takes you to the lovely beach at *Anse Trabaud*. The islands of Îlet Hardy, Îlet à Toisroux, Îlet Burgaux, and Îlet Percé are sea bird nesting sites and landing ashore is prohibited.

Îlet Chevalier

Waypoints:
Îlet Chevalier- ¼ nm SE of entrance channel
14° 25.80' N, 60° 49.20' W

Îlet Chevalier offers a wonderful protected anchorage, but the entrance is limited to vessels with drafts of under 5' as there is a rocky bar with a depth of just under 4' (actually 3.8') at MLW. Vessels with drafts of 4'-4½' must play the tides to enter and leave this anchorage, and don't forget, never try to enter this anchorage in strong easterly conditions that can cause your vessel to bounce off the bottom.

Navigational Information

If approaching from *Baie des Anglais*, keep well off a line between Îlet Hardy and Îlet Chevalier to avoid the reef system that lies between them and southeast of Îlet Chevalier. As shown on chart MAR-20, a waypoint at 14° 25.80' N, 60° 49.20' W, will place you approximately ¼ mile southeast of the entrance channel. To enter from the waypoint, put the light on Pointe à Pommes (Q W/R/G, 30' 7-10M) on your bow steering for it on an approximate heading of 305° T. Take the green buoy to port and immediately turn back to the southwest keeping the red buoy lying south of Îlet Rat to starboard. Between the green and red buoy, try not to drift too far away from your course as the water shallows both north and south of the courseline. Once in the deeper water in the lee of Îlet Chevalier you can anchor west of Îlet Chevalier or Îlet Rat. Never try to enter the anchorage from the southwest of Îlet Chevalier, the bar is far too shallow, only 1'-3' in places. This pass is also open to the ocean and can be extremely dangerous when seas are running.

What You Will Find Ashore

The anchorage itself is lovely, but it is sometimes crowded, especially on weekends. Although the island is protected, ferries carry hikers and picnickers back and forth from the mainland of Martinique to Îlet Chevalier.

Îlet Petite Grenade to Cul-de-Sac Fregate

Waypoints:

Passe de Caye Pinsonelle- 2 nm E of
14° 36.20' N, 60° 47.50' W

Îlet Petite Grande- ¼ nm NNE of entrance
14° 34.80' N, 60° 49.65' W

Navigational Information

Heading north along the eastern shore of Martinique you will truly be entering some rarely visited waters (by most cruiser's standards) with numerous offshore reefs and currents with which you must deal. The best time to transit this coast is during periods of settled weather with lighter trade winds and seas, and with good visibility a must. I prefer to run well offshore here to avoid the inshore reefs as much as possible, and then to venture into their lee when I have the opportunity. Leaving Îlet Chevalier behind, the next anchorages of any note that can handle larger boats and offer good protection lie north of Pointe du Vauclin as shown on Chart MAR-21. Smaller, shallow draft vessels (4' and less) can anchor off the town of Le Vauclin (south of Pointe du Vauclin and not shown

on the chart), but vessels drawing more than that are confined to an anchorage area that is far less than ideal and very choppy in any winds therefore I am not showing it here. A reminder, some of these entrances are never to be attempted in heavy following winds and seas, and none are to be attempted at night!

The first anchorage on your northward bound cruise is at *Le Cul-de-Sac Petite Grenade* off Îlet Petite Grenade as shown on Chart MAR-21. As you head north from Îlet Chevalier, stay a minimum of two miles offshore to avoid the huge reef system, *Cayes Pariades*, lying east of Martinique between Pointe du Ducassous and Pointe du Vauclin as shown on Chart MAR-1. Although the shoal is deeper than one fathom north of Pointe du Vauclin in places, it is recommended that for safety's sake you proceed northward a bit to enter into the lee of the reef system at *Passe de Caye Pinsonelle* as shown on Chart MAR-21, this will allow you access to the anchorage at Îlet Petite Grenade and Baie du Simon.

As shown on Chart MAR-21, a waypoint at 14° 36.20' N, 60° 47.50' W, will place you approximately 2 miles east of *Passe de Caye Pinsonelle*. To access the anchorage off Îlet Petite Grenade, from this waypoint head west past the reef systems shown as *Cayes Pinsonelle* (to starboard) and *Petite Pinsonelle* (to port). Heading west, once past *Petite Pinsonelle*, turn southward toward Îlet Petite Grenade as shown on the chart. Heading south, once past *Petite Pinsonelle* steer more east of south to avoid the reefs lying east of Îlet Petite Grenade but keeping clear of the shoal shown as *Cayes du Sans Souci*.

A waypoint at 14° 34.80' N, 60° 49.65' W, will place you approximately ¼ mile north/northeast of the entrance channel leading into the anchorage area between two reefs that are usually breaking. The depth is good between the outer parts of the reefs, but the channel is only about 100 yards wide. The controlling depth for this channel is just a hair under 6' so keep that in mind if you plan to enter and do not put the safety of your crew and vessel in jeopardy by being anything less than extremely cautious. One boat made the mistake of thinking the channel was more to the north than it was because the skipper mistook a place on the northern reef where the seas were not breaking to be the entrance. Jérôme Nouel suggests that cruisers take up a heading of 200° T on the conspicuous red roof that lies on the point south of Îlet Petite Grenade. Pass between Îlet Petite Grenade and the small point off the mainland lying south of the island and you'll be in water that's generally 6' in depth in most places, a bit more in others.

You can anchor behind the point just off the mainland and south of Îlet Petite Grenade called Trou Cochon in 10' (a great anchorage by the way), or pass westward and round up behind Îlet Petite Grenade to anchor off its western or northwestern shore in

The dock at Le François

the Baie des Mulets. North of Îlet Petite Grenade is a small anchorage in *Baie de Sans Souci*, entry is straightforward and easy and the protection behind the reef at the southern end of the bay is fair to good. Ashore is a small fishing community at the western end of Baie des Mulets and a road on the mainland south of Îlet Petite Grenade will lead into Le Vauclin, a pretty fair hike.

The next group of anchorages lies to the north of *Baie Sans Souci* in *Baie du Simon*. From the waypoint 2 miles east of *Passe de Caye Pinsonelle*, enter as described above past *Cayes Pinsonelle* (to starboard) and *Petite Pinsonelle* (to port) angling a bit north of west to enter *Baie du Simon* via *Grand Passe du Simon* as shown on Chart MAR-21. On the northern side of *Grand Passe du Simon* are two small anchorages off Îlet Long.

One anchorage lies east of Îlet Long and the shoal that extends southeastward from it and south of Îlet

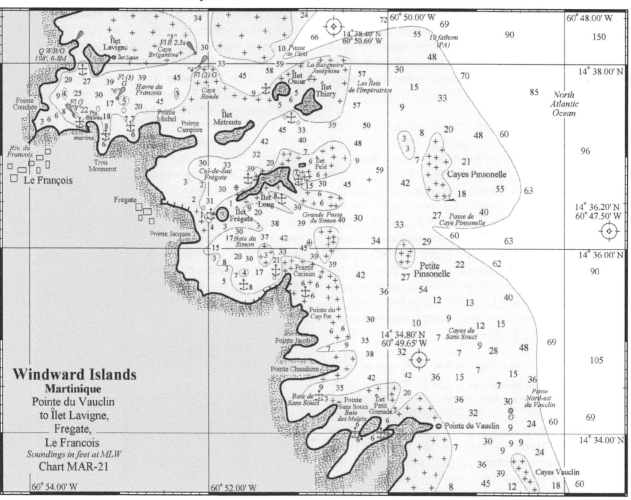

Pelé, and the second anchorage lying south of the island in the lee of that same reef as shown on the chart. These reefs are easily seen in good light and visibility; they're usually breaking as well. To enter the anchorage at Îlet Pelé, you'll have to clear a bar with only 6' over it at MLW, but once inside you'll have 7'-10'. Make sure your anchor is set well here, the bottom is a mixture of sand and grass and if the wind picks up you won't want to drag.

Proceeding westward via *Grande Passe du Simon* into the *Baie du Simon*, a skipper can find a good anchorage in the lee west of Pointe Cerisier as shown on Chart MAR-21. The easiest way to access this anchorage, and the one at the south end of *Baie du Simon* is to pass between the reefs off Pointe Cerisier and the large unnamed reef lying in the center of *Baie du Simon* northwest of Pointe Cerisier.

If you're planning to anchor west of Pointe Cerisier watch out for the small reef in the center of the anchorage, a small stake sometimes marks it. Small, shallow draft vessels can work their way into the lee of the reef system east of Pointe Cerisier to actually anchor east of Pointe Cerisier and northeast of Pointe du Cap Est. Access is by a narrow, shallow channel just off the point that is sometimes marked by stakes; this anchorage will get choppy in a good breeze.

The next group of anchorages lies north of *Baie du Simon* in *Cul-de-Sac Frégate* as shown on Chart MAR-21. This area is more developed than the anchorages from Pointe du Vauclin to *Baie du Simon* and there are some facilities ashore. To enter the anchorage areas let's backtrack once again to the waypoint lying two miles east of *Passe de Caye Pinsonelle* and the instructions for heading west past the reefs of *Cayes Pinsonelle* (keep it to starboard) and *Petite Pinsonelle* (keep it to port). When *Petite Pinsonelle* is on your port quarter you can turn your bow northward passing between *Cayes Pinsonelle* (to starboard) and the reefs that stretch northeastward from Îlet Long and Îlet Pelé.

The entrance into *Cul-de-Sac Frégate* is wide and deep, with a couple of doglegs that you must negotiate to achieve the inner anchorage off the town of Frégate. As you begin working your way into *Cul-de-Sac Frégate* you'll find a nice anchorage south of Îlet Thiery (watch out for the two small shoals in the anchorage area), which, with Îlet Oscar makes up *Les Îlets de l'Impératrice*, named after the Empress Joséphine who is said to have bathed in the shallow *fond blanc* called *La Baignoire Joséphine* which lies just north of Îlet Thiery.

What You Will Find Ashore

Let me take a moment to explain about a certain Creole custom. It is not unusual to see folks standing waist deep in water, sipping a rum drink and chatting the day away. What you may not be used to is that these folks are doing this well offshore in places such as *La Baignoire Joséphine (Joséphine's Bath)* or on some of the offshore reefs such as *Loup Garou*. *Fond blancs* are white sandbanks protected by reefs and they usually only have about 3' of water over them. Originally begun by the white plantation aristocracy enjoying their Sundays, entrepreneurs got the idea that it would be of interest to tourists as well as locals, so, starting about mid-morning you'll see small boats full of happy people headed offshore to spend a day in the water.

On Îlet Oscar you can dine at *La Maison de L' Îlet Oscar*, a sort of Robinson Crusoe theme restaurant. You can be picked up by boat from your vessel or the shore and the cost will be deducted off your check if you have lunch for two; this restaurant is said to have been won by the owner in a poker game. On both Îlet Oscar and Îlet Thirey there are small houses that have been converted into hotels.

Navigational Information

Okay, back to the anchorages of *Cul-de-Sac Frégate*. Continuing westward into the bay past Îlet Thiery you will find an anchorage on the northwestern shore of Îlet Long in the lee of the small point, and in the extreme southern part of *Cul-de-Sac Frégate* in the lee of Îlet Frégate. Watch out for a few isolated reefs on your way into this anchorage from Îlet Long. In the community of Frégate you can find a small market if you need a few groceries.

Hâvre du François

Waypoints:
Passe de l'Est, Hâvre du François- ½ nm NE of 14° 38.40' N, 60° 50.60' W

The next stop on our northward journey is at *Hâvre du François* and the town of Le François, the largest city on Martinique's eastern shore with over 17,000 residents (not the most populous, but certainly the largest). Sailors will probably like to know that Le

François is known for its team of *yoleurs*, sailors who race the small sailboats unique to Martinique called *yoles rondes*. Don't miss a race if one is going on while you're visiting.

Navigational Information

As shown on Chart MAR-21, a waypoint at 14° 38.40' N, 60° 50.60' W, will place you ½ mile northeast of *Passe de l'Est* (*East Passage*). Once again you will have to negotiate a nearly two-mile long twisting passage between reef systems, but at least this one will have some markers to guide you.

From the waypoint head southwest to pass between Îlet Oscar (to port) and the massive reef system to starboard. You can also head northward around this reef system to enter the harbor through the marked *Passe du François* (not shown on this chart). Though better marked, there is a green buoy at the northwestern end of this reef system that you take to port to head southward to the first set of buoys lying west of Îlet Oscar as shown on the chart (the buoys mark *Caye Brigantine* and *Caye Ronde*), the channel is a tad shallower, but it is safer if the winds and seas are up; never attempt *Passe de l'Est* in strong following winds and seas or if the afternoon sun is in your eyes.

Anyway, proceeding westward in *Passe de l'Est* with Îlet Oscar to port, it is possible to anchor off the southwestern tip of Îlet Oscar in settled conditions. Still heading west you will want to pass between the markers of *Caye Brigantine* ("3," red-keep it to

starboard) and *Caye Ronde* ("4," green-keep it to port) as you enter *Hâvre du François* where you'll want to pass north of the unnamed reef marked by a lighted green buoy ("6").

Once past this reef you can turn a bit to starboard to anchor in the lee of Îlet Lavigne, or proceed into the southern part of *Hâvre du François*, avoid a couple of small shoals, to anchor in *Trou Monnerot*, the small unnamed cove east of *Trou Monnerot*, or off the town of Le François in the lee of Pointe Bateau and southeast of green lighted buoy "8."

Here you'll find a small marina, *Club Nautique du François*, where you can get diesel and gas at their gas dock (depth here is only 6' and maneuvering is tight) as well as ice; however the slips are all private.

What You Will Find Ashore

In Le François you'll find several places to provision, three pharmacies, and a Laundromat. The magnificent church in the heart of town is the *Église Saint-Michel-du-François*, the sixth church to occupy this site on *Place Charles-de-Gaulle* with its World War I memorial. There is also a nice bakery, the *Boulangerie-Pâtisserie Roasanne*, near *Place Charles de Gaulle*, and behind the bakery is a tiny restaurant, *La Kreyole*. The nearby town hall has come under a lot of criticism for its daring futuristic architecture. If you need to provision, try *Champion Supermarket* at the edge of town on the road to Le Lamentin, and there is also another market next to the *Tourist Office* downtown.

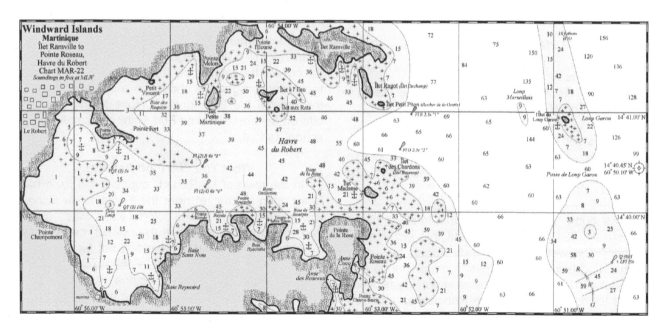

On the road from town to the harbor you'll find *La Riviera Hotel and Restaurant* in a large white house that's unmistakable; the food here is affordable and delicious, especially their melon omelet. *Frégate Bleue* is the closest thing to a European bed and breakfast on the island of Martinique and it's the perfect place if you want to spend a nice quiet night.

In Le François you'll want to visit the *Bally* rum distillery. *Bally* operated in Le Carbet on the northeastern coast until 1978 when production moved to Le François. The company has received many awards for several of its products with the same square bottle and distinctive label that has been in use since 1924.

Just outside of town on the road from Sainte-Espirit is the *Domaine de l'Acajou*, or as it's better known, *Habitation Clément*. Originally founded as a rum distillery in 1917 and producer of some of the finest Martinician rums until around 1988, the *rhumerie* has now moved to Simon, about 4 miles from Le François on the road to Le Vauclin. The beautifully restored 18th century residence was the site of a summit meeting between President George Bush and Francois Mitterand during the Gulf War in 1991, and was a favorite haunt of French President Jacques Chirac and the opera singer Barbara Hendricks. Also between Le François and Le Vauclin, just off *N6*, is *Au Village*, a recreation of an early 20th century village with actors in period costumes complete with bamboo shacks and displays of coffee and cotton growing. On the same road is a nice restaurant, *Les Brisants*, located in a lovely wooded area near the shore.

Hâvre du Robert

Waypoints:
Hâvre du Robert- ½ nm E of Passe Loup Garou
14° 40.45' N, 60° 50.10' W

"*This is one of the most beautiful natural harbours imaginable, able to accommodate any size of fleet so comfortably that even the largest vessels can cast anchor in many places...*"

This quote by Père Labat, the founder of Le Robert in 1694, says it all about this picturesque harbor. The waters of *Hâvre du Robert* are home to many protected anchorages, a small marina and haul-out yard, and the extensive shoreside facilities of the town of Le Robert. Le Robert was attacked by the British in 1809 when Admiral Villaret-Joyeuse surrendered; this paved the way for British troops to cross inland to attack *Fort Royal* in Fort-de-France. A century later, after the eruption of *Mt. Pelée* in 1902, many plans were drawn up to make this area a huge commercial port to replace St. Pierre, but nothing ever came of it.

Navigational Information
Heading north from the waypoint east of *Passe de Caye Pinsonelle*, you will have to stay a bit further offshore, about three miles off, to work your way to the next waypoint at *Hâvre du Robert*. As shown on Chart MAR-22, a waypoint at 14° 40.45' N, 60° 50.10' W, will place you approximately ½ mile east of the *Passe de Loup Garou*. From the waypoint head west in the pass, and if you like, take a detour to the north to anchor off l'Îlet du Loup Garou, a good place to enjoy the tiny beach in settled weather. Continuing westward into *Hâvre du Robert*, you will pass between the two outer markers, "1" and "2" and once abeam of Îlet Madame you will need to turn a bit more to the southwest to split the next two markers "3" and "4." If you don't wish to continue further into *Hâvre du Robert*, you can turn to the north to anchor off Îlet Ramville, Îlet Ragot (sometimes shown as Îlet Duchamp), Îlet à l'Eau, Îlet Petite Martinique, and in the lee of Pointe Melon. Îlet Ramville is home to the ruins of an old pottery factory that is now overrun with iguanas and several nice houses that are not overrun with iguanas.

If none of these anchorages appeal to you and you wish to proceed further into *Hâvre du Robert* past "3" and "4," continue southwestward until abeam of Pointe Fort when you may turn back toward the north to anchor in the anchorage in the lee of the point or in the cove to the west off the town of Le Robert. Both of these anchorages are choppy in a breeze; however the one off the town dock is close to the services offered ashore; at Pointe Fort there is a small sailing school ashore.

What You Will Find Ashore
In the town of Le Robert, opposite the town hall is an open-air market near the *Fontaine du Robert* with its swans, shells, and colorful water lilies. If you can't find what you need at the market, nearby is a modern *8 à Huit* grocery store and not far away are two pharmacies and a laundry. For a quick snack, try *La Yole Bleue*, a beachfront pizzeria that also serves crepes or if you are in search of a more substantial

meal, near the town dock is *Chez Fofor* whose second floor dining room offers a lovely view of *Hâvre du Robert*. On the road between Le Robert and Le François is the *Miramar*, a pizzeria in a hotel that transforms into a piano bar on Friday and Saturday nights.

At the southern end of *Hâvre du Robert*, south of the town, are three good anchorages and a marina. As shown on Chart MAR-22 you can anchor at *Baie Reynoird, Baie Sans Nom*, and at the extreme southwestern end of *Hâvre du Robert* just off the marina entrance.

Baie de Trésor

La Marina de Robert lies up a creek at the southwestern end of *Hâvre du Robert* and is set in the old sugar mill of Le Robert as shown on Chart MAR-22. Small and basic, the marina offers *Texaco* diesel and gas, water, a mechanic, and they can even supply a mobile crane for a haul out (the controlling depth in the creek is 4' at MLW, and I've seen boats as large as a *Catana 44* hauled out here). If you cannot access the creek you'll have to anchor outside in the lee of the shoal that lies to the west of *Baie Reynoird*. The town of Le Robert is about a 1½ miles away but there are places to eat nearby. The houseboat rental company located on the marina's grounds, *L'Aqua Location*, rents "aqua-homes," floating houses with four cabins that accommodate couples nicely, they are really glorified houseboats but good if you just want to go spend a couple of days on the *fonds blanc*.

Along the southern shoreline of *Hâvre du Robert* are several more protected anchorages as shown on Chart MAR-22. East of *Baie Sans Nom* in order

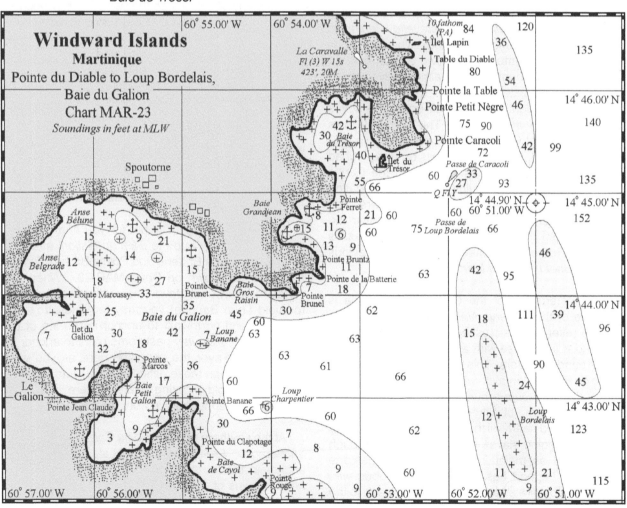

are the small cove east of Pointe Royale called *Baie Royale*, the small anchorage in *Baie Hyacinthe* (buggy), *Baie Saintpée,* and the anchorage in the lee of Îlet Madame. Some folks anchor in the lee of Îlet des Chardons but I find it a bit choppy with a breeze blowing. You can tie your dingy up at the small dock at Îlet Madame to access the picnic tables ashore; the island is busy on the weekends. On the eastern side of Îlet Madame is a narrow, shallow channel between Îlet Madame and Îlet des Chardons that is only recommended for smaller boats. *Baie Royale* is an extremely sheltered anchorage, small yet with good holding.

Baie du Galion;
The Caravelle Peninsula

Waypoints:
½ nm ENE of Passe de Loup Bordelais
14º 44.90' N, 60º 51.00' W

From Le Galion to La Trinité, the area is called *Presqu'Îlet la Caravelle*, the *Caravelle Peninsula* (*presqu'Îlet* means *almost an island*). The peninsula, once a haven for smugglers known as *Cabesterre*, juts out into the Atlantic Ocean almost seven miles and the shoreline, with its sheer cliffs and sparse vegetation, is indented with small bays and coves and several nice anchorages. The peninsula was the site of the last Carib war on Martinique. Up until his death in 1658, Governor Jacques du Parquet had done his utmost to maintain peace with the Caribs avoiding bloodshed that would hinder the propagation of the French colony on Martinique. Two years later, in 1660, French colonists decided to take over the peninsula from the Caribs and what started out as an invasion turned into a massacre (see the previous section *A Brief History of Martinique*).

The eastern end of the Caravelle Peninsula is the home of the *Réserve Naturelle de la Caravelle*, a nature reserve criss-crossed with numerous hiking trails and a lighthouse with an extraordinary view of the surrounding waters. This area is the site of the old *Dubuc de Rivery* plantation where you can still visit the ruins of *Château Dubuc*, built around 1770. This was the ancestral home of Aimée Dubuc whose family at one time owned nearly all the peninsula and were said to have smuggled slaves and merchandise through here as well as maintaining a working sugarcane plantation. Legend has it that Aimée Dubuc was taken at sea by pirates and later sold as a slave to the

Turks. Eventually Aimée became a mistress to the *Sultan of Constantinople* and gave birth to *Mahmud II* who later became the *Sultan* of the Ottoman Empire in Turkey. At the entrance to the reserve you can dine on Creole cooking at *Le Trésor*.

Navigational Information

The *Baie du Galion* is said to be named after a Spanish Galleon that stopped here to take on water on its way to Peru and was the haunt of many pirate ships that anchored in these waters. When heading northward along this stretch of shoreline, keep three miles off to avoid *Loup Bordelais*. As shown on Chart MAR-23, a waypoint at 14º 44.90' N, 60º 51.00' W, will place you approximately ½ mile east/northeast of *Passe de Loup Bordelais*. From the waypoint head southwest until past the flashing yellow light that marks *Passe de Caracoli* when you'll need to turn to the south/southwest to clear Pointe de la Batterie. To starboard just past the yellow light is the entrance to the wonderful anchorage in *Baie de Trésor*, watch out for the many shoals inside the bay. The bay became a marine park in 1999 and cruisers can access the moorings in the northeastern part of the bay for day use only, no anchoring is permitted. At the time of this writing the powers that be were in the process of planning the placing of the moorings, if the moorings are not installed when you arrive you will be permitted to anchor. A trail ashore leads to the lighthouse that was built in 1861. The anchorages in *Baie Grandjean* should only be used in settled weather and with no swells running as the waters here are very open. The southern cover offers the best protection but you must wind your way through some reefs to achieve it.

So if *Baie de Trésor* is not for you and you wish to continue further into the *Baie du Galion*, after you clear Pointe de la Batterie and Pointe Brune you may turn west as shown on Chart MAR-23. When you clear Pointe Brunet (favor the northern shore a bit to avoid *Loup Banane*) you may turn more towards the north and northwest to anchor in the lee of the point or work your way past some reefs to anchor off Spoutorne. Favor the shoreline here as you wind your way through these difficult to see reefs, fish trap makers, and old mooring floats. There is a small grocery store about ½ mile from the dock.

At the southern end of *Baie du Galion* are two good anchorages. From Pointe Brunet steer southwest to anchor in the lee of Pointe Marcos where you can see the ruins of the only sugar mill still in operation on Martinique. Just to the east of Pointe Marcos is *Baie Petite Galion*, an excellent, well protected anchorage.

Hâvre de la Trinité

Waypoints:
Hâvre de la Trinité- 2 nm NNW of
14° 46.50' N, 60° 57.00' W

Navigational Information

The anchorages in *Hâvre de la Trinité*, although excellent in normal tradewind conditions, are not to be considered when northerly swells are running. From *Hâvre de la Trinité* to the northern coast of Martinique and around to the northwestern coast there are no more usable anchorages.

As shown on Chart MAR-24, a waypoint at 14° 46.50' N, 60° 57.00' W, will place you approximately 2 miles north/northwest of *Hâvre de la Trinité*. As you round the Caravelle Peninsula, stay at least two miles north to clear *Loup Ministre* (see the chart) whose center lies approximately at 14° 46.70' N, 60° 56.45' W before heading to the waypoint. There are several offshore shoals here with depths of 9'-25' and heavy seas will become steeper on these shoals so try to make this leg on a calm day.

From the waypoint head south/southwest between *Banc Mitan* and Îlet St. Aubin and the reef system called *Le Banc de Sable*. Once abeam of the southern edge of *Le Banc de Sable*, turn and work your way southward keeping between the red buoy off Port de Cosmy to starboard and the large reef off Pointe de la Batterie to port. Continue southward keeping red "7," the light at *Loup Fort* to port and green "6" to starboard, and then in turn, red "9" to port and green "8" to starboard to anchor off the town of La Trinité in the *Baie des Raisiniers*, or, in my favorite spot, on the eastern side of the harbor between "G6" and "G8." On shore, the large white building is the *Ecole d'Apprentisage Maritime* where you can tie your dinghy to their dock to walk to town, they usually don't mind but ask first.

On the western side of *Hâvre de la Trinité* lies *Port de Cosmy*, a fishing center that caters to smaller craft. The entrance to the anchorage (choppy with a good breeze due to the fetch) is between two small markers as shown on the chart. Fuel can be jerry-jugged or you can pull up to the dock if you draw less

than 5'. There's a small grocery store on the road north of Port de Cosmy.

Customs and Immigration
If you anchor at the southern part of the bay off the town, you'll find the *Customs* office just across the road (open from 0800-1200 everyday).

What You Will Find Ashore
La Trinité is a very clean, beautiful town with almost every kind of store and restaurant along the waterfront where the most popular pastime is strolling down the promenade and wandering in and out of the little shops and kiosks. You can pick up provisions at the *Match* supermarket located on the main street facing the waterfront; nearby is the local open-air market. *Chez Titine* has a great view of the harbor and serves up good salads and fresh seafood as evidenced by their lobster tank. The seaside restaurant *Le Vieux Galion* offers greet seafood in a nautical setting complete with a crashing surf serenade.

Just south of La Trinité on *N1*, the east coast highway, you'll find the *Usine du Galion*, the only Martinician sugar refinery that is still in operation. If you head towards the center of the Caravelle Peninsula from La Trinité on *D2*, you'll come to the town of Tartane where you can visit the *Rhumerie Hardy* for a free tour and samples. On the northern side of the peninsula is the lovely beach at *Anse l'Étang* where you can treat yourself to a pizza at the *Mini Golf Beach Club*. Just below the *Caravelle Panoramique* hotel at Anse l'Étang is a unique restaurant, *La Mandarine*, whose shark with sweet cider is unbeatable.

In Tartane on the Caravalle Peninsula, you can grab a bite at the *Ti-Carbet*, a sort of Caribbean Tiki-hut at the east end of *Plage de Tartane* at *Hardy La Brèche* beach. Across from the beach, at the site of the old *Hardy* distillery, you can get grilled meats, crepes, or pizza at *Kalicoucou*. Next to the *Le Madras* hotel in Tartane you can get a grilled sandwich under the awning at *Banga Snack*. One the waterfront you can dine at *Le Dubuc*, a very popular spot. The *Le Madras* hotel also has a very nice restaurant on its premises that serves up a tasteful blend of French and West Indian cuisine. On Friday and Saturday nights you can party at their beach barbeque parties while on Sundays live music will accompany your meal.

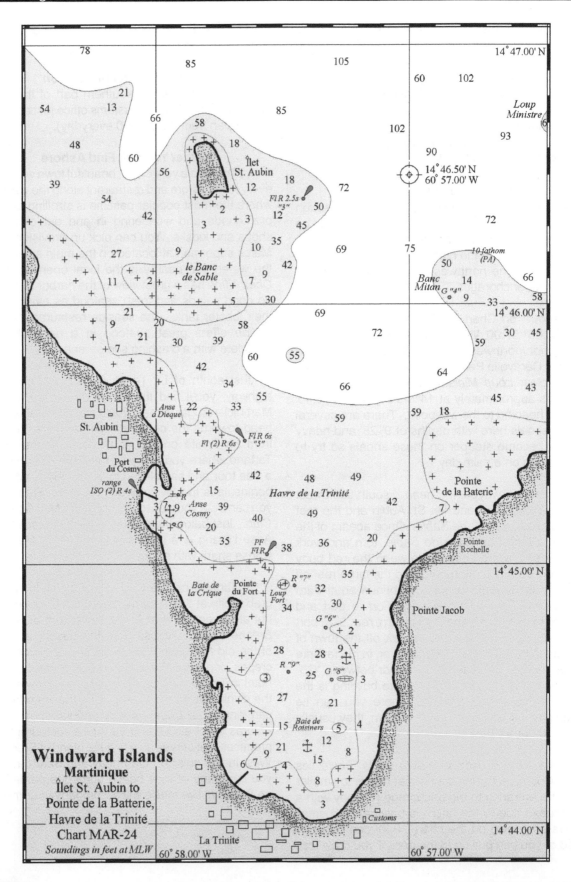

Windward Islands
Martinique
Îlet St. Aubin to
Pointe de la Batterie,
Havre de la Trinité
Chart MAR-24
Soundings in feet at MLW

Touring Inland Martinique

The best way to see the beauty that is Martinique is by renting a car and exploring the island (but isn't that true anywhere you travel?). Martinique has an excellent, well-maintained highway system, above average for a Caribbean Island. Most of the major thoroughfares in the busier areas such as Fort-de-France are four-lanes, and very nice two lane roads cover most of the island. If you're American or Canadian, a valid driver's license from home will suffice to rent a car in Martinique, while European citizens are advised to acquire an *International Driver's License*. There are two main types of roads on Martinique, *Routes Nationales*, designated by an *N* and then the highway number, are usually the larger, multi-lanes roadways. The *Routes Départementales* are generally narrower, perhaps even one lane in some places, and are denoted by a *D* before the highway number.

There are two types of buses operating on Martinique. The regular buses are called *Grands Bus*, hold about 40 passengers, and go anywhere within the city limits of the island. Martinique does not have an extensive island-wide bus system; however the *taxis collectifs* can provide transportation to nearly every other town on the island. These minivans leave the area of the cruise ship docks at Pointe Simon in Fort-de-France and pick up and let off passengers along the way to the outlying towns. These *taxis collectifs*, which are identified by their *TC* tags, are usually full, especially during rush hours. They begin very early in the morning, around 0600, rarely follow a regular schedule, and usually stop running at 1800. It is not unusual to see people hitchhiking on Martinique and it is fine to pick them up, it'll give you a chance to meet new people, learn a bit about the island and her people, and perhaps make a new friend. While this is not the United States where it is not customary to pick up hitchhikers due to the danger involved, use caution here just to be on the safe side, attacks by hitchhikers are rare, but not unknown.

Let's begin our tour of inland Martinique by leaving Fort-de-France and driving to Le Marin. Heading south on the national highway, *N1*, you'll come to *N5* and the airport located at Le Lamentin. Le Lamentin, which received its name from the large manatees that once inhabited the mouth of its canal, is the second largest city on Martinique, but it is heavily industrialized (including an oil refinery) and little is attractive to the

average cruiser except perhaps a visit to the rum factory, *Rhumerie La Favorite*, where you can enjoy a free tour and rum tasting. *La Favorite* received its name from Madame de Pompadour, the mistress of Louis XV, who was quite fond of the rum produced here.

After the rum tasting you can trek to the huge *Centre Commercial la Galleria* mall just off *N1* to giddily spend all your money (of course you wouldn't really do that, would you?). The mall is similar to your typical American mall with an American-style food court, but with a heavy dose of Caribbean soul tossed into the mix. Here too is a huge supermarket, *HyperU*, several restaurants, and over a hundred businesses in this modern complex. You can dine at the extremely French *Le Verger* restaurant at *Place d'Armes*. Many Martinicians take the short drive in the country to Le Lamentin to dine at *La Plantation*, where you can feast on such treats as Brazilian lobster or roast pigeon. There is an excellent hospital in Lamentin, the *Hôspital Pierre Zobda Quitman* (0596-75 15 15).

Heading west on *D7* through *Trois Îlets* and Domaine de la Pagerie, you will find the road quite picturesque to say the least. If you take the coastal road to Le Diamant, *D37*, you'll be rewarded with scenic views of Diamond Rock lying just off the southwestern tip of Martinique. From Le Diamant, home of the longest beach on Martinique, the highway will take you along the southern shore through *Trois Rivières* and Ste. Luce to Le Marin.

Now let's discuss the scenic route from Fort-de-France northward on the *Route de la Trace*, the *Trail Route*, a twisting, turning road that leads all the way to Martinique's eastern shore. The *Route de la Trace* was cut through the rainforest by Jesuit priests back in the 1700s as a means of bypassing the *Pitons du Carbet,* that series of peaks lying south of *Mt. Pelée.* No visit to Martinique is complete without taking the wheel of a car and traveling down this road through the luxurious tropical vegetation of the island's rainforest, past singing birds and cascading waterfalls. Cruisers should rent a car just for this experience if for no other reason. The national park service of Martinique, the *Parc Régional de la Martinique*, ensures that the area will be developed in harmony with nature and has also cut many hiking trails through the rainforest enabling you to get well off the beaten path and explore to your heart's content.

In Fort-de-France the *Route de la Trace* begins life as *Boulevard Allègre* which soon turns into *N3*. Take *N3* northward through the hills to Balata-Tourte where you already begin see the signs of the rainforest. The *Église de Balata is* a twin to the famous *Basilica du Sacré Coeur* located in Paris. North of Balata-Tourte look for *Halte Panoramique*, a scenic viewing area on the estate of *Habitation La Liot*, as fine a spot to view the *Pitons du Carbet*, the Caribbean Sea, and the Atlantic Ocean as can be found. The small admission price includes a drink. The *Jardin de Balata* is a lovely botanical garden that is worth viewing.

Following *N3* northward into the mountains you'll find yourself at an elevation of round 2,000' before winding down into the Rivière Blanche gorge, complete with picnic tables and vendors. If you take a westbound detour at *D1* toward Fond St. Denis, you'll pass through a tunnel and then see a sign pointing to the *Trace des Jésuites,* the *Jesuits Trail*, a great hiking trail and named for the *gommier*, or white gum, tree that the Jesuits would extract sap from for their incense. Also on *D1* you can stop at a rest area next to a waterfall, the *Cascade Saut de Gendarme* or take the road that leads to *Canal Beauregard*, a 200-year-old canal built to supply water to four sugar mills in the *Carbet River Valley.*

In *Fond St. Denis* you will find that the village and the roadsides are absolutely covered with flowers, they are everywhere, in fact, the residents here compete with nearby L'Ajoupa Bouillon to see which town has the most flowers. On the road between Fond St. Denis and St. Pierre is *Le Fromager*, an award winning restaurant with a scenic view of *Mt. Pelée*. Another pleasant stop for a meal is A*uberge du Mont Béni* for Creole cooking. In front of the church is a war memorial dedicated to the soldiers of World War I, a large base with a statue of a soldier barely a foot tall. The statue was only the model for the intended monument, but when the citizens who had to pay for the monument realized it was too costly they decided that the model would suffice.

A final stop in Fond St. Denis could be the *Observatoire du Morne de Cadets*, built to monitor the volcanic activity of *Mt. Pelée*. Here a seismograph monitors the volcano's slightest activity, but it is only one part of a network of 20 such monitoring stations that continually feed data to the main computer also located here. East of the *Route de la Trace* sits steep sloped Morne Jacob, one of the oldest volcanoes

on Martinique. Several trails lead from the large anthurium plantation on its western flank to the summit.

Continuing northward on *N3*, the *Route de la Trace*, you'll find yourself descending gradually through banana plantations as you approach Le Morne Rouge, almost on the shoulder of *Mt. Pelée* and a good spot to begin an exploration of the mountain. Le Morne Rouge was destroyed a few months after St. Pierre by another eruption in which 1,500 people were killed. Le Morne Rouge was virtually wiped off the map after that eruption and again during the years from 1929-1932 when *Mt. Pelée* again erupted forcing the residents to flee. Every August 30th, the date of the second eruption, many Martinicians make a pilgrimage to the Catholic church here to pay homage to the Virgin Mary. There is a *Champion* grocery store on the road into town, but if you'd like to dine close to the volcano, visit *La Refuge de l'Aileron*, the snack bar at the start of the hiking trail up the mountain. You can also grab a bite a *Le Bambou* on the southern side of town, at *Le Gita Péléen* right in the heart of Le Morne Rouge, *Barbecue du Nord* (economical), and *Auberge de la Montagne Pelée*, for a truly awesome view some 2,600 feet up.

From Le Morne Rouge you can take the road down to St. Pierre. From St. Pierre southward through Le Carbet, Bellefontaine, Case Pilote, and Schoelcher, the road stays right along the coast and offers excellent views of the Caribbean. South of St. Pierre you'll pass through a tunnel, *Le Trou Caraibe* (*The Caribbean Hole*) built in 1854. When you begin to enter the suburbs of Fort-de-France in Schoelcher, you'll find that your view of the water is blocked, not only by large houses, but also by huge walls that give you the feeling that the owners are attempting to keep the view to themselves. The attractions along this coast have already been discussed in their respective sections, and now we find ourselves back where we started in Fort-de-France. So let's go back to Le Morne Rouge and the *Route de la Trace*.

Continuing on the *Route de la Trace,* you will now enter L'Ajoupa Bouillon, a quaint little town lying virtually in the shadow of *Mt. Pelée*. The town is named after a man named Bouillon who built a shack here, the Carib word for which is *ajoupa*, meaning a *hut made of branches*. Just to the west of town is a small park, *Gorges de la Falaise*, where a trail leads down to a gorgeous waterfall. Hiking to the falls requires you to get wet, bring a swimsuit or some extra clothes, and a waterproof bag for your camera. Part of the hike goes through a section of deep water so if you can't swim, avoid those sections of the trail. North of town on the eastern side of *N3* is *Les Ombrages* where you can hike a trail leading to a botanical garden and an old sugar mill and rum distillery. If you are hungry and haven't stopped for lunch yet, try *L'Universium* in the center of town or *L'Abri* for a good meal in a romantic setting surrounded by flowers.

Just before you reach Martinique's eastern shore, *N3* intersects with *N1*, the eastern shore road, and if you take a left and go north you'll come to the birthplace of Aimé Césaire, Basse Pointe. Aimé Césaire, born in 1913, was a renowned poet, playwright, and longtime mayor of Fort-de-France. Born into poverty, Césaire studied in France and was one of the three founders of *Négritude*, a term he invented to designate the black culture as a whole and a movement that encouraged blacks to promote their racial heritage. In 1945 he became the mayor of Fort-de-France and later became a member of the *National Assembly* and founded the *Parti Progressiste Martinquais,* the *PPM* or *Progressive Party* in 1957. Under Césaire's leadership Martinique avoided falling into the same rut as Guadeloupe whose independence movement caused widespread violent riots in the 1980s. In 1983, the *Conseil Régional de la Martinique* was created and Aimé Césaire was elected its first president. In 1995, Aimé Césaire was voted back into power at the age of 82 retaining the office of Mayor of Fort-de-France that he held since 1945, a truly amazing record.

Near Basse Pointe, is the 18th century *Plantation de Levyritz*, where U.S President Gerald Ford met with British Prime Minister James Callaghan, West German Prime Minister Helmut Schmidt, and French President Valéry Giscard d'Estaing in 1976. The plantation is also home to the *Musée des Figurines Végétales* where you can view locally made dolls of banana grass representing famous French women such as Marie Antoinette and Madame Curie. If you're hungry, the restaurant here would be hard to beat, but there is an alternative, *Chez Mally* or *Le Petit Palais* right in the heart of the town itself. Further north along the northeastern shore is Macouba, a Carib word for a fish that was prevalent in pre-Columbian times. Once a thriving tobacco growing center, today the town is known more for the outstanding views of the Caribbean that you can enjoy while visiting the

rum distillery *JM Crassous de Medeuil* which offers free tours and sampling of some of the excellent *rhum vieux* (reason enough to visit Macouba!). A good place to grab a bite is *Pointe Nord*. To the west of Macouba you'll cross a metal bridge high over the *Rivière Potiche*, a dizzying experience.

The next town is Grand Rivière, the end of the road and a surfer's delight. The town has a very nice spot to eat, *Yva Chez Vava*, where owner Vava and her daughter Yva will serve you food that has earned them a near-legendary reputation. In 1992, *Gault Millau*, a high-class French culinary guide, awarded *Yva Chez Vava* a *Gold Key* designating the eatery as one of the finest French restaurants in the world. It is also here in Grand Rivière that hikers can pick up the ten-mile trail that leads through the rainforest to Le Prêcheur on the western shore.

If you arrive at the eastern shore on the *Route de la Trace* and don't wish to head north, you can turn right at *N1* and head southward along Martinique's beautiful, absolutely breathtaking eastern shore. All along the eastern shoreline you'll be reward with stunning views of the Atlantic Ocean and the offshore reefs breaking under the trade-wind driven swell. The rolling hills and fields of the countryside look almost manicured while the houses and towns along Martinique's eastern shore are neat and tidy, not at all like the shacks and shanty towns seen on other Caribbean islands such as St. Lucia and St. Vincent

Heading southward on *N1*, the first town you'll come to is Le Lorrain, a nice touristy town with a long black beach, a prominent cathedral, and a casino. Le Lorrain was the birthplace of novelist Raphaël Confiant and was once known as Grande Anse. If you would like to grab a sandwich here, the *Délifrance* chain has a store in Le Lorrain, but the best place to eat here is the *Relais des Isles* just north of town. The next town south is Le Marigot with its small harbor for small fishing boats. A short distance north of Marigot is a large aquaculture farm where shrimp are raised. If you take a detour up *D15* you'll find scenic views from *Pain de Sucre*, *Sugar Loaf*, named for its similarity to the *Sugar Loaf* in Rio de Janeiro. South of Le Marigot, about three miles north of Sainte Marie, is a very popular restaurant, *La Découverte* (*Chez Tatie Simone*) lying hidden in the forest. Here *Tatie* (*Auntie*) Simone Adelise welcomes you to her restaurant and the hiking trail along the coast for those wishing to walk off their meal.

The next stop south is Sainte Marie with its open, attractive waterfront that offers no protection save in the lee of a tiny island, Îlet Ste. Marie, whose shallow anchorage is usually full of small fishing boats. At low tide it is possible to walk across to Îlet Ste. Marie, easily recognizable by the cross atop the island. A visit to the *Distillerie St. James* and rum museum may be called for here if you're not burnt out from all the other distillery tours that you've taken while driving around Martinique, but let's face it, a visit to Martinique would not be complete without at least several tours of *rhumeries* to sample their wares and offer your own opinions as to which one is best and why. For a bit more information on rum and Martinician rum in particular, see the section *Rum* in the chapter *The Basics*.

The *Distillerie St. James* originated in the hills above St. Pierre and moved to Sainte Marie after the eruption of *Mt. Pelée* in 1902. *St. James* is the oldest brand of rum on Martinique and in the distillery's gift shop you can purchase a bottle of century-old rum or if that doesn't suit you, try the seafood in the restaurant. In town you can dine in the elegant *Habitation Lagrange*, one of the best restaurants on Martinique. South of Sainte Marie, turn west on *D25* and head for Morne des Esses, once a hideout for escaped slaves and now a center for native African and Caribbean culture. If you want to try some truly creative Creole cooking, visit *Le Colibri* (*The Hummingbird*) in Morne des Esses, the *vannerie* (basket weaving) capital of Martinique.

Our next stop is the Caravalle Peninsula, which juts out into the Atlantic almost 7 miles and offers many places to anchor and explore (see the previous sections on *The Eastern Coast of Martinique*). Heading south you will come to Le Robert and Le François where you'll see banana plantations surrounded by huge man-made hedges.

Le François is the island's fourth largest district in terms of population and is home to the unique architectural lines of *Église Saint Michel du François*, a daring break from the normal churches seen on Martinique. It was designed as a replacement for the original church that was ravaged by fire in 1973 and is actually the sixth church to be built on the site. In between Le Robert and Le François you can dine at the pizzeria in the *Miramar* hotel. On Friday and Saturday nights the restaurant is transformed into a piano bar.

From here it's a short hop to Le Vauclin, known as the *Capital of the South*. Le Vauclin is named after the Compte de Vauclin who settled here in at the turn of the 18th century. The fishing port that grew up around de Vauclin's plantation, once the site of a Carib settlement, soon became known as Le Vauclin. A great spot to dine here is *Cabana Plage* where children and pets are welcome to dine with you in this open-air seaside restaurant. If true open-air dining is what you seek, try *Sous des Cocotiers* where the only thing above your beach-side table may be an umbrella. From Le Vauclin it's a lovely drive through beautiful rolling countryside to Marin. Driving through here it's easy to let the mind wander and think that you truly are in France, however a simple glance to the east, to the offshore reefs, will bring you back to reality.

St. Lucia

Port of Entry: Rodney Bay (*Rodney Bay Marina*), Castries, Marigot Bay, Soufrière, and Vieux Fort
Fuel: Rodney Bay, Vigie, Marigot Bay
Haul-Out: Rodney Bay
Diesel Repairs: Vigie, Marigot Bay, Rodney Bay
Outboard Repairs: Vigie, Marigot Bay, Rodney Bay, Vigie
Propane: Gros Islet
Provisions: Castries, Vigie, Rodney Bay, Marigot Bay
Important Lights: See *Appendix A*

How I love St. Lucia! To condense it into a few words, *Marigot Bay* and the Pitons, either one of which could qualify for the finals in a "Most Breathtaking Spot In The Caribbean" competition (and I'd bet the Pitons would win). Like most Caribbean islands, St. Lucia (pronounced Saint Loo-sha) is lush and mountainous, and is blessed with tremendous natural beauty, over 19,000 acres of tropical rainforest.

St. Lucia, the second largest of the Windward Islands, is roughly 15.5 miles wide by 28 miles long, and its leeward coast offers some fine anchorages, a great hurricane hole at *Marigot Bay*, and quality whale-watching for the eco-tourists among us. Over 20 different species of whale including humpbacks, pilot whales, and sperm whales (from December to March) have been spotted off the coast of St. Lucia. The sperm whales in particular have been known to come close to shore with their calves as they orient them to their migratory patterns.

If approaching St. Lucia from Martinique, sailors will have an enjoyable reach from Ste. Anne to *Rodney Bay*. From Fort-de-France the route can often be a bit more on the wind and heading for *Marigot Bay* would ease that beat. Northbound skippers arriving from St. Vincent will also have a nice reach, though beware that the winds at the northern tip of St. Vincent can be quite strong and gusty, better to reef and stay inshore until about five miles or so north of St. Vincent where the conditions should moderate a bit and you can shake out the reef.

Ashore, electrical service is 220 volt, 50 cycle AC. Many restaurants will include a 10% tip so be sure to check your bill, and take note that you'll also be charged an 8% government tax where applicable. Spearfishing is not permitted in the waters around St. Lucia

A Brief History of St. Lucia

The first known inhabitants of St. Lucia were Arawaks who arrived on the island from the Orinoco delta region of Venezuela around 200 AD. Hot on their heels, between 800 and 1200 AD, were the Caribs who, immediately upon arrival, proceeded to decimate the Arawak population by killing the men, enslaving their women, and castrating and fattening the young boys for later consumption until by the turn of the 16th century the Arawaks were but a footnote in St. Lucia's history. The Caribs named the island *Iouanalao*, or *Land of the Iguanas*, and this name was later corrupted to *Hiwanarau*, and finally to *Hewanorra*, which is now the name of St. Lucia's international airport.

Although it has been suggested that Columbus "discovered" St. Lucia on his fourth and final voyage to the New World in 1502, no reference to the island exists in the Admiral's records leaving some critics to speculate whether or not he actually ever viewed the island. The island is named after St. Lucie, an Italian saint whose feast day is December 13, and this date was celebrated for years as St. Lucia's *Discovery Day*. Columbus' log reveals that the *great discoverer* was elsewhere on Dec. 13, 1502.

The man that actually discovered St. Lucia may well have been Juan de la Cosa, a Spaniard who accompanied Columbus on his first two voyages. During an independent expedition in 1504, de la Cosa sighted St. Lucia and named it *El Falcón* on his famous map of the New World. Although the Spanish never attempted to colonize St. Lucia, the island later appeared on a Spanish *Royal Cedula of Population* as St. Lucia in 1511, and later was included on a Vatican map of the New World in 1520. St Lucia has also been called the *Fair Helen of the West Indies*, after Helen of Troy.

The Spanish claimed St. Lucia in absentia after Juan de la Cosa's visit in 1504, but the first non-Amerindian settler is reputed to be a pirate, Francois le Clerc, also known as *Jambe de Bois* (Wooden Leg), who is said to have used Pigeon Island as a base for attacking Spanish ships. In 1600, the Dutch set up a reprovisioning outpost at Vieux Fort, which was soon

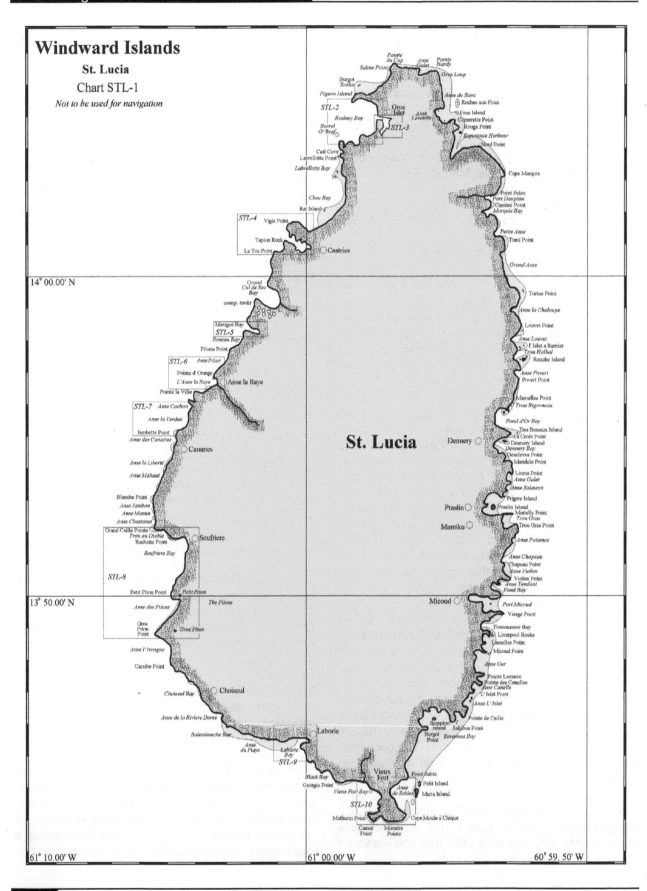

Windward Islands

St. Lucia

Chart STL-1

Not to be used for navigation

St. Lucia

destroyed by the Caribs and the survivors driven from the island. In 1605, and quite by accident, British settlers established a colony at the southern end of the island. The settlers were on a ship called the *Olive Branch* (sometimes shown as the *Olive Blossom*) and were bound for Guyana when they were blown off course, landing on St. Lucia. The 67 settlers met with the Caribs to arrange shelter and were shortly thereafter attacked. After a month of battle, 19 of the colonists survived by fleeing in stolen Carib canoes. In 1625, the Dutch built a fort in the same vicinity, which eventually led to the name of the present day town of Vieux Fort.

The British again attempted to colonize the island in 1639 under the leadership of Sir Thomas Warner, and actually lasted almost two years before being wiped out by the Caribs. For the next dozen years St. Lucia was the site of many skirmishes between Caribs and settlers, with the Caribs coming out on the winning end in each instance.

In 1651, Governor du Parquet of Martinique purchased the island and the French, or to be more precise, the *French West India Company*, attempted to colonize St. Lucia. The French built a fort on the Vigie peninsula just to the north of what is now the capital city, Castries. The French encampment, Le Carenage, was on the banks of a small creek that led into the bay. The French fought many battles with the Caribs, but were finally able to come to terms with their enemy and signed a peace treaty with them in 1660.

A dispute soon arose over ownership of the island between the French and the British (who were firmly entrenched in Barbados), both of whom were intent on increasing their holdings in the Caribbean. A long era of hostility persevered between the two nations as both used the Caribs as mercenaries in their conflicts. Missionaries attempted to convert the Caribs and those who would not convert were often killed as a systematic annihilation of the Caribs was undertaken by the British who captured as many as they could find and shipped them off to Dominica.

During this period St. Lucia was like a ping-pong ball, changing hands 14 times in the next 150 years. France settlers moved in along the southern coast at Soufrière in 1743 (which later became the capital of St. Lucia in 1746) and began setting up vast sugarcane plantations and importing large numbers of West African slaves to work their fields.

While all this was going on, the American colonies were rebelling against British rule, and France, taking sides with the rebels, earned even more disfavor with the British who attacked the settlements of St. Lucia in 1778. After four long years of fighting, British Admiral George Rodney established a fort and naval base at Pigeon island from which he attacked French forces at Iles de Saintes. The British victory at what is known as the *Battle of the Saints*, was the beginning of the end of French domination in the Caribbean although the French in St. Lucia was not yet ready to relinquish their island.

The *Treaty of Paris* in 1783 secured French control of the island and within six years the French Revolution changed the island forever. Most of the settlements were renamed, French nobles were guillotined in the streets, and the Republicans freed the slaves, the work force of the plantation owners. As if this was not enough, the British and the French were still fighting on the island and the slaves were drawn into the struggle. Although some slaves opted to stay on the plantations, many fled into the interior and formed loose-knit guerrilla-style freedom fighters known as the *Brigands*. The *Brigands* were a thorn in the side of the British, attacking and destroying their plantations, and generally terrorizing the British settlers. After a slave rebellion in 1748, a group of *Brigands*, fled to the mountains in the vicinity of Fond Gen Libres, (*Valley of the Free People*) where their descendants still live today.

In 1795, a group of *Brigands* captured Pigeon Island and were able to hold it for several weeks before being overpowered by the superior British forces. During these years, most of the island's settlements were destroyed, and a great center of conflict revolved around *Ft. Charlotte* in the hills above Castries. Tough British troops attacked the fort in 1796 and after a fierce two-day battle, captured the fort that marked that would rapidly bring about the end of French rule on St. Lucia. By 1798, many of the Brigands, their numbers reduced and their supplies depleted, also surrendered to the British and returned to a life of slavery.

In 1814, the *Treaty of Paris* brought St. Lucia under permanent British control as a Crown Colony. British law was established in 1827, and later, in 1838, St. Lucia became a member of the British Windward Islands. English was established as the official language of the island and the official seat of government was moved to Barbados. During these years of peace, the economy of St. Lucia fostered until the abolition of slavery in 1834.

Although many slaves stayed on as indentured servants, there was not enough of a work force to successfully work the plantations and the St. Lucian economy fell apart until the 1860s when Castries came into its own as a coal supply center for ships in the Caribbean. Indentured servants from India were brought in to bolster the work force and St. Lucia thrived for about 70 years. Before World War II, diesel fuel replaced the coal used by the older steamers and St. Lucia's coal warehousing went belly-up as the economy took a downward turn again. Trade unions were formed and these led to political parties that were to shape the future of St. Lucia.

By the 1950s, independence from Britain was a hot topic on the island and in 1958 St. Lucia joined other British colonies in the West Indies Federation, a political grouping whose aim was to win independence for its members. After the withdrawal from the federation of the more economically stable islands of Jamaica, Trinidad, and Tobago, the federation dissolved in 1962, but St. Lucia kept plodding along on the road to independence. In 1967, St. Lucia was granted full self-government and a two-party governmental system developed, the United Worker's Party (UWP), and the more liberal St. Lucia Labour Party (SLP).

Britain was besieged by years of lobbying and finally granted independence to St. Lucia on February 22, 1979. Today St. Lucia remains a Commonwealth country and a constitutional monarchy with the British sovereign as the titular head of state. St. Lucia now enjoys a more balanced economy, thanks in no small part to tourism, the nation's number one employer with one out of three workers involved in the field.

Today, St. Lucia is home to the most endangered snake on the planet. The tiny Maria Islands Nature Preserve, off the northern coast of St. Lucia, is home to the St. Lucia racer, of which 18-100 remain. The snakes were decimated on St. Lucia by the introduction of the mongoose in the late 1800s, but the Maria Islands are mongoose free and the St. Lucia racer lives there without fear of that fierce reptile hunter.

In 1936, the St. Lucia racer was declared extinct as none were found on the island, but in 1973, a researcher found one on Maria Island. By the end of

2011, eleven St. Lucia racers had been verified and outfitted with tiny data recorders that observers used to determine that the St. Lucia racer population was between 18 and 100. Researchers are attempting to help the meter long snakes make a comeback as did the Antigua racer when 50 snakes were counted in 1995, and a decade later their numbers grew to 900.

Customs and Immigration

Ports of Entry: Rodney Bay (*Rodney Bay Marina*), Castries, Marigot Bay, Soufrière, and Vieux Fort

Upon arrival, skippers are required to notify *Customs* and *Immigration* of their arrival and intent to visit other ports on the island and to acquire a permit for this purpose. Skippers will need to bring along their vessel registration papers, their clearance for the last port and a valid passport for all aboard. No passengers may disembark from your vessel until clearance is granted. If you plan to stay only three days or less, you may clear in and out at the same time.

Citizens of the United States, Canada, Britain, Australia, and Russia can enter St. Lucia without a visa and stay up to 42 days. All visitors are required to have a passport. Citizens of New Zealand, the Dominican Republic, Jordan, Syria, Lebanon, Iraq, Iran, Nigeria, and the People's Republic of China are required to obtain a visa prior to arrival. *Immigration* extensions cost EC$100 for 21 days; for extension information call *Immigration* at 758-454-6239.

Fees
Current entry fees are:
EC$10: Pratique (for vessels up to 10 tons)
EC$15: Navigational Aids
EC$5: Clearance for vessels under 40' LOA
EC$15: Clearance for vessels over 40 LOA
EC$20: Charter boats under 40' LOA
EC$30: Charter boats between 40'-70' LOA
EC$40: Charter boats over 70' LOA
EC$15: Charter fee per passenger
EC$68: Departure Tax if leaving by plane

Regular visitors now have the opportunity to pay a semi-annual fee equivalent to only four times the occasional fee.

Firearms
All firearms must be declared upon arrival. If

staying less than three days no action is necessary; if staying over 72 hours all firearms must be sealed on board by a *Customs* officer.

Fishing

Sportfishing boats will need to purchase a fishing license, but sailboats are permitted to troll a line without a permit. No SCUBA diving is permitted without a St. Lucian guide. Spearfishing is not permitted in the waters of St. Lucia.

Pets

All pets must have an import permit before entering St. Lucia. Cats and dogs must be microchipped, be over 3 months old, and have a valid health and rabies inoculation certificate. For more information contact the *Chief Veterinary Officer* at chiefvet@slumalffe. org.

Clearing Out

Duty-free fuel may be purchased after clearing out. This is most easily accomplished at *Rodney Bay* and *Marigot Bay*. Vessels are now permitted to stay for up to 72 hours after clearing out. This allows cruisers to enjoy the beautiful anchorages in the southern half of St. Lucia such as Anse des Pitons, Anse Chastenet, and Anse Cochon without having to return to a POE for clearance.

Getting Around on St. Lucia

Taxis and Buses

Transportation is easy on St. Lucia, and a good way of getting around the island is by taking the local busses, identified by their "H" license plates. But don't be confused as taxis also have an "H" plate. Make sure that the vehicle you're on is a bus or taxi as there is a tremendous difference in their fares. The easy way to spot a bus is to look for a small van that has some sort of graphics displayed across the top of the windshield, usually a name or nickname of the owner, or a particular tenet of his. Busses are privately owned and are inexpensive. Generally, there are set bus stops, but if you see a bus go ahead and flag it down, they'll usually stop for you. Be advised that taxis charge more between 2220 and 0630 and for more than three passengers.

If you wish to rent a car, there are companies all over the island for your convenience, see *Appendix C* in the back of the book for more information. You will need a St. Lucia driving permit issued by the police at Gros Islet, at the airports, and by most major rental car firms at a cost of EC$54.

Ferries

If you wish to visit St. Lucia from another nearby Caribbean island, *L'Express des Iles* is a high speed passenger ferry that runs from Castries to Guadeloupe with stops in Martinique and Dominica. For more information call 758-452-2211. There is also a smaller ferry that runs from Le Marin in Martinique to *Rodney Bay Marina* on St. Lucia.

Rodney Bay and Gros Islet

Waypoints:
Rodney Bay- ¼ nm NW of
14° 05.20' N, 60° 58.50' W

This entire area, the northern tip of St. Lucia, is usually referred to as the *Quarter of Gros Islet* and it includes the town of Gros Islet, as well as *Rodney Bay* with its marina complex, and hotel lined *Reduit Beach*. The *Quarter* hosts St. Lucia's largest concentration of hotels, restaurants, and tourist offerings. The village of Gros Islet is probably best known for its *Friday Night Jump Up*, a huge street party with loud music and lines of stalls with street vendors selling everything from barbeque to handmade crafts. Take the appropriate security measures here as you would anywhere.

Navigational Information

As shown on Chart STL-2, a waypoint at 14° 05.20' N, 60° 58.50' W, will place you approximately ¼ nautical mile northwest of horseshoe-shaped *Rodney Bay* (named after Admiral George Brydges Rodney). From the waypoint, you can enter the bay and anchor just south of the causeway that connects Pigeon Island to the mainland in what is sometimes shown as the *St. Croix Roadstead*. You can also approach the entrance channel to the inner lagoon and *Rodney Bay Marina* dropping the hook off beautiful and popular *Reduit Beach* by the *Royal St. Lucian Hotel* south of the well-marked channel.

Another anchoring alternative, although not viable when northerly seas are running, is to tuck up into *Trou Gascon* in the extreme southern portion of *Rodney Bay*. Whichever anchorage you choose, keep your eyes open as *Rodney Bay* has lots of fish traps marked with small plastic bottles, not easily seen until almost upon them, especially in the early morning as you approach with the sun in your eyes.

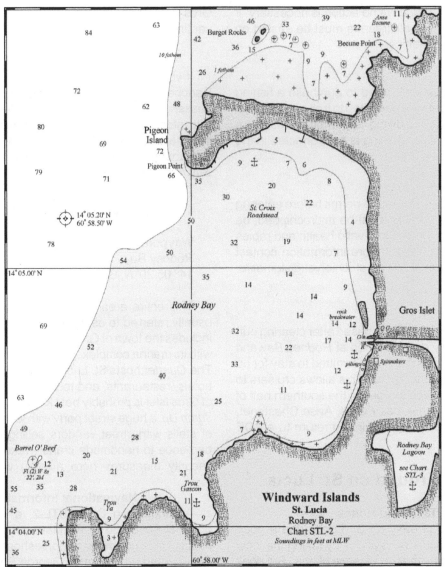

Windward Islands
St. Lucia
Rodney Bay
Chart STL-2
Soundings in feet at MLW

View from atop Pigeon Island looking east

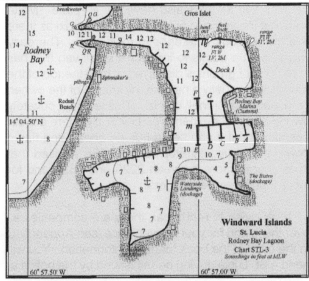

Windward Islands
St. Lucia
Rodney Bay Lagoon
Chart STL-3
Soundings in feet at MLW

If you are approaching *Rodney Bay* from the south, keep a sharp lookout for the shoal called *Barrel O' Beef*. If you do not wish to pass north of the *Barrel O' Beef* you can pass between the shoal and the mainland in 8'-35' of water.

A lot of cruisers tend to favor *Rodney Bay Lagoon* and the facilities that *Rodney Bay Marina* has to offer. To enter the lagoon and the marina, make your way to the marked entrance channel as shown on Chart STL-2, and in detail on Chart STL-3, passing between the lighted jetties in 10'-14' of water. Continue along the channel past the *Eagle's Inn* seafood restaurant (check it out after you've cleared in and tied up or taken a mooring) on your starboard side and you'll enter the inner lagoon.

In the inner lagoon, to the southwest of *Rodney Bay Marina*, you might be able to get a slip at *Waterside Landings* (they seem to stay full).

Anchoring is no longer permitted in the inner lagoon. There are several *IGY* marina installed and maintained moorings for your convenience.

What You Will Find Ashore
There is a daily VHF net in *Rodney Bay* on ch. 68 at 0830, Monday through Saturday, where you can pick up on the latest news on who's arriving and departing, what businesses are having specials and happy hours, and where you can even get help in obtaining parts and services.

Customs and *Immigration*
Rodney Bay Marina is chock full of facilities for the cruiser including a *Customs* and *Immigration* office located in the central building on the ground floor facing the marina. The offices are open from 0800-1200 and 1330-1630, and until 1800 on Thursdays and Fridays; overtime (EC$10-EC$15) is charged outside of regular office hours (weekends, during the lunch hour, or after 1545 during the week). Only the captain may come ashore; all crew must stay on the vessel while the skipper clears. If you need to clear when the facilities are closed, you can phone the office in Castries at 758-468-4859 for instructions.

Getting Around
Public transportation is easy to access; buses can be found across from the marina and there is a taxi stand on marina property. There is another taxi stand located at *JQ Mall*. Water taxis can also be found on

VHF ch. 16 (I recommend Marley; his phone number is 758-486-2874).

Internet
Lime (*Cable & Wireless*) has an office in *Rodney Bay Marina* with hard-wired Internet access as well as Wi-fi and cell phones for sale. Also located in the marina is *Rent A Ride* where you'll find email access, fax service, and several phones for international calls (including *USA Direct*).

Restaurants such as *Café Ole, H2O, Pizza Pizza, and Red Snapper* have free Wi-fi as does *Jambe de Bois* on Pigeon Island (located near the dinghy dock, they also have a computer station with Internet access).

Marine Facilities
Marinas
Rodney Bay Marina
IGY Rodney Bay Marina, formerly a United States Army base and today a *Port of Entry* as well as the finish line for the *Atlantic Rally for Cruisers ARC*, boasts 253 slips (floating docks) and can accommodate vessels up to 280' LOA with drafts up to 15'. Please note that Dock 1 is for mega-yachts and offers 110/220/380 volt electric (including 3-phase) in both 50 and 60 cycle AC and high-speed fueling capabilities (duty-free if the vessel has cleared out). Docks A-E offer 220 volt, 50 cycle electric while docks F, G, and J offer 100 volt 60 cycle AC.

The marina also has water, cable TV, laundry services, ice, and can arrange for propane fills (although you can refill your tanks yourself at the *Shell* station in Gros Islet). Marina guests are also allowed use of the pool, but beware of loud music on Friday and Saturday nights. Garbage can be taken out to the large bins near the road that runs in front of the marina. There's also a place to deposit your used motor oil, ask at the marina office. Most days you may have a visitor who'll bring his palm frond-covered boat alongside yours to sell you fresh fruits, vegetables, and anything else he might have and that you might need.

Waterside Landings
At the southern end of *Rodney Bay* you'll find a smaller marina, *Waterside Landings*, an informal and friendly marina offering 15 slips with water, electric, Wi-fi, and showers. The ambiance can't be beat!

Marine Haul-Out

As you turn to the south, on the east side of the inner lagoon lies the 4.5 acre *Rodney Bay Marine Boatyard* whose fuel dock is open from 0800-1300 everyday. The boatyard monitors VHF ch. 68 and has a 75-ton TravelLift, a 40-ton boat trailer, and can accommodate vessels to 85', LOA with a 27' beam, and 13' draft. Duty-free fuel is available to vessels that have cleared out.

Marine Services

If you're hauled out at the yard, check with the office for tech help. The yard can handle all repairs or put you in touch with local contractors who can do the job for you (some of whom may not be listed here).

Electrical/Electronics

For electronic problems, try *Regis Electronics* if you need some quality electronic or watermaker repairs. Another electronic repair option is *Marin Tek* who can also service your genset and refrigeration. *Marin Tek* are also dealers for *Volvo Penta*, *Northern Lights*, and *Kohler*. Matthew at *Amtec* can handle most any electronic repair (Matthew monitors VHF ch. 72). For metal work and fabrication try *ARC Dynamics* also at the marina.

Inflatables/Life Rafts

The *Liferaft and Inflatable Center*, an *Avon* dealer, can repack your life raft or sell you a new one, they'll even turn your dinghy into a survival dinghy! They have a great dock with 10' alongside!

Mechanical and Refrigeration

Destination St. Lucia, *DSL*, is multi-talented, they can repair your boat, your engine, and your refrigeration, and if they can't handle the repair, they'll direct you to the right person for the job.

For mechanical repairs you can also contact *Quick and Reliable Mechanical Services*, probably the best of the lot of service companies in *Rodney Bay*. They are agents for *Caterpillar*, *Onan*, *Fischer Panda*, *Northern Lights*, *Yanmar*, and *Perkins*. Another highly qualified mechanic is Tony George at *Tony's Engineering*.

Outboard Repair

For outboard repair try *Mac's Marine*, a *Mariner* dealer with a nice little dinghy dock. Nest to *Mac's* is *Island Marine Supplies*, agents for *Mercury* and *Mercruiser* and work on all brands of outboards. Across from the marina, *Johnson's Marine Center*

is an agent for *Mariner* outboards. The *Liferaft and Inflatable Center* also repairs outboards (ask for Steve). *Marin Tek* can also repair your outboard.

Rigging and Sails

Rodney Bay Sails is located in the marina and can handle your sail repair, canvas work, and rigging needs. *RBS* also handles *Doyle* sails from Barbados and carries furling systems. *RBS* cannot do swaging but they will arrange for Ian Cowen, the local rep for *Furlex*, *Profurl*, and *Selden* to handle that chore.

Welding and Fabrication

Nearby *Ryte Weld Enterprises* can handle all your metal working needs. In the boatyard, Lawrence (*Chinaman* on VHF ch. 16) has a welding and fabrication shop.

Woodworking/Hull Repair

For hull repair and joinery try *Mermaid Repair* located in the boatyard. *Cox Enterprises* can handle repairs as well as new construction of boats.

Marine Supplies

Located at *Rodney Bay Marina* is an *Island Water World* outlet (758-452-1222). Here you will find all types of marine supplies and hardware, as well as electronics, outboards (*OMC, Mercury,* and *Yamaha*), and dinghies (*Caribe* and *Walker Bay*), everything you could need. If they don't have it, they'll have it shipped in. Bring your paperwork and get duty-free marine supplies. Across from the marina, *Johnson's Marine Center* offers marine supplies and hardware in their huge outlet. They sell all manner of marine supplies and are agents for *Mariner* outboards.

Rodney Bay Marine Hardware offers duty-free marine supplies for visiting yachtsmen.

Medical Help

The *Rodney Bay Medical Clinic* is just across from the *Super J* and a dentist, Greg Glace, is available at his office near the *JQ Mall*.

Provisions

I suppose the first stop for most folks who take a slip at the marina will be *Top Shelf*, open from 0700-2100, Monday through Saturday, and on Sundays from 0800-1400. Nearby is the *Bread Basket* (a favorite of mine for an early breakfast) offering all manner of freshly baked goods. If you need spirits, *Bryden and Partners* have a small outlet on site.

For larger provisioning needs try the *Super J* located in the southern end of *Rodney Bay* at *Rodney Bay Village*. *Super J* is open Monday-Thursday from 0700-2200, Fridays and Saturdays from 0700-2400, and Sundays from 0700-1600.

If you need to supply your larder with frozen meats or veggies, contact *Island Food Ltd.*, in Gros Islet at 758-50-0405, they deliver to your boat.

For gourmet Med fare try the deli located at *Delirious*, just behind the restaurant. Specializing in yacht provisioning, they are open weekdays from 1100-1900 and on Saturdays from 1700-1900.

Further south, towards Castries, is *JQ Mall* with a *KFC*, a *Post Office*, *JQ Market*, *JQ Hardware*, *Cool Breeze*, a photo shop, and the *Gourmet Kitchen Deli*...all worth a stop. Across the small side street is a medical/dental clinic if you need their services. Further south still is the *Gablewoods Mall*, with all sorts of shops, not the least of which is *Choice Meats* for a good selection of meats and deli products.

Dining

There are SO MANY places to eat in the area, I could pen a whole chapter on that subject. Sometimes it's best to ask those who've been there a while for their opinions, they've usually tried them all and will steer you to what's hot and away from what's not, no matter what may be written about them elsewhere. Bear in mind, if I mention a place here, I've dined there, for good or bad, and my words are not guided by any ads placed in my books.

As I mentioned, *Nick's Bread Basket* is a favorite of mine for an early breakfast and offering all manner of freshly baked goods. Across from the marina is *Café Ole* for breakfast, quality coffees, and great sandwiches (they also have Wi-fi so bring your laptop). Also with Wi-fi (and a swimming pool), is *H2O*, the largest restaurant on marine property. You'll also want to try *Bosun's*, *Elena's*, and *Captain Mike's*.

At the southern end of *Rodney Bay,* across from *Waterside Landings*, you'll find *Pizza Pizza* and the *Red Snapper*, a great seafood restaurant with a view.

If you take the road in front of the marina and head south (either by rental car or bus), towards Castries, you'll immediately find *The French Restaurant* and *The Bistro*, both of which are reachable by dinghy. At *The Bistro* you might find a slip if one is available; however the slips are shallow, varying in depth from just under 4' to almost 7'. *The Bistro* has a great Friday night happy hour for cruisers as well as locals and it's a great hangout, a good place to meet your fellow cruisers. The new managers are very friendly and eager to please so stop by and check out *The Bistro*.

Further south you'll soon come to one of my favorite spots, *Key Largo*, where you can sample their excellent wood-fired oven baked pizza, it's as good as it gets.

At the far southwestern end of the inner lagoon is *Shamrock's Pub* where you can dinghy in and tie up to enjoy their fare and take a walk around and access such locations such as the *Big Chef Steak House*. If you tie up on the seawall at the field that lies between the condos on the eastern shore of the inner lagoon, you can take a short hike to the *JQ Mall*. A short walk to *Reduit Beach* will bring you to a popular yachtie hangout, *Spinnaker's*. For a more casual atmosphere, try the *Half-Yellow Moon*, where you can catch live music on their large stage. Some nights you'll even get to hear owner Rod Taylor blowing some notes on his saxophone.

For some good jazz and blues, try the *Jazz Lounge and Restaurant* right in the heart of *Rodney Bay*, just a couple of streets over from *JQ Mall*, you'll see the signs.

Discovering *Rodney Bay*

On Pentecost Sunday, you'll find the *Gommier Race* from *Rodney Bay*, St. Lucia, to Martinique. *Gommiers* are narrow sailing boats with the keel and lower hull made out of the trunk of a gommier tree. The mast, boom, and other parts are made of bamboo. The gommiers are sailed with 10-man crews that hike out well over the water on boards to maintain the boat's balance. If you're in the area, try to watch the start; it's a real treat.

Just north of *Rodney Bay* is Pigeon Island where Arawakan artifacts were discovered that date back over ten centuries. The pirate Francois Leclerc is said to have stashed some of his treasure on the island in the mid-sixteenth century when he used the island as a base for five years. Pigeon Island was originally named *Le Gros Islet* (Big Island) on a French map created in 1717. In 1782, Colonial hero Admiral George Rodney established a fort atop the island from which he was able to watch French activity on the island of Martinique from atop *Signal Hill.*

In April of 1782, the French fleet under the command of Admiral Francois de Grasse sailed from Martinique to meet up with a Spanish fleet at Cap Francois, Haiti, and thence attack Fort Charles in Jamaica. Rodney foiled this attempt by sailing his fleet to the Dominica Passage between Guadeloupe and Dominica where his ships engaged de Grasse's fleet in what has come to be known as the *Battle of the Saints* after the group of islands (Iles des Saintes) lying in that body of water. After a three-day battle, Rodney emerged victorious capturing de Grasse and seven of his ships. The victory sounded the death knell for French power in the Caribbean and earned Rodney a barony bestowed by King George III of England (today there is an excellent audiovisual recreation of the battle housed in what used to be the old officer's barracks on Pigeon Island; other interactive exhibits and a gift shop make this a delightful and informative stop). The new *Hyatt Hotel* on Pigeon Island (look for the bright blue roofs), has a dinghy dock for your convenience.

A decade later, in 1792, the post-revolutionary French named the island *La Revolution*. The island changed hands some 14 times before being ceded to the British for good in 1814 when the island's name reverted to *Le Gros Islet.* It is unclear, but at some point the island was named Pigeon Island after the pigeons that carried messages back and forth from Martinique.

During World War II, the United States, seeking to protect its interests in the Caribbean, built a naval airfield at the nearby village of Gros Islet. Engineers attempted to fill in the swamp south of Gros Islet for a naval base but were unsuccessful. Today that swamp is *Rodney Bay* Lagoon, home to *Rodney Bay Marina* and Pigeon Island is connected to the mainland by a causeway constructed in 1971. The island itself is now a 45-acre national park with excellent hiking trails and the ruins of the old fort from which you'll get great views of *Rodney Bay* and Martinique. In the waters of *Rodney Bay*, you can still see the remains of an old concrete seaplane ramp from those days.

Pigeon Island's busiest time is each May when the island plays host to the *St. Lucia Jazz Festival.* At this time stages are set up among the old ruins. If you wish to visit Pigeon Island and don't want to take your dinghy, taxi, or rent a car, you can take a ferry from the marina with one operator offering day-long picnic trips. A very popular spot on Pigeon Island, *Jambe de Bois,* formerly the *Snooty Agouti,* has a small dock and offers a cyber café, coffee and snacks, it has a nice book swap, and is a bit of an art gallery and boutique. Another good spot to eat and drink is the *Captain's Cellar Pub* with its daily happy hour from 1700-1800 and jazz music.

A short trip southeast of Gros Islet is the small village of Babonneau, settled early on by Joseph Tascher de la Pagerie, the father of Marie-Joseph de la Pagerie, better known as Empress *Joséphine*, Napoleon's better half. Many St. Lucians claim that the Empress *Joséphine* was born in a small estate here called *Paix Bouche* (sometimes this is shown on some maps and not Babonneau), but the folks in Martinique will disagree with them forever and the dispute can get quite hot at times, especially for those St. Lucians steeped in national pride. Though no birth records exist, St. Lucians will tell you that *Joséphine* was conceived in Martinique and born and reared on St. Lucia for her first seven years before returning to Martinique. A few miles east from Babonneau is the *Union Nature Trail*, an agricultural center, small zoo, and hiking trail that is maintained by the *St. Lucia Department of Forest and Lands*. Nearby Grand Anse Beach is well known for turtle watching.

Castries and Vigie

Waypoints:
Castries- ¼ nm NW of entrance to harbor
14° 01.30' N, 61° 00.60' W

Castries, the capital of St. Lucia, is a typically modern Caribbean city, especially noticeable in the cruise-ship area and the government offices. Small, yet home to over 60,000 people, one-third of the island's population, the city is at times busy and hectic, at other times, almost sleepy in comparison. Castries has a significant history dating back to 1651, when built a small fort on the Vigie Peninsula, just north of what is today known as Castries. The community grew steadily until around 1767 when the population moved south a bit to the banks of a river leading into a harbor that they called *Petit Cul de Sac.* In 1785, the settlement was named Castries in honor of the Marquis de Castries, a naval minister and the driving force in French military efforts in the Caribbean

Port Castries as seen from atop *Morne Fortune*

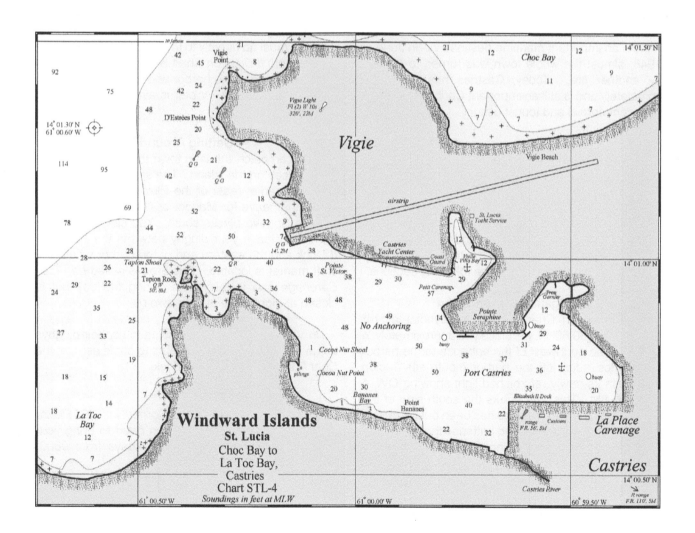

Castries flourished as a port and was marred by a succession of four fires, several hurricanes, and the French Revolution. During that period French Republicans rounded up members of the French nobility and set up a guillotine in the *Place d'Armes*. At that time the place was called Promenade Square, and later *Columbus Square* in 1892. A century later, in 1993, the area was renamed *Derek Walcott Square* in honor of St. Lucia's Nobel Laureate for literature; it is a place to find a bit of nature in downtown Castries concrete and hustle and bustle.

In later years, Castries became an important 19th century refueling port for coal-burning steamships and a convenient stopover for all shipping. As Castries became more and more of a commercial harbor, the town's infrastructure grew and grew, new docks, piers, and warehouses, all made of wood, sprang up through the 20th century. In May of 1927, a huge fire decimated the port, destroying over half of Castries, fueled by the same wooden docks, piers, and warehouses that helped Castries become and remain an important maritime destination. In June of 1948, almost the whole town was turned to cinders by another fire. Today, Castries has recovered completely and is still an important Caribbean port for both commercial and tourist usage.

As is the norm, most cruisers are deeply concerned with security in the Caribbean. With that in mind I am pleased to inform you that the St*. Lucian Marine Police*, based in Vigie, monitor VHF ch. 16 twenty-four hours a day...I hope you never need their help.

Most of the marine services and restaurants are located in Vigie, located on the northern shore of the harbor, and will be covered in the following sections.

Navigational Information

As shown on Chart STL-4, a waypoint at 14° 01.30' N, 61° 00.60' W, will place you approximately ¼ nautical mile northwest of the entrance to the harbor at Castries. Just off the harbor mouth sits Tapion Rock with its newly refurbished light showing QW, 1 sec, 50', 8M. This light marks the south side of the entrance to Port Castries and has been out for quite a while as the solar panels and batteries that controlled the light were constantly being stolen.

From the waypoint head generally southeast keeping the green-lighted buoy south of D'Estrées Point to port. Proceeding roughly southeastward,

keep the red lighted buoy the sits just northeast of Tapion Rock (watch out for *Tapion Shoal*) to starboard while keeping the green lighted buoy that marks the end of the airport runway to port. As you pass Tapion Rock and enter the harbor, you'll notice the ruins of gun placements on the mainland to starboard as you enter Port Castries.

You can anchor past the cruise ship docks at the far eastern end of Port Castries, or you can turn to port just before the cruise ship docks to anchor in *Vielle Villa Bay* (sometimes just called *Vigie Creek*) where most cruising boats anchor. Do not think that *Vielle Villa Bay* is a hurricane hole, far from it, it gets uncomfortable even when strong northerly swells are running.

What You Will Find Ashore
Customs and *Immigration*

Castries is a Port of Entry although it is far easier to clear in at *Rodney Bay* or *Marigot Bay*, either one would be my first choice. Yachts wishing to clear in at Castries must go directly to the *Customs* dock (shown as *Elizabeth II Dock* on Chart STL-4) or anchor at the far eastern end of the harbor and dinghy in if there is no room at the dock. Water is available at the dock if needed.

Getting Around

You can catch a bus in town that will take you to most places on the island. The station is behind the produce market (east of the Elizabeth II dock. The buses that leave for Marigot or Canaries leave from *Victoria St.*, two blocks south. You can usually find a place to leave your dinghy between the *Elizabeth II Dock* and the eastern end of the harbor where the craft market is located. This area is called *La Place Carenage* and is fairly safe during the day but is closed at night. Use at your own risk.

In Vigie, Cruisers are welcome to tie their dinghys to the *SLYS* fuel dock after hours to come ashore; the *Coal Pot* also has a dinghy dock.

Internet

In town, *The Business Corner* in *MC PLaza* has internet access stations (no need to bring your computer). They are open weekdays from 0800-1700.

Marine Facilities
Fuel

St. Lucia Yacht Services, *SLYS*, located at the

northern end of *Vielle Villa Bay,* has a fuel dock that also offers water and is open weekdays from 0800-1600 and on weekends from 0800-1400.

Marine Services

At the northern end of *Vielle Villa Bay* is *St. Lucia Yacht Services* with their fuel dock where you can also pick up water or even rent a car. On the road into Castries is the local *NAPA* store which is also an *OMC* dealer. In Castries itself you'll find *Valmont & Co.*, the local *Yamaha* dealer who can handle any outboard repairs required as well as sell duty-free outboards to cruisers in transit.

Johnson's Hardware on *Micoud St.* in Castries offers marine and fishing items including charts and some painting needs.

Provisions

Located near the produce market east of the *Elizabeth II Dock*, is *Super J*, easy to get to and not far from the dinghy landing at La Place Carenage. The Carenage is also home to a number of small shops including duty-free liquor stores. The market east of the Carenage has many small shops offering the freshest of produce and the tastiest local fare.

You can also find provisions at *JQ's* at the roundabout by the airport runway, a good spot for just about anything to fill the ship's larder.

Dining

For dining, try the *Coal Pot*, right on the water at Vielle Villa Bay, and has its own dinghy dock. Also on site is the *Café au Lait* and the *Mango Moon Gym* to work off the gastronomic delights that you partake of in those other places. Just across the bay is the popular *Froggie Jacks* where France meets the Caribbean, good food is almost guaranteed here.

On *Brazil Street* in Castries you will discover a wonderful restaurant called *Chez Paul*, formerly *Rain*, which dates back to 1885; and just a few doors down is the two story *Creole House* restaurant with its ornate verandah. On *Cox Street* you might wish to have lunch at *The Pink Elephant*, there's a bit of a crowd but the food is economical and good. On *Chauseé Road* is the *Natural Café*, a health food store and restaurant.

Discovering Castries

Little of the historical architecture of Castries has survived the city's numerous fires and consequently Castries is not noted for its sightseeing tours, rather it is noted more for its duty-free shopping and restaurants at places like *La Place Carenage* at the *North Wharf*. The city is spread about the harbor where cruise ships offload some 300,000 visitors every year at the huge, modernistic shopping complexes, hotels, and restaurants of *Pointe Seraphine* on the Vigie Peninsula.

The heart of Castries is the, vibrant, alive, *Central Market* where you'll have a ball on Saturday mornings searching the stalls for fresh produce and fish. Besides the *Central Market* you'll find small stalls in many places around town where you can spend your money on fresh food and crafts. A good place to eat is the *Panach Café* opposite the *Derek Walcott Square*. The square itself is home to a huge 400-year old Saman tree, sometimes called a "rain tree." A small gazebo next to the tree is used for concerts and public meetings and there is small plaque dedicated to the St. Lucians who gave their lives in the world wars at the western end of the square.

South of *Walcott Square* is *Brazil Street*, Castries' West Indian architectural showcase that has somehow survived the destruction of the fires and hurricanes that plagued Castries over the years. It is on *Brazil Street* that you'll find a marvelously preserved white Victorian home with green trim and white gingerbread fretwork.

Just off the eastern side of *Derek Walcott Square*, at the corner of *Laborie* and *Micoud Streets* is the imposing *Cathedral of the Immaculate Conception*. The vast majority of St. Lucians are Roman Catholic, a legacy of the French colonial years on St. Lucia, and the cathedral, which seats over 2,000, is the seat of Catholicism on the island. The building itself was home to several churches dating back to the 1700s, all of which were destroyed by various fires and storms. The current structure dates back to 1894, but was not completed until 1931. The church became a cathedral in 1957 and hosted Pope John Paul II on his visit to the Caribbean in 1986. You are welcome to visit the cathedral to have a look around whenever Mass is not being celebrated. The wall murals are by local artist Dunstan St. Omer who painted them in 1985 prior to the Pope's visit.

Overlooking Castries from the south is *Morne Fortune*, which was an important military base where today barracks and gun batteries can still be seen in several locations. The *La Toc Battery*, built in the 1800s on a hillside overlooking the harbour, is a thick walled fortification with many mysterious underground rooms and corridors.

Near the summit of *Morne Fortune* is *Government House*, the residence of the Governor General, a fine example of Victorian architecture. Atop *Morne Fortune*, *Good Luck Hill* in French, sits *Fort Charlotte*. Originally fortified by the French in 1768, the hill was re-taken by the British in 1803 and renamed *Fort Charlotte*.

North of Castries, along the *Peninsular Road* and parallel to *Vigie Beach*, you'll find the *Choc Bay Cemetery* just before the airport. Here you'll find a special section called the *War Cemetery* where forty memorial stones stand about a large white cross. These stones are dedicated to the local sailors who lost their lives in World War II when in March of 1942, a German U-Boat entered the harbor and torpedoed two British ships.

Also north of Castries, in the middle of *Choc Bay*, you can visit Rat Island (by dinghy), a former quarantine station for scarlet fever and smallpox. In pre-Columbian times, the island was occupied by Arawaks as evidenced by several pottery finds. Today, Rat Island is on the drawing board to become home to an artist retreat so that its "extraordinary solitude" can be fully utilized. *Choc Bay* is also home to several nice little beaches and an equal number of small resorts and hotels.

An interesting place to visit lies east of Castries at Morne Pleasant, the *Folk Research Centre (Plas Wichès Foklò)* a museum and cultural center set in an old estate. The museum offers exhibits of St. Lucian folklore, music and musical instruments, and the library contains many books, papers, and photographs relating to St. Lucia's cultural heritage.

If you wish to further explore the history of St. Lucia and her national resources, I would suggest that you visit the *St. Lucia National Archives* and the *St. Lucia National Trust*, just off the Peninsular Road at the western end of the Vigie Peninsula.

Marigot Bay

Waypoints:
Marigot Bay- ¼ nm W of
13° 58.10' N, 61° 02.10' W

Navigational Information

When headed south from Castries, keep at least ½ mile offshore until you pass the conspicuous yellow buildings with green roofs that sit on the point about ½ mile south of Tapion Rock. At this point, you can pass a bit closer in towards shore, keeping ¼ mile off to clear any dangers.

As shown on Chart STL-5, a waypoint at 13° 58.10' N, 61° 02.10' W, will place you approximately ¼ mile west of the entrance to this most impressive harbor. The entrance to *Marigot Bay* is marked by a conspicuous red-roof high on a hill on the south side of the entrance to the bay. The entrance lies approximately 1¼ miles south of the conspicuous green tanks of the *Hess Oil* plant at *Cul de Sac Bay* (which itself lies approximately two miles south of Castries). The entrance is easy to miss, so easy that a French fleet passed right by an anchored British fleet that camouflaged their rigging with palm fronds.

From the waypoint head in on a southeasterly course, the exact course is not important here, you simply wish to avoid the shoal off the northern shore of the outer cove. As you head in, keep center channel until the headlands are abeam, then favor the southern shoreline following the dark blue water towards the entrance. There is a lighted buoy (Fl G) south of the resort and just before you reach the spit of land separating the inner and outer coves; keep this buoy well to port. Pass between the spit of land and the southern shore and anchor wherever your draft allows.

You can also anchor in the outer cove on either side of the channel making sure you keep the channel clear for the big charter cats that pass through here on a daily basis. If you wish to anchor in the inner cove, keep clear of the small dock on the spit of land at the entrance as a small ferry runs back and forth across the entrance every few minutes, whenever somebody needs to cross. Also, do not anchor directly in the area of the entrance to the inner harbor as there are electric and telephone cables here, and avoid the swing radius of vessels using the moorings in the bay. Be sure to anchor out of their way. The marina

Marigot Bay

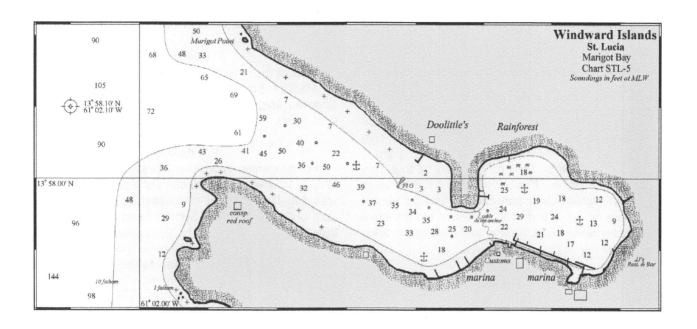

has 20 moorings here (white with a blue stripe) that are suitable for a three boat raft-up (up to 60 tons). Be wary of some folks who will offer you un-official moorings, always ask for a receipt.

What You Will Find Ashore

Dinghy docks can be found at the *Marina Village*, *Chateau Mygo*, *Hurricane Hole*, *Doolittles*, and at *JJ's*. Bear in mind that there is a 4-knot speed limit in the inner lagoon.

If you wish to travel by car south of *Marigot Bay*, the road passes through one of the largest banana plantations on the island in the *Roseau Valley* and is home to the island's largest rum distillery, the *Roseau Sugar Factory*, in nearby Roseau. The distillery offers interesting tours showing the transformation from raw sugar cane to rum, but they don't tell you that most of their raw material is not grown on the island, instead it is shipped in from Guyana in the form of molasses. To the east of the distillery lies the *Roseau River* with several excellent waterfalls, but you'll need a guide and I can recommend one, Benjamin Paul, who can be reached at 451-4521. The walk is rough and you can't swim in the water due to chemical runoff from the nearby banana plantations, but the scenery is beautiful and unique.

Customs and *Immigration*

Marigot Bay is a Port of Entry and the *Customs* office is upstairs in the *Marina Village*. *Customs* is open from 0800-1200 and then from 1300-1615. Next to the marina offices is *SLASPA* and they collect all entry fees. You can tie up your dinghy to the *Customs dock*, it's located next to the marina's fuel dock.

Getting Around

Marigot Bay has several thrifty ferries and water taxis to carry you from your boat to shore and back again. For more info, and for a land taxi, give *Chateau Mygo* a hail on VFH ch. 16. *Taxi Service Marigot*, available on VHF ch. 16, can be found by the *Customs* office. If you walk about a mile up to the main highway you can catch a bus to almost anywhere on the island. On the return trip the drive will usually take you all the way to the *Customs* office for a small fee.

Marine Facilities
Marinas
Marigot Bay Marina

On the south side of the inner lagoon (sometimes

called *Hurricane Hole*, and yes, it is an excellent hurricane hole) sits the *Marigot Bay Marina* and *Marina Village*. The marina offers moorings in the lagoon, stern-to dockage, and a few alongside slips and can accommodate vessels to 250' LOA. Mega-yacht slips have high-speed fueling while smaller vessels must use the fuel dock (diesel and gasoline) which is located next to the *Customs* dock. Slips have full electric (110/220 volt, 50 and 60 cycle, while the mega-yacht slips also have 410 volt 3-phase available) and pump outs. There is a full/self-service laundry in the *Marina Village*.

Chateau Mygo

On the southern shore of the outer bay is *Chateau Mygo* marina offering 6 stern-to berths with water and electricity, a small chandlery, and a laundry service that will return your clothing the next day, sparkling clean and folded.

Marine Services

Check with the Shaid, the manager of the charter fleet (*Bateau Mygo*) at *Chateau Mygo Marina*, he has several good techs on hand to keep up the fleet and he can help with your repairs. Across the inner lagoon from the marina is *Complete Marine Services* with a barge and crane. Although their primary focus is marine construction, the can also handle underwater and other assorted repairs.

Marine Supplies

There is a small chandlery located at *Chateau Mygo* that carries some boating basics and fishing gear.

Internet

Most of the inner bay is covered by Wi-fi courtesy of *Marigot Bay Marina*. Nearby, *Doolittles* and *Chateau Mygo* have Wi-fi while the *Marigot Beach Club* offers stand alone internet stations.

Provisions

For groceries, your first stop will probably be the *Marina Village* where you can shop at *Mari Gourmet* with duty-free spirits and cigarettes. They're open from 0800-1900 except Sundays and holidays when they are open from 0800-1300. Nearby, the *Baguette Shop* has great breads and sandwiches. If you can't find what you need take a taxi to the main highway where you can shop at the *Promise Supermarket*.

Be advised that when anchored in *Marigot Bay* you will be approached by some local entrepreneurs trying to sell you bananas and other goodies at prices often considerably higher than what you would pay at the local market.

Garbage

Garbage can be dropped at the marina or you can can give it to Johnson who will come by your vessel and haul off your bags of refuse for a slight fee.

Dining

The restaurant located at *Chateau Mygo, Le Spa*, is one of the most popular eateries in the area and a great spot just to hang out and lime. Their fare is excellent and a specialty are their thin crust pizzas. Many bars have a Happy Hour, *Le Spa* has a Happy Day with two-for-one drinks anytime. Dinghy in or give them a hail on VHF ch. 16 and they'll come out and pick you up at your boat.

On the northern shore of the inner lagoon, just below the *Marigot Beach Inn*, is the *Rainforest Hideaway*, rated as one of the top ten Caribbean restaurants. This is indeed a special place and proper attire is requested, as are advance reservations.

At the eastern end of the *Marigot Bay Marina* you'll find the *Hurricane Hole Bar*, a casual place with a great view of the lagoon. Next door you'll find the more upscale *Boudreau Restaurant*.

At the far eastern end of the bay is *JJ's* dock and the *King's Mangrove Grill* with plenty of room for dinghies at their dinghy dock. Up the hill is the old *JJ's* and the village of Marigot where you can still party till the wee hours and stagger back down the hill in high fashion. In the village you can choose from the *Tipsy Bar*, *Henry's Fish and Tings*, *JJ's Pearl*, and *Julietta's Restaurant* located just down the road.

On the northern shore of the outer lagoon is the *Marigot Beach Resort* where you'll find *Doolittle's Restaurant,* THE spot for truly elegant dining in *Marigot Bay* with live entertainment most nights during the winter season. This area was the site of some of the filming of the 1967 movie *Dr. Doolittle* with Rex Harrison.

St. Lucia's Marine Parks, *SMMA* and *CAMMA*

From *Marigot Bay* south to Gros Piton, cruisers seeking privacy and serenity are in luck. The waters of St. Lucia's marine parks offer well-maintained moorings in some of the most awesome settings along the western shore St. Lucia and particularly in the area of the Pitons. Skippers will be charged a mooring fee based on vessel size and the fee is used for coral reef conservation, but make sure you've cleared in before picking up a mooring.

Over the last decade a change for the better has come over the southwestern coast of St. Lucia, particularly in the area of Soufrière and The Pitons, one of St. Lucia's premier attractions for the cruising yachtsman. Horror stories exist from the older days of boat boys who would pull alongside your boat long before you arrived, hang on uninvited, and almost demand that you let them take your line ashore... this was little more than strong-arm extortion to some people. Skippers who refused their services were often cursed by these intruders who threatened to cut the vessels lines. Ashore, visitors were constantly badgered by "guides" and other hangers-on to the point that nobody desired to come ashore.

On top of this, fishermen resented the yachts that anchored where they normally set their nets while eco-groups complained that cruisers damaged the reefs by anchoring right on top of them. The area was being damaged, tempers were rising, and the fishing was declining...something had to be done.

In 1994, the *SMMA, Soufrière Marine Management Area* was created to protect the marine environment and to resolve the conflicts between visiting boats and the local populace. With the help of the *Tourism Department*, some educational programs, and the local police, visiting Soufrière is again a pleasure. The *SMMA* soon had a dialog going with all users of the area...the hoteliers, divers, fishermen, water taxis, cruisers, community groups, and the government and finally negotiated a creative solution to all of the problems as well which also ensured the long-term protection of the marine environment.

So successful has the *SMMA* been that in 1998 the *SMMA* received the *British Airways Tourism for Tomorrow Award for National Parks and Protected Areas*. In fact, the *SMMA* has been so successful that in 1998, a spin-off area was added, the *Canaries to Anse La Raye Management Area, CAMMA*, that is largely administrated under the same management as the *SMMA*. In 2001 the *SMMA* was selected as a world "flagship" coral reef management demonstration

Roseau

The Pitons

Vigie airport

Soufrière and Petit Piton

The anchorage at the Pitons

Roadside wood carver, Soufrière

Roadside guides and vendors, near the Pitons

site under a special program of the *UN Environmental Program, UNEP.*

The *SMMA* has divided the shoreline into priority areas, setting some aside as marine reserves designed to increase fish stocks yet offer quality dive sites. In addition, recreational areas were set aside where cruisers can take a mooring and other areas reserved for commercial fishing purposes. *SMMA* licensed water taxis are now available to take you ashore, while licensed yacht guides are available to take your line ashore or attach your line to a mooring. These folks are very professional and all carry *SMMA* ID cards and it is really a pleasure to deal with them. Also, during the hurricane season, Peter, the chief warden for the marine parks, gives the yachts the latest weather forecasts by VHF. The *SMMA* can be contacted on VHF ch. 16 and 08 and can give you excellent information on water taxis, shoreside taxis, and all sorts of other relevant information. You can phone the *SMMA* at 481-2158.

Divers wishing to check out the underwater scenery in the SMMA dive areas must, according to *SMMA* regulations, dive with a guide. If you have your own equipment, diving guides are available at most dive shops, though a guide will be cheaper if you go through the *SMMA*. There are dive shops with guides available at Anse Chastanet and Jalousie.

Notes on anchoring: In the area covered by the *SMMA*, anchoring is prohibited except in five mooring areas listed below:
1. Between Anse Chastanet & Anse Mamin
2. Rachette Point
3. Soufriere Jetty
4. Malgretoute Beach
5. Beausejour

A special mooring maintenance program has been designed and all moorings are equipped with a special yellow tag indicating the last date of service on that particular mooring. All this information, plus what type of maintenance was performed, is kept in a log at the *SMMA* office in Soufrière.

The 60 moorings available are white with a blue stripe and are designed for vessels to 70' LOA while some moorings can accommodate vessels to 120' LOA. There are over 20 moorings north of Petit Piton at Malgretoute. Orange buoys are for dive vessels or dinghies while yellow buoys are reserved for

private vessels. White and orange cylindrical buoys demarcate the marine reserves.

Fees for the management areas are as follows:
EC$2: per person per day Entrance Fee
EC$40: 1-2 days for vessels up to 40' LOA
EC$54: 1-2 days for vessels 40'-70' LOA
EC$162: daily rate for vessels over 70' LOA
EC$80: weekly rate for vessels up to 40' LOA
EC$108: weekly rate for vessels 40'-70' LOA

Diving fees are as follows:
Daily dive fee: EC$13.50
Annual dive fee: EC$40.50
Snorkeling fee: EC$3.00

All fees collected go into the *Coral Conservation Fund.*

L'Anse Pilori to *L'Anse La Raye*

Waypoints:
L'Anse Pilori- ¼ nm W of anchorage
13° 57.00' N, 61° 02.90' W

Trou l'Orange- ¼ nm WNW of anchorage
13° 56.70' N, 61° 03.20' W

L'Anse la Raye- ½ nm W of
13° 56.50' W, 61° 03.50' W

Navigational Information
Along the leeward coast of St. Lucia, south of *Marigot Bay* to Soufrière, are several nice anchorages, some of which can only be used during daylight hours of 0900-1700. Two of these are shown on Chart STL-6, *L'Anse Pilori* and *Trou l'Orange*. As shown on the chart, a waypoint at 13° 57.00' N, 61° 02.90' W, will place you approximately ¼ mile west of the anchorage at *L'Anse Pilori,* while a waypoint at 13° 56.70' N, 61° 03.20' W, will place you approximately ¼ mile west/northwest of the anchorage at *Trou l'Orange,* well north of the small cay that sits off Point d'Orange. These anchorages have very nice beaches and are popular with the day charter cats out of *Rodney Bay* so don't expect much solitude here, but they are worth a stop.

Just south of Point d'Orange is a very nice anchorage at *L'Anse La Raye* as shown on Chart STL-6. A waypoint at 13° 56.50'N, 61° 03.50' W, will place you approximately ½ mile west of the

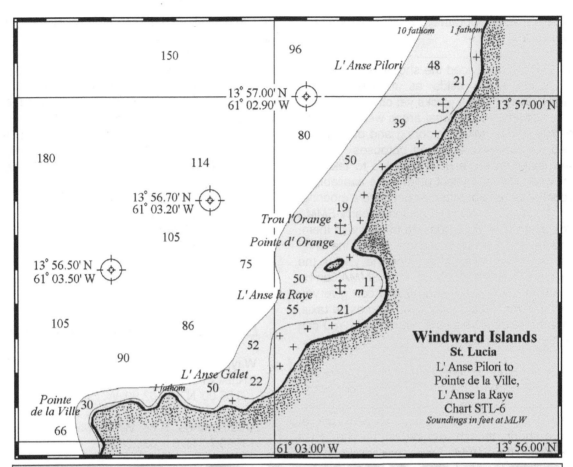

150

96

10 fathom *1 fathom*

L' Anse Pilori 48

21

13° 57.00' N
61° 02.90' W   13° 57.00' N

39

80

50

180   114

50

19

13° 56.70' N
61° 03.20' W

105

Trou l'Orange

Pointe d' Orange

75

13° 56.50' N
61° 03.50' W

50

50   11
m

L' Anse la Raye

55   21

105   86

52

L' Anse Galet

90

1 fathom   50   22

*Pointe
de la Ville*   30

66

Windward Islands
St. Lucia
L' Anse Pilori to
Pointe de la Ville,
L' Anse la Raye
Chart STL-6
Soundings in feet at MLW

61° 03.00' W   13° 56.00' N

L'Anse La Raye

anchorage off the town dock. Favor the central and southern portions of the bay where you can anchor in 20' or less as the northern part of the bay shoals. A pleasant anchorage in most conditions (never attempt to anchor here if northerly swells are expected), you can tie up to the town dock and visitors are asked to bring their papers to the *Police Station*, a courtesy and nothing more.

What You Will Find Ashore
L'Anse La Raye is a delightful little fishing village where on Fridays you can partake in *Seafood Friday*, a street party that features the very best of the local catch. Just up from the dock is *Rankin's Bar*, a good spot to grab a bite to eat in a lively atmosphere. A bit further into town is a delightful little restaurant called *La Sikwee*, set amid the remains of an old sugar mill and well worth the short walk. Here you can view historical re-enactments of life during the plantation era in the 150-year-old mill. The stage itself is built into a hill and local entertainers perform before and after the re-enactments. You'll want to phone ahead first as *La Sikwee* is not always open.

A metal bridge spans the *L'Anse La Raye River* and a short 20 minute hike upriver will bring you to a lovely waterfall almost 50' high with a pool at the base that is usually used by the young folks from town.

At the northern part of town is a well-marked road that leads to the more touristy *River Rock Falls*. The falls and the surrounding facilities are well tended and the pool at the bottom of the falls is lined with concrete in places. You'll also find tables and benches here as well as changing rooms for those who wish to take a dip in the pool.

A few miles south of *L'Anse La Raye* a road turns off and leads into Canaries winding east along the *Canaries River*. The road then dead-ends in the heart of the rainforest. From here it's a short walk to three different waterfalls and an area known for its concentration of boa constrictors (relax, they're harmless to humans!). You might wish to ask in town for a guide if you wish to visit the falls.

Anse Cochon

Waypoints:
Anse Cochon- ½ nm W of
13° 55.75' N, 61° 04.20' W

Navigational Information
Approximately three miles south of *Marigot Bay* is the anchorage at *Anse Cochon*. As shown on Chart STL-7, a waypoint at 13° 55.75' N, 61° 04.20' W, will place you approximately ½ mile west of the anchorage. Small, and usually deserted, the bay is marked by the conspicuous red roofs of the buildings ashore. The moorings in the bay are for daytime use only and you'll be sharing them at times with the large charter cats that frequent this anchorage.

The moorings on the northern side of the bay are for commercial vessels only. The moorings at the southern end of the bay and the ones stretching southward past *Petit Trou* all the way to *Anse La Verdue* are all good for overnight stays (see Chart STL-7). If the moorings are all taken, you may anchor in the bay off the beach for a lunch stop, but you'll have to move if requested by the local fishermen.

There are several moorings available at Canaries (as shown on Chart STL-1) but these often go missing.

What You Will Find Ashore
Heading south on the road towards Soufrière the road bends past Bouton where you will come to one of the most impressive sights you will ever see, the Pitons, said to be the most famous mountain pair in the world, Petite Piton and Gros Piton. At the more scenic overlooks you'll likely be hounded by young men hawking all sorts of native crafts and offering to guide you to the sulfur springs and other tourist spots. If you don't need their services simply let them know, firmly, as some, but not all, cannot comprehend the meaning of the word "No."

At *Anse la Liberte* (south of Jambette Point-Chart STL-7) you'll find a new eco-friendly campsite south of Canaries. Encompassing some 133 acres, the resort is home to several old caves where Brigands once hid. The name *Anse la Liberte* (as shown on Chart STL-1) means the *Bay of Freedom*, because there was a great Brigand celebration here when emancipation came in the 19th century.

Diving
If you wish to do some serious diving, *Island Divers* is right on the beach at *Anse Chastanet* and they can take you to the best dive sites in the area. Also on the beach at *Anse Chastanet* is a nice little beach bar and a couple of boutiques in case you have some extra

money to spend. Here you'll also find *Biking Jungle Adventure* where you can rent bicycles to explore the surrounding areas via a series of wilderness trails.

There is an interesting wreck in the center of the bay at *Anse Cochon*. In 1986 the 165' freighter *Lesleen M* was intentionally sunk in 65'-70' of water here to create an artificial reef and it's working.

Dining
Located on the beach, *TiManje* (VHF ch. 16 or 456-8110) is perched above the rocks and will serve you on their deck or even deliver to your boat.

Located on the southern edge of the bay is *TiKaye* with a nice dock that unfortunately is not a good spot to land with any sort of swell running. Atop the hill is *Kai Manje*, complete with a breathtaking view of the bay and a menu equally as special.

Canaries is home to a wonderful street festival/food fair every other Saturday from 1500-midnight. For more information on the festival call Margaret Edwards at 459-4402. Margaret is also the owner of *La Maison Estate* located a ten minutes away on the road to Castries.

Anse Chastanet

Navigational Information
Further south, as shown on Chart STL-8, two anchorages are available before reaching the area of Soufrière and the Pitons. You can take a mooring at Chamin Cove and at *Anse Chastanet* and partake of some excellent snorkeling on the reefs here.

What You Will Find Ashore
The *Anse Chastanet Beach Bar* is a good spot for a quick bite, but if you are interested in slightly more formal dining there's a restaurant just up the hill. Those interested in SCUBA diving will be happy to learn that one of the largest dive operations in the Windward Islands, *SCUBA St. Lucia*, is located in Anse Chastanet (they do not fill tanks).

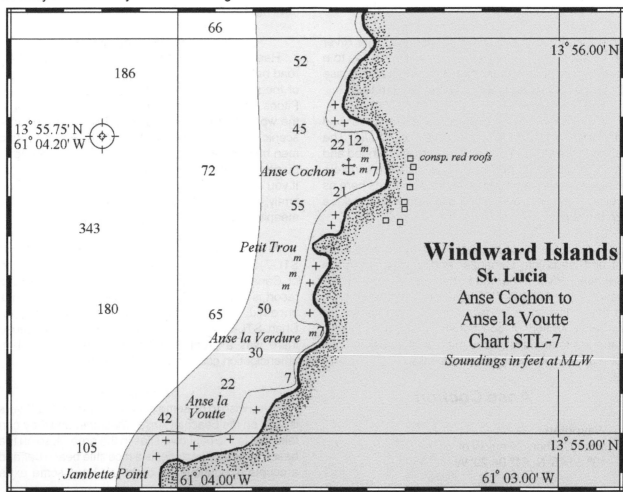

Soufrière

Waypoints:
Soufrière- 1½ nm W of
13° 51.25' N, 61° 05.25' W

Without a doubt, the area around Soufrière and the Pitons is the most popular area for sightseeing on the island of St. Lucia, and the Pitons are an icon for Caribbean cruising. If you remember the movie *Superman II*, the Man of Steel flew between the Pitons. The triangular spot on the St. Lucia flag represents the Pitons, symbolizing the "rising hope of a new nation." There's even a beer named after the Pitons...how about that beer lovers!

The town of Soufrière was once the French capital of the island and the town square once had its own guillotine. As you walk around you'll notice the charming, photogenic old Creole buildings and the old waterwheel at the *Soufrière Estate* that still works. In recent years, Soufrière has appeared in the movies *Water* and *White Squall*. Hurricane Lenny destroyed the original town dock in 1999, but has for the most part it has been rebuilt to accommodate the charter cats from *Rodney Bay*.

When visiting this area, please don't forget that the entire area from *Soufrière Bay* to Gros Piton Point (see Chart STL-8) is a marine reserve set aside by the *SMMA*.

Navigational Information

If you're approaching from the north, give the reef south of *Anse Chastanet* at Grand Caille Point a wide berth, if you go aground here you can be fined heavily for damaging the reef.

As shown on Chart STL-8, a waypoint at 13° 51.25' N, 61° 05.25' W, will place you approximately 1½ miles west of the moorings off Soufrière and *Hummingbird Beach* at the northern part of *Soufrière Bay*.

The area off *Hummingbird Beach* used to be a very popular anchorage, but anchoring here is no longer permitted (as the signs onshore will attest), so five moorings have been installed at nearby Rachette Point and the Bat Cave. However, in periods of inclement weather vessels are allowed to anchor off the beach. Vessels within the *SMMA* will be notified via VHF radio when the beach is open to anchoring.

There are four moorings just south of town but the two farthest south are for small boats, under 30', larger boats will collide when the vessels swing during the night.

From the waypoint, you can head toward Rachette Point or the Bat Cave to pick up a mooring.

You can use the dock at *SMMA* for landing the dinghy or the larger boat if needed.

What You Will Find Ashore
Clearing *Customs*

If you need to clear in, Soufrière is a *Port of Entry* and the *Customs* office is located in the *SMMA* facilities on the waterfront near the *Police Station* and is open 7 days a week 0800-1200, 1300-1630. Overtime rates apply after 1630 daily. *Immigration* is located in the *Police Station* and is therefore always open (but expect an overtime charge from 1630-0800).

Marine Facilities
Fuel

There are three docks onshore; the southermost dock is the main town dock, just north of it is the yacht mooring dock, next is the fuel dock, and in the northern corner of the beach is a small dinghy dock. You can get diesel and gasoline, as well as water, ice, and fresh fish at the fishing boat dock from 0630-1800 daily.

If you wish to jerry jug your fuel, the *Cool Breeze Texaco* station at the head of the dock and garbage bins are located everywhere for your convenience. *Cool Breeze* also has ice and offers care rentals.

Marine Facilities
Marine Services

In Soufrière there is a *Water Taxi Association,* which is instrumental in turning the local boat boys into certified *Yacht Guides* by educating them and helping ease their aggressive vending habits. Several trustworthy water taxi operators are available to take you to shore and back, arrange for taxis or tours, and even arrange for technical help for your problems. One of the best is Charles Richards, *Mystic Man* (VHF ch. 16), who also repairs outboards in the fishing harbor.

Mega-Yacht agents, *Ben's Yacht Services* and *Benny's Harmony Yacht Services*, can work all of St. Lucia's anchorages offering fuel, provisioning, and

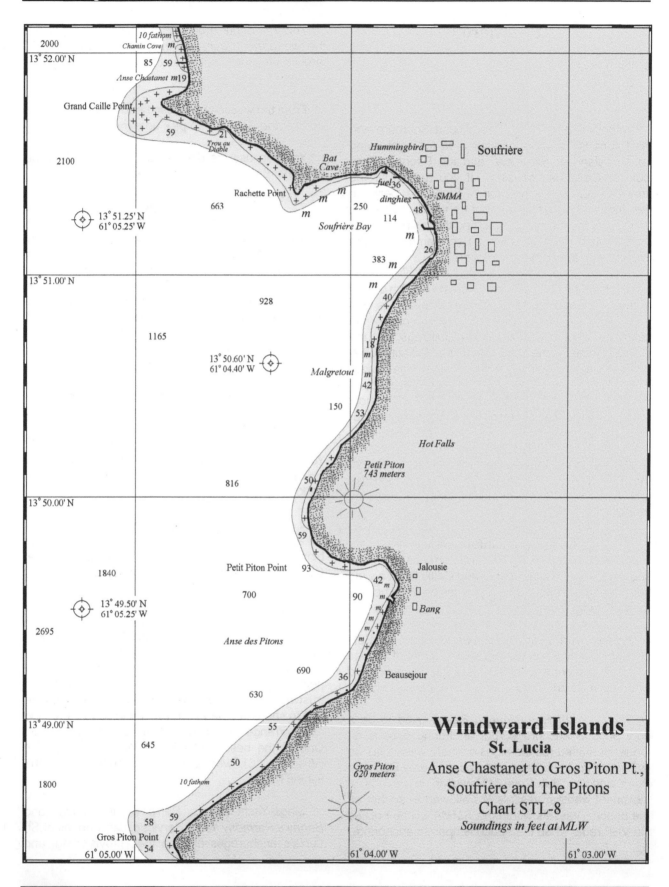

Windward Islands
St. Lucia
Anse Chastanet to Gros Piton Pt.,
Soufrière and The Pitons
Chart STL-8
Soundings in feet at MLW

numerous other services necessary for a comfortable stay while on St. Lucia. *Benny's* also does laundry and can pick up yours at your boat.

Internet Access
On the northern edge of town, the *Hummingbird Resort* offers free *Wi-fi* for their customers. The resort can also help you place an overseas call or send/receive a fax.

Benny at the *Harmony Beach Restaurant and Bar* located at Malgretout has free *Wi-fi* that covers the waters off Soufrière from Malgretout to the Bat Cave. The *Wi-fi* is free for customers of Benny's restaurant. If you need your laundry done, Benny can handle the job.

There is an Internet access point at the *SMMA* office in town as well as a bookswap. In the nearby *Excelsior Plaza*, visit *Diamond.Net* for web surfing, computer repairs, parts, or purchases. *Tas Café*, located between the *Hummingbird Resort* and Soufrière, has *Wi-fi* as well as a laptop their customers can use.

Dining
At the northern end of the bay is the elegant *Hummingbird Restaurant* which is VERY cruiser friendly and has free showers for diners as well as dinghy security and usage of the swimming pool. Any skipper who brings in five or more diners gets a house selected meal for free. Cruisers also can receive discounts on rooms and handmade batiks. Owner Joyce can also arrange a taxi or tour for you and your party. Joyce also owns the *Hummingbird Bamboo Beach Bar* with their popular happy hour from 1700-1900.

Captain Hook's is another good spot for a meal, they are situated behind the *Hummingbird Restaurant*.

Provisions
For provisions try *Eroline's Supermarket* on Church Street who'll deliver to your boat if needed. A few doors down is *Maison Salaizon* where you can pick up fresh cuts of meat.

For fine wines visit *Tas Wine and Coffee Shop*.

Dining
For dining, your first stop could be right at the head of the town dock is *Petit Peak* located at *The Old Courthouse* (it was actually the courthouse a century ago). Across the street is *Antonia's Waterfront Restaurant* with a great view of the harbor.

Just north of *Eroline's Supermarket* is *La Mirage* and *Fedo's*. *La Mirage* is a guesthouse and restaurant that offers local dishes with a continental flair while *Fedo's* is simply another great local place to eat that is only open for lunch.

A pair of the most popular spots for cruisers is *Skipper's* and *Archies*, a couple of restaurant/bars just down from *SMMA*. Nearby, behind the church is *Sunset Pizza*.

A must stop while visiting Soufrière is the *Dasheene Bar and Restaurant* at the *Ladera Resort*. Perched on the edge of a 900' high ridge and looking straight down between the Pitons, *Dasheene's* has the most spectacular view in the Windwards, and perhaps the entire Caribbean. It's a heck of a walk to the site, but a taxi makes it much easier. Another stop with an excellent view is the *La Haute Plantation* on the Castries road. You can catch the Castries bus to get there, but remember that reservations are suggested for dinner.

Discovering Soufrière
Between Soufrière and the *Ladera Resort* lie the *Sulfur Springs*, which claim to be the world's only drive-in volcano. Some 40,000 years ago this area was a volcano some ten miles in diameter before it erupted and collapsed in on itself. Theoretically it could still erupt; however it is classified as a *solfatara*, meaning that it emits gases and vapors rather than lava and hot ash.

A short walk off the road you'll find bare earth colored in many different hues with hissing steam vents and over 20 bubbling pools with a strong sulfur stench. The Arawaks called this place *Qualibou*, the *Place of Death*. If you bring a bathing suit you can lounge in the hot waters of the natural springs where it is said the Empress Joséphine Bonaparte is said to have bathed as a young girl when she came to visit her father's plantation nearby. In 1785, King Louis XVI ordered the construction of baths over the springs so that his troops could benefit from the curative powers of the waters.

Much more pleasant are the *Diamond Botanical Gardens* waterfall, mineral baths, and old mill with waterwheel. Established in 1748, this estate was one of the oldest on the island and was part of 2,000 acres granted to the Devaux brothers by King Louis XIV in 1713. Baron De Laborie built the original mineral baths in 1784 for the use of French troops stationed nearby and you can see the ruins of these old baths as you hike back from the waterfall. Take a towel to the *Diamond Baths* and ask for the upper bathhouse. Here, in a private room, you'll have two huge tubs with giant valves that will fill the tubs with hot water straight from the volcano.

Hikers could spend days in the area. St Lucia's best rain forest starts in the hills behind Soufrière. You can call the forestry department for a guide to take you on a hike such as the 2½-hour loop tour, which includes the *Maho Waterfall*. Hikers as well as rock and mountain climbers will find plenty to pique their interests at Petit Piton and Gros Piton. Guides are available in Soufrière and at Jalousie or you can call Rupert Mynns at 459-5526.

Malgretout

Waypoints:
Malgretout- ¼ nm W of moorings
13° 50.60' N, 61° 04.40' W

South of Soufrière is Malgretout, a nice spot to pick up a mooring just off the *Anse Mitan Restaurant* on the beach. At the southern end of the beach is the *Harmony Beach Restaurant and Bar*. The owner's brother Jah I, acts as a guide for those interested in climbing the Pitons and he can also take you to what was once his secret hot waterfall. What a treat it was to lie back against a cliff while hot water cascaded down over your body. Today, the new owner has felt the need to "improve" the site and has constructed concrete pools all but destroying the former ambiance and quite a bit of marine flora as well.

Navigational Information
A waypoint at 13° 50.60' N, 61° 04.40' W, will place you approximately ¼ nm W of the moorings at Malgretout. The two outer moorings are for vessels to 120', and if you're smaller than that, you should take a mooring closer to shore. Check with the *Harmony Beach Restaurant and Bar* (VHF ch. 16) to see if the larger moorings are booked, if they're not booked, smaller vessels can tie to them.

If you take a smaller mooring, one closer to shore, you'll need to secure a line ashore. They'll be plenty of folks to help you and the going rate for such assistance is about EC$15. But if you call Benny at the *Harmony Beach Restaurant and Bar*, he will come out to tie you up for free (please be sure to thank him by dining in his restaurant).

Benny is very helpful to cruisers. He monitors VHF ch. 16 day and night and will help if you need assistance. I remember one night when two vessels slammed into each other on the moorings off Jalousie when the currents were swirling, Benny came on and instructed the owners on what to do to relieve the situation, he's a huge help in this area.

What You Will Find Ashore
Now if you're worried about security at *Malgretout,* there's no need to take your dinghy in here, Benny the owner of *Harmony Beach*, will send a pirogue out to get you and make sure that your boat is secure while you are ashore! North of *Malgretout* is the new *Stonefield Estate Restaurant* with its own pool and a garden with ancient Carib petroglyphs. The view from here of the bay is magnificent and the food is of no less quality as well.

Internet Access
Benny at the *Harmony Beach Restaurant and Bar* has free *Wi-fi* that covers the waters off Soufrière from Malgretout to the Bat Cave. The *Wi-fi* is free for customers of Benny's restaurant. If you need your laundry done, Benny can handle the job.

Dining
Without a doubt, *Harmony Beach Restaurant and Bar* is the best spot for food and ambiance. Located almost at the foot of Petit Piton, you won't have to dinghy in for a meal, owner Benny will come out and pick you up and return you to your vessel when you've finished your meal. Even if you don't wish to dine here, and are worried about the safety of your vessel, speak to Benny. Benny can place a trustworthy guard aboard your vessel for 2.5 hours for E$30. Benny also has a taxi which you can use to visit his rum shop in town, the *Harmony Inn*.

The *Anse Mitan Restaurant* is located on the beach at Malgretout that specializes in seafood from 1130 daily. However, if there are no customers they'll usually close mid-afternoon.

Up the hill above the anchorage, the *Stonefield Estate* has perhaps the best view of the mooring area as well as a swimming pool for customers and guests.

Jalousie

Waypoints:
Jalousie, between the Pitons- 1½ nm W of
13° 49.50' N, 61° 05.25' W

Navigational Information
If you wish to moor "between the Pitons," south of Petit Piton at Jalousie, head to a waypoint at 13° 49.50' N, 61° 05.25' W, as shown on Chart STL-8 which will place you approximately 1½ miles west of the mooring field. Again, take a mooring here, the best being those to the south. The three outer moorings are for larger vessels, to 120' LOA.

The more northern moorings are far too close and one night I witnessed a large motoryacht bump against a smaller sailboat as the vessels rode on their moorings. There are some nice heads inshore of the moorings that are worth a snorkel. If you need help picking up a mooring don't fret, there's usually a water taxi operator around that will be glad to give you a hand as the currents here can get squirrely at times. It was everything I could do to manhandle my line and secure my boat under the watchful eyes of a water taxi operator who, had he bet against me, would have lost big time.

What You Will Find Ashore
Ashore at Jalousie you'll find the *Jalousie Plantation*, one of the Caribbean's fanciest resorts, and the remains of what was once their marina. As it stands, you can dinghy in to the hotel dock to tie up your dink and take the shuttle that runs all over the resort compound. The resort offers four restaurants, *The Pier* (dinner on the beach), *The Plantation* (fine dining located in the main building), *Bayside* (right on the beach-lunch). All the restaurants are open for visiting cruisers and don't miss the all-you-can-eat Sunday brunch. Visitors can pay a day use fee and have access to the beach chairs and other facilities including saunas, hot tubs, tennis courts, billiards, a children's center, and other hotel amenities.

Next door is one of the most interesting facilities on the island, *Bang*. *Bang is* currently closed but hopefully it will reopen by the time this guide is published. It is the child of Lord Glenconner, one of the developers of Mustique in the Grenadines. The eccentric Lord had constructed five island creations, including a house and a restaurant before his passing on August 27, 2010.

While on a visit to Dublin years ago, Lord Glenconner was so taken with a baby elephant that he purchased her and shipped her to St. Lucia where he named her Buppa. Unfortunately, Buppa only lived to be 10 years old and was so sorely missed that Lord Glenconner had a life-size statue made of her that today stands on his St. Lucia grounds.

Bang has always been well known, and Lord Glenconner took great pride in cooking and produced a series of Caribbean inspired cookbooks. Lord Glenconner personally taught his own assistants and often added touches of his own to the meals being prepared. He was adamant about people having a good time and often invited calypso bands, fire-eaters, and limbo-dancers to perform for his guests. He was a true island character and will be sorely missed.

Just south of Jalousie and *Bang*, sits majestic Gros Piton, and on the side of the mountain is the small community of Fond Gen Libres, easily accessed by car or on foot. From there, it is a four hour hike to the top of Gros Piton and back. You can pick up a guide in town to make your trek that much more interesting. Try Jimmy Haynes (489-0136). Fond Gen Libres means "valley of the free people" and the residents there are descendants of the Brigands who fled to the mountains in the slave rebellion of 1748.

Laborie

Waypoints:
Laborie- ½ nm S of entrance to bay
13° 44.52' N, 61° 00.00' W

Southeast of the Pitons, and just a couple miles north of *Vieux Fort Bay*, is the small harbor at Laborie. Rarely visited, the bay offers a good lee anchorage in most conditions, but the entrance often intimidates some skippers. Laborie was once called *Îlet a Care, Turtle Island*, after the turtles that frequented the bay. The town was named after Governor Baron De Laborie and has a lovely beach with an almond grove behind it.

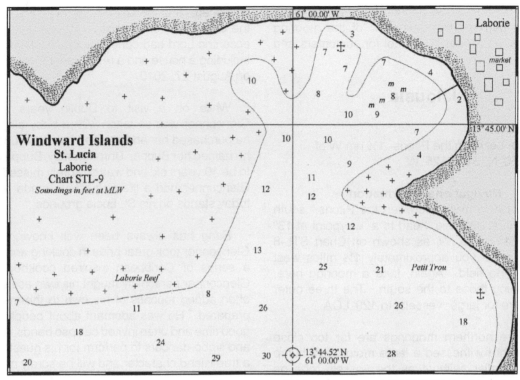

Windward Islands
St. Lucia
Laborie
Chart STL-9
Soundings in feet at MLW

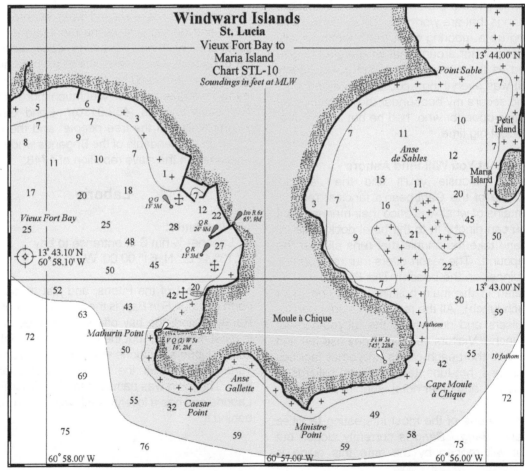

Windward Islands
St. Lucia
Vieux Fort Bay to
Maria Island
Chart STL-10
Soundings in feet at MLW

Navigational Information

When approaching from the north, care must be given to avoid the reefs lying offshore between Choisel (well to the northwest of Laborie) and Laborie as shown on Chart STL-1, stay at least a half-mile offshore here (and yes, it is a beat to windward). As shown on Chart STL-9, a waypoint at 13° 44.52'N, 61° 00.00' W, will place you approximately ½ mile south of the entrance to *Laborie Bay*. From the waypoint head in generally in a northerly direction until past the reef system that lies off the point to starboard. Then you can turn to starboard and anchor off the town in 7'-10' of water. A word of caution, in certain conditions the anchorage can get a bit rolly as do most of the lee anchorages in the Caribbean, you'll probably be used to the roll by the time you get this far south.

What You Will Find Ashore

Laborie is your typical colorful fishing village with a wonderful seaside market for you to explore.

On the main road, just north of the village turnoff, a sign points up a steep, rocky hill to the *Le Blanc Nature Heritage*. The road is best suited for 4-wheel drive vehicles, but the view from atop *Mt. Blanc* is worth it. Sweeping panoramas of Vieux Fort and the southeastern to southwestern coasts of St. Lucia await you, and don't forget your camera! There are two viewing platforms here, but exercise caution as they have not been kept up in years.

On the road north of Laborie, just south of Choisel, is the 200 year-old estate house of *Balenbouche Estate* where you can enjoy a truly elegant meal served on the verandah of this historical estate. Although full of period furniture, the house is not a museum, it is a working resort built on 150 acres of an old sugar plantation, a truly fascinating place to visit. Part of the acreage is still farmed and you can explore the ruins of an old water wheel and an old sugar mill. The estate's grounds stretch to the sea and if you walk around you can hike along the *Balenbouche River* where you'll find several interesting stones with hollowed out tops that are said to be wash basins used by the Arawaks here centuries ago.

If you continue further inland, you'll find several sites with petroglyphs dating back to Arawakan times. You are permitted to wander around the estate by yourself, with a personal guide, or with a guided tour, the choice is yours; however the estate asks for a EC$3 donation if you wander about by yourself.

Choisel itself is a small picturesque little village that is best known for its *Arts And Crafts Development Center* (which is actually in La Fargue just past *Miss Lucy's Mini Guesthouse*), a co-op where locally made crafts are offered for sale as well as cold drinks and snacks. Choisel's center is its large church and beachside fish market, both of which are worth a stop. Just to the north of Choisel is Caribe Point which was home to St. Lucia's last Caribs until the latter part of the 19th century when intermarriage made a pure Carib ancestry a thing of the past. From Choisel you can head to Morne Sionor Cafiere for some very nice locally produced baskets and weavings.

Dining

The *Big Bamboo Café and Wine Bar* is the new kid on the block in Laborie. They're open for lunch and dinner Tuesday through Sunday. Across the way is the *Market Place Restaurant*, while just over the bridge to the west is the *A&A Restaurant*. My favorite is *Adisha's Blue Water Bar* just to the west of the fish market. *Adisha's* is truly local in flavor and cuisine where you dine on healthy portions outside on the waterfront, and pay much less than you would expect.

On Sunday, take a bus headed to Soufrière and get off just down the road from Laborie at *Debbie's Home Cooking* for their not-to-be-missed Sunday buffet.

Vieux Fort Bay

Waypoints:
Vieux Fort Bay- ½ nm W of anchorage
13° 43.10' N, 61° 58.10' W

Vieux Fort is St. Lucia's second largest town and you'll probably be able to tell that by the amount of traffic and vendors that fill the streets. The city is a commercial center and nearby *Hewanorra Airport* only adds to the congestion. Up until the early 1600s the only inhabitants were bands of Arawaks until a band of Dutch settlers built a small fort east of town at Point Sable. Within a century large sugar cane plantations sprang up in the surrounding areas with their fertile soil. These plantations survived the slavery years and even as far as the 1920s when sugar prices plummeted and poverty ruled. A short bit of prosperity returned during World War II when Allied forces leased 1,000 acres of land and built an airstrip (which is now the *Hewanorra Airport*).

Please note that there has been a recent spate of break ins of vessels in the southern anchorages as well as along the harbor wall. If you cannot leave someone aboard at all times you might wish to move to Laborie.

Navigational Information

As shown on Chart STL-10, a waypoint at 13° 43.10' N, 61° 58.10' W, places your vessel approximately ½ mile west of the anchorage. The best spot to anchor is south of the commercial dock, although the anchorage at the northern part of the bay by the fishing harbor offers easier dinghy access. Be aware of the large shoal lying west and northwest of the fishing harbor.

If you wish to tie your dinghy up in the fishing harbor, do so on the western or northern walls and don't leave anything of value in it. If you choose to anchor south of the commercial dock, stay south of the markers. If you anchor south of the commercial dock, you can use the commercial dock to tie your dinghy to only if a ship is not expected. Call *Moule a Chic* on VHF ch. 16 for docking information.

Marine Facilities
Customs and *Immigration*

If you need to clear in, *Customs* is located at the head of the large commercial dock though you might have to take a taxi to the airport to clear *Immigration*.

Marine Facilities
Fuel

Gas can sometimes be purchased in the fishing harbor (and also ice at the easternmost dock), if they don't have it, a gas station is within walking distance. The nearby mall has a *NAPA* store that carries oils and some limited marine supplies

Marinas

There is not a marina available in *Vieux Fort Bay*, but you can sometimes find dockage inside the fishing harbor stern-to on the NW wall. There is no electricity here and you will be charged EC$20 for a night's stay. Figure on 6'-7' at MLW here.

What You Will Find Ashore

The focus of life in Vieux Fort is *Clarke Street*, lined with all sorts of shops and homes in the classic gingerbread design. There is a small grassy square just off *Clarke Street* where each May, *St. Lucia Jazz Festival* concerts are held.

At the southern end of *Vieux Fort Bay* you'll find Moule à Chicque, a rugged mass of rock, home to the world's second highest lighthouse.

Internet Access

In town there is a small Internet café, *Jemann* as well as *The Document Center*, both of which offer Internet access. Located at the *Courtyard Mall* is *Wegosite.com*, another Internet café. *Kimatri, The Old Plantation Yard*, and *The Reef* restaurants all have *Wi-fi* for their customers.

Provisions

Shopping in Vieux Fort is a pleasure! *Mike's Frozen Foods* will cut, freeze, and deliver to your boat whatever cut of meat you desire. *Il Pirata*, an excellent Italian restaurant well worth a meal or two for your deserving crew and mate, is located only a mile west of town on the bus route to Laborie or Choisel. Just a few miles further on is *Gablewoods South Mall,* another good spot to reprovision.

Dining

Just a short walk up from the commercial dock, on the left, sits the *Kimatrai Hotel and Restaurant* on a hill overlooking *Vieux Fort Bay*. This is the perfect place for a sunset meal. Bring your laptop as the restaurant has free *Wi-fi* .

The Old Plantation Yard is located on Commercial Street and is as noted for its ambiance as it is for its food. Here you dine in a courtyard amid breadfruit trees while your food is cooked in large earthenware pots, also in the courtyard. The restaurant also has free *Wi-fi* for its customers.

The Reef is the spot for the best local cuisine as well as free *Wi-fi* . The owner, Cecille, is a windsurfing instructor and next door is her *Reef Kite 'n Surf Center*.

The Eastern Coast of St. Lucia

The eastern coast of St. Lucia has no viable anchorages, but for those willing to travel by car along this shoreline the scenery is superb and there are several places of interest to visit. Let's start our tour from south to north and you can follow your progress on Chart STL-1.

The *Pointe Sable National Park* begins at Point Sable, as shown on Chart STL-10, and continues northeastward along the eastern shoreline of St. Lucia and encompasses the *Cape Moule à Chique* promontory, *Anse des Sables Beach*, the *Maria Islands*, the *Man Kotè Mangrove* and *Savannes Bay Nature Reserves*. Still in its infancy, the park is yet to pass legislation banning visitors so please be advised to use caution in these areas. Take nothing but photographs and leave nothing but footprints.

Atop the *Cape Moule à Chique* promontory you'll have marvelous views of *Vieux Fort Bay* and the Maria Islands as well as the interior of St. Lucia. The only access here is by car from *Vieux Fort Bay*. *Anse des Sables Beach* is a great spot for a swim, the best beach on the island and one that is also popular for windsurfers. At the southern end of the beach is a nice museum, the *Maria Islands Interpretive Center* where you can also arrange a trip to the offshore Maria Islands.

The beach is also home to a few hotels and beach bars, and a *Club Med* which is restricted to non-paying visitors. You can however use the rest rooms and get a cold drink at the *Sandy Beach Club* nearby as well as sample the fare at a great restaurant, *The Reef*.

To the east of Vieux Fort and Moule à Chique, lie the Maria Islands. The Maria Islands, shown on Chart STL-10, are nature reserves and home to two species of reptiles found nowhere else in the world. The Kouwes snake, the world's rarest snake, about 3' long with dark green and brown markings, once thrived on St. Lucia, but was nearly wiped out by mongooses introduced by the cane planters to kill offending snakes and mice. Today they number only about a hundred and inhabit Maria Island, sometimes called Maria Major.

Another rare reptile, the Zandoli Te lizard, shares the island with the Kouwes snake. The male of this species can grow to over a foot long and has a bright blue tale with a yellow belly, while the female is brown with darker vertical stripes. The Maria Islands are off limits to visitors unless with a guide provided by the center on Anse des Sables beach. Don't fall prey to local fishermen who will offer to take you to the island, make sure your guide is certified.

About 6 miles northeast of the Maria Islands along the eastern shore you'll find Micoud at the eastern edge of the rain forest reserve. From here, many hikers like to travel the *Descartiers Trail* which extends to Fond St. Jacques. Micoud itself was once home to some nine groups of Arawaks owing to its harbor and fresh water supply. Micoud is also the birthplace of St. Lucia's first Prime Minister, John Compton.

In Praslin, local builders still fashion canoes in the traditional way, being carved out of a single tree. In nearby Mamiku, just a bit south of Praslin, you'll find the *Mamiku Gardens*. Here Veronica Shingleton-Smith has longed to incorporate the ruins of the old *Micoud Estate House* into a botanical haven called *Mamiku Gardens* on the 500-acre estate where her family farms bananas and other fruits. The original estate burned to the ground in 1797, and with the help of Veronica's daughter-in-law Louise, who found several artifacts including an old French musket barrel, the project finally got underway with professional help and today over 500 artifacts have been recovered from the site.

The story of the *de Micoud Estate* begins in 1794 when British troops and naval forces captured the island from the French. The French Revolutionary government declared all the slaves free and they took to the forests to become guerrilla fighters, *Brigands*. The Brits sent a large army under the command of Lt. Gen. Sir Ralph Abercromby (the same man who later took Trinidad) to try to recover the neighboring islands which they succeeded in doing in 1796.

England finally took control over the island in 1814 in the *Treaty of Paris*. Abercromby left Sir John Moore and some 5,000 men to maintain control on St. Lucia and Moore set up military posts throughout the island, one of them at the home of Baron de Micoud and his wife. In 1797, Brigands attacked the estate, fortified by 70 men from the *Guadeloupe Rangers* commanded by Capt. de Marchay. Surprised at three in the afternoon, the group was overwhelmed and de Marchay and 15 of de Machay's men were killed. De Marchay was asleep at the time of the attack and most of the men were washing in the river. The men on guard were either asleep or drunk and were bayoneted without resistance. De Marchay committed suicide when he realized that he had no choice but retreat. The Brigands then burnt the *de Micoud Estate* to the ground.

Just a bit northeast of Praslin lie the Frigate Islands, a nature reserve designed for frigate birds to nest. But Frigate birds are not the only inhabitants of these islands, they are also home to several other avian species as well as a species of boa constrictor that can grow to 12' and the poisonous *Fer de Lance*, but it's highly unlikely you'll spy one of these reclusive creatures as visitors are not allowed on the islands.

A couple miles north of Praslin is the *Errard Plantation*, a working plantation that offers guided tours featuring a 70' waterfall and a lunch featuring fruit juices made from fruit grown on the plantation. The next stop is probably going to be Dennery where the coast road runs out and you'll have to make your way back south or westward to Castries. Once known as *Anse Canot*, the town received its name from the island's Governor, Count D'Ennery, who visited the area in 1768. The primary attraction is Grand Anse Beach, just north of town, where leatherback turtles come to lay their eggs in season, March through July. The *St. Lucia National Trust* arranges turtle watching tours that leave daily from *Derek Walcott Square* in Castries for this spectacular and memorable event.

Barbados

Port of Entry: Bridgetown, Port. St. Charles
Fuel: Port St. Charles
Haul-Out: Bridgetown

Diesel Repairs: Bridgetown, Guinea
Outboard Repairs: Bridgetown, Guinea
Propane: Bridgetown, Port St. Charles
Provisions: Bridgetown, Port St. Charles
Important Lights: See *Appendix A*

*To confess truly, of all the islands that I have seen
unto this day, not any pleaseth me so well.*
Sir Henry Colt, 1631

Barbados is the most windward of the Windward Islands, lying over 90 miles to windward from the rest of her sister islands that arc south and southwestward from Martinique to Grenada. It has been said that sailing to Barbados is best done by heading to Bermuda, then across to the Azores, southerly to the Canaries, and then across the *Atlantic Ocean* to avoid the windward beat from anywhere else in the eastern Caribbean. True enough, it will be a beat, but the rewards are worth it. By waiting on weather you can certainly choose a window of lighter winds and seas, and leaving from Charlotteville, Tobago when the winds are east or south of east, or from La Désirade off Guadeloupe when the wind is well north of east, also eases the thrash to windward.

Some experienced Caribbean skippers prefer to leave from the northern tip of St. Lucia at *Rodney Bay* or the southern end of Martinique, from Ste. Anne. Either way it will be a windward beat and you will be fighting a northwesterly setting current of varying strength.

If arriving from the east, from Europe, South Africa, or South America, it is a good idea to make Barbados your first landfall in the Caribbean; however you must beware of both the southern and northern coasts. Both of these shorelines have reef systems lying well offshore, up to a half-mile and more, and well over a mile on the southeastern coast at *Cobbler's Reef*, give these areas a wide berth (see Chart BAR-1). Then there are those that knowingly nod and say there's nothing that goes to weather better than a *747*.

However you make your way to Barbados, you'll find a wonderful island, steeped in a distinguished British tradition (with afternoon tea and cricket being very popular), yet certainly Caribbean in nature, with gently rolling hills, marvelous beaches, great sailing, and good protection when the wind and seas pick up. So lovely is this island that it played a co-starring role with Grenada in the movie *Island in the Sun* with Harry Belafonte.

One of the biggest draws for cruisers to the island of Trinidad is *Carnival*. Trinidad may have *Carnival*, but Barbados will not be outdone in the party arena that much is for sure. The biggest bash on Barbados is *Crop Over*, a five-week-long celebration that is only slightly less of a bacchanal than *Carnival*. *Crop Over*, originally an annual event that dates back to the 1780s, celebrates the final sugarcane harvest of the year. Although the celebration died away during the 1940s, it was revived in 1974 and today the fete has evolved into a massive party featuring costumed celebrants from throughout the Caribbean. During *Crop Over* food stalls offer every Bajan dish imaginable along with plenty of rum and cold beer while local vendors hawk their jewelry, carvings, handicrafts, and T-shirts. *Crop Over* begins with the ceremonial *Delivery of the Last Canes* and the crowning of the *King and Queen of the Festival*, the most productive cane-cutters of the season.

At night, Calypso rules with musicians from all over the Caribbean vying for a chance to reign as the *Calypso Monarch* at *Cohobblopot*; a huge carnival-like show complete with stunning costumed entertainers and a packed house. Calypso performers are organized into *tents* with names such as *Conquerors*, *Untouchables*, and so on, which are sponsored by Bajan businesses. The performers vie for titles such as the *Party Monarch*, the *Road March Monarch*, and the *Pic-O-De-Crop Monarch*.

The celebration climaxes on *Kadooment Day* (Bajan for a *big to-do*) when the *Calypso Monarch* is crowned along with the winners of the costumed band contests. The party ends with a frenzied march through the streets of Bridgetown, from the *National Stadium* to Spring Garden, with revelers dancing every step of the way.

In days past, Bridgetown and *Carlisle Bay* was the only worthwhile stop for visiting yachts, but Barbados now offers the cruising yachtsman a very nice alternative. The *Port St. Charles* development on the northwestern coast of Barbados, just north of Speightstown, offers a marina with dockage inside a dredged, protected cove, *Customs* and *Immigration* have offices on site, and the marina offers fuel, water, full electric, cable TV, and phone service at each slip.

Barbados has a very reliable bus system that reaches almost every part of the island, some are government operated, and some are privately owned. Fares are BDS$1.50 and buses run along the coastal highways for cruisers needing transportation. In Bridgetown there are two bus stations, one off *Fairchild St.*, and a smaller station near the *Post Office*. If you are headed north, catch your bus at the *Post Office* station, if you're headed anywhere else on the island, you can catch your bus at the *Fairchild St.* station.

A Brief History of Barbados

Barbados is less than one million years old, being created by the collision of the Atlantic and Caribbean plates, along with a volcanic eruption. Barbados is geologically unique, being actually two landmasses that merged over the years. As with all the islands of the Caribbean, the first settlers on Barbados were Amerindians that arrived on the islands somewhere between 2000-1500 BC. Recent radiocarbon dating of shell tools place the first Arawakan settlers in the vicinity of Heywoods, just south of the *Port St. Charles* development, around 1630 BC, this of course means that area in and around Heywoods has been inhabited

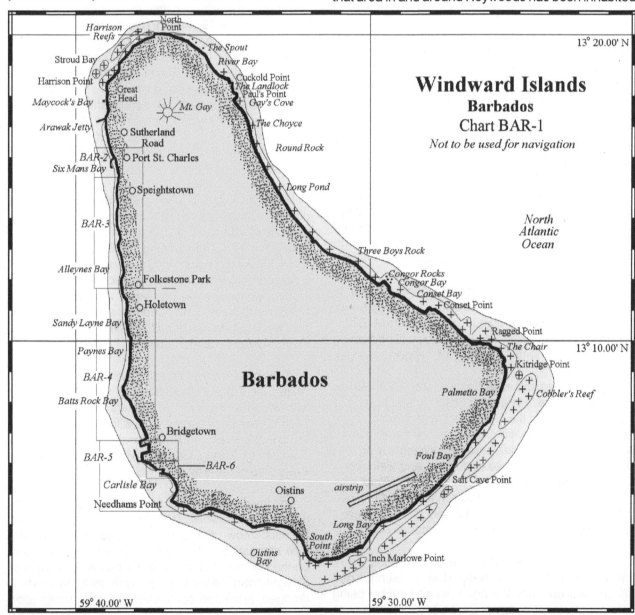

for over 3,600 years! By now, you probably know that the Caribs followed the Arawaks up the chain of islands, killing them and enslaving their women. However no evidence of Carib inhabitation has been found on Barbados, leading some experts to theorize that the Caribs only visited the island from nearby St. Vincent or St. Lucia. The Caribs continued to visit Barbados even after the British arrived on the island and who documented some of the Caribs' comings and goings.

Interestingly, unlike most of the other islands of the Caribbean, Columbus never "discovered" Barbados. There is no record of the *Admiral of All Oceans* even sailing by the island and the early Spanish explorers ignored Barbados in their search for gold. The first mention of the island in recorded history is on December 23, 1511, when King Ferdinand of Spain permitted Spanish slaving expedition to *Los Barbudos*. It was a group of early Portuguese explorers that named her *Los Barbudos* after the "bearded" fig trees that they found there. Other tales tell of a race of bearded men who were said to be Barbados' pre-European settlers. Experts point out that this is unlikely as the Arawaks were not bearded, while other "experts" say the bearded men were of African origin, which opens up all sorts of theories about how these people got to Barbados in the first place.

The British arrived in 1625 when Captain John Powell landed near today's Holetown and claimed Barbados for the King of England, James I, who unbeknownst to Powell had passed away on his voyage across the Atlantic. Two years later the first true attempt at colonization was funded by a London merchant, Sir William Courteen, and on February 27, 1627, 80 mostly male British settlers let by Captain John Powell's brother Henry, and 10 slaves who were captured from a Spanish vessel, arrived on the leeward coast of Barbados near Holetown and named their settlement Jamestown.

These first settlers did not own land; rather they kept small plots of land and a slave or a white indentured servant to work the land. At this time, only people with social connections and good financial backgrounds were allocated land in Barbados proving once again that it's not what you know, but who you know. The indentured servants agreed to work for a period of up to ten years for a small plot of land or a sum of money payable at the end of their indentureship to get the workers started. Many of these indentured servants

were white men and women who signed an agreement to serve a particular planter for a period of 5-7 years. Most employers reneged on their agreements and the majority of the indentured servants moved on to North America or other Caribbean islands. Many of the indentured servants that remained, called *Red Legs*, still live in Barbados today in the *St. Martin's River* area and other eastern shore regions. Besides slaves and indentured servants, some of the Bajan workforce of the day were kidnapped, while others were convicted criminals who chose a life in the cane fields of Barbados over life in a British prison.

The settlers at Jamestown were successful in their efforts and the profits from their tobacco, indigo, cotton, and ginger crops went directly to their expedition's financial backer, the island's "owner," Sir William Courteen. Courteen was an able administrator, but his successor, the Earl of Carlisle was quite the opposite, ambitious and driven. In the 1630s, the Earl of Carlisle succeeded in convincing King Charles I to grant him certain rights to Barbados, which conflicted with Courteen's own agreements. The Earl of Carlisle then sent his own band of settlers to the southwestern tip of Barbados in the vicinity of Bridgetown setting up a confrontation between himself and Courteen and which later became known as the *Great Barbados Robbery*. Stunned by the turn of events, Courteen turned to his friend, the Earl of Pembroke, to assist him in getting his rights to Barbados restored. King Charles I agreed and then in a turnabout, re-granted ownership to Carlisle who had pulled many strings to achieve his goal.

Political parrying between Courteen and Carlisle continued and the islanders suffered as they also had to deal with a drought and a decrease in food production. Across the pond in England, Carlisle pushed for an increase in his export profits at the expense of the islanders and as a result the 1630s became known as the "starving time." In 1639, Carlisle appointed Henry Hawkley as Governor of Barbados who was described as relentless and scheming and not at all well received by the local planters. To appease the powerful planters Hawkley set up a *House of Assembly* making many of the white landowners representatives. Barbados at this time, being far from Britain and out of the reach of treaties and enforcement, became a bit of a haven for gamblers, fortune hunters, political outcasts, and all manner of rogues. A local Captain complained about Hawkley's appointments to the island's Judge saying,

"If all the whore-masters were taken off the beach, what would the Governor do for a council?"

The population increased on Barbados until by 1643, there were some 37,000 whites and 6,000 black slaves on the island, nearly all engaged in farming. In 1647 a yellow fever epidemic swept Barbados which took both plantation owners as well as slaves, several plantations were left to whomever could manage them as their owners passed away.

The 1640s brought the English Civil War and Bajans did their best to remain neutral. When Oliver Cromwell took over England and Charles I was executed in 1649, the *Royalists (Cavaliers)*, who were in the majority on Barbados and who opposed Cromwell, began open hostilities with the opposing *Roundheads*. During this period, if any Bajan called another Bajan a *Cavalier* or *Roundhead* as a joke, they had to invite their victim and all who had heard the jest to dinner. Eventually the *Roundheads* were deported to England where they reported to Cromwell that the *Royalists* were involved in trading with the Dutch who were enemies at the time. In retaliation, Cromwell sent a fleet carrying 4,000 troops to Barbados in 1651 and Bajan Governor Lord Willoughby and his troops surrendered to the British forces after a fierce battle at Oistins. The year 1652 saw the enactment of the *Charter of Barbados* in which the islanders had to pledge allegiance to the Crown, but were allowed the right of self-government and free-trade. This latter agreement did not last long as Cromwell reinforced a previous trade act banning foreign trade, which seriously damaged the burgeoning sugar industry on Barbados. After years of protests from the Bajan planters, a compromise was reached in 1663, which allowed free trade, but added in a 4.5% export tax which lasted until 1837.

So, by the 1650s, sugar had made its appearance on the island and most of the forests had been removed to make way for large sugar cane plantations. Barbados entered a period of great prosperity and for the white upper class Bajans the island became "the brightest jewel in the English Crown" as Barbados became the first country in the New World to plant sugar and export it on a large scale. The man accredited with the birth of the sugar industry on Barbados was a Dutch Jew named Pieter Blower who had learned the sugar cane business in Brazil and brought this knowledge with him to Barbados in 1637.

During this sugar boom, more and more slaves arrived on the island, delivered by Portuguese and Dutch slavers who brought slaves from many diverse tribes that hailed from West Africa. As I mentioned, in 1643 there were approximately 6,000 slaves on the island, but by 1685, the numbers increased to 60,000 slaves, outnumbering the white Bajans by over three to one. Strict laws were enacted for the capture and punishment of runaway slaves, even passing laws, which prohibited slaves from playing drums, blowing horns, and assembling in any sort of group. For those slaves who broke the law, the actions of the trained militia was said to be particularly brutal. The *British Parliament* granted planters in the West Indies the right to "...fight, kill, slay, repress and subdue all such as shall in a hostile or mutinous manner...disturb the peace." On top of all this, Royalist prisoners from the recent Civil War were sold into slavery on Barbados and a group of these white slaves plotted a revolt that failed and 18 of the white slaves were summarily executed.

Slave revolts were occurring all over the Caribbean during these years, with many runaway slaves hiding in the mountainous interiors of islands such as Jamaica and St. Vincent. In Barbados revolts occurred in 1675, 1683, 1686, 1692, and 1702, but Bajan topography was not conducive to successful hiding. In 1807 the slave trade was abolished by *Parliament* and in 1815 a bill was passed that declared that all slaves in the West Indies had to be registered so as to control any black market slave trading activity and which led to another slave rebellion. Bajan planters saw this registration law as a threat to their self-government, however the slaves mistakenly thought the law was intended to free them and their resentment of their white owners grew. A slave named Bussa (now a Bajan *National Hero*), a ranger on Bayley's Plantation in St. Phillip, started an uprising on Easter Sunday, April 14, 1816, on the Bayley Plantation which quickly spread to other plantations across the island. After troops from St. Ann's Fort squashed what came to be known as *Bussa's Rebellion*, hundreds of slaves, including Bussa, had been killed and a fifth of the Bajan sugar crop had been destroyed.

Bussa's Rebellion was a victory of sorts for the slaves as it triggered reforms and was one more step on the road to Emancipation. Abolitionists took up the cause and in 1834 slavery was abolished and the 84,000 slaves on Barbados suddenly found themselves apprentices, which meant that they would continue to work for their plantation masters, with food, clothing, and shelter provided in exchange for a 45-hour workweek. In reality, the freed slaves weren't much better off than before. The planters did not wish to lose their labor force, they feared that the freed slaves would immigrate to other Caribbean islands and so they did what they could to convince them to stay on Barbados. The planters finally realized that they could realize greater profits with a freed labor force than with their apprenticed help for whom they had to provide.

On August 1, 1838, the former slaves were freed from their apprenticeships however a law was passed binding the freed slaves to their plantations as tenants. The planters would house the former slaves in tiny houses and charge them rent, virtually stripping the workers of their rights. This kept the Bajan sugar industry from a decline of the planter class as had happened on other Caribbean islands with Emancipation and allowed the Bajan plantation economy to grow steadily between 1838 and the 1870s. In 1843, Samuel Jackson Prescod, the son of a white planter and slave mother, became the first non-white Member of Parliament. Prescod was a powerful voice for the plight of the downtrodden on Barbados and helped found the Liberal Party. Five years after Prescod's death in 1871 Barbados found itself in the middle of a governmental shake-up that pitted whites against blacks and the rich against the poor

In 1876, Britain proposed that Barbados link with the other Windward Islands and Bajan Governor John Pope Hennessy tried to accept his fellow Bajans to accept this idea. However, many Bajans wanted no part of this scheme having self-governed for over two centuries. Plantation owners feared losing their work force to planters on other islands that paid higher wages while Bajan workers favored the union for the very same reason. The arguments for and against the move grew heated and blood was spilled when riots erupted in April of 1876 as black workers reacted violently against the stubborn planters. Hennessy took the heat for these riots and was transferred to Hong Kong and the planned Windward Islands association was shelved and by the end of the 1800s the plantation system with its cheap labor was still dominant on Barbados.

The twentieth century brought the end of the sugar boom on Barbados as cheap European sugar beets priced Bajan sugar right out of the market. Planters, who owned over 90% of the island, had to lay off

workers, most of whom had no choice but to emigrate. Between 1904 and 1914, over 20,000 Bajan workers left for Central America to build the Panama Canal while others left for Brazil, Guiana, Trinidad, Curacao, and anywhere else that showed the promise of steady employment. Many canal workers were successful and were able to send money home to their families until finally returning to Barbados with U.S dollars in every pocket. Some of these returning canal workers purchased land from the planters who were forced to sell off their part or all of their properties to pay their mounting debts during the early part of the 1900s when the number of plantations dropped from 437 to 305 in twenty years while large portions of some estates were converted into villages where anybody was free to reside.

Starting around 1850, planters hired chemists, botanists, and all sorts of researchers to develop new and better fertilizers which would result in a new type of sugar cane, which could open a new market for the depressed sugar economy and there were certain advances made with profitable results. A hurricane in 1898 killed 80 people, blew down some 18,000 houses (mostly worker's shacks), and increased incidences of dysentery and typhoid. In the aftermath of the 1898 hurricane, £50,000 was granted to Barbados for plantation repairs and Barbados began to gain a bit from the British and U.S. sugar markets. A cholera epidemic in 1854 killed over 15,000 Bajans, and a smallpox epidemic in 1902, followed by a yellow fever epidemic in 1908, struck the poorer labor force hard although the upper class Bajans were hardly affected.

The depression of the 1920s was felt hard in the Bajan work force, especially those who had returned from the Panama Canal construction projects in 1914 and were used to having a bit of money. A lot of the work force returned to a tenant status and wages during these years for plantation workers were the same as those of almost a century before, one-shilling (five pence) per day. New political movements arose during these years in response to the people's need. Charles Duncan O'Neal, a doctor, devoted his life to the improvement of the lives of the Bajan masses much as Samuel Prescod had done a century before. In 1924, O'Neal formed the *Democratic League*, the first of several political forces that were to shape Barbados' future. The *Democratic League* was popular among middle class non-white Bajans and many won seats in the *Barbados House Of Assembly* including O'Neal himself in 1932. O'Neal, also was instrumental in forming the *Workingman's Association* in 1925 which, along with the *Democratic League*, were influential in the formation of the *Barbados Labour Party* in 1938 and the *Barbados Worker's Union* in 1941, both of which fought for Bajan worker's rights.

Marcus Garvey (see the section on *Rastafarians* in the chapter entitled *The Basics*) brought his message to the dissatisfied segment of the Bajan population and brought about riots in the streets in 1937. Sparked by an orator named Clement Payne (a Trinidadian by birth though his parents and siblings were born on Barbados) who advocated trade unions in defiant speeches in Bridgetown, Bajan authorities deported him on July 16, 1937. Crowds gathered to protest his deportation and the outrage they felt exploded into violence that lasted for three days and moved into the rural areas as well with protesters bemoaning the fact that over 70% of the population of Barbados was not allowed to vote.

But the riots of 1937 were not in vain, a new movement was born of the unrest with Grantley Adams at the helm. Adams, the son of a Bajan teacher, studied law at Oxford before returning to Barbados in 1925. In 1934, he was elected to the *House of Assembly* and in 1938, Adams helped form the *Barbados Labour Party* with Charles O'Neal and C.A. Braitwhite. The *Labour Party* won its first victory in 1940 when it gained five seats in the *House of Assembly* and Adams and his *Labour Party* set about to modernize the Bajan political system changing it from a feudal plantocracy to a modern democracy even though the *Legislature* was still controlled by white planters giving every Bajan adult the right to vote in 1951. Within two decades, Barbados made significant strides towards independence while leaders of other British West Indian islands were again speaking of federation. In 1958, Adams represented Barbados in the formation of the *Federation of the British West Indies*. The federation never truly gained momentum partly because each member nation had different ideas for the direction of the union and its goals and the short-lived effort dissolved after only four years.

In 1961, Errol Walton Barrow, the nephew of Charles O'Neal and Adam's foil in political circles, succeeded Adams and with his *Democratic Liberal Party*, the *DLP*, Barrow took over the reins of Bajan government and instituted reforms lacking during the years of governmental rearrangement. Barrow

also instituted a program of public works that was designed to provide relief for unemployed Bajans. In 1966, Barbados achieved independence and Barrow was elected the first Prime Minister. Barrow would later be voted out of office in 1976, but was reinstated as Prime Minister in a landslide in 1986, a year before his untimely death.

The 1990s brought a nosedive to the Bajan economy partly due to the recession that was occurring in the United States. In 1994, Owen Arthur became Barbados' fifth Prime Minister as the *BLP* returned to power and his policies renewed the confidence of investors in the island and the Bajan economy soared to new heights. Today Barbados has a new economy and an increased standard of living for all, in fact, at the end of the 20th century, the *United Nations* ranked Barbados as the most prosperous small state in the Caribbean and one of the top ten developing countries in the world. Not bad, not bad at all!

Customs and *Immigration*

Ports of Entry
Bridgetown
Port St. Charles

Upon arrival in Barbados, skippers are required to report to *Customs* and *Immigration* at either *Bridgetown Harbour* at the southwestern corner of the island, or at the new Port St. Charles complex located about ten miles north of Bridgetown. Bridgetown is a commercial port and clearance at Port St. Charles is much easier, and safer, for the cruising yachtsman. You are not permitted to anchor out and dinghy in; contact *Customs* via VHF ch. 16 (*Signal Station Port Control* in Bridgetown, or *Barbados Customs* at Port St. Charles on ch. 16 or ch. 77)) for directions to where to tie up. At Port St. Charles you may tie up at the marina (at the fuel dock), in *Bridgetown Harbour* you need to tie to the seawall (use plenty of fenders).

Immigration
Immigration allows stays of 90 days and extensions are available for a modest fee, bring your boat papers and proof of financial support, to the *Immigration* office at *The Wharf* in Bridgetown (426-9912), but be prepared for a long wait. If you have crew flying in, they will need a document signed by the Captain stating their status as crew, and it is recommended that the skipper meet his/her crew at the airport with the vessel's papers to ease the clearance procedure.

Cruising Permit

You will need a cruising permit in Barbados. If you clear at Port St. Charles and wish to visit Bridgetown and *Carlisle Bay*, you will need a permit to do so and *Customs* will want to know your itinerary (and the reverse is true if you enter at Bridgetown and wish to visit Port St. Charles). There are several other anchorages along the leeward (western shore) that are well worth a stop, however at this time *Customs* is hesitant to allow yachts to anchor in most places.

Barbados has severe penalties for yachts anchoring in coral. The fine is US$25,000 and a prison term is possible for convicted skippers.

On the Barbados charts in this guide, I show several anchorages where it is sometimes possible for vessels to anchor provided they obtain permission first, at Speightstown on Chart BAR-2 and at *Payne's Bay* on Chart BAR-4. Plans call for a few locations to be marked by buoys where visiting yachts will find a nice sandy bottom to anchor in and a chart of these areas will be available from the *Port Authority* (hopefully) by the time this guide is published. As to the other areas, there may be a way to obtain that permission if you know somebody at the *Barbados Yacht Club* who could vouch for you...it's worth a try! It would be a shame to miss the leeward coast. In addition, if a Bajan official reads this, please open up your coastline to us cruisers, we wish to enjoy the beauty that is your birthright! And we'll promise to anchor in the sand!

Fees

When you check in with *Customs* and *Immigration*, you will also need to speak to the representatives of the *Barbados Port Authority* and the local health official. *Customs* does not charge for clearing in, but there is a BDS$100 for clearing out (the going rate is BDS$1.98 to US$1.00 and most businesses are happy to take U.S. dollars). You will also have to pay an anchoring fee to the *Port Authority* of BDS$8.33. After 2200, overtime fees are in effect.

Firearms, Fishing, and Parts Importation

If you have firearms aboard, you will need to turn them in to *Customs* for safekeeping during your stay. Non-commercial fishing is permitted for cruisers except in designated marine parks. If you need parts shipped in, check with your local *Customs* officer; the parts can enter duty-free.

Pets

Barbados is rabies-free and pets are not allowed on the island unless they have gone through a quarantine period. Cruisers must keep their pets aboard under all circumstances. For advance information on pet regulations, you can write the *Senior Veterinary Officer, Ministry of Agriculture and Rural Development*, Pine, Plantation Road, Barbados, 246-427-5073, fax 246-427-2143.

Port St. Charles

The Port St. Charles complex is a rather new infrastructure and very comfortable for any skipper and crew. While under construction, an ancient piece of pottery was found while workers were on a coffee break and the owners of *Port St. Charles* brought in archeologists from England to excavate each area before workers began construction on each of the complex's five phases. Some of the pieces that were dug up showed to be almost 4,000 years old! In 1997, and again in 2001, the marina played host to the finish of Sir Chay Blyth's *Atlantic Rowing Race*.

The *Port St. Charles* complex is designed for the wealthy, have no doubt about that. It has been described in its brochures as the "ultimate reward" and is the brainchild of three investors, two Bajan brothers, Cow and Bizzy Williams, and Bjorn Bjerkman who has lived in Barbados almost all his life. The complex has been designed to be eco-friendly with a garbage incineration system and an inner lagoon that is designated as a marine sanctuary.

Navigational Information

If you're approaching from the north, or if you simply wish to clear in without having to tie to the high dock at Bridgetown, *Port St. Charles* should be your landfall. As shown on Chart BAR-3, a waypoint at 13° 15.75' N, 59° 39.25' W, will place you approximately ½ mile west of the entrance to the *Port St. Charles* complex and marina. Before attempting to enter the marina contact the dockmaster on VHF ch. 16 or 77 for instructions on entry and remind him that you'll need to clear *Customs*. You will be directed to a berth or to the fuel dock to tie up while clearing *Customs*. If the dockmaster does not respond to your hail try to contact *Customs* directly on VHF ch. 16 or 77.

From the waypoint shown on Chart BAR-3, head a bit south of east keeping the southern tip of the marina breakwater (marked by a light, Fl G) to port. For entry to the complex see Chart BAR-2 below which shows the marina in greater detail. Pass between the breakwater to port and the line of red buoys to starboard that mark the western edge of *Tom Snooch Reef* and you'll see the marina's docks to port. If you only plan to clear in you'll likely be directed to the 60' fuel dock just across from the reef as shown on the chart. Anchoring is not permitted in the private inner lagoon.

What You Will Find Ashore
Customs and *Immigration*

Port St. Charles is a Port of Entry, one of two on Barbados. After you have contacted the marina and been directed to a slip or dock, the skipper, crew, and guests must remain on board until all of the officials have arrived and you have been granted clearance. If you plan to visit Bridgetown or *Carlisle Bay* before clearing out you will need to get a cruising permit.

Marine Facilities
Marina

The *Port St. Charles Marina* can accommodate six transient vessels (with lengths of up to 200') and offers both diesel and gasoline at its fuel dock. The docks have water, telephone service, and cable TV hookups. Fifty-cycle electricity is available at 415, 240, 208, and 120-volt single phase AC, and at 415 and 208 volt three phase AC.

Holding tanks are mandatory and no pump out of sewage, waste, fuel, or oil is permitted in the harbor. Ashore you'll find offices for *Customs*, *Immigration*, and the *Police*.

Marine Facilities
Marine Services

There is not a wealth of marine services at Port St. Charles, however, *Bajan Ocean Yacht Sales*

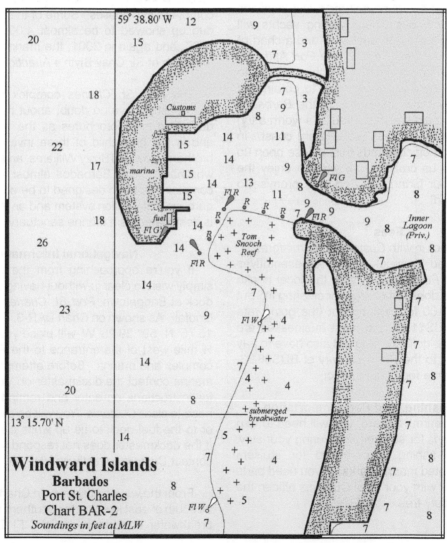

and Services does an excellent job of repairing and maintaining many of the vessels that dock there.

Internet Access
If you need Internet access you can have one of the marina technicians hook up a phone line to your boat or you can visit the *Port St. Charles Reception Office* and use one of their computers for a small fee.

Provisions
Port St. Charles lies about a mile north of Speightstown and the best shopping will be found there at *Eddies* and *Jordans*. Just south of Holetown is *Sunset Crest*, a sprawling complex of condos and shopping centers where the new *Super Centre* has established an online shopping service (there's also a branch in Warrens).

Dining
There is very good dining to be found in the marina complex at Port St. Charles. *La Mer* is a nice restaurant overlooking the complex with a great Sunday buffet lunch that is not to be missed. The *Sunset Isle Pool Bar* has been around for a few years now and is a popular stop for guests of the marina. There is also a small gym of sorts on the property with treadmills and other workout equipment.

Speightstown

About a mile south of Port St. Charles, Speightstown is Barbados' second largest town and was named after William Speight, a landowner and a member of Barbados first *House of Assembly*. During the sugar cane era Speightstown was a thriving port when sugar from here was transported to Bristol in England, earning Speightstown the nickname *Little Bristol*. Other ships would carry freight and passengers to and from Bridgetown.

Just north of Speightstown is *Almond Beach Village*, an all-inclusive resort and the sister of the *Almond Beach Club* in St. James. The 300-room resort stretches northward to the *Port St. Charles* complex.

Navigational Information
As shown on Chart BAR-3, a waypoint at 13° 14.90' N, 59° 39.25' W, will place you approximately ½ mile west of the lee anchorage off Speightstown. You cannot anchor here unless you first obtain permission from *Customs* and you must anchor only in the sand

south of the fisheries dock. Anchoring on reef will result in a very hefty fine! Bear in mind that even if you have permission to anchor at Speightstown or at *Payne's Bay*, these anchorages are not tenable when northerly swells are running. A very nice anchorage, if you can get permission to anchor there, is at Gibbs Beach as shown on Chart BAR-3.

What You Will Find Ashore
Provisions
The best shopping will be found in Speightstown at *Eddies* and *Jordans*. Just south of Holetown is *Sunset Crest*, a sprawling complex of condos and shopping centers where the new *Super Centre* has established an online shopping service (there's also a branch in Warrens).

Dining
Right on the waterfront you can dine at *The Fisherman's Pub* for typical Bajan fare, or at *Mango's By The Sea* which has a more romantic setting. *Mangos* is also home to *Mango's Fine Art Gallery* which exhibits a very nice collection of brightly colored silkscreens by Michael Adams.

Speightstown Mall opened in 1980 and has several stores, a bank, and even a *KFC*.

South of Speightstown, and north of Four Winds, are two lovely beaches, *Mullins Beach* and *Gibbs Beach*. *Mullins Beach* is by far the most popular of the pair, owing in part to the *Mullins Beach Bar and Restaurant* which sits right out over the water on stilts.

Historic Speightstown
On the corner of *Church* and *Queen Streets*, you'll find one of the oldest churches on the island, *St. Peter's*. Built in 1630, the church was rebuilt in 1837 and then again in 1980 when a fire left nothing but the walls and tower.

Also on *Church Street* is the tall, 17th century *Arlington House*, now being rebuilt by the *Barbados National Trust (The Barbados National Trust* is dedicated to the preservation of Bajan historic treasures and opens many of their properties to you at reduced rates with their *Heritage Passport*, for more information call 436-9033, or 888-*BARBADOS*). The *Arlington House* bears a startling resemblance to South Carolina buildings of the same era. Why is that you ask? Well, I'll tell you. Between 1670 and 1700, hundreds of Bajans and their slaves settled in and around the Charleston and Goose Creek, South Carolina areas (I'm told that the coastal South Carolina dialect of Gullah is remarkably similar to Bajan). This is why in 1997, Speightstown was twinned with Charleston, South Carolina, for the role that Bajans played in developing South Carolina in the late 1600s.

In the center of town are the remains of the *Denmark Fort* and the *Orange Fort*, which once boasted 23 cannons between them, some of which overlook the sea on the *Speightstown Esplanade.* Many of the old homes and buildings in Speightstown are slated for renovation by the *Barbados National Trust.* Hikers will want to investigate the *Arbib Nature and Heritage Trails.*

Folkestone Park and Holetown

Navigational Information

As shown on Chart BAR-4, at *Folkestone Park,* you'll find the *Folkestone Park and Marine Reserve.* Here you can check out the *Visitor's Center,* which includes a marine museum and a saltwater aquarium. In the waters off the shore is a buoyed recreational area where snorkelers can follow an underwater trail around *Dottin's Reef,* a seven-mile long reef. If you're not into snorkeling you can hire a glass-bottom boat to carry you to the reef, and SCUBA divers can hire a guide to the best spots on the reef.

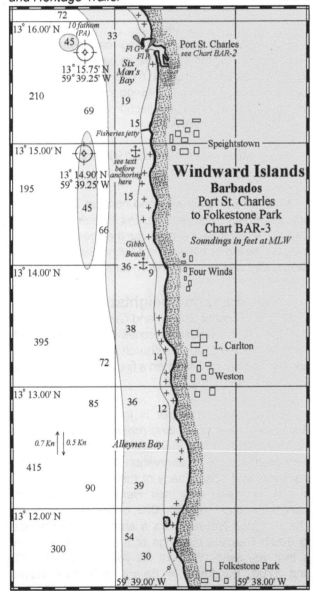

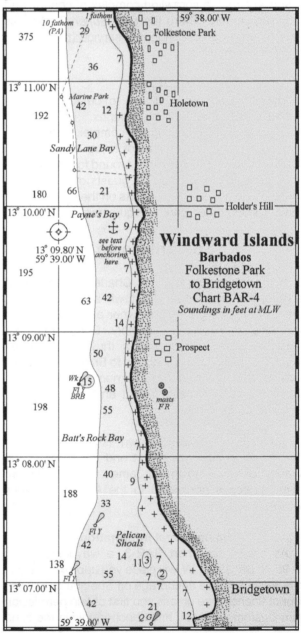

What You Will Find Ashore

Next to *Folkestone Park* is the *Bellaire Research Institute*, an affiliate of *McGill University* of Canada. The goals of the institute are to improve the agriculture and fisheries of Barbados and most of the marine biological studies of Bajan waters are made here.

Just north of Holetown is the *St. James Parish Church*, parts of which date from 1660. The date of the tower and its spiral staircase is unknown, but the baptismal font is dated 1684, while the King William Bell is dated 1696.

Holetown is where Captain John Powell first landed on Barbados on May 14, 1625, and claimed the island for King James I who had perished while Powell and his settlers were in mid-voyage to Barbados. They named the town St. James Town, later changing the name to Holetown because only shallow draft ships could enter the river at this point reminding them of The Hole on the River Thames. In mid-February every year is the *Holetown Festival* celebrating the discovery of Barbados and Holetown's streets are filled with vendors, dancers, showmen, and revelers all weekend.

Provisions

Just south of Holetown is *Sunset Crest*, a sprawling complex of condos and shopping centers where the new *Super Centre* has established an online shopping service.

Dining

In town, a dozen bars and restaurants are concentrated on First and Second Streets making Holetown a popular spot for Bajan nightlife. *Angry Annie's* is quite unique and well worth a stop, while *The Sitar* offers Indian food and *Sakura* serves up fine Japanese fare. *Mins* and *Tams Wok* offer good Chinese cuisine while if you wish to be seen *Olive's* and *The Mews* is the place to be. Just a bit south of *Olive's* is *Indigo*, a late-night spot with truly fine cuisine.

A bit south at Holetown, sitting behind the *Police Station*, are the remains of *James Fort*, which once protected this coastline when the first settlers established Jamestown here in 1627. Little remains of the fort, which stood until well after the Napoleonic Wars, just part of a wall and one gun. Nearby you can dine at two beach restaurants, *Surfside*, also behind the *Police Station*, or *Cocomos*, about a hundred yards further south, and both serve up great food.

Payne's Bay

Navigational Information

Payne's Bay is named after Clement Payne, a Bajan national hero and a fiery orator whose speeches and deportation helped incite the riots of 1937. As shown on Chart BAR-4, Payne's Bay is one of the two places where you might be able to receive permission to anchor. A waypoint at 13° 09.80' N, 59° 39.00' W, will place you approximately ½ mile west of the anchorage area. From the waypoint, head eastward and make sure you anchor in the sand!

What You Will Find Ashore
Dining

Just a bit north of *Payne's Bay*, at a place known as The Garden, is *The Lone Star*, not to be confused with a Texas-style diner. *The Lone Star* rivals *The Cliff* for choice dining. Once a garage, *The Lone Star* offers an upstairs *Sushi* bar and lounge with dining downstairs just above the water. Both *The Cliff* and *The Lone Star* are not your casual, thrifty eateries; they are elegant and can be quite pricey if you desire Cuban cigars and expensive wines.

For fine dining right on a lovely terrace overlooking the beach at *Payne's Bay*, try *Fathoms* for a taste of some delicious Bajan fare. Just east of *Payne's Bay* is Derricks, near Holders Hill, where you can dine in one of the best Bajan restaurants on the western coast of Barbados, *The Cliff*. *The Cliff* is an elegant three-level coral building overlooking a small, secluded beach with the lowest level directly on the top of a cliff and surrounded by flaming torches for a special ambiance. Also in Derricks is *Nico's Champagne and Wine Bar* offering dining amid a tropical garden.

Nearby Prospect, a few miles south of *Payne's Bay*, offers some excellent dining opportunities for the hungry skipper and crew. *Carambola* will serve you at tables atop a cliff overlooking the sea, while *The Rose* specializes in Bajan seafood and is well known for their lobster.

Bridgetown and *Carlisle Bay*

Bridgetown is the capital of Barbados and *Carlisle Bay* the only anchorage available to cruisers. *Carlisle Bay* is a very nice anchorage, though it can be a bit noisy at times when three local nightclubs blast away with music until the dawn.

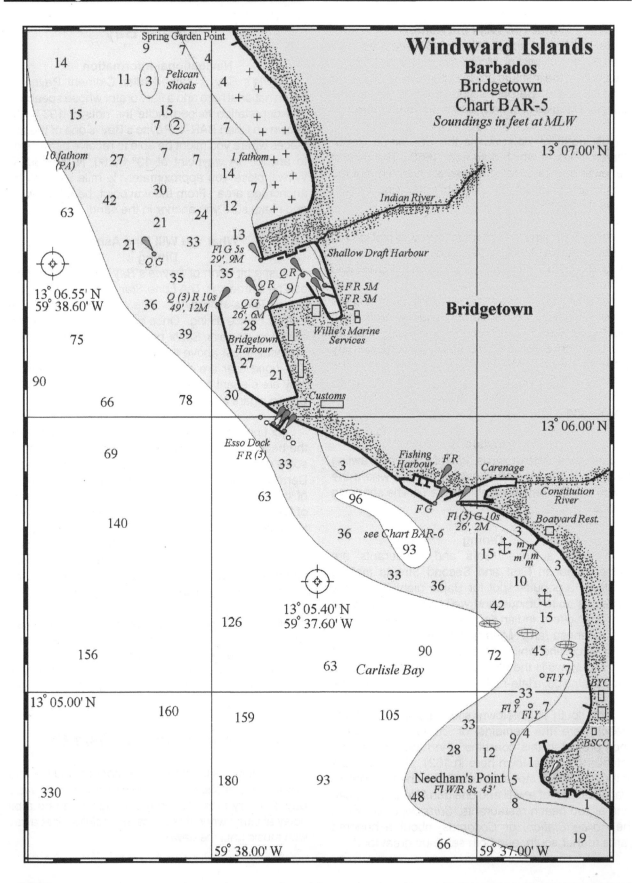

Windward Islands
Barbados
Bridgetown
Chart BAR-5
Soundings in feet at MLW

Spring Garden Point

9   7

14   4

11   ③   *Pelican*
Shoals   4

15   15
7   ②   7

10 fathom   27   7   7   *1 fathom*
(PA)

14
42   30   7

63   21   24   12

21   33   13

QG   *Fl G 5s*
29', 9M   *Shallow Draft Harbour*

35   35
QR   QR
9

Q (3) R 10s   QG   *FR 5M*
49', 12M   *26', 6M*   *FR 5M*

36   28   *Willie's Marine*
Services

39   *Bridgetown*   **Bridgetown**
Harbour

75   27

21

90   30

66   78   *Customs*

13° 06.55' N
59° 38.60' W

13° 07.00' N

Indian River

13° 06.00' N

69   *Esso Dock*
F R (3)

33   3   *Fishing*
Harbour   *F R*   *Carenage*

63   *Constitution*
River

96   F G   *Fl (3) G 10s*   *Boatyard Rest.*
26', 2M

140   36   *see Chart BAR-6*   3

93   15   m m
m 7 m
m

33   3

36   10

140   42   15

156   45   3

126   *13° 05.40' N*
59° 37.60' W

72

90   *Fl Y*   7
63   *Carlisle Bay*   BYC

13° 05.00' N   33
160   159   105   *Fl Y*   7

33   9   4
28   12   BSCC

180   93   1

Needham's Point   5
330   48   *Fl W/R 8s, 43'*   8
1

19

59° 38.00' W   66   *59° 37.00' W*

The city of Bridgetown was founded on July 5, 1628, when Charles Wolverstone and 64 settlers sent by the Earl of Carlisle landed here. The indigenous Amerindians built a bridge over the nearby *Constitution River* and the settlement was called *Indian Bridge*, which eventually evolved into *Indian Bridgetown*, *The Bridge*, and finally *Bridgetown*. The area now known as the Carenage was an important trading center for passing ships who could enter the mouth of the river to careen themselves and carry out bottom repairs. Today however the only ships you'll see are a few freighters and cruise ships, not to mention the numerous private yachts and charter boats.

Navigational Information

As shown on Chart BAR-5, a waypoint at 13° 05.40' N, 59° 37.60' W, will place you approximately one mile west of the anchorage area in *Carlisle Bay*. From the waypoint head generally eastward to anchor well inside Needham's Point just off the lovely beach, home to the *Barbados Yacht Club* and the *Barbados Sailing and Cruising Club*. Do not anchor off the *Yacht Club* with the local boats, you will be asked to move. The *BYC* offers free water if you jerry-jug it, a great Friday night beach party, and the *BYC* will hold mail for cruisers, as well as sending and receiving email.

Just a bit to the north of *Carlisle Bay* is the entrance to the *Carenage* and the *Constitution River* as shown on Chart BAR-6. Here you'll notice quite a few boats tied up along the seawall, you can check with the *Barbados Port Authority* for slip availability and rental here. There is a fishing harbor to the north of the *Carenage* that is not available to cruising yachts, however you can take on diesel here. As you enter the harbor and steer to port, you'll notice two T-docks on your starboard side (see Charts BAR-5 and BAR-6), these are the fuel docks, *Esso* and *Texaco*. Use caution, the harbor is small and the channel narrow. Beware of the shoal area at the southern end of *Carlisle Bay* that is marked by white buoys, with yellow lights.

Vessels wishing to clear in at Bridgetown must proceed to *Bridgetown Harbour*. As shown on Chart BAR-5, a waypoint at 13° 06.55' N, 59° 38.60' W, will place you approximately ½ mile west of the entrance to the harbor. From the waypoint, head generally eastward passing between the green-lighted buoy (QG) and the end of the jetty, which is also lit (red). Do not enter the harbor before contacting *Customs* (see next section, *Clearing Customs*).

There are several orange moorings available for rent in *Carlisle Bay*. Rental is BD$10 per night or BD$60 per week. For more information phone Peter Hoad at 246-820-1060. Do not anchor near the local vessels by the yacht club as you will be asked to move.

What You Will Find Ashore
Customs and *Immigration*

Upon arrival in Barbados, skippers are required to report to *Customs* and *Immigration* at either *Bridgetown Harbour* at the southwestern corner of the island, or at the new Port St. Charles complex located about ten miles north of Bridgetown. Bridgetown is a commercial port and clearance at Port St. Charles is much easier, and safer, for the cruising yachtsman (due to possible damage to your vessel from surge at the seawall). You are not permitted to anchor out and dinghy in; contact *Customs* via VHF ch. 16, *Signal Station Port Control* in Bridgetown, for directions to where to tie up; in *Bridgetown Harbour* you need to tie to the seawall (use plenty of fenders).

Once you have secured your vessel head over to the *Customs* and *Immigrations* offices in the building located at the southern side of the harbor for clearance (they are on duty until 2200 daily, if you arrive later you will need to wait until they open the next morning). Once you have been granted clearance you should move to *Carlisle Bay* to anchor. If you need them, there are plenty of telephones just outside the port building.

Internet Access

Bridgetown has several locations to access the Internet, and most of the larger hotels have *Wi-fi* for their guests. *Connect* is located in the center of Bridgetown, while the *Global Business Center* has two locations, on at the *West Coast Mall* one at the *Quayside Centre*. In Hastings you can get online at *A&R Computer Services* and at the *Osterly Inn* on *Maxwell Main Road*, you can access the net at *Netsurf Internet Café*.

Marine Facilities

Most of Bridgetown's marine services are centered in and around *Bridgetown Harbour*. If you need to haul out, *Willie's Marine Services* is located at the southern end of *Shallow Draft Harbour*, well inside *Bridgetown Harbour*. Owner Willie Hassell, an experienced cruiser himself, has a 45-ton *TravelLift* that can handle yachts with drafts to 7'. Just a short walk away is *Porthole Marine Supply* where you can meet owner Derek Johnson, a diesel mechanic who will be happy to help with any problems you may have. *Porthole Marine Supplies* carries basic marine needs, but for a more complete selection visit *Fisherman's Corner* or call them on VHF ch. 06. You can also find marine services outside the downtown Bridgetown area.

In Wildey, you'll find *McEnearney's*, a *Ford* dealer that also sells and services *Ford*, *Kubota*, *OMC* outboards, *Boston Whalers*, and *Apex* inflatables. If you need *Yamaha* parts or service, try *Star Products* on *Baxters Road* in Bridgetown, while *DI Manufacturing* in Guinea, St. John Parish, handles *Mercury*, *John Deere*, Yamaha, and *Mariner* products.

The very well known *Doyle Sails* is located in the parish of St. Philip at Six Cross Roads. Roger

Edgehill (*Edge Hill Sails*) in Hastings, just a couple of miles southeast of Needham's Point, can repair your sails and boat canvas, you can telephone Roger at 246-429-5800. *Undercover* also does sail and canvas work.

You can take on fuel in the fishing harbor north of the *Carenage* or fuel can be jerry-jugged from the *Esso* station next to the *Boatyard Restaurant* or from the *Shell* station across from the *Barbados Yacht Club*.

At the northern end of *Carlisle Bay* is the *Boatyard Restaurant* which is very cruiser-friendly (see Chart BAR-6). The owners are members of the *Barbados Yacht Club*. The restaurant has just finished a huge 300'+ dock where you can tie your dinghy up to explore Bridgetown (for a small fee) or pull your big boat alongside to fill up your water tanks though no

Bridgetown, Barbados

Chamberlain Bridge, Bridgetown

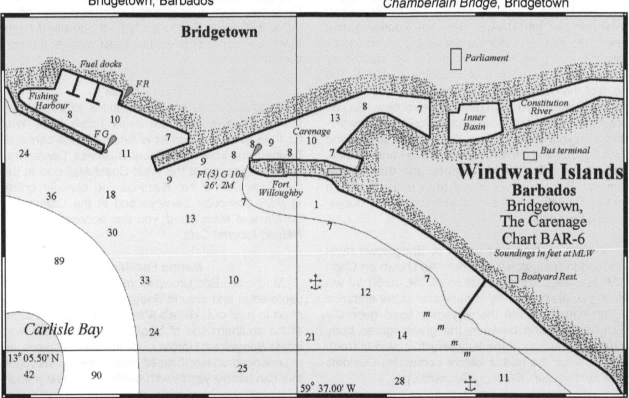

dockage is available. The restaurant allows visitors to use their showers and garbage bins for a fee of US$20 per day. Just a note, their dinghy dock is a real plus as there are no other dinghy docks in *Carlisle Bay*.

Cruisers are also welcome at the *Barbados Yacht Club* (see Chart BAR-5) where you can receive a week's pass to use their facilities. Please dress appropriately here. If you need fuel, you can carry your jerry-jugs to the *Shell* station across the street from the yacht club. The yacht club will hold mail for visiting cruisers. The yacht club has a weekly Friday night beach party and a daily happy hour from 1730-1830. You can dine at their beach restaurant or enjoy their buffet in the clubhouse during the week and on the beach on Sundays.

Just south of the large hotel is the more laid back *Barbados Sailing and Cruising Club*, usually just called the *Cruising Club*, where you can avail yourself of the showers when the club is open (they are closed on Tuesdays and Thursdays, but the bar IS open on those days).

Getting Around
Taxis or buses are the best way to get around unless you'd rather rent an automobile. Barbados has a very reliable bus system that reaches almost every part of the island, some are government operated, and some are privately owned. Fares are BDS$1.50 and buses run along the main coastal highways for cruisers needing transportation. In Bridgetown, there are two bus stations, one off *Fairchild St.*, and a smaller station across from the fishing harbor next to the *Post Office*. If you are headed north, catch your bus at the *Post Office* station, if you're headed anywhere else on the island, you can catch your bus at the *Fairchild St.* station.

Provisions
If you need to provision and do not wish to venture very far, you can take your dinghy into the Carenage and visit *Julien's Supermarket* for all your needs. *Julien's* is on the north side of the Carenage just past the old swing bridge (the *Chamberlain Bridge*). There is a nice fish market behind the fishing harbor and across from the bus terminal. Downtown Bridgetown has several excellent markets, pharmacies, and gift shops.

South of the *Constitution River* and east of the *Pierhead* peninsula is *Fairchild St.*, home of one of

Bridgetown's two bus stations and the large *Fairchild Market*, one of two large public markets in Bridgetown. The street by the market borders a rough part of town, one of Bridgetown's red-light districts, called *Raccoon Quarters*.

Across *Broad Street* from the fishing harbor is the *Cheapside Market*, the second of Bridgetown's two open markets.

Dining
I have already mentioned the *Boatyard Restaurant* and the *Barbados Yacht Club* in the previous *Marine Facilities* section as favorite eateries of mine, but there is much more to Bridgetown dining.

For a good dining experience with a view, try the *Waterfront Café* right on the waterfront with a fine view of the Carenage. Tuesday you can feast on a Caribbean buffet while listening to a steel band.

Another good stop is the *Rusty Pelican* on an upper floor near the bridge. Both are located on the southern side of the Carenage on a small peninsula of land that is also home to *Ft. Willoughby* and a new development called *Pierhead*. *Ft. Willoughby* was built by one William Withington who was paid 80,000 pounds of sugar for his labor. Although today it is part of the mainland, this entire peninsula was once an island called Little Island.

On *McGregor Street*, just off *Broad Street*, sits *Mustor's Harbour Bar and Restaurant*. If you wish to dine on traditional Bajan dishes such as flying fish (a Bajan specialty), you cannot go wrong here. If you favor BBQ make your way to *Baxter Road* where every night you can find vendors grilling seafood.

For those with more refined tastes head to St. Lawrence Gap (sound end of Barbados) where you can dine at *Pisces* (superb seafood), *Bellini's* (great Italian fare), and *Café del Sol* (Mexican cuisine).

Historic Bridgetown
Across the river to the north are the Parliament buildings and *Trafalgar Square*, now known as *National Heroes Square*. In the center of the square is a stature of Lord Nelson that has caused a lot of controversy in Barbados. Many consider Nelson a British hero, not a Bajan hero, and wish him moved while others say that the statue that has resided there since 1813 is part of their Bajan heritage and

should remain. It has been suggested that Lord Nelson's statue be moved to the *Naval Heritage* site at *Ft. Willoughby*, I don't know where this argument will end, but it will be interesting to see how this is resolved. East of the square is the *Dolphin Fountain*, built in 1865 to commemorate the introduction of running water to Bridgetown in 1861. The nearby *War Memorial* was built in 1925 to honor those Barbadians who gave their lives in World War I.

In Bridgetown, you'll find the *Bush House*, the home where George Washington stayed in 1751. Young Washington, then 19, came to Barbados with his brother-in-law, Lawrence, a tuberculosis patient who thought that the climate in Barbados might be beneficial for his affliction. Barbados was chosen because Lawrence's father-in-law had married a prominent Bajan and because Lawrence had a wife and young children; Washington was chosen to accompany Lawrence for the duration of his stay. Within a few weeks of his arrival, the future President of the United States contracted smallpox, a small stroke of luck it would seem. Years later, when many of his Revolutionary War troops would contract the same disease, Washington was immune and was able to continue his campaign.

It was established in the 1980s that the *Bush House* was actually the house that Lawrence and Washington stayed. For many years, a house on Bay Street was mistakenly introduced as the *Washington House*. Today, the *Bush House* at The Garrison, the 17th century military compound outside Bridgetown, has been completely restored as the original home of Washington and his ailing brother-in-law thanks to the efforts of the *Barbados National Trust*.

There is a large Jewish community in Barbados and Bridgetown is home to one of the oldest synagogues in the Western Hemisphere. Built in 1654, the synagogue was destroyed by a hurricane in 1831, it was rebuilt, eventually fell into disrepair, and was sold in 1929. In 1983, the synagogue was purchased by the Bajan Jewish community who restored it to its present state. Today it is again an active synagogue, a *Barbados National Trust* protected building, and a winner of the *American Express Preservation Award.* The first Jewish settlers arrived on Barbados in 1654, from Recife, Brazil, where the Dutch persecuted them. They were skilled in the sugar industry and quickly introduced the crop to the island and passed on their skills in cultivation and production to the Bajan

plantation owners who soon came to see sugar cane as their new cash crop.

A bit inland in the heart of Bridgetown is the *Garrison Savannah*, one of the finest parade grounds in the Caribbean. At the northeastern corner, you'll find the *Barbados Museum* situated in a 19th century garrison, home to a fine collection of Bajan history. Dating back to the early 1800s, the museum was once a military prison. And what guide to Barbados would be complete without a mention of rum, particularly *Mount Gay Rum*? Just outside of Bridgetown, off the *Spring Garden Highway* north of Bridgetown, is the *Mount Gay Rum Visitors Centre*, where visitor can learn the ins and outs of making rum the Bajan way. *Mount Gay Rum* is said to be the oldest rum on the island, and possibly in the world, with evidence of rum manufacturing dating back to 1703 on the *Mount Gay Estate* in St. Lucy Parish. Samples are provided for visitors, now what cruiser can resist that offer? The word *rum* is said to have been born in the taverns of old Bridgetown. Here sailors and locals alike would drink to their heart's delight and the evening would often end in a *rumbullion*, and old English word for a brawl.

Touring Inland Barbados

The beauty that is Barbados is best viewed inland, or along the windward or southern coasts where cruising boats never go. As you have seen, the western coast of Barbados is quite modern and offers nearly everything the cruiser/tourist needs. The southern coast is similar, but with no anchoring possibilities, while the northern and eastern coasts tend to be more rural, more Bajan in feel. Let's begin our discussion with the southern coast and work our way around Barbados counterclockwise, finishing up in the interior.

From Bridgetown, through Oistins, and eastward to Garrison, the southern coast is the most developed shoreline on the island. Here you'll find towns like Hastings, Dover, or Worthing, named after the English towns that were home to the first Bajan settlers. The whole coast is full of hotels, malls, apartment complexes, restaurants, and bars where you'll find places like *Fat Andy's* (in Hastings), a 50s Art-Deco diner, or *Bubba's Sports Bar* (in Rockley) boasting a dozen televisions and three 10' big screen TVs to catch any sporting event in the world. A meeting of old and new? No, not really, more new than old. The southern coast is THE place for nightlife on Barbados, and if you're looking for peace and quiet, you probably won't find it here (except perhaps at Sandy Beach... read on).

Heading East from Bridgetown on *Hwy. 7*, the main road along the southern shore, you'll soon come to Hastings where you'll spy some old red buildings lining the road. These were once army barracks for nearby *St. Ann's Fort*. Construction on *St. Ann's Fort* was begun in 1704, never completed, and little remains today save a few ramparts. Today the *Barbados Defence Force* uses the grounds as a base, and the red buildings you saw as you entered Hastings are now pricey private apartments. *The Kirby Gallery* sits across the street from the *Savannah Hotel* and is the largest commercial art gallery on Barbados. Car nuts will want to visit the *Mallalieu Motor Collection* in Pavilion Court, to view their collection of vintage cars. East of town is the club field of *The Wanderers*, Barbados' oldest cricket team who came together in 1877.

The shoreline from Hastings to Oistins has some of the most beautiful beaches on the entire island of Barbados, but you will only be able to access them by bus, taxi, or car rental, not by anchoring off. In Worthing is *Sandy Beach*, an almost perfect little cove, great for a bit of peace and quiet. The *Carib Beach Bar* is nearby to serve you food or drink whenever you desire. In Rockly you can visit the studio of famed sculptor, Bill Grace, at his studio. For more info call 435-6398. Bill works primarily in glass, ceramics, and stone, and focuses his work on the reef structures of the sea.

An oasis of calm amid the clamor of the southern coast is the *Graeme Hall Swamp* and the *Graeme Hall Bird Sanctuary* at St. Lawrence Gap. Once visited only by hunters and fishermen, the area is now a sanctuary for the over 150 species of migratory birds that pass back and forth between North and South America including some extremely rare birds such as the Eskimo curlew or the purple heron. Two walk-through aviaries offer a close-up look at many varieties of Caribbean and South American birds. Just east of St. Lawrence Gap is *Dover Beach*, home to the *Malibu de Conga-Line Carnival*. The 6-day event features arts and crafts, good local food, music, rum, and is capped off by a *May Day* parade from Independence Square in Bridgetown all the way down *Hwy. 7* to the roundabout at Dover. This is not your normal parade mind you, it is thousands of revelers forming what may be the world's longest Congaline with trucks blasting out tunes for the participant's happy feet.

The next stop is Oistins, whose name came from an early settler named Austin because it sounded like Oistin in the unique Bajan accent. In 1652, Oliver Cromwell's navy was anchored in the bay and the Charter of Barbados was drawn up in Oistins and signed in a tavern called *Ye Mermaid's Inn*. Oistins is known as the fishing capitol of Barbados because for generations Bajans came from all over the island to purchase fresh fish here from women standing on the roadside yelling "Fish! Fish!" This changed in the mid-1970s when several shopping malls sprang up and the government built a huge fisheries terminal. Now vendors approach you even as you park your car to coax you to their stalls. If you need fish, the best time to visit is around 1600 when the day's catch is being brought and the fish filleted. If you just want to eat some fresh fish, try the Friday night *Oistins Fish Fry*, or the larger *Oistins Fish Festival* in April. Silver Sands Beach, south of Oistins, is a favorite for windsurfers. East of Oistins is the Chancery Lane where Amerindian artifacts have been dated to 600 AD. At nearby *Long Beach* are two huge rusty cannons and the wreck of a DC3 airplane.

Now let me tell you about the Dancing Coffins of Barbados. Overlooking Oistins is the *Christ Church Parish Church* and the parish graveyard with its well-known *Chase Vault*. It all started on August 9, 1812, when Col. Thomas Chase was laid to rest in the vault. Two coffins already inside the vault were noticed to be in unusual positions, while the smaller coffin of the infant Mary Ann Chase, had been moved from one corner to another. The coffins were rearranged and later, in 1816, and again in 1817, the coffins had been found in different locations than those in which the workmen had left them. On July 7. 1819, the Governor of Barbados, Viscount Combermere had masons cement the door closed and the Governor then used his seal to mark the fresh cement around the door. Nine months later the Governor checked that the seal was intact and had a workman break the seal and enter the vault. Inside the workman found that one large coffin was upright against the middle of the stone door and Mary Ann Chase's coffin had been relocated to the far end of the chamber with such force that it had damaged the wall of the vault. The Chase family moved the coffins and today the vault remains empty.

The southeastern tip of Barbados is comprised mostly of St. Philip's Parish, the largest of Barbados' 11 parishes. The area is far different from the hectic southern coast, it will seem isolated compared to the area around *Hwy. 7*. Today St. Philip is changing, in the last decade alone it has become one of the fastest growing parishes due to the low-cost land available. St. Philip is becoming THE place for Bajans to build their dream home, far from the hustle and bustle of Bridgetown or Oistins. *Hwy. 6* is the main thoroughfare through St. Philip, and any road leading away from *Hwy. 6* at *Six Cross Roads*, will take you someplace interesting.

In the heart of St. Philip parish is the huge *Woodbourne Oil Field*, discovered in 1966 and nationalized by the government in 1982. Just past the oilfield you'll come to the *Rum Factory and Heritage Park*, a good stop if you are interested in rum production (and what cruiser isn't?). Set on 7 acres of a 300 year old sugar cane plantation, the park boasts the most modern rum distillery in the world and the first environmentally friendly distillery in the Caribbean. Here you can watch workers produce *Field White Rum*, *Doorly's*, and *Old Brigand Rum*, bottled by hand, the way it has been done for over a century, and the newer high-tech way, by machines bottling over 25 bottles a minute. The old cane pit where the harvested cane was stored is now an amphitheater where concerts and shows are regularly staged.

Further east, atop a craggy cliff, is the *Crane Beach Hotel*, a must-stop for the view itself. You've probably seen the hotel before in fashion magazines, its oceanfront pool has been used as a backdrop for countless photo shoots and the small entrance fee is redeemable at the bar. The hotel received its name from the old crane that stood at the end of the bay in the 1700s when sailboats plied the waters between *Cobbler's Reef* and Bridgetown every day carrying sugar and other goods. A railroad was built in 1881 which led to the demise of the port and the crane. A mile or so further on is *Sam Lord's Castle*, named after the notorious Sam Lord, a Bajan wrecker whose profits paid for the construction of this grand mansion. At the far eastern end of Barbados is Ragged Point, with its spectacular scenery that is not to be missed.

The northeastern and northern coasts of Barbados, from Ragged Point northwestward towards North Point at the extreme northern tip of the island, and then around towards Speightstown, is far removed from the southern and western coasts. The northeastern shoreline is simply mile after mile of small towns, scenic windward views, roaring waves, and steady trade winds blowing across from Africa. If you take *Hwy. 3* and *3B* you'll come out at *Hackleton's Cliff*, 100' above sea level where you can get a panoramic view stretching from Ragged Point in the south to Paul's Point in the north.

A few miles northwest of Ragged Point, you'll come to a long palm tree-lined drive leading to Codrington College standing atop a 360' cliff above *Conset Bay*. Christopher Codrington, a former Governor of the Leeward Islands in Antigua, founded this theological college in 1710. The college really didn't get underway until 1748 because it was hard to find professors and teachers who would be willing to work at the college under Codrington College's monk-like vows of poverty, chastity, and obedience. If you take a stroll out the front gate and down the twisting path to the beach at Conset Bay you might catch a glimpse of a group of green monkeys that live in the overhanging trees. Heading north from Codrington College, you can take a left (marked by a sign) that takes you up a steep hill to *St. John's Church*. The church, first built in 1660, was destroyed by fire and rebuilt only to be destroyed by a hurricane. The present church was built in 1836 and boasts a beautiful pulpit constructed of six different types of wood, and is all that is left from the original church of 1660. A bit more to the north is Clifton Hall, named after a man who committed suicide by riding his horse off a cliff into the sea.

Martin's Bay is a quaint fishing village known for its lobster catches. The rock pools on the beach are a good spot to take a dip. This entire area is known as Glen Burnie and it is almost unspoiled by the modern civilization that has taken over the southern coast of Barbados. This whole area, from Ragged Point northward to North Point was designated a nature conservation area in 1985. Two miles north of Glen Burnie is the *Andromeda Botanical Gardens*, situated on a cliff and littered with fossil-encrusted boulders. Overlooking nearby Tent Bay is the *Atlantis Hotel* sitting at the end of what has been described as the world's steepest driveway. One of the oldest hotels on the island, this simple, pleasant rest stop has some of the best views of any hotel room on Barbados.

Further north still is the large town of Bathsheba, a fishing village where a number of wealthy Bajans own homes. The town is noted for its *Soup Bowl*, a spot in the bay off the town where the surf is foamy with waves large making Bathsheba a favorite for the hordes of Bajan surfers that flock here for the annual *Soup Bowl* surfing championships.

Just inland from *Morgan Lewis Beach* is the only intact Barbadian windmill left on the island, the *Morgan Lewis Windmill*. Originally built in 1727 by Dutch Jews who came to Barbados from Brazil, the windmill ground sugar cane for over two centuries until 1945, and is one of two intact and restored windmills in the Caribbean, the other one being on the island of Antigua. The windmill was rebuilt in 1997 and is now in perfect working order. The old plantation house is well worth a visit; its walls are comprised of boulders held together by a mixture of egg-white and coral dust as there was no cement at this time. The nearby *Grenade Hall Forest and Signal Station* was restored in 1992, it was once part of the colonial signaling system in the early 1800s and had visual contact with *Dover Fort* to the west, and *Cotton Tower* in the southeast.

A short distance away is the *Barbados Wildlife Reserve* and the *Barbados Primate Research Centre;* both are set in a gorgeous, lush, tropical woodland. Here you can view indigenous green monkeys in their natural habitat. A bit inland is the *Farley Hill National Park*, the home of the *Paint It Jazz Festival* that is held every January on Barbados. A bit northeast sits St. Nicholas Abbey, in the parish of St. Peter. Built in 1660, the abbey is one of only three genuine Jacobean mansions in the Western Hemisphere, two of which are located on Barbados (see the section on Drax Hall). Visitors here can view an extremely rare film made in 1930 that shows life on a sugar plantation. The abbey was built by Col. Benjamin Berringer and is not without its share of tragedy. Berringer's neighbor, Sir John Yeamans was far too interested in Mrs. Berringer and a dispute evolved between Col. Berringer and Sir John which culminated in a duel in which Col. Berringer was killed. Sir John soon married the widow Berringer and claimed the abbey as his. A later court ruling returned the property to Col. Berringer's children and the abbey was named after the husband of Col. Berringer's granddaughter, George Nicholas. Sir John and the former Mrs. Berringer left Barbados in 1669 and helped to start a colony in what is now South Carolina with Sir John eventually becoming Governor in 1672. Sir John died in 1674 and the former Mrs. Berringer remarried.

On the northeastern coast, *Pico Teneriffe* is an unusual pillar-shaped white cliff approximately 260' above sea level. Just north at Paul's Point you'll find another remote, scenic promontory with another spectacular view of the wild Atlantic, it seems that Barbados has no shortage of these views.

At the extreme northern tip of Barbados, near North Point, you can visit the *Animal Flower Cave,* named after the tiny sea anemones that lived in the small rock pools in the cave. The sea anemones looked like small flowers when they stretched their tentacles, hence their name, however few survive today. The area around the cave was once called the *Animal Flower Plantation* where sugar cane was grown. At *Maycock's Bay* you can view the ruins of *Maycock's Fort* and search for the treasure reported to be buried there.

Okay, so we've covered the coasts, now let's see what you'll find inland, in the highlands that make up the northern interior and the lowlands that are the central and southern Bajan interior. We'll start in the north and work our way south.

The northern highlands are rugged in places, with steep, winding, uneven roads. From Eagle Hall just outside Bridgetown, you can take *Hwy. 2* and wind your way northeastward toward Belleplaine. Heading out from Eagle Hall you'll come to the Warrens Roundabout where you can view the second-oldest baobab tree on the island, over 250 years old, sitting in what is left of a plantation that dates back to 1686. A mile or so further on is the *Sharon Moravian Church*, built in 1799 by Moravians who had settled on Barbados in 1765. The Moravians were the first missionaries to bring Christianity to the Bajan slaves and the first to admit slaves to their congregation.

A few more miles further on is the *Edgehill Great House*, home of the *Future Centre Trust*, a non-profit, non-governmental entity whose focus is to safeguard the Bajan environment for future generations. Manned by volunteers and financed by donations, the *Centre* opened in 1998 and houses this hemisphere's largest organic garden, and a kid's interactive learning center. Future plans include a simulated undersea walk as well as some small business projects. Nearby is *Earthworks Pottery* and the *Potter's House*, a pottery gallery featuring Bajan craftsmen.

Further north is the *Welshman Hall Gully* (sometimes shown as *Welchman Hall Gully*), a tropical preserve where lush foliage abounds in a ¾ mile long ravine. The area is named for its original owner, a Welshman named Asygell Williams who was banished to Barbados when the Royalists lost in the English Civil War. There is an old Bajan legend that tells us that the grapefruit was born in Barbados in *Welshman Hall Gully* in the 1700s. The fruit is said to have been a hybrid between *Shaddock* and *Sweet Orange* and was known as the *Forbidden Fruit*. The name was later changed to grapefruit because the fruit grew in large, grape-like clusters.

Almost next door is the breathtaking splendor of *Harrison's Cave*, said to be the only one of its kind in the Caribbean. A small, electrically powered tram takes you for a mile long ride though this subterranean wonderland, a must-see in anybody's book. Once a hideout for runaway slaves, the caverns have been known for over 200 years, but it wasn't until 1970 that a Danish speleologist, Ole Sorenson, who was commissioned by the Barbados National Trust to map the cave, discovered one of the most fascinating parts of the entire cave system, the *Crystal Cavern*. The caverns house several passages and large rooms, countless stalagmites and stalactites, and even an underground waterfall into a blue-green lake deep below the surface.

At the end of *Hwy. 2* is Belleplaine which also served as the end of the old Bajan railway when until the 1930s, Bajans celebrated life on train excursions from Bridgetown to Belleplaine, complete with traveling bands, and stops along the way where other musicians would entertain the travelers. Nearby is the highest point on the island, *Mt. Hillaby* at 1115', where the surrounding hillsides sweep down to the eastern coast far below. *Highland Outdoors Tours* (438-8069) is located nearby and offers walking, horse, and jitney tours.

The southern part of the interior of Barbados is sugar cane country and is sometimes just known as the *St. George Valley*. Although some plantations are still active, the boom years ended in 1967 and today's crops are less than a quarter of the annual production in the decade before the decline of the sugar industry. Oddly enough, almost all of the Barbados crop is exported to Europe, while Bajan sugar needs are met by a cheaper South American product.

Hwy. 4 is the route we'll follow out of Bridgetown as we head into the *St. George Valley* and see what we can find. Once past the *Charles Rowe Bridge*, the road becomes steeper rising up towards Gun Hill where you will find the *Gun Hill Signaling Station* overlooking the *St. George Valley*. Guarding the entrance is a 7' tall, sculpted lion that dates to 1868. The station itself is one of a chain of such stations, two of which still exist, that were to warn of the approach of passing ships. On the drive along *Hwy. 4* you'll find one sugar plantation after another, several guest houses, and a few restaurants if you're hungry. One plantation, the 878-acre *Drax Hall Estate*, is still owned by the same family that owned it in the 1600s and was the first to cultivate sugarcane on Barbados. The estate is said to have been built by the Drax brothers, William and James, in the 1650s was one of the earliest and largest sugar producers on Barbados. The estate is classic Jacobean architecture with steep gabled roofs, corner finials, casement gable windows, and a Jacobean staircase with a carved archway.

I've tried to cover most of what you may find on Barbados to pique your interest, but just remember that anywhere you go on Barbados, you'll find something of interest. If you plan to rent a car, do so for several days, take your time exploring this most British of Caribbean islands.

St. Vincent and The Grenadines

Port of Entry - St. Vincent: *Blue Lagoon*, Chateaubelair, Wallilabou, Kingstown, *Young Island Cut*

Port of Entry - The Grenadines: Port Elizabeth (Bequia), Clifton (Union Island), *Grand Bay* (Mustique), Charlestown (Canouan)

Fuel: *Ottley Hall Marina, Lagoon Marina*

Haul-Out: *Ottley Hall Marina*

Diesel Repairs: St. Vincent, Bequia, Mayreau, Union Island

Outboard Repairs: St. Vincent, Bequia, Mayreau, Union Island

Propane: St. Vincent, Bequia

Provisions: St. Vincent, Bequia, Clifton (Union Island), *Grand Bay* (Mustique), Charlestown (Canouan)

Fuel: *Ottley Hall Marina*

Important Lights: See *Appendix A*

Without a doubt, St. Vincent, Vincy, is one of the lushest and most beautiful islands in the Eastern Caribbean. And when I say "lushest" I mean that the interior of St. Vincent gets 150 inches of rainfall a year making the area rich in flora. From Kingstown northward, a series of irregular mountain ranges extend up into the center of St. Vincent from *Mt. St. Andrew* to Richmond Peak just south of the *Soufrière Mountains* in the north. The southern mountain range is dominated by two peaks, *Grand Bonhomme* and *Petite Bonhomme*, which, at over 3,000' form the heads of two valleys, the *Buccament Valley* on the western side of the island, and the *Marriaqua Valley*, or *Mesopotamia Valley* to the east.

La Soufrière, the 3,000' volcano that dominates the *Soufrière Mountains* is one of the most active volcanoes in the eastern Caribbean. Eruptions were recorded in 1718, 1812, 1902, 1971, and 1979, but archeological evidence suggests that it may have erupted as early as the second century AD. Today the volcano is safe to climb with trails leading to the summit from both the eastern and western sides of St. Vincent. The eastern trail starts about one mile north of Georgetown while the western trail begins at Chateaubelair and is the more demanding and scenic of the two trails. This 18½ mile long by 11¼ mile wide island is home to over 113,000 people.

A Brief History of St. Vincent

The first settlers in St. Vincent and The Grenadines were a group of hunter-gatherers called the *Ciboneys*, (sometimes spelled *Siboneys*) who arrived here from South American approximately 7,000 years ago, around 5000 BC, before the time of the Pharaohs. Later settlers on these islands assimilated the Ciboneys, who used rough hand-made tools but did not make pottery, and the Arawaks, who settled in the islands about 200 BC and were also of South American origin. Peace reigned in the eastern Caribbean for many years until the arrival of the Caribs who killed their male enemies and enslaved their victim's women. The Caribs, who were cannibals, castrated and fattened the young male captives for their later pleasures. The Caribs were prevalent in the Eastern Caribbean inhabiting almost all the islands at one time or another and to them St. Vincent was known as *Hairoun*, or *Youroumei*, meaning *land of the blessed.*

The Admiral of All Oceans, Christopher Columbus, discovered the island on Jan. 22, 1498, and named it *St. Vincent* after the Spanish saint whose feast day it was. Although a few missionaries did live among the Caribs on St. Vincent after the turn of the 16th century, it was not until almost two centuries after Columbus that the Europeans were able to establish any kind of permanent settlement on St. Vincent. Early attempts at landing on St. Vincent were met with fierce resistance from the indigenous Caribs who fiercely resisted the imposition of the European community upon them.

Sir Walter Raleigh anchored off St. Vincent in 1595 and reported that "savages and cannibals" inhabited the island. The first European settlers were two French missionaries that are thought to have established a camp near Chateaubelair. One, Father Aubergeon, was actually invited to the island by the Caribs in 1653 for his role in the release of captured Caribs who had been abducted for questioning. The two priests took an informal census and estimated that there were over 10,000 Caribs on the island. Soon thereafter, a lack of communication led to a slaughter of the missionaries and the burning of their mission. When word of this reached Martinique, a trio of ships full of troops sailed to St. Vincent and many Caribs were slaughtered and their crops burned.

The Caribs lived in the mountainous interior of the island of St. Vincent, well protected by the topography. Many Caribs who were defeated on other islands fled

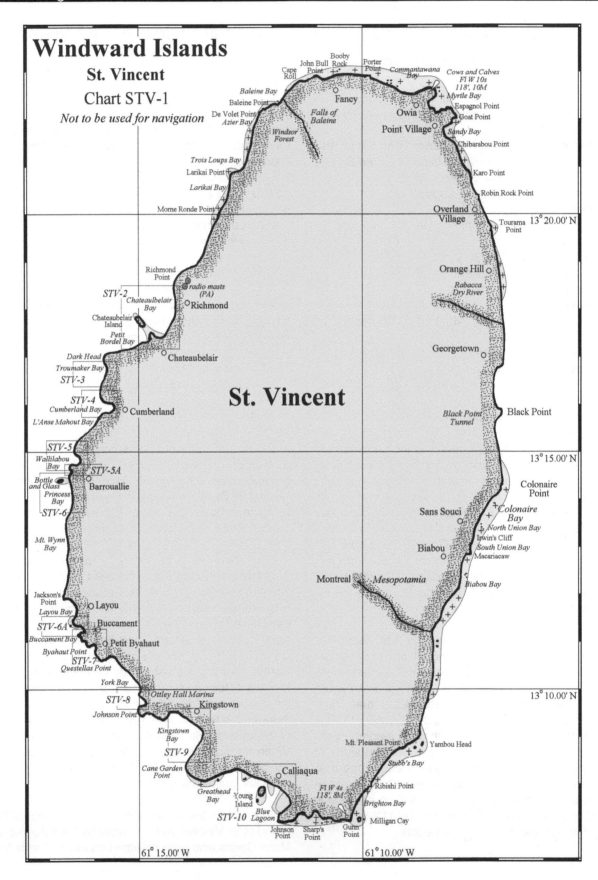

Windward Islands

St. Vincent

Chart STV-1

Not to be used for navigation

Cape Roll
John Bull Point
Booby Rock
Porter Point
Commantawana Bay
Cows and Calves
*Fl W 10s
118', 10M*
Baleine Bay
Baleine Point
Fancy
Myrtle Bay
Espagnol Point
De Volet Point
Goat Point
Azier Bay
Owia
Windsor Forest
Falls of Baleine
Point Village
Sandy Bay
Chibarabou Point
Trois Loups Bay
Larikai Point
Larikai Bay
Karo Point
Robin Rock Point
Morne Ronde Point
Overland Village
Tourama Point
13° 20.00' N

Richmond Point
Orange Hill
Rabacca Dry River
STV-2
radio masts (PA)
Chateaulbelair Bay
Richmond
Chateaubelair Island
Petit Bordel Bay
Georgetown
Dark Head
Troumaker Bay
Chateaubelair
STV-3
St. Vincent
STV-4
Cumberland Bay
Cumberland
Black Point Tunnel
Black Point
L'Anse Mahout Bay
STV-5
13° 15.00' N
Wallilabou Bay
STV-5A
Bottle and Glass
Princess Bay
Barrouallie
Colonaire Point
STV-6
Sans Souci
Colonaire Bay
North Union Bay
Mt. Wynn Bay
Irwin's Cliff
South Union Bay
Biabou
Macariacaw
Montreal
Mesopotamia
Jackson's Point
Biabou Bay
Layou
Layou Bay
Buccament
STV-6A
Buccament Bay
Petit Byahaut
Byahaut Point
STV-7
Questellas Point
York Bay
13° 10.00' N
STV-8
Ottley Hall Marina
Kingstown
Johnson Point
Kingstown Bay
Mt. Pleasant Point
Yambou Head
STV-9
Stubb's Bay
Cane Garden Point
Calliaqua
Ribishi Point
Greathead Bay
Young Island
Brighton Bay
STV-10
Blue Lagoon
Fl W 4s 118', 8M
Johnson Point
Sharp's Point
Gunn Point
Milligan Cay
61° 15.00' W
61° 10.00' W

to St. Vincent for the protection offered and the Carib population increased rapidly, swelled even further by escaped slaves from Barbados and St. Lucia as well as shipwreck survivors. In 1675 a Dutch ship carrying settlers and slaves wrecked in the waters between St. Vincent and Bequia. The slaves were the only survivors and were accepted by the Caribs. They eventually intermarried and were later joined by escaped slaves from St. Lucia and Grenada. They became known as the Black Caribs (sometimes called the *Garifuna*), as opposed to the Yellow Caribs, those of pure Carib descent, and St. Vincent was divided between the two groups with the western side of St. Vincent being allocated to the Yellow Caribs and the eastern side to the Black Caribs.

Even with this sharing of the island, their differences eventually led to a civil war among the Yellow and Black Caribs in 1700. Fearing domination at the hands of the Black Caribs, the Yellow Caribs sought help from the French and allowed French settlers to build a small community on the island in 1719 where the settlers sought to live in harmony with both tribes of Caribs. In reality, the French considered St. Vincent theirs and wished to remove the British from the island and they foresaw a way of acquiring new slaves through the conflict. The British, had earlier moved into St. Vincent in 1627 by way of a series of royal grants and treaties when Charles I granted St. Vincent's rule to the Earl of Carlisle. However, the first real attempt at British colonization came nearly a century later, in 1722, when King George I gave St. Lucia and St. Vincent to the Duke of Montagu and a Captain Braitwaite was sent to St. Vincent to start a settlement at which point the series of private land treaties between the French and the Caribs were declared null and void.

Both the British and the French sought to use the tension between the Yellow and Black Caribs for their own causes by enlisting their help in battle. Seeing that the Black Caribs were the more successful soldiers, winning several battles with British settlers in the early 1700s, the French farmers provisioned the Black Carib leaders with wine, cognac, and weapons, which in turn encouraged more trade with the French and caused the Black Caribs to take up the French language, some of their customs, and even some of their names.

In 1748, the *Treaty of Aix-la-Chapelle* officially made St. Vincent a neutral territory. A few years later,

in 1762, the *Treaty of Paris* allocated certain territories to the British, and in 1763, after the first Carib War, the British took control over the island and settlement began in earnest. In 1773, George II drafted a peace treaty with the Caribs and the two dozen Carib chiefs who signed the treaty could not read English so it was not until later that the true meaning of the treaty manifested itself as the Caribs were unknowingly restricted to smaller and smaller areas of the island.

Hostilities renewed and in 1779, the Black Caribs requested assistance from the French in Martinique. So it was that a French ship sailed to St. Vincent with 500 troops and the French took over St. Vincent with little resistance. The British soldiers were all at the northern end of the island working on the Governor's plantation, and no one could find the key to the battery. The French won in a matter of a few minutes and were able to keep the Black Caribs from massacring the British settlers, troops, and the Governor.

The *Treaty of Versailles* gave the island to the British in 1783, and the island was restored to British control. In 1795, the Black Caribs, with the aid of the French, went on the offensive in what is called the Second Carib War, sometimes called the *Brigands War*. A French radical, Victor Hughes, after a successful uprising in Guadeloupe, incited two Black Carib chiefs, Chatoyer and Duvalier (sometimes spelled Duvallé), to attack the British and drive them from the island. Duvalier's forces burned British plantations along the eastern coast, often putting the owners themselves through the gears of their own sugar mills, while other Black Caribs under their great chief Chatoyer, killed many people without destroying property and forced British forces southward along the western coast to Kingstown. In short order, the two chiefs met in the hills above Kingstown when Duvalier took Dorsetshire Hill, removed the British flag, and replaced it with the French Flag. British troops stormed Dorsetshire Hill and in a battle that lasted ten days, Chatoyer was killed in a swordfight with a British officer, Major Leith. Today Major Leith's remains lie buried under the chandelier in the Anglican Cathedral in Kingstown, and on Dorsetshire Hill there is an obelisk memorializing the great chief Chatoyer.

The Black Caribs, although deprived of their great leader, continued to fight for a year after Chatoyer's death. General Abercrombie had already taken St. Lucia where the Black Caribs, without the assistance of the French, were quickly overcome and surrendered. Abercrombie then moved his troops to St. Vincent where the British soldiers destroyed the Black Carib villages and crops, and a year later, delivered an ultimatum to the Black Carib chiefs that the Black Caribs would be shipped to the Bay Islands off Honduras. Only 280 Caribs surrendered for the shipping, arriving at Balliceaux enroute to Honduras. The British then hunted down over 5,000 Black Caribs who were deported to Roatán, off the coast of Honduras. Meanwhile, the Yellow Caribs, who had not taken part in the hostilities, moved to the northern part of St. Vincent, near Sandy Bay, where they were given some land and where their descendants still live today. A few of the hardiest of the Black Caribs escaped into the wooded areas of Greiggs and were, years later, granted a reservation near Petit Bonhomme. A few Caribs attempted to remain at Morne Ronde but fled just before the 1812 eruption and a few went as far as Trinidad.

Because of the two centuries of Carib hostilities, St. Vincent never really shared in the sugar boom that so many islands in the Eastern Caribbean enjoyed even though slaves continued to enter into the islands to work the plantations until 1834 when the slave trade was abolished. The year 1838 saw an influx of Portuguese settlers who soon were running shops and other small trading ventures and in 1861, indentured servants from India took the place of the slaves and many of Portuguese, Lebanese, and Syrians established successful businesses in the islands while many Scottish mariners and shipwrights emigrated to the islands of The Grenadines.

In 1871, St. Vincent became part of the British colony of the Windward Islands. In 1969, St. Vincent became a *British Associated State*, and a decade later, on October 27, 1979, St. Vincent and The Grenadines became an independent state within the British Commonwealth.

Today, St. Vincent is constructing a new international airport that is scheduled to be completed in 2013.

Customs and *Immigration*

Ports of Entry:
   St. Vincent- Blue Lagoon, Chateaubelair, Wallilabou, Kingstown, Young Island Cut
   The Grenadines- Port Elizabeth (Bequia), Clifton (Union Island), Grand Bay (Mustique), Charlestown (Canouan)

All vessels entering the waters of St, Vincent and The Grenadines must report to *Customs* and *Immigration* within 24 hours of arrival. There is a EC$20,000 fine for not clearing in.

Immigration
Citizens of the US, Canada, and the UK, can stay in St. Vincent for 6 months with a valid passport. Citizens of all other nationalities must have a passport and visa, and anybody arriving by air must have an ongoing or return ticket. If you're flying out of St. Vincent and The Grenadines there is a departure tax of EC$40.

Private Vessel Fees
Cruisers must pay EC$35 per person per month upon entry. If you leave within that month and return, you must pay the fee again when you clear in again. Clearing outside of normal working hours, Monday-Friday from 0800-1200 and from 1300-1600, requires an overtime charge.

Charter Vessel Fees
St. Vincent has a new set of entry fees, which only affects charter boats carrying fare-paying passengers. Charter boats now pay a license fee of EC$5 per foot per month. The occasional charter boat pays a flat fee of EC$125.

Fishing
A license must be purchased for pleasure fishing in St. Vincent and The Grenadines, for more information contact the *Fisheries Department* upon arrival at 784-456-2738. If you fish only for your own consumption you don't need a permit, but spearguns are not permitted. Protected areas where no fishing is allowed are the northeast coast of Bequia, the area around Devil's Table in Bequia, Isle de Quatre, Mustique, the eastern coast of Canouan, the Tobago Cays, Mayreau, Palm Island, and Petit St. Vincent and her reefs. If you have a hunger for lobster, don't take or buy one out of season (the season is Oct. 1- April 30), fines can be extreme.

eSeaClear
eSeaClear is a service that provides vessel operators the ability to submit electronic notifications of arrival via the Internet to participating *Customs* offices in the Caribbean. Registered users can access the system to enter and maintain information about their vessel and crew. Prior to arrival at a new country the vessel operator simply insures

that the information is accurate and submits a new notification. Upon arrival, *Customs* can access the notification information to process your clearance more efficiently and without the need for the Ship's Master to fill out the declaration forms. *eSeaClear* is currently in use in St. Vincent and The Grenadines. For more information visit the *eSeaClear* web site at https://www.eseaclear.com/PAN/index.cfm.

Firearms

Firearms must be declared on arrival, and can be sealed on board, but if a vessel has no suitable locker, the firearms will be held in the custody of *Customs* or the police until the vessel's departure.

Pets

Pets from the UK, New Zealand, and Australia are allowed into St. Vincent and The Grenadines on presentation of a health certificate to the Government Veterinary Office. Pets from all other countries require a 6-month quarantine except those aboard private yachts. These pets must remain onboard at all times until the above requirements are met. Pets must be microchipped and have current health and rabies inoculation certificates. For more information you can email the Chief Veterinary Officer at animalhealth.svg@hotmail.com, or write to him at the Ministry of Agriculture, Richmond Hill, Kingstown, St. Vincent and The Grenadines.

Mustique Moorings

There is a EC$50 charge for the first night on a mooring at Mustique, subsequent nights are EC$25 each.

What's Prohibited

Jet-skis and waterbikes are banned in St. Vincent and The Grenadines. The wearing or importation of camouflage clothing is also prohibited in St. Vincent and The Grenadines.

Chateaubelair

Waypoints:
Chateaubelair Bay- 1 nm NW of anchorage
13° 18.50' N, 61° 14.90' W

Approaching from the north, you will notice how the huge volcano, *Mt. Soufrière* dominates the topography of St. Vincent's northern portion. Here beautiful mountains and valleys lead down to the sea on both the windward and leeward coasts of St.

Vincent and the leeward coast is inundated with small coves of which several are suitable for extended stays. The most northern anchorage is in *Chateaubelair Bay* as shown on Chart STV-2.

Caution: In early 2011, the *St. Vincent Coast Guard* began suggesting to yachts anchored at Chateaubelair to move elsewhere: *Troumakar Bay*, *Cumberland Bay*, Wallilabou, *Keartons Bay*, or Barrouallie. There have been several security issues in Chateaubelair over the last few years and they are uncertain that the area is stable. Be advised, listen in to the *Safety and Security Net*, and anchor here at your own risk.

Navigational Information
As shown on the chart, a waypoint at 13° 18.50' N, 61° 14.90' W, will place you approximately one mile northwest of the anchorage area in *Chateaubelair Bay*. From the waypoint you can take up an approximate southeast heading into the anchorage areas. Although not the place to be when northerly swells are running, *Chateaubelair Bay* is excellent in the normal Caribbean trade-wind conditions.

As with most eastern Caribbean leeward anchorages, Chateaubelair is deep, but good holding can still be found. The best spot is in the sandy area just off the *Beach Front Bar* off the town, while some folks like the protection given by the cliffs along the eastern shore of the bay. Make sure your anchor is set well in sand here as the bottom is rocky in places. Heading south from Chateaubelair you can pass north of Chateaubelair Island (good snorkeling here) or between it and the mainland in the narrow, deep (35' minimum depth) channel as shown on Chart STV-2.

You can tie up to the town dock, but keep the dock (and other parts of the anchorage when asked) clear for the fishermen and those others who move their goods out of here.

What You Will Find Ashore
Customs and *Immigration*
Chateaubelair is a Port of Entry, the first you will come to when heading south along St. Vincent's western shore. If you walk up from the dock and take a right, *Customs* is a short walk away. *Immigration* is located in the *Police Station*. From the dock, head up the road and take the uphill left turn and the station is on your right (see chart). *Customs* is open Monday-Friday from 0800-1600 and on Saturdays from 0800-1200.

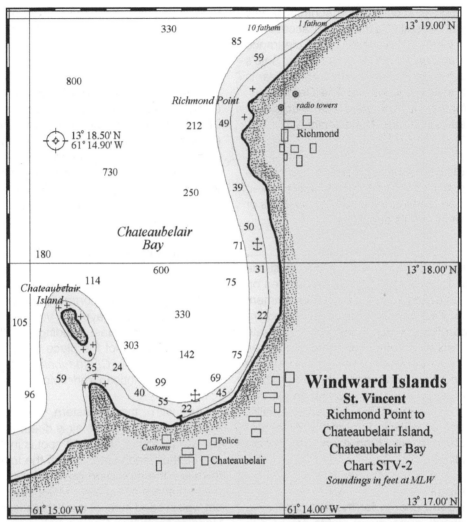

330   10 fathom   1 fathom   13° 19.00' N
85
59
800
Richmond Point
radio towers
212   49   Richmond
13° 18.50' N
61° 14.90' W
730
250   39
Chateaubelair   50
Bay   71

180   13° 18.00' N
114   600   75   31
Chateaubelair
Island   330   22
105   303   75
142
35   24   69
59   99   45
96   40   55   22
Customs
Police
Chateaubelair

Windward Islands
St. Vincent
Richmond Point to
Chateaubelair Island,
Chateaubelair Bay
Chart STV-2
Soundings in feet at MLW

61° 15.00' W   61° 14.00' W   13° 17.00' N

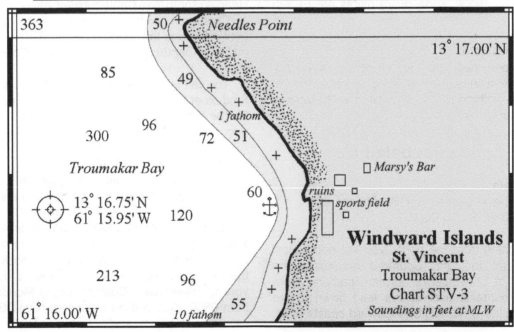

363   50   *Needles Point*
13° 17.00' N
85   49
96   72   51   1 fathom
300
Troumakar Bay   Marsy's Bar
13° 16.75' N   ruins
61° 15.95' W   120   60   sports field
Windward Islands
213   96   **St. Vincent**
Troumakar Bay
55   Chart STV-3
61° 16.00' W   10 fathom   *Soundings in feet at MLW*

The *Beach Front Bar and Restaurant* sits at the northern end of the long beach (where else would a beach front bar sit?). Here you can get breakfast (starting at 0800), lunch, or dinner featuring West Indian fare as well as the usual bar food, burgers and such. Vegetarians can even dine here on the *Beach Front* selection of fruits, vegetables, and salads. The Friday night happy hour begins at 1900 and never seems to end, often there's live music for your enjoyment. The *Beach Front* monitors VHF ch. 16 and 68 and is also the place to get a taxi or a tour guide to the hiking trails that lead inland from here.

From Chateaubelair and Richmond, you can hike up *La Soufrière*, the massive volcano that takes up the northern third of the island and stands over 4,000' high. *La Soufrière* is one of the most energetic of Caribbean volcanoes, having erupted in 1718, 1812, 1902, and 1979, although carbon dating suggests eruptions from 160-350 AD.

After the 1812 eruption, *La Soufrière* had two craters, one of which was home to a small lake some 1,200' below the crater's rim. At this time a narrow ridge separated the two craters and the volcano was quite for ninety years.

The 1902 eruption began in February with some slight rumblings that the people living in the area ignored. However, on May 7, nineteen earthquakes caused the people of Wallilabou, Richmond, and Morne Ronde to flee to safer territory. When *La Soufrière* finally did erupt, even Kingstown and the southern coast of St. Vincent were not spared as showers of stones fell upon these areas as well as the windward coast of the island. In all, some 2,000 people were killed in St. Vincent and the eruption coincided with the eruption of St. Pierre in Martinique that claimed 30,000 lives.

In 1971, there was a minor eruption that formed a lava island in the crater-lake. On April 13, 1979, Good Friday (and Friday the 13th), *La Soufrière* erupted again, five times on that one day. Some folks didn't decide to flee until after the second or third eruption. In all, between April 13 and April 25, there were a total of 20 eruptions, but no serious earthquakes. There was no loss of life, but the banana crops were hit hard, and many roads and forests were lost.

North of Chateaubelair is the small community of Richmond where you can set out on a 4-hour round-trip hike through the rainforest up the *Wallilabou River* to *Trinity Falls*, one of the most beautiful waterfalls in St. Vincent, about 4 miles from the *Richmond Vale Academy*. If you wish to shorten the hike you can take a taxi part of the way.

Troumakar Bay

Waypoints:
Troumakar Bay- ¼ nm W of anchorage
13° 16.75' N, 61° 16.95' W

Sometimes shown as *Troumaca Bay*, this small but pleasant anchorage, only about a mile or so south of *Chateaubelair Bay*, was once home to Arawak Indians as evidenced by the relics found nearby. The town sits perched on the hillside above the bay and about ¼ mile south of the anchorage is a nice black sand beach. *Troumakar Bay* is another one of those deep leeward anchorages that is not tenable in northerly swells.

Navigational Information
As shown on Chart STV-3, a waypoint at 13° 16.75'N, 61° 16.95' W, will place you approximately ¼ mile west of the anchorage area. From the waypoint head east to anchor off the town and playing field. You'll have to anchor close to shore as water here is deep, you might even have to take an anchor or line ashore by the ruins of the old block plant to keep you in place.

What You Will Find Ashore
Ghetto Man monitors VHF ch. 16 and 68 and will take you to his restaurant, *Marsy's Bar and Restaurant,* sometimes called *Under The Rocks,* sitting on the hill overlooking the bay. *Ghetto Man*, Alstar Mars, will be happy to serve you dinner if you give him advance notice (458-2879).

Cumberland Bay

Waypoints:
Cumberland Bay- ¼ nm NW of entrance to bay
13° 16.10' N, 61° 16.00' W

Cumberland Bay has a lot going for it. It's well protected (though not the place to be when northerly swells are running), it's near Wallilabou if you wish to clear *Customs*, and it is a very secluded anchorage where lush, rich green mountains and valleys surround you and no resorts taint your view.

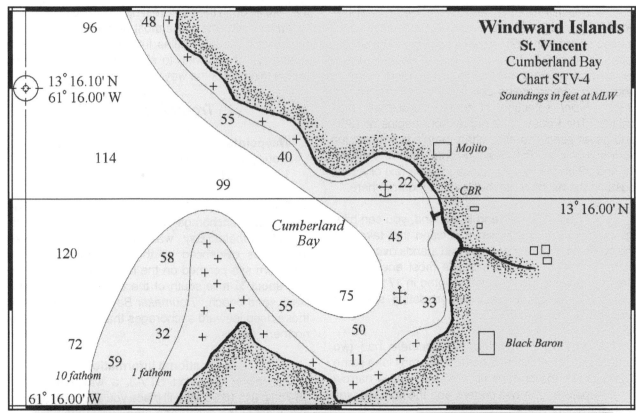

Windward Islands
St. Vincent
Cumberland Bay
Chart STV-4
Soundings in feet at MLW

96   48

13° 16.10' N
61° 16.00' W

55

114

40

99

22

Mojito

CBR

13° 16.00' N

Cumberland Bay

45

120   58

75

55   33

32   50

72   59   11

10 fathom   *1 fathom*

Black Baron

61° 16.00' W

Lower part of *Cumberland Bay* as seen from the north, *Black Baron* is approximately left of center

While there have been security problems here in the past, the locals have worked hard to change things and their efforts are working, but still take normal precautions, locking your vessel when not aboard, and locking your dinghy.

Navigational Information

As shown on Chart STV-4, a waypoint at 13° 16.10'N, 61° 16.00' W, will place you approximately ¼ mile northwest of the bay. From the waypoint steer generally southeast trying to avoid the boat boys who'll want to come alongside.

You must use caution to avoid the reefs that work their way northward from the point at the southwestern tip of the bay. When anchoring you may need to take a line ashore. If you need the services of a water taxi hail *Carlos* on VHF ch. 16.

What You Will Find Ashore

The *Cumberland Beach and Recreation Park*, *CBR* on Chart STV-4, offers a dock, water and ice for sale, a laundry, showers (EC$5 includes a towel), and a welcome center. Plans call for a restaurant in the near future. There is 6' at MLW at the head of the dock if you wish to come in for water. The staff puts on a great BBQ at 1400 on the last Friday of every month, the cost is EV$10 per person and it's worth it.

Dining

Ashore you can stop by *Beni's* located right on the beach. Owner Bennett is a good cook and he offers live music on Wednesday nights. Bennett can also arrange a hike and guide to the nearby attractions and has a taxi if you need one. Be careful, his dinghy dock seems to stay in a state of disrepair but he fixes it up every now and then.

South of town is the *Black Baron*, a pirate-themed restaurant. They are open every day during the winter season and offer French and Creole fare made with local produce. You can even order a whole suckling pig if you so desire. Next door is *Joseph's Place*, a great place to enjoy a fresh seafood barbecue.

At the northern end of the bay is *Mojito* with a great view of the bay and an even better menu featuring above average, almost gourmet food. If the skipper of the vessel brings five guests, he or she dines for free.

Wallilabou

Waypoints:
Wallilabou Bay- ¼ nm NW of anchorage
13° 15.00' N, 61° 16.60' W

Wallilabou, pronounced *wally-la-boo,* was the star of a *Disney* film, *Pirates of the Caribbean*, back in 2003, and is one of the most popular anchorages on this stretch of coastline. The *Wallilabou Anchorage Restaurant* still has some of the old movie props on their property and have a room dedicated to souvenirs of the movie that are definitely worth viewing.

Navigational Information

As shown on Chart STV-5, a waypoint at 13° 15.00' N, 61° 16.60' W, will place you approximately ¼ mile northwest of the anchorage area in *Wallilabou Bay*. From the waypoint steer generally southeastward towards the town dock and anchor either north or south of the dock; you'll see some conspicuous white pointed roofs north of the dock that you can anchor off. You might have to run a line ashore to a tree, the dock, or some dock ruins that lie in the northern part of the bay. In the center of the bay, you can pick up a mooring set out by the *Wallilabou Anchorage Restaurant*. The mooring fees are EC$20 and are applied to your bill if you eat ashore.

If northerly swells are running you might be able to tuck up snugly into the northeast corner of the bay, but it won't be comfortable if the swells have any westerly component to them.

You will have to deal with boat boys here, it's a popular spot for cruisers and boat boys...just thought I'd mention that. The most popular boat boys are the twins, Ron and Ronnie, as well as Speedy and Bagga. The fee for line handling is EDC$10.

There has been a bit of theft in the bay recently. I suggest you anchor close to the *Anchorage Hotel*, they have a night watchman.

What You Will Find Ashore

If you feel like a dip in fresh water, walk to the road, take a left, and look for the falls about a mile on your right. Divers and snorkelers will enjoy the anchorage and the surrounding waters. The snorkeling is excellent around the rock arch on the northern shore of the bay, and north of the point are some small caves along the shore.

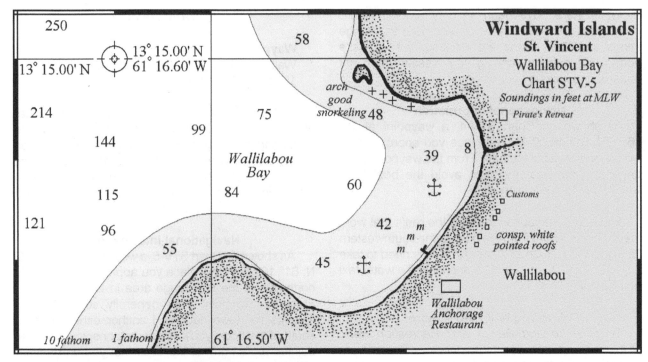

Windward Islands
St. Vincent
Wallilabou Bay
Chart STV-5
Soundings in feet at MLW

□ Pirate's Retreat

250

13° 15.00' N
61° 16.60' W

13° 15.00' N

58

214

75

*arch
good
snorkeling* 48

99

144

8

*Wallilabou
Bay*

39

115

84

60

Customs

121

96

42   *m*
     m
        m

*consp. white
pointed roofs*

55

45

Wallilabou

*Wallilabou
Anchorage
Restaurant*

10 fathom   *1 fathom*   61° 16.50' W

Rock Side Café, Keartons Bay

Keartons Bay

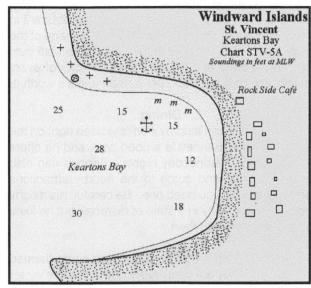

Windward Islands
St. Vincent
Keartons Bay
Chart STV-5A
Soundings in feet at MLW

Rock Side Café

25   15   *m* *m*
                      m

15

28   12

Keartons Bay

30   18

Customs *and* Immigration

Wallilabou is a Port of Entry and you can clear *Customs* here, but only between the hours of 1700-1800, and overtime is usually charged. You can clear with *Immigration* at the *Police Station* in Barrouallie, but you'll have to clear *Customs* here in Wallilabou or further south at Kingstown. *Customs* is on the northern part of town just up from the dock.

Internet Access
The *Wallilabou Anchorage Restaurant* has *Wi-fi,* accessible easily onsite, possibly even at anchor. The cost is extremely minimal, only US$5 per year.

Dining
At the southern end of the bay, the *Wallilabou Anchorage Restaurant* monitors VHF ch. 16 and 68 and offers moorings, water, ice, showers, free garbage service, fax and phone service, and has a very nice restaurant and bar with a daily happy hour from 1700-1800 and sometimes live music, usually on Tuesdays and Thursdays.

Just up the road is the *Golden Spoon Restaurant* owned by the twins, Ron and Ronnie. At the northern end of the bay, past the buildings with the conspicuous white, pointed roofs, is the *Pirate's Retreat* serving local food and strong libations with interesting conversation courtesy of the owner, Shadow.

One of the most interesting stops is *Morna's Craft Shop* where you can pick up some of their special guava liqueur. *Morna's* is located on the main road as you walk toward the waterfall.

Keartons Bay

Navigational Information
The next bay south, *Keartons Bay*, now has 5 moorings installed by the *Rock Side Café*, a bar on the northern shore of the bay (as shown on Chart STV-5A). As you enter the bay, give the café a hail on VHF ch. 68 and Orlando will come out and help you secure your vessel. This is not as simple as picking up a mooring line, you will be tying off bow and stern with your bow into the swells that work their way into the anchorage. You will have 15'-25' of water in the mooring field.

What You Will Find Ashore
The *Rock Side Café* has moorings, *Wi-fi,* Internet access, laundry, showers, and water provided to the moored vessels via a long hose, all for the use of their dinner guests. If you want to dine in their restaurant they will pick you up at your boat. If you would like to pick up some fresh produce, just ask the owners, Rosi and Orlando.

The restaurant is open air and has a great view of *Keartons Bay*. The food is excellent but they'll need advance notice. If you're a diver, Orlando is also

and he can guide you to the best dive and snorkeling spots in the area.

Barrouallie

Waypoints:
Princess Bay- ½ nm WSW of anchorage
13° 14.20' N, 61° 16.90' W

Barrouallie, pronounced *bar-relly*, was once the capital of St. Vincent and is home to an ancient Carib Indian altar. Once a whaling settlement, whalers still set out from here, but today they go after blackfish, a small pilot whale. Most of the catch is sold fresh or on ice. Some of the catch is salted, cut into strips, and dried on bamboo. The blubber of the blackfish is usually boiled to a crisp in large vats to extract the oil. The remains, the "blackfish crisps," are sold and can be a tasty snack.

Navigational Information
The primary hazard to navigation here, and probably the major hazard along this leeward coast of St. Vincent, are the small cays known as the *Bottle and Glass* (see Chart STV-6). When approaching from the north, or if you are heading north from *Princess Bay* and Barrouallie, give this shoal a wide berth as the shallow water extends a bit west of the westernmost cay as shown on the chart.

As shown on Chart STV-6, a waypoint at 13° 14.20' N, 61° 16.90' W, will place you approximately ½ mile west/southwest of the anchorage off Barrouallie in *Princess Bay*. From the waypoint steer a bit north of east to anchor north of the town dock, between the dock and Pint Rock, this gets you out of any swell that may work its way around *Bottle and Glass*, however do not think you can stay here if northerly swells are running, it will not be wise. Holding is fair to good here, but it's best to take a line ashore.

What You Will Find Ashore
The architecture of the fishing village of Barrouallie reflects a strong French influence and the Barrouallie *Police Station,* dating back to the 1700s, is one of the oldest buildings on the island. Just south of Barrouallie is a coconut plantation where the trees grow right down the hillsides to the water's edge.

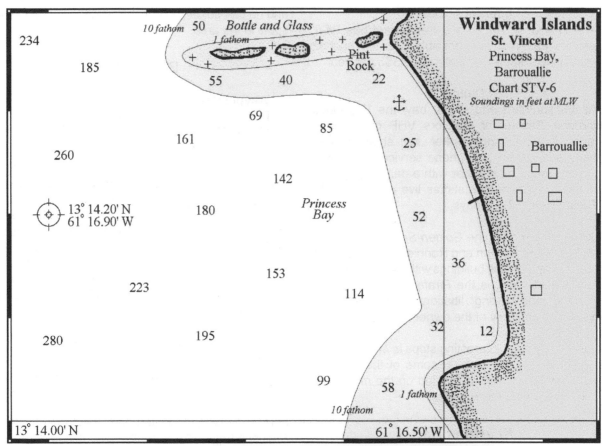

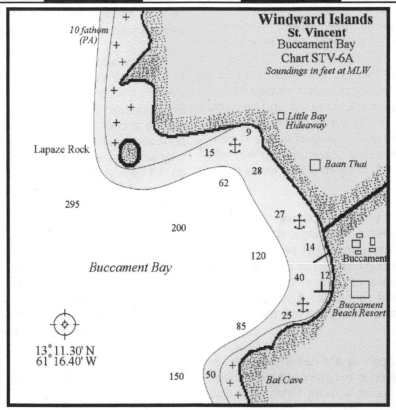

Layou

Your next stop on a southward voyage along the leeward coast of St. Vincent could be either Layou, *Buccament Bay*, or Petit Byahaut.

For years Layou had been threatened by the sea; years of wave action seriously eroded the coastline threatening the highway and access to the communities that lie north of town. In the late 1990s three storms wreaked havoc on the Layou waterfront and the government of St. Vincent finally decided to help the residents of Layou rebuild their waterfront. In 2006 this project was complete and today Layou has a beautiful waterfront even though the town is not geared to the yachtsman and leans more toward commercial interests and fishing.

Navigational Information
Just north of *Buccament Bay* is the seaside town of Layou just south of Jackson's Point as shown on Chart STV-1. Give the point a wide berth and anchor off the town, the best spot is in the southeastern end of the bay.

What You Will Find Ashore
In Layou you can see 1,300-year-old petroglyphs on the side of a large 20' rock. The petroglyphs are on private property, about ¼ mile off the main road by the river, so it's best to make arrangements to see them through the *Tourist Bureau* in Kingstown, or ask permission when you arrive. The owners, Victor Hendrickson, or his wife, will be happy to guide you to the site for US$2. East of Layou is the *Emerald Valley Resort and Casino* if you're into a bit of gaming at a family-friendly resort. The resort is open Wednesday-Monday from 0900-0300.

Buccament Bay

Waypoints:
Buccament Bay- ¼ nm WSW of anchorage
13° 11.30' N, 61° 16.40' W

Buccament Bay is a pleasant anchorage and one that will get a bit busy as the *Buccament Bay Beach Resort* nears completion and boat traffic from the resort increases.

Navigational Information
The next anchorage to the south, just south of Lapaze Rock (give it a wide berth) is *Buccament Bay*.

As shown on Chart STV-7 and in more detail on Chart STV-6A. A waypoint at 13° 11.30' N, 61° 16.40' W, will place you approximately ¼ mile west/southwest of the anchorage at the southern end of *Buccament Bay*. From the waypoint head generally north of east to clear the point and anchor in the southeastern part of the bay in 12'-40', a bit rolly at times, but comfortable in settled conditions. The anchorage in *Buccament Bay* is affected by northerly swells but well-protected from southerly seas.

Besides anchoring off the resort, you can anchor at the north end of the bay by the *Little Bay Hideaway* Restaurant, or in the middle of the bay by *Baan Thai Restaurant*, convenient locations if you plan to dine in either of these establishments.

What You Will Find Ashore
The *Buccament Bay Beach Resort* is located in the southeast corner of the bay and is recognizable by the conspicuous red roofs of the cottages on the site. Although still under construction, the finished resort will have a mixture of properties, from studio apartments to four bedroom plantation houses on their own landscaped grounds.

If you take the road that veers eastward up the *Buccament River Valley you will* pass the former *Pembroke Estate*, an old 1,000 acre plantation with a sugar mill and aqueduct that form a backdrop for the modern *Aqueduct Golf Course*. Staying on the road you'll soon come to the *Vermont Nature Trails*. The trails are well-marked and lead you in a loop along the 1,000' and 2,000' levels of *Grand Bonhomme* through an evergreen forest and into a tropical rain forest. The flora and fauna are amazing, and you might get lucky and spot a rare St. Vincent parrot from a viewing area.

As you drive up the road towards the *Nature Trails*, you'll pass *Table Rock*, a great picnic area about a tenth of a mile to the right off the main road. Table Rock is a long sheet of lava rock in the bed of a river where the water has carved channels and basins ideal for swimming. Never try to swim here after heavy rains as the force of the water will be too strong.

Dining
Located on the shore midway in the bay, is the *Baan Thai Restaurant*. Open Tuesday-Sunday for lunch and dinner, this is the best place to dine in *Buccament Bay*.

At the northern end of the beach, is the Little Bay Hideaway and features local seafood with at least a 3-hour advance notice.

The *Bat Cave*

Located on the point southwest of the *Buccament Bay Resort*, the *Bat Cave* is unique and a must see if you're in this area and are not afraid of bats. The snorkeling is good as you approach the cave where you will find about 3' of water at the entrance. The cave itself is full of bats, hence the name, so don't enter if you are fearful of the creatures, you will not enjoy your visit. But if you can handle seeing the bats you will enjoy watching them as hundreds of them hang from the ceiling and walls.

You have no reason to fear the bats, the two species that call the cave home only eat fruit, fish, and insects. Please do not bother the bats and do not use a flashlight or take photographs when in the cave.

If you look to the left upon entry, you'll see a bit of light which is the end of a tunnel 30' long and about 4' wide. If the seas are down it will be safe to traverse the tunnel to a huge fissure 30' high and 40' in depth. You can follow the fissure to emerge in the open sea on the other side where the water colors are breath-taking.

Petit Byahaut

Waypoints:
Petit Byahaut- ¼ nm WSW of
13° 10.85' N, 61° 16.30' W

Navigational Information
As shown on Chart STV-7, a waypoint at 13° 10.85' N, 61° 16.30' W places you approximately ¼ mile west/southwest of *Petit Byahaut*. From the waypoint head in a general east/northeast direction steering to the center of the bay to drop your hook. You can anchor here in 20'-30'. If southerly swells are present you might not wish to anchor here or if you do you'll need to set a stern anchor and use a bridle to keep your bow into the swells.

What You Will Find Ashore
The *Petit Byahaut Resort* is now closed, but in its prime it was a sort of luxurious camp for adults. You could stay in a tent (only 5 available for up to ten adults), but not quite a regular tent, you had all the amenities such as a bed with fresh linen, but you also had a bathroom open to the sky and only shielded by a huge flowering hibiscus. The refrigeration, lighting, and pressure water were all supplied by solar panels and there were no telephones to interrupt your musings in paradise. Sadly the resort is closed and is available for lease and is for sale for US$3.5 million.

Ottley Hall Marina

Waypoints:
Ottley Hall Bay- ¼ nm SW of entrance to marina
13° 09.45' N, 61° 15.10' W

Ottley Hall Marina and Shipyard lies west-northwest of Kingstown, at the foot of 636' high *Fort Charlotte*, and below the conspicuous large white satellite dishes on the hillside, easily seen from offshore.

There is a large rock on the shoreline north of *Ottley Hall Marina* with a large white cross atop it. This marks the grave of the former owner who wished to be buried standing up so that he could see the sea.

Navigational Information
As shown on Chart STV-8, a waypoint at 13° 09.45' N, 61° 15.10' W, will place you approximately ¼ mile southwest of the entrance to the marina. From this waypoint you can head in a northeasterly direction to pass between the mainland to starboard and the jetty to port as shown on the chart. The marina is deep and there is a bit of a surge at times so keep that in mind if you're thinking about a stay here.

As shown on Chart STV-8, a waypoint at 13° 09.45' N, 61° 15.10' W, will place you approximately ¼ mile southwest of the entrance to the marina. From the waypoint, pass between the jetty/seawall/dock on your port side and the point of land on your starboard side and enter the marina. Be sure to call on VHF ch. 16 before entering the marina.

What You Will Find Ashore
Ottley Hall Marina is a large, full-service marina with 22 slips for vessels up to 200' in length with full electric, water, *Wi-fi*, laundry, and showers. The marina has a covered dry-dock and can haul vessels up to 200' LOA, a 36' beam, and 1,000 ton displacement. The maximum draft at the fuel dock is 16'.

The yard has a 500-ton lift, a 40-ton *Travel Lift*, a 20-ton crane, a chandlery, and can handle jobs such as sandblasting, welding, painting, electrical repairs,

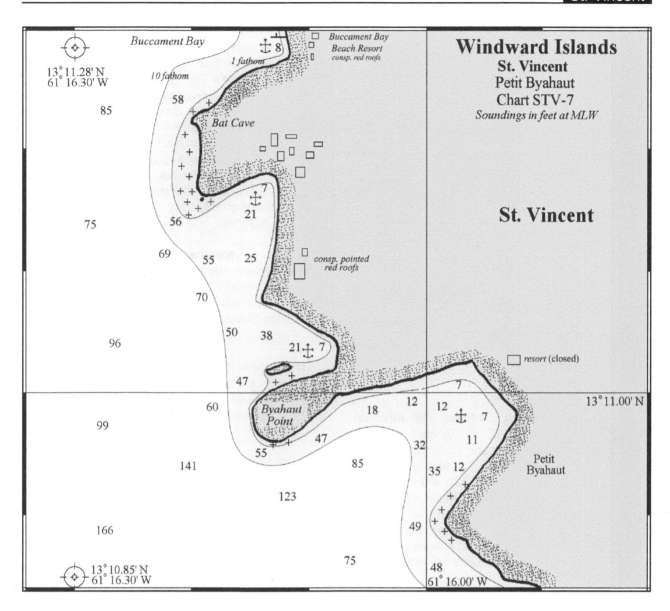

Buccament Bay

Buccament Bay
Beach Resort
consp. red roofs

Windward Islands
St. Vincent
Petit Byahaut
Chart STV-7
Soundings in feet at MLW

13° 11.28' N
61° 16.30' W

85

1 fathom

10 fathom

58

Bat Cave

75

56

69

55   25

consp. pointed
red roofs

70

96

50   38

21 ⚓ 7

47

St. Vincent

resort (closed)

13° 11.00' N

Byahaut
Point

60

18   12   12   ⚓   7

99

55   47

11

141

85   32

35   12

123

Petit
Byahaut

166

49

75

48

7

21

13° 10.85' N
61° 16.30' W

61° 16.00' W

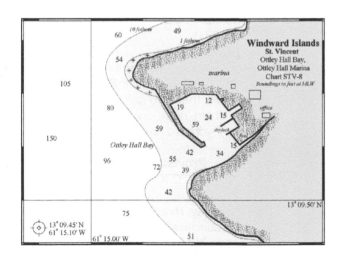

60   10 fathom   49

1 fathom

Windward Islands
St. Vincent
Ottley Hall Bay,
Ottley Hall Marina
Chart STV-8
Soundings in feet at MLW

105

54

marina

80

19   12

office

150

59   59   24   15

drylock   fuel

Ottley Hall Bay

42   34   15

96   55

72   39

13° 09.50' N

42

75

51

13° 09.45' N
61° 15.10' W

61° 15.00' W

Ottley Hall Marina as viewed from atop *Ft. Charlotte*

mechanical repairs (agents for *Cat, Yanmar,* and *Volvo Penta*), refrigeration repairs, and offers storage on the hard for those interested in leaving their boats in St. Vincent for a while. They even have a large machine shop if you need any metal or wood fabrication. The marina also has a small hotel available if you need somewhere to stay while your boat is being repaired. You are also permitted to stay on your vessel while it is on the hard. You can do your own work or you can use their sub-contractors.

There is a duty-free grocery store on site operated by *Gourmet Food Service,* suppliers of wholesale foods and fresh produce on a major scale on St. Vincent and in The Grenadines. You can reach the marina offices by phone at 784-457-2178, or by email at ottleyhall@caribsurf.com.

Kingstown

Waypoints:
Kingstown Bay- ¼ nm W of docks
13° 09.00' N, 61° 14.00' W

Kingstown, not to be confused with Kingston, Jamaica, is the capital of St. Vincent and The Grenadines and all the major government offices are here including Parliament. In fact, a quarter of the island's population of over 100,000 lives in the Kingstown area. While not very popular with cruising yachtsmen, who seem to prefer the Young Island/ *Blue Lagoon* anchorages to Kingstown, there is a lot to see in town. Provisioning and shopping is good, and several marine service centers are located here.

Navigational Information
As shown on Chart STV-9, a waypoint at 13° 09.00' N, 61° 14.00' W, will place you approximately ¼ mile west of the docks in *Kingstown Harbour.* From the waypoint head north/northeast to anchor northwest of the fish market and the bus station.

What You Will Find Ashore
Customs and Immigration
If I'm headed south, I prefer to clear in at Wallilabou and if I'm headed north I prefer to clear at Young Island, but if you need to clear with *Customs,* head for the inner part of the cruise ship dock at the south of the main docks and tie off to clear or pick up parts and provisions. *Customs* is located to your left at Kingstown's main docks; *Immigration* is located at the *Police Station* north on *Bay Street.*

Getting Around
The first thing you'll probably do in Kingstown is explore, either by foot, taxi, or bus. Taxis are easy to come by; *Sam's Taxi* Service is one of the best around and they'll even organize a trip to La Soufrière for you. You can reach *Sam's Taxi* on the VHF ch. 16/68, or phone them at 784-456-4338. Buses run all over the island and start their routes at the station in Kingstown (see chart) and you travel both the leeward and windward coasts for only US$1. If you wish to visit The Grenadines, but not take your own boat, you can catch a daily ferry in Kingstown to Bequia, Canouan, Mayreau, and Union Island.

Medical Assistance
If you need medical assistance, the *Kingston General Hospital* can be reached at 784-456-1185, or if the problem is not major, you can try the *Medical Associates Clinic* at 784-457-2598/2819.

Internet Access
There are several Internet cafés in Kingstown. Just across from the cruise ship dock is the *Port Authority Internet Café* which is open daily from 0700-1900. On *Egmont Street* you can get online at *Computec.*

Marine Facilities
Fuel, ice (available at the fish market), and water (for a small fee) can be taken on at the small dock off the fish market as shown on the chart. Before approaching the dock call, *St. Vincent Signal Station,* on VHF ch. 16 for a phone relay to let them know you're coming.

Ace Hardware in town near the bus station (see Chart STV-9) is a *Yamaha* dealer and sitting between the *Botanical Gardens* and the Prime Minister's mansion is Carlton King's machine shop if you need welding or fabrication. Carlton can be reached by phone at 784-457-9311.

Across the street from the small market north of the cruise ship docks is *St. Vincent Sales & Service,* the local *NAPA* store that also carries limited marine supplies such as chain, rope, anchors, batteries, and can also make up hydraulic hoses for you.

Provisions
For provisioning, try *C.K. Greaves Supermarket* on *Bay St.* Greave's gives a charter yacht discount and is open Monday-Thursday from 0800-1700, on Fridays and Saturdays from 0800-2100, and on

Misty morning, Kingstown as seen from *Ft. Charlotte*

Botanical Gardens, Kingstown

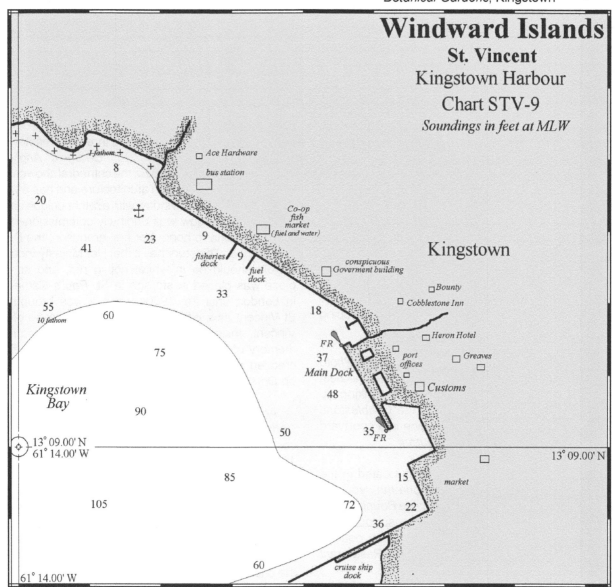

Windward Islands
St. Vincent
Kingstown Harbour
Chart STV-9
Soundings in feet at MLW

1 fathom

Ace Hardware

bus station

8

20

Co-op
fish
market
(fuel and water)

Kingstown

9

41

23

fisheries
dock

9

fuel
dock

conspicuous
Goverment building

Bounty

Cobblestone Inn

33

18

55

10 fathom

60

FR

Heron Hotel

37
Main Dock

port
offices

Greaves

75

48

Customs

Kingstown
Bay

90

50

35
FR

13° 09.00' N
61° 14.00' W

15

market

13° 09.00' N

85

105

72

22

36

61° 14.00' W

60

cruise ship
dock

Sundays they're open from 0800-1100. If you visit the store from *Young Island Cut*, you might be able to talk the manager into delivering your provisions to your point of origin.

Aunt Jobe's Market is fairly new, stylish, large, and a pleasure to shop. The market is located in a mall about a ten minute walk out of town on the main road just past the hospital. Besides your usual market goods they have a very nice deli. *Aunt Jobe's* is open Monday-Saturday from 0700-2130 and on Sundays from 0700-1400.

Just south of the *Customs* office is the *St. Vincent Marketing Board's Food City*, a large market where you can pick from a great selection of fresh fruits and veggies. Just outside of town is the *Gourmet Meat Market* whose name says it all.

If you need to refill the bar aboard your vessel, visit *Gonsalves Liquor*, open Monday-Friday from 0800-1700 and on Saturday from 0800-1300. *Gonsalves* will deliver to the dock for you.

Dining

Now that you have filled the larder aboard your vessel, let's discuss where to dine in Kingstown.

The *Cobblestone Inn*, built in 1814 as a sugar warehouse, is home to a wonderful, popular restaurant, *Basil's*, offering candlelight dinners, excellent buffet lunches, a Friday night Chinese buffet, and yes, this bar is owned by the Basil of Mustique fame. Kingstown has several cobblestone streets, and the 19th century alley at the *Cobblestone Inn* separates the two streets that make up the heart of the shopping district, *Bay Street* and *Middle Street*.

Opposite the inn and upstairs from *Roger's Photo Studios*, *Vee Jay's Rooftop Dining Club* has the best views of Kingstown Harbour. If you're walking up Bay St. from the south, just before the *Cobblestone Inn* is *The Heron*, where you can dine in a courtyard verandah in their *Nicefoods Restaurant*.

In the red-brick *Troutman Building* located in the center of town behind the *Cobblestone Inn*, you can join local business people at lunch at the *Bounty*. Here the staff is friendly, the food good, the surroundings simple, and the prices economical. Another popular spot with the office lunch crowd is *Juliette's Restaurant* across from the *National Commercial Bank*.

The *Rooftop Restaurant and Bar* does a thriving business from its location three stories above Kingstown on *Bay St.* Wednesday and Friday are Karaoke nights and Saturday is Family Night complete with a barbecue and a steel band. *Aggie's* sits opposite the *Sardine Bakery* and this casual second floor bar and family restaurant is good for local Creole cooking. The *Green Parrot* on *Halifax St.* (the same street where the *Post Office* is located) is great for breakfast and *Cham's*, also on *Halifax St.* serves up good West Indian cooking.

Discovering Kingstown

The center of town is *Market Square*, just west of the wharf at *Bay St.* and *Bedford St.* *Bay Street* is the colorful center of Kingstown's waterfront, and is wall-to-wall shops with a few hotels thrown in for good measure. The market, which opened in February of 1990, is packed on Fridays and Saturdays with people selling fresh fruits, vegetables, meats, fish, and is sometimes called *Little Tokyo* because the funding for the market originated in Japan.

West on *Grenville Street* sits three of Kingstown's most famous churches. *St. George's Anglican Cathedral*, built around 1820, the cathedral showcases brightly painted Georgian architecture and has a well-known stained glass window with a rather unique angel in red. The window was originally commissioned by Queen Victoria to honor her first grandson, the Duke of Clarence. The story has it that Her Majesty thought angels should be in white, not in red, and so the piece was placed in storage in *St. Paul's Cathedral* in London until the 1930s when it was brought to St Vincent as a gift to the bishop and diocese of St. Vincent. Inside the cathedral is a memorial plaque in memory of Major Alexander Leith, the British officer credited with killing the great Carib chief Chatoyer on *Dorsetshire Hill* during the *Brigands War* of 1795.

Across the street and just a bit west of the *Anglican Cathedral* is *St. Mary's Catholic Cathedral*. Originally constructed in 1823, the cathedral was rebuilt in the 1930s by a Flemish monk and features a myriad of styles including Moorish, Romanesque, and Georgian, all fashioned out of volcanic sand bricks. Across the street and just a bit south of the *Anglican Cathedral* is the *Kingstown Methodist Church* with its small cemetery. The brightly colored interior of this church is a must see, especially the massive pipe organ in the choir balcony.

A must visit is the *Botanical Gardens*, just a short walk from town, Founded in 1765 as a 20-acre garden, the *Botanical Gardens* (see photo) are the oldest of their type in the New World. The *Gardens* were established to propagate plants used in medicine and for trade. Here you can see the endangered St. Vincent Parrot, the national bird. Estimated 500 left in the wild, but there are over two dozen of them at the *Garden's Parrot Breeding Center.*

Within the *Botanical Gardens* is the *St. Vincent National Museum*, founded by Dr. Earle Kirby and home to many pre-Columbian artifacts some of which date from 4,000BC including stone and shell tools, jewelry, the prow of a war canoe, and some stones with petroglyphs inscribed onto them. Christian Daniel is a good and trustworthy tour guide here, but you'll find several other fellows standing around wanting to help you. Whoever you choose, make sure that you negotiate a price beforehand. Christian is a Black Carib and is one of the most knowledgeable and likable persons you could meet. He can show you, and tell you the history of all the flora and fauna here, including the "screw palm," a native of Vietnam. The center of his tour is the breadfruit tree grown from one of the original plants brought here by Captain Bligh. In 1787-1788, Captain Bligh made his ill-fated voyage on the *HMS Bounty* to Tahiti to collect breadfruit and other useful plants for the people of the West Indies and after a well-publicized mutiny finally completed his mission in Kingstown on January 23, 1793. And the breadfruit you see today are direct descendants of Bligh's cargo. What I've told you in this paragraph only scratches the surface of what you can learn at the *Botanical Gardens*, so don't miss a tour with the energetic Christian Daniel.

On *Berkshire Hill*, west/northwest of town and overlooking *Ottley Hall Marina*, sits *Fort Charlotte,* 636' above the harbor. The fort was built by the British in 1806 as a defense against the French and was named after King George III's wife. At its peak the fort housed 600 soldiers and 34 cannon. The only death that occurred at the fort was that of an officer killed by an enlisted man. The museum in the old barracks depicts a bit of the history of the Black Caribs on its walls, paintings by Lindsay Prescott. At the foot of the fort, along the shore, are the remains of an old leper colony. At the top of the twisty, climbing, narrow road, you'll meet one of the local (and official) guides, Anthony Huggins, or you can call Anthony at 457-1602 to set up an appointment for a tour.

Three miles west of Kingstown is the *Industrial Estate* at Campden Park. Thirty-acres in area, the *Industrial Estate* is home to most of St. Vincent's manufacturing, including the *St. Vincent Brewery Ltd.*, home of the gold medal winning *Harioun Lager* and *Harioun Ginger Ale*.

As I discussed in the section on *Buccament Bay*, about 5 miles northwest of Kingstown, the road veers eastward up the *Buccament River Valley* passing the former *Pembroke Estate*, an old 1,000 acre plantation, and an old sugar mill and aqueduct that form a backdrop for the modern *Aqueduct Golf Course*. Staying on the road you'll soon come to the *Vermont Nature Trails*. The trails are well-marked and lead you in a loop along the 1,000' and 2,000' levels of Grand Bonhomme through an evergreen forest and into a tropical rain forest. The flora and fauna are amazing, and you might get lucky and spot a rare St. Vincent parrot from a viewing area. As you drive up the road towards the *Nature Trails*, you'll pass *Table Rock*, a great picnic area about a tenth of a mile to the right off the main road. *Table Rock* is a long sheet of lava rock in the bed of a river where the water has carved channels and basins ideal for swimming. Never try to swim here after heavy rains as the force of the water will be too strong.

For a good day trip, take one of the small boats that goes from Kingstown upriver to the *Falls of Baleine*, which can best be reached by boat (sometimes you may have to swim to shore!). The most beautiful waterfall on the island, there is a large rock-lined pool at the base of the 70' high cascade that is perfect for swimming and photography, it's a popular spot for both. *Baleine Falls* is designated as a wildlife reserve. Serious hikers can pick up a trail at Fancy, which skirts the north coast of St. Vincent to the falls, but I warn you, it is an extremely rugged hike.

Stamp collectors will want to pick up some stamps of St. Vincent and The Grenadines (some of which are strictly collector's items) at the *Philatelist Club*.

Young Island and *Young Island Cut*

Waypoints:
Young Island- ½ nm WSW of anchorage
13° 07.90' N, 61° 12.50' W

Calliaqua Bay- ½ nm SW of entrance
13° 07.30' N, 61° 12.30' W

Blue Lagoon

Ft. Durvernette

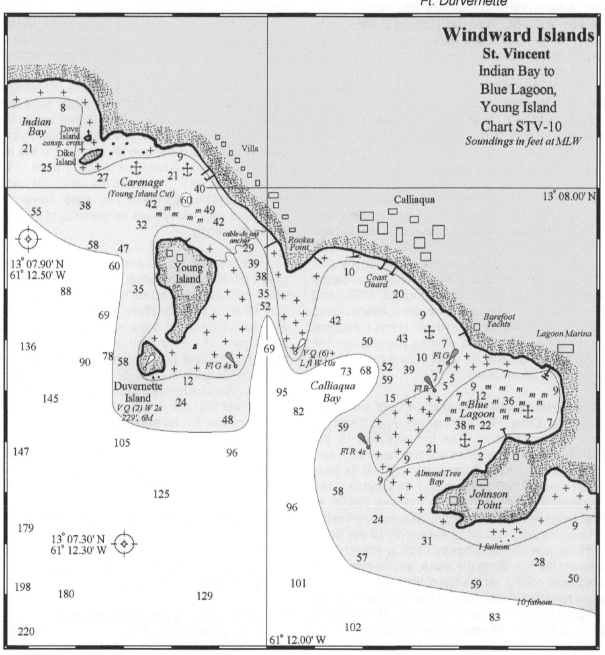

Windward Islands
St. Vincent
Indian Bay to
Blue Lagoon,
Young Island
Chart STV-10
Soundings in feet at MLW

The southern end of St. Vincent, from Arnos Vale to Prospect, is the primary residential area of St. Vincent, and that stretch of coast that encompasses the waters of Young Island, *Calliaqua Bay*, and *Blue Lagoon* is especially popular with cruisers to the mainland of St. Vincent. Close to Kingstown and Calliaqua, this area is less secluded than the anchorages on the western shore of St. Vincent north of Kingstown and offers easy access to the best marine services and restaurants on the island.

According to legend, Young Island was a gift from a Carib chief to a Governor of St. Vincent who had given the chief a fine horse. In the 1700s, Sir William Young, then Governor of St. Vincent met with a Carib chief who admired the governor's horse. Feeling particularly generous that day, Young gave the horse to the chief. Later, the chief happened by the Governor's house in Calliaqua and found Sir Young staring at Young Island. The chief, also feeling generous, seeing that the governor had an interest in the small island, gave it to him.

Just south of Young Island lies *Ft. Duvernette* (see photo), which still has the original cannon and mortar that were used during the battles between the French and the English and the Caribs. Built around 1800, the fort was constructed 190' above the sea to defend *Calliaqua Bay*. There are two batteries on the island (one facing inland and one facing to sea) one at the summit, and one approximately 40' below the top, and both contain 24-pound guns and an 8" mortar. Until recently there were 250 steps leading to the top, however they are now in a state of severe disrepair and it is extremely difficult at best to gain the top. However, if you find a way to climb to the top take a look at the gun emplacements, you will marvel at the effort involved with getting the armaments up to the top of this rock. You can catch a water taxi from Villa to the dock at *Ft. Duvernette* and Young Island.

Navigational Information

When heading south from Kingstown, give Cane Garden Point a wide berth before turning to the east/southeast and entering *Great Head Bay* as shown on Chart STV-1; there is shallow water and a submerged rock lying about 200' off the point.

As shown on Chart STV-10, a waypoint at 13° 07.90' N, 61° 12.50' W, will place you approximately ½ mile west/southwest of the anchorage area in Carenage, usually called *Young Island Cut*.

From the waypoint, steer a bit north of east to enter the cut between Young Island and the mainland; be sure to give the shallows north of Young Island and the shoal water south and east of Dike Island a fair berth. If you are approaching Young Island from the south, you can head for the above waypoint, or steer to a waypoint at 13° 07.30' N, 61° 12.30' W, which will place you approximately ½ miles southwest of the entrance to the eastern channel leading to *Young Island Cut* from *Calliaqua Bay* as shown on Chart STV-10. From this waypoint, steer well to the east of Young Island keeping the green marker at edge of the reef east of Young Island safely to port and the white light marking the shoal to that lies south of Rookes Point to starboard as you head northward in the deeper water of the channel east of Young Island.

Bear in mind that there is a westward setting current along the southern coast of St. Vincent that can be as strong as two knots. This current may reverse during the early stages of a flood tide and can create rough seas depending on wind speed and direction.

You can either anchor in *Young Island Cut* or pick one of several moorings. If you anchor, don't forget that the current is fickle here and that you'll need to set out a stern anchor to keep from spinning in a circle and running into your neighbors. Don't anchor too far south on the eastern shore of Young Island as there is a submerged cable leading to the mainland from the northeastern tip of Young Island as shown on the chart.

Because the cut is so deep and anchoring can be difficult at times, I recommend that you pick up one of the moorings available, but if you take a mooring remember that competing companies (two taxi drivers) have placed moorings here and the competition between the two has been heated at times, though usually nothing more than posturing and a few angry words. I have no personal experience with this rivalry, however other cruisers have warned me that there have been occasions where one company's mooring lines were sabotaged and boats were set adrift as a result; so use caution. To avoid any conflict it's best to give the owners a shout on the VHF before picking up a mooring. Try hailing *Charlie Tango* or *Sam's Taxi*, my personal favorite, on VHF ch. 16 or 68). The owners feel that if you rent their mooring you are obligated to use their taxi. At the time of this writing mooring fees are US$15 for boats up to 89' in length, and US$25 for vessels over 90'.

What You Will Find Ashore
Customs and *Immigration*

If you need to clear *Customs* and *Immigration* from *Young Island Cut* you can catch a bus on the main road, or have *Sam's Taxi Service* take you into Kingstown to handle that matter. You can also pay *Sam's Taxi* to handle clearance for you leaving you free to enjoy yourself. Sam's clearance charges are US$60 for vessels up to 80'; US$100 for vessels up to 129'; and US$200 for vessels over 130'. Sam can also arrange to get your imported parts through *Customs* with little if any red tape. *Charlie Tango* can also take you into Kingstown to clear. You can contact *Sam's Taxi Service* or *Charlie Tango* on VHF ch. 16 or 68.

Getting Around

Sam's Taxi can also arrange car rentals and guided tours for you, *Charlie Tango* owns the other group of moorings in *Young Island Cut* and also runs a taxi and tour service that can be of great assistance to cruisers. If you are headed to Bequia you'll be happy to know that *Sam's Taxi* offers service there.

Internet Access

Sam's Taxi operates an excellent Wi-fi system that you can easily pick up aboard your vessel in *Young Island Cut*.

Marine Facilities

Sam's Taxi Service is who you need to call to handle your laundry and propane needs (even though if you rent a car you can take your own bottles to the *Texaco* station by the airport in nearby Arnos Vale (steel tanks only, aluminum tanks are sent to Bequia for filling). Sam can also arrange duty-free fuel in large amounts for mega-yachts. *Sam's Taxi Service* also broadcasts two daily weather forecasts at 0900 and 1730 with announcements on VHF ch. 16/68 before moving to ch. 06 for the weather. Sam can also dispose of garbage, EC$5 per bag.

Charlie Tango also offers help in matters relating to laundry, fuel, garbage, and propane.

Provisions

Shopping in southern St. Vincent focuses on the area around the airport. Just across from the terminal is the *Sunrise Supermarket*, a large and well-stocked market that is part of the *C.K. Greaves* family. On the road to Calliaqua is *Aunt Jobe's Supermarket* and an *Ace Hardware* store. Not to be outdone, *Delco* offers groceries and hardware. In Calliaqua you'll find *Gourmet Food* with an excellent selection of hard to find food items. If you feel like fresh fish, visit the fish market in Calliaqua in the afternoons.

Dining

Young Island is home to one of the most successful first-class hotels in the eastern Caribbean, the 32-acre *Young Island Resort* (monitors VHF ch. 68). The restaurant requires reservations if you wish to dine in luxury on their imported meats and poultry. On Saturday nights check out the barbecue with live steel band music.

For gourmet French dining with a West Indian flair, try *The French Verandah*, usually just called *The French*. Said to be the absolute best restaurant on St. Vincent, if it's not, it has to be in the top two or three.

A lively, popular eatery is *Xcape*. Here you can enjoy the upstairs open-air view of *Young Island Cut* and eat a great meal at an even better price. Friday nights are loud and packed with live music for your enjoyment. Another favorite local hangout is *The Boat Club* with a pool table and Karaoke. They're open daily from 0700 until late.

Beachcomber's is another casual spot but with a twist; *Beachcomber's* offers rooms and has a spa/gym on site as well. *Sunset Shores* is a small hotel just off the western end of the beach next to *Beachcombers*. With a good view of *Young Island Cut* and a pool, the happy hours make for good limin'. The *Paradise Beach Hotel is* on the opposite end of the beach and is strong on live music and Friday night Captain's barbecues.

Northwest of *Young Island Cut* is *Indian Bay*, home to the *Grand View Beach Hotel* with their *Grand View Grill* where you can dine and view the art of owner Caroline Sardine. *Wilkie's* is the hotel's restaurant, an excellent place to dine after enjoying the hotel's gym or tennis courts.

Calliaqua Bay and *Blue Lagoon*

In Calliaqua, every Friday evening the street comes alive in the *Calliaqua Culture Pot*. This is a community organized event, a street fair if you will, featuring local cuisine, loud music, singing, dancing, and all sorts of sidewalk barbecues and locally made crafts. Just outside Calliaqua, on the road to Ribishi, is the *Harmony Hill Sugar Mill,* where you'll find a windmill tower that dates to the late 1800s.

Blue Lagoon is a popular place for cruisers as well as charter boats. Several charter boat companies are located here including *TMM, Sunsail,* and *Barefoot Yacht Charters.*

Navigational Information
East of Young Island is *Calliaqua Bay* and *Blue Lagoon.* Approaching from *Young Island Cut* you can follow the channel alongside the eastern shore of Young Island using caution to keep in the center of it as it curves between the shoals east of Young Island marked by a green light, and the shoals to the south of Rookes Point that are marked by a white light as shown on Chart STV-10. Once clear of *Rookes Point Shoal* light turn to east to enter *Calliaqua Bay.*

A waypoint at 13° 07.30' N, 61° 12.30' W, will place you approximately ¼ mils southwest of the entrance to *Calliaqua Bay.* From the waypoint, head generally northeast to enter *Calliaqua Bay* as shown on the chart. You can anchor in the northern part of *Calliaqua Bay,* but some cruisers prefer to anchor at the eastern end of the bay near the *Barefoot Yachts* facility. The *St. Vincent Coast Guard* station stands by on VHF ch. 16/68 and if you're lucky you might see the *Captain Mulzac* or the *George MacIntosh* at the dock if they're not out on patrol.

Blue Lagoon is a pleasant, yet busy anchorage that lies just east of *Calliaqua Bay.* As shown on Chart STV-10, the western entrance into *Blue Lagoon* is shallow, but well marked with a pair of red and green-lighted markers. Pass between the marks, red-right-returning, and you'll pass over a shallow spot with a bit over 5' over it at MLW. You can hail Lagoon Marina on VHF ch. 68 for the latest information concerning the depth of the entrance channel. *Lagoon Marina* informs me that the cut carries 5'9" at low water, and almost 7½' at high water, but I found just a little bit less when I passed through last time.

Once inside *Blue Lagoon* you can get a slip at the marina or pick up one of the moorings that are available. It's possible to anchor here but there are so many moorings in the bay that there is little room to anchor with any swinging room. The red moorings belong to *TMM Charters* while the moorings with a stripe or bare foot on them belong to *Barefoot Charters*

(EC$15 per night). Both companies stand by on VHF ch. 16 and 68.

If possible, try to anchor or get a mooring as far to the eastern side of *Blue Lagoon* as you can to avoid some of the swells that work their way over the reef off Johnson Point. The swells are not dangerous, just a bit irritating at times.

There is a southern entrance to the lagoon that is wider and deeper (7' at MLW) than the marked entrance that you should use. The southern entrance is hard to see and if the seas are up it is not the place you'll want to be with reefs close on both sides of you.

What You Will Find Ashore
Marine Facilities
Marinas
The *Lagoon Marina and Hotel,* sometimes called *Sunsail Marina* since *Sunsail Charters* is based there, offers 40 slips with 110/220v 50-cycle electricity, water, fuel, showers and head ashore, ice, mechanical advice and repairs, 19 hotel rooms, a bar and restaurant, a small but well-stocked market, currency exchange, car rentals, Internet access, a laundry service, 2 swimming pools, phone and fax service and they monitor VHF ch. 16/68. If you need to dispose of some garbage, take your trash to the green building at the north end of the hotel's property.

Marine Facilities
Marine Services
Barefoot Charters is outside *Blue Lagoon* as shown on Chart STV-10, and they have 6 moorings in *Calliaqua Bay* and 20 inside *Blue Lagoon.* They are an *ASA* sailing school and have a fuel dock, water, ice, and fax and Internet service. If you need mechanical repairs the folks here can handle the work for you. Also on site is a sail loft, agents for *Doyle, Harken,* and *North.* Electronic repairs can also be handled here as they are also agents for *Raymarine* and *Tacktic.*

Barefoot Charters and Marine Center has become one of the premier marine facilities on St. Vincent. Located on the northeastern shore of *Calliaqua Bay,* just before the entrance to *Blue Lagoon,* the site is conveniently on the main highway and offers dockage as well as moorings (located in *Blue Lagoon*), a dinghy dock, a 20-boat charter fleet, a laundry, a small boutique, available taxis, Internet service, phone and fax service, free mail drop, ice, water, an excellent restaurant and bar, a book exchange, showers for guests, car rentals, and guided tours.

Also in *Calliaqua Bay* is the *St. Vincent Yacht Club* with a dock that has '6-7' of water. There is water and electricity at their dock and they are completing a fuel dock as of this writing. Also on the drawing board is a haul-out yard.

TMM has about 20 moorings in *Blue Lagoon* and can send a guide to lead you through the pass into the lagoon. They're open between 0800-1600 daily and also offer a fax service.

The *Blue Lagoon* area is home to a pair of chandlers and fabrication specialists. The two chandlers are *KP Marine*, a *Yamaha* and *Apex* dealer that sells duty-free outboards and general marine parts and *Howard's Marine*, an *OMC* and *Yanmar* dealer (two companies, same owner) just across from *KP*.

Nichol's Marine is located here and they are alternator and starter specialists as well as welders (stainless steel and aluminum) and fabricators. *Nichol's* can also pick up and ship to *GYE* in Bequia. A short jaunt from *Nichol's* is *Oscar's Machine Shop* for fabrication, engine and winch repairs.

Internet Access
TMM and *Sunsail* both have *Wi-fi* while *Barefoot Yacht Charters* and has a computer on site so you can check your email.

Provisions
In Calliaqua you'll find *Gourmet Food* with an excellent selection of hard to find food items.

Shopping in southern St. Vincent focuses on the area around the airport. Just across from the terminal is the *Sunrise Supermarket*, a large and well-stocked market that is part of the *C.K. Greaves* family. On the road to Calliaqua is *Aunt Jobe's Supermarket* and an *Ace Hardware* store. Not to be outdone, *Delco* offers groceries and hardware. In Calliaqua you'll find *Gourmet Food* with an excellent selection of hard to find food items. If you feel like fresh fish, visit the fish market in Calliaqua in the afternoons. And don't forget that *Blue Lagoon Marina* has a nice market on site.

Dining
Barefoot's Driftwood Restaurant sits above the bay with an excellent view of the surrounding waters including nearby Bequia. *Barefoot's* is open for breakfast, lunch, and dinner and offers specials to long-term guests. The *Surfside Restaurant* (VHF ch. 68) is located at the *St. Vincent Yacht Club* and features everything from pizza to pasta and from seafood to chicken.

Touring Inland St. Vincent

St. Vincent has a bit of a limited roadway system with the best roads lying in the more populous southern third of the island. Elsewhere the roads tend to be narrow and winding, but quite adequate to explore this scenic island. There are very few roads in the northern third of St. Vincent and no road completely encircles the entire island and on the northern coast, there is no road west of Fancy, which lies at the northernmost tip of St. Vincent and is only accessed by a road from the eastern shore. From Fancy there is only a narrow and difficult trail that works its way along the northwestern shore of St. Vincent down towards Richmond on the western shore of St. Vincent. Public transportation is available to Fancy, but taxis and private vehicles rarely go beyond Orange Hill and some don't like to go north of Georgetown.

On the western coast, the *Leeward Highway* winds north from Kingstown to its end at Chateaubelair. Although some maps show this road going on to Richmond Point, it is a rough road more suited for 4-wheel drive vehicles. Beyond Richmond Point the road becomes almost a path at times, while at other times it is virtually nonexistent in this, the most inaccessible part of St. Vincent.

The northern part of St. Vincent is dominated by the *Rabacca Dry River*, a unique area of volcanic rock that has to be constantly cleared to make and remake the road to the Carib villages of Orange Hill, Overland, *Sandy Bay*, Owia, and Fancy. In 1902, 2,000 people died in these villages when the volcano erupted and they were cut off by the river, which was no longer dry, and they found themselves trapped by the flow of lava. The people who live here today are descendants of the original Amerindian settlers of these islands, the Carib Indians. Once occupied by the old *Orange Hill Estates*, the original 3,200 acres have been subdivided into 350 subplots and are today known as *Rabacca Farms*. The old *Orange Hill Estate* was once one of the largest coconut plantations in the world and today coconut trees remain a part of the landscape here. The grand old estate house is now the headquarters for an agriculture diversification program. Here you'll find Chinese from Taiwan instructing the local farmers in the proper methods of growing new crops such as grapes and orchids, and teaching interested craftsmen to use bamboo and other indigenous materials. There is a small stone building dating to the days when the estate grew sugarcane and when the volcano erupted in 1902, the only survivors of the estate's work force were 40 people who crammed in here. Those who chose to occupy the estate house during the eruption died there.

In Owia, a must-see is the *Owia Salt Pond*, a series of natural pools in volcanic rock that originated from the La Soufrière volcano long, long ago. You must visit this beautiful area and take a dip in the pools, the climb down may be a bit daunting, but the overall experience is worth it. Owia is the location of the *Owia Arrowroot Processing Factory* where workers process the spice used in sauces and cookies and which has recently come into demand as a finish on computer paper. On the way to Owia stop at Georgetown, the old capital of St. Vincent (once a thriving sugar town and home to the defunct *Mount Bentinck Sugar Factory*) and eat on the verandah at *Ferdi's Restaurant*.

Between Fancy and Owia is an outcropping called Jumby Point (sometimes shown as Jumbie Point) that is named after supernatural creatures called *jumbies*. In St. Vincent and The Grenadines, *jumbies* start their mischief at nightfall. Those who fear *jumbies* will close their doors and windows at night to keep out these mischievous creatures. Men that must travel by night do so with a protective supply of tobacco in their pockets to ward off the *jumbies* while women will wear their underwear inside out as protection. St. Vincentians may also place a heap of sand at their doorstep to keep out the female witch *Cocomar* who must count each and every grain of sand before she can enter. This usually takes until dawn when she must leave, foiled in her attempt to enter the house. Livestock are often seen on St. Vincent adorned with red ribbons whose owners placed around their necks to prevent the devil from taking their form, or to protect them from spells cast upon them by neighbors. Similarly, black beads are often sewn into a person's clothing to protect them from evil as well.

On the eastern side of St. Vincent, east of the *Buccament Valley*, lies the *Mesopotamia Valley*, or *Mespo*, one of the richest and most productive agricultural areas on the island. *Mespo* is planted all around with banana trees, breadfruit, sugar cane, and almost every other fruit that grows in these islands. This is a must-visit area with unsurpassed views of St. Vincent's mountain ridges dominated by the 3,181' Grande Bonhomme. Several streams come together here to flow southeastward to cascade over the rocks into the sea in the Yambou Gorge. North of Mesopotamia is Montreal, not a settlement, rather it's just a spot on the map, but it has great views of the mountains to the sea. *Montreal Gardens* is a series of well-tended gardens with a romantic picture-book rental cottage sitting on the edge of a lovely stream.

On the windward side of the island, north of Montreal, you'll find the *Black Point Tunnel*, constructed in 1815 by Colonel Thomas Browne with the help of Caribs and slaves at a cost of 5,000 pounds. The 350' long tunnel links Grand Sable with *Byera Bay* and was built to hasten the shipment of sugar from the estates on the northern end of St. Vincent.

St. Vincent to The Grenadines
When heading south to Bequia from St. Vincent, be aware of the strong west/northwest setting current in the *Bequia Channel*. When the tidal current runs counter to the above-mentioned current, the current is lessened however particularly nasty seas can result in the right conditions (or would that be the wrong conditions?). Another curious effect when this occurs is currents setting in two different directions. For instance, the current close in the St. Vincent shoreline, and the current close in the northern Bequia shoreline may be most affected by the tide and consequently flow in an east/southeast direction, while the central axis of the current in the *Bequia Channel* will still set in a west/northwest direction.

The Grenadines

Port of Entry: Bequia (Port Elizabeth), Union Island (Clifton)
Fuel: Bequia, Union Island
Haul-Out: None
Diesel Repairs: Bequia, Canouan, Mayreau, Union Island
Outboard Repairs: Bequia, Canouan, Mayreau, Union Island
Propane: St. Vincent, Bequia
Provisions: Bequia, Union Island, Mustique, Canouan, Mayreau, Petite Martinique
Important Lights: See *Appendix A*

The Spanish sailors who first sighted the Grenadines in the late 1400s, called these islands *Los Pajaros*, *The Birds*, because when on the horizon the cays looked like tiny birds in flight. Over the next two centuries, the name was changed to *Grenadinos*, meaning *Little Grenadas*, which also originated with the Spanish sailors. When the English took control they adopted the name that had then came to be the Grenadines.

The Grenadines are probably the most popular cruising destination in the Eastern Caribbean, with cruisers from America, Europe, and South Africa making this fifty-mile long chain of 32 islands their primary destination. There is a large winter cruising community here, not to mention the ever-present charter fleet, and even in summer, these islands are extremely popular due to their location at the southern end of the hurricane belt.

The Grenadines are politically part of St. Vincent and The Grenadines, and were created as a result of a volcanic eruption of Grenada. The largest of the Grenadines, Carriacou and Petite Martinique are politically part of Grenada and we'll discuss Carriacou in the next chapter on Grenada.

Ports of Entry in the Grenadines are at Bequia (Port Elizabeth in *Admiralty Bay*), and at Clifton on Union Island. One can clear in or out of St. Vincent and the Grenadines in either place. Be advised that jet skis and spearfishing are prohibited in the Grenadines. For a chart of the northern Grenadines, see Chart GND-1, Bequia to Canouan; the southern Grenadines are shown on Chart GND-7, Canouan to Carriacou.

If you are on St. Vincent and wish to visit the Grenadines by some other means than your own boat, you can take either of two ferries, the M/V *Barracuda* (784-455-9835) or the M/V *Gem Star* (784-526-1158), that sail daily from St. Vincent to Canouan, Mayreau, and Union Island with stops at Bequia on Tuesdays. For more information visit the *Tourist Office* at the main dock.

The Northern Grenadines

Bequia

Bequia, pronounced "Beck-way," comes from the Carib word, *Becouya*, meaning *Island of the Clouds*, is the northernmost of the Grenadines lying approximately 9 miles south of St. Vincent and is roughly 7 square miles in area. A lot of Bequia's population of almost 5,000 is of strong Scottish descent (and a few of French descent) and you'll find folks with surnames such as Wallace, MacIntosh, Ollivierre, Quashie, and Simmons.

In general, the islanders have a deeply rooted history with the sea, whalers, traders, and boat builders who have constructed hundreds of wooden vessels on the island over the years. The largest boat built in the Caribbean was the *Gloria Colita*, a 131' schooner that traded in the Caribbean and Atlantic from Venezuela to the United States. The schooner was owned by Reginald Mitchell whose family has owned the *Frangipani Hotel* in *Admiralty Bay* since the early years of the 20th century when it was their private home and the downstairs was used as a storage room for the schooner's gear.

As a side note, in 1940, the *Gloria Colita* was found drifting in the Bermuda Triangle with no crew aboard, one of many strange stories about this strange place. In more recent years, Bob Dylan's 68' schooner, *Water Pearl*, was built on the beach in Bequia by Californian Chris Bowman and a crew of Bequia shipwrights headed up by Nolly Simmons and Albert Crosby. *Water Pearl* was the last of the two-masted gaff-rigged schooners built on the island. A 25' sailboat, *Plumbelly*, built by Bequia's Loren Dewar and German born Klaus Alverman, later circumnavigated with singlehander Alverman aboard.

Bequia is the largest and most developed of the Grenadines and with a new airport that opened in the last decade, more and more tourists are discovering

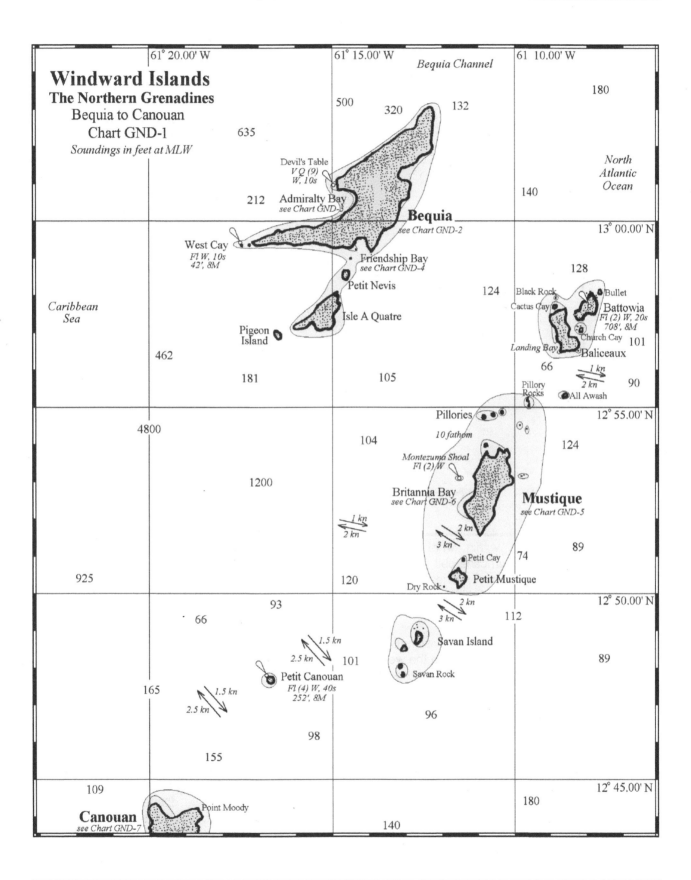

Windward Islands
The Northern Grenadines
Bequia to Canouan
Chart GND-1
Soundings in feet at MLW

61° 20.00' W

61° 15.00' W

61 10.00' W

Bequia Channel

180

500   320   132

635

*North
Atlantic
Ocean*

Devil's Table
*V Q (9)
W, 10s*

140

212   Admiralty Bay
see Chart GND-3

Bequia
see Chart GND-2

13° 00.00' N

West Cay
*Fl W, 10s
42', 8M*

128

124   Black Rock   Bullet
Cactus Cay   **Battowia**
*Fl (2) W, 20s
708', 8M*

Friendship Bay
see Chart GND-4

Petit Nevis

Church Cay   101

*Caribbean
Sea*

Isle A Quatre

Landing Bay   **Baliceaux**

66   1 kn
2 kn   90

Pigeon
Island

Pillory
Rocks   All Awash

462

181   105

12° 55.00' N

4800

104   Pillories

124

10 fathom

*Montezuma Shoal
Fl (2) W*

1200   Britannia Bay
see Chart GND-6

Mustique
see Chart GND-5

1 kn
2 kn   2 kn   89

3 kn

925   120   Petit Cay   74

Petit Mustique

Dry Rock

12° 50.00' N

2 kn
3 kn   112

93

66

1.5 kn

Savan Island   89

2.5 kn   101

165   1.5 kn   Petit Canouan
*Fl (4) W, 40s
252', 8M*   Savan Rock

2.5 kn

96

98

155

109   12° 45.00' N

Canouan
see Chart GND-7   Point Moody   180

140

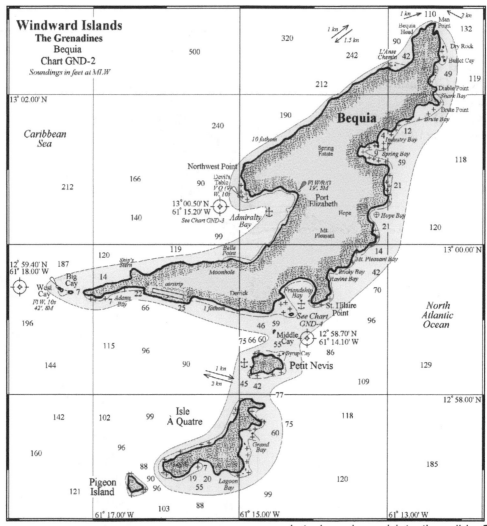

Windward Islands
The Grenadines
Bequia
Chart GND-2
Soundings in feet at MLW

Caribbean Sea

Bequia

North Atlantic Ocean

her charms. Although within what insurance underwriters view as the hurricane belt in the North Atlantic Ocean, Bequia has not experienced a major hurricane in over 50 years as most threatening storms pass north of the island.

The two harbors of interest for cruisers visiting Bequia are located at *Admiralty Bay*, located on the western shore of Bequia, and at *Friendship Bay* on the south coast of the island. There is a lee anchorage at Petit Nevis that's best used as a daytime anchorage only.

For those of you who are windsurfers, *Industry Bay*, on the northeast coast of Bequia offers good snorkeling and windsurfing for beginners, while further south, *Hope Bay* offers windsurfing for those who are definitely not novices. The *Old Hegg Turtle Sanctuary* at Industry is also worth a stop. There is a small fee for entrance, but it goes to a good cause, the preservation of small sea turtles until they are old

enough to be released into the wild. The kids will love it.

Admiralty Bay (Port Elizabeth)

Waypoints:
Admiralty Bay- ½ nm W of
13° 00.50' N, 61° 15.20' W

When heading south to Bequia from St. Vincent, be aware of the strong west/northwest setting current in the *Bequia Channel*. When the tidal current runs counter to the above-mentioned current, the current is lessened however particularly nasty seas can result in the right conditions (or would that be the wrong conditions?). Another curious effect when this occurs is currents setting in two different directions. For instance, the current close in the St. Vincent shoreline, and the current close in the northern Bequia shoreline may be most affected by the tide and consequently

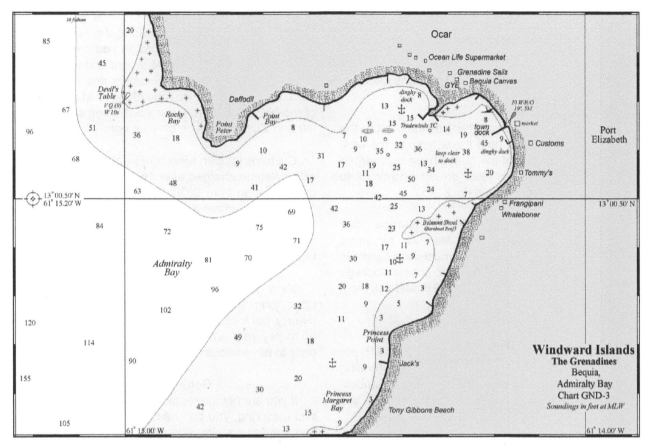

The chart shows Admiralty Bay, Bequia, with numerous depth soundings in feet at MLW. Labeled features include: Ocar, Ocean Life Supermarket, Grenadine Sails, Bequia Canvas, GYE, dinghy dock, Tradewinds YC, town dock, market, Customs, Tommy's, Frangipani, Whaleboner, Belmont Shoal (Bareboat Reef), Devil's Table VQ(9) W 10s, Daffodil, Rocky Bay, Point Peter, Point Bay, Admiralty Bay, Princess Point, Jack's, Princess Margaret Bay, Tony Gibbons Beach, Port Elizabeth. Coordinates marked: 13° 00.50' N 61° 15.20' W, 61° 15.00' W, 61° 14.00' W. Box legend: Windward Islands, The Grenadines, Bequia, Admiralty Bay, Chart GND-3, Soundings in feet at MLW.

flow in an east/southeast direction, while the central axis of the current in the *Bequia Channel* will still set in a west/northwest direction.

St. Vincent lies over your stern and you're reaching to *Admiralty Bay*. The chances are that long before you reach *Admiralty Bay* you'll be met by a young man in a small inflatable, in fact, you may hear him before you actually see him if you're not paying attention. Do not wave him off, the man is not a boat boy wanting to help you tie up to one of his moorings, the man is Kenmore Henville, and he is on a mission. Kenmore will likely appear out of nowhere, and even if you don't see him, you might hear him and mistake his whistle for an alarm going off on your boat. You'll notice the young man harnessed into his dinghy in the surging waters, blowing a whistle, and aligning himself with the light to snap a photograph of your boat as you approach Bequia (so make sure your sails are full and that you're looking good for posterity).

Twenty-six year-old Kenmore learned his craft from Tim Wright, an English photographer who spends a good bit of time on the island, and today Kenmore greets visiting yachts well offshore, in all sorts of seas,

bashing about trying to get the best shot of your boat. Later, after you're anchored, Kenmore will drop by to offer to sell you the photo, with or without a frame, and believe me, he does good work. Who wouldn't want one of his 8" x 10" glossies of their boat bashing through the waves on a close haul into Bequia? The prices are fair, especially when you consider that Kenmore virtually risks his life at times, then has to dash ashore and develop the photos, make prints, frame them, and then find you before you raise anchor and head elsewhere.

Navigational Information

As shown on Chart GND-2, and in detail on Chart GND-3, a waypoint at 13° 00.50' N, 61° 15.20' W, will place you approximately ½ mile west of the anchorage area in *Admiralty Bay*. If you are approaching from the north, St. Vincent, give the *Devil's Table* off Northwest Point a wide berth.

If you are approaching from the south, give a wide berth to West Cay at the southwestern tip of Bequia. A waypoint at 12° 59.40' N, 61° 18.10' W, will place you approximately ½ mile west of West Cay and clear of any dangers. From this point, you can parallel the shoreline close in past *Moonhole* (see Chart GND-2) to anchor in *Admiralty Bay* (see Chart GND-3). When anchoring avoid blocking the ferry dock and *Belmont Shoal*. Use caution to avoid the shoals on the eastern shore of *Admiralty Bay*, from *Tony Gibbons Beach* to *Belmont Shoal*.

Avoid the large ship buoys lying off the point by the *Tradewinds Yacht Club* (and the wrecks to the west of the buoys). Some of the buoys have submerged hoses running to them. Also, do not anchor as to block the channel to the town dock.

Slips are available at *Bequia Marina*, see the section *Marine Facilities, Marinas*, for more information. Please note that you must clear *Customs* and *Immigration* before attempting to access dockage at the marina or hail the marina on VHF and ask them for permission to dock before clearing.

Moorings are available, call *Daffodil* on VHF ch. 67. At the time of this writing the fee was US$15 per night. There is some question as to the legal standing of the moorings other than those offered by *Daffodil*. Use caution when picking one, dive to check it, and always get a receipt.

There is a 5-knot speed limit in *Admiralty Bay* that applies to ALL vessels including water taxis and dinghies. The only place where speeds greater than 5 knots are permitted is in the shipping channel in the center of the harbor.

What You Will Find Ashore
Port Elizabeth is a very friendly town, very lively with lots of people mingling about and some just liming. Cruisers will enjoy the daily *Cruiser's Net* at 0800 on VHF ch. 68.

Dinghy Docks
There are several places to tie up your dinghy in Port Elizabeth, the most popular being the small dock off the market that sits just north of the large ferry dock. To the south of the ferry dock is a small "L" shaped dinghy dock that sits just across from the *Bequia Bookstore* and south of the *Customs* building. On the extreme northern shore of *Admiralty Bay* is another dinghy dock that services the marine facilities along that shore in the area known as Ocar.

Customs and *Immigration*
Either of the two docks in town (not the one in

Ocar) will be within a hundred yards or so of the *Customs* building. If you tie up to the northernmost dock, tie off as close to shore as you can and walk to the road. At the road take a right and within a few yards, you'll come to the *Customs* and *Immigration* office that sits on the left side of the road at the head of the ferry dock. From the southernmost dock, turn left and *Customs* will be on your right.

Customs is open Monday-Friday from 0830-1800 with overtime charged after 1600. On Saturdays the office is open from 0830-1200 and then from 1500-1800 when overtime is charged. Sundays and holidays they are open from 0900-1200 and from 1500-1800 with overtime charges in effect at all times. *Customs* in Bequia is now using the *eSeaClear* system.

It's a good idea to clear in early here, there are often long lines, not for *Customs* or *Immigration* usually, but for the cashier where you too will have to go to pay your entry fees as many locals come here daily to pay various bills.

Getting Around
If you are not interested in walking around Bequia and exploring, you can hail a taxi on VHF ch. 68 or find a driver hanging about under the almond tree in Port Elizabeth. There are local buses that can take you to various parts of the island or you can rent a car or scooter in town (see *Appendix C5: Service Facilities in the Grenadines*). If you need a water taxi, they hang out on VHF ch. 68. Rates for 1-4 people range from EC$20-EC$25.

Internet Access
There is good *Wi-fi* coverage in *Admiralty Bay* courtesy of *HotHotHotSpot, Mega, Bequia Tech*, and *Sam's Taxi*, and you should not have a problem getting online.

Located on *Front Street*, Port Elizabeth, next to *Bagos Pizza Hut*, *Bequia Tech* offers high speed Internet access, international phone calls, wireless hotspot, fax services, laptop connections, PDA hookups, photocopies, computer parts and repairs, and some publishing facilities. *Bequia Tech* is also a *Digcell* dealer.

Several businesses such as the *Gingerbread Café, Frangipani, Maria's French Terrace, The Fig Tree Restaurant*, and *Sail Relax Explore* have free *Wi-fi* for their customers.

If you need to use a computer you can visit *RMS* (just across from the market), *Bequia Land and Home*, *Bequia Technology Center* next to *Andy's*, or *ACS Computer Services* next to *Coco's Place* (they manage the *HotHotHotSpot* system in *Admiralty Bay*).

Marine Facilities
Marinas

Bequia Marina (VHF ch. 16 and 68) is located at the tip of the spit shown on the chart as *Tradewinds Yacht Club* (the marina is owned by *Tradewind Cruises*).

The marina, besides being home to the owner's fleet, is also open to the public, but there are times, usually the weekends, when there is no room at the dock for transients due to the charter boats enjoying Port Elizabeth. However, the marina also has two moorings located about 100' off their dock.

As you approach the marina, give them a hail on VHF ch. 16 (if you have not cleared in yet, you must take care of that formality before getting a slip at the marina or hail the marina on VHF for permission to dock).

The fuel dock is open Monday-Fridays from 0800-1600, and Saturdays from 0800-1500. You can also pick up ice and water here. I prefer to buy my diesel here due to the purity of the fuel compared to that offered by other vendors around the bay who tend to sell cheaper, imported (Venezuelan) fuel. If you wish to jerry jug fuel from town, just to the right of the market is a *Shell* station where you can get gas or diesel.

Marine Facilities
Marine Supplies

The area along the northern shore of *Admiralty Bay* where *Bequia Marina* is located is known as Ocar, and is home to many of *Admiralty Bay*'s marine services (see chart GND-3) with several good dinghy docks available.

Cruises will enjoy dealing with the folks at *Daffodil Marine Services* for water, ice (cubed and block), garbage removal, filtered diesel, and laundry. *Daffodil* monitors VHF chs. 67/68 and has moorings for rent in the harbor. *Daffodil* also offers electrical repairs and has rooms for rent.

The best chandlers in Port Elizabeth are located in Ocar. *GYE, Grenadine Yacht Equipment*, are agents for *Evinrude* and can handle repairs on all brands as well as filling propane tanks, offering block ice and fax service, a book swap, and carrying a good selection of marine hardware and rigging. *GYE* monitors VHF ch. 16 and 68. *GYE* can have your fabrication needs sent to *Oscar's Machine Shop* in Calliaqua, St. Vincent, and if you have a starter or alternator that needs reworking, they can ship it to *Nichols Marine* (also in Calliaqua, St. Vincent) for repair.

Nearby is *Wallace & Co.*, the place to go for fishing and diving supplies. *Wallace & Co.*, an *Icom* dealer, also has a nice book swap with all donations going to the *Sunshine School for Disabled Children*.

Located underneath *Alick's Sail Loft* is *Piper Marine* carrying a good line of marine hardware, paints, fittings, and rigging items (they also handle rigging repairs-see Don Lewis), and they even rent mountain bikes.

Lulley's Tackle Shop is a good stop for fishing supplies, bait, and some marine goods including foul weather gear, courtesy flags, and wire and rope.

If you require specialized woods, visit Caribbean woods for South American hardwoods with a good woodworking shop on site.

Marine Facilities
Marine Services

Near *Wallace & Co.* you'll find *Simpson Engineering* better known as *Fixman Engineering*, a full-service repair facility offering diesel repairs, fabrication, stainless and aluminum welding, and electrical and electronic repairs.

For mechanical help call Tyrone at *Caribbean Diesel* (VHF ch. 68), agents for *Perkins* and *Northern Lights*. Tyrone is also familiar with *Cummins, Detroit Diesel, GM's*, and *Yanmar*, and can help with your electrical problems.

For general repairs ranging from diesel engines to watermakers, starters, alternators, refrigeration and electrics and plumbing, try *KMS Marine Services*. Owner Kerry also welds and can arrange for specialty welding or fabrication from St. Vincent.

For refrigeration repairs, try *Knock Refrigeration* located a couple of doors up from *GYE.*

Marine Facilities
Sail and Canvas Repairs
If you need canvas or sail repairs, *Ocar* is the place to go. Here you'll find *Grenadines Sails* just across from *Bequia Marina*, where you can get repairs completed or a new sail built. They are agents for *North Sails* and monitor VHF ch. 16 and 68.

Bequia Canvas, located near *GYE*, handles strictly canvas work from awnings to dodgers and everything in between including upholstery (indoor and outdoor) and monitors VHF ch. 68.

Alick monitors VHF ch. 68 and is located a street over from the dinghy dock (they used to be located in Ocar). Alick handles sails, awnings, cushions, and boat covers, at reasonable prices and has a good selection of materials from which to choose.

Sews Simle is a small sewing shop located behind *Island Things.* Owner Cassandra can repair your wardrobe and even make some new curtains for your boat or perhaps some bags to help you carry your grocery items back to the boat.

Garbage
Free garbage drop off is available at the dumpsters by the market at the head of the dinghy dock. *Daffodil* will take away your garbage from boatside for EC$3/small bag and EC$5/large bag. You can also drop off your garbage at *Bequia Marina* for EC$5 per bag.

Medical Needs
The Government of St. Vincent and the Grenadines appoints a doctor to serve Bequia. This doctor attends his clinic every day except Sunday from 1600-1800, and there is even a private physician on the island. The clinic/hospital in Port Elizabeth can deal with minor emergencies and illnesses, but the more serious cases are sent to Kingstown on St. Vincent for treatment.

Propane
You can drop off your propane bottles at *Grenadine Yacht Equipment* and pick them up the next day.

Laundry
Daffodil will do your laundry for EC$25 per 10 lbs. *Lighthouse Laundry* will also do your laundry, picked up and delivered for only EC$20 a load, and they have same day service as well as a taxi if you need one. Both of these services monitor VHF ch. 68 and *Daffodil's* also monitors VHF ch. 67.

Miranda's Laundry monitors VHF ch. 68 and will pick up and deliver to your boat. Miranda can be reached by phone at 784-530-6865. *Lighthouse Laundry* (VHF ch. 68), is also available for boatside laundry pickup and delivery. They have a Laundromat in town by the power generating station and offer showers for a small fee. Nearby, *Handy Andy* has washers and dryers available for your use.

You can also hail *Papa Mitch* on VHF ch. 68 for laundry service or phone him at 784-458-7222. His laundry is located next to the *Bequia Bookstore*.

Provisions
Without a doubt, Bequia is the best place in the Grenadines to provision your vessel, and you can do it yourself or have someone do it for you. *Sail Relax Explore* offers a provisioning service and can even bring in items from St. Vincent if they cannot be found locally.

When anchored in *Admiralty Bay*, at some point you will likely meet a vendor in a small boat offering ice, water, baked goods, and fresh produce or fish. Use your judgment as to what is a good deal, prices and quality varies from boat to boat.

As with most islands and ports, there is a fresh market here just ashore of the main dock. Just inside the northernmost dinghy dock, right on the side of the road, you'll find the fresh fish and produce market (a few yards north of the market is a dumpster for your garbage). Sadly, over the last few years the vendors have been getting more and more aggressive and today a lot of folks skip the market and head for one of the town's several fine grocery stores.

A few yards to the north of the main dock is *Mauvin's Model Boatshop* (see photo next page-a MUST stop in Port Elizabeth), and just behind *Mauvin's* is *Doris' Fresh Food & Yacht Provisioning,* once known as *Doris Fine Foods* (monitors VHF ch. 16 and 68). Just as Bequia is the best place for provisions, *Doris' Fresh Foods* is the best place to provision. *Doris' Fresh Foods* has the best selection of frozen meats, fresh produce, and baked good on the island.

Not to be outdone, the *Shoreline Mini-Market*, which is connected to the restaurant of the same name, is open the same hours as the restaurant and will even open on Sundays (their day off) if you give them advance notice. You can land your dinghy on the beach just outside the market.

On a quiet back street, the road above *Frangipani*, by *Alick's,* is *Euroshopper* (VHF ch. 68), a small market that gives bulk wholesale prices. Next to the *Bistro* is *Select Wines* (sometimes called the *Select Store*) for those seeking to refill their spirits locker as well as pick up some nice deli items such as cheeses, meats, bread, and canned goodies.

Lina's Delicatessen offers some very tasty freshly baked items in the *Shoreline Plaza* just south of the *Customs* office. You can also grab a sandwich and a cup of coffee here as well as a large number of specialty foods.

Just below *Coco's* is a branch of the St. Vincent establishment, *Gourmet Foods* (in Calliaqua on the southern end of St. Vincent near *Young Island Cut*).

Next to *Shell* station is another open air market where you can pick up T-shirts and crafts. Across the street is *Knight's Supermarket*. Although they don't carry fresh produce, *Knight's* has many good deals and lots of freshly baked goods. They'll even deliver to the dock for you.

Mauvin's Model Boatshop, Port Elizabeth, Bequia

The beach at *Admiralty Bay*, Bequia

If you require organic produce, free from pesticides, visit *Nature Zone* in Lower Bay.

Dining

As far as restaurants go, I could turn this cruising guide into a restaurant guide if I wasn't careful here. You have your choice of numerous places to dine, I could write a paragraph about each restaurant and probably the only effect it would have would be to use more paper and drive up the cost of this guide. Besides, it's fun to check out all the best places to eat, don't go by my opinion, formulate your own! I'll just highlight my favorite places to dine here in Port Elizabeth.

The *Devil's Table Bar and Restaurant* at *Bequia Marina* always serves top-of-the-line food on a delightful deck over the waters of *Admiralty Bay*, it's a good yachtie-type hangout, The restaurant opens daily at 1500 and is closed on Sundays.

Bequia's favorite (and oldest) rendezvous, the *Frangipani Hotel*, features a great Thursday night barbecue. *Frangipani Yacht Services* monitors VHF ch. 68 and has a mail drop, telephone, fax, and email service, and is here to help the visiting boater. The hotel has been owned by the Mitchell family for over a century and the current owner, Son Mitchell, is the former PM of St. Vincent and the Grenadines, and his daughter, Sabrina, is the manager.

For ambience, it takes a lot to beat the pleasant seating under the trees at *Gingerbread* in Bequia. *Gingerbread*, also managed by Sabrina Mitchell from *Frangipani*. *Gingerbread*, which is open for breakfast, lunch, and dinner, has an elegant upper level dining area with a fantastic view of *Admiralty Bay* and often has live music for your enjoyment. While you're here you might want to visit *Maranne's* for gourmet ice cream, yogurt, and sorbet, all homemade.

A shady spot, Port Elizabeth, Bequia

Next to *Frangipani* is the *Whaleboner Inn* with its own dinghy dock. Here you can dine on authentic island dishes or sit down at a bar that is carved from the jawbone of a whale with barstools made from a whale's vertebrae. While here check out their wonderful boutique for handmade clothing.

The Old Fig Tree, now called *The Fig Tree* (located next to *Mac's Pizza*-the BEST pizza on the island), and the *Sunny Caribee* are two excellent restaurants in Port Elizabeth, and are almost as old as the *Frangipani*. *The Fig Tree* has re-opened under the management of Cheryl Johnson, the manager of the *Bequia Bookshop* (another stop you MUST make while in Port Elizabeth).

A very popular spot for locals as well as visitors, and with the largest book swap on the island, is the *Porthole*, owned by Noeline Taylor.

Located behind *Bequia Marina* is *Coco's*, a popular spot with live music on Tuesdays and Fridays, and a Sunday buffet lunch that should not be missed.

In *Lower Bay*, just south of *Tony Gibbon's Beach*, don't miss *Mango's Beach Bar and Grill*, open daily from 0900. Great ambiance, superb fare, and crowded on the weekends.

Moonhole

Moonhole is a very interesting area lying just a bit southwest of the anchorage in *Admiralty Bay* and west of Paget Farm. Made famous in National Geographic magazine, *Moonhole* is a private development of 17 houses built by American Tom Johnston. Here, beautiful large homes are built of rock and are nestled in and on the cliffs along the water's edge. The area gets its name from the natural arch formation at the

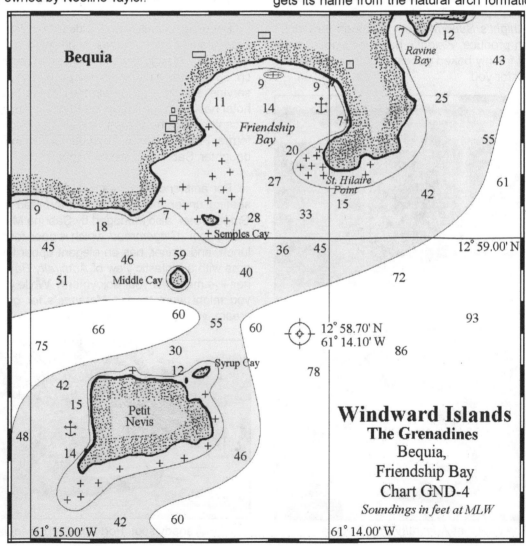

water's edge. The sky seen through the arch is said to resemble a moon peaking through the arch, hence the name. You can take a tour of the *Moonhole* development (EC$40 per person, contact *Moonhole* on VHF ch. 6), check with the taxi drivers in town for the latest info on times and dates. The original house in the development is now empty, the result of a large boulder crashing into the owner's bedroom one night. A convincing reason to move elsewhere.

Paget Farm

At *Paget Farm*, on Bequia's southern coast, you can meet Sam McDowell, one of the world's top scrimshanders who maintains a winter home at Paget Farm. Scrimshaw is the traditional seaman's art of etching seafaring scenes on whale's teeth, bones and other hard materials like oak wood and a maker of scrimshaw is called a scrimshander. Sam McDowell hails from Carmel, California and has formal training as an artist. He first came to the Caribbean on board the charter schooner *Ramona* during the 1960s and he became interested in the deep maritime history of the region. In the early 1970s, Sam built a house above a beach overlooking Isle a Quatre (pronounced *Oily Cot* by Bequians).

Scrimshaw is a painstakingly delicate work, and McDowell's worktable reflects that. The large magnifying glass and light give him adequate magnification and light to create his intricate carvings. As with the seaman of yesteryear, Sam McDowell's work reflects the sea, as do his paintings, yes, he's not just a scrimshander, he paints as well. Now before some of you go screaming about whales being protected and just where does Sam get his teeth, let me just say one word; micarta, an imitation ivory. Today Sam creates micarta pieces, including knives, which can go for upwards of $500.

But whales teeth and knife handles are not Sam's only products. With his wife Donna's assistance, the couple create a form of 19th century sailor's art called the *Sailor's Valentine*, unique gifts made of seashells inlaid in a small box. If you get over to Paget Farm, look up Sam McDowell at his *Banana Patch Studio* and check out his art. You can also pick up some of Sam's work at the *Bequia Bookstore*.

Friendship Bay

Waypoints:
West Cay- ½ nm W of
12° 59.40' N, 61° 18.10' W

Friendship Bay- ½ nm S of entrance
12° 58.70' N, 61° 14.10' W

Friendship Bay is the center of whaling activity on Bequia, and a pleasant, secure, if not rolly anchorage. It's a great place to hide when northerly swells are running (preferable to *Admiralty Bay* in that regard), and a good spot to begin a cruise to Mustique.

Navigational Information
As shown on Chart GND-2, and in detail on Chart GND-4, a waypoint at 12° 58.70' N, 61° 14.10' W, will place you approximately ½ mile south of the entrance to *Friendship Bay*. From the waypoint head a bit west of north staying mid-channel between the reefs off Semples Cay (sometimes shown as Semplers Cay) and the reefs off St. Hilaire Point to anchor on the eastern side of *Friendship Bay*. Beware of the wreck that lies about 300 yards west of the docks and only 200 yards or so off the beach.

If you are approaching from St. Vincent or Mustique, you should have no problems passing to windward of Bequia, just watch out for the currents at the northern tip of Bequia. If you're approaching from *Admiralty Bay*, pass along the southern shore of the bay towards West Cay as shown on Chart GND-2. Once past West Cay, you'll be turning to port, to windward, and heading for the gap between Petit Nevis and the mainland of Bequia. You can pass between Petit Nevis and Middle Cay, or pass north of Middle Cay between Middle Cay and Semples Cay. I prefer to pass south of Middle Cay and avoid getting too close to the reefs off Semples Cay.

What You Will Find Ashore
Internet Access
The *Bequia Beach Hotel* has Wi-fi in their *Bagatelle Restaurant* so you'll want to bring your laptop with you.

Dining
At one time, the social activity in *Friendship Bay* revolved around the *Friendship Bay Resort* on the hillside above the bay. Sadly the resort has closed and I have no idea when it may reopen. I will post

an update on www.seaworthy.com if it does reopen however, as of the Spring of 2013 it is still closed.

Today, the *Bequia Beach Hotel's Bagatelle Restaurant* sits right on the beach where you can dine on local or European fare, tastefully prepared and served.

On the road to La Pompe is the *Diamond Bar Fish Food*, a popular local establishment with good food at great prices.

Petit Nevis

Navigational Information

Vessels can anchor in the lee of Petit Nevis as shown on Chart GND-4. From *Friendship Bay*, exit the bay and turn to starboard, heading west to pass between Middle Cay and Petit Nevis until you can turn to port to pass into the lee of Petit Nevis. The whale rendering facilities are worth exploring as is the reef that stretches well to the southwest of the island.

Bequia and Whaling

No publication can bypass the history and importance of the controversial subject of whaling and Bequia. The whaling season here lasts from February to May, just as it has been for centuries. The *International Whaling Commission* provisions for indigenous traditions granted a quota of 4 whales per year to the whalers of Bequia. Although some years Bequian whalers do not make any kills, the kills that they do bring in result in much needed income for the islanders as well as providing meat for the table.

On the lower floor of the blue and white house on the hill at Paget Farm, overlooking *Friendship Bay*, you'll find the *Bequia Whaling Museum*. As you walk through the entrance made from the sun-bleached bones of whales, you find exhibits featuring whaling tools, harpoons, and other various implements used in the processing of the humpback whales that breed on the Grenada Bank. If you're lucky, you might meet Athneal Ollivierre, the "last harpooner" as he's called here, a whaler for over 60 of his over 77 years. I can sit there all day and listen to his whaling stories.

Athenal's grandfather Joseph Ollivierre, was one of the first whalers on Bequia, and who, with William Thomas (Bill) Wallace, started the industry in the last half of the 19th century. Wallace learned the trade in New Bedford and when he arrived in Bequia with his new bride, he started the first whaling company in the Grenadines in 1870. The company was not too successful at first because of the Norwegian whalers who were there in great numbers. Wallace shut down his operation and went to Scotland where he studied the share basis system of whaling.

Wallace returned to Bequia in the 1880s and joined up with Frenchman Joseph Ollivierre who owned *Paget Farm Estate* and who had already maintained a whaling station at nearby Petit Nevis (which has thrived for over a century and is still used today). By 1890, six whaling stations were operating in Bequia, along with one at Frigate Rock, and one at Canouan. By the 1930s humpbacks were becoming scarce and the whaling industry went into a decline.

Today, Athneal's nephew Bentley is the new harpooner and his recently made his first kill. The responsibility of a long tradition is upon this young man. The whalers use two, 26'-long wooden boats that have been reported to reach speeds of 15 knots under sail while surfing (no engines are allowed). Launched from *Friendship Bay* with rocks for ballast, the whalers normally head for Mustique, the two 6-man crews keep a sharp eye out for any sign of whales (as do the spotters perched atop *Monkey Hill* on Bequia). When a kill is made the whale's mouth is sewn shut so that the creature will not take on water while it is towed to Petit Nevis where it will be processed.

Mustique

Waypoints:
Britannia Bay- ¾ nm W of Montezuma Shoal
12° 52.60' N, 61° 12.30' W

Mustique, pronounced *mus-teek*, derives its name from the French word for mosquito. In 1835, the Hazell family acquired the island and kept it for over a century before selling it to a wealthy Scottish nobleman, the Honorable Colin Tennant, now known as Lord Glenconner in 1958 (see the section on *Soufrière and the Pitons* in the chapter on *St. Lucia*). Lord Glenconner, who is sometimes called *Lord of the Revels*, is the grandson of Charles Tenant, the Scottish chemist who invented bleach and whose company once rivaled *DuPont* a century ago. Lord Glenconner bought Mustique for £45,000 as a wedding present for his wife, Lady Anne Coke, the daughter of the 5th Earl of Leicester and a Lady-in-

Waiting to Princess Margaret. Tennant had a vision of creating an exclusive hideaway for the rich and famous, and along with Oliver Messel, who designed the *Covent Garden Opera House* in London, England, built several "gingerbread houses" on the island in the 1960s and 1970s. Sinking most of his fortune into the island, he created a playground for the rich and famous, for the likes of Mick Jagger, David Bowie, Bryan Ferry, Raquel Welch, Paul Newman, Lord Lichfield, Roddy Lewellyn, Tommy Hilfiger, Prince Andrew, and of course, Princess Margaret. Lord Glenconner and Princess Margaret maintained a lifelong friendship and were so close that Glenconner gave the Princess a 5-acre peninsula on the island as a wedding present in 1960.

A reckless businessman, Lord Glenconner was eventually forced to sell his share of Mustique for £1 million in 1979 to a Martinican, Cuy de la Houssaye, and later moved to the northwestern end of the island. Here Lord Glenconner built what has been described as a Maharaja's palace in the middle of a palm grove, unknowingly right on top of some of the oldest prehistoric settlements in the Caribbean.

However, don't think that the life of the rich and famous jet-set crowd is strictly the way Mustique is today. The island is far more rustic than many people believe and some of the rich and famous have moved off-island to make room for more of the new rich and famous. David Bowie sold his mansion to *Maxim* publisher Felix Dennis, and Princess Margaret gave her estate, *Les Jolies Eaux*, to her son, Lord Linley, who sold it to an American couple for £2.5 million who later demolished it to build something "bigger and better." Lord Glenconner settled between the Pitons on St. Lucia with an elephant named Buppa (see the chapter on St. Lucia) and opened *Bang*, his version of a Caribbean dining experience. If you wish to know more about Mustique, and particularly Lord Glenconner, there is a film about him, *The Man Who Bought Mustique*, a documentary by director Joseph Bullman and producer Vikram Jayanti (*When We Were Kings*).

In 1979, a Venezuelan industrialist, Hans Neuman, bought Mustique and along with *The Mustique Company*, the private institution that oversees the island for its shareholders, and the government of St. Vincent and The Grenadines, agreement was reached on a development plan for the island which included the formation of the *Mustique Indigenous Peoples Association* to address the problems of those who were actually born on Mustique. In 1989, the government of St. Vincent and the Grenadines established the *Mustique Company Limited Act*. This act designates this privately owned island as a conservation area that extends to 1,000 yards offshore. In compliance, cruisers are asked to anchor or moor on one of the 34 moorings in *Britannia Bay*.

Navigational Information

If you're heading from St. Vincent to Mustique, your sail will be anywhere from a beat to a reach and the seas can be quite strong close to the northern shore of Bequia around Bequia Head. Watch out for the strong current here that will push you westward towards Bequia. Heading to Mustique from Bequia the sail is almost always a beat, directly into the wind and seas with the only danger being *Montezuma Shoal* near *Britannia Bay*. Cruisers must beware of the shoals and reefs that jut northward from *Sandy Bay* along the northern coast of Mustique as well as the shoals the lie east of the island and off the southwestern coast from South Point to *Britannia Bay* (see Chart GND-5).

As shown on Chart GND-5, and in greater detail on GND-6, a waypoint at 12° 52.60' N, 61° 12.30' W, will place you approximately ¼ mile south of *Montezuma Shoal* and ¾ mile west of the anchorage in *Britannia Bay*. From the waypoint head generally east towards shore and either pick up a mooring or anchor south of the jetty as close to shore as your draft allows. If you choose a mooring, make sure you have plenty of depth and allow for swinging room. Leave a channel open to the dock and be prepared for a little roll here my friends. Divers will want to investigate the wreck of the 90' dredge, Jonas, lying in 6 fathoms on the eastern side of *Montezuma Shoal*.

Mustique Company Regulations

The *Mustique Company* regulates usage of the waters of Mustique and has installed 30 moorings in *Brittania Bay*. Yachts are only permitted to moor in *Britannia Bay* and there are 30 moorings installed there for visitors. Yachts under 50' are required to use a mooring while larger vessels must contact the Harbormaster, Berris Little, by hailing *Mustique Moorings* on VHF ch. 16 or 68, for anchoring directions. Anchored vessels pay the same fees as moored vessels. Please do not anchor as to block the dock or interfere with moored vessels.

Mustique beach

Basil's Bar, Mustique

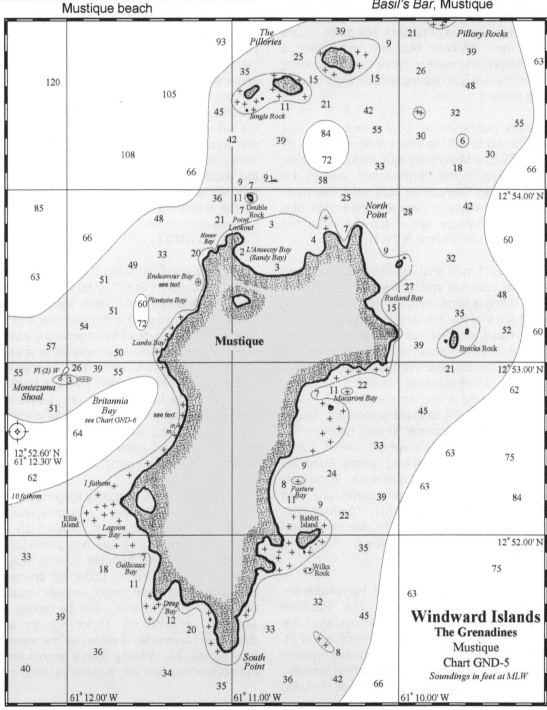

Mooring fees for a 3 consecutive night stay are EC$200 for vessels to 70'; EC$300 for vessels from 71'-85'; EC$400 for vessels from 86'-100'; and EC$500 for vessels over 100' in length.

Cruisers wishing to anchor in *Endeavour Bay* must contact Harbormaster Berris Little before heading for the bay. This anchorage is generally reserved for charters wanting a lunch stop.

What You Will Find Ashore

When strolling around Mustique, please use courtesy. Do not photograph the residents and please respect private property, stick to the paths. If you would like the convenience of a taxi contact *Boom* at 455-2084.

On Mustique the main roads are surfaced, but there are few cars, most people travel about on motorbikes or golf carts they lovingly call *mules*. You can rent a *mule* by calling *Mustique Moorings* on VHF ch. 16 or 68, or if you'd like you can rent a real, flesh and blood horse to ride; hail the *Mustique Company* on VHF ch.

16 or 68. If you don't rent a horse or mule, you'll probably be walking and getting around is no problem on Mustique, it's not far to most locations

Internet Access

If you need Internet access, or if you need to send a fax, the *Mustique Community Library* can help. They also carry the latest books and magazines if you just wish to read a while.

Marine Facilities
Garbage

If you need to dispose of bagged garbage, bins are available at the head of the dock.

Provisions

Corea's General Store carries champagne, caviar, French cheeses, and other delicacies as well as regular groceries, fresh produce, liquors and toiletries. *Basil's Gourmet Store* carries fine wines, cheeses, coffees, and special food items.

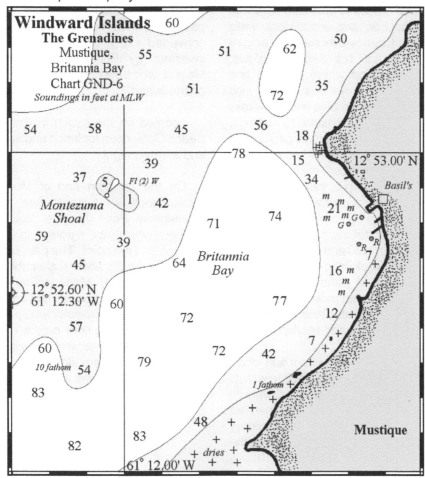

Across the road from *Basil's* is the *Sweetie Pie Bakery* (VHF ch. 68) where you'll find freshly baked breads, croissants, cakes, and brioche. Northwest of *Basil's Bar* is the fish market, a good spot to pick up on a fresh catch. On Tuesdays, Wednesdays, Friday, and Saturdays, you'll find a fresh veggie stall set up next to *Basil's*.

Shopping is certainly unique in Mustique, it's above scale compared to most Caribbean islands. Just north of *Sweetie Pie* in what is sometimes called Lovell Village, is a trio of small shops; *Treasure Fashion* (the *Purple House*) where you can pick up something elegant and exotic to wear while on Mustique, *Treasure* (the *Pink House*), more of your usual Caribbean boutique with casual and beach wear, toys, snorkeling gear, gifts, magazines, and postcards, and *Ali's Café*, a nice stop for lunch or just to pick up some baked goodies.

Dining

Overlooking *Britannia Bay* on Mustique's western coast, *Basil's Bar* has been drawing customers since 1976. Basil's is indeed castaway chic complete with thatched roof, bamboo bar, and windowless walls open to the sea. Basil Charles oversees his empire consisting of his restaurant, his *Basil's Boutique*, and his nearby gourmet shop where he sells fine wines, cheeses, and other gourmet treats. Basil also has a small antique and collectibles store, *Across Forever*, that features Balinese furniture, furnishings, fine accessories, and all sorts of unique gifts and is well worth a stop. At *Basil's* you'll find some of the world's most famous "upper crust" mixing with the locals and visiting yachties while sampling one of Basil's *Mustique Whammys* or some of his tropical entrees. Wednesday night is *Jump Up and Barbecue Night* with the barbecue buffet starting at 2000 with live music beginning about 2130 and lasting until late. Basil also hosts the two-week long *Mustique Blues Festival* featuring the likes of Dana Gillespie, Dino Baptiste, and Steve Clayton with most events at this fete being free. Divers will be interested to know that *Basil's Bar* can arrange *SCUBA* and snorkeling trips.

A popular spot in Mustique with visitors and locals alike is *Firefly*, the island's upscale guesthouse with its excellent restaurant. It's a bit of a vertical climb with a scenic view of Britannia Bay that makes the hike worth it. But if you don't feel like a cardio-pulmonary workout, don't sweat it; *Firefly* will pick you up at the dock if you'd prefer (*Firefly* monitors VHF ch. 10).

However, the focus on Mustique is at an 18th century sugar mill now called the *Cotton House Hotel* and *Veranda Restaurant*. Dining here has been described as barefoot elegance, and you'd better wear that nice dress or suit you packed away deep in your lockers, this is the place for it. Serving lunch and dinner, the ambiance is exclusive, expensive, and reservations are required. The *Cotton House Boutique* is located in the original sugar mill and features Caribbean garments, jewelry, hand painted swimwear, and leather accessories.

The *Cotton House* has undergone a revival over the last few years and has been featured in many hip/escape/hotel books and the operators know how to treat their guests. Where else can you find a bottle of *Laurent Perrier* champagne in your room, exotic flowers scattered about, a pillow menu, and the unpacking of your suitcase and the pressing of its contents upon arrival. The hotel consists of 20 rooms/suites/cottages spread about the estate and the colonial style Great House serves as the dining room and bar and has a wrap-around terrace that overlooks an estate grounds full of frangipani, hibiscus, and palm trees. The building was restored and originally converted into a guesthouse for potential property investors by British theatre set designer Oliver Messel, who also designed many of the original villas on the island.

Located on the beach in *Endeavour Bay* is the *Beach Café*, open for lunch and sometimes for dinner and a movie night.

On the northern end of Mustique is the wide public beach at *L'Ansecoy Bay*. Just offshore, past Cheltenham Point, lies the hulk of the cruise ship *Antilles*, which ran aground in 1971 between the Pillories and the point. The passengers were rescued by the *Queen Elizabeth II* after she diverted course to come to their aid. Many stories abound about how varied interests hoped to salvage the wreck. One tells of an Oriental investor who purchased the wreck for one dollar, but died before deciding how to go about dismantling the wreck, a stipulation in the bill of sale. On the eastern side of the island is one of the most popular beaches at *Macaroni Bay*. Snorkeling at *Gelliceaux Bay*, *Lagoon Bay*, *Britannia Bay*, and *Endeavour Bay* are first class.

Canouan

Waypoints:

Jupiter Head - ½ nm NW of
12° 44.60' N, 61° 20.40' W

Charlestown Bay - ½ nm NW of entrance
12° 42.90' N, 61° 20.60' W

Canouan, pronounced "Can-no-wan," means *Island of Turtles* in the Carib language. Boot shaped Canouan is an island of hills and panoramic views, perfect for hiking, with waters that are blessed with superb snorkeling. When heading towards Canouan from the north the topography of the island can be deceiving as *Glossy Hill*, on the southwestern tip of Canouan, usually appears as a separate island at first, until you get close enough to pick up the low land that joins the hill to the mainland of Canouan.

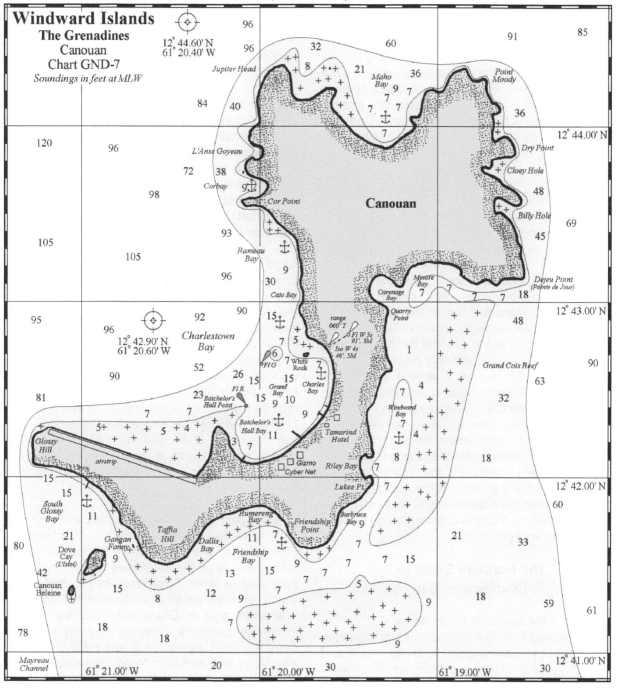

Although there are only about a thousand full-time residents that rely mostly on farming and fishing, there are two major hotels and the gated *Canouan Resort Development* on the northern part of the island. The resort maintains 52 villas, 180 rooms, a golf course, tennis courts, a beachfront bar and restaurant, a pool, and even a casino. The resort takes up almost the entire northern half of Canouan and all visitors must have permission to enter. Although claiming half the island and selling lots. the resort has brought some prosperity to the residents of the southern half of the island and that is not a bad thing.

The centerpiece of Canouan is the 900' high *Mount Royal,* which has not and will not be developed. The area around *Mount Royal* is now a nature reserve with an excellent hiking trail that takes you straight to the top of the hill for a spectacular view. Canouan is surrounded by lovely beaches, especially on the windward side, and at the northern end of the island at *Maho Bay.*

Canouan was the birthplace of the shipbuilding industry in the Grenadines when after the abolition of slavery in the mid-1800s, the owner of the island enlisted British shipwright Benjamin Compton, who together with William Mitchell, influenced the shipbuilding industry throughout the Eastern Caribbean and particularly on Canouan, Bequia, and Carriacou. Canouan, like all the islands of the Eastern Caribbean, is steeped in history, unfortunately development on the island over the last two decades has destroyed a lot of Canouan's history. One old 18th century church is now a storage building, its old cemetery bulldozed, and in another instance, somebody stole the oldest prehistoric rock carving in the Grenadines from Canouan. However, the ruins of an old church on the north side of the island stands as testament to the former glory of Canouan. Although a 1921 hurricane destroyed the village and the survivors moved to the center of the island, the bells of the old church were distributed to other churches on Canouan, as the church's original location became the equivalent of a ghost town.

The Northern Coast to
Charlestown Bay

Navigational Information
Approaching Canouan from Bequia or Mustique is a great sail, usually a beam to broad reach, and occasionally a run. There is a strong west/northwest setting current in the channel just north of Canouan, between Canouan and Mustique. The current's strength varies between 2-3 knots as shown on Chart GND-1. The current can also be quite strong in the vicinity of Jupiter Point at the northern end of Canouan.

As shown on Chart GND-7, a waypoint at 12° 44.60' N, 61° 20.40' W, will place you approximately ½ mile northwest of Jupiter Head at the northwestern tip of Canouan. This waypoint is just southeast of a 16' deep shoal area located approximately at 12° 44.90' N, 61° 20.64' W; use caution if seas are building up here (this area is normally rougher than surrounding waters).

From this waypoint, you may pass south along the western shore of Canouan towards the waypoint west of *Charlestown Bay.* Anchorages can be found along the western shore at Corbay (well protected but not very roomy, especially when it is being used to offload supplies for the *Canouan Resort),* *Rameau Bay* (holding is fair to good here in places) and *Cato Bay* (see Chart GND-7) for those so inclined, however the best and most popular anchorage is in *Charlestown Bay.* If you're not ready to head for *Charlestown Bay,* and if the weather is settled in the east to southeast, you can anchor in lovely *Maho Bay* at the northern end of Canouan (see Chart GND-7), home to one of the prettiest beaches on the island. This anchorage is best for daytime use and can be quite rolly at times.

As you sail south in the lee of Canouan, you will work your way towards a waypoint at 12° 42.90' N, 61° 20.60' W, which will place you approximately ½ mile northwest of the entrance to the anchorage in *Charlestown Bay.* As shown on Chart GND-7, you can head in to *Charlestown Bay* keeping the green light to port (it marks a shoal with just under 6' at MLW) and the red light to starboard that marks the shoals off Bachelor's Hall Point.

Once past these dangers you may anchor in any of three locations. *Charlestown Bay* is actually made up of three bays, *Grand Bay* (where the main anchorage is located just off the large town dock), *Charles Bay* southeast of White Rock, and *Bachelor's Hall Bay,* which lies at the extreme southern end of *Grand Bay.* The anchorages in *Charlestown Bay* are very nice in normal conditions, however northerly swells can make this area unpleasant to say the least. Another alternative is to anchor in *Nens Bay* (although you're still open to northerly swells here), west of Bachelor's Hall Point, however you must use caution when entering as you'll need to avoid the shoals lying off Bachelor's Hall Point.

Vessels are not permitted to anchor within 200 yards of the beach fronting the *Tamarind Beach Hotel* (see Chart GND-7).

Marcus, VHF ch. 16, rents mooring in the bay for EC$40 per night, they are the white moorings in front of the *Tamarind Beach Hotel*. Marcus also has a taxi and sells ice, water, gasoline, and diesel.

If you notice other moorings in the bay, particularly moorings with two painters, do not pick one up, they belong to *The Moorings* (VHF ch. 165) and are for the use of their charter fleet.

What You Will Find Ashore
Marine Facilities
As you enter *Charlestown Bay* you will notice several docks. Local boats use the small dock at the southern end of the bay, the large dock in the middle of the bay is the town's ferry dock. The *Tamarind Beach Hotel* has their own dock, and the other dock belongs to *The Moorings* and is not available for cruisers. None of the docks should be used if any swells are present. There are some very small garbage bins on the road across from the ferry dock. The *Tamarind Beach Resort* requests that cruisers please not throw garbage overboard because it always seems to land on their beach. Gas and diesel can be jerry-jugged from the gas station located at the southern end of the beach.

Marine Services
At the southern end of the bay is *Gizmo Marine* where owner Earl can deal with just about any repair you need aboard your vessel, from electrical to inboards and to outboards. *The Moorings* can assist in an emergency and also posts daily weather reports at their office.

Customs and *Immigration*
If you need clearance, *Customs* and *Immigration* are located at the airport.

Internet Access
You can get online at the *Tamarind Beach Hotel,* or at *Cyber Net*, located along the road past *Canouan Food* at the southern end of the bay.

Provisions
Located on the main road in town, *Canouan Food Limited* has a good selection of foods including fresh produce. They are open Monday-Saturday from 0800-2000 and on Sundays from 0900-1200 and then from 1600-2000.

In town there are several small mini-markets and food stalls including one behind the *Police Station*. The *Tamarind Beach Hotel* also sells ice and fresh bread.

Dining
You can use the *Tamarind Bay Resort* dock to land your dinghy, especially if you plan to visit one of their two beachfront restaurants, the informal *Pirate's Cove* (opens at 1600-bare feet and shorts are welcome) and the larger and more elegant *La Palapa Fanicie* (reservations requested). If you're interested, the *Pirate's Cove* cooks a mean pizza after 1900.

Just to the left of the ferry dock is a restaurant owned by Marcus' sister, Phyllis, that is open for lunch and dinner. *Frontline* is opposite the dock and features local fare and fresh baked bread.

Elsewhere in town (called *Retreat Village*) you can grab a bite to eat at the *Honey Crome Bar* which also doubles as a food store and sits just behind the *Police Station* (open for dinner only by request).

The Southern Coast of Canouan

Navigational Information
South of *Charlestown Bay* is the *Canouan Beach Hotel* in *South Glossy Bay* as shown on Chart GND-7. From *Charlestown Bay*, give the shoals of *Taffia Bay* a wide berth and round the very conspicuous Glossy Hill at least ¼ mile off to enter *South Glossy Bay*. Although quite rolly at times (with a bit of current as well), you can anchor off the hotel to savor the water and the beach, one of the nicest on the island. The resort is elegant and French, but cruisers are welcome (dress nicely folks). The restaurant serves excellent French and West Indian food with a great buffet lunch and dinner. If you don't care to anchor in *South Glossy Bay*, take a taxi over from *Charlestown*.

East of *South Glossy Bay* is *Friendship Bay*, a daytime anchorage only, it is in the lee of a large reef system but can still get rolly. It's a good spot to anchor to explore the reefs south of Canouan. Further east still is another daytime anchorage that is best in relatively calm conditions in *Windward Bay* between the barrier reef and Canouan itself as shown on Chart GND-7.

The Southern Grenadines

Mayreau

Mayreau, pronounced "My-row," and sometimes shown as *Mayero*, is the smallest of the inhabited Grenadines, being only about 1½ square miles in area and a population of only about 300 permanent residents, most of whom live in the village on the southwest corner of the island at *Saline Bay* atop *Station Hill*. There is only one road, a handful of cars, and a church atop *Station Hill* with a black Christ, one of several such in the Caribbean. There

also is a top-notch resort on the northern end of the island at *Saltwhistle Bay* with its mile-long beach that is connected to *Saline Bay* by a small trail for those inclined to hiking. And if you ARE inclined to hiking, you'll find that Mayreau has several good hiking trails offering great views of the Grenadines.

The original settlers of Mayreau were French, the St. Heliers, a descendant of which was the recent Governor General of St. Vincent and The Grenadines. Mayreau was more recently owned by the Eustace family of St. Vincent, but government programs in the last few decades have allowed the 262 islanders (at last count) to invest in their land.

Please note that Mayreau is part of the *Tobago Cays National Park* although no anchoring fees are collected. However, if you wish to dive in the waters

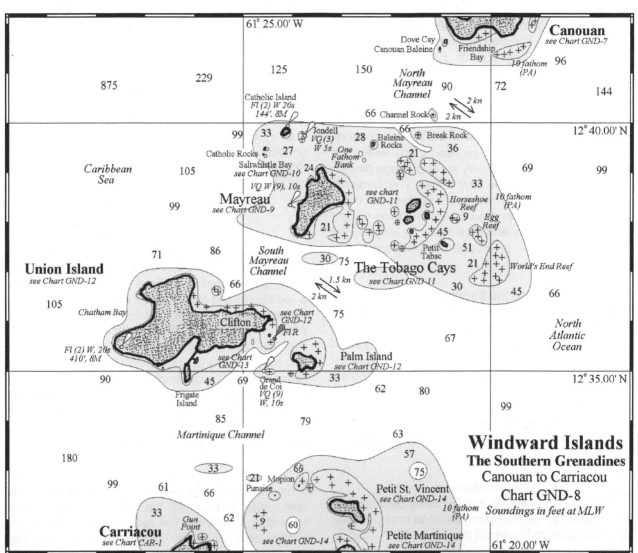

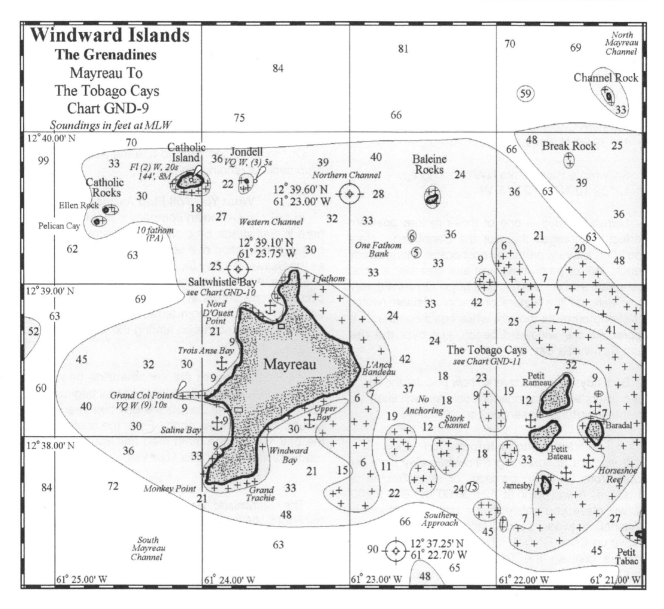

Windward Islands
The Grenadines
Mayreau To
The Tobago Cays
Chart GND-9
Soundings in feet at MLW

North Mayreau Channel

81   70   69
84
Channel Rock
75   66   59   33

12°40.00'N   70
99   33   Catholic Island   Jondell   39   40   Baleine Rocks   24   66   48 Break Rock   25
        Fl (2) W, 20s 144', 8M   36 VQ W, (3) 5s
Catholic Rocks   22   Northern Channel   39
Ellen Rock   30   12°39.60'N 61°23.00'W   28   36   63   36
Pelican Cay   18
        27   Western Channel   32   33   21   63   36
10 fathom (PA)   12°39.10'N 61°23.75'W   30   One Fathom Bank 6 5   36   6   20   48
62   63   25   33   33   9   7
12°39.00'N   1 fathom
69   Saltwhistle Bay see Chart GND-10   33   42   7
63   Nord D'Ouest Point   24   25   41
52   21   7
45   Trois Anse Bay   Mayreau   24   The Tobago Cays see Chart GND-11   32
60   32   30   L'Ance Bandeau   42   18   23   19   Petit Rameau   9
40   Grand Col Point VQ W (9) 10s   9   37   No Anchoring   18   9   12   7 Baradal
30   Saline Bay   Upper Bay   6 7   Stork Channel   19   12
12°38.00'N   9   30   19   12   Petit Bateau
36   33   Windward Bay   6   11   18   33   Petit Bateau
84   72   Monkey Point   21   15   Horseshoe Reef
        Grand Trachie   33   22   24 75   Jamesby   Horseshoe Reef
        21   48   Southern Approach   7   27
South Mayreau Channel   63   66   45   45   Petit Tabac
90   12°37.25'N 61°22.70'W   65
61°25.00'W   61°24.00'W   61°23.00'W   48   61°22.00'W   61°21.00'W

Saline Bay, Mayreau

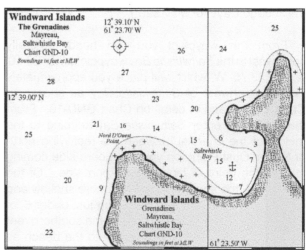

Windward Islands
The Grenadines
Mayreau,
Saltwhistle Bay
Chart GND-10
Soundings in feet at MLW

12°39.10'N
61°23.70'W

25
26   24
27
28
12°39.00'N   23   20
21   16   14
25   Nord D'Ouest Point   15   6   3
20   Saltwhistle Bay   15
9   12   7
Windward Islands
Grenadines
Mayreau,
Saltwhistle Bay
Chart GND-10
Soundings in feet at MLW
22   61°23.50'W

around the island you must dive with a local dive shop.

Saltwhistle Bay

Waypoints:
Northern Channel
12° 39.60' N, 61° 23.00' W

Saltwhistle Bay - ¼ nm NW of anchorage
12° 39.10' N, 61° 23.75' W

Saltwhistle Bay is one of those picture postcard perfect anchorages that dot the Caribbean. Here you'll find a lovely, protected anchorage, a long sandy beach, lots of palm trees and sea breezes, a good restaurant ashore...and no boat boys. Divers will want to investigate the waters of Catholic Island (watch for strong currents though) while beachcombers will appreciate the windward beach, just over the rise from Saltwhistle Bay.

Boat boys have discovered how popular the bay is for cruisers as well as charter boats and will likely vie for the opportunity to service you.

Navigational Information
If you are approaching Saltwhistle Bay from the north, from Canouan perhaps, or even Bequia or Mustique, a waypoint at 12° 39.60' N, 61° 23.00' W, will place you safely in the middle of Northern Channel, between Jondell and Baleine Rocks as shown on Chart GND-9. (This is important as many cruisers confuse the Tobago Cays with Mayreau and the results of that can be disastrous. Viewed from Canouan, Union Island lies behind Mayreau so skippers often mistake Mayreau for Union Island and the Tobago Cays for Mayreau.)

From this waypoint you can head generally southwest to the Saltwhistle Bay waypoint at 12° 39.10' N, 61° 23.75' W, which will place you approximately ¼ mile northwest of Saltwhistle Bay as shown on Chart GND-9 and in detail on Chart GND-10. From this waypoint, enter Saltwhistle Bay keeping to the middle of the channel between the reef lying north of Nord d'Oust Point (on your starboard side coming in) and the point of land to your port side. Of the two shoals, the southern reef is far more shallow and dangerous, the northern shoal being just under 6' at MLW. Use extreme caution here as the southern reef is a boat killer. Anchor in as close to the beach as

your draft allows in a sandy patch, watch out for the grass which may foul your hook; you might need to set a stern anchor or a bridle in some conditions to lessen roll, especially if northerly swells are present. If northerly swells ARE present, I usually head over to the protection offered by the Tobago Cays (see the next section).

Cruisers are permitted to use the Saltwhistle Bay Club dock for landing the dinghy.

What You Will Find Ashore
In 1972, a Canadian company bought some land here in Saltwhistle Bay, and Undine and Tom Potter began construction of a secluded resort to be known as the Saltwhistle Bay Club. Today the resort consists of 8 large, airy double rooms, each with its own name, circular stone showers, ceiling fans, batiks, a good selection of books, room terraces, wooden shutters, and hammocks scattered among the palm trees and tropical shrubbery.

If you wish to visit the windwardside beach and sample the beachcombing there, a trail begins at the southern end of the Saltwhistle Bay beach and goes around the inland salt pond. From the south dock in the bay, walk to the main road and you'll find a dirt road heading east, this is your trail.

Dining
The Saltwhistle Bay Club Bar and Restaurant (monitors VHF ch. 16 & 68) is an open-air dining experience with 10 stone tables, each with its own thatched roof, and there is also a small boutique. The restaurant serves breakfast, lunch, and dinner and there is a dinghy dock in place for cruiser's convenience with the trail to Saline Bay beginning here. Near the dock is another small bar/restaurant.

If you're heading south, leave Saltwhistle Bay giving a good berth to the reef off Nord l'Oust Point, and proceed down the leeward side of Mayreau. There is a fair anchorage between Saltwhistle Bay and Saline Bay at Trois Anse Bay that is untenable in northerly swells.

Saline Bay

Saline Bay was a pre-Columbian settlement with many precious artifacts having been found here including a number of hand-hewn axes. The site of the dig has since been covered by construction by the *Princess Cruise Line* that leases much of the land here for their passengers.

Navigational Information
If you are approaching from the north, from *Saltwhistle Bay*, give the long reef off Grand Col Point a wide berth; the shoal is marked by a light on its western edge, don't round it too closely as the light sits in shallow water. As shown on Chart GND-9, once past Grand Col Point you may steer generally eastward to anchor off the town dock where the best holding is west of the main dock in sand, not grass. Also, be advised that the southern part of *Saline Bay* is very uncomfortable when northerly swells are running and rolly when strong easterly swells are present.

When the cruise ships are present the pace will be quite hectic in the bay, but they never stay long, they're usually gone by dusk.

What You Will Find Ashore
If you tie up your dinghy to the dock, you can hike up the winding, concrete road that leads straight up to *Station Hill*, the main settlement on Mayreau, about a 20-minute walk. As you approach the settlement, you'll notice small shops lining the road selling gifts, handicrafts, and T-shirts.

Marine Facilities
Marine Services
The first house on the road as you approach *Station Hill* is the home of Arthur Roach, a good mechanic if you need somebody to help with your outboard or inboard problems.

Internet Access
Dennis' Hideaway Restaurant offers an internet connection.

Provisions
The best you'll find on Mayreau are some basic grocery items at any of several small stores such as *First Stop Supermarket* or *J&C*.

Dining
By far, the largest business on Mayreau is *Dennis' Hideaway Restaurant* where you can get a great meal, lime while listening to some live music in the open air bar by the pool with all the other cruisers who lime here, or get a room and stay the night. Dennis monitors VHF ch. 68 and his place is easily seen from the anchorage. Dennis also has a desalinization plant

on the waterfront by the main dock and sells water. Dennis also has a 44' charter yacht for cruises to the Tobago Cays.

Just across from Dennis is the *Combination Café and First Stop Supermarket* featuring a rooftop bar. They're open for breakfast, lunch, and dinner, and also offer freshly baked breads. Nearby is *Friendship Rose* open for lunch and dinner.

A bit further uphill is the *J&C Bar and Restaurant*, who, along with a great view, serves up excellent seafood and island dishes in a light atmosphere. *J&C* (Jean and Claude) monitors VHF ch. 68 and has a small boutique and supermarket on site, and offers a water taxi service if your dinghy is up on the davits or if you just want a boat-side pickup service.

One of the most laid-back spots on the island is *Robert Righteous & de Youths Seafood Restaurant & Bar*. Robert "Righteous" Lewis is a Rastafarian and his dedication to Bob Marley is obvious upon entry when you spy the walls covered with posters and other Marley memorabilia. The name tells you what the fare is, and the ambiance is low-key local as well as cruiser.

At the top of the road is the *Island Paradise Restaurant and Bar* where James Alexander, the owner, will greet you, seat you, and fill you up with some of the best seafood in the Grenadines. James also has a small 2-bedroom house for rent for US$20 per day (at the time of this writing) and he monitors VHF ch. 68. During the season look for Friday night barbecues and live music; if you want a ride up the hill, give James a hail on VHF ch. 68.

Windward Bay

Navigational Information
Besides the two anchorages already mentioned, *Saltwhistle Bay*, *Trois Anse Bay*, and *Saline Bay*, there is another anchorage on the eastern shore of Mayreau that is great for those wishing to check out the reefs. Although open to the south, and normally a bit rolly, this anchorage is an alternative when westerly or northerly swells are running. As shown on Chart GND-9, there is a small, reef protected anchorage on the southeastern shore of Mayreau in Upper Bay. From *Saline Bay* pass south of Monkey Point and Grand Trachie Point (giving the inshore reefs a wide berth) to enter *Windward Bay*. Work your way

up into the small pocket known as *Upper Bay* that is protected by the mainland of Mayreau to the west and north, and by a reef to the east and southeast.

The Tobago Cays

Waypoints:
Southern Approach, 1nm SW of Jamesby
12º 37.25' N, 61º 22.70' W

Over the years I've heard a lot of cruisers who have commented that the Caribbean is not as nice as The Bahamas when it comes to beautiful, serene anchorages in gin-clear turquoise waters, good holding sandy bottoms, scenic coral reefs, all caressed by the constant trade winds. Most seem to think that it's better in The Bahamas, with one exception, the

Tobago Cays, quite possibly the most beautiful spot in the Caribbean, that is if you like that sort of thing (and who doesn't?).

The Tobago Cays, one of the most popular stops for Caribbean cruisers as well as charterers and cruise ship passengers, is now a national park and visitors are asked to do their part in keeping this area pristine. It took a long time for the park to come into being starting in 1987 when the Government of St. Vincent and The Grenadines designated a *Conservation Area* in the southern Grenadines centering on the Tobago Cays. In 1993, at the request of the Government of St Vincent and The Grenadines, an agency of the French government, the *French Mission for Cooperation in the Lesser Antilles*, undertook a study called the *Tobago Cays Marine Park Project*. The Government

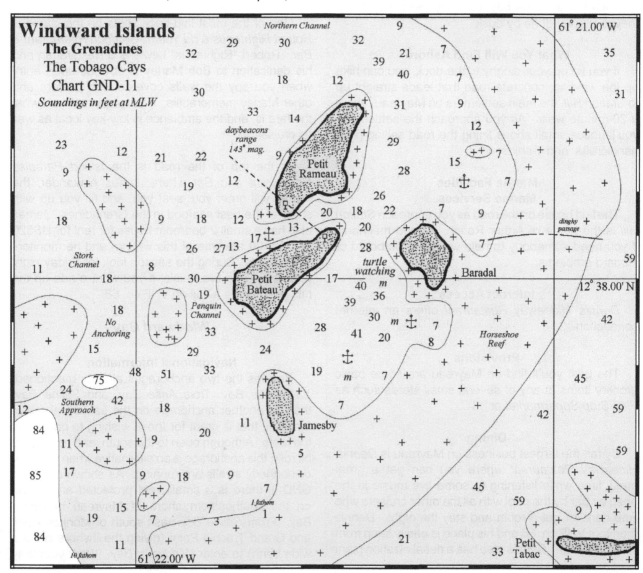

Windward Islands
The Grenadines
The Tobago Cays
Chart GND-11
Soundings in feet at MLW

of St. Vincent and the Grenadines gave approval in June 1995 to a proposal submitted by the *Ministry of Agriculture and Labour* (the ministry responsible for the parks and beaches of these islands) for the establishment of the Tobago Cays as a *National Marine Park*.

In 1997, legislation was enacted and the Tobago Cays became a national park in 1998. When the plans were finalized, one important point was that no commercial activity would ever be allowed on the Tobago Cays (a good idea if you ask me). So why the delay in becoming a national park? Well, it seems that the Government of St. Vincent and the Grenadines did not actually own the Tobago Cays until quite recently. The Tobago Cays were once owned by the Eustace family of St. Vincent, the same family who owned nearby Mayreau. Over 40 years ago, the Eustace family sold the Tobago Cays to private owners from the U.S. Finally, after a decade and a half of negotiations, the Government of St. Vincent and the Grenadines acquired the islands from the *Tobago Cays Holding Company* on April 12, 1999 for just over one million dollars for 58.5 acres of land. I am told that one day soon Park Wardens will be patrolling the Tobago Cays and a usage fee structure will be in place with the fees gathered going into the coffers of the *Tobago Cays National Park* itself. Bear in mind that fishing is not allowed in the Tobago Cays and you are requested to use the dinghy moorings available instead of anchoring in the coral on the reef systems.

Navigational Information

Let me begin by reminding mega-yachts to call ahead for advice on where to anchor before entering the park (hail the national park rangers on VHF ch. 16). Next, let me remind you that eyeball navigation is vital in these waters, proceed with caution.

As shown on Chart GND-9, which gives you an overview of the Tobago Cays in relation to their neighbor, Mayreau, there are two entrances to access this Caribbean playground. Approaching from the north, or perhaps from the leeward side of Mayreau, head for a waypoint in the *Northern Channel* at 12° 39.60' N, 61° 23.00' W, which places you in deep water safely between Baleine Rocks and Jondell as shown on GND-9. From this waypoint you'll steer generally in a southeast direction, approximately 143° magnetic on a range consisting of two black and white day markers on Petit Rameau and Petit Bateau as shown

in detail on Chart GND-11. You'll be piloting between the reefs lying just to the northeast of Mayreau and the *One Fathom Bank* shown on Chart GND-9.

Once in the lee of Petit Rameau you can pass between Petit Rameau and Petit Bateau and anchor east of these cays and in the lee of *Horseshoe Reef* north or south of Baradal or northeast of Jamesby. You can also anchor in the channel between Petit Rameau and Petit Bateau, but you'll need two anchors here due to the current; watch out for day charter traffic here as well.

If you are approaching the Tobago Cays from the south, a waypoint at 12° 37.25' N, 61° 22.70' W, will place you approximately 1 mile southwest of Jamesby as shown on Chart GND-9. From this position you'll have a bit trickier piloting job than coming from the north, but luckily the shoals are easily seen; never try to enter the Tobago Cays at night. From the waypoint you'll be heading in a general northeast direction. You can use the western tip of Petit Bateau lined up with the eastern tip of Petit Rameau in the background as a range, but you'll still have to keep a sharp lookout to void the reefs lying southwest of Petit Bateau. If you are uncomfortable with this route, I suggest that you pass to the west and then north of Mayreau to enter the Tobago Cays from the northwest.

You'll notice several national park moorings available in the anchorages of the Tobago Cays, including the turtle watch area off Baradal. Fees are EC$45 per night.

National Park Fees and Regulations

You may only anchor in sand, not in coral or in sea grass beds. Fees for anchoring in the Tobago Cays run EC$10 per person per day, children are only EC$5 per child per day, and park rangers will come by your boat to collect. Mayreau is part of the park but no fees are currently collected in the anchorages of Mayreau.

Fishing and/or the taking of any marine life is prohibited. This includes corals and shells. Take only photographs, leave only footprints. No fires are permitted ashore.

To the west of the beach on Baradal is a turtle watching area and no anchoring is allowed here, However, national park moorings are available for EC$45 per day. You are permitted to carefully pull your dinghy onto the beach to dive in the waters to watch the turtles, but drifting with your dinghy in tow is not permitted.

Holding tanks are required, you are not permitted to discharge any waste into the water nor leave any garbage on any of the land masses in the park.

There is a 5-knot speed limit in the *Tobago Cays National Park* that applies to all vessels with the exception of kite-boarders and sail-boarders in the area north of Petit Rameau.

Divers are charged a fee of EC$10 per dive and may only dive with a local dive shop.

What You Will Find Ashore

You'll find plenty of beaches here to frolic on, as long as the cruise ships aren't using them. Petit Rameau has a nice beach on the southern side of the cay as does Barabal, and Petit Bateau has a nice beach on its northern shore and another on the eastern side of the cay.

Jamesby, once home to a large colony of iguanas, has one of the nicest beaches in the group on its eastern shore. As shown on Chart GND-11, there is a small cove on the northwest side of Petit Tabac that is fair for a day anchorage in calm weather. You'll sometimes see fishermen camping on Petit Tabac.

You will probably be approached by vendors while anchored in the Tobago Cays. My favorite, Mr. Fabulous, will usually have some of the nicest fresh fish and lobster to be had, though I believe he overcharges if he thinks he can get away with it. He can also arrange a beach BBQ for you.

In 1983, a whale erred in its navigation and found itself in the center of the Tobago Cays with no way out. Charter boats would anchor and wait for the whale to come by so their charterers could swim with it...the whale seemed unafraid of humans. One boat tried to communicate with it by playing a tape of Judy Collins' whale songs to the creature. After a few months of this insanity the whale finally found its way back out to sea.

Union Island

Union Island is the southernmost Port of Entry for St. Vincent and The Grenadines and because of its mountainous topography has been likened to the island of Tahiti.

First settled over 2,000 years ago, Union Island had a deeply religious meaning for its Amerindian settlers of which there is evidence of a settlement on Point Lookout. Today Union Island is home to more than 3,500 people and is known for its lovely beaches which ring the island and its peaks with their scenic views. *The Pinnacle*, the highest peak on the island at 995', is one of the most popular spots for tourists as is 450' *Fort Hill* on the northeastern side of Union Island just north of the airport. Built by the French in the 1600s, today *Fort Hill* is a prime spot to sit and gaze out over the *Caribbean Sea* and *Atlantic Ocean* from St. Vincent to Grenada.

The two main settlements are Clifton and Ashton, which sit beneath *Mt. Parnassus*. Just to the west of *Mount Parnassus* is *Mt. Toboi*, at nearly 1100' it is the highest peak in the Grenadines. Both Clifton and Ashton are said to have been settled by Bristol sailors because their names reflect those of towns just outside Bristol in the U.K.

Chatham Bay

Waypoints:
Chatham Bay- ¾ nm west of anchorage
12° 36.00' N, 61° 27.75' W

Chatham Bay lies on the western shore of Union Island and offers a good, well protected lee anchorage with a beautiful, long, sandy beach to enjoy.

Navigational Information

As shown on Chart GND-12, a waypoint at 12° 36.00' N, 61° 27.75' W, will place you approximately ¾ mile west of the anchorage area. From the waypoint head eastward into *Chatham Bay* and anchor wherever your draft allows. The best place to anchor is in the northern part of the bay, but bear in mind that you may have to move when the local fishermen are seine netting.

On the southern side of *Chatham Bay* is *Aqua*, a wonderful bar and restaurant with moorings for rent. Nearby you'll find a family of four rays that are so easygoing you can swim along with them.

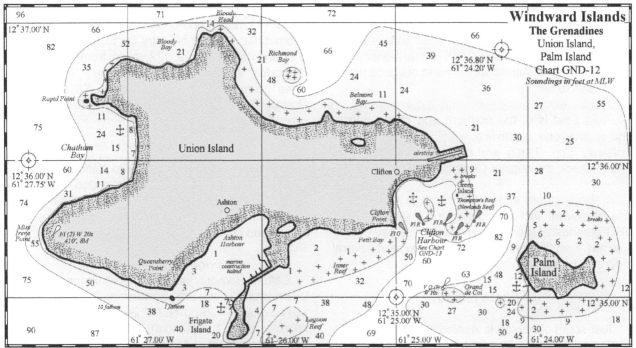

Aerial view of *Clifton Harbour*, Union Island

Clifton Harbour as viewed from the east

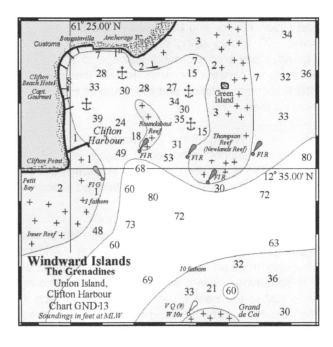

What You Will Find Ashore
Customs and *Immigration*

It is possible to clear Customs from *Chatham Bay*. You'll have to find a local boater to run you into town, the going rate for this service is around EC$150.

Provisions

There are no markets here, but every morning the *Palm Leaf* boat will come around with fresh bread and ice for sale. Other local boaters will come around trying to entice you into dining in their establishment.

Dining

During the winter months look for weekly beach barbeques in any of a number of small shacks on the beach. The BBQs charge EC$65, a little higher if you order the lobster. Almost all will need advance notice if you wish to eat.

Palm Leaf is at the northern end of the beach, and is only one of several small eateries such as *Bullhead*, *Sun, Beach, and Eat*, *Pleasure's Bar*, and *Shark Attack*, the original *Chatham Bay* beach BBQ.

At the southern end of the beach is *Aqua*, a bar and restaurant with their own pool, quite unlike the BBQ eateries at the northern end of the bay. *Aqua* also has a small dinghy dock, fresh water, and several moorings for rent.

Frigate Island

Just south of Ashton is *Ashton Harbor* (as shown on Chart GND-12). The harbor and nearby Frigate Island have suffered much during the last few years. In 1994, a developer planned to construct condominiums, closed the cut between Frigate Island and Union Island, and built docks to accommodate some 300 yachts using part of Frigate Island as fill. After doing considerable damage to a delicate ecosystem, construction was halted thanks to a UNEP recommendation and the future of the project remains bleak.

Navigational Information

You can anchor in the lee of Frigate Island (see Chart GND-12), but don't go too far in towards the old marina construction as there is no dredged channel.

What You Will Find Ashore

Lagoon Reef lies southeast of Frigate Island and is still good snorkeling I am happy to say. And on the northern coast, *Belmont Bay,* or *Water Break* as it is sometimes called, also offers good snorkeling while just to the west of *Belmont Bay* the beach at *Richmond Bay*, although lined with manchineel trees, is popular with children due to its shallow water.

Clifton

Waypoints:
Clifton- ½ nm S of Grand de Coi Reef
12° 35.00' N, 61° 25.00' W

Clifton is THE place on Union Island and the center of cruising and charter activity in the southern Grenadines. A Port of Entry for St. Vincent and the Grenadines, Clifton is 122 miles from Bridgetown, Barbados, 40 miles from St. George's Grenada, 35 miles from Kingstown, St. Vincent, 95 miles from *Rodney Bay*, St. Lucia, 110 miles from *Chaguaramas Bay*, Trinidad, and 171 miles from Porlamar, Isla Margarita, Venezuela.

The approach and entrance to *Clifton Harbour* is not difficult, but a bit of piloting is needed to avoid the nasty reefs that lie to the east of and in the center of the harbor. Do not try to enter this harbor at night unless you are extremely familiar with the entry.

Navigational Information

Clifton Harbour lies on the southeastern tip of Union Island, if you are approaching from the north, a waypoint at 12° 36.80' N, 61° 24.20' W, will place you approximately 1 mile north of the channel between Thompson's Reef and Palm Island as shown on Chart GND-12.

From this waypoint head generally south, keeping the markers demarcating *Thompson's Reef* (sometimes shown as *Newlands Reef*) well to starboard and Palm Island well to port. As you approach the southern tip of *Thompson's Reef,* see Chart GND-13, you can follow the markers on your starboard side around to the west to enter the harbor itself either to the east or west of *Roundabout Reef.*

If you are approaching from the south, a waypoint at 12° 35.00' N, 61° 25.00' W, will place you approximately ½ mile south of the entrance to *Clifton Harbour* and a bit over ¼ mile west of *Grand de Coi Reef* as shown on Chart GND-12. From this waypoint, keep well marked *Grand de Coi Reef* to starboard and proceed a bit east of north to enter *Clifton Harbour* either east or west of *Roundabout Reef* as shown on Chart GND-13.

Holding in *Clifton Harbour* can be anywhere from good to poor depending on where you anchor, usually it tends to be more on the poor side. Behind the reef the anchorage appears to be good sand, but it is quite hard and difficult to get an anchor to set in at times as the bottom is scoured in many places. The large white mooring buoys that appear empty are really not, by evening the returning day charter catamarans will be picking them up so give those buoys a wide berth (these moorings are usually in the northeast corner of the harbor, in the lee of *Thompson's Reef*). *Clifton Harbour* is, sadly, having a problem with unscrupulous mooring owners, problems from poor installation to downright fraud (securing your vessel to a charter mooring, charging you, and then leaving before you are told to vacate the mooring by the real owner). All in all, it's best to lie to your own anchor, just make sure it is set well.

Bougainvilla (monitors VHF ch. 16), has stern-to berthing for 20 boats and may have room for you.

What You Will Find Ashore

There are several dinghy docks around the harbor, but there are also several water taxi services available for EC$10-EC$20 per trip ashore. If you dine at *Lambi's* you will receive a free round-trip water taxi ride.

Customs and Immigration

Vessels wishing to clear *Customs* and *Immigration* will find the procedure simple and painless. The *Customs* office is located just up from the main dock in the fishing complex. I usually use the large dinghy dock at the *Bougainvilla* complex to land my dink and clear. The *Customs* office is open from 0830-1630 except for Sundays and holidays at which time you will find a *Customs* officer on duty at the airport.

From *Customs* you must head for *Immigration* in the new tourist building just across from the market. If *Immigration* is not in; you can find them at the airport, a short, pleasant five-minute walk. The main road runs right behind the *Customs* building, take it to the right and continue to the airport to clear.

Internet Access

Internet access is very good in Clifton. At the *Bougainvilla* complex try *Erika's Marine Services*. Erika handles emails, provisioning, telephone and fax service, computer sales, underwater photo rentals, bike rentals, mail, and even does laundry. You can even get cash on your credit card here. A great service that Erika performs for cruisers is the posting of the current weather fax and weather forecast at her shop each morning. Erika has a nice book exchange and is the local *UPS* agent as well. You can also access the Internet at *Unicom* on the airport road, a few hundred yards from the entrance to the airport. Erika also offers *Wi-fi* in the anchorage area, as does the *Internet Café* just above *Buffalo Trading*. The *L'*

Aquarium restaurant and *Captain Gourmet* also offer free *Wi-fi* for their customers.

Marine Facilities
Marine Services

The focus for cruisers in Clifton is at the *Bougainvilla* complex at the northwestern end of the harbor; you can tie stern-to at their dock where there is room for up to 20 boats and where you can pick up fuel (diesel and gas), water, and ice, or just use their dinghy dock to access town. The complex is chock full of restaurants and shops, most of which will be utilized by cruisers at some time or another, even those just wishing to visit the unique tropical garden. There are even a couple of charter companies based here, *Switch Charters* and *Wind and Sea Charters*.

For welding and fabrication needs, visit *Unitech Marine Services* (monitors VHF ch. 16). The folks here can handle outboard or inboard repairs, fill propane tanks, stock marine supplies in their chandlery, and rent kayaks. They also can fabricate metal and weld stainless and aluminum.

Across the street is Earl Allen's *Island Marine Special*. With over 25 years experience, *Island Marine* can handle almost all your diesel and outboard repairs as well as sell you parts to do it yourself. Earl's small shop also carries some basic marine supplies.

The *Anchorage Yacht Club* sits on the northern edge of the harbor, just north of *Roundabout Reef*. Here you can tie stern to a floating dock with room for up to 12 boats. The marina monitors VHF ch. 16 and 68 and offers water, showers, laundry, ice, telephone and fax service, a mechanic, and can send and receive mail for you.

On the western side of the bay, is the *Clifton Beach Hotel*, Skippers can tie up stern-to to pick up ice, water, dine, or arrange for laundry service. There is about 8'-9' at the end of the dock at MLW.

Next door is the *Lambi* complex with its own dock. Here you can pick up water at their fuel dock, visit *Lambi's Supermarket*, *Lambi's Hardware*, or dine at the casual *Lambi's Restaurant*. Caution, the fuel dock only has about 4'-5' at MLW alongside.

You can leave bagged garbage in the dumpster by the fishing docks. The *Lambi's* boat will haul your garbage for a small fee.

Clifton Harbour, Union Island as seen from the south

Palm Island with *Clifton Harbour,* Union Island in background

Provisions

Provisioning is good in Clifton, besides the street vendors and market, there are several fine places for full provisioning. *Island Green* has the freshest locally grown produce.

On the western side of the harbor is *Captain Gourmet* (near the *Clifton Beach Hotel*) with a good selection of meat, cheese, wine, yogurt, baked goods, and prepared frozen meals made to your specifications (and free *Wi-fi*). The owners offer delivery to your dock and a full provisioning service if required.

The *Grand Union Supermarket* and *Lambi's* both carry all the basics including fresh fruits, veggies, fish, and the occasional chicken.

Cash and Carry is also good for groceries, but it is their fresh baked bread that is the real attraction.

Dining

The *Anchorage Yacht Club Restaurant* offers good French/Creole food for breakfast, lunch, and dinner, with live music on Fridays and Saturdays. A pleasant distraction is the pool in front of the yacht club where you can view nurse sharks. Another nice spot is *Sydney's*, on the road to the airport next to the *Anchorage Yacht Club's* gate where you can dine on good Creole food, pasta, and the usual bar snacks. *Sydney's* also has rooms to rent and monitors VHF ch. 68.

One the western edge of the harbor is the *Clifton Beach Hotel and Restaurant* (monitors VHF ch. 16), serving fine West Indian cuisine from 1930-2200 daily with yacht captains dining for free. Next door in the *Lambi* complex with their fine restaurant featuring live music.

A good stop is the *West Indies Restaurant and Bar* for fine French cuisine and local dishes and they have their own dinghy dock. They're located on the waterfront next to *Grenadines Dive*.

Besides the places already mentioned for dining out, you should try the *Boll Head Restaurant and Bar* near the *Clifton Beach Hotel*. Casual, with outdoor seating, the local dishes are good and reasonable. Both the *T&N Bar and Restaurant* and *Jennifer's* offer West Indian cuisine at good prices.

Located in the *Bougainvilla* complex, *L'Aquarium* boasts a lobster tank, Italian cuisine, and free *Wi-fi*.

Just across from the main dock, *Ciao Pizza* not only serves up the best pizza and pasta, but quality seafood as well and should not be missed. Next door is the laid back, locally flavored *Twilight*.

My new favorite is *Janti's Happy Island*, built by hand out on the edge of the reef using a lot of old conch shells. The fare is local, inexpensive, and absolutely delicious!

Palm Island

Waypoints:
1 nm N of channel between Thompson's & Palm
12° 36.80' N, 61° 24.20' W

Palm Island, once called Prune Island, is one of the most popular stops in the Grenadines for one reason, John and Mary Caldwell. The story behind Prune Island and how it became Palm Island will be told in the next section, The Story of Coconut Johnny, but for now, let's talk about how to get there and what you'll find when you arrive.

Palm Island is a bird-watcher's paradise. Five beaches ring the island, the best being Casuarina Beach, which runs the entire length of the western shore of this 135-acre paradise. Palm Island caters to those who like barefoot informality, friendly people, warm sun and clear water. There are several private villas for rent, there's also a boutique, tennis court, a game room complete with TV, and even a ping-pong table. The island is ringed by *Highway 90*, John Caldwell's walking/jogging/fitness trail that helped keep him so fit into his 80s.

Navigational Information
As shown on Chart GND-12, the anchorage is off the western shore of Palm Island, just off the dock. Approaching from the north, a waypoint at 12° 36.80' N, 61° 24.20' W, will place you approximately 1 mile north of the channel between *Thompson's Reef* and Palm Island. From the waypoint steer generally east of south avoiding *Thompson's Reef* to starboard, and the reef system lying north of Palm Island to your port. When off the dock anchor in sand wherever your draft allows; expect the anchorage to be crowded. Watch out for the shoals lying southwest and west/southwest of the anchorage area. Note that this anchorage can be a bit rolly.

What You Will Find Ashore

Tie your dinghy to the dock (leave plenty of room please) and if you walk southeast you'll come to a small boutique next door to the *Sunset Grill*, an informal and cruiser friendly establishment that monitors VHF ch. 16.

Located in the hotel is the more upscale *Royal Palm Restaurant & Bar*, where you can experience intimate gourmet dining in three different areas, giving you the ultimate in privacy for breakfast, lunch and dinner. The hotel and restaurant are both a bit more formal than most similar Caribbean haunts as you will learn when you notice that every afternoon at precisely 1600 tea is served in the private patios and at the gazebo. For those wishing to tie the knot, Palm Island has its own special wedding ceremonies, ask about them at the hotel. The hotel also puts together tours of various areas, ask at the office. Also, don't forget that T-shirts, flip-flops, and sneakers and not permitted during the evening meals in either of the restaurants on Palm Island.

The Story of Coconut Johnny

The late John Caldwell and his lovely wife Mary are responsible for the transformation of Prune Island into one of the loveliest islands in the Eastern Caribbean, now known as Palm Island. So, where does the Palm Island story begin, and who was Coconut Johnny. Permit me to explain...

The tale begins in Fort Worth, Texas, the birthplace of John Caldwell in 1919. John suffered from tuberculosis until his mid-teens when his father, an alcoholic, left the family. John and his part-Cherokee Indian and a nurse by trade, moved to Los Angeles where John toiled at all manner of odd jobs to support his mother and five younger siblings. John never went beyond 8th grade, but he did manage to enroll in what is now the University of California at Santa Barbara and quit in 1943, two years after the outbreak of World War II. John served in the U.S. Merchant Marine during the remaining war years and while in Australia he met Mary who soon became his wife. John's ship then returned to America and the adventures John had in returning to Mary in Australia was to become the book that made him famous, *Desperate Voyage*.

Upon his return to the States after the war, John Caldwell found that he had no other way to get from California to Australia except to take a steamer. He hopped on a ship bound for Panama where he hoped to find another to take him across the Pacific to his Mary. Finding none, John bought a 29' wooden sloop named *Pagan* that he hoped would be the means to reunite him with his wife. John did not know how to sail, but he set off anyway with two cats for crew and a book on navigation when lo and behold, he found himself in the midst of a hurricane which all but sank his vessel. Adrift for 49 days without food, he washed up on the shore of Tuyutha in the Fiji Islands where he was cared for by the islanders who nursed him back to health until he was able to catch a freighter several months later.

Reunited with his Mary at last, the couple returned to California where John published *Desperate Voyage* (Little Brown, 1948) and graduated college with a major in Sociology. John has been called to task many times concerning some of the stories in his book and the truth behind them, but as Tristan Jones once said, "Why let the truth get in the way of a good story?"

In 1954, John, Mary, and their two sons, sailed for Australia on a 36' double-ended John Hanna designed ketch in a tale that is told in *Family at Sea*, John's second book (Little Brown, 1956). *Family at Sea* is the amazing story of their voyage and their strength in the light of the fact that their second son, 8-month old Stevie, was retarded and had an immune deficiency. After planning the voyage for years, doubt crept in over their new son's condition. Finally, their friend, actor Sterling Hayden, recommended a physician who counseled the Caldwells to take their son offshore where he could breathe clean air and live free of the contaminants in our industrialized society.

As they voyaged throughout the islands and atolls of the South Pacific, the Caldwells rarely took their son ashore, so much did they fear infection. Sadly, after reaching Australia they had to take him ashore and he soon died at the age of 3½, far too young in anybody's book. Remaining in Australia, John and Mary had another son and built a 46' ketch, *Outward Bound,* on which they began a circumnavigation in 1958. When the family arrived in Antigua in 1960, their cruising kitty was extremely low and they began taking charters up and down the Eastern Caribbean for Desmond Nicholson, the dean of Caribbean charter skippers. As they sailed up and down the island chain John would carry sprouting coconuts aboard and would stop and plant some at nearly every island the couple visited, earning John the nickname *Coconut Johnny*. And it was while planting coconuts that John first set foot on Prune Island, then hardly more than a mosquito infested swamp.

John and Mary had a vision for Prune Island, a hotel. In 1966, John began to talk to representatives of the government of St. Vincent and the Grenadines that eventually led him to leasing the island for 99 years for the sum of $1 per year. At this time, the government was leasing barren islands such as Mustique, Petit St. Vincent, and Young Island, to entrepreneurs who applied with hotel designs and promises of employment for the local populace. Once secure on Prune Island, John created the *Palm Island Hotel Company* and set about draining the swamp, planting hundreds of palm trees, and building his hotel (knowing as much about running a hotel as he did about sailing the first time he set off across an ocean). John's vision, the *Palm Island Beach Club,* opened in December of 1967 and the Caldwell's cruising days were over. For the next three decades John, Mary, and their children and grandchildren ran the hotel and adjacent properties. At one time there were rumors that Donald Trump was interested in purchasing the property, but John held on to his dream.

John Caldwell is said to have planted thousands of palm trees up and down the Caribbean, probably most of the ones you'll see on your cruise in these waters were carefully planted by his own hands. Coconut Johnny passed away in November of 1999 at the age of 80. Today, new owners are continuing John and Mary's dream and Palm Island is evolving into the elite world class destination whose potential John and Mary saw long ago. Rest in peace Coconut Johnny.

Petit St. Vincent and Petite Martinique

Waypoints:
Punaise/Mopion- ½ nm NNW of pass between
12° 33.00' N, 61° 24.20' W

Petit St. Vincent - ½ nm W of anchorage
12° 32.00' N, 61° 23.50' W

Petite Martinique- ½ nm ESE of Petite Dominique
12° 30.30' N, 61° 23.40' W

The two tiny islands of Petit St. Vincent and Petite

Martinique are, with the exception of Mustique, probably the most exclusive islands in the Grenadines. Petit St. Vincent (PSV) is world-renowned thanks to the efforts of Haze Richardson, the current owner, and his former partner Doug Terman. After careers in the U.S. Air Force, the two pooled their money and headed for the Caribbean on an old wooden yacht. Here they met Willis Nichols who gave them the inspiration to buy a Caribbean Island, which is now one of the world's most exclusive resorts. There are no phones on this 113 acre island, and if you need something you raise a yellow flag and put your list in the bamboo mailbox, somebody will soon be by to pick up your list and deliver your goodies back to you. If you raise a red flag, nobody, and I mean nobody, will come by to bother you.

Petit St. Vincent is part of St. Vincent and The Grenadines, while its neighbor Petite Martinique, although geographically part of the Grenadines, is actually part of the nation of Grenada and was settled by the French at the same time as Grenada.

Petit Martinique (PM) is volcanic in origin (it is actually the tip of a volcanic cone), covers 586 acres (450 of which were once farmed), and is dominated by a 750' high mountain at its center with great views of the Grenadines, Carriacou, and Grenada. PM was once owned by a Frenchman, his wife (Madame Pierre), and their children and slaves. The small village is called *Madame Pierre* after the owner's wife.

Navigational Information
As shown on Chart GND-14, a waypoint at 12° 32.00' N, 61° 23.50' W, will place you approximately ½ mile west of the anchorage off Petit St. Vincent, and approximately ½ mile northwest of the anchorage at Petite Martinique. However, getting to this waypoint requires usage of other waypoints and a bit of piloting between shoals.

Approaching from the north, or from Windward in Carriacou, you can make your way to a waypoint at 12° 33.00' N, 61° 24.20' W, which will place you about ½ mile north/northwest of the passage between Punaise and Mopion (meaning *bedbug* and *louse*). From the waypoint, pilot between the two small sandbar/islands to the waypoint off PSV and PM.

Lots of cruisers enjoy anchoring at Mopion, but many are damaging the coral when they drop their

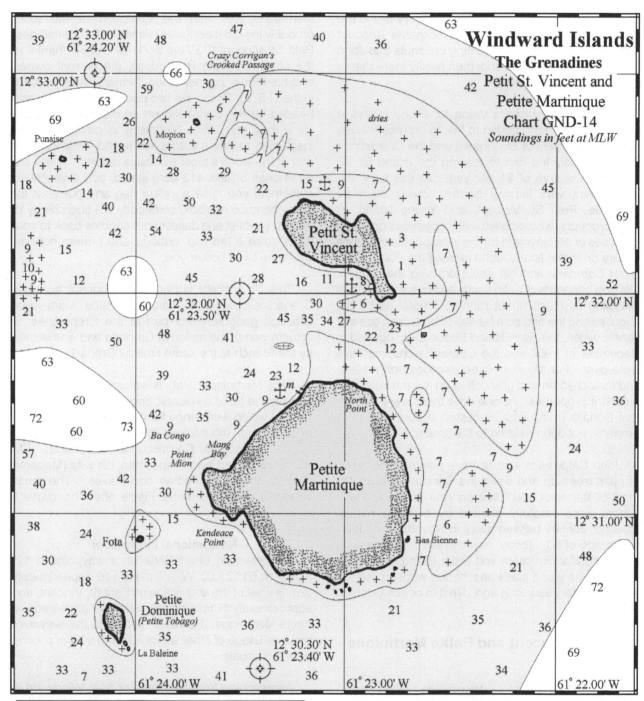

Windward Islands
The Grenadines
Petit St. Vincent and
Petite Martinique
Chart GND-14
Soundings in feet at MLW

39 12° 33.00' N
61° 24.20' W

48   47   40   36   63

Crazy Corrigan's
Crooked Passage

42

66

12° 33.00' N

59   30   30

63   26   Mopion   6   7   dries

69   22   7   7

Punaise   18   14   7   7   45

18   28   29

12   15   ⚓ 9   7   69

18   30   22   1

14   40   42   50   32   3   39

21   54   33   21   Petit St.   7   52

42   30   27   Vincent   1

9   15   45   28   16   11   ⚓ 8   1   12° 32.00' N
61° 23.50' W

10   12   63   60   12° 32.00' N   6   9

9   61° 23.50' W   30

21   33   45   35   34 27   23   7

50   48   41   22   12   33

63   39   24   23   12

60   33   33   ⚓ m   7   5   36

72   60   42   9   9   North   7

60   73   35   Point   7   24

57   Ba Congo   9

Point   Mang   7   15   50

40   Mion   Bay   Petite   7

36   33   30   Martinique   9

38   15   6   12° 31.00' N

24   Fota   Kendeace   7   48

30   33   Point   33   21   72

18   33   33   Bas Sienne

35   22   Petite   21   35

Dominique   36   33   36

24   (Petite Tobago)   35   33

33   7   33   La Baleine   33   41   12° 30.30' N   36   34   69
61° 23.40' W
61° 24.00' W   61° 23.00' W   61° 22.00' W

Petit St. Vincent (left) and Petite Martinique (right)

Mopion

hook off the south side of the small sandbar. I prefer to anchor off the western shore of Petit St. Vincent and dinghy over to Mopion.

If you are approaching from the south, you can steer for a waypoint at 12° 30.30' N, 61° 23.40' W, which will place you approximately ½ mile southwest of Petite Martinique and approximately ½ mile east/southeast of Petite Dominique (sometimes shown as Petite Tobago). From this waypoint steer between Petite Dominique and Petite Martinique where you can then pass on either side of the tiny island of Fota. Passing to the west of Fota is safest as there are reefs of the southwestern shore of Petite Martinique at Kendeace Point. Once past Fota you can turn to the northeast to the waypoint off PSV and PM. If you wish to anchor off Petite Martinique, the best spot is just southwest of the docks in soft mud. Keep an eye out for the wreck of a freighter that went down in 1998, it's marked on Chart GND-14 and is located about ¼ mile north/northwest of the dock. The *Palm Beach Restaurant* has two red moorings available, free if you dine at their establishment.

If you choose to anchor off Petit St. Vincent, you may anchor west of the docks, but keep an eye out for the shoal that works out westward from PSV as shown on Chart GND-14. Be advised that there is a good bit of current here and when the wind dies, you will swing on your hook.

What You Will Find Ashore
As I mentioned, Petite Martinique is politically a part of Grenada, but if you have cleared out of St. Vincent at Union Island, nobody will say anything if you visit PM before heading to Carriacou or Grenada to clear for entry. The same is true if you're heading north and have cleared out of Carriacou.

The people of Petite Martinique have a rich seafaring heritage including boat building, fishing, sailing, and many of the men have had careers in the cargo industry. PM has one church, a school, bank, *Post Office*, health center, gas station, and several small grocery stores with telephone service close to the dock.

Marine Facilities
Fuel
Hurricane Lenny destroyed the fuel dock on PM in 1999, but it has long been rebuilt. Here you can take on diesel, gasoline, water, or ice at the new dock (16'

water depth) by contacting *B&C Fuels Enterprise*, call *Golf-Sierra* on VHF ch. 16, or phone 473-443-9110.

Marine Facilities
Marine Services
A short walk up the main road from the dock on PM is *E&B Hardware*, just above *E&B Supermarket*. Besides normal hardware, they also carry some marine hardware and other items such as resin, fiberglass cloth, and fishing tackle. You can also get your outboard repaired here. Local boatbuilders, the Clement brothers, are invaluable if you require some assistance with any type of repair; they often respond to charter boat problems in the area.

Internet Access
On Petite Martinique you can get online at *Millennium Connection*, a small boutique located at *Matthew's Shopping Center*. The *Palm Beach Restaurant*, also on PM, has free *Wi-fi* for their diners.

Provisions
A short walk up the main road for the dock on PM is the *E&B Supermarket*. On the beach at Petite Martinique is the *Seaside View Supermarket* where you can get some provisions, a room, or rent *SCUBA* gear and get a tank refilled. Also on PM you can choose from the *Standing Wave* for food, rum, and snack foods, and the *M&M Market* for fruits, veggies, and dry goods as well. You can pick up spirits at *Matthew's Shopping Center* just up from the dock.

Dining
The resort at Petit St. Vincent is really only set up to accommodate its guests, however cruisers are welcome, but it is advisable to make reservations for dinner well in advance. This place is so popular that if the bar is too crowded; you may be met at the dinghy dock and refused entry unless you have a reservation.

For dining on Petite Martinique, try the *Palm Beach Restaurant* (VHF ch. 16) with its elegant waterfront atmosphere featuring West Indian cuisine and of course specializing in seafood. If you're anchored at Petit St. Vincent, they offer a water taxi service, a great offer that one cannot refuse, especially if you are able to pick up one of the red moorings that are free for their customers. Nearby is *Melodies Guest House Restaurant and Bar* (*Tasha P Radio* on VHF ch. 16), which also offers a water taxi service.

Grenada

The independent nation of Grenada, pronounced *Gre-nay-da*, comprises three main islands: Grenada, Carriacou, and Petite Martinique (which was covered in the previous chapter *The Grenadines*). The main island of Grenada's 133 square miles is home to over 100,000 people, 45 beaches, and co-starred with Barbados in the movie *Island in the Sun* with Harry Belafonte.

Grenada is known as the *Island of Spices* and in fact has more spices per square-mile than any other place on earth...nutmeg, cinnamon, vanilla, clove, mace, ginger, as well as cocoa and bananas. In fact, Grenada produces a third of the world's nutmeg and is second only to India in the production of that particular spice. It's hard to go anywhere in Grenada, a bar or restaurant, without finding a unique drink or entree that is specially seasoned with nutmeg.

In the appendices at the end of this guide, there is as complete a listing of the marine services in Grenada as I could compile, but in addition Grenada now offers a *Marine Services Directory* that is available free of charge at most marinas and chandlers on the island.

Grenada has a marine trades association called *MAYAG* (www.mayag.org, 473-416-7135) and they can be called upon for help with any matters of dispute while you are in the waters of Grenada.

A Brief History of Grenada

Christopher Columbus "discovered" Grenada in 1498 on his third voyage to the New World, but never set foot upon her shores. Columbus named the island *Concepción*, but that name was short lived. Years later, Spanish sailors passing by, seeing her rolling hills, named her Granada after their hilly homeland in Spain. The French changed this to Grenade, and the British changed that to Grenada. But Grenada's history begins centuries before Columbus voyage by the island.

Grenada shares a similar history with her sister islands in the Eastern Caribbean, being settled first by the peaceful Arawaks who were followed by the Caribs who named the island *Camerhogne*. Earlier, the Calivignoid Indians inhabited the island, their only remains being some pottery with strange geometric designs. The Caribs had a strong presence on the island until the mid-1600s when the French settlers, after years of bloody skirmishes, managed to get the upper hand.

In 1609, British settlers attempted to settle on Grenada, but were chased off by the savage Caribs. In 1650, a French expedition from Martinique traded beads, knives, and hatchets to the indigenous Caribs for extensive tracts of land. However fighting soon broke out between the French settlers and the Caribs, which resulted in the last 40 Caribs jumping to their deaths from Sauteurs 100' cliffs rather than submit to French rule in 1651. Today the place is called *Leaper's Hill*, or in French, *Place le Morne de Sauteurs*.

The British and the French battled for the next 90 years for possession of Grenada; Fort George and Fort Frederick, both overlooking St. George's Harbour, are of that era. The British finally overwhelmed the French in 1762 and Grenada was ceded to Britain in 1783 by way of the *Treaty of Versailles*. No sooner had this been done than African slaves were imported as the primary work force on the plantations until Emancipation came in 1834.

To replace the former slaves, indentured servants from India arrived in 1857 followed by English settlers from Barbados. These folks settled in the hilly area known as Mt. Moritz just outside St. George's, keeping to themselves and growing fruits and vegetables. Over the centuries many ships called at Grenada to take on spices, and in return left ballast stones. These stones can be seen as the primary building material in many old houses on the island.

In 1877, Grenada became a *Crown Colony* and in 1967, an associate state within the *British Commonwealth*. On February 7, 1974 Grenada gained her independence under the leadership of the late Sir Eric Gairy. Sir Eric was quite a character; he believed in UFO's and even stated that he had communicated with them. In 1979, while Gairy was off the island, his political opponent, the Marxist Maurice Bishop, staged a coup and took control of the government and attempted to create a socialist/communist state.

Over the next four years the radical Bishop and his *New Jewel Movement* (*Joint Endeavor for Welfare, Education, and Liberation*), formed the *People's Revolutionary Government* and established strong ties with Cuba (and Bishop's mentor, Fidel Castro) and the Soviet Union. The island became home to Cuban soldiers and the airport was being expanded to allow jet aircraft to use the facilities.

In 1983, a group of Bishop's ruling *New Jewel Movement*, led by Deputy Prime Minister Bernard Coard and Army Commander Hudson Austin, staged another coup placing Bishop under house arrest and taking control of the government. Soon Bishop and several of his aides were executed in St. George's causing widespread unrest on the island.

A short while later, at the request of the Governor General, US military forces (along with troops from Jamaica, Barbados, and the Eastern Caribbean States led by Dominica's Eugenia Charles) invaded the island on October 25, 1983 under the pretext of rescuing 100 stranded US citizens at the *St. George's University Medical School*. However, the true aim of the invasion was to restore democracy and shortly order was restored as Coard and Austin were arrested. Elections were held in December of 1984 and the late Hubert A. Blaize became Prime Minister.

Blaize turned Grenada around, reorganized her economy to emphasize agriculture, light manufacturing, and lately tourism. Soon the roads of Grenada were being rebuilt and a direct-dial telephone system installed.

Today Grenada is again a stable democracy with a steady stream of tourists enjoying what she has to offer, and the medical school, near the *Renaissance Grenada Hotel* at Grand Anse Beach, is somewhat of a tourist attraction though it is still in operation with many U.S. students in attendance.

Now that you're familiar with the history of the *Isle of Spice*, let's begin our exploration in Carriacou and then work our way southward along the Grenada shoreline.

Customs and *Immigration*

Ports of Entry:
Carriacou - Hillsborough
Grenada - St. George's (*Grenada Yacht Services*), Prickly Bay (*Spice Island Marina*), St. David's Bay (*Grenada Marine*), Petite Calivigny Bay (*Le Phare Bleu Marina*), Grenville

Customs has offices at *Hillsborough Bay* on Carriacou, and on Grenada at St. George's (at *Grenada Yacht Services*), *Prickly Bay* (*Spice Island Marina*), *Mt. Hartman Bay* (*The Moorings Marina*), St. David's Bay (*Grenada Marine*), and at the primarily commercial port of Grenville on the eastern shore of Grenada. Clearing in at *Hillsborough Bay*, Carriacou, is accepted as clearance into Grenada and no further checking in is required.

Fees
Grenada has a new cruising permit fee structure in place that is to take the place of the *Port/Navigation* fees. The fees are EC$50 for vessels up to 50', EC$75 for vessels from 50'-60', EC$100 for vessels from 60'-79', and EC$150 for vessels over 80'. These fees are to be charged at your time of check-in and are to be monthly for the duration of your stay.

There are also port charges of EC$8.10 per person excluding the skipper. Vessels hauled out for a complete calendar month will be exempt for the cruising permit fees for that month upon presentation of yard documentation.

Customs hours are 0800-1145, and 1300-1600, and 1300-1700 of Fridays. Vessels are not permitted to anchor anywhere in *Grand Anse Bay,* the *Carenage* in St. George's, or in the mangrove lagoon at the northern end of *Tyrrel Bay.* Yachts are also not allowed to anchor within 200 meters of any beach in Grenada, Carriacou, or Petit Martinique.

A coastal permit is required to visit other harbors on the island; there is no charge for this permit.

If you are clearing in Grenada (not Carriacou) you can use an agent such as *Henry's Safari Tours* or *Spronks Mega Yacht Services*, they can clear you from any harbour on the island. Both agents monitor VHF Ch. 16 (*Henry's*: 473-444-5313, safari@spiceisle. com; *Spronk:* claire@spronksprovisioning.com, 473-407-3688)

Pets
Animals are not permitted ashore without an import permit and a valid rabies certificate. Proper health documents (vaccination records) must be produced and a Government Veterinary Officer must be notified as to your port of entry and time of arrival.

Firearms

Firearms must be declared and, at the *Customs* officer's discretion, will be either sealed in a locked locker aboard (whereupon you give the *Customs* officer the key) or removed from your vessel and placed in a secure locker ashore (don't forget to ask for a receipt).

Fishing

Spearfishing is not permitted in the waters of Grenada. Purchasing lobster out of season is prohibited (the season runs from Oct. 31- April 30). SCUBA diving is permitted without a Grenadian dive master.

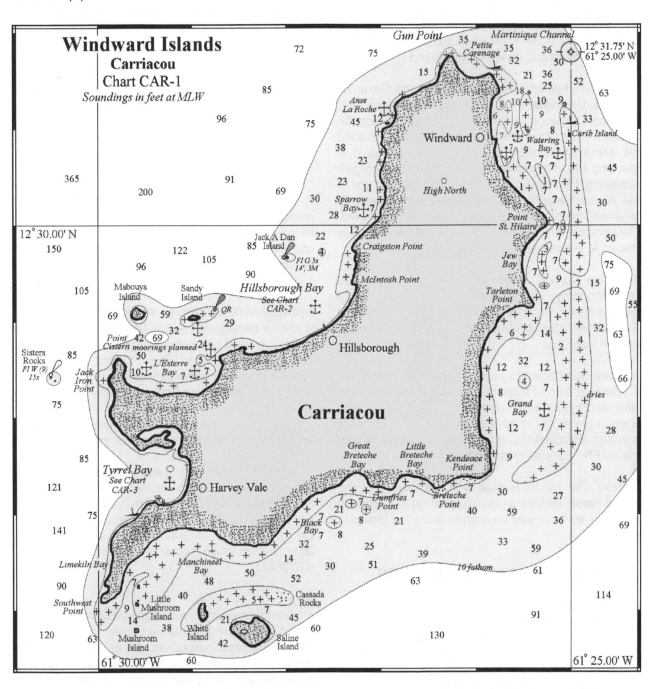

Windward Islands
Carriacou
Chart CAR-1
Soundings in feet at MLW

Carriacou

Port of Entry: Hillsborough
Fuel: Tyrrel Bay
Haul-Out: Tyrrel Bay
Diesel Repairs: Tyrrel Bay
Outboard Repairs: Tyrrel Bay
Propane: Tyrrel Bay
Provisions: Hillsborough, Tyrrel Bay
Important Lights:

Jack A Dan	Fl G 5s
Sandy Island	Q R
Sisters Rocks	Fl W (9) 15s

Although geographically part of the Grenadines, Carriacou is actually a territory of Grenada and home to roughly 5,000 people. The name *Carriacou* is said to derive from a Carib word for *land surrounded by reefs*, a fitting name judging by the reefs along the eastern and southern shore of this largest of the Grenadian Grenadines. Approximately 7 miles long and 4 miles wide at its broadest point, Carriacou is irregular in shape with a central, wooded ridge running its length and averaging approximately 750' in height. Sailing movie fans will probably know that many scenes from the movie *White Squall* were filmed on Carriacou.

Carriacou is dotted with small picturesque settlements, one gas station, over 100 rum shops, and is probably one of the most laid-back islands in the Caribbean, a sea known for its surplus of laid-back islands. A quiet island, Carriacou is the type of place where time has little meaning, unless you plan to catch the ferry. A place where you go to bed with the setting sun and arise with the dawn; a place where you share the roads and walkways, and yes, even the boatyard's grounds, with cows, goats, and donkeys.

The people of Carriacou are friendly, open, and quite industrious. Carriacou is one of the only places where I contracted a man to do a small job for me and trusted him when he told me "Don worry, it won't cost much." As it turned out, it didn't cost much! Now used to being shaken down by the more expensive establishments that love to gouge us cruisers, I was pleasantly shocked to say the least.

How the people of Carriacou love to lime and party! Besides Carnival, there are two big annual parties on Carriacou, the annual *Carriacou Regatta* in August (DO NOT MISS THIS EVENT!), and the *Fisherman's Birthday*. The *Fisherman's Birthday* is a three-day fete during which everyone joins in swimming races, tug of war, domino games, as well as the usual partying and dancing. So, if you like quiet, no hustle, no bustle, and with nobody whose sole purpose is to drain your wallet (of course *Customs* and *Immigration* officers everywhere are exempt from this statement), you'll love Carriacou.

As with her neighbors, Carriacou was first settled by Arawaks and has a well-documented Taino history with a large number of artifacts being found on the island. A recent dig in Harvey Vale unearthed several complete skeletons, burial masks, and a drinking well. Other digs produced ceramic body ornaments and loom weights that researchers speculated dated back over a thousand years. From more recent history, French built roads dating to the 1600s, crisscross Carriacou making great walking trails for visiting cruisers out for a day's hike. In other areas, plantation remains dating to the 1700s are evidenced by the remains of great houses and outbuildings in what is today pastures and woodlands.

High North Peak rises over 930' above sea level and is the highest spot on the island. A national park, *High North Peak* contains important watersheds for the northern part of the island and its forests lead down to *L'Anse la Roche* (where you can find a decent day anchorage as shown on Chart CAR-1), the most scenic and private beach on Carriacou while the estate ruins overlooking L'Anse la Roche Bay date back to the early 1800s. Current plans call for *High North National Park* to be recommended as a *Biosphere Reserve* with *UNESCO*, and a bird sanctuary is touted for *Petit Carenage* at the far northern tip of Carriacou.

At Belair, located in north central Carriacou at a height of 719' (with a great view of Carriacou), are the remains of the old English *Belair Estate*. John Reid owned the plantation in 1784 and in 1809, a great house was built on the property. Next to the great house are the remains of an even older French house. The estate boasts the finest sugar mill and wind mill foundations on Carriacou. At first the *Belair Estate* was a sugar cane plantation and the mill was supported by the crops grown on the grounds, later however cotton became the dominate crop and the cane was phased out. The *Belair Cultural Landscape* once served as a headquarters for the *People's Revolutionary Army* (see *A Brief History of Grenada*). At the time of the

U.S. and Caribbean Forces intervention on Grenada, a large explosion occurred at the house that remains a mystery to this day.

About ¼ mile inland along the northeastern section of Carriacou are the *Dover Ruins*, the site of the first church in Carriacou. Here square cut rocks form the foundation of Father Maissoneuve's church, an important meeting and worship place for the early French settlers of Carriacou.

Windward

Waypoints:
Windward- ½ nm N of windward reef
12° 31.75' N, 61° 25.00' W

Windward, on the northeastern tip of the island, is protected by a reef system and offers a good anchorage in most conditions even though open to the strength of the trades. Windward is a working harbor where you may actually see a locally built boat sailing in and out between the various reefs. Here, men with Scottish surnames, share a history of boatbuilding that dates back almost two centuries. In fact, one of the last of the Caribbean top-masted schooners, the *Ruby C*, was built here by the Comptons in 1948.

Navigational Information
As shown on Chart CAR-1, a waypoint at 12° 31.75' N, 61° 25.00' W, will place you approximately ½ mile north of the windward reef with the conspicuous wreck near its northern tip. Use extreme caution when piloting here as the reefs may be hard to see in some conditions.

From the waypoint, head a bit west of south to pass between the outermost windward reef (the one with the wreck) and the inner reef as shown on CAR-1. The inner reef is usually marked by a stake near its southern end, just as you enter *Watering Bay*. There is another inner reef here, but the water between it and the mainland of Carriacou is less than 6' at MLW (see Chart CAR-1). You'll see a lot of the local craft anchoring here, even a shallow draft cruiser or two at times.

If you anchor behind the reef with the stake, you can pass north of the reef with good visibility and a rising tide, to head out of *Watering Bay* as shown on Chart CAR-1. You can dinghy in to the town dock and tie off to explore.

What You Will Find Ashore
As I mentioned, Windward is the focus for boatbuilding on Carriacou although some boats are built in *Tyrrel Bay*. Here too you can view the fishing fleet under sail, unique to this island.

South of Windward sits Point St. Hilaire in central eastern Carriacou, a place steeped in Carriacou history. Here you can visit the ruins of the *Limlair Estate* that dates back to 1778. Once a livestock development area, there is a large, 30'x20'x20' well here and high rock walls as well as several cemeteries with tombs dating back to the 1700s.

On nearby Tarleton Point is an old cannon resting on a cliff and looking quite out of place. It seems that portable cannons were quite high-tech from a military standpoint in days of yore. These portable cannons could be moved about freely to surprise the enemy, be it the British, the French, or whomever, during the years when France and Britain fought for dominion over the islands of the Caribbean.

Hillsborough

Waypoints:
Hillsborough Bay- ¾ nm NW of
12° 29.90' N, 61° 28.60' W

Hillsborough is the center of Carriacou, both governmentally and socially. A *Port of Entry*, you can clear in at Hillsborough for all of Grenada, and then head south to the mainland of Grenada, to St. George's, Hog Island, or *Prickly Bay*, and from there clear out to head to Trinidad or Venezuela. You must anchor in Hillsborough to clear *Customs* and *Immigration*, anchoring in *Tyrrel Bay* and taking a taxi to Hillsborough can result in a steep fine.

Navigational Information
As shown on chart CAR-2, a waypoint at 12° 29.90'N, 61° 28.60' W, will place you approximately ¾ mile northwest of *Hillsborough Bay*. From the waypoint pass south of Jack A. Dan Island and anchor off the town dock. One can pass between Jack A. Dan Island and the mainland of Carriacou, but you must beware of the small shoal with about 4' over it that lies just east of the center of the channel between the two landmasses.

The town dock hosts the *Osprey Lines Ferry* that runs from Grenada to Hillsborough, and to Petite

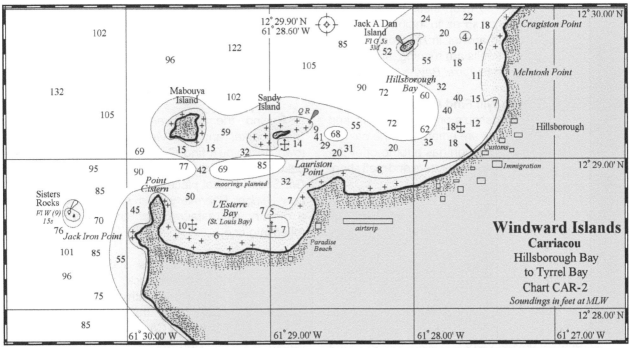

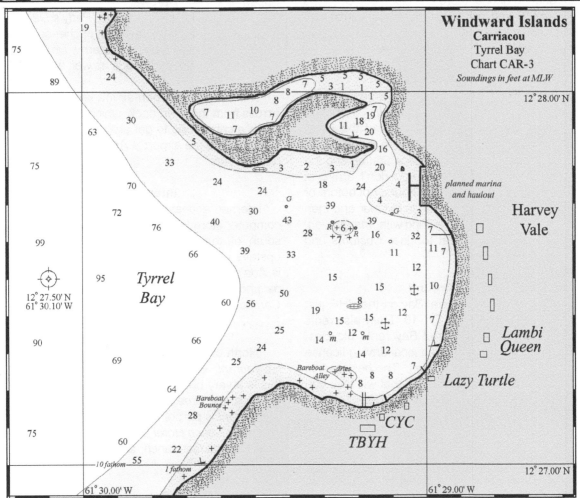

Martinique twice daily, so keep clear of its coming and goings, don't anchor so as to inhibit the ferry's movement. Don't try to anchor in *Hillsborough Bay* when strong northerly swells are running, at that time it's better to move down to *Tyrrel Bay*.

What You Will Find Ashore

Hillsborough is Carriacou's only true "town," and although some storefronts are empty, and the paint is peeling on others, Hillsborough has a lot to offer the cruiser besides the normal grocery store and craft shop.

Cruisers who enjoy history will want to visit the *Carriacou Historical Museum* on *Paterson Street* in Hillsborough. Set in the ruins of an old cotton gin, the building was restored in the style of an early 1800s museum and displays Amerindian, African, and European artifacts relevant to Carriacou's history.

Customs and *Immigration*

Hillsborough is more open than *Tyrrel Bay*, and if it is too rough to anchor there and clear, call *Customs* on VHF ch. 16 and ask for permission to anchor in *Tyrrel Bay* and take a bus to Hillsborough to clear. Do not go to *Tyrrel Bay* unless you have permission from *Customs* to do so.

After anchoring in *Hillsborough Bay*, tie up to the town dock's dinghy landing to clear in. Although *Customs* is in the building at the foot of the dock, you will need to go across the street to the blue and white building that houses the *Police Station* and the *Immigration* office. Make sure you don't arrive at their office except during working hours, not before or during lunch, as they'll invite you in to clear and then charge you overtime. After clearing with *Immigration*, head back across the street to clear *Customs* and you're all set.

Getting Around

Taxis can be found in *Tyrrel Bay* on the VHF, just call *Linky Taxi* or *Bubbles* on Ch. 16. *Linky* also rents jeeps. *Lambi Queen* in *Tyrrel Bay* rents bicycles. Cruisers will have to purchase a local driving license (EC$30) and must drive on the left. The best deal to be found is the buses on Carriacou that will take you just about anywhere on the island for EC$3.

Provisions

Just south of the *Immigration* office is a nice supermarket and fresh produce can be picked up at the stalls in front of the *Police Station*. Just south of the

blue and white building that houses the *Immigration* office and *Police Station*, is *Bullen's Market*, a good place to pick up a few provisions, hardware, tools, and even duty-free fuel and lubricants. *Bullen's* monitors VHF ch. 16 and their call sign is *VBS Agency*. *Bullen's* is also a *Western Union* agent.

Behind the *Immigration* office is the *Unity Supermarket* and the *Victoria Bar*. North of the town dock you'll find *Gramma's Bakery* (all sorts of baked goods and ice cream), *Sandisland Café and Gift Shop* (a great place for breakfast), a gas station, *Low Budget Pharmacy*, and *Ade's Dream* which is a guesthouse-restaurant-bar and grocery store all rolled into one.

There are crafts shops such as the *Master Craftsman* (left from the dock), boutiques such as the *Mahogany Boutique* with its book exchange, and a couple of good markets; *John's Unique Resort Supermarket* on *Church St.*, and *Mattheson's Supermarket and Hardware*, also on *Church St.* (they will deliver to the dock for you). *Patty's Deli* is not to be missed with a great selection of cheese, cold cuts, and freshly baked goodies! Nearby, *De Pastry Shop* also has freshly baked goods as well as sandwiches.

There is a small open-air market (just a few stalls) across from the town dock, which is also the place to catch a cab or bus to get around the island. A short walk towards the airport is *Annie's Roti* to satisfy your roti cravings.

Internet Access

Internet access can be found at *Digi-Soft*, a computer store located upstairs in the *M&M* building south of the dock. *Bullen's* has internet access upstairs at *Services Unlimited*. Near the town dock is *Ade's Dream* with his own computer room as well as phone and fax services. You can also try the *Carriacou Yacht Club*.

Dining

North of town is the Swedish owned *Green Roof Restaurant*, dinner reservations are suggested as this is a very busy place. A nice upscale restaurant is *Lyme and Dine* at *Silver Dining*. The *New Wave Restaurant* is part of *Ade's Dream*. Nearby you'll find the *Silver Beach Hotel* a good guesthouse/restaurant serving breakfast, lunch, and dinner, and continental dishes.

Further north, at the foot of *High North Peak*, is the *Caribbee Country House*, where you can dine on fine authentic French Creole dishes. They have an elegant dining room, or if that does not suit your taste, you can chow down in the informal tropical garden.

South of the town dock the road leads eventually to Harvey Vale and *Tyrrel Bay*, but in the immediate area south of the dock you'll find *John's Print Shop* upstairs next to *Barclay's Bank*, *Millie's Guesthouse*, *M&M* and *Dollarman Hardware* (both good hardware stores).

A short ten-minute stroll south of town is the *Green Roof Inn* right on the shore. The restaurant and bar are located on the verandah with a scenic view of *Hillsborough Bay*.

Fuel

You can arrange for fuel through *Bullen's Supermarket*.

Sandy Island and *L'Esterre Bay*

One of the best snorkeling spots in the Caribbean can be found off the southwest coast of Carriacou at Sandy Island. Lying about 1¼ miles west of the town dock at Hillsborough, the small anchorage south of Sandy Island is surrounded by some nice reefs and the tiny island itself is home to a gorgeous beach. Turtle nesting sites have been found on the island and the entire area is excellent for birdwatching. A bit further west is volcanic Mabouya Island, part of *Protected Seascape*. Little is here save some thorny scrub vegetation, cactus, and frangipani. Cruisers please note that spearfishing is not permitted in the waters around Sandy Island.

Navigational Information

If approaching Sandy Island, simply head west/northwest of the town dock and anchor on the southern side of the island, just east of the shoal that works its way out from the southwestern tip of the island. Use caution when approaching this reef, it is made up of dead coral in spots that are hard to discern if the water is not crystal clear. Watch out for the reef that extends east and east/southeast from the eastern tip of Sandy Island as well. This is a small anchorage so make sure your hooks are well set, if you drag, it will likely be onto that western reef, unless a neighbor's boat stops you.

You can anchor off the mainland of Carriacou in *L'Esterre Bay*, sometimes shown as *St. Louis Bay*. As shown on Chart CAR-2, head into the bay and you can anchor in the eastern end just off the small dock at *Off The Hook on Paradise Beach*.

What You Will Find Ashore

At the southwest end of *Paradise Beach* in *L'Esterre Bay* is *Off The Hook*, a wonderful little restaurant open for breakfast, lunch, and dinner, from 0900-2300. If you need a haircut, Curtis, the owner, is a barber!

At the northeastern end of the bay is *Fidel's*, a fantastic little gift and craft shop that is not to be missed. Next door is Joan's, a small bar and restaurant that serves up lunch and dinner (with advance notice).

Tyrrel Bay

Waypoints:
Tyrrel Bay- ¾ nm W of anchorage
12° 27.50' N, 61° 30.10' W

Navigational Information

As shown on Chart CAR-3, a waypoint at 12° 27.50' N, 61° 30.10' W, will place you approximately ¾ mile west of the anchorage area in *Tyrrel Bay*. If you're approaching from *Hillsborough Bay*, you may pass south of Sandy Island to round Point Cistern and Jack Iron Point, keeping in the channel between Carriacou and Sisters Rock as shown on Chart CAR-2. Here you can keep at least ¼ mile offshore as you work your way into *Tyrrel Bay*. The best anchoring is on the more southern side of the bay, anywhere between the town dock to the north, and the *Tyrrel Bay Yacht Haulout* dock to the south. Keep an eye out for the reef on the northern side of *Tyrrel Bay* that has almost 6' over it at MLW and is marked by a red buoy.

At the extreme northern end of *Tyrrel Bay* is the entrance to a mangrove lined lake that is a good spot to secure your vessel in the event of a hurricane. The entrance is straightforward as shown on Chart CAR-3, but once past the second point of land to port, you must favor the northern shore of the lake, that is where the deeper water lies (about 5' at MLW). Vessels are not allowed to anchor here unless it is an emergency; there are oyster beds here that must not be damaged. Carriacou is famed for its mangrove oyster which comes from these waters and this area may one day soon become protected. It is currently illegal to take oysters without a license.

What You Will Find Ashore

Tyrrel Bay is one of my most favorite spots in the Caribbean...I don't know why...perhaps because it has a great boatyard, several good restaurants, and hurricane protection in the mangroves north of the bay, or simply because it's just a nice, pleasant anchorage with a great ambiance. The town itself is called Harvey Vale, and offers a bit of shopping, though true provisioning should be done in Hillsborough or south at Grenada.

Getting Around

Taxis can be found in *Tyrrel Bay* on the VHF, just call *Linky Taxi* or *Bubbles* on Ch. 16. *Linky* also rents jeeps and *Lambi Queen* rents bicycles.

Internet Access

Tyrrel Bay is covered with Wi-fi based at *TBYH* and sponsored by the *Carriacou Children's Educational Fund*. Check at the *TBYH* office to link up. The *Lazy Turtle* offers free Wi-fi.

Marine Facilities
Marine Services

I am pleased to give a stunning recommendation to the haulout facility in *Tyrrel Bay*, the *Tyrrel Bay Yacht Haul Out* (473-443-8878). *TBYH* is a newly established yard, only about 3 years old, and the service and prices are superb. To call it rustic might be an understatement...you have to share the yard with wandering goats, chickens, and the occasional cow. Just walking to the shower you have to dodge goat and cow droppings (difficult to do in the dark), but that just adds to the ambiance. Owners Jerry Stewart and the Alexis family have a great yard with a marine railway and a 50-ton Travel Lift (they can haul up to an 18' beam with an 8' draft), and while you can't get spray painting here, you can certainly sand and paint your bottom, or have the yard do it for you at very, very reasonable rates. The yard can import parts from *Budget Marine* or *Island Water World*. If you need a slip the yard can handle up to seven boats.

If you need help with your labors, you can hire the yard's personnel or a local entrepreneur. I chose Kenroy Noel, who, for a very modest hourly wage helped me sand and paint my boat from the deck to the keel. For expert fiberglass repair you can contact George Schmitt at *Arawak Divers* and for fabrication, Dominique (on his trimaran workshop anchored just off the yard) or Uwe at *Tool Meister*, who also works on diesels. There is a sailmaker on site, check with *In Stitches*.

The yard itself is very eco-friendly. There are drains completely encircling the yard that empty into a huge tank. All debris, sandings, barnacles, old paint, etc., that comes off boats all winds up in the tank where it settles and is disposed of instead of being allowed to run off into *Tyrrel Bay* (which has poor circulation for flushing something of this magnitude). I painted *IV Play* there and was happy with the prices and service, even with getting help to pull my rudder from an already overworked yard manager. All in all, if you're planning to haul out in Venezuela, try Carriacou first, it's on the way and it's just as cheap.

Next door to *TBYH*, is the *Carriacou Yacht Club*, *CYC*, a popular meeting spot for cruisers. Here you can shop their small store, dine in their restaurant, use the phone, send a fax, check out the book swap, receive mail, shop in their mini-mart, grab a shower, have your laundry done, get a room, or simply relax and enjoy the bar and restaurant.

Fuel

You can arrange for fuel through *Bullen's* supermarket in Hillsborough.

Laundry

You can have your laundry done at *My Beautiful Launderette next to the Alexis Supermarket*. Next to *Lambi Queen* is *Jack's Shorebase Services*, a laundry with a small chandlery on site as well as a small market.

Garbage

You can drop off your garbage at the *Yacht Club* for a small fee per bag. Alternative dumping spots are at the dump north of the town dock, or the can on top of the hill above the *Tyrrel Bay Yacht Haulout*. You'll see other garbage bins located around town.

Provisions

As I mentioned, the *CYC* has a small market on site. The *Twilight Supermarket* in the center of Harvey Vale monitors VHF ch. 16. Nearby *Alexis Supermarket* is run by the same family that runs *TBYH*. If you need meat, try *Uncle George and Sons*, on the right side of the road just south of the yacht club. *After Ours* offers a 5% discount on orders over US$150.

Dining

Now let's discuss where to get a drink or something to eat in *Tyrrel Bay*. My first stop is usually *Saraca* at the *Carriacou Yacht Club*. Next door is

Slipway in a building icarefully crafted from the old slipway building; it is a great spot for lunch and dinner (Tuesday-Saturday) or a Sunday brunch.

The *Lazy Turtle* is a popular spot and they have their own dinghy dock (careful, it's a floating dock and it can be tricky, you can also tie up the dinghy at the *CYC* or town dock). Italian fare and pizzas are the focus here but an added bonus is their free Wi-fi.

In the center of town is *Scraper's Restaurant* run by *The Mighty Scraper*, who was once known as the *Calypso King of Carriacou*. In the center of the harbor you'll find *Hallelujah*, a green and white power boat that's also a floating restaurant and party vessel that you should not miss! Their seafood barbecue is nothing short of delicious.

Next to *In Stitches* is *Natasha's Bayside Restaurant* with one waterfront table just across the road, a unique floor plan. Ronnie, who is known as *The Mighty Runaway*, is an ex-policeman and former security guard at TBYH who has his own bar and restaurant, *Runaway's Hideaway*, high on the hill east of *TBYH*. Just look for the red flag flying from Ronnie's roof.

The *Twilight Restaurant and Bar* offers fine local fare including mangrove oysters in an intimate atmosphere. Another one of my favorite places is the *Lambi Queen,* a popular spot for locals as well as cruisers serving up seafood, fine wine and other spirits, and is just a great place to lime (Friday night is *Steel Pan* night). *After Ours* is a new spot and quite popular.

Exploring Southwest Carriacou
At La Pointe, at the southwestern tip of Carriacou, you'll find the *Fossil Beds Natural Landmark* which exposes millions of years of archeology in the sedimentary and igneous layers of the outer crust. The *La Pointe Cultural Landmark* is situated on the southwestern peninsula and contains the ruins of an old French estate house as well as being home to a group of curious iguanas.

Carriacou to Grenada

White Island and Saline Island

Navigational Information
Located about one mile south of Carriacou as shown on Chart CAR-1, lie White Island and Saline Island, possibly one of the future's outstanding scenic and tourism sites in Grenadian waters. The island pair are geologically fascinating and a bit unusual for the Grenadines. Both have pyroclastic volcanic plugs and deposits that indicate major volcanic activity in the past. These plugs, more like a dome in shape and fractured in places into tall columns, rise over 200' in height and are deeply undercut by wave action.

While there is really no place for a cruising boat to anchor overnight here, you might find a bit of a lee to drop the hook and explore. In mild conditions you should be able to find a spot in the lee of Saline Island, between Saline Island and the reef that extends eastward from White Island to Cassada Rocks.

What You Will Find Ashore
White Island is surround on three sides by pristine beaches untouched by the masses of tourists that congregate a few miles to the north in the Tobago Cays. Iguanas were common here until the 1960s and today are rarely seen. The vegetation on White Island is said to be unusual for the Lesser Antilles, being more in character with flora found in the Greater Antilles and the Bahamas.

Saline Island has a brackish salt pond surrounded by mangroves where shorebirds search for food; this area is one of Grenada's finest natural settings. There are various lookout points on the island pair that offer panoramic views of the reefs close in along the shoreline of Saline Island and the vast reef stretching from White Island to Cassada Rocks, some of the largest and most diverse reefs in Grenadian waters. Look for this are to be developed for tourism in the future; hopefully only eco-tourism.

There is good snorkeling on the northeastern side of the anchorage at Saline Island even though much of the island's reefs are dead and/or dying.

Cruisers will want to note that spearfishing is not permitted in the waters surrounding White Island and Saline Island, both of which are underwater parks.

Île de Ronde

Waypoints:
Île de Ronde- 1½ nm W of
12° 19.00' N, 61° 37.00' W

Hillsborough Bay, Carriacou

Building a schooner, Tyrrel Bay

Tyrrel Bay Yacht Haulout

Windward Islands

Carriacou to Grenada

Île de Ronde,
Kick Em Jenny
Chart CAR-4
Soundings in feet at MLW

Kick 'Em Jenny
Underwater
Volcano (582)

210   114   150

12° 19.00' N   149   12° 20.00' N
61° 37.00' W   Diamond Rock
                 (240)   59   (Kick Em Jenny)   160
                         52
                    42   Île de   105
         166   Ronde
              109   11
   180   202   20   90   Dry Rock
          Corn Store   ⊙
            Bay   120
   162 102   (39)   90   Les Tantes
                                                          1 fathom
   366   The Sisters
                                          3 knots
        240   184   10 fathom   1.5 knots
                265   (33) Caille   25
                              Island   Whale
   1800   315   75   Bay
                                                  120   150
              310
   554   1 knot   180
              275
                         2.5 knots

61° 40.00' W   61° 35.00' W

Navigational Information

About halfway between Carriacou and the mainland of Grenada, lie a small group of islands, Île de Ronde being the largest and the only one with an anchorage to speak of. As shown on Chart CAR-4, a waypoint at 12° 19.00' N, 61° 37.00' W, will place you approximately 1 ½ miles west of the anchorage on the western shore of Île de Ronde. From the waypoint steer generally eastward towards Île de Ronde to anchor in *Corn Store Bay*, the small cove created by the elbow of the island. You can anchor here in 15'-40' of water with a sandy bottom, but be prepared to roll a bit, as is the case in most lee side Caribbean anchorages. Divers and snorkelers will truly enjoy the waters around Île de Ronde, the Sisters, and Diamond Rock (sometimes shown as Diamond Islet or Île Diamante) where you can view pristine reefs full of color and sea life.

What You Will Find Ashore

A lot of folks call Diamond Rock "Kick 'Em Jenny," but Jenny is actually the name of the underwater volcano lying approximately 3¼ miles west of Île de Ronde. For more information on *Kick 'Em Jenny* read the next section.

Just south of Île de Ronde is Île de Caille, a 400-acre paradise that is tied in with John Caldwell's Palm Island and where plans call for private home sites. Ruins found on the island place a Calivignoid Indian settlement on the island in the 11th century.

Kick 'Em Jenny

"On November 18, 1867, five o'clock in the afternoon, the water in the harbor dropped five feet. The reef in front of the lagoon was exposed. Then the water in the harbor rose quickly to four feet over normal height and rushed up to the head of the Carenage. This happened three or four times. Much damage was done to boats and buildings but fortunately no lives were lost."

Frances Kay
This Is Grenada

The tsunami in Grenada, described by Frances Kay in the above quotation, was caused by an earthquake in the Virgin Islands in 1867. However, there is an increased interest in tsunami awareness in the region due to *Kick 'em Jenny*, an underwater volcano off Grenada's north coast. *Kick 'em Jenny* is the name that is attributed to the underwater volcano

lying approximately 3¼ miles west of Île de Ronde as shown on Chart CAR-4, but on some charts it is shown as the name of the island also known as Diamond Rock (sometimes shown as Diamond Islet or Île Diamante). Nearby Caille Island (see chart CAR-4) is actually made up of two youthful craters and lava flows. The area around Diamond Rock is known for its rough waters as it's the area of convergence of three distinct currents and you can almost always be assured of a lively passage through here, not always mind you, but a good bit of the time.

No one is certain where the name *Kick 'Em Jenny* came from, but Grenadian yachtsman, Laddie McIntyre, in his book *Isles Of The Caribbees* writes: "Nobody knows where the name comes from. Maybe it's a corruption of the French *cay que gêne*, or *the troublesome cay*, because the currents around it gave the old sailing ships such a hard time. Some say it's *Kick 'Em Jenny* because it kicks like a mule." That last line, as you may find out, is quite true at times.

Kick 'Em Jenny is the southernmost active volcano in the Lesser Antilles and, although a number of dive sites such as *Champagne* in Dominica and the *Mayreau Gardens* near the Tobago Cays have streams of bubbles that trickle up from the bottom signaling volcanic activity, *Kick 'Em Jenny* is the only active submarine volcano in the lower Eastern Caribbean. The 1939 eruption sent up a black cloud almost 900' into the air while the 1974 eruption caused the sea above the volcano to boil violently, spouting steam and killing numerous fish that were later found drifting to leeward of *Kick "em Jenny*.

Kick 'Em Jenny has a base with a diameter of about 3 miles and its summit rises about 4,300' above the sea floor and has been rising steadily over the years. In 1962, its summit was 770' below the sea surface and twenty years later, in 1982, it was recorded at being only 492' below sea level. In 1988, the depth to the summit was documented at 480', however the 1990 eruption may have blown off part of the summit as a recorded depth taken in 1997 placed the summit at 566' below sea level. On March 12, 2002, the R/V Ronald H. Brown placed the center of the crater at 12.3004° N, 61.6378° W, or approximately 12° 18.02' N, 61° 38.26' W. Images created from soundings show the crater as being almost perfectly circular with a diameter of approximately 1066'. The highest point of the crater rim was measured at approximately 582' below sea level with the crater floor being approximately 256' below the rim. In light of the rate of ascent of the summit, researchers have estimated that *Kick 'Em Jenny* could emerge above sea level in the early part of the 21st century.

Kick 'Em Jenny has erupted 10 times since 1939 according to records kept by the *Smithsonian Institution*. On July 24, 1939, *Kick 'Em Jenny's* first recorded eruption, which was also the largest eruption in the last 60+ years, was witnessed by a large number of people in northern Grenada and lasted for over 24 hours. At the height of its seismic activity, *Kick 'Em Jenny* spewed a column an estimated 900' above sea level and generated a series of tsunamis which reached a height of over 6' in northern Grenada and the southern Grenadines and was felt as far away as Barbados where waves washed across the west coast road.

Kick 'Em Jenny's last eruption was in 1990 and as late as the winter of 2002-2003, was having increased periods of activity with yachts sailing right over it on a daily basis. Several years ago the *Grenada Coast Guard* gave out a security warning to give this entire area a berth of at least 6 miles, but this is not enforced, and for the most part, curious cruisers ignore it. I myself am guilty as I wanted to sail right over it. When I did pass over what I believed to be the crater's location, I didn't even know that I had passed over an active volcano; there was nothing to be seen, heard, or smelled. Disappointed I counted my blessings when I later learned of Montserrat's volcanic activity. Will I tempt fate again? I can't say.

So what does all this have to do with tsunamis and cruisers? Well, it seems that each eruption brings the summit of the volcano closer to the surface of the sea. When the summit is deep, the pressure of the seawater on the summit has a damping effect on the energy released in an eruption (although some have broken the surface). But when the summit approaches sea level, the pressure upon it by the weight of the seawater has a far less damping effect, which may result in more violent eruptions and the increased possibility of a tsunami. But DON"T PANIC!!! Don't get hysterical and cancel plans to visit the Caribbean! Sure, you'll hear stories of sailors who sailed by Île de Ronde and claimed that the seas they encountered were due to *Kick 'Em Jenny*, but these should be attributed to the currents that earned the area its name rather than an eruption. *Kick 'Em Jenny* is monitored by seismograph stations throughout the

Caribbean and the experts advise us that there is no need to worry at this time however, because future eruptions are expected, increased monitoring of *Kick 'Em Jenny* is being undertaken.

Those whose job it is to worry, theorize that if a tsunami was generated by *Kick 'Em Jenny*, the islands most affected would be Grenada, Carriacou, St. Vincent and the Grenadines, Tobago, and Barbados and the tsunami's effects could also be felt as far away as Puerto Rico and Venezuela. It seems that tsunamis do not radiate evenly from their source, but are affected by islands and the shape of the ocean floor. It has been suggested that a tsunami generated from *Kick 'Em Jenny* could be funneled by the Aves Ridge toward St. Martin, Anguilla, and the Virgin Islands.

So how strong could an eruption of Kick 'Em Jenny be? Certainly not as strong as Krakatoa whose volume was estimated to be 90 times the estimated worst-case scenario volume of an eruption of *Kick 'Em Jenny*. Estimates in a hypothetical worst-case scenario have suggested 120' waves in the Grenadines while more conservative estimates put the wave heights at about 45' while the most likely scenario (and the most realistic) puts the wave heights at about 10' on Grenada's northern coast diminishing to about 3' by the time the tsunami reaches Trinidad.

Fortunately modern seismographic technology will likely give us some warning of an eruption and subsequent tsunami as the volcano needs time to build up to a full eruption. The *Caribbean Development Bank* has recently provided a grant of US$170,000 for the establishment of a means of continuous monitoring of *Kick 'Em Jenny*. Some monitoring devices are already in place on Mt. St. Catherine and additional equipment is to be installed at Île de Ronde, Carriacou, and at Sauteurs on Grenada.

So what can we as cruisers do in the event of an eruption of *Kick 'Em Jenny*? As Tony Buxo of Grenada's *National Emergency Advisory Council* recommends, "If you feel a big rumble, don't bother to pick anything up, just head for higher ground. If you're on a boat, head offshore."

For more information on *Kick 'Em Jenny*, visit the *Volcano World* website at http://volcano.und.nodak.edu.

Grenada

Port of Entry: St. George's (*Grenada Yacht Services*), Prickly Bay (*Spice Island Marina*), St. David's (*Grenada Marine*), Petite Calivigny Bay (*Le Phare Bleu Marina*), Grenville

Fuel: St. George's, Prickly Bay, St. David's, Petite Calivigny Bay, Grenville

Haul-Out: Prickly Bay, St. David's Bay

Diesel Repairs: St. George's, Prickly Bay, St. David's, Petite Calivigny Bay, Grenville

Outboard Repairs: St. George's, Prickly Bay, St. David's Bay, Petite Calivigny Bay, Grenville

Propane: St. George's, Prickly Bay, Clarke's Court Bay, St. David's, Petite Calivigny Bay, Grenville

Provisions: St. George's, Prickly Bay, St. David's Bay, Petite Calivigny Bay, Grenville

Important Lights: See *Appendix A*

Grenada lies at the southern end of the Windward Islands, and is without a doubt one of the loveliest islands in the eastern Caribbean and is one of my personal favorites (it seems that each and every island is a personal favorite in some way or another). The coast of Grenada offers several all weather harbors as well as excellent hurricane protection for those rare occasions when a named windstorm traverses this area.

Quite a number of cruisers are now calling Grenada their summer home instead of heading further south to Trinidad, which is losing ground rapidly to the draws of Grenada's anchorages and her growing marine services industry. Watch Grenada closely, the potential for growth in Grenada's marine services sector is wide open. By the time this guide is published, you will probably be able to pick up a copy of a locally produced *Grenada Marine Services* directory in any marina or chandler in Grenada and which will be a great help to all cruisers.

Like most islands of the Caribbean, Grenada is volcanic in origin, and even today mariners must beware of Kick 'em Jenny, an underwater volcano lying north/northwest of the island between Carriacou and Grenada and west of Isle de Ronde. Grenada

is mountainous, with a ridge that rises to over 2,000' along the spine of the island. Here you'll find several old crater basins and a peak that rises to 2,756'.

The mountainous terrain makes for challenging driving, a lot of ups, downs, switchbacks, and 180s along narrow roads with buses and trucks whizzing by with only inches to spare. However the picturesque landscape with the quaint small towns more than makes up for the roads. By the way, if you're planning to rent a car in Grenada you'll need a local driver's permit (EC$30), but don't fret, most car rental companies will handle that for you, and don't forget to drive on the left.

Grenada is a modern tourist destination with all the amenities for cruisers as well as tourists. Electricity is 220 volt, 50 cycle AC so plan accordingly if you're used to U.S. 110 volt, 60 cycle AC. And, don't be surprised by an 8% tax at hotels and restaurants, Grenada's economy depends in a large part on her tourism industry.

The Northern Coast of Grenada

The northern coast of Grenada offers no anchorages with all around protection, however there are a few places you can anchor overnight and enjoy the scenery, the reefs around *Grenada Bay*, and the facilities ashore at Sauteurs.

Sauteurs

Navigational Information
At the extreme northern tip of Grenada lies the small community of Sauteurs. The anchorage here is used primarily as a stopover for cruisers when it is used at all. As shown on Chart GRE-1, you can anchor in the small cove off the town in the lee of the point of land and shoal that lies north of the point. Many cruisers use Sauteurs as a overnight anchorage to get a better angle on the wind before heading north to Carriacou the next day.

What You Will Find Ashore
The 100' promontory alongside *St. Patrick's Roman Catholic Church* is a cultural landmark, *Leaper's Hill*. Here Carib Indians leapt to their death in 1651 rather than surrender to the French whose policy was extermination of the Caribs. In fact, *Sauteurs* is French for *leapers*. At the church you'll

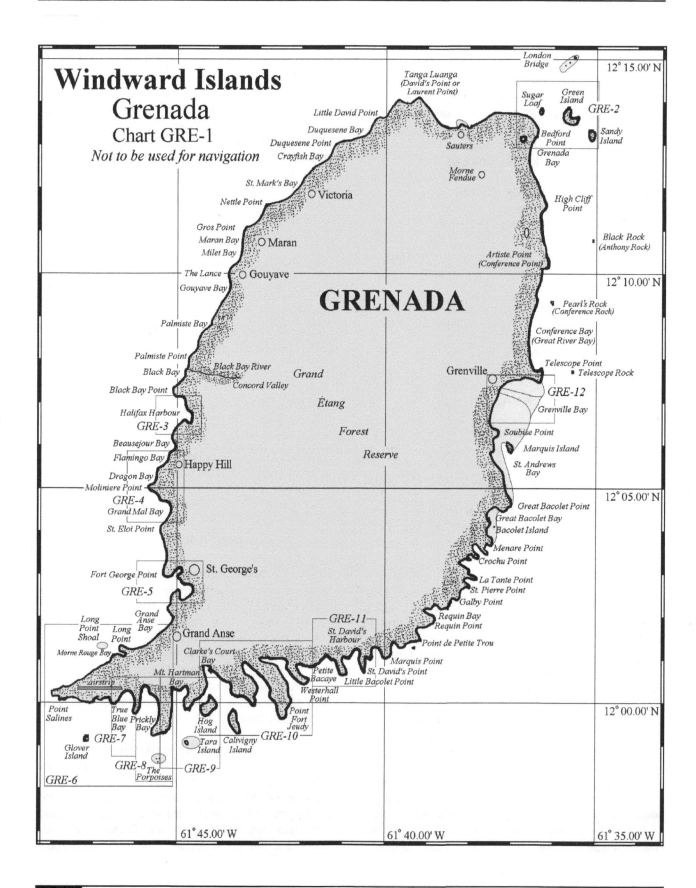

Windward Islands
Grenada
Chart GRE-1
Not to be used for navigation

London Bridge

12° 15.00' N

Tanga Luanga
(David's Point or
Laurent Point)

Sugar Loaf

Green Island

GRE-2

Little David Point

Duquesene Bay

Duquesene Point

Crayfish Bay

Sauters

Bedford Point

Grenada Bay

Sandy Island

St. Mark's Bay

Victoria

Morne Fendue

High Cliff Point

Nettle Point

Gros Point

Maran Bay

Maran

Milet Bay

Artiste Point
(Conference Point)

Black Rock
(Anthony Rock)

The Lance

Gouyave

12° 10.00' N

Gouyave Bay

GRENADA

Palmiste Bay

Pearl's Rock
(Conference Rock)

Palmiste Point

Conference Bay
(Great River Bay)

Black Bay

Black Bay River

Grand

Grenville

Telescope Point

Telescope Rock

Black Bay Point

Concord Valley

Étang

GRE-12

Halifax Harbour

Grenville Bay

GRE-3

Forest

Beausejour Bay

Soubise Point

Flamingo Bay

Reserve

Marquis Island

Happy Hill

St. Andrews Bay

Dragon Bay

Moliniere Point

12° 05.00' N

GRE-4

Grand Mal Bay

Great Bacolet Point

St. Eloi Point

Great Bacolet Bay

Bacolet Island

Menare Point

Crochu Point

Fort George Point

St. George's

La Tante Point

GRE-5

St. Pierre Point

Galby Point

Grand Anse Bay

Requin Bay

Long Point Shoal

Long Point

GRE-11

Requin Point

Grand Anse

St. David's Harbour

Point de Petite Trou

Morne Rouge Bay

Clarke's Court Bay

Marquis Point

Mt. Hartman Bay

Petite Bacaye

St. David's Point

airstrip

Little Bacolet Point

Westerhall Point

Point Salines

True Blue Bay

Prickly Bay

Hog Island

Point Fort Jeudy

12° 00.00' N

GRE-7

Tara Island

Calivigny Island

GRE-10

Glover Island

GRE-8

GRE-9

The Porpoises

GRE-6

61° 45.00' W

61° 40.00' W

61° 35.00' W

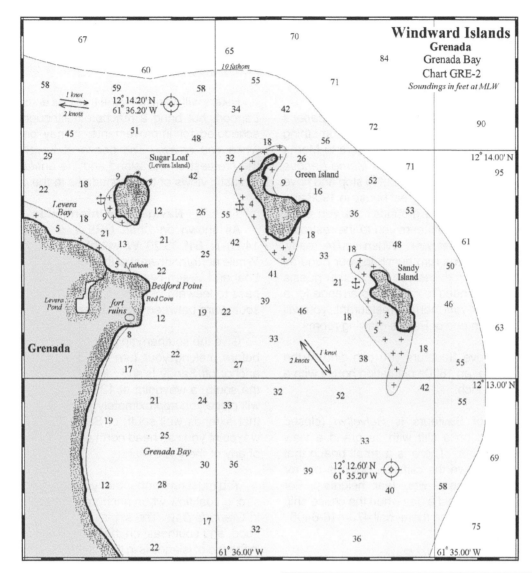

Windward Islands
Grenada
Grenada Bay
Chart GRE-2
Soundings in feet at MLW

67   70   84

65
60   10 fathom   71
58   59   58   55   90
  1 knot   12° 14.20' N   34   42   72
  2 knots   61° 36.20' W
45   51   48   56
                18
29   32   26   71   12° 14.00' N
  Sugar Loaf   Green Island   95
9   (Levera Island)   42   9   52
22   18   16
22   Levera   12   26   36   53
  Bay   18   9   55   4   18   61
5   21   42   18
13   21   25   33   48   50
5   1 fathom   22   41   Sandy   46
  Levera   fort   Red Cove   21   Island
  Pond   ruins   12   19   39   18   63
Grenada   8   22   46   18   3
  22   33   5   18
17   27   2 knots   1 knot   38   5   55
                42   12° 13.00' N
21   24   32   52   55
19   25   33   33
  Grenada Bay   69
30   36   39   12° 12.60' N
12   28   61° 35.20' W   58
  17   40
  32   75
22   61° 36.00' W   36   61° 35.00' W

Halifax Harbour, note low-hanging power lines

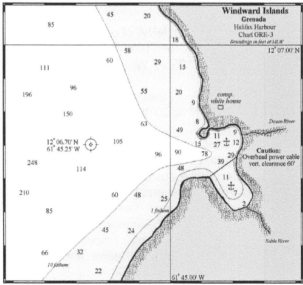

Windward Islands
Grenada
Halifax Harbour
Chart GRE-3
Soundings in feet at MLW
12° 07.00' N

85   45   20
                18
111   58   29   15
196   60   20   *consp.*
  96   55   *white house*
  150   9   *Doyce River*
  63   8
12° 06.70' N   49   11   9
61° 45.25' W   105   15   27   12
248   96   90   78   29   *Caution:*
  114   48   39   *Overhead power cable*
  vert. clearance 60'
210   60   48   11
  85   25   7
  45   24   2   *Sable River*
66   32   1 fathom
  10 fathom   22
  61° 45.00' W

also find a workshop of the *Young Grenadians United Crafts Workers Association* where candles and batik are created and sold. If you need a car try *D' Key's Car Rentals* in Sauteurs, their phone number is 442-9294

If you want to dine in Sauteurs, try the *Leaper's Hill Restaurant & Bar*, but if you wish for something a bit more special head south of Sauteurs to Morne Fendue, the home of Betty Mascol's *Morne Fendue Plantation Great House*, a good spot to stop and have lunch. Betty's father built the great house in 1908 and lovely flowers surround the grounds. As you enter the restaurant a lady who steers you to the restroom to "freshen up" will greet you. When you're ready, Betty herself will place a rum punch in your hand as she seats you and introduces you to the other guests at your table. You'll need to call first to arrange for a meal, Betty's is not your normal restaurant, you will actually be dining in one of Betty's drawing rooms.

In the hills above Sauteurs you can dine at the *Mt. Rodney Estate*, an 1800s plantation house with a very good buffet lunch.

To the east of Sauteurs is *Helvellyn* (closed Sundays) perched on a cliff with as grand a view as you could imagine. There is a small beach that is worth the hike down the cliffside, but it is not for the squeamish or those who fear heights. For reservations, and to avoid a day when the cruise ship sends their patrons to dine there, call 473-418-6405.

Grenada Bay

Waypoints:
Grenada Bay- ½ nm NNW of passage between
 Sugar Loaf & Green Island
12° 14.20' N, 61° 36.20' W

Grenada Bay- ½ nm S of shoal off Sandy Island
12° 12.60' N, 61° 35.20' W

East of Sauteurs, at the northeastern tip of Grenada, is the *Levera National Park*, one of the most scenic coastal areas on the island of Grenada. This rustic area has several beautiful beaches lined with sea grapes and palm trees and is a favorite haunt for Grenadians on the weekend. The park also has a large mangrove swamp, fascinating offshore reefs, and all manner of flora, fauna, and epifauna. Here the offshore islands in *Grenada Bay*, Sugar

Loaf (sometimes shown as Levera Island), Green Island, and Sandy Island, are breeding grounds for the reclusive Audubon's Shearwater, or as it is known locally, the *jablotin*.

Hikers will want to try the trail that encircles *Levera Lagoon*, but bring a machete…although the trail is scheduled for improvements, it may be overgrown when you arrive. The beach at Levera is one of the prettiest on the island and the entire area offers fantastic views of the Grenadines to the north.

Navigational Information
As shown on Chart GRE-2, a waypoint at 12° 14.20' N, 61° 36.20' W, will place you approximately ½ mile north/northwest of the passage between Sugar Loaf and Green Island. From this waypoint you can pass to leeward of Sugar Loaf to anchor or continue southward between Sugar Loaf and Green Island.

Give the southern tip of Green Island a wide berth before making your turn to the east if you plan to anchor off Sandy Island. If you're approaching from the south, a waypoint at 12° 12.60' N, 61° 35.20' W, will place you approximately ½ mile south of the reef that extends well south of Sandy Island. From this waypoint you can head northwest to anchor in the lee of any of the three islands.

You must remember that you will be dealing with a strong tidal flow when anchored at any of the islands in *Grenada Bay*. The set is usually northwest on the flood, and southeast on the ebb. The best anchorage in the trio of islands is in the lee of Sandy Island where you can anchor in depth of 10'-25' of water. Use two anchors as there is a good bit of current here.

Green Island, although not the best spot to anchor due to the current and the depth along the western shore, does have some very nice beaches and some interesting snorkeling off its southern shore. At Sugar Loaf, the best holding is west of the hill sometimes shown as Sugar Loaf Peak. The holding is fair to good here but a strong tidal flow will affect you.

What You Will Find Ashore
Leatherback turtles are returning once again to lay their eggs on Grenada's beaches. Starting in March and lasting through the end of July, Bathway and Levera beaches are popular spots to view, but not disturb these creatures. For more information contact *Ocean Spirits* at 473-444-3442 to view the

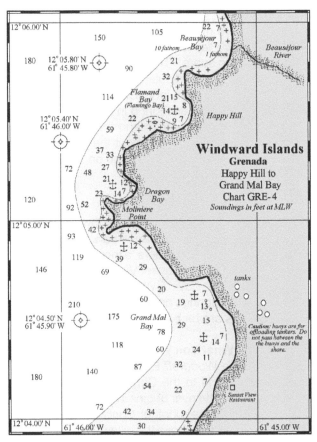

turtles. A total of one hundred and eleven nests were laid on those two beaches last year and 73% were destroyed by people taking the eggs.

The Western Coast of Grenada

The western coast of Grenada is the second most popular cruising grounds, the southern coast being the choice of most cruisers. Yet there are several good anchorages here that will pique the interest of almost any cruiser.

Gouyave

Gouyave is the fishing capital of Grenada and home to some of the most eccentric folks on the island and the town's reputation is raucous at best. It's not unusual to drive through here and find many people up all night burning the midnight oil, not just the fishermen, but other residents as well. The town of Gouyave was the site of the first British landing in 1609 when the Caribs repelled the invading troops. There's also a fishing museum in Gouyave that is closed now, but I am assured it will reopen...we'll see. Gouyave is home to the *Gouyave Nutmeg Processing Cooperative* where a worker will guide you on a ½

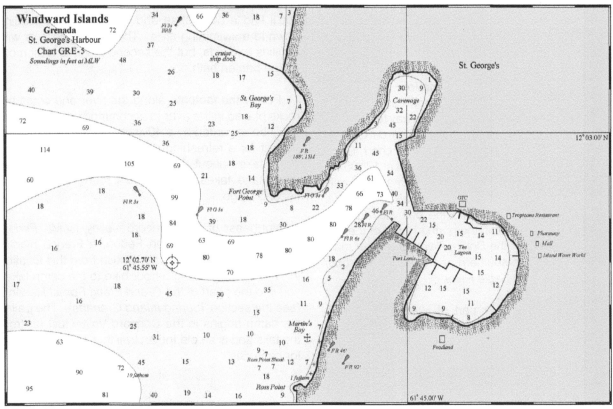

hour tour of the three-story facility that produces over 3 million pounds of nutmeg per year. Here you'll see ladies hand sorting thousands of nutmegs by the hour, a nearby handwritten message stating: "*God looked at my work and was pleased. Then He looked at my salary, bowed His head, and sadly walked away.*"

Navigational Information

The anchorage at Gouyave sits just off the town, you'll see the small fishing boats. Ashore is a *Texaco* station where you can fill your jerry jugs with either diesel or gas. Nearby *Land and Sea Marine Supplies* is a small chandlery and you can get a bite to eat at *Kelly's Hot Spot Restaurant & Bar.*

What You Will Find Ashore

Gouyave is home to Al Bernadine (473-444-8016), THE man to see if you're having problems with your alternator, starter, or power tool.

Just north of Gouyave is Victoria where you can pick up the trail to the summit of *Mt. St. Catherine,* Grenada's highest peak. It's best to get a guide for this hike as the trail is not well-defined in several places.

Halifax Harbour

Waypoints:

Halifax Harbour- ¼ nm WNW of entrance
12° 06.70' N, 61° 45.25' W

Navigational Information

Halifax Harbour is sometimes shown as *Black Bay,* however *Black Bay* is actually the next bay to the north (just north of *Black Bay* Point as shown on GRE-1) and is not shown on the *Halifax Harbour* chart, GRE-3. As shown on Chart GRE-3, a waypoint at 12° 06.70' N, 61° 45.25' W, will place you approximately ¼ mile west/northwest of the entrance to *Halifax Harbour.* From the waypoint head into the bay steering just south of east to anchor in the northern part of the bay just off the mouth of the *Douce River,* or, if your mast is not too tall, in the southern part of *Halifax Harbour* off the mouth of the *Sable River.*

CAUTION: the lower part of *Halifax Harbour* is crossed by a high tension power line with a vertical clearance of only 60' at high water. I've spoken to people in the village, and I've spoken to people who work for the power authority, and nobody can give me the exact vertical clearance of the power lines, so I'm

going to say 60' for safety's sake, but don't take a chance if you're mast is anywhere near that height. The mast on *IV Play* is 55' off the water and I cleared with very little to spare. The holding in the lower bay is rocky in places, particularly on the southern and western shore. A particular nuisance in the area, and the only drawback to anchoring in this protected bay, is the nearby garbage dump and the accompanying flies. For more information about the fly problem in Grenada, see the upcoming section on *The Grenada Superfly.*

Halifax Harbour, as well as Happy Hill (*Flamingo Bay*), *Dragon Bay,* and the area northwest of *Grand Mal Bay* are now part of a marine park so you should find moorings in the harbours although you are still permitted to anchor off Sunset View in *Grand Mal Bay* and in *Beausejour Bay.* PWCs are not permitted in the park. Red moorings are for the day charter boats, white moorings are for private vessels.

What You Will Find Ashore

Right by the *Woodruff Estate* in *Halifax Harbour,* a road turns inland to the Concord Valley along the *Black Bay River* (the river begins in *Black Bay,* north of Black Bay Point), the runoff of *Concord Falls,* a triple stage cascade. Just above the village of Concord the road stops directly in front of the falls first stage where you'll find a bathhouse and concrete steps leading down to a swimming area. This area is popular with families and kids, but the second stage is a bit more off the beaten path.

Follow the footpath along the river and cross the rocks placed in the river to accommodate visitors and you'll be rewarded by a 40' waterfall and a deep pool perfect for a refreshing dip The hike to the second stage takes about 45 minutes while the hike to the third stage takes over 3 hours round trip from the second stage.

Northeast of the Concord Valley is *Mt. Fedon,* once the camp for Julian Fedon, a French planter who led a revolt against the British from this location in 1795. The grueling 5-hour hike to the camp takes you into the heart of the *Grand Étang Forest Reserve* (see the section *Touring Inland Grenada*). The trail to the camp begins in the Concord Valley just up from the falls and is an old Indian trail that has been in use for centuries.

Flamand Bay to *Grand Mal Bay*

Waypoints:
Flamand Bay- ½ nm NW of anchorage
12° 05.80' N, 61° 45.80' W

Dragon Bay- ½ nm NW of anchorage
12° 05.40' N, 61° 46.00' W

Grand Mal Bay- ½ nm W of anchorage
12° 04.50' N, 61° 45.90' W

Navigational Information

Just a few miles south of *Halifax Harbour* are several nice anchorages before you arrive at St. George's. As shown on Chart GRE-4, the northernmost anchorage is located at *Flamand Bay* (sometimes shown as *Flamingo Bay*) and the town of *Happy Hill*. As shown on Chart GRE-4, a waypoint at 12° 05.80' N, 61° 45.80' W, will place you approximately ½ mile northwest of the anchorage.

From the waypoint steer into the bay keeping in the center between the reefs off the points to the north and south of you; anchor in the center or northern part of the bay, as the southern part is rocky. The local fisherman may ask you to move if you're in their way, be courteous as this is how they make their living.

As with most of the leeward anchorages in this book, this particular anchorage is not advisable when northerly swells are running.

Halifax Harbour, as well as Happy Hill (*Flamingo Bay*), *Dragon Bay*, and the area northwest of *Grand Mal Bay* are now part of a marine park so you should find moorings in the harbours although you are still permitted to anchor off Sunset View in *Grand Mal Bay* and in *Beausejour Bay*. PWCs are not permitted in the park. Red moorings are for the day charter boats, white moorings are for private vessels.

The next anchorage to the south is the popular *Dragon Bay*. A waypoint at 12° 05.40' N, 61° 46.00' W, will place you approximately ½ mile northwest of the anchorage. From the waypoint head for the center of the bay keeping an eye out for shoals along the northern and southern shores. The bay is small, and that is part of its charm, that and the good snorkeling of Molinière Point where you'll find an underwater statue park with a dinghy mooring.

The next bay south is *Grand Mal Bay* and as shown on Chart GRE-4, a waypoint at 12° 04.50' N, 61° 45.90' W, will place you approximately ½ mile west of the anchorage area in the bay. *Grand Mal Bay* has a bit of industry ashore and this turns off many cruisers, but the anchorage is still nice, as long as you anchor out of the shipping lanes, either north or south of the main dock. Do not approach the two buoys shown on the chart, they are used for offloading tankers and pipes run from the buoys to the shore. You can pick up a mooring on the northern side of the bay near Molinière Point.

What You Will Find Ashore

Ashore, you can dine at the *Sunset View Restaurant and Beach House* on an open-air terrace. You can even jerry jug water from the *Sunset View* dinghy dock, or just pump it right aboard if your draft is shallow enough and the hose long enough.

St. George's

Waypoints:
St. George's Harbour- ¼ nm WSW of entrance
12° 02.70' N, 61° 45.55' W

Navigational Information

Besides being the capital of Grenada, St. George's is home to the most protected harbor on the island's western shore. As shown on Chart GRE-5, a waypoint at 12° 02.70' N, 61° 45.55' W, will place you approximately ¼ mile west/southwest to the entrance to St. George's Harbour and south of the center of the two outer buoys.

Approaching from the north you'll want to pass on either side of the buoy From the waypoint the approach is fairly easy, simply head for the harbor mouth keeping between the outer red and green lighted buoys as you work your way inside the entrance to the harbor.

To port lies the *Carenage* which is off limits for anchoring, to starboard lies the *Lagoon* where you'll want to drop the hook or get a slip at the *Grenada Yacht Club*. To enter the lagoon follow the red buoys keeping them to starboard. You will run parallel to the ship dock until past its southern end when the channel doglegs to the east, to port. When you arrive at the last red buoy you'll see a green marker to port, just off the *Grenada Yacht Club*. Pass between the green marker and the last red marker to starboard and you are in the Lagoon. Keep clear of the two red buoys that lie between the green buoy and the dock at *GYC*, they mark a small shoal and it is best to avoid them.

Anchor in the *Lagoon* wherever your draft allows, but don't forget that in the *Lagoon* anchorage there are some odd currents that are most noticed on nights with no wind when you'll find yourself swinging round and round your anchor just as your neighbor is doing to his. Careful anchoring will allow you uninterrupted sleep and keep you from banging into the boat that was to windward of you when you anchored earlier in the day. If you need to clear *Customs*, the office located in the *Grenada Yacht Services* (*GYS*) complex on the western shore of the *Lagoon*.

What You Will Find Ashore
To me, St. George's is the quintessential Caribbean city. Colorful buildings perched on the steep hills high above an active and protected harbor, the streets busy with folks walking here and there and cars honking their horns as they zoom along the bay-front road. I'd be willing to wager that St. George's is one of the most photographed harbors in the Caribbean, and now it's yours to enjoy once the anchor is down.

St. George's has a cruiser's net, Monday through Saturday, on VHF ch. 66 at 0730. Jonathon from *Island Water World* gives the daily weather on the net and local news is also featured. The net utilizes a repeater so there should be coverage to the southern anchorages.

Customs and *Immigration*
The *Customs* office is located in the *Grenada Yacht Club* but you can expect it to move to the *Port Louis* complex. Office hours are 0800-1200 and 1300-1600 weekdays, and 0800-1200 on Saturdays.

Internet
Island Water World provides Wi-fi access in the harbour for no charge (but donations are cheerfully accepted. *Port Louis* offers plug-in internet service.

Marine Facilities
Marinas
Grenada Yacht Club
The *Grenada Yacht Club*, *GYC* (VHF Ch. 16 & 06), is a revered institution on the island of Grenada, founded in 1953 by 12 local yachtsmen and businessmen who each donated $375 to start the organization. In 1954, a formal request was made to

the government for lands on which a clubhouse could be constructed and a plot of land was granted next to a shed that was used to store bananas at the port of St. George's. Today that shed is still in place and is used by workmen employed by the *Grenada Port Authority*.

GYC members immediately began raising funds to erect a clubhouse and dock and since money was in short supply, they did much of the early work themselves. One prospective member offered a large prefabricated building in lieu of membership fees and *GYC* members soon found themselves working on their new clubhouse.

Their joy was short lived however as *Hurricane Janet* destroyed *St. George's Pier* along with most of the new *GYC* clubhouse in 1955. In 1957, the rebuilding of St. George's began and the *GYC* was notified that the land allotted them was to be returned to the Port Authority for this project. In way of compensation, the *GYC* was offered a 25-year lease on a piece of land known as *The Spout*. New plans were drawn, more funds were raised, and in 1960 the *GYC* had a new clubhouse.

Today the *GYC* has just gone through a major renovation, adding a 180' extension to their main dock, along with a smaller dock and 43 slips. The *Grenada Yacht Club* offers transient slips with a maximum draft of 14', 24-hour security, duty-free fuel (gas and diesel), water, 110/220 electricity, showers, laundry service, fax, propane refills (on Tuesdays and Thursdays), a taxi service, a book swap, Internet services at the bar, ice, phone cards, garbage disposal (free to guests), and a dinghy dock ($1 charge redeemable at the bar), and *The Marine View Restaurant*.

The yacht club also hosts the annual *La Source Grenada Sailing Festival*. You can phone the *GYC* at 473-440-3050, fax at 473-440-6826, or email them at gyc@spiceisle.com. And best of all, the GYC offers guests a free *Westerhall* rum drink upon arrival. A few steps to the east of the GYC is the *Tropicana Restaurant* with its own dinghy dock. The fare is a combination of Chinese and West Indian and is very economical.

Port Louis Marina
Across the harbor is the *Port Louis Marina and Resort* (VHF ch. 16 & 14) complex, owned by *Camper and Nicholson*, that can handle up to 10 boats of 300'

LOA (and 20' draft), 16 boats up to 120" LOA, and 144 slips for smaller vessels. Each slip boasts full electric (up to 600 amp, 220v and 240V and some 60 cycle), cable TV, an Internet connection, pump outs, 24-hour security and of course fresh water. Creature comforts include a laundry, the *1782 Bar and Restaurant*, and *Spronks Mega-Yacht Services*.

Marine Supplies

On the eastern side of the *Lagoon* are several businesses that are of interest to cruisers. Here you'll find the *Island Water World* store, as well stocked a chandlery as you could expect to find. On the first Tuesday of every month IWW hosts a book/DVD swap and coffee party for charity.

Marine World is located in the Carenage on *Melville St.* and offers fishing and snorkeling gear as well as charts.

Napa and *Ace Hardware*, once located next door to *Island Water World,* have now moved to *Maurice Bishop Highway* behind True Blue.

In the waterfront area of the Carenage you can find *Hubbard's Hardware* for your common hardware items, *Arnold John* for tools and household goods, and *Julien's* for chain and related hardware items.

Marine Services

If you have refrigeration problems, contact *Lagoon Marine Refrigeration* at 473-440-3381. For fabrication and welding needs, call *Tech Metal Works* at 473-440-2895, or Albert Lucas at 473-440-1281.

Grenada Boat Services at *Port Louis* repairs inflatables, electronics, fiberglass, as well as inboard and outboard motors

Turbulence Sails can handle all your sail, rigging, and electronics repairs and installations; they have an office at *Port Louis*.

For yacht management try *Horizon Yachts* at *Port Louis* or *Island Dreams* (who also have an office at *Phare Bleu Marina*).

Fuel

As previously noted, you can get fuel at both *GYC* and *Port Louis* marinas, but larger vessels can also arrange for low sulfur diesel through *Supply Source Grenada*, call them at 473-440-0011.

Propane

Henry's Safari Tours (VHF ch. 16) will pick up your empty propane bottles from *GYC* on Mondays and Wednesdays and return with filled bottles the same day. He also supplies propane to those at *Port Louis*. You can also get propane at *Texgas* in St. George's.

Provisions

At the south end of the *Lagoon* is the *Foodland* dinghy dock, a good spot to tie up and hit the *Foodland* store directly across the street. *Foodland* is open late most nights, a plus if you arrive in St. George's late in the day and find you have little for your arrival dinner. *Foodland* is open until 1900 Monday through Thursday, until 2000 on Friday nights, and they're open until 2100 on Saturday nights.

A good market, the *Food Fair*, has a location at the Carenage. Also at the Carenage, at *Church St.* take a right and cruise down Market Hill to the foot of *Young St.* and visit *Market Square* where you'll find a vendor to sell you nearly anything. Open Monday through Saturday, the market is best visited on a Saturday morning when the usual *Saturday Morning Caribbean Market Madness* takes hold. You can pick up fresh fruits and vegetables, spices, sauces, and other Grenadian products at the *Marketing and National Importing Board* on *Young St.*

Located at the *Port Louis* complex is a the new *Marry Bakery* selling the best in fresh breads and baked goodies along with meat filled pastries, pre-cooked meals, and home-made ice cream. On Friday's they offer a special hamburger barbecue!

For spirits, you can visit the *Best Little Liquor Store*, the monitor VHF ch. 16 and respond to "Rhum Runner Base." They offer duty-free prices on case lots but you must allow 48 hours for processing. They will also deliver large orders to *Prickly Bay*. The *BLLS* is also a *DHL* and *Western Union* agent.

On the western side of the Carenage is *Food Fair* and you can tie up your dinghy nearby. *Food Fair* offers a 5% discount to charter vessels.

Just outside St. George's is the *Springs Shopping Center* which is open on Sundays and Holidays, a plus if you need provisions in a pinch; they're also open late, until 2200 Monday through Thursday, and until 2300 on Friday. You can even phone in your order and have *Springs* deliver it to the dock at *GYC*.

Laundry

If you need somebody to do your laundry, other than those people who approach your vessel in small boats, contact *Super Kleen* at 473-440-8499. *Super Kleen* will pick up and deliver your laundry in St. George's or in *Prickly Bay*.

Dining

Most cruisers make their first stop the *Marine View Restaurant* at the *GYC* while others head for the *1782 Restaurant* at the *Port Louis Marina*. They both serve excellent food and you won't go wrong at either place.

The Nutmeg is a very popular spot for a meal in St. George's and is located right on the *Carenage* at the foot of Scott St. The restaurant features a killer rum punch with a good view of St. George's harbor from their second story dining room.

Also, on the waterfront at the Carenage is *Portofino Ristorante Italia*, a very homey Italian restaurant. Nearby you can sample the fare at *BB's Crab Back* or the *Ocean Grill* with their huge open-air deck.

Between St. George's and *Grand Anse*, one of the most popular places to eat is at *Patrick's Home Style Cooking* where you will be served a 20 course dinner. Patrick, who monitors VHF ch. 09, serves great rum drinks including his own special concoction that he swears will put lead in your pencil.

Discovering St. George's

Ft. George is home to three forts, *Ft. George*, *Ft. Matthew*, and *Ft. Frederick*. *Ft. George*, built in 1705 by the French and later expanded by the British, is a classic siege fort laced with many tunnels and narrow passageways where, amazingly, no shots were ever fired until 1983. *Ft. George* was at the center of the October 19, 1983, political disturbance when Maurice Bishop and part of his cabinet were executed by a faction of the *People's Revolutionary Government*. Today the fort is the headquarters of the *Royal Grenada Police Force* and is open for sightseeing. *Ft. Matthew* was built by the French in 1779 and is another classic siege fort.

Ft. Frederick, built in 1791 on *Richmond Hill* commands a great panoramic view of St. George's and Grenada as well. This fort was the headquarters of the motorized division of the *People's Revolutionary Army* during the 1983 intervention and from the fort you can get a good view of the prison that houses the perpetrators of that event atop an adjacent hill.

The botanical oasis of *Bay Gardens* sits in the suburb of St. Paul's on the grounds of an old sugar estate about ½ mile from *Ft. Frederick*. Here you can stroll paths lined with nutmeg shells that wind through a tropical paradise complete with fish-ponds and a turtle aquarium. East of the garden is the *Tower House*, the estate house of a working fruit and spice plantation and one of the few that is open to the public. The house itself is constructed of lava rock and is surrounded by tropical gardens and offers displays of Carib artifacts and antiques. Also in St. Paul's you can visit the *De la Grenada* spice processing plant to see spice processing first hand and purchase some of their award winning nutmeg products.

Some of the best shops, shopping, and dining in St. George's is focused in the area immediately around the Carenage. As you walk around the Carenage you'll probably notice the old cannons that were removed from the forts and are currently used as bollards for ships. The red fish-scale tiles that roof several of the buildings around the Carenage were originally used as ballast on European trading vessels.

The *Grenada National Museum* sits at the corner of *Young* and *Monckton Sts*. With many displays of Caribs, whaling, and the 1983 debacle artifacts, the most popular display is the Empress Josephine's bathtub. Also on *Young St.* is the *Batik Shop*, where you can buy batik fabrics or watch it being created. Walk up *Young Street* from the Carenage and at the crossroads, take a right onto *Church Street* by *Barclay's Bank*.

As you approach the Anglican church, sneak a peak through the black iron railings and you will find a beautiful little pink-walled garden with a yellow "gingerbread" house just behind it. Known as *The Priory*, the house dates back earlier than 1788 when it was a chapel for the Church. The garden is full of tropical pants from zinnias to bougainvillea, including a dwarf Golden Apple Tree, a bright blue Tropical Sweet Pear, and a Silver Bush.

Further down the *Carenage* is the boutique *Tikal*, one of the most interesting shops in St. George's and located on *Young St.* Upstairs is *Jim Rudin's Art Gallery* featuring Rubin's work as well as many other local artists. Nearby you'll find the *Yellow Poui Art Gallery* where you can pick up one of local artist Canute Caliste's works.

Next door to *Tikal* is the *National Museum*, which was originally erected as an army barracks in 1704, and later served as a women's prison before being reincarnated as the *Antilles Hotel* for a while. Opposite *Tikal* is *Pebbles Jazz Club* with live jazz on Tuesdays and Saturdays.

Just past the Carenage is the *Sendall Tunnel,* built in 1895, and named after an early governor of the island, the tunnel is 12' high and 340' long. Just north of the tunnel is the huge fish market and bus terminal.

Grand Anse

Grand Anse is a huge touristy area just south of St. George's along the western shore. With its lovely, long beach, one can easily understand the draw here. Many of the places that you'll visit while in Grenada are located in Grand Anse or between Grand Anse and St. George's and *Prickly Bay*; markets, restaurants, bakeries, malls, even a marine service center is located in this area. All the facilities mentioned here are not very far from each other and easy to get to by rental car, taxi, or bus.

On the beach itself is the world class *Spice Island Beach Resort* offering 66 luxury suites located right on the 2-mile stretch of beach (no, you are not permitted to anchor off the beach although you can anchor south of *St. George's Harbour* at *Martin's Bay*, as shown on Chart GRE-5, and take the dinghy to Grand Anse Beach to tie up at the floating dock near the *French Restaurant*). This eco-friendly resort is involved with several environmental programs and is a leader in the fight to promote sustainable tourism in Grenada.

Internet
You can find internet access at both *Cyber Connect* and *Onsite Software Support* in *Marquis Mall*.

Marine Facilities
Outboard Repairs
Also located in Grand Anse is the *ANRO Agencies*, dealers for *Mercury, Mercruiser, Mariner,* and *Yanmar*. ANRO will come by your dock to pick up your outboard for repair. On the airport road near

True Blue is *McIntyre Brothers,* diesel mechanics that can handle any problem you might encounter with your power plant. *McIntyre Brothers* are also agents for *Yamaha* outboards and can deliver a new motor to your dock at duty-free prices.

Provisions
The shopping in Grand Anse is focused on several nice malls. The *Spiceland Mall* is home to the *Real Value Supermarket,* a candy store, the *Wine Shoppe* a hardware store, a food court, and several other small shops. The *Grand Anse Shopping Center* is where you will find *Magic Photo*, the *Food Fair, Mitchell's Pharmacy, Hubbard's Home Center, Scotia Bank*, and the *Serendipity Company* where you can access the Internet and check your email.

For wholesale prices on provisions go to *CK's Super-Valu Food Depot* at the Sugar Mill Roundabout opposite the *NCB House*. CK's offers free delivery to yachts and if you buy three bottles of any brand of spirits you get wholesale pricing. *La Boulangerire French Bakery and Pizzeria Marquis Mall* offers free delivery to *Prickly Bay*, call them at 444-1131.

In the *Excel Mall* you find *Value Garden* with their excellent selection of local products and produce; they're open Sunday mornings too!

Dining
At Grand Anse Beach you must dine at *La Belle Creole* at the *Blue Horizon Cottage Hotel*. One of the best restaurants on the island of Grenada, the menu features upscale West Indian cooking and reservations are required for dinner for those who are not guests of the hotel. Also at Grand Anse is *Tabanca* on a hill at the southern end of the beach, a good spot for dinner. *Rudolf's*, the fine restaurant whose *Young St.* location was destroyed by fire, has reopened in Grande Anse at *Cinnamon Hill*. Next to Island *Center* you can get a good burger or rôti at *The Fountain*.

For Chinese food try the *Bird's Nest*, for fish and chicken try *Fish & Chick* in the *Old Sugar Mill Building*. Also in the *Old Sugar Mill Building* is *Le Sucrier*, the place for live jazz on Thursdays. For pizza and ice cream, visit *Sugar and Spice* at the *Grand Anse Shopping Plaza*. If you wish to sample some very nice French food, visit *Coconut's Beach*, also known as *The French Restaurant*, located right on the beach in an old house with loads of ambiance, casual and romantic.

St. George's, Grenada

Ruins of an old sugar mill near *Mt. Rose*

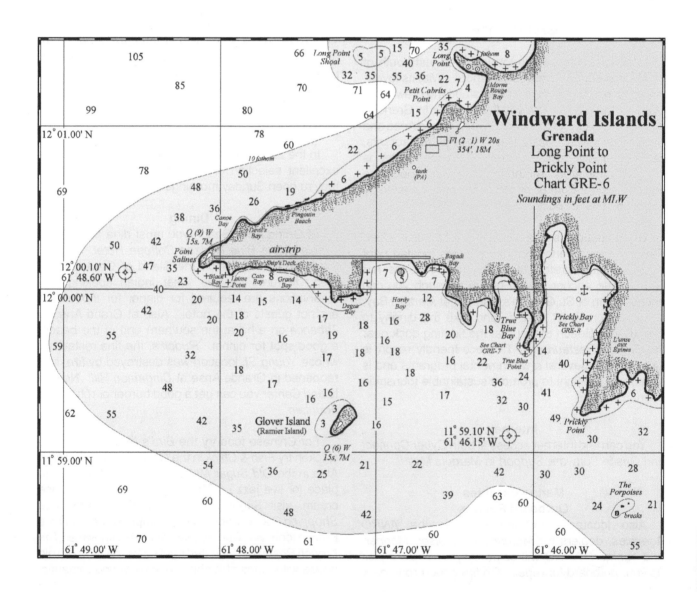

Medical

If you need medical help, it too can be found in the malls of Grand Anse. Dr. Mike Radix is opposite the *Spiceland Mall* in *Ocean House* along with Dr. Robbie Yearwood, a surgeon. If you need a dentist try Dr. Roxanne Nedd at the *Sunshine Dental Clinic* next to the *Excel Mall*. Opposite the roundabout is the *Island Dental Clinic* above *Gittens Drug Mart*.

The Southern Coast of Grenada

Waypoints:
Point Salines- ½ nm W of
12° 00.10' N, 61° 48.60' W

The focus of Grenadian cruising is on the southern coast of the island. Here you'll find some of the best anchorages in the Caribbean and two excellent mangrove encircled coves offering excellent hurricane protection. Facilities are not far away from most of these anchorages, and there's always a large, friendly cruising community ensconced in the harbors of the southern shore sitting out hurricane season or simply enjoying these wonderful cruising grounds, some of the best in the Caribbean.

When leaving St. George's for the southern coast, you must give Long Point at the off-lying *Long Point Shoal* a wide berth as shown on Chart GRE-1. You may also pass between the shoal and the point in good water, but it is safer to just go west a bit and clear all the hazards involved. As you round Point Salines at the southwestern tip of Grenada you will find yourself dead into the wind and current as you head eastward along this shore as shown on Chart GRE-6. A waypoint at 12° 00.10' N, 61° 48.60' W, will place you approximately ½ mile west of Point Salines.

From this waypoint you can work your way eastward along the southern shore of Grenada keeping between Glover Island and the shoals lying just off the southern coast. Unless you like a beat, I suggest that you run this leg early in the morning before the trades pick up. From Point Salines, Prickly Point is conspicuous as the distant piece of land on the horizon appearing to be the southernmost tip of Grenada, which it actually is.

Glover Island was a Norwegian whaling station until about 1925 and ruins of the facility can still be found there.

True Blue

Waypoints:
True Blue Bay- ¼ nm W of True Blue Point
11° 59.60' N, 61° 46.27' W

Navigational Information

As shown on Chart GRE-7, a waypoint at 11° 59.60' N, 61° 46.27' W, will place you approximately ¼ mile west of True Blue Point and southeast of the entrance to *True Blue Bay*. From the waypoint, steer towards the center of the bay before turning to the north to pick up a mooring (free if you dine at the marina restaurant) or anchor off the marina. A bit of roll seems to be prevalent in *True Blue Bay* as well as *Prickly Bay* so you might wish to set a stern anchor or a bridle to keep your bow into the direction of the surge. The moorings are close enough together that it is possible to tie off between two for the same purpose.

What You Will Find Ashore

In the 1700s through the early 1800s the area surrounding True Blue was an indigo plantation that went belly-up when the price of Indigo dropped. In the late 1960s the surrounding roads were constructed to accommodate exhibitors and visitors to the World Trade Fair held in True Blue. Today you can look along the western shore of *True Blue Bay* and see the conspicuous orange roofs of *St. George's University and Medical School*, one of the largest medical schools in the Caribbean.

Marine Facilities
Marinas
True Blue Marina is the base for *Horizon Yacht Charter* and they offer dockage, moorings, diesel, water, ice, laundry, Internet access, phone and fax service, a boat watch service, propane service, and showers. The marina, which monitors VHF ch. 16, is the center of activity in True Blue as evidenced by the charter fleet, car rentals, laundry service (*Henry's Safari Tours*) and a dive shop.

Internet
Besides the marina, *Bananas* has Wi-fi (free) and the *True Blue Hotel* has a fax service as well as a high speed email connection.

Provisions
A short walk from *True Blue Marina* toward *Spice Island Marine Services* is the *Bananas* complex

where you'll find a small mini-market while upstairs you can shop at the *Gourmet Store,* a place that is appropriately named. There's also a pharmacy on site.

Dining

At the southeast end of the dock is the *Dodgy Dock*, the restaurant located in the hotel with its own dinghy dock. The bar and restaurant is a good spot to hang out and enjoy the ambiance. The staff offers a *Grenadian Night* on Tuesday, a *Latin Night* on Friday, and on Sunday they serve up a roast beef brunch (reservations are suggested). During the season, Saturday nights are set aside for live music. They also have a daily happy hour from 1700-1800. *Bananas* is home to a sports bar, the *Carib Cave* (for wood-fired pizza), *Club Bananas* (for *Latin Nights*), and *Delicious* (Italian fare). Across the bay, Options Food Court boasts several food vendors.

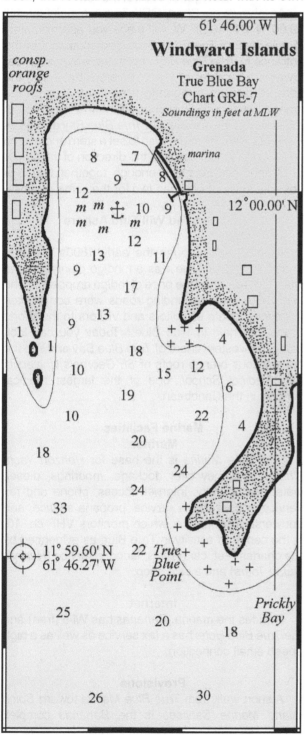

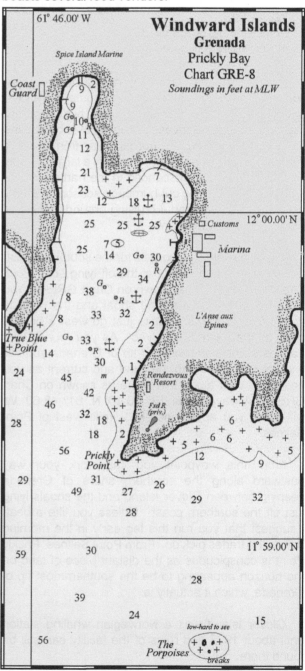

Prickly Bay

Waypoints:
Prickly Bay- ½ nm W of Prickly Point
11° 59.10' N, 61° 46.15' W

Prickly Bay is one of the most popular stops on the southern coast of Grenada, and rightly so. There is an excellent marina and haul-out yard here, a new *Budget Marine* store, restaurant, Internet access, a great bar, and easy access to town. Entrance is very straightforward with few dangers for the prudent mariner, it can even be entered and left at night if need be. This is a boon for the cruiser bound to Trinidad who wishes to make a daylight arrival at the Bocas.

Navigational Information
As shown on Chart GRE-6, a waypoint at 11° 59.10' N, 61° 46.15' W, which will place you approximately ¼ mile south/southwest of the entrance to *Prickly Bay*. Night entry is facilitated by a fixed red light at Prickly Point. This privately maintained light is atop a conspicuous green tower with a pointed red roof and is a good daymark as well as a nighttime navigational aid. Bear in mind that this is a privately maintained light and may or may not be working when you need it to be.

From the waypoint, head into the harbor keeping approximately halfway between True Blue Point and Prickly Point (Chart GRE-8). The entrance is wide and deep and offers no hazards at this point, but you must avoid the shoals lying just off those two points, and especially the reefs along the eastern shoreline. Proceed up the harbor and anchor wherever your draft allows. There is an unmarked shoal area about mid-way across the harbor from the marina, and a wreck that is marked by a float and small pennant. The wreck is deep and does not pose a threat to navigation, but several cruisers have fouled their anchors on it so it now is marked.

Do not anchor within 100 meters of the beach at the northern end as it is reserved for swimmers. The biggest complaint about the anchorage here is the roll; it does get rolly here at times and the best solution is to set a bridle to keep your bow into the surge. If you find that you cannot handle the roll, simply move a mile or so to the east to anchor off Hog Island or in *Mt. Hartman Bay.*

Another problem in *Prickly Bay* is the flies, and let me make this perfectly clear, *Prickly Bay* has a lot of flies. The government only sprays once a year so there is a bit of a problem with the critters. Fly strips help, and a fly swatter (hard to find on the island) gives a bit of tension release, but the best defense is simply keeping the trash empty and off the boat, and keeping the head clean, flushed dry, and the lid closed (see the upcoming section: *The Grenada Superfly*).

What You Will Find Ashore
There is a VHF net on Monday, Wednesday, and Friday mornings at 0730 on VHF ch. 68. Patterned after the same net in Trinidad, weather will be given, announcements made, and "treasures of the bilge" will be up for trade or barter.

Customs and *Immigration*
If you need to clear *Customs* and *Immigration*, their office is located at *Spice Island Marina*. Tie up to the wall south of the marina docks between the docks and the Travel Lift dock, or along the wall just north of the marina docks. The *Customs* office is located left of the restaurant and bar (north), and you can enter by walking up the stairs, or heading out onto the small roadway and entering by the front door.

Getting Around
There are several car rental companies that will deliver a car to the marina for you, or as an option, there's a small shack between the restaurant and the *Customs* office where a man will call a taxi for you (sponsored by the taxi-drivers association and answering to *Boatyard Taxi* on VHF ch. 16). You can also hail a taxi on VHF; try calling *Blue Diamond* or *Funseeker Tours* on ch. 16, or *Selwyn Maxwell* on ch. 16/68. *Henry Taxi* has an office at the marina and *McIntyre Brothers* rent cars (on the road past the boatyard).

For a quick trip into town, the best ride is to take the daily buses. There are two buses running every morning at 0845 and 0900 GMT (*Grenada Maybe Time*) and they'll return you at 1300. Walk up the driveway from the marina to the road to catch it. The bus will stop first at the *Moorings Secret Harbour* in *Mt. Hartman Bay* and then come by to pick you up at the entrance to *Spice Island Marine* or *Prickly Bay Marina.*

Marine Facilities
Marinas
Prickly Bay Marina has a lot to offer the visiting cruiser. Dockage for vessels to 200' and drafts to 17' along with 110v and 220v 50-cycle electric, water, and diesel and gasoline. The office can arrange propane fills for you or you can visit *Henry's Safari Tours* located on site. Also on site is *Enza Marine*, the *Marina Tiki Bar and Restaurant*, and the *Essentials* mini-mart. Look for the marina to expand in the future and offer condos for sale.

Marine Services
Spice Island Marine Services is located in the extreme northwestern tip of *Prickly Bay*, just past the Coast Guard station. The yard has room for 200 vessels and their Travel Lift can handle boats to 70 tons with a 25' beam. The current depth at the dock is 10' but plans are in the way for dredging to 12'. The yard offers hurricane preparation with mast removal and tie downs. Here you can also find quality fabricators, electronic and electric specialists, and top-notch mechanics or you can do-it-yourself. For marine supplies there is a *Budget Marine* outlet located in the yard. Also on site is *Turbulence Grenada* (for your sails and rigging needs) and *TechNick Yacht Services* for your fabrication and mechanic needs.

Johnny Sails and Canvas is just down the highway that leads north from *Spice Island Marine Services*. On the same road is *Anro Services*, great outboard and inboard mechanics as well as dealers for *Yanmar, Perkins, BMW, Subaru, Mariner,* and *Mercury* engines. The highway is a popular spot for you can also find *McIntyre Brothers* here in walking distance of the boatyard. *McIntyre Brothers* can repair any inboard and are agents for *Yamaha* outboards. *McIntyre Brothers* also rents cars.

Enza Marine at *Prickly Bay Marina* can handle all manner of yacht repair from electrical to mechanical. For marine joinery and carpentry visit *Cottle Boat Works* also at the marina.

Laundry
Beneath the *Customs* office is a laundry where the ladies will handle your washing and drying needs at a fair price. If this does not suit you, try *Henry's Laundry Service* at 473-444-5313, *Spice Isle Cleaners* at 473-444-4747, or *Super Kleen* at 473-440-8499. *Spice Island Marine Services* has coin operated machines on site.

Internet
Boats and Harbours, located at *Prickly Bay Marina*, offers a high-speed Internet connection, you can use their computers or bring in your own. They offer Wi-fi that covers the marina area and docks. If you are further out in the bay you might be able to receive Wi-fi from *HotHotHot Spot*. *Spice Island Marine* offers computers for their guests and patrons. Several restaurants in the area offer Wi-fi for their guests (*Dodgy Dock* and *Bananas* in True Blue, *De Big Fish*, *Linzee's*, and *Mocha Jumby*).

Garbage
Garbage disposal at *Prickly Bay Marina* is free for guests, and non-guests must pay from EC$1-$5 per bag. All around Grenada you will see garbage bins every hundred yards or so imploring you to keep Grenada clean. If you have a car you can take your garbage with you and dump it in one of these bins for no charge, but if you leave it at the marina don't forget that they have to pay somebody to come by to pick it up, hence the charges

Provisions
The *Essentials* mini-mart at *Prickly Bay Marina* has a nice supply of foods, frozen meats, cold drinks, ice cream, and some very good fresh baguettes (and they're even open Sundays until 1300).

A lot of folks enjoy taking the bus to *Spiceland Mall* in Grand Anse, home of the *Real Value Supermarket*, a very nice grocery store and a popular stop.

Another good stop for provisioning is *CJ's Super Valu* at the roundabout a little over a mile from the marina. Here you can get good prices on bulk goods.

Dining
Marina Tiki Bar and Restaurant at *Prickly Bay Marina* is a very popular spot with great pizzas and a pleasant happy hour (1700-1800).

At the southeastern end of *Prickly Bay*, at the last small dock, is the entrance to the *Rendezvous Beach Resort*. A great place to unwind on their terraced bar and restaurant, the resort also offers Internet access, a small market, a laundry, and a weekly Sunday barbecue. Cruisers who dine at the restaurant are also allowed access to the swimming pool. There is a dive shop on site for those interested in experiencing some of the local diving. If you are interested in picking up some quality wines, try *North South Trading* located between *Prickly Bay* and *Mt. Hartman Bay*. They offer numerous fine wines and will even deliver to the dock for you as well as instruct you as to which wine you should choose and why.

On the road into St. George's is one of the finest restaurants on Grenada, the *Red Crab*. The award-winning chef George Mueller, serves great steaks and seafood which is why the *Red Crab* is so popular with local Grenadians, students from the medical college, and cruisers. Nearby is a great Chinese restaurant, *Choo Light*, an informal and economical place with very good food, a favorite of mine. *Castaway's* is a bit livelier with live bands on Friday nights. The place is not open on Sundays, but after all the fun you'll have on Friday and Saturday, you'll need a day to rest as well.

De Big Fish is located at the boatyard and is another popular cruiser's hangout as is the nearby *Linzee's*.

Mt. Hartman Bay

Waypoints:
Mt. Hartman Bay- ¼ nm SSW of entrance
11° 58.90' N, 61° 45.05' W

Mt. Hartman Bay, sometimes called *Secret Harbour*, is a lovely little anchorage just a bit east of *Prickly Bay*. Home to the *Martin's Marina (formerly The Moorings At Secret Harbour)*, you can get fuel here (diesel and gas), as well as a slip or mooring.

Navigational Information
Entrance to *Mt. Hartman Bay* should never be attempted at night, and caution must be exercised if visibility is poor and the reefs are not visible. As shown on Chart GRE-9, a waypoint at 11° 58.90' N, 61° 45.05' W, will place you approximately ¼ - ½ mile south of the entrance that begins west of Tara Island. If approaching this waypoint from offshore, extreme care must be used as you must avoid the Porpoises, a small series of low-lying rocks that are difficult to see in good weather, and almost impossible to see in heavy weather. To avoid them, never approach the above-mentioned waypoint from the south to the west/ southwest. It might be better to head for the *Prickly Bay* waypoint at 11° 59.10' N, 61° 46.15' W, and then head a bit south of east towards the *Mt. Hartman Bay* waypoint, keeping safely between Prickly Point and the Porpoises (see chart GRE-6).

From the waypoint head generally northward keeping the red buoy that marks the western edge of the Tara Island shoal to starboard (Chart GRE-9). Bear in mind that any and or all of these markers may not be there when you arrive so don't panic if you don't see them, the reefs are visible in good light and with no glare on the water such as is sometimes encountered on cloudy days. The entry gets deep as you pass Tara Island, 60' in places, and once past Tara Island keep an eye out for the large shoal to starboard that is marked by two small red markers that may or may not be there. Ahead of you will be a large buoy topped with a green daymark, keep it to port. It marks a large shoal area. Actually, the buoy sits atop a shallow spot of about 6' and the reef lies a bit west of it. Although there is a narrow channel between the reef and the buoy that carries 27'-32', it's easier and safer to just keep the green buoy to port. Just south of Mt. Hartman Point you'll see a large red buoy, keep it to starboard as you pass between it and a second green marker north/northwest of the first green one that you've just passed.

Once past here the anchorage is open with no hazards save a submerged rock along the western shore and a reef off the point across from the marina. One can pass between the reefs with the green markers and the western shoreline, but only in good visibility as you must pilot your way through here, never try this route in anything less than excellent visibility and calm seas.

The anchorage itself is not as rolly as *Prickly Bay* gets at times, and it does get a bit less wind that can be fluky. Some spots in the harbor get the wind while some don't; this causes boats to sometimes turn this way and that during the course of an average 24-hour period. If the wind is up and from the southeast this is not much of a problem unless you're tucked into the cove on the eastern shore. Don't anchor too close to the point directly across from the marina as there is a rocky shoal there that should be avoided if you draw over 4'. If you anchor too close in a northeast or east wind, you might find yourself on the shoal if the wind shifts southeast.

The marina has a small fuel dock and if you come along side, you'll have to center its approximately 12' width amidships. If the wind is blowing from the east it will pin you to the dock and make leaving a tricky maneuver unless you have a bow thruster. The marina sells duty-free fuel with a 300-gallon minimum.

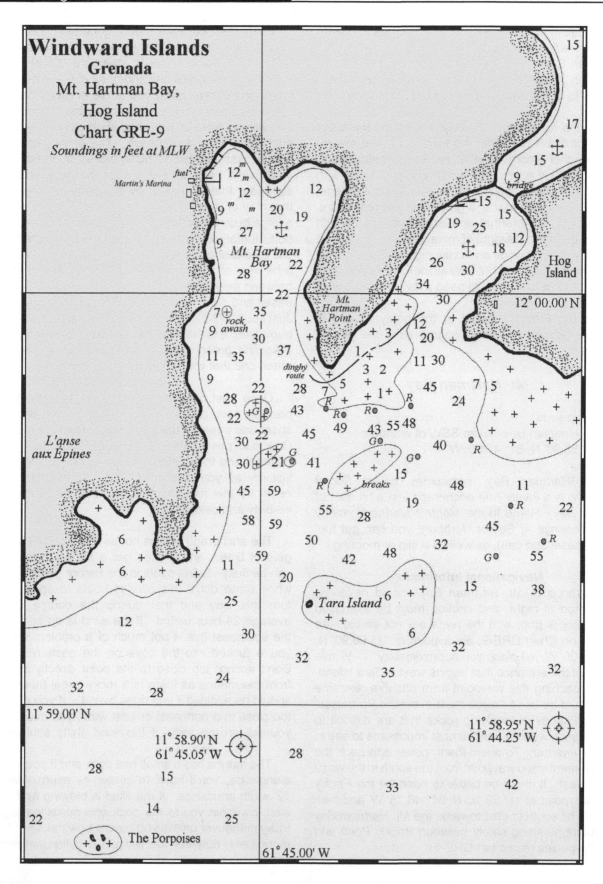

Windward Islands
Grenada
Mt. Hartman Bay,
Hog Island
Chart GRE-9
Soundings in feet at MLW

Every morning there is a bus to town that will pick you up at the marina (at the top of the hill on the road) at 0830 and 0900 GMT (*Grenada Maybe Time*) to take you into St. George's and return you to the marina at 1300 for EC$5.

What You Will Find Ashore

Customs and *Immigration*
If you need to clear, contact *Martin's Marina* (VHF ch. 71) and they can arrange to have an agent handle your clearance.

Marine Facilities
Marinas
Martin's Marina is located in the northeast corner of the bay and offers 53 slips (depths to 20'), several moorings, duty-free fuel, water, full electric (110/220/380 volt 50 cycle), showers, telephone service, Wi-fi, fax services, a laundry service, and a dinghy dock (EC$5 for visitors unless you use the bar).

Marine Services
Martin's Marina has a number of contractors on site and can arrange for others as needed to fulfill your needs.

Propane
Hail George (*Survival Anchorage* on VHF ch. 16), a taxi driver who can arrange propane fills for you. George is also happy to do underwater repairs, serve as extra crew for an overnight passage to Trinidad if needed, perform pilot duties, and take customers for a day sail in his own vessel.

Dining
Martin's Pub, located at the marina, is open every day from noon till 2200 and boasts a terrific Friday night barbecue!

At the *Calabash Hotel*, L'Anse aux Épines, *Cicely's* restaurant is dining in an elegant setting with impeccable service. The award winning chefs will dazzle you with dishes that they have created for royalty such as Prince Charles and Princess Diana.

Hog Island

Waypoints:
Mt. Hartman Bay- ¼ nm SSW of entrance
11° 58.90' N, 61° 45.05' W

Hog Island- ½ nm SSE of entrance to anchorage
11° 58.95' N, 61° 44.25' W

Hog Island is one of the most popular anchorages on the island, and a favorite of those who like to spend hurricane season in Grenada, especially families. Although you cannot enter and leave at night (although some will attempt it with the proper bearings, but I cannot recommend it), the anchorage is well-protected with a small beach for swimming, and a great little bar, *Roger's Pirate Bar*, the best beach bar in the Caribbean. You'll find fewer flies here, no roll, and lots of wind for ventilation and for powering those wind generators. Private interests are developing the island so expect the demise of *Roger's Pirate Bar* to be on the horizon.

Navigational Information
As shown on Chart GRE-9, if you are approaching Hog Island from the west, you can use the waypoint for *Mt. Hartman Bay* at 11° 58.90' N, 61° 48.05' W, which places you approximately ¼ mile southwest of Tara Island. From this waypoint you can pass either north or south of Tara Island and the large surrounding reef structure that lies well to the east of the island. If you pass south of Tara Island you have to deal with far fewer shoals. Once past Tara Island you can turn to the north to work your way into the harbor off Hog Island keeping between the shoals on both sides of you as shown on the chart. This is fairly easy in daylight when the shoals are quite conspicuous; in overcast periods or in poor light the shoals are not so easy to discern. If passing north of Tara Island, you can pass either north or south of the small reef to the north of Tara that is marked by two red buoys along its northwestern edge. When you are past the reef that lies on the western edge of the channel into the harbor at Hog Island, you can enter the channel with its small dogleg to enter the harbor and anchor where ever your draft allows.

If you are approaching Hog Island from the east or the south, a waypoint at 11° 58.95' N, 61° 44.25' W, will place you approximately ½ mile south/southeast of the entrance channel to the anchorage. From the waypoint head toward the channel keeping the Tara Island reef well to port as you approach the entrance to the harbor.

What You Will Find Ashore
The focus of social activity in the Hog Island area is located on the beach at *Roger's Bar*. Sometimes

Roger will bring fresh produce to the bar in the mornings, you'll hear it on the VHF net in the mornings as someone usually announces it. Roger's Sunday barbecue's are not to be missed, as is the informal music that follows when cruisers as well as locals bring their instruments to play for anyone wishing to listen.

Enjoy the Hog Island anchorage while you can. I have been told that plans have been developed to construct a golf course and villas in the area of Mt. Hartman Point and then a bridge over the small cut to Hog Island. You can imagine what this will do to this wonderfully serene anchorage, this wonderful, magical place that is dear to the hearts of so many cruisers. Such is the price of "progress" I suppose.

Most cruisers anchored at Hog Island will at one time or another dinghy over to Woburn at the northwestern tip of *Clarke's Court Bay*. I'll discuss what is available there in the next section.

Clarke's Court Bay

Waypoints:
Clarke's Court Bay- ½ nm S of entrance channel
11° 58.95' N, 61° 43.80' W

Moving eastward, just around the corner (so to speak) from Hog Island is the entrance to *Clarke's Court Bay*, one of the south coast's most popular and protected anchorages. Once an anchorage for ships taking on cargo, today the bay is primarily the haunt of cruisers seeking to get away and get a bit of solitude and yet not be isolated.

Navigational Information
As shown on Chart GRE-10, a waypoint at 11° 58.95' N, 61° 43.80' W, will place you approximately ½ mile south of the entrance to *Clarke's Court Bay*. From the waypoint head generally northward passing to the west of Calivigny Island keeping a sharp eye out for the reefs that you'll want to take to port, passing between the reefs and Calivigny Island. Once past the reefs and the shoal off the eastern tip of Hog Island, you can anchor in several places inside the bay. Immediately upon entry you'll notice a small cut at the north end of Calivigny Island and the mainland at Petit Calivigny Point. The cut is shallow and blocked by coral and rock and offers a fair lee where you can anchor in most conditions. To the north is a small unnamed cove where you can also drop the

hook. Some folks like to anchor off the northwestern end of Hog Island on the *Clarke's Court Bay* side of the small cut between *Clarke's Court Bay* and the harbor at Hog Island.

You can also anchor northeast of Calivigny Island in the small bay to the east of *Clarke's Court Bay* between Petit Calivigny Point and Point Egmont, but you must access the anchorage by taking Calivigny Island to port upon entry as shown on Chart GRE-10; give the south end of Calivigny Island a wide berth to avoid the off-lying reef and then stay between the reefs east of Calivigny Island and the reefs that surround Adam Island.

What You Will Find Ashore

Woburn, usually called Lower Woburn, is the place to go for cruisers in the Hog Island/*Clarke's Court Bay* area. Sometimes called *Conch Village* due to the huge conch shell mound located nearby, here you'll find a nice dinghy dock to tie to as you visit town or catch a bus or taxi in St. George's.

Marine Facilities
Marinas
Clarke's Court Bay Marina
On the northwestern side of the bay, across from Woburn, is *Clarke's Court Bay Marina* (VHF, ch. 16 & 74). The marina boasts 56 slips (to be expanded to 110 in the near future), water, full electric (110/220 volt, 50 cycle). The marina has some hurricane moorings for rent during the winter and spring. Owner Bob Blanc is happy to watch your vessel while you travel for several months or more. The marina has 15' of water at the outer docks and 7' at the inner docks.

Whisper Cove Marina
On the northeastern side of the bay is *Whisper Cove Marina* that can handle vessels to 60' with a 10' draft and provides 220v electric (110v with a transformer), and water thanks to a rather long hose. The marina also has hurricane moorings that are available to rent during the winter and spring. The mooring is free if you dine in their restaurant. There is a dinghy dock, a laundry, and a do-it-yourself shop located here.

Internet
Both *Clarke's Court Bay Marina* and *Whisper Cove Marina* have Wi-fi and plug in Internet connections (just bring in your computer).

Provisions

Whisper Cove Marina has a nice little mini-market with a fantastic selection of meat, sausages, and smoked fish, some say the best on the island.

If you turn right at the end of the dinghy dock you can walk up to the road where, if you take a left, you'll come to *Nimrod's Store* with a limited selection of groceries, but with cold drinks to serve you.

Dining

As usual, the marina restaurants such as the *Oasis Bar* at *Clarke's Cove Marina* and the French flavored restaurant at *Whisper Cove Marina* are the most popular stops for everyday dining and liming.

Tying off in the mangroves in Port Egmont

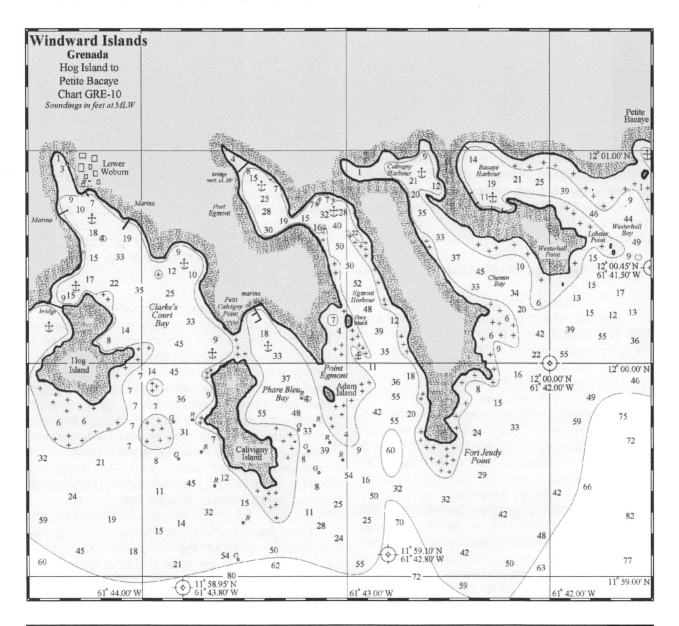

Nearby is the *Little Dipper Restaurant*, a small but impressive restaurant that will be happy to pick up diners from the docks at *Prickly Bay* or *Mt. Hartman Bay* on Thursdays for no charge.

Garbage

If you need to dispose of garbage, dinghy northward past the town where you'll find a small dinghy dock at the extreme northwestern tip of the bay. Land here and step onto the road where you'll find a garbage dumpster about 50 yards to your left.

Phare Bleu Bay

Waypoints

Egmont Harbour- ½ nm S of entrance
11° 59.10' N, 61° 42.80' W

Just to the west of *Clarke's Court Bay* is *Phare Bleu Bay*, home to the *Phare Bleu Marina* and the *South Grenada Regatta* every February.

Navigational Information

From the waypoint at 11° 59.10' N, 61° 42.80' W, as shown on Chart GRE-10, head in a NNW direction to enter the marked channel leading to the marina. Be sure to give the red marker on the shoal inside the bay (see the chart) a wide berth taking it well to starboard when entering the bay. Proceed to the marina or anchor where your draft allows.

What You Will Find Ashore

Customs and Immigration

Customs is located at the marina, office hours are 0800-1600 daily, however on the weekends the hours are up to the discretion of the attending officer.

Marine Facilities
Marinas

Le Phare Bleu Marina is located at the northern end of the bay and boasts 50 slips with room for vessels to 100' LOA. Slips have water, electric (110/220 volt, 50 cycle), diesel and gasoline, and free Wi-fi for guests.

Marine Services

Island Dreams is located here, having moved from *Clarke's Court Bay* and Woburn. *Island Dreams* are project managers and absentee owner agents and have their own moorings. *The Canvas Shop* can handle your canvas and upholstery repairs. *Palm Tree Marine* is well-known for their mechanical and electrical expertise; they are agents for *Caterpillar* and can handle all manner of fuel polishing as well as welding and fabrication. *Underwater Solutions* are based here and they are up for all underwater repairs you may have.

Dining

Le Phare Blue Restaurant is open for dinner and the *Pool Bar Restaurant,* located near the beach, is open for lunch and dinner.

Port Egmont, Calivigny Harbour, and *Bacaye Harbour*

Waypoints:

Westerhall Bay- ¼ nm SSE of entrance
12° 00.45' N, 61° 41.50' W

Chemin Bay- ¼ nm SSE of entrance
12° 00.00' N, 61° 42.00' W

Egmont Harbour- ½ nm S of entrance
11° 59.10' N, 61° 42.80' W

Between *Phare Bleu Bay* and St. David's are three small harbors that are rarely visited but offer excellent protection should a major storm threaten. Although this area is technically out of the hurricane zone, at least as far as the insurance carriers are concerned, named storms are not unknown and protection should be sought as soon as possible in the event of the approach of a storm.

Navigational Information

The first of these anchorages, when approaching from the west, is *Port Egmont*, whose entrance is through *Egmont Harbour* as shown on Chart GRE-10. A waypoint at 11° 59.10' N, 61° 42.80' W, will place you approximately ½ mile south of the entrance to *Egmont Harbour*. From the waypoint head generally north avoiding the reefs east of Adam Island and the reefs lying off the land to the east, on your starboard side; favor the Fort Jeudy Point side of the channel. You'll continue up *Egmont Harbour* past Gary Island until you get to the head of the bay, a pleasant anchorage in itself, and turn to port to enter *Port Egmont*.

Once inside *Port Egmont* you can anchor almost anywhere or tie off into the mangroves if you choose. Don't get too near the small bridge at the northern end, you would not want to blow into that should the worst case scenario occur. The bottom is a bit grassy in places here so make sure your anchor is set well. If you walk up to the main road you can catch a bus into Woburn and St. George's.

A bit further east lies *Calivigny Harbour* at the north end of *Chemin Bay*. This is another enclosed anchorage, very similar to *Port Egmont*, only smaller. From the waypoint head south of *Egmont Harbour* as shown on Chart GRE-10. Work your way south of Fort Jeudy Point keeping an eye out for the dangerous reefs south of the point, to a waypoint at 12° 00.00' N, 61° 42.00' W, which will place you approximately ¼ mile south/southeast of the entrance to *Chemin Bay* and south of Westerhall Point.

From this waypoint you must thread the needle between two shoals that can be difficult to see at times. Never attempt this passage in heavy following seas! Once inside *Chemin Bay* head up the bay until you can round the point to starboard and anchor in *Calivigny Harbour*. The nearby *Westerhall Estate* is home to *Aubrey's Restaurant and Bar*. The nearby *Westerhall Rum Distillery* dates back to the 1800s and if you continue east on the main road you'll come to a small market.

Still eastward is another small bay, *Bacaye Harbour* (at the northwestern end of *Westerhall Bay*), not as sheltered as the two already mentioned, but certainly worth a stop. From the waypoint south of Westerhall Point as shown on Chart GRE-10, make for a waypoint at 12° 00.45' N, 61° 41.50' W, which will place you approximately ¼ mile south/southeast of the entrance to *Westerhall Bay*.

From this waypoint keep the rocks off Lobster Point well to port as you enter *Westerhall Bay* and then turn to the northwest to again thread the needle between two reefs as you work your way into *Bacaye Harbour*. Westerhall is known for its beautiful villas, the expensive, elegant homes of local business people and European and American retirees with stunning views of the sea.

Petite Bacaye is a small harbor lying east of Westerhall as shown on Chart GRE-11. It is not recommended for an overnight stop except in settled weather as it can get quite rolly. The small *Petite Bacaye Hotel* welcomes cruisers and the restaurant and bar is a good place to stop for a cold one on a hot day.

St. David's

Waypoints:
St. David's Harbour- ½ nm S of entrance channel 12° 00.40' N, 61° 40.60' W

Approximately 1¼ miles east of Westerhall Point lies the entrance to the harbour at St. David's.

Navigational Information
As shown on Chart GRE-11, a waypoint at 12° 00.40' N, 61° 40.60' W, will place you approximately ½ mile south of the entrance channel into *St. David's Harbour*. From the waypoint head northward towards the mouth of the entrance channel lying between two reef systems. Here you'll pick up lighted markers to guide you in as shown on the chart.

What You Will Find Ashore
St. David's Harbour is another popular stop for cruisers on the southern coast of Grenada, and usually it is because of the good reputation enjoyed by *Grenada Marine*, the local yard.

Customs and *Immigration*
St. David's is a Port of Entry for Grenada. *Customs* is located at *Grenada Marina* at the extreme northern part of the bay and is usually onsite 0800-1600 from Monday-Thursday. *Immigration* does not maintain an office on site but will come as needed.

Marine Facilities
Marinas
Grenada Marine (monitors VHF ch. 16/14) offers 60 slips with 30amp and 50amp 110/220volt 50-cycle electricity, phone and fax service, moorings in the harbour, Wi-fi, ice, a chandlery, diesel and gas, bus service, car rentals, showers, a laundry, and a picnic area. The docks can handle drafts to 26'.

Marine Services
Grenada Marine offers engine and sail repairs, electronics, a diving service, fiberglass and wood repairs, a 30 ton Travel Lift that will haul boats up to 32' wide with a 12' draft, and all of it protected by 24-hour security. Paint sheds are in use and the workers are experienced with *AwlGrip*. Hurricane tie-downs are available and mast removal is no problem.

Grenada Marine is one of the best yards in this part of the Caribbean and offers competition to the yards in Trinidad. They can handle any type of mechanical or electrical repair, hull work, osmosis treatments, sail repair, rigging work, underwater repairs, welding and fabrication of all kinds, and yacht management for absentee owners.

Near *Bel Air Plantation* is *Fred's Shipwrights* with their own dock. Fred's can handle hull work and joinery and specializes in teak decking and wooden vessels of all types.

Marine Supplies

Island Water World has a branch at *Grenada Marine* if you need anything marine related. They are not quite as well-stocked as their branch in St. George's but they can bring in the items for you very quickly.

Internet

Both *Grenada Marina* and *Bel Air Plantation* (located on the eastern side of the bay) have free Wi-

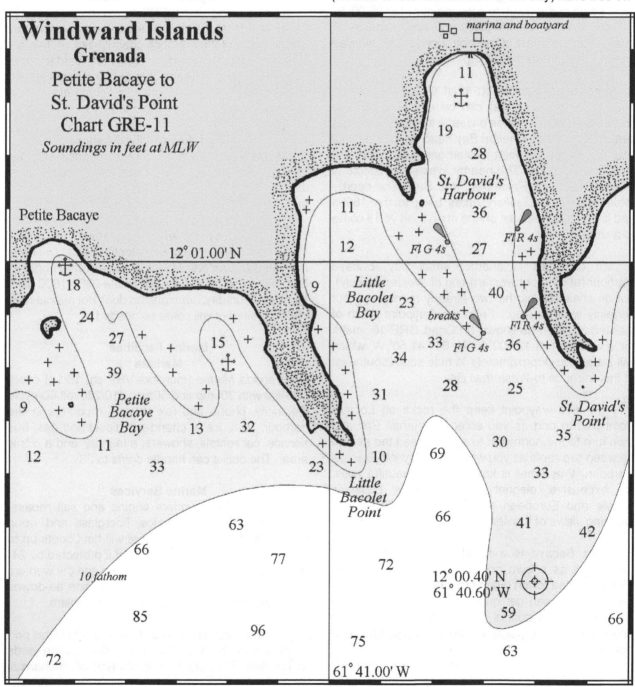

fi. If you don't have a computer to use check with the marina office and they can assist.

Provisions
Located at Bel Air Plantation, *The Deli* is well-stocked with quality meats and basics.

Dining
The *Grenada Marine Bar* is popular both with cruisers and techs from the boatyard and overlooks the harbour. *Bel Air Plantation* has a wonderful upscale restaurant on site with their own dinghy dock.

To the east of the harbor, you can dine at the *La Sagesse Restaurant* at the *La Sagesse Nature Center*, a small hotel located in St. David's. On a romantic beach, this is one of the most casual places to dine on the island yet the cuisine is anything but casual. The restaurant loves vegetarians and caters to their special dietary needs as well. A couple of miles from here you can visit the *Herb and Spice Garden*, one part of a marketing co-op to promote Grenadian spices and herbs. It's a good spot to take a pleasant stroll and learn what herbs and spices are what in Grenada.

The Eastern Coast of Grenada

Grenville

Waypoints:
Grenville- ¼ nm SE of entrance channel
12° 06.90' W, 61° 36.40' W

Grenada's windward coast offers only one good anchorage, and that is at the commercial port of Grenville, Grenada's second largest city and a fishing and boat-building center. The entrance is a bit tricky, a dogleg between two reefs, however it is generally well marked and the anchorage, although wide open to the trades, is protected by two reefs. Never try this entrance at night or with a large following sea running.

Navigational Information
As shown on Chart GRE-12, a waypoint at 12° 06.90'N, 61° 36.40' W, will place you approximately ¼ mile southeast of the entrance channel. From the waypoint head in between the first pair of lit markers (remember, red-right-returning in Grenada), and follow the marked channel taking the dogleg to starboard through *Luffing Channel* (keep *Barrel of Beef* to port upon entry) to anchor north of the town

dock. Used caution as the sun will be in your eyes and you will have difficulty seeing the reefs after 1400 and if leaving in the morning, the sun will again be in your eyes until about 1030-1100.

What You Will Find Ashore
Customs is ashore and Grenville is modern with tons of shopping, a laundry, several grocery stores, a pharmacy, the *Grenville Cooperative Nutmeg Association* (the island's largest nutmeg coop), a huge basket weaving district where everybody weaves, and even a one-hour photo all within an easy walk from the town dock. Saturday is market day in Grenville and a great time to tour the spice factory where nutmeg is prepared for export. This is a perfect time and place to try *Mauby*, the island's local drink made from tree bark. Directly on the waterfront is a good fresh fish market open every day.

Six miles north of Grenville is *The Lake Antoine National Landmark*, a 16-acre lake lying within an extinct volcanic crater. One mile southeast of the lake, and located on the *River Antoine*, is the *River Antoine Rum Distillery* (and you know how cruisers love rum distilleries, especially if you've visited Martinique), the oldest functioning rum distillery in the Caribbean and one that still uses equipment unchanged since the 19th century. You are welcome to take a tour and purchase any of the products made on site. To find the distillery, drive down the runway at the old airport and then north on the road to Tivoli. Turn east to La Poterie then north across the River Antoine where the road becomes a narrow single lane that leads to the lake.

Although *Lake Antoine* gives the impression of great altitude as it sits nestled among the peaks, it is actually only 20' above sea level. Also nearby, about three miles from Grenville, is St. Andrews where you can visit the *Dunfermline Rum Distillery*, built in 1797.

The nearby small settlement of Sea Moon has quite a history. A former sugar plantation, the area also grew coconut and limes and in years past was known for its horse racing and large musical events. Today however it is known for a different reason, Sea Moon's participation in the expanding world of techno-industry. *Call Centres Grenada* has opened a 20,000 square-foot office with over 1,000 telemarketing agents in the area giving quite a boost to the local economy.

Just south of Grenville, as shown on Chart GRE-1, lies Marquis Island, a naturalist's delight. Marquis Island was once part of the mainland of Grenada and is home to the magnificent frigate bird, but its real significance is that ash layers are visible in the geological structure of the island that were formed by eruptions from as far away as *Grand Étang*, far to leeward. You can anchor for the day in the lee of Marquis, just west of its western tip in a small cove south of Soubise Pt. accessed from *St. Andrew's Bay* south of Marquis Island.

Touring Inland Grenada

As is the case in all the Eastern Caribbean islands, some of the most scenic vistas, historical and unusual locations, and the friendliest people live inland, far from the anchorages that cruisers frequent, and the only

way to access these treasures is by car rental, a guided tour, bicycles, buses, or as a last resort, hitchhiking. If you don't wish to rent a car, another option it to take a tour with Dennis Henry. *Henry's Safari Tours* will take you on an all-day excursion leaving at 0900 from your marina or anchorage area and will return you around 1700. If you have a particular destination in mind, don't forget to tell Dennis and he will customize his trip to suit your needs.

Taking the road from St. George's to *The Grand Etang Forest Reserve* in the center of Grenada a short half-detour at Constantine is definitely called for if you like waterfalls. Here you can visit *Annandale Falls*, the most accessible of the waterfalls that carry the water away from the *Grand Etang* catchment. *Annandale Falls* are only a few feet off the road and a set of concrete steps will guide you to them. The

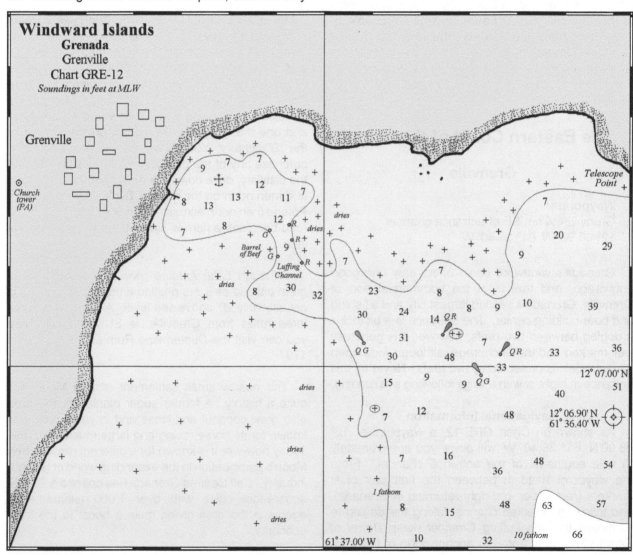

hill next to the falls is being developed as a spice and herb garden to enable visitors to view firsthand Grenada's main crops.

One of the most popular stops is the Hermitage at St. Patrick's, home of the *Grenada Chocolate Factory*, a wonderful coop making some of the best chocolates you'll ever taste. Most of the machinery here is either antique or hand made, some of it is even solar-powered. Their dark chocolate is highly prized and one of the best in the world. For more information visit their website: www.grenadachocolate.com

The Grand Étang Forest Reserve is a national park that encompasses the mountain range in the center of Grenada which includes *Mt. St. Catherine* at 2,757' to the north, *Mt. Qua Qua* near the center at 2,373', and *Mt. Sinai* at 2,305' on the southern end of the range. The road leading across the island passes hillsides thick with bananas, cocoa, and nutmeg before crossing the center of the mountain range at 1,910'. *The Grand Étang Forest Center* sits within a few hundred yards of *Grand Étang Lake*, the site of an extinct volcano whose crater is filled with water (*Grand Étang* is French for *Great Lake*). The 30-acre lake sits at 1,740' above sea level and folklore claims that the lake is bottomless. On the northern side of the lake *Mt. Qua Qua* is easily visible and on clear days you can see *Mt. St. Catherine*.

There are several trails that are worth investigating. Directly behind the visitor's center is the start of the *Morne LaBaye Trail*, an interpretive trail featuring twelve points of interest explained in the brochure that you'll take with you on the trail. The 15-minute walk will take you to a lookout where you can get a view of Grenada's eastern coast and *Mt. Sinai* to the south. The *Mt. Qua Qua Trail* is about a 1½ hour hike that passes the lake trail junction where the trail gets steeper as it follows the contours of the ridge.

The *Ridge and Lake Circle Trail* is a 30-minute hike along the shores of *Grand Étang Lake*. Beginning at the visitor's center the first half of the trail is basically the same trail as the *Mt. Qua Qua Trail,* but then it branches off towards the lake. The *Seven Sisters Trail* is one of the most interesting trails and begins southwest of the lake and leads to an area of seven waterfalls alive with local flora and fauna. A guide is recommended for this 3-hour tour (I can't believe I actually wrote "3-hour tour"). Other waterfalls of interest are the *Royal Mt. Carmel Waterfall* in St.

Andrews, the island's highest waterfall which is actually two falls cascading 70' into a crystal clear pool. In St. Mark visit the *Victoria Falls* at the foot of Mt. St. Catherine on the western coast of Grenada. This recently discovered waterfall is only accessible by foot.

Snorkelers and divers will find the waters of Grenada rich in sea life among the many dive and snorkeling sites ringing the island. There is good snorkeling off *Grand Anse Beach*, Molinère Point (St. George's), and at *Dragon Bay* on the western coast of Grenada. Just west of St. George's lies the *Halifax-Molinère Wall*, a great wall dive (20'-90') made that much more so for being so close to shore. Probably some of the best snorkeling in Grenada can be found off Molinère Point, north of St. George's.

At *Grand Anse Bay* the inner reef system has for the most part been destroyed, but there is still a lot of marine life to see, large sea fans, and there are still many living corals. *Boss Reef* is a 6-mile long reef that stretches from *Grande Anse Bay* to *Canoe Bay* and offers several good dive sites. Just west of *Boss Reef* is *Wibble Reef* where slow, lazy drift dives are the order of the day.

A bit west of *Grand Anse Beach* lies what may possibly be the largest wreck in the Caribbean, the cruise ship *Blanca C*. The 600' cruise ship sank on October 24, 1961, after lying at anchor for two days off St. George's while it burned, the result of a boiler explosion. Every boat in St. George's rushed to the rescue of the crew and passengers and for their bravery the *Costa Cruise Lines* presented Grenada with the statue, *Christ of the Deep* located in the Carenage. As the hulk of the *Blanca C* was being towed out of the shipping lanes it sank in 90'-170' of water where it lies today for only the most intrepid of divers as the depth does not allow much time for exploration, but enough perhaps to visit the 350lb. grouper (jewfish) that lives in the smokestack. Just of Pt. Salines is the *Spice Island Reef*, where good diving and snorkeling can be found in 20'-80'.

From Grenada to Trinidad and Tobago

Vessels headed to Trinidad and Tobago, from Grenada or Carriacou must deal with the fluky northwest set of the *Guyana Current* that flows between Trinidad/Tobago and Grenada. Here you'll find the current pushing you westward at 2 knots or more at times, while at other times you would have to look hard to find any current at all. If you set your autopilot to steer directly for the waypoint at *Boca del Monos*, you'll sometimes find your autopilot steering 185°, while at other times it will be steering your vessel at 140°, so strong is the current in places. As a rule of thumb, the current can be strongest closer to Grenada.

Although cruisers often head for Tobago from the southern coast of Grenada, *Prickly Bay* or Hog Island, it is not recommended unless you have a good engine or simply like tacking. A better idea would be to head northward to Carriacou and then sail to Tobago from the northeastern tip of Carriacou or Petite St. Vincent. Another option is to sail to Tobago from Barbados to lay the island on one tack. Of course, those of us that don't like to go to weather might suggest that you head to the Azores and then down to the Canaries and back across the Atlantic to avoid headwinds. The choice is yours.

Vessels heading for Trinidad from Grenada should be aware of a natural gas platform approximately 25 miles north of the Bocas that began operation in August of 2001. The platform, called *Hibiscus*, lies almost on the rhumb line from *Prickly Bay* to *Boca de Monos*, at an approximate position of 11° 19.30' N, 61° 42.40' W. The platform, called *Hibiscus*, is easy to see in daylight, and well lit at night, however the large tenders that are moored just off the platform are not so easily seen at night so give the platform a wide berth. There is a second platform approximately four miles to the east of *Hibiscus*.

The Grenada Superfly

Without their knowledge, cruisers are currently involved in an ongoing and heretofore secret insect breeding program on the Caribbean island of Grenada. Here, amid the snug, protected anchorages along the southern shore of the Island of Spice, cruisers are unwittingly helping to create a new, super-intelligent and possibly threatening species of fly, the Grenada *SUPERFLY*.

Innocent cruisers, who are besieged on a daily basis by the local fly population, seek only to eradicate the pests that invade their boats. However, all they are actually accomplishing is a culling of the fly population by destroying the weak, the slow, and the stupid, those unable to escape the fly-swatter, hanging flypaper, and various poisonous gas attacks which leads to a stronger, quicker, more toxin-resistant insect

The scenario is typical and varies little from day to day. As reliable as clockwork, the typical cruiser will be asleep in his or her bunk, snugly anchored in *Prickly Bay*, or off Hog Island, and then at exactly 0545, give or take 30 seconds, they are awakened by a fly landing on their face. They will swat at the fly and it will only laugh. It will land again and again on their victim's nose, cheek, and forehead, dancing its little fly-dance until the cruiser arises, cursing and swearing and looking for an implement of destruction with which to attack the vile creature. But folks, this is only the beginning.

These pests are extremely fast and they will be long gone when the skipper's fly swatter makes contact with the mate's nose. These flies have shown that they understand the concept of a fly swatter, and as soon as a human hand grasps one, they are nowhere to be found. Research has shown that the fly is actually hiding in some remote, darkened alcove, snickering as their victim/prey stalks them without a clue as to where they are while the mate screams fiendish curses at the skipper's ancestors for his or her stupidity. Of course, as soon as the fly swatter is placed on a table or berth and is rendered harmless, the fly will zoom across the cabin and land squarely in the middle of it, dancing its fly-dance and taunting its victims in barely audible fly-talk.

If all this was not bad enough, there is some speculation that these creatures are telepathic. Some of these superior flies have been noticed to seek shelter at the very moment the thought of a fly swatter enters the mind of their victim.

These flies make use of devious strategies of concealment and evasion. When a fly swatter is hefted, the flies will leave the immediate cabin only to return when their victim looks for them elsewhere. In hundreds of documented cases, cruisers sought to destroy the flies that appeared in their aft cabin, only to discover the flies were no longer present. Turning around the cruisers notices that the flies are now in the main salon and upon stealthily approaching that cabin, discover that the flies are now somewhere else. This game of hide and seek has been known to drag on for hours until the frustrated cruiser surrenders and leaves the boat for a well-deserved happy hour libation.

As the day wears on more and more flies arrive, often up to two dozen per vessel. A small percentage fall to fly-swatters, while flies with lesser mental capacities fall victim to sticky fly-tape that dangles from overhead fixtures and snares not only the stupid flies, but stupid cruisers as well.

Gas warfare has been used in defense of these airborne invaders for quite some time aboard cruising boats. It did not take long for the local markets to sell out of their stocks of flying insect sprays and soon the sounds of "pfffftttttt" could be heard emanating from almost all the boats in Grenada. At first this defense was quite successful, dead flies soon littered saloon soles, but this victory was short-lived. Soon the flies appeared wearing tiny gas masks for protection. Shortly thereafter, the wee critters acquired immunity to the poisonous vapors and the flies actually seemed to enjoy the gas attacks. Now these insects invite the attacks and have been seen inhaling deeply while flying through the noxious clouds. The only effects noticed on the more recent strands of the species is a certain giddiness, increased appetite, and short term memory loss.

The one good bit of news is that the flies cease their mischief at dusk and refrain from making appearances until 0545 the next morning. Researchers are attempting to discover what part night plays in their program, and if it can be used as a defense against this growing menace.

What do these flies want? What is their purpose? These questions remain a mystery. Theories range from the cunning to the mundane. It has been suggested that their intent is driving cruiser's from their boats so the flies can commandeer the vessels to carry their swarms far across the ocean to propagate their species elsewhere, while others believe the flies are simply creating havoc for havoc's sake. At this point in time, one theory is as good as another as no proof exists to support either one...yet.

While the forces controlling this breeding program remain unknown, there has been some concern that some wily Grenadian is behind the scheme hoping to corner the market on fly-swatters. However merchants on Grenada normally do not sell fly swatters, few even know what one is. More recent research shows that it may be the flies themselves behind this nefarious evolutionary plot, and if that is so they are far further along in their development than previously imagined. For now, more research is being planned while cruisers must be made aware of their part in this sordid affair. Mankind can only hope that the mosquitoes don't catch on...

I have found a new defense, which is actually an old method of keeping away flies in the Southern United States, and upon my return to Grenada I will certainly try it. The defense is quite simple actually. Take a gallon-size plastic baggie, fill it about halfway with water, and attach it above the companionway or open hatchway so that it hangs down a bit. How does this work you ask? Well, the theory seems to be that the fly approaches the baggie filled with water and sees his/her own reflection in the bag, magnified many times in size by the water filled baggie. The invading fly immediately seeks safer territory far from the huge creature it barely escaped from in your companionway. If you try this let me know how it turns out, but I fear that the Grenada Superflys will quickly figure out a way around this defense, and I certainly hope the little buggers don't read about it here. Good luck and happy hunting!

Trinidad and Tobago

The island of Trinidad has become a major cruising destination for vessels in the Caribbean, and with good reason. Trinidad's marine service industry has blossomed over the last decade, and if you tie that in with the fact that the islands of Trinidad and Tobago are technically out of the hurricane zone (at least the insurance underwriters treat them that way), you have an attractive combination for seasonal visitors.

Trinidad/Tobago is a polyglot of cultures, the most diverse spectrum of people in the entire Caribbean. The population of the islands is a melting pot made up primarily of the descendants of freed slaves and the indentured East Indians that replaced them. The population is fairly evenly divided between those of African and East Indian descent, both about 40% of the population of 1.3 million people, while approximately 18% of the population is of mixed descent, and the rest of the population is made of Chinese, Arabic, Spanish, and other nationalities.

Nowhere is this mix of cultures more apparent than in downtown Port of Spain, Trinidad. Here you'll find the Savanna, a huge park that is the center of Carnival activities. Surrounding the park you'll find everything from a US staple (TGI Friday's) across the street from a Victorian mansion that sits majestically next to a building that you would swear resembles a Moroccan palace. Farther outside of town, you might see a Hindu temple on one corner and just down the road a Mosque sitting across the street from a Catholic Church.

The island of Trinidad has a strong magnetic quality about her that has become an accepted fact among veteran cruisers, many of whom call these islands home. There are so many vessels that initially call at Trinidad planning to stay a week, or a month, and wind up staying many times longer than they had originally planned. The *Immigration* officers know this, and if you don't ask for the maximum stay allowed, they might give it to you anyway to save you and them the hassle of an extension when you realize that your stay will be a bit longer than you first imagined, and trust me, that will likely happen. It happened to me and I don't know how many other skippers.

What is the attraction? Well, I've tried, but I can't quite define it. I think that it may be different for each and every person. Some like the haulout facilities so

they can leave their boat on the hard while they return home for a visit. Others like the fact that they can get just about anything repaired or fabricated for their boat at a very good price. Some like the shopping, or the camaraderie of hundreds of other cruisers, the get-togethers and pot-lucks that go hand-in-hand with the cruising lifestyle. But, let's not limit ourselves to what is attractive in services and social events. There is a LOT more to Trinidad and Tobago.

First and foremost is what is possibly the greatest party in the world...CARNIVAL! All else pales in comparison to that colorful, highly energetic celebration of life.

The topography of Trinidad ranges from the mountainous tropical rain forests in the north to the rolling hills of the southern island. On both the east and west coasts are huge swamps with a tremendous range of creatures large and small. The *Cocal* along the southeastern shore is not to be missed, miles and miles of coconut trees backing up a beach that stretches for miles. Tobago has its own rain forest along with scenic mountain views and diving and snorkeling opportunities to rival any in the Caribbean.

Before departing for Trinidad or Tobago, I suggest you spend about eight minutes watching a very well made video online at http://www.facebook.com/video/video.php?v=102211779824410. This video will show you some great footage of what we will be discovering in the following chapters.

Okay, okay, I'll stop...I'm starting to sound like a tourist publication. Besides, you'll learn about all these things within the pages of this guide. But one of the greatest treasures of these islands, and one that I can't put on paper here, is the endearing quality of the people that reside there. Known far and wide for their simple, open friendliness, Trinidadians, Trinis for short, are welcoming and quick to make one feel at home. They will create many warm memories of your visit here, something to look back on one day and smile about. Whether you come here for a week, for a month, for a season, or for years, you will one day leave Trinidad, even if just for a while, but Trinidad will never leave you.

A Brief History of Trinidad and Tobago

Centuries before the birth of Christ, the first settlers in Trinidad arrived upon her shores making the island the first of the Caribbean islands to be populated. Springing from the middle Orinoco around 2100 BC, they moved downriver to the Guyanas, and then up the West Indies chain. During the past half-century, fresh finds, techniques of dating artifacts, and some heated debate, have refined our cumulative knowledge of these people into a sketchy history extending as far back as 5000 BC. In 1971, the remains of Banwari Man were found. Discovered in southern Trinidad, near the town of Banwari Trace, the bones were carbon dated and show that the fellow lived around 5000 BC.

The most famous of these groups were the Arawaks and Caribs, who crossed the waters in their dugout canoes and established villages on the island as they progressed up the island chain towards the Bahamas. The people of southern Trinidad kept close cultural ties with their cousins in Venezuela and trade with people far south as the Guyana's, while the people of northern Trinidad and Tobago maintained ties with the peoples of the Windward Islands.

Up until the early 1500s, more and more Amerindians came to Trinidad, the island they called *Ieri*, land of the hummingbird. In fact, up until the 19th century Amerindians ventured to Trinidad to trade, walking up the long footpath from the southern shore to the mission at *Savanna Grande*, which today is called the "Indian Walk" (near Princes Town). By the end of the 15th century, there were some 35,000 people inhabiting the islands ranging from the Kalina (sometimes called the Kalinargo) in Tobago to the Yao, Nepoio, Shebaio, and Carinepagoto tribes on Trinidad. Perhaps I should explain something here. All these peoples are Arawaks. An Arawak is simply an Amerindian that speaks the Arawakan language and covers many tribes from the Lucayans in the Bahamas, to the Tainos in Puerto Rico, to the Kalina in Tobago, and the Caribs who were to be found on all the islands of the Caribbean. Today, their only pure relatives are the Lokono Arawaks in the Guyanas.

On July 31, 1498, Christopher Columbus "discovered" Trinidad on his third voyage to the New World, saying a prayer as he spied the southern hills of Trinidad in the distance after a long spell at sea with dwindling water rations. Columbus, named the island *La Trinite*, after the *Blessed Trinity* to whom he prayed. Columbus traveled along the southern shore anchoring at Moruga, the entire passage there now being shown as *The Columbus Channel* on some tourist maps (but not on any official charts). Just off the southwestern tip of Trinidad, Columbus was approached by a boatload of Amerindians armed with bows and arrows. Columbus ordered music so his sailors could dance to entertain the visitors. The Indians mistook this for a war dance and let loose with a volley of arrows to which the Spaniards responded in kind causing the Indians to flee. The next day Columbus headed north, never setting foot on the island of Trinidad. Columbus later sailed by Tobago, which he named *Assumpcion* and Grenada, which he called *Concepcion*.

Shortly thereafter Spanish slavers arrived searching for divers for the pearl beds off Margarita and Cubagua, and began what is little less than genocide. At first the Indians were skeptical about fighting back, they were unsure if a white man could be killed. A *cacique* (chief) named Brayoan had an idea. He and his men found a Spaniard passing through their area and offered to escort him and carry him across a river on their shoulders. Once in deep water the Indians threw the Spaniard into the water and held him under until he drowned, proving that the white man could indeed be killed. Try as they may, the Indians were unsuccessful in their fight for survival and in a few short years the Spaniards decimated the indigenous population until by 1510 there were declared to be no peaceful Indians on the islands. In 1511 the King of Spain forbade slave trading on the islands of Trinidad and Tobago, but this was reversed sometime around 1532. Today all that remains of these first inhabitants are bits of their language, the names of various places, rivers, and mountains on the islands of Trinidad and Tobago.

For almost three hundred years after Columbus there were no settlers on the island save the Spaniards who used Trinidad as a base for exploring the upper reaches of the *Orinoco River* where they believed that *El Dorado*, a mythical city of gold, could be found. Along with the Spaniards came Capuchin monks who tried to convert the Amerindians that were not enslaved and removed them from the island. As you will soon learn, the Spaniards were attacked time and time again over the years. Once by Sir Walter Raleigh, himself on a quest for *El Dorado*, who sacked the town of St. Joseph, the old capital of Trinidad that lay 12 miles east of today's capital, Port of Spain. A later invasion by the Dutch resulted in the Spanish survivors becoming nudists for a while as the invaders took all their possessions, including their clothes.

The Spaniards allotted a number of Amerindians to work on the local plantations where missionaries attempted to convert the Indians to Catholicism. On December 1, 1699, three missionaries were slain by Amerindians at the mission of *San Francisco de los Arenales*. The "peaceful" Indians also killed the Governor and several soldiers who arrived later to restore order. The bodies of the martyrs were brought to the church in St. Joseph's and interred under the floor and the Spaniards gathered their forces and set off after the Indians who had committed the deed. The Indians, pursued by the Spanish, fled across the island to the eastern coast where they committed suicide by leaping off a cliff into the huge breakers at Toco at the northeastern tip of Trinidad. The plantation owners realized that the Missions were not working and they were eventually abolished by 1708, although four remained at Savanna Grande (now Princes Town), Guayria (now Naparima), Savanetta, and Montserrat.

The Spaniards were growing tobacco on the island by this time as the drug had become quite popular in Europe although it was not legal at the time. Dutch and English smugglers moved the illicit drug until a Spanish fleet destroyed all foreign ships in the Gulf of Paria in 1610 (Am I the only one that thinks this whole scenario sounds familiar, an illegal smoking drug, illicit trade, Caribbean based?). American tobacco growers began to dominate the tobacco market so the Trinidadian plantation owners began to grow cocoa until a disease wiped out the cocoa farmers in 1725 and a smallpox epidemic further decimated the local population. The remaining Spanish settlers concentrated themselves in St. Joseph until a coup by members of the town council in 1745 almost destroyed the settlement. The resident Governor was taken hostage and order was only restored after a Spanish military force from Venezuela arrived. In 1757, the governing body in Trinidad moved from St. Joseph, 12 miles westward to a small fishing village on the coast at *Puerto de Espana*, Port of Spain where within two decades the town had grown to about 80 houses, one church, and a battery consisting of several cannons.

At this time Trinidad was still trading with other nations, but foreign settlers were not permitted on the island. However, in 1776, Governor Manuel Flaquez sought to attract Roman Catholic immigrants to Trinidad, particularly French planters, and offered land grants and tax incentives. But was it the planters or their African slaves that were really in demand? These laborers had brought so much already to the islands of Barbados and Haiti, and it is believed that Flaquez was a man of foresight and realized what this labor force could do for Trinidad. Soon Frenchmen from Grenada, unhappy with their new British rulers, began to trickle into Trinidad. One of them, Roume de St. Laurent, suggested the *Cedula of Population*, which proposed that any European white of the Catholic faith, be welcome in Trinidad.

In 1783, the King of Spain agreed to the Cedula and between 1783 and 1797, thousands of French settlers and their African slaves arrived in Trinidad and set up vast sugar plantations. Each white settler was granted 130 acres for each member of his family and 65 acres for each slave he brought with him as well as special tax exemptions. There were a few free black settlers who were granted half as much as their white counterparts. The only restrictions were that the settlers had to be Roman Catholic and from a nation on good terms with Spain.

Tobago at that time was going through several changes of leadership over the years, changing Kings some 31 times, and currently being ruled by the French. Tobago was originally settled by the British in 1625 when the first group of settlers were wiped out by the indigenous Kalina Indians. In 1628 the Dutch arrived, but a combined force of Indians and Spaniards from Trinidad arrived in canoes and killed off the Dutch settlers, the only time that Trinidad and Tobago ever went to war with each other. In 1639 the British arrived again, only to be run off again by the Kalina. Charles I gave the island to his godson the Duke of Courland (in Latvia) and another settlement was established at Plymouth in 1642 by the Courlanders. Again the settlers made like a ping-pong ball being chased off by the Indians, returning in 1650, and again in 1654. At this time the Dutch returned and claimed dominion of the island until they were driven off by the British who were in turn driven off by the French who destroyed the settlements and abandoned the island.

In 1674, Tobago was ceded to the Dutch and the ownership of the islands bounced back and forth between the French, Dutch, Latvian, and English for many years. The United States briefly ruled the island for a period in 1778, just before the French regained possession, which for so many years was no more than a base for pirates. In 1783, in a move to thwart the Spanish government in Trinidad, the French got on the bandwagon and offered a similar *Immigration* policy with large cash compensations to attract French settlers away from the Spanish colony.

Between 1783 and 1797, the population of Trinidad grew from 4,500 to over 16,000 people, including slaves, but the Amerindian population declined during the same period from 1,900 to about 1,000. It is estimated that the slaves outnumbered the freemen by a ratio of 2 to 1 during these years.

Trinidad had a new governor at this time, Don José Maria Chacon (the national flower, the *Chaconia*, is named after him), who embraced the new colonization policies of the island. The island itself, though under Spanish rule, became increasingly French in flavor and customs with more and more French settlers taking important administrative posts with only one-third of the governing body, the *Cabildo*, being Spanish. The predominant language was French on the streets of Port of Spain, and Carnival originated about this time among the planters.

About this time Britain and France were engaged in the Napoleonic Wars which even affected Trinidad, half-a-world away, with British and French warships battling in the Gulf of Paria. In 1796, British sailors from *HMS Alarm*, fresh from sinking French privateers in the Gulf, arrived in Port of Spain and became involved in fighting with some of the French inhabitants of the capital city. Governor Chacon petitioned Madrid for reinforcements and while awaiting help was offered assistance by the French emissary, Victor Hughes. Chacon declined saying he that if he were unsuccessful in his conflict with the British, he would rather the colony fall into the hands of the British than into the hands of the French settlers. In September of 1796, five Spanish ships under the command of Admiral Ruiz de Apodaca sailed from Puerto Rico to Trinidad with over 700 soldiers, most of whom immediately were beset with yellow fever. A month later Spain declared war on Britain citing the incident with the *HMS Alarm*.

On February 16, 1797, 18 British ships under the command of Sir Ralph Abercromby and Sir Henry Harvey, sailed into the Gulf of Paria with the intent of capturing Trinidad. Outnumbered by over 2 to 1, Governor Chacon decided not to offer any opposition to the British fleet. However, not wishing to allow his ships to fall into British hands, Chacon ordered Admiral Apodaca to set fire to the Spanish fleet anchored in Chaguaramas Bay and the Governor surrendered the next day. The terms of surrender were very generous. Chacon's soldiers were allowed to return to Spain, administrative officers were to remain at their posts, and Spanish law was to be maintained. Port of Spain then became the capital of the British colony (and remained the capital until August 31, 1962 when Trinidad and Tobago gained independence), and everybody was required to swear loyalty to the Crown and having done just that, were permitted to keep their property and holdings. Those who still considered themselves as French citizens were given safe conduct off the island to another colony.

Abercromby appointed Thomas Picton as governor and took his fleet and left, beginning Picton's infamous six-year rule. Intimidation, torture, and executions were the rule of Picton's term, and the slaves bore the brunt of his terror. Picton's policies were not in line with British standards as he attempted to foster an illegal trade with Venezuela through Port of Spain. Picton even assisted Venezuelan rebels and eventually the Governor of Cumana placed a bounty on Picton's head of 20,000 pounds. In return, Picton offered a reward of twenty pounds for the head of the Governor of Cumana. In 1801, the Crown praised Picton's zeal, but a year later denounced him as an embarrassment for promoting a slave colony (Britain wanted a free white colony). In 1803, Picton was indicted for torturing a young black girl and the office of Governor of Trinidad was up in the air.

At this same time Tobago changed hands for the last time as the British claimed the island and were backed up by the Congress of Vienna in 1815. Between the British and French, Tobago became a major exporter of sugar and cotton thanks to slave labor. Up until about 1774, Tobago was plagued with almost annual slave revolts until a savage retaliation quelled any thoughts of revolt for the rest of the century. Tobago's population at this time was around 15,000, quite populous for such a small nation when you consider that the much larger Trinidad had not that many more settlers. A planned slave revolt in 1801 was exposed and some 200 slaves from 16 different plantations arrested. Within two weeks six rebel leaders were executed (burnt alive), four banished, and the rest flogged and return to their plantations. This quieted slave matters for decades to come.

In 1834, the abolition of slavery brought new problems to the plantation owners. As freed slaves moved off the plantations a new labor force was required. The plantation owners were recompensed for their property losses, and slaves were apprenticed to their former owners for periods of 2-4 years. Slaves protested in Port of Spain and the militia moved in to calm things down, at least until 1837 when some 40 rebels, mutineer members of the First West Indian Regiment, lost their lives, their leaders summarily executed in St. Joseph's. By the time the former slave's apprenticeship periods ended early in 1838, the plantation owners required a new labor force. The plantation owners, seeking to maintain a dependable workforce, offered former slaves housing and wages, but most of the slaves left. Many settled in and around the towns and began eking out a living as best they could. Others squatted illegally on lands they could not afford to purchase.

The Crown, refusing to distribute Crown Land to those who were landless, could do nothing to prevent squatting. In 1846 the Sugar Duties Act allowed cheaper foreign sugar into Crown lands which naturally enraged the sugar planters in Trinidad and Tobago. The sugar economy fell in the islands, many sugar plantations were abandoned (and many new cocoa plantations sprang up), but most survived and recovery was only going to come with a dependable work force. At this time some 3,000 Africans from Sierra Leone arrived in Trinidad, but they eventually abandoned their duties on the sugar plantations. Portuguese from Madeira and Chinese arrived and set up shops on the island. One day in May of 1845, the *Fatel Rozack* docked at Port of Spain with the answer to the plantation owner's woes, 225 immigrants from Calcutta.

India at this time was a British colony with a large destitute population who were used to a tropical climate and agriculture. Unfortunately, the first immigrants soon left the plantations in Trinidad and the answer became apparent; an indentureship contract, just another form of slavery some would later claim. In 1848, the Crown agreed to sponsor the immigration of indentured laborers from India, an act that would have an impact on the economy as well as the future of Trinidad and her culture. By 1851 a steady flow of Indians entered Trinidad and continued until 1917

when the Indian government stopped the practice. But by then some 144,000 Indians had arrived in Trinidad, many quarantined on Nelson Island (in the Five Islands area just south of Carenage), Trinidad's version of New York's Ellis Island.

The indentureship agreement bound the workers to the plantation owner for a period of three years followed by a two-year "industrial residence" period during which the worker was permitted to re-indenture to any plantation or find another occupation provided they pay a special "occupation tax." After five years the worker was given what was known as "free paper," but if they wanted free passage back to India they had to remain in the colony for another five years. After 1895, indentured workers were required to pay a portion of their return passage. As one would imagine, thousands of East Indian workers stayed in Trinidad after their contracts were fulfilled, their descendants making up approximately 40% of Trinidad's current population.

At that time Tobago was going through some extremely hard times as the island found itself bankrupt as of Emancipation Day. Wages were too low to attract laborers from Barbados, convicts, freed slaves from the Americas, or Africans from Sierra Leone. If that were not enough Mother Nature gave a helping hand by devastating the island's crops in 1847. Tobago was becoming increasingly unattractive to planters as well as workers. And then somebody came up with what's known as the *Mertaire System*, whereby workers took no pay, instead sharing in the profits of the crop with the land owner. This oral arrangement worked find until the 1870s when the sugar industry declined and planters reneged on their agreements leading to riots by workers. The Belmanna riots, named after a Corporal who was sent to arrest the riot's leaders, convinced the planters that the Metaire System was not working. Tobagans realized that British rule was preferred to the self-governing, almost feudal system that was currently in effect so in 1877 Tobago became a British Crown Colony. Twenty years later Tobago became a "ward" of Trinidad and united the two islands forever. Soon sugar would fall by the wayside as the prime element in the Trinidadian economy, to be replaced by oil.

The first oil well in Trinidad was drilled at La Brea in 1857, but it was over half-a-century later when the first oil refinery was constructed at Point-a-Pierre at the beginning of the first World War. Trinidadian soldiers volunteered for active duty and at first were refused until King George intervened. They formed a West Indian contingent that was not a part of the real British Army and received lower pay for simply being black. At this time only whites were eligible for commissions as officers. Though generally kept from combat with Europeans, some units saw action in Egypt against the Turks. After countless instances of racism from their military peers, the disgruntled Trinidadians returned home after the war.

Over the years many oil wells were drilled in the southern areas of Trinidad at Guayaguayare, Palo Seco, Erin, Siparia, Tabaquite, and Rousillac. One of the pioneers of the oil industry was a Brit named Randolph Rust who immigrated to Trinidad in 1881. There is a small bay named after him on the island of Chacachacare. Even with the burgeoning oil industry, the post war years brought hardship and high inflation to Trinidad. A dockworker's strike in 1919 almost turned into a national movement for higher wages. And as one would expect, the depression years affected Trinidad as well as unemployment rose and those that did have jobs, found shrinking wages and greater workloads. The oil industry was growing but workers were striking for more money and riots seemed to be the order of the day with both strikers and policemen dying as protests turned fatal.

The advent of World War II brought the Americans to the island nation. In 1940, Great Britain leased to the United States several Crown Lands including the western coast of Trinidad at Chaguaramas for a period of 99 years. In return the Crown received 50 antiquated warships as part of FDR's *Lend-Lease* program.

Trinidad was a hub of Allied and Axis activity due to its strategic location. Over 80 ships were sunk by German U-boats in the waters surrounding Trinidad. Two German U-boats entered Port of Spain and sunk two ships at King's Wharf. Another U-boat entered Chaguaramas Bay and shelled the surrounding shoreline. This activity caused the placement of a steel submarine net stretching from Chacachacare westward north of Patos Island almost to the Venezuela shoreline.

During the war years, the United States stationed over 50,000 troops on Trinidad and within 8 years they were for the most part....gone...leaving a skeleton crew at the Chaguaramas Naval Base. These years created a boom in employment on Trinidad as thousands of people found well-paying positions in an economic balloon that was to burst shortly after the war's end. But is was not just the labor force that benefited, land and home owners received inflated rents and hotels, restaurants, garages, taxi drivers, and bars also did a thriving business. All across the island roads and bridges were constructed, large areas of land leveled, and ugly spots transformed into scenes of beauty. In the medical field, Trinidad gained much from American health authorities whose talents, expertise, and knowledge were years in advance of the existing conditions in the prevention, treatment, and cure of disease, as well as hospital administration and supervision.

One benefit turned out to be a double-edged sword. Trinidad gained from the influx of large numbers of workers from Barbados, St. Lucia, Grenada, and St. Vincent, who came to Trinidad seeking employment on the American military bases. However, when the military left mounting unemployment plagued the islanders that remained, the majority of whom decided to take up permanent residence in Trinidad. Another sad by product was the racial prejudice the Americans brought with them. In 1945, *Life* magazine reported instances where U.S. military personnel would keep a brown paper bag at the door of their parties. Those that were lighter than the bag were considered "white" and allowed to enter.

But the economic boom was just an upside to a social downside, the family life suffered and few gains were made in education and agriculture during these years, nothing lasting. But one of the greatest gifts the American gave to Trinidad and her people would soon make her people, culture, and musicians, world famous.

The Americans left untold numbers of oil drums behind. Some inventive musicians in the Port of Spain area formed these oil drums into musical instruments that are now symbolic with almost all Caribbean music and its own form known as *Pan*. *Pan* music also helped to transform Carnival into a world class event instead of a local festival, today Carnival is known as possibly the greatest party in the world.

On July 4, 1973, Trinidad signed the *Treaty of Chaguaramas* establishing *the Caribbean Community and Common Market, CARICOM*. The treaty was signed in Chaguaramas at an old military barracks that the Trinis rebuilt in six weeks. That barracks was again restored in 1999 and today is known as the *Chaguaramas Hotel and Convention Center*. For the *CARICOM* signing, works of local artists were used to decorate the building and some are still present on the site.

The founding members of *CARICOM* were Barbados, Guyana, Jamaica, and Trinidad and Tobago. Over the years Belize, Dominica, Grenada, St. Lucia, St. Vincent and the Grenadines, Montserrat, Antigua, St. Kitts, Nevis, and Anguilla joined in. The Bahamas signed on also, but is not a member of the *Common Market*. The BVI and the Turks and Caicos are *Associate Members* and Haiti is a *Provisional Member.*

On August 1, 1976, Trinidad and Tobago became an independent republic and the 70s saw an economic boom in Trinidad with rising oil prices the world over. The 1980s however turned out just the opposite as oil prices fell worldwide.

Today Trinidad and Tobago are seeing an increase in the tourism industry that along with the strong petroleum industry offers a bright future to the dual-island nation.

Carnival

This is it! If you come to Trinidad for no other reason, it should be to experience Carnival. Do you like a parade? Do you like a party? If you do, you'll love Trinidad as the entire island focuses on parades and parties the week of Carnival and the six weeks leading up to it. This is it, Carnival, the big one, the biggest party of them all.

I can only touch upon the basics of Carnival here, but cruisers in Trinidad wanting to learn more about Carnival are in luck. For over 8 years now, Jack Dausend, publisher of *The Boca*, has been putting on the "Taste of Carnival" seminars in Chaguaramas.

Carnival revelers, Trinidad

These seminars are geared toward educating the visiting cruiser about Carnival and assisting them to become participants instead of observers. Jack's works have been met with great success and a definite "must-do" when in Trinidad. Check with Jack in his office next to *Immigration* at *CrewsInn* or listen to the daily VHF net for times and places. You can also check the section on Internet access later in this chapter for some interesting Carnival related websites. Your best bet for finding out about what events are occurring and where is to watch the local newspapers, *The Guardian*, or *Newsday*, for the latest Carnival schedules.

Most of the festivities are centered in Port of Spain and to a lesser extent in San Fernando, Arima, and other towns all over the island nation. Cruisers and their vessels can get in the Carnival spirit together in the *Carnival Fun Race* sponsored by the good folks at *TTSA* at the Carenage. Choose a Carnival theme and decorate your boat and crew accordingly, the more outrageous concept the better, and enter the race and join the party. After the race prizes are given for the best costume, both local and cruiser, and there is live entertainment and a healthy dose of favorite beverages (all boats entering receive a bottle of the sponsor's rum). For more information check with *TTSA*.

A mixture of French and African celebrations, Carnival season actually begins on Boxing Day, the day after Christmas, and the momentum and excitement builds to a crescendo ending at midnight on Carnival Tuesday, the eve of Ash Wednesday, the first day of Lent. Trinidadians from all over the world return to their homeland at his time to engage in the fete will all their kinfolk, friends, and neighbors and, yes, even the cruisers are invited to *mas*, to don a costume and join the throngs parading through the streets. Carnival is not a show put on for tourists, it is a participatory event and you should be thrilled to take part and interact, it will be an event, and a period of your life that you will never forget. And Carnival is not just for adults, everywhere you go you'll see children parading in their own Carnival costumes with each school being represented and Saturday activities geared towards the youth of Trinidad.

Some trace Carnival (*carne vale*-farewell to the flesh) back to roots in the Bacchanals of ancient Greece, others to the Roman fetes of Saturnalia. But one cannot put aside the timing of Carnival which is Christian in tone, being a prelude to the weeks of Lent's abstinence. Carnival was initially a festival of white French plantation owners in the late 1700s. During the few days before Ash Wednesday, the Creole establishment would invert their roles taking on the guise of field laborers and slaves. The slaves too celebrated Carnival, but in secret, until their emancipation in 1834 when they took it to the streets of Port of Spain mimicking and satirizing the colonial gentry. The characters created then are still alive today and *Viey La Cou* (*old yard*) is an organization dedicated to keeping the old traditions and characters alive by utilizing the "yard" at Queen's Hall as a performance spot.

In the first few years after Emancipation, the freed slaves had protection at Carnival time, *batonniers*, or *stickmen*, who carried bamboo sticks similar to what was used in the cane fields to put out fires. Today, stickfighting is still one of the many faces of Carnival and you'll still see many characters from folklore as well as satirized locals personalities. You'll meet *Midnight Robbers* whose orations are designed to intimidate you into parting with some money, devils called *Jab Jabs*, clowns called *Pierrot Grenade*, human donkeys called *Burrokeets*, giants on stilts called *Moko Jumbies*, *Dame Lorraines*, caricatures of Creole plantation wives, *Jammette's*, the local prostitutes (no they are not prostitutes, they are playing a character), *Jamets*, the "sweet men" or kept lovers, and the cross-dressing *Pisenlets*. The lewd actions of the early characterizations did not sit well with the powers to be and in an effort to crackdown on the sexual nature of Carnival resulted in a riot in 1881.

But Carnival was not to be subdued and a toned down version appeared over the next few years. In the 1890s a music competition was introduced and in the 20th century more and more aspects of Carnival became competitions. World War II brought a temporary cessation to Carnival, but when the celebration returned, it arrived with a new sound... Pan. The original pan drums were made from old 55-gallon oil drums left behind by the U.S. military and were hammered into musical instruments. Today Pan music is a worldwide phenomenon and with Calypso has become the score for Carnival.

Between Christmas and Ash Wednesday, as if you won't have enough to do learning about Carnival, making a costume, and attending Jack's seminars, you'll likely find yourself caught up in an ocean of fetes. Fetes are parties, some private, some quite public, some free, some quite costly, either way, you will have FUN! Fetes are get-togethers where you can lime (Lime you ask? Read the section on *Culture*.) with the best, eating and drinking (some ticket prices are all-inclusive and the proceeds of some may go to charity) and listening to live bands or a DJ playing the best in Calypso, Soca, and Rapso. Most fetes sell out early, most are outdoors, and some can get quite rowdy. Either way, Carnival without attending a fete will be lacking my friends.

Speaking of lacking, what would carnival be without Calypso? Calypso songs parody the issues and events of the day and the Calypso poet has open license to offer satirical, scathing, and sometimes risqué commentaries that will leave audiences laughing uproariously. Competition between Calypsonians is fierce and throughout the Carnival season you'll find the top Calypsonians showcasing their talents nightly in *Calypso Tents*. The *Calypso Tents* are showcases for these performers and the audiences eagerly await their performances.

A performer may engage in *Extempo*, an ad-lib event in which he or she must compose and perform a Calypso song off the top of their head on a suggested topic. Sometimes two Calypsonians will trade verses back and forth, quite often insulting and always extremely funny, each trying to outdo the other in an event called *Picong*. Don't forget to buy your tickets early for one of the Calypso tent festivities and remember that some events may offer a *Ladies Night* with two for one admissions. There are often amateur and junior Calypso competitions around the island at this time that are also fun to attend and can be just as entertaining as the pros and the adults. Now let's discuss what else is going on during Carnival.

Panorama is a nation-wide steel band competition featuring some large pan bands with upwards of 100 musicians. Regional competitions are held and the finals are held at the Savanna, the park in Port of Spain. Here you can buy a ticket and find your spot in the grandstands (bring a cooler and a cushion for comfort) and sit back and watch people and listen to Pan music. The grandstands themselves are as much a show as the performers, each area being one huge party.

Dimanche Gras, *Fat Sunday*, is held on the Sunday night before *J'Ouvert*. The show features the King and Queen of the *Band Final Competition*, performances by the Panorama champions, as well as the Extempo winners and the Junior Monarch. Between acts the show does not stall as other performers show their talents while the next act is preparing. This show usually lasts until 0200, the beginning of *J'Ouvert*.

J'Ouvert, pronounced *joo-vay* means *daybreak* in French, is the official start of Carnival and is the one event you MUST NOT MISS! To begin with, let me warn you, if you plan to attend *J'Ouvert*, don't wear white, or anything you cannot afford to get dirty, muddy, and wet. All night long, revelers in homemade costumes, will dance in the streets till dawn. Mud and paint rule, and if you're clean, prepare yourself for a hug from a person covered with mud from head to toe. Better to simply jump right in and enjoy, you can always wash off in the morning...if you're not covered in mud, you haven't experienced *J'Ouvert*. *The Bomb* steel band competition takes place on Monday morning.

Mas, or *playing mas*, is what the costumed revelers are doing during Carnival, either playing their chosen character, or themselves, and you too are invited to *play mas*. First you'll need to register with a mas camp and purchase a costume. Today's costumes tend toward the *bikini mas*, generally a bikini style with sequins, feathers, and whatever other creative notions occurs to the costume maker. Remember, you'll be partying in the tropical heat, best to wear as little as possible. The Woodbrook area of Port of Spain is home to numerous *mas camps* and is a hotbed of pre-carnival activity starting as early as November.

One of the most popular of the *mas* groups is Peter Minshalls Callaloo *mas camp,* now in Chaguaramas (see Peter's website at www.callaloo.co.tt), where you can register to play with Peter's group, numbering around 3,000 festive masqueraders. Peter designs the group's costumes and one will set you back about TT$800 and up. To his credit, Peter helped design and choreograph the festivities at the 1992 *Olympics* in Barcelona.

On Carnival Monday, *Pretty Mas* begins with costumed bands and lasts well into the night. Today the bands take to the streets giving you a sample of what you can expect on Carnival Tuesday, the climax of the celebrations with the *Parade of Bands*. Tuesday, beginning early in the morning, bands of costumed revelers march pass the judging booths and break down into sections, each section with its own particular costume theme. The band with the most energy, spirit, and visual impact wins the prestigious *Band of the Year* competition. The focus of this last event is *Queens Park Savanna* in Port of Spain and is the one event that most people attend.

There are several things you'll need to know when attending Carnival, I'll mention a few here, and Jack will give you the details when you attend his seminars. First off, Carnival, although not a public holiday, will find many businesses closed so bear that in mind. Make sure you have plenty of TT's (Trinidad/Tobago dollars), and keep your money in your shoe, don't carry a wallet or jewelry, Carnival really brings out the pickpockets. And speaking of shoes, make sure they're comfortable as you'll be in them for a long time, especially if you join a parade. Don't take a drink from somebody you don't know and either bring your own food or buy from vendors with proper food badges. Stay with your friends, there is strength in numbers. If you have to wander off to relieve yourself, don't go alone. And don't try too hard to have fun, it is possible to have TOO much fun; pace yourself, especially if you're not used to staying up long hours and partying hard.

Currency

If you head south to Trinidad and Tobago you'll need Trinidad/Tobago dollars or *TT*s as they're commonly called. Paper currency comes in denominations of $1, $5, $10, $20, and $100 (a "blue one"), while coins come in 1¢, 5¢, 10¢, 25¢, and 50¢ pieces.

ATM's are happy to spew out *TT's* for you. Although the *TT* is the official currency in Trinidad and Tobago, many businesses will accept U.S. dollars for payment...check first however. Also, if you're ever unsure as to whether or not you've been quoted a price in TT$ or US$, ask!

Trinidad/Tobago adds on a *VAT* (*Value Added Tax*) of 15% on all goods and services except those marine services (and materials) relating to yachts in transit. Materials purchased not in relation to a service will not be *VAT* free. For instance, if you contract *Power Boats* to paint your bottom, there will be no *VAT* on the paint or the labor. However, if you enter *Budget Marine* and purchase a gallon of bottom paint, you will have to pay the *VAT*, but if *Power Boats* then applies the paint, there will still be no *VAT* on the service. Although you may not notice it on a receipt,

rest assured that the *VAT* has been collected. If a merchant offers a "*VAT* free" item, it simply means that the merchant is giving you a 15% discount on the goods and that the item is NOT "*VAT* free."

Hotels always include a 10% service charge as well as a 10% *Hotel Room Tax*. If leaving by plane a *Departure Tax* of TT$100 (must be paid in *TT*'s) will be assessed.

Dining in Trinidad and Tobago

The multi-cultural nature of Trinidad is nowhere more noticeable than in her cuisine, a blend of African, Creole, East Indian, Amerindian, Chinese, Middle Eastern, and European flavors. There is not another island in the Caribbean that offers as diverse a cross section of exotic food as Trinidad. Everywhere you go, almost every town has a fresh fish or produce stall making it easy to find these most plentiful of resources. *Kingfish* is one of the most plentiful, and popular fish in Trinidad. The *cascadura* is a river fish that is allegedly responsible for luring Trinis back home from wherever they are. *Curry crab n' dumplin* is crab served in the shell with curry sauce and dumplings and is primarily a Tobago specialty. *Buljol* is a blending of saltfish, onions, tomatoes, lime juice, and peppers. Served with avocado and light rolls called *hops*, *buljol* is usually served for breakfast.

While you won't be able to find it on the menu in Chaguaramas, bush meat is popular though hard to find. *Quenk*, the wild boar that roams the bush on Trinidad, is a very popular dish, and in the more rural areas you might find iguana, agouti, and manitou.

Today many towns in Trinidad and Tobago have fast food restaurants such as *KFC* and the local flavored favorite, *Royal Castle*. But there is a lot of street food available, and the most popular is probably the *roti*, and there are *roti* stands everywhere, in every small town and even the most remote hamlet. A *roti* could be considered a complete meal in a handy package. A flattened Indian bread called *dhalpourri* is filled with curried beef, chicken, shrimp, fish, or goat, along with potatoes or chick peas. The bread is folded over the filling and the creation resembles a large crepe. *Rotis* are everywhere, they're cheap, they're good, and some might be a bit hot for the unaccustomed palate.

You'll find a lot of *curry* being used in Trinidadian dishes, (it's practically the national spice if there was such a thing) due to the huge East Indian influence. *Curry* is a ground blend of ginger, turmeric, fenugreek seed, cumin, coriander, fennel, pepper, cinnamon, cloves, and as many as 16-40 other herbs and spices.

Along the water's edge, especially in *Maracas Bay* which is famous for this, you'll find *Shark n' Bake*. A roll made from a dough that resembles a doughnut, is filled with shark (you can also get kingfish if you'd like) and deep fried. Then you have your choice of condiments to add to it and that is a real treat, all sorts of hot sauces, sweet, hot, some made with mustard, some with papaya, many made with the local yellow pepper, and all tasty. Like most places, if you're looking for the best food head for the stall with the longest line.

Doubles are usually breakfast and lunch snacks, though it's not improper to eat them at any time, it's just that the *doubles* shops in Port of Spain usually close after lunch. *Doubles* are very saucy, curried chick peas spread between two breads called barahs. You've got to be careful when eating these as they can be quite messy, and have something to drink handy as they're a tad on the hot side. *Aloo pies* are pastries filled with meat or cheese and are a very popular snack though there's usually more pastry than filling. You'll often see vendors selling boiled or roasted corn on the cob, but be warned, it may be a bit tougher than you're used to.

A newcomer to the fast food market in Trinidad is the Rastafarian *Ital*. Very wholesome, the Rasta-inspired foods (no meat) are fresh fruits and vegetables prepared with no additives and little if any salt.

Dining out in Trinidad and Tobago can be an experience in itself if you don't know what you're ordering. If you're not sure of the dish, don't be afraid to ask as people are happy to educate you in their offerings. To begin with, many places offer Creole cooking, which is primarily African and French in flavor.

Pelau is a classic Creole dish that can have two faces. Some places serve it as a rice and peas mix, others have it as chicken based entree. Either way it consists of rice, peas, garlic, onions, mixed vegetables and in some instances cinnamon, coconut milk, and red wine.

Callaloo is made from the leaves of the dasheen plant and is usually served as a very tasty soup though it can also be a sauce laid on rice or meat. *Mas* master Peter Minshall once made *callaloo* a theme for his Carnival program. *Callaloo* is often served with Coocoo, a creation similar to grits or polenta. Corn flour and okra are mixed, steamed with coconut milk into a cake and allowed to cool and is usually served with gravy.

Driving along the roads you're likely to see vendors selling all sorts of sweets and candies out of glass jugs called *safes*. The *Maracas Bay Scenic Overlook* on the northern coast is a good spot to sample a large selection of these wares though most towns have somebody selling them. Here you'll find safes full of coconut or currant rolls, pone (a sweet cassava bread), and beer pies. Coconut sweets are prevalent, probably due to the fact that coconuts are so plentiful, and the tooloom is a coconut concoction that dates to slave days. The *tamarind ball* is a mixture of tamarind, salt, and sugar, and takes some getting used to. The *kurma* is Indian in origin. A sweet dough, the *kurma* is fried in oil until crisp and is a very popular treat in Trinidad.

Farine is a quite ordinary cereal that you can purchase in almost any market, but few know that it dates back to pre-Columbian times. The Amerindians who inhabited the islands then made the same cereal from the cassava plant, which is still popular today.

Those in search of liquid refreshment will not find Trinidad and Tobago lacking. Rum is everywhere and is very economical. Both light and dark (called "red") rums are popular here. The most popular local brands are Vat 19 and *Old Oak* while *Royal Oak* and *Angostura Premium White* are at the upper end of the rum spectrum. *Angostura* is by far the most famous of the Trini produced alcoholic beverages. *Angostura Bitters* dates to 1824 when Dr. J.G.B. Siegert left his native Germany to assist Simon Bolivar in his fight for Venezuela independence.

Bolivar's troops were plagued with stomach ailments and the good doctor began a search for a remedy. His secret formula, now known as *Angostura Bitters* is named after the Venezuelan town where Bolivar was based. Sailors brought news of the drink to England and the beverage was first exported in 1830. The production facilities were soon moved to Trinidad where it still is today. The distillery in Laventille offers daily tours including lunch and sampling. You can phone Glenn Davis at 623-1841, ext. 170, for more information.

Aloo Pie

Lining up for *Doubles* in Port of Spain, Trinidad

Vendors selling sweets at the *Maracas Bay Scenic Overlook*, Trinidad

A final note on the formula that you might find interesting ... so secret is the formula that only two people know the entire mix. Five people have memorized particular parts of the formula, but none of the five are allowed to travel together or even enter the blending room together, each doing his part in the process and sending it on.

Fauna and Flora

At one time, over 10,000 years ago, Trinidad and Tobago were a part of the South American continent. As the earth's forces heaved and churned beneath the sea, a mountainous chunk of land was torn from the continent and Trinidad and Tobago were formed. The fauna and flora on these new islands were the same as those found on the mainland of South America, separated by a small body of water just a few miles wide. Today little has changed in this regard, the plants and animals to be found in Trinidad and Tobago are little different from their mainland cousins giving the islands a diversity of fauna and flora disproportionate to their size.

Habitats on the islands include tropical rain forests, savannas, semi-deciduous forest, mangrove swamps and marsh lands. Tobago's rain forest is the oldest protected rain forest in the Western Hemisphere. Tobago's western end is alive with marshes and its northeastern end and offshore islands are bird sanctuaries.

On its eastern coast, Trinidad boasts the *Nariva Swamp*, home to the maniteel, a cousin to the Florida manatee, as well as large water snakes, caimans, various parrots, ducks, and many species of fish and birdlife. It's been said that large crocodiles have even turned up here after crossing the *Gulf of Paria* after being washed down the *Orinoco* in a flood. The western shore of Trinidad, just south of Port of Spain, is home to the *Caroni Swamp* where tour operators will happily take you to view the beautiful Scarlet Ibis, the national bird of Trinidad.

Of all the flora to be found on the islands, you must become aware of one in particular, the Manchineel Tree. This tree is very toxic, even its sap, don't stand under one when it's raining, better to get soaking wet. The Manchineel can grow to over 40' and it resembles an apple tree with green fruit and flowers.

Of course, the prolific mangrove will be found in many places along the shore, as will the seagrape and Indian almond tree with its symmetrical branches. Its nuts can be eaten after they turn brown, but don't expect them to taste like the almond with which you are familiar. Of course palm trees are numerous, especially in the cocal, an old coconut plantation that stretches for miles along the eastern shore of Trinidad from Guayaguayare to Manzanilla.

All over the islands you are likely to run across bromeliads, orchids, and over 2,300 varieties of flowering plants. The most colorful are the hibiscus, bougainvillea, torch ginger, the ginger lily, 40 vividly colored varieties of balisier, and the colorful bird of paradise, a blue and purple flower that resembles a bird's head.

In addition to possessing the flora and fauna of South America, these islands are also influenced by their geographic location, being a perfect stopping point for northern or southern migratory birds, butterflies or anything drifting in the ocean or wind currents. Over 430 species of birds, and over 600 species of butterflies have been recorded in Trinidad and Tobago. Of these, 250 species of birds breed in Trinidad and Tobago while over 150 species migrate here on an annual basis from North and South America.

I have already mentioned the scarlet Ibis, but Tobago has its own national bird, the cocorico, a pheasant that is often viewed as little more than vermin. You're also likely to spot any of a number of parrots, toucans, egrets, peregrine falcons, hawks, tanagers, boobies, pelicans, frigate birds, bananaquits, and the most prolific of them all, and usually seen around Chaguaramas and *TTSA*, the vulture.

One of the most unusual of the Trinidad/Tobago avian species are the oilbirds. These birds are nocturnal, feeding primarily on fruit. Eating the fruits whole, during flight they regurgitate the seeds helping with the reforestation of Trinidad. With a wingspan over 3', and a loud, raucous call, they are an impressive sight at night. Their young have a high fat content and the Amerindians and Capuchin monks would boil them down for their oil hence their name. One of the eight known colonies of these birds on Trinidad is on Huevos Island in the Bocas.

Mammals are represented on Trinidad and Tobago by over 100 species, including armadillos, deer, wild hogs, silky anteaters, ocelots, capuchin monkeys, otters, West Indian manatee, and the one species that you will most likely encounter, especially if anchored at *Scotland Bay*, the howler monkey. You'll know them when you hear them, they roar like lions, especially after a rain. Fewer today, in the last decade they were stricken with a disease that killed off over 90% of the howler monkey population. Another mammal that you'll encounter, and most likely in the same anchorage, is the fruit bat. These can be quite the pest when they fly into your boat at night to dine on fruit left in the open (and leave layers of guano in their wake). The way to combat them is to keep screens in place at night and keep a light shining in the cockpit, though this is not necessarily a guarantee to keep them away. Anchored at *TTSA*, at night you can see the bats in the early evening crossing the road to dine for the night.

Reptiles, especially the dangerous ones, are rarely seen except well off the beaten path. Trinidad is home to over 45 different snakes including the boa constrictor, the anaconda (usually only seen deep in the swamps), two small coral snakes, and two highly poisonous snakes, the Fer de Lance, and the Bushmaster. Both of these really don't pose a danger to the cruiser unless you take to hiking inland, in the forests and swamps of the island. There are many varieties of lizards from small anoles all the way up to large iguanas. One of the most interesting is the 3' long, brown matte lizard. This speedy lizard will raise itself up on its hind legs and can accelerate from 0-10 mph in 2 seconds. In the swamps and rivers you might come across a caiman, a small, about 3' long, relative of an alligator with an elongated, pointed snout.

One final note on sea creatures that will have an immediate effect upon your vessels. First and foremost are the small jellyfish, especially in Chaguaramas that love to block off water flow to your air-conditioner. The jellyfish are not always around, usually from Easter until June or July, so you get some relief in that regard. I've seen them quite thick at Chacachacare. *TTYC* does not suffer from the problem as much, though you might see a lot of jellyfish as you approach *TTYC,* inside the jetty the numbers of creatures are far less than what you will experience in *Chaguaramas Bay*.

Another creature you'll have to deal with is the barnacle. These are fertile waters and barnacles are plentiful. Even if you have new bottom paint, if you're sitting at a marina with your air-conditioner running, over a period of time, within six weeks or so, they'll build up inside your intake, seacock, and strainer to immense proportions, diminishing your water flow to almost nothing. Maintenance, a periodic cleaning of the system, is probably the best preventative.

Ferries

Trinidad and Tobago are connected by a regular ferry so, if you don't feel like beating to windward to visit Tobago, you can hope the ferry for a 5½ hour trip. The ferry costs TT$60 per person for a round trip ticket and cabins, when available, can be picked up for TT$180 round trip. You can even bring a car with you and costs around TT$200 for a small car and drive on a one-way trip. You need to make car reservations two weeks in advance. If you're taking the ferry from Port of Spain, plan to be there at least two hours before sailing and be prepared for a crowd. It's best to book tickets in advance as they are often sold out. Once aboard you can relax in chairs on deck or hang out in the bar or restaurant. For more information call the *Port Authority Ferry Service*s in Port of Spain, Trinidad at 625-4306, and in Scarborough, Tobago, at 639-2416. The ferry departs from Port of Spain M-F, at 1400, and from Scarborough at 2300. On Sundays the ferry departs Port of Spain at 1100 and Scarborough at 2300. There is also a passenger and cargo ferry that travels regularly between Port of Spain and Isla Margarita, Guiria, St. Vincent, Barbados, and St. Lucia.

Getting Around

Getting around in Trinidad and Tobago is not difficult. There are several car rental companies if you are so inclined. Cruisers that possess a valid driver's license issued in the U.S, Canada, France, U.K., Germany, and the Bahamas, may drive for up to three months.

Driving is on the left due to the British influence on these islands. Many drivers appear to enjoy the middle of the road, but these are few and far between. Driving in Trinidad is quite a thrill, a challenge to some. Cars dart in and out to pass slower vehicles, or cars stopped to let somebody out, or simply to stop and chat with a passerby. However the oncoming traffic is very cordial and road rage is unheard of here. When driving the twisting-turning mountain roads, as are found on the northern sections of Trinidad and

Tobago, it's a good idea to sound your horn when you approach a corner or curve so oncoming cars will know you're coming. This is important, as the roads are so very narrow in many of these places.

Other vehicles are not the only hazard to roadway navigation. In the more rural areas it's not uncommon to share the road with chickens, goats, sheep, or even cows. In more urban areas, humans are known to share the road with you so drive with care.

If you don't care to rent a vehicle and try your hand at driving, you can take a taxi or rely on public transportation. All commuter transport vehicles will have a license plate that begins with the letter "H" (vehicles with the letter "H" are for hire, "P" are private vehicles, a plate that starts with a "T" is obviously a truck, and "R" plates designate a rental vehicle). Buses serve main commuter routes and are differentiated into two services, the transit and express commuter services (ECS). ECS service, white and red-striped mini-vans, is available to points east of Port of Spain and runs along a dedicated transit highway system that only these mini-vans can use.

The most popular mode of public transport is the maxi-taxi. In Trinidad these are color-coded mini-vans. All are white and those with yellow horizontal bands run in the Port of Spain and Chaguaramas areas; red bands are for eastern Trinidad; green bands for southern Trinidad; black bands run in the Princess Town area; and brown bands run from San Fernando to the southwestern tip of the island. All vans run regular routes and the white/yellow vans that you will use in Chaguaramas have a centralized base in Port of Spain across from the port, and run every few minutes so you won't have to wait long for a ride.

Simply stand at a bus stop and as the van approaches you must put out your hand or else the taxi will not stop. The usual fare is TT$2-$5, but for a few dollars more they'll usually take you a short way off their route to get you to your destination. There are larger buses that run at regular intervals, usually a couple of hours apart.

These buses do not take cash, instead you must pre-purchase tickets which can be found at most marinas in Chaguaramas. A good idea is to buy a couple and keep them in your wallet or purse in case you need them. If you're headed to Chaguaramas

from Port of Spain, make sure you board a taxi that says Chaguaramas on it as some don't go past Carenage.

In Scarborough, Tobago, the road in front of the ferry terminal, *Carrington Street*, is where you'll want to go to catch a taxi to anywhere on the island. The *Tobago Taxi Owners and Drivers Association* (639-2692) has an office next door to the *Customs* office.

In Scarborough, Tobago, there is a temporary bus station at *eTec Mall* off *Sangster Hill Road*. As of 2011, it's been open for 2 years already and there is no indication from the authorities as to when a new station will be built. If you plan to ride a bus to anywhere on the island, you must buy the ticket at the station before boarding your bus. Do not forget that if you are waiting at a designated bus stop, the bus will not stop for you unless you hold out your hand.

Leaving Your Boat in Trinidad

Many skippers have insurance policies with "named windstorm" clauses necessitating the vessel be out of the maximum risk zone for hurricanes by a certain date, usually July 1st. Some clauses use the latitude of 12° 30.00' N, which is approximately in the middle of Prickly Bay, Grenada. Either way, Trinidad is well south of this latitude and is a favorite spot for yachtsmen to leave their boat during hurricane season.

Chaguaramas, as you will learn, has several large yards with hundreds of boats on the hard for long periods of time. You too can take advantage of this hurricane-free paradise, but there are certain steps that must be taken.

First, your boat must be left in the care of a yard or marina, and a letter prepared by the marina or yard, called a *Temporary Importation of Foreign Yachts Form*, along with an inventory of items aboard, must be taken to the *Customs* office for approval. The captain and crew must also submit letters for *Immigration* approval, this is extremely important if the crew remains while the captain leaves the country. The ships storage papers will need to be presented upon the captain's or owner's return. For more information, see the section on *Customs and Immigration* in the chapter on Trinidad.

Provisioning

Trinidad is a great place to provision, especially if heading back up-island or to Venezuela. Although some things in Venezuela will be cheaper, your selection of items in Trinidad, at least for Americans and Canadians, will be brands that you will recognize and with which you are familiar. In Venezuela you'll find a lot of brands that you've never seen before, a lot of items manufactured in Venezuela with Spanish labels, so brush up on *su Espanol* before shopping in Margarita.

Jesse James' *Members Only Maxi-Taxi Service* offers several good shopping trips for those interested in bulk purchasing. On Friday's Jesse normally runs to the *Tru Valu* store at *Long Circular Mall,* a popular grocery shopping expedition that is free (cruisers also get a 3% discount on their purchases). On the road that parallels the covered parking lot there is a small open-air market where you can pick up fresh produce.

Occasionally Jesse makes runs to the *Grand Bazaar Mall* for shopping at the *X-tra* store, another good grocery store. On Saturdays, very early, Jesse makes a run to the fresh veggie and fish market in Port of Spain, this is a must for a good deal on fruits, vegetables, fish, and meat. Jesse also makes occasional trips to the *Food Giant* in Barataria. For more information call Jesse or his wife Sharon, *Member's Only* on VHF ch. 68.

I know a lot of you may think that I'm making a big deal by pushing Jesse's service. Let me explain. I take no ads. I receive no perks. I receive no freebies. Neither do I seek them. Jessie has given me nothing for mentioning his service. To the best of my ability I relate to you, the cruiser in need of information, what is available, and Jesse does the cruising community a great service, and is the only person that does this.

Tides and Currents

Vessels heading to Trinidad or Tobago from points north, particularly from Grenada or Carriacou, will encounter strong and fluky currents in the stretch of water between Grenada and Trinidad and Tobago. The *Equatorial Current* (Guyana Current) flows northwestward between Trinidad/Tobago and Grenada and to say it is unpredictable would be an understatement.

Heading for a waypoint at Boca del Monos from Grenada, you will find that the current is pushing you westward at over 2 knots at times, while just a few minutes later the current will appear to be non-existent. The strength of this current is lessened somewhat on an ebbing tide which flows southeast.

This current makes sailing from Grenada to Tobago difficult at best. A better suggestion would be to head for Tobago from Petite St. Vincent, or even Barbados. Entering the harbor at Scarborough on Tobago, you might encounter an eastward flowing current, an eddy that has spun off the westward setting *Equatorial Current.*

The current flows northwestward between Tobago and Trinidad and then westward closer in along the northern coast of Trinidad and sometimes attains a velocity of 2-3 knots. At places along the northern coast you can sometimes pick up a bit of an easterly flow when the tide ebbs and flows southeast between Tobago and Trinidad.

Approaching the northwestern tip of Trinidad at the Bocas del Dragon, you will want to exercise caution when entering Boca del Monos, the normal passage for yachts heading into *Chaguaramas Bay* (try to time your arrival for daylight hours here). When the prevailing winds and seas are up, and the tidal flow is heading north through the bocas, you can have some heavy sea action well into the boca as the current sometimes flows northward through here at up to 4 knots on the flood. On the other hand, no matter the tide, the current rarely if ever has a noticeable southerly flow through the Bocas. The current that flows through the Bocas, and for a distance along the northern coast as far as Macqueripe, is known locally as *L'Remous.*

Don't take the currents at the Bocas lightly. I've heard tales of sailboats without engines taking three days trying to tack their way through the Bocas. On more than one occasion I've left Boca de Monos heading to Grenada or Tobago and seen a stream of churning white water snaking northwards for ten miles. Only about a quarter of a mile wide, the windward side of the rip was quite calm, while a hundred yards to leeward, right in the middle of the choppy water the story was quite the opposite. Exercise caution if you're approaching the Bocas and experience this.

The current along the western shore of Trinidad, as well as the tides, are impacted by the weather conditions in Venezuela. Heavy rains and flooding in the Orinoco delta region releases tremendous amounts of water and energy into the Gulf of Paria. This force has nowhere to go except towards Trinidad and can make itself apparent in the form of higher tides, stronger swirling currents, and lot of flotsam and jetsam approaching from the Gulf. The entire western coast of Trinidad, from the Bocas to Icacos, is washed by a southerly-southeasterly eddy of this northward flowing current.

Chaguaramas has its own particular problems with currents as well. Sometimes, anchored boats will spin and turn and bounce off each other, so use caution when anchored in *Chaguaramas Bay*. In *TTYC*, you'll often rock slightly when the tide changes and the wind dies, but this won't last long.

Entering Port of Spain, the current flows at a velocity of about ½ knot southeast on the flood and 1½ knots on the ebb. This is due to an eddy action of the main flow of current, which runs generally northeast through the Bocas.

The current along the southern shore of Trinidad is extremely strong, usually 3-5 knots, and I've been told by local mariners that they've seen it flow as strong as 7 knots. The tidal range in Trinidad and Tobago is approximately 3'. Tide tables can be found in the *Trinidad and Tobago Boaters Directory* available free at most marinas and chandleries. The buoyage system in Trinidad and Tobago is *IALA B*, that is red-right-returning my friends.

Trini Talk

Let's talk about talking. Let's touch upon the words that will grace your ears in Trinidad. Many cruisers have problems understanding the Trinis at times. They look questionably with wide eyes as someone speaks and wonder "What language do they speak here?" Well, they speak English here, the same as most of us do. Correction, not quite the same. At one end of the spectrum is standard English, at the other end is Caribbean Creole, which differs from standard English in syntax, and a Trini may speak anywhere between the two.

Generally, when speaking standard English, it is spoken a bit faster and the words sometimes shortened

and corrupted to the point where downtown comes out as dunton, and gone is gorn. Don' panic mon', you'll get the hang of it. I wish I had a dollar for every time that I've had to ask a Trini to please repeat what he or she said as I couldn't understand a word since the first word passed their lips. Oddly enough, if you listen long enough, you'll notice differences between Tobago Creole and Trinidadian Creole. Experts say that the Tobagan Creole is more akin to the Jamaican Creole.

You'll probably notice a French influence in the language, but it is a bit different than that spoken in the northern Caribbean such as Nevis where there is more of a Portuguese influence. There is also a considerable Hindu influence that extends to everyday language in the names of things and places.

VHF in Trinidad

Usage of the VHF radio in Trinidad/Tobago is similar to usage rules in most other places in the Caribbean. Channel 16 is used as a hailing and distress frequency and ch. 70 is for digital use only. Most cruisers in TT tend to use 68 has a hailing channel though it is also often used by local commercial vessels and the TT *Coast Guard*.

In Chaguaramas there is a daily net beginning at 0800 on channel 68 and lasting for about 20 minutes or so. This is an informative net for newcomers, and a place to ask for assistance in finding parts and services. During the *Treasures of the Bilge* segment, you will be allowed to advertise those items you don't need and wish to trade or barter (it is illegal for cruisers to sell anything in Trinidad/Tobago, but foreign flag vessels may trade or barter between themselves.

Cruisers are quested not to use the following VHF channels in Chaguaramas for boat to boat communications as they are in use by the following businesses or agencies:
01 Echo Marine
8-17 Coast Guard
11 Tidewater Tugs
68 TTSA, TTYC, IMS
69 Peakes
72 Power Boats
74 Caribbean Dry Dock
77 Crews Inn
25-28, 78 North Post Radio
84-88 Public Correspondence/Marine Operator

The recommended general usage channels are: 1, 5, 7A, 18A, 19A, 21A, 22A, 23A, 61, 62, 63, 65A, 66A, 71, 78A, 79A, 80A, 82A, 83A, 85A, 88A.

As you approach Trinidad from Grenada listen for *North Post Radio's* strong signal on VHF ch. 16 for notices to mariners.

YSATT

While Trinidad is known far and wide in the cruising community for its plethora of marine services and the quality of the work performed in both the construction and repair/maintenance fields, the marine industry is actually very young on the island.

In 1994, a gentleman named Donald Stollmeyer, who also opened *Power Boats* in the early 1990s, founded *YSATT*, the *Yacht Service Association of Trinidad and Tobago*. *YSATT*, pronounced "y-sat," is a non-profit organization established by the boatyards and marinas in the Chaguaramas peninsula to ensure the proper and controlled growth of the marine service industry in Trinidad and Tobago.

YSATT is intent on maintaining and improving the quality of services provided to visiting boaters in Trinidad by screening, training, and monitoring its members, as well as advising government agencies of the *YSATT* position on relative legal issues. The organization also keeps a database of correspondence received from cruisers about their experiences while in Trinidad.

YSATT also has a formal process to deal with complaints against and by boatyards and cruisers. People with a complaint, whether it's a cruiser that received a slipshod repair, or a member that has not received payment, *YSATT* will go to work on the problem.

But don't just run to *YSATT* with your problem. You must first bring the complaint to the attention of the member and give them the opportunity to rectify the matter. If this fails you should then submit a written complaint to *YSATT*.

YSATT also has worked with *Customs* and *Immigration* to smooth entry and clearance procedures for boat parts. *YSATT* also operates a water taxi in *Chaguaramas Bay*.

For more information on the services provided, call (868-634-4938), email (ysatt@trinidad.net, www.ysatt.org), or visit the *YSATT* office at the *CrewsInn Marina*.

Trinidad and Tobago Index Charts

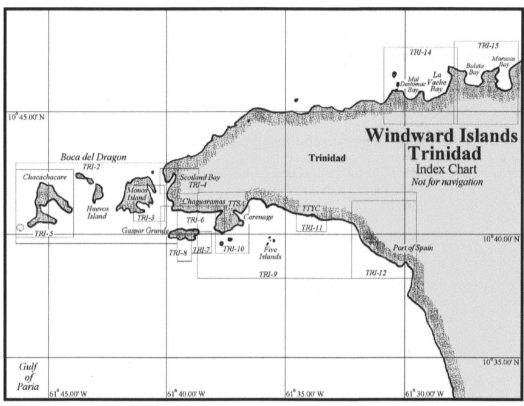

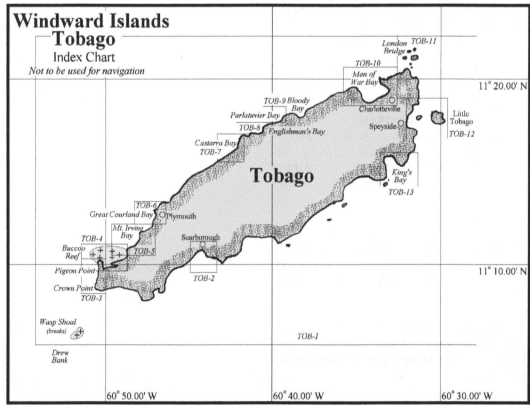

Trinidad

Port of Entry: Chaguaramas, Port of Spain
  Point-a-Pierre (currently not available)
Fuel: Chaguaramas
Haul-Out: Chaguaramas
Diesel Repairs: Chaguaramas
Outboard Repairs: Chaguaramas
Propane: Chaguaramas, Port of Spain
Provisions: Chaguaramas, Port of Spain
Important Lights: See *Appendix A*

The islands of Trinidad and Tobago, the southernmost of the Lesser Antilles, form one nation lying just off the northeastern tip of the South American continent to which they were once attached. Although officially called *Trinidad and Tobago*, most refer to them as *TT* for short. Trinidad is approximately 1864 square miles in area and has a rugged mountain range spanning the northern breadth of the island with its highest peak rising to 3,085'. The center of the island, a flat central plain where the bulk of the sugar cane crop is raised, is bordered by rolling hills to the south. The proximity to the *Rio Orinoco* delta region of Venezuela across the *Gulf of Paria* is

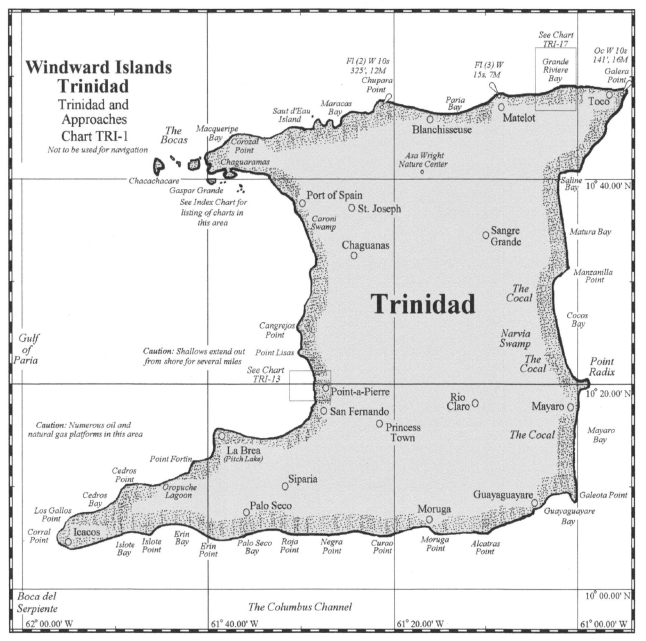

why the waters of the island tend to be silty and the visibility generally poor.

Vessels heading for Trinidad from Grenada should be aware of a natural gas platform located approximately 26 miles north of the Bocas. The platform lies close to the rhumb line from *Prickly Bay* to Boca de Monos at an approximate position of 11° 19.30' N, 61° 42.40' W. The platform is easy to see in daylight and well lit at night, however the large tenders that are moored just off the platform are not so easily seen at night so give the platform a wide berth.

Customs and *Immigration*

Ports of Entry
Trinidad- Port of Spain, Chaguaramas, Point-a-Pierre (currently not available)
Tobago- Charlotteville, Scarborough

Entering the Country's Waters
Vessels are required to clear with *Customs* and *Immigration* immediately upon arriving in the waters of Trinidad and Tobago (12 nm). This is a very simple process as there are only a few Ports of Entry in this dual island nation. Nearly all cruisers arriving in Trinidad clear at Chaguaramas (*Customs* and *Immigration* are open 24 hours here) and this is recommended. There is a *Customs* office in Port of Spain, but they will recommend that you clear at Chaguaramas. When clearing anywhere, appropriate attire should go without saying.

Although the *Customs* and *Immigration* offices in Chaguaramas are open 24 hours a day, their normal working hours are 0800-1600 Monday through Friday (except holidays). New regulations permit arriving outside of these hours without paying overtime fees as long as you clear in first thing in the morning during regular office hours, otherwise overtime fees are TT$100. Overtime fees are payable if you require the services of an *Immigration* officer outside of office hours or on weekends or holidays. The fee of TT$100 is payable for each service only if you present yourself at the office outside of office hours.

In Chaguaramas you must proceed directly to the *Customs* Dock which is located just past the *CrewsInn Marina* docks (you MUST tie up at this dock unless you wish to pay a hefty fine). Vessels are not permitted to anchor or visit any other area before clearing in at the dock. After your vessel is secure, head down the dock; at the corner walk up the steps, and then climb the stairway to the second floor of the building on your immediate left, this is the *Immigration* office where you must clear first. *Immigration* will want to see all crewmembers upon arrival and departure.

Visiting *Immigration*
In the *Immigration* office the master of the vessel will be required to complete the following forms:
1: Form 10 - *Arrival Report* (4 copies)
2: Form 11 - *Crew List* (4 copies)
3. *Health Declaration* (1 copy)

These completed forms, together with the clearance forms from your last port of call, along with passports for all crew are presented to the *Immigration* officer who will sign you and your crew into the country.

Immigration Extensions
Extensions are available for three months to one year and cost a minimum of TT$150. Staying for hurricane season or having work done on your vessel are valid reasons for extensions.

All extensions of *Entry Certificates* are handled by the *Immigration* office and you must apply for an extension before your current *Entry Certificate* expires. One week before expiration you should present yourself to *Immigration* and complete the *Application for Extension of Landing/Change of Status* form.

Upon completion of this form you will be given an appointment for an interview with an *Immigration* officer. Your reasons for requesting an extension can be as simple as the fact you enjoy the island, wish to stay during hurricane season, or are having work done on your vessel (probably the most common reason given for an extension).

Extensions can be granted for up to 90 days for a fee of TT$150. You can apply for a further extension beyond 180 days but this is granted solely at the discretion of the *Immigration* officer and there needs to be a valid reason.

Visiting *Customs*
From the *Immigration* office head back down the steps and about 50' to your right is the *Customs* building. Here you must fill out additional paperwork in duplicate. The forms will ask you about your ship's inventory including how many engines you have (outboard or inboard). Be truthful in your answers. If

your boat is to remain in the water there is a harbor fee depending upon tonnage and length of stay. This fee is waived if your boat is to go on the hard.

Firearms and Pets

You will be required to hand over all firearms for the duration of your stay and you will have to show current vaccination records for all dogs and cats (and they will be quarantined aboard your vessel for the duration of your stay). You may not walk your pet ashore under any circumstances.

If you wish to leave by plane and take your pet with you, you will need a transit permit from the Veterinary services (622-1221). Once you have the permit you will be required to obtain a Quarantine Guard (622-5986). *Jesse James Member's Only Taxi*, or *Ian's Taxi*, can help you arrange this.

Transiting the Coast of Trinidad

When you clear in with *Immigration*, you must inform the officer of your plans on which anchorages you plan to visit on Trinidad and receive your *Temporary Certificate* for coastwise navigation.

The captain of the vessel must go to *Customs* with the ship's arrival document so that *Customs* officer can mark the intended location of the vessel and the date it left *Chaguaramas Bay*. This information is written on the document and then stamped. Upon return to Chaguaramas the procedure must be repeated. Note that this is not a new regulation, it has been on the books for many years, and only recently been exercised.

Transferring Crew to Another Vessel

Crew members wishing to transfer from one vessel to another may do so provided the crewmember signs off the vessel he arrived on and signs on to the vessel he is leaving aboard. Crew cannot sign on to a vessel that is staying longer than the vessel he or she arrived on. Arriving crew members need to have two copies of an *invitation letter* from the captain stating that he or she is part of the crew. The marinas on Trinidad can assist you with this process and the letters. The marinas can also assist you with the paperwork necessary to keep your vessel in storage in Trinidad. This paperwork will need to be stamped by the *Customs* officer in Chaguaramas. Be sure to keep one copy for your return.

Crew Leaving and Rejoining a Vessel

Crew leaving and rejoining a vessel will be required to undergo the same procedure as outlined above for signing off a vessel and for signing on to a vessel and a *letter of invitation* will need to be prepared by the master of the vessel. If the master of the vessel is leaving then they should prepare a letter indicating who will be acting as master in their absence; especially if the vessel needs to leave the waters of Trinidad/Tobago.

If the entire crew (including the master) are departing then a further letter (2 copies) detailing who will be in charge of the vessel in your absence will be required and endorsed by *Immigration*. A copy of this letter should be presented to *Immigration* upon return to the country.

Removal of Crew Members from Crew List

If you have a member of your crew departing and leaving the country, the master of the vessel and the crew member should present themselves to *Immigration* 48 hours before their flight leaves in order to avoid departure tax. The departing crew member will need to provide proof of repatriation to the issuing country of their passport (i.e. a plane ticket). Upon receipt of this proof the crew member will be removed from the *Crew List* of the vessel.

Signing on Additional Crew Members

If you plan to take on additional crew, prior to the arrival of the crew members you need to inform *Immigration*. The master of the vessel will need to present to the *Immigration* officer two copies of a letter of invitation which includes details such as the name of the joining crew member, their passport number, where they plan to stay in Trinidad, when they plan to leave, together with an undertaking by the master of the vessel to repatriate the crew member to the issuing country of the crew member's passport.

This letter will then be endorsed by *Immigration* and a copy should be forwarded to the crew member that is joining the vessel so that it may be presented to *Immigration* upon arrival at the airport. Crew joining a vessel will be given a two day *Entry Certificate*. Prior to the expiration of this certificate the master of the vessel and the joining crew member should present themselves to *Immigration* at a Port of Entry to be added to the vessel's crew list.

Flying In and Out of Trinidad

If you are planning to leave your boat in Trinidad, fly out, and return on a one-way ticket, you will need a special form stamped. You can get the form from the marina or boat yard where your vessel is located. The form will need to be stamped by *Immigration* and you will need to present it to the *Immigration* office at the airport when you arrive back in Trinidad. After you return and clear in at the airport, you will still need to appear at the *Immigration* office located at *CrewsInn* to go back on the crew's list.

If you are returning to Trinidad just to check your boat and are in possession of a round-trip ticket, you are not required to appear at the *CrewsInn Immigration* office. If this is the case, when you clear in at the airport you will be asked for your form and where you plan to stay. At this point present your form and round-trip ticket to indicate that you are not leaving aboard your vessel but by air. Please note: if leaving by plane a *Departure Tax* of TT$100 (which must be paid in *TT's*) will be assessed.

Importing Boat Parts With You

When returning to Trinidad, take the boat parts you bring with you (and the list of parts that you have brought with you), if any, to the *Customs* office in Chaguaramas (the officers here are alerted by phone when you leave the airport so don't try to visit your boat first) where an officer will go through your list with you.

No overtime will be paid by incoming cruisers importing boat parts via airplane as long as the check in with *Customs* immediately upon arriving in Chaguaramas from the airport.

Items Shipped to You in Trinidad

To have items shipped to you in Chaguaramas you can send them to you at the following address: Yacht In Transit, your boat name, Captain's name, marina (if applicable), Chaguaramas Terminal Point Gourde, Trinidad, West Indies. When your package arrives you must pick it up at the *Customs* office and present your passport and boat papers including your inward clearance.

Downstairs at the *Customs* office is their storage room for packages arriving for cruisers. When you expect your package to arrive, please check with *Customs* and pick it up promptly. If you are picking up items at the airport, check with *Customs* beforehand. After picking up the package you must take the item

directly to the Chaguaramas *Customs* office, you are not permitted to visit your vessel first. If you are confused check with *Customs* first.

Departing Trinidad for Tobago

This next part is VERY IMPORTANT! If you have cleared into Trinidad and expect to visit Tobago you must go to *Customs* and *Immigration* at Chaguaramas and present your papers, your *Temporary Certificate* from *Immigration*. When you arrive at Tobago you will need to report to *Customs* and *Immigration* at Scarborough or Charlotteville for another stamp on your *Temporary Certificate* "as soon as practically possible." If you are on Trinidad and plan to go Tobago and leave Trinidad/Tobago from there, you must report to *Customs* and *Immigration* at Chaguaramas to collect your papers to take with you to your Port of Entry on Tobago.

Clearing Out

When you clear out of Trinidad, take the paper the marina gives you stating the time your vessel was in storage so that you are not charged the monthly cruising fee for that period.

When you clear out the captain and all crew must report to the *Immigration* office in Chaguaramas to sign out. You will be required to fill out the following forms.

1: Form 5 - General Declaration (4 copies)
2: Form 16 - Notice of Approximate Time of Departure (4 copies)
3: Form 27 - Grant of Clearance (4 copies)

There is a new regulation in effect in Trinidad and Tobago that gives you 24 hours to depart after you have cleared out. If you cannot depart within 24 hours you must return to your Port of Entry and clear in again.

Boca del Dragon

Usually just called the "bocas," these islands and passes off the northwestern tip of Trinidad are the gateway to Chaguaramas for vessels approaching from Grenada or Tobago. Columbus named these cuts the *Boca del Drago*, the *Dragon's Mouth*, when he sailed north through them in 1498.

As shown on Chart TRI-2, there are three islands lying west of the Chaguaramas peninsula, Monos Island, Huevos Island, and the westernmost,

Chacachacare Island, and each has its own unique bit of history behind it. The islands of the bocas, actually the tops of undersea mountains, are said to be the easternmost of the Andes. These islands have been popularized as a holiday resort and many Trinis still visit them for that purpose. Visiting this compact archipelago is called going "down de islands" and cruisers will find good anchorages at Chacachacare, Monos Island, and on the mainland, at lovely *Scotland Bay.* The Bocas are usually numbered by local mariners. Boca de Monos is the first Boca, Boca de Huevos is number two, and Boca de Navios is number three.

Monos Island

Waypoints:

Bocas del Dragon, Boca del Monos- ½ nm N of
10° 43.00' N, 61° 40.50' W

Monos Island, Morris Bay- ½ nm SSE of
10° 41.40' N, 61° 40.20' W

Monos Island, Grand Fond Bay- ½ nm SE of
10° 40.60' N, 61° 40.40' W

Approaching the northwestern tip of Trinidad at the *Bocas del Dragon,* you will need to exercise caution

when entering *Boca de Monos,* the normal passage for yachts heading into *Chaguaramas Bay* (try to time your arrival here for daylight hours). When the prevailing winds and seas are up, and the tidal flow is heading north through the bocas, you can have some heavy sea action well into the boca as the current sometimes flows northward through here at up to 4 knots on the flood. On the other hand, no matter the tide, the current rarely if ever has a noticeable southerly flow through the Bocas.

The current that flows through the Bocas, and for a distance along the northern coast as far as Macqueripe, is known locally as *L'Remous.* Don't take the currents at the Bocas lightly. I've heard tales of sailboats without engines taking three days trying to tack their way through the Bocas. On more than one occasion I've left *Boca de Monos* heading to Grenada and seen a stream of churning white water snaking northwards for ten miles. Only about a quarter of a mile wide, the windward side of the rip was quite calm, while a hundred yards to leeward, right in the middle of the choppy water the story was quite the opposite. Exercise caution if you're approaching the Bocas and experience this.

Navigational Information
As shown on Chart TRI-2, a waypoint at 10°

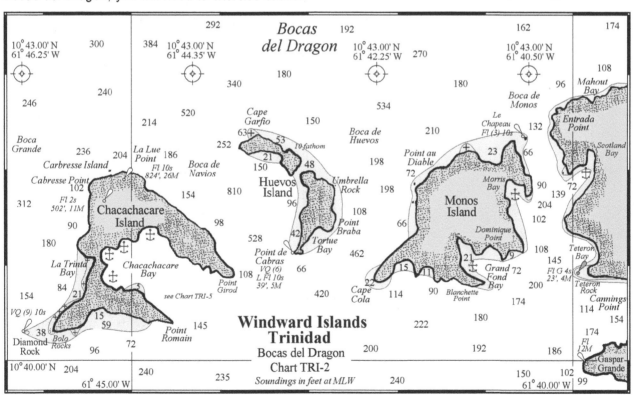

43.00' N, 61° 40.50' W, will place you approximately ½ mile north of the entrance to *Boca de Monos*. As I mentioned, try to arrive here in daylight and use caution if the sea conditions are creating rough seas in the boca. The passage is wide and quite deep as you pass between the mainland of Trinidad to port, and Le Chapeau, the small rock that lies northeast of Monos Island. If entering at night, Le Chapeau has a light that flashes white (3) every 10 seconds. Soon, as the effects of the seas north of the bocas fade away, the waters in the *Boca de Monos* will become calmer.

To port the entrance to *Scotland Bay* will open up just past the small off-lying rock on your port side (for more information on *Scotland Bay* see the next section). Continuing on past Teteron Rock (Fl G, 4s, 23', 4M) you can make your turn to port to enter *Chaguaramas Bay*. On the eastern shore of Monos Islands are two anchorages, *Morris Bay* and *Grand Fond Bay*. Although open to the southeast, both anchorages are remarkably calm in light to moderate southeast winds.

The anchorage at *Morris Bay* lies northwest of Dominique Point as shown on Chart TRI-3. Upon entering give the shallow bar south of Dominique Point a wide berth and head towards the northwestern corner of the bay for the best holding. The houses onshore are private and visits should be by invitation only.

The anchorage at *Grand Fond Bay* lies northwest of Blanchette Point as shown on Chart TRI-3. Head towards the northwestern corner of the bay to anchor in 15'-25' of water. You'll notice some old pilings here that date to World War II when the owners of this island called the cove *Allies Bay* to distance themselves from any association with the Axis powers. *Grand Fond Bay* is sometimes called *Turtle Bay* due to the leatherback turtles that nest here.

What You Will Find Ashore

Monos was originally named by the Spanish and it means *apes*, probably due to the howler monkeys that share the island with a few Trinis who have private homes here. There was once a thriving whaling station on Monos and I'm told that if one searches in the shallows off the point at *Grand Fond Bay* you can see the remains of the old cauldrons that were used

Boat anchored in *Scotland Bay*

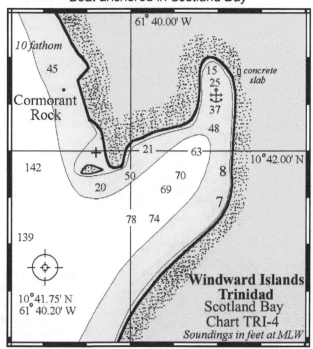

to render the whale blubber. I've looked for them and cannot find them, but perhaps I've been looking in the wrong place. If anybody knows where they are I'd appreciate a pointer.

Today, part of the island is owned by the well-known Gatcliffe family. Tommy Gatcliffe is said to be one of two people who knows the secret formula for the world-famous *Angostura Bitters*.

At the southeastern end of Boca de Monos you'll find *Teteron Bay*, the home of the *Trinidad and Tobago Naval Station*. The bay is restricted and anchoring is not permitted. The house on the point was turned into a bar called the *Crow's Nest* by the U.S. military during WW II.

Scotland Bay

Waypoints:
Scotland Bay- ¼ nm SW of entrance
10° 41.75' W, 61° 40.20' W

Navigational Information
Scotland Bay is one of the loveliest anchorages in Trinidadian waters and is my personal favorite. As shown on Chart TRI-2 and TRI-4, *Scotland Bay* lies on the mainland side of *Boca de Monos* and works its way deep into the surrounding mountains.

As you enter the bay you'll likely see boats anchored off the beaches on your port, or off the mainland to your starboard, but the best anchorage is tucked up in the northern tip of the bay in 20'-40' of water. Drop your hook between the small beach on your left and the concrete slab to your right where people sometimes camp. The bottom here is mud and the holding is good.

You'll find that you'll rarely be alone here, especially on the weekends when local boaters come here to get away from it all for a while. A good idea is to anchor bow to the south and set a stern anchor to the north or tie a stern line to a tree on shore.

What You Will Find Ashore
Scotland Bay is wonderful for observing wildlife. Here you'll hear the lion-like roar of the howler monkeys, especially after a good rain. At night, you will need to put up screens and set a light in your cockpit to help keep away the fruit bats. They've been known to enter boats at night, feast on whatever fresh fruit may be laying around, and leave a layer of nasty, slick, guano all over everything.

Huevos Island

Navigational Information
As shown on Chart TRI-2, Huevos Island lies in the middle of the *Boca del Dragon* between Chacachacare Island and Monos Island. The 84-acre island was originally named *El Delfin* (the dolphin) by Christopher Columbus because of it appearance.

It is said that Christopher Columbus, while anchored off Chacachacare on August 12, 1498, sent two skiffs to Huevos in search of water and the returning sailors told of finding an abandoned fishing village on the island. Many years later, Spanish settlers changed its name to *Huevos* (eggs) because of the large number of hawksbill turtle eggs laid on the island's beach.

What You Will Find Ashore
In 1900, Huevos Island was owned by Johnny Wehekind, a keen fisherman who loved the piscatorial action in the surrounding waters. In 1927, Huevos Island was sold to Carl Boos for $1 including the M/V *El Pao*, by the headman of Seville in Venezuela, Jefé Seville.

The Boos family's hospitality was known far and wide and they hosted Royalty and world leaders such as the Duke and Duchess of Kent in 1935, Princess Margaret in 1958, and Franklin Delano Roosevelt who came here to fish during WWII. Today the island is still owned by the Boos family.

Huevos is actually two islands, and the break between the two is called *Boca Sin Entrada* (*Mouth with no Entry*). There is a group of submerged rocks abreast of the break that is said to be haunted. It is said that on calm moonlit nights you can hear the sound of a chapel bell and the solemn chanting of ancient Latin hymns. Legend has it that a Spanish galleon was wrecked here and during the last moments, a prince, a passenger aboard the vessel, and his chaplain summoned a group of choirboys that were aboard to beg God for deliverance from the danger.

If you remember reading about oilbirds, you might be interested to know that one of their eight known colonies on Trinidad is on Huevos Island.

Chacachacare Island

Waypoints:

Bocas del Dragon, Boca Grande- 1 nm N of
10º 43.00' N, 61º 46.25' W

Bocas del Dragon, Boca de Navios- 1 nm N of
10º 43.00' N, 61º 44.35' W

Chacachacare Island- ¼ nm SE Chaca. Bay
10º 40.40' N, 61º 44.00' W

Usually just referred to as Chacachacare, this 900-acre island is the westernmost of the *Boca del Dragon* chain and the last bit of Trinidad before you

reach the coastline of Venezuela some 7 miles to the west.

Anchorage and ruins at Chacachacare Island

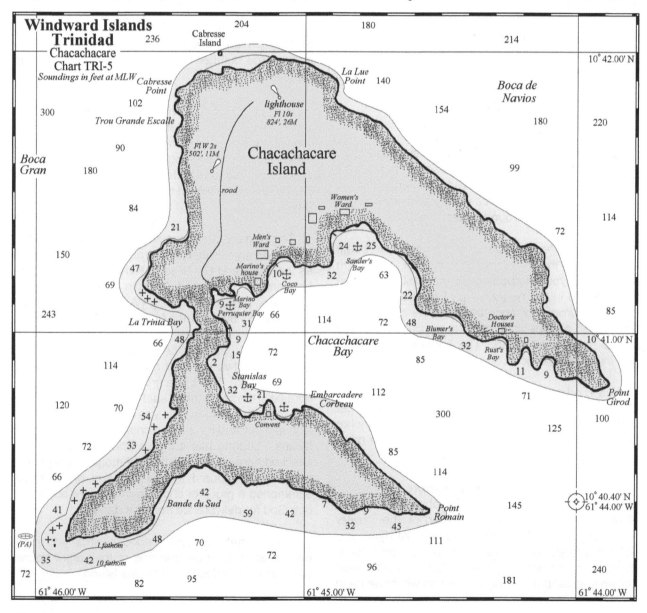

Navigational Information

As shown on Chart TRI-2, a waypoint at 10° 43.00' N, 61° 44.35' W, will place you approximately 1 mile north of *Boca de Navios*, the passage between Huevos Island and Chacachacare. Pass between the two in deep water and after passing south of Point Girod you can turn to the west to anchor in one of the small bays off *Chacachacare Bay* as shown on Chart TRI-5.

These anchorages are exposed to the southeast, but *Stanislas Bay*, and especially *Sanders Bay*, give the best protection from that direction. Unfortunately the bays here are deep and shelve rapidly, and if that's not enough, the holding is generally fair to poor and the bottom rocky. It's best to set an anchor and run a line ashore.

What You Will Find Ashore

And what will you visit while ashore? Of course, the leper colony ruins (see the next section, *Historical Chacachacare Island*), but other treasures also await you (see Chart TRI-5). Trek to the operating lighthouse for a fantastic view of Trinidad and Venezuela. But if your visit to the lighthouse is not enough, visit the salt pond at the southwestern tip of the island at Bande du Sud. Divers might wish to explore the waters around Bolo Rocks where three wrecks are reported to lie, the *Samuel* in 1809, the *Pirata* in 1892, and the *Dr. Sigert* in 1895.

The island is wonderful to explore, but caution must be exercised, as there are Manchineel trees growing on the island. If you are not familiar with Manchineel trees, learn about them. Their sap is toxic and it's inadvisable to even stand underneath one, especially if it is raining. A hint...the Manchineel and its fruit resembles an apple tree. Luckily for you however, they tend to congregate close to the water and not far inland, so keep your eyes open for them.

Historical Chacachacare Island

Mountainous and wooded, Chacachacare is named after the native cotton that grows on the island, *chaca* (sometimes written as *chac-chac*) in Amerindian. Artifacts have placed the earliest settlers on Chacachacare between 100-700AD. The first European to sight Chacachacare was Christopher Columbus who anchored here on August 12, 1498. He named the bay he anchored in *Puerto de Gato* for the wild cats that he heard on shore. Those wild cats were actually the howler monkeys and they DO sound like wild cats. Columbus named the island *El*

Caracol, the snail, because of the island's angular shape. On the western shore of the island is *La Tinta Bay* (*Ink Bay*), named by the Spanish for the black sand of its beaches, which used to be a popular spot for smugglers and is now a popular sunbathing spot for Trinis on the weekend.

The Spaniards grew cotton on the island and established a whaling station and by the 1700s, Chacachacare had a sizable population. In the late 1700s, Chacachacare was given to an Irishman, Gerald Fitzpatrick Carry, for services rendered to the King with the proviso it would be returned if needed by the King. Carry used the island for agriculture and took to growing sugar apples and cotton on the island. In 1813, Venezuelan patriot Santiago Marino used Chacachacare as a base to launch an invasion of Venezuela during its war of independence. The ruins of Marino's house still stand on the point by *Marino Bay*.

In the 1800s, Chacachacare was used as a health spa and retreat for Trinidadians and then by the end of the 19th century this idyllic paradise was to change quite abruptly. In 1880, Dominican nuns built *St. Catherine's Church*, a school, and a convent on land that was willed to the Church in 1842. In 1896, a lighthouse was built on the island (Fl 10s, 824', 26M). Once the highest lighthouse in the world, it stands like a sentinel high above the surrounding waters.

Today the lighthouse is the second highest lighthouse in the world, the highest lighthouse is now located in Russia. The only full-time inhabitant of Chacachacare is the light-keeper that lives in the century-old building atop the hill. In a way it's sad that tradition of lighthouse keeping is quickly falling by the wayside around the world as more and more lights are turning to automatic operation. The lighthouse keeper on Chacachacare enjoys guests and stands by on VHF ch. 10, he'll often give visitors a ride to the lighthouse if he's not busy, but please don't bother him if you're just too lazy to take the short hike.

Chacachacare is best known for the leper colony that existed on the island for over half a century, or perhaps more. Dates are unclear concerning the timeline here. There has been speculation among Trinidadians that I have spoken with that the concept of a leper colony on Chacachacare was brought forth in the late 19th century, but remained dormant for almost 40 years. I have seen literature that states the leper colony was established on Chacachacare in 1877, while another reports the year as 1887. However, newspaper clippings from the early 20th century report that in the early 1920s, the British government decided to separate the lepers of Trinidad from the rest of the population.

At that time the lepers were contained at a hospital in Cocorite, and the authorities, in an action that resembled a raid rather than a transfer, moved the lepers to Chacachacare and the lepers, as well as their families, had no idea if they would ever see each other again. By the mid-1920s, most of the infrastructure was complete and the colony housed some 250 patients.

Most of the lepers lived in small groups in several buildings scattered about the island. They were basically on their own, including having to feed themselves. The Sisters used food shipped over from the mainland to induce patients to secure treatments at the clinic. Those lepers who could not care for themselves were confined to the 260-bed *Sunda Bay Hospital* in the small village on the island.

The Dominican nuns, who unselfishly cared for the lepers, strictly forbid any contact between the sexes and as you would expect, this segregation raised a protest. The nuns eventually relented and allowed intermingling during certain hours, but things being as they are, more than one baby was born on the island, and those that were uninfected were transferred to an orphanage on the mainland.

U.S. and Puerto Rican Marines occupied part of Chacachacare during WW II, separating themselves from the leper colony with a barbed wire fence. During the war years the lighthouse was unused as German U-boats were quite successful in their hunting in the waters around Trinidad, sinking some 80 Allied ships.

At one point a steel submarine net stretched westward from Chacachacare almost all the way to Venezuela across Boca Grande and the north entry to the *Gulf of Paria*. Chacachacare has always been a good source of fresh water and during the war years ships would pull in here to take on water. There are still the remains of viaducts and piping on the island.

In 1950, the Dominican nuns left the island and were replaced by a local nursing staff. Over the years, several of the Sisters died of the same disease as their patients and were buried in the cemetery on the island. Today, just up the hill from the convent, you can still visit the old graveyard where 12 nuns from age 28-88 are buried.

In 1984, the leper colony closed and the remaining patients, some of whom had spent over 4 decades on the island, returned to Trinidad to try to live some semblance of a normal life. The amazing thing about the ruins on Chacachacare is that it looks as if everybody just walked away and left everything behind.

As you explore the wards and the doctor's house you'll find desks, filing cabinets with patients records, part of an X-ray machine with a patient's X-rays nearby, and even a typewriter. The hospital still has beds and a pharmacy containing bottles of medication. There's even a theater with an old movie projector.

You can't help but wonder as you stand there staring at the mass of items left behind, why did everybody just leave like that? It's said that some of the buildings are haunted, and writings on the walls bear testament to this. Some say it's the ghost of a Dominican nun who took her own life after becoming pregnant by a local fisherman For a while the *Trinidad Coast Guard* used the old buildings for living quarters and as administrative offices, but it is said that the *Coast Guard* left Chacachacare after only six months because of the haunted buildings.

Along with the ruins of the leper colony, you'll find an old Catholic Church as well as a Hindu temple. And don't just stay to the path or road, if you wander around in the brush you might be surprised at what you'll find. Don't forget to bring plenty of bug spray, the mosquitoes can be vicious.

There are a lot of caves along the northwestern shore of Chacachacare that were used by smugglers for years. One gentleman I spoke to recalled wandering through the caves as a boy and finding a case of whiskey.

Today, Chacachacare is overseen by the *CDA*, the *Chaguaramas Development Authority*, and they have proposed constructing hotels on the island as well as preserving the remains of the leper colony.

The Western Coast of Trinidad

Chaguaramas Bay

Waypoints:
Bocas del Dragon, Boca del Monos- ½ nm N of
10° 43.00' N, 61° 40.50' W

Chaguaramas Bay- 1 ½ nm W of anchorage
10° 40.50' N, 61° 40.00' W

This is it, the Mecca of Eastern Caribbean cruising. Cruise central. Chaguaramas! At the end of the 1980s, the only place in Trinidad for a cruiser to get a slip and spend the season, was at *TTYC*, the *Trinidad and Tobago Yacht Club* in Bayshore. But over the last two plus decades Chaguaramas has become the center of marine services in the lower Caribbean. You can find anything you need here, and if you can't, you can get it shipped in with no duty due. Chaguaramas, being technically out of the hurricane zone, is a huge draw for vessels wishing not to deal with hurricanes and yet still enjoy the Caribbean and the camaraderie of other like-minded cruisers.

Historical Chaguaramas
The peninsula was named Chaguaramas by its original Amerindian inhabitants (100-700AD), after the majestic Royal palms which once flourished here. This natural harbor has been favored for its depth and shelter for centuries. *Chaguaramas Bay* offered sheltered moorings for Spanish, French, and British ships, which fought over Trinidad for over two hundred years. The Spaniards burned their fleet here when the British invaded in 1797.

During the plantation years, the area saw coffee, cocoa, and cotton estates worked by slave labor and later by indentured servants. World War II saw the area leased to the American military in exchange for 50 old destroyers as part of the *Lend-Lease Program*. During this period the area was closed to all civilians, and the inhabitants were moved to what is now Carenage. Today, most of the large buildings you see, especially those that line the road from *TTSA* to Carenage, were constructed for military use during the war years.

As the independence movement grew in Trinidad, Chaguaramas became a focal point. In April of 1960, thousands of residents marched in the rain to solicit the return of Chaguaramas to the people of Trinidad.

The beaches of Chaguaramas were always a draw, and in 1961 the area was returned to the citizens and the Government of Trinidad immediately set aside most of the region as *Chaguaramas National Park*, which remains today (from the *Tucker Valley* to Chacachacare). In 1962, the *CDA*, the *Chaguaramas Development Authority* was established with the purpose of maintaining the natural resources of the area and encourage the growth of a business infrastructure.

Today, the town of Chaguaramas is the area of large buildings between *TTSA* and eastward to *KFC*. The *CDA* is located here and they offer guides and hikes through the surrounding area such as the hike through the *Tucker Estate*, the first citrus plantation on Trinidad. The *Covigne River* tour is hike through a majestic gorge ending up at a waterfall with a deep pool at its base, perfect for a cool dip after the hike.

Birdwatchers will appreciate the hike to *Mount Catherine*, and everybody will enjoy the tour to *Edith Falls*. *Edith Falls* can be arrived at by road if you prefer to go on your own in a rental car. Take the *Tucker Valley Road* to the well-marked turn-off to the falls at *Bellerazand Road*. There is a small and poorly marked trail just before the golf course and *Edith Falls* waits patiently for you a short 30 minute hike away. If you wish to camp, *CDA* will rent a tent to you for your stay.

Navigational Information
The entrance to *Chaguaramas Bay* really doesn't need a waypoint, as you approach from the north, through the first Boca (*Boca de Monos*-Chart TRI-2), but if you need one I'll be happy to give you one. A waypoint at 10° 40.50' N, 61° 40.00' W, will place you 1½ miles west of the anchorage area as shown on Chart TRI-6. If you don't need a waypoint, as you head south in the Boca you'll pass Cannings Point at which point you can turn to port to pass either side of Gasparillo Island to proceed to the anchorage west of *CrewsInn Marina*. On most charts Cannings Point is called Point Delgada, or Delgada Point. Either way, it is known locally as Cannings Point and that's good enough for me, so that's what I'll show it as.

Keep an eye out for the submerged rock just off the point. Called Teteron Rock, it is marked by a lit buoy, but if the light should not be on station, give the point a wide berth, at least ¼ mile, to be on the safe side. Just before Teteron Rock you'll notice

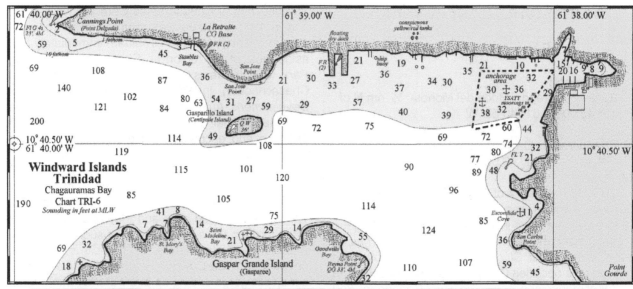

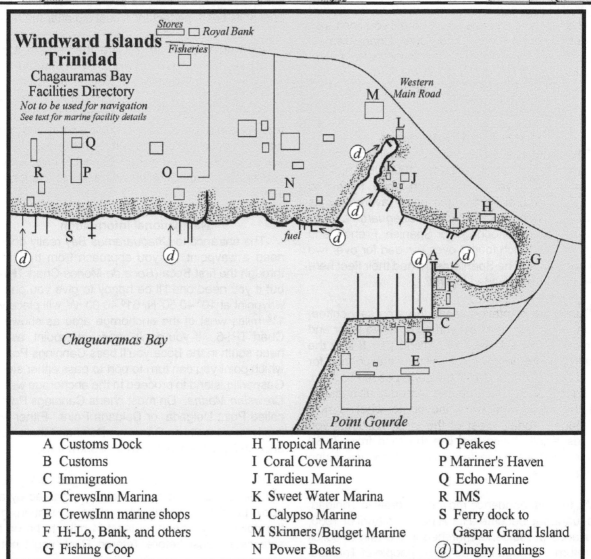

A Customs Dock	H Tropical Marine	O Peakes
B Customs	I Coral Cove Marina	P Mariner's Haven
C Immigration	J Tardieu Marine	Q Echo Marine
D CrewsInn Marina	K Sweet Water Marina	R IMS
E CrewsInn marine shops	L Calypso Marine	S Ferry dock to
F Hi-Lo, Bank, and others	M Skinners/Budget Marine	Gaspar Grand Island
G Fishing Coop	N Power Boats	(d) Dinghy landings

Teteron Bay, the home of the *Trinidad and Tobago Naval Station*. The bay is restricted and anchoring is not permitted. Gasparillo Island is known locally as Centipede Island for the huge centipede population that controls the island. The largest centipede ever captured, 14 inches, was caught on Gapaillo Island.

The anchorage in Chaguaramas, as outlined by a dashed line on Chart TRI-6, is deep, usually 25'-30' and more, the holding isn't the best, and the area is beset with currents. You'll soon notice that your boat will swing to the swirling currents and vessels nudging into each other at these times is not unusual. Keep a good anchor watch and try to give yourself enough swinging room. Do not anchor close to the large shipwright's building at *CrewsInn*, or close along the southern shore below *Peake's*, *Power Boats*, and *Sweet Water Marinas*. Do not anchor as to block commercial vessels that use the harbor's facilities.

YSATT has moorings in *Chaguaramas Bay* lying west of the *CrewsInn Marina* docks and stretching westward. The large orange floats are east to see with *YSATT* painted on them. If you wish to rent one, pick up a vacant mooring and check in at the *YSATT* office at *CrewsInn Marina* or somebody may come by to collect the mooring fee. The moorings are on a first-come/first-served basis.

Vessels needing to clear in should continue past the *CrewsInn Marina* docks to the *Customs* dock, which can usually accommodate two, and often three, vessels. Although some cruisers will anchor first and then dinghy in to clear, *Customs* officers stress that it is not permitted.

What You Will Find Ashore
Customs and *Immigration*
Customs in Chaguaramas monitors VHF ch. 16. After you tie up to the *Customs* dock, walk down the first row of boats and at the end of the dock, walk up the stairs and to your left are the steps leading up to the *Immigration* office, your first stop (*Immigration* my or may not wish to see all crew and passengers). When you have cleared with *Immigration*, walk down the stairs and just off to your right is the *Customs* office, your next stop. When you have completed your clearing-in process proceed to the marina of your choice or anchor wherever you choose.

For more information on rules and regulations, see the earlier section, *Customs and Immigration*.

Getting Around
Getting around Chaguaramas requires little more than a good dinghy and a nice pair of shoes as everything is within walking distance of a dinghy dock. If you don't wish to use your dingy, *YSATT* operates a shuttle that stops at all of the marinas and yards in *Chaguaramas Bay*. The service operates Monday-Saturday from 0900-1900 and costs TT$5-10. You can contact the shuttle on VHF ch. 68 (*YSATT*).

There is also a water taxi service in the bay, *Skizzo's Water Taxi*, and they operate from 0800-2300 daily. *Skizzo's* can be hailed on VHF ch. 68 and can arrange pickups at any time of the day or night with prior notice.

Ashore, car rentals are numerous and reasonable, but the preferred mode of transportation is the maxi-taxi. If you don't care to rent a vehicle and try your hand at driving, you can take a taxi or rely on public transportation. All commuter transport vehicles will have a license plate that begins with the letter "H" (vehicles with the letter "H" are for hire, "P" are private vehicles, a plate that starts with a "T" is obviously a truck, and "R" plates designate a rental vehicle). Buses serve main commuter routes and are differentiated into two services, the transit and express commuter services (ECS). ECS service, white and red-striped mini-vans, is available to points east of Port of Spain and runs along a dedicated transit highway system that only these mini-vans can use.

The most popular mode of public transport is the maxi-taxi. Maxi-taxis run regular routes from Port of Spain to Chaguaramas and back (as well as many other routes to other parts of Trinidad). Maxi-taxis are color-coded mini-vans. All are white and those with yellow horizontal bands run in the Port of Spain and Chaguaramas areas; red bands are for eastern Trinidad; green bands for southern Trinidad; black bands run in the Princess Town area; and brown bands run from San Fernando to the southwestern tip of the island. All vans run regular routes and the white/yellow vans that you will use in Chaguaramas have a centralized base in Port of Spain across from the port, and run every few minutes so you won't have to wait long for a ride.

Simply stand at a bus stop and as the van approaches you must put out your hand or else the taxi will not stop. The usual fare is TT$2-$5, but for a few dollars more they'll usually take you a short way off their route to get you to your destination. There are larger buses that run at regular intervals, usually a couple of hours apart. These buses do not take cash, instead you must pre-purchase tickets which can be found at most marinas in Chaguaramas. A good idea is to buy a couple and keep them in your wallet or purse in case you need them. If you're headed to Chaguaramas from Port of Spain, make sure you board a taxi that says Chaguaramas on it as some don't go past Carenage and *TTSA*.

One of the most pleasant Trinidadians that you will meet is Jesse James, who, with his wife Sharon Rose, are owners of *Members Only Maxi-Taxi* (VHF ch. 68). Jesse's fleet is based at *Tropical Marine* and you can listen to the daily VHF net (0800 on VHF. ch 68) for the latest on his routes and special trips to places like the *Asa Wright Center Nature Center*, shopping outings to places like *Price Mart, Hi-Lo*, and the Saturday morning produce market. Jesse can even arrange visits to other parts of Trinidad, any place you would like to visit Jesse can take you.

Trump Tours, next to *Immigration* in the *CrewsInn Marina Village*, is another travel agency that can arrange tours to any part of Trinidad and even to Tobago.

Marine Facilities
Marinas and Haul Out Yards

There are several marinas available here and they might be full so give them a call on the VHF to check on slip availability before you arrive. Most marinas monitor VHF ch. 68 and have dinghy docks available (see the *Chaguaramas Bay Facilities Directory* map). Some of these marinas offer use of their facilities for a small weekly fee for those who are anchored or moored in the bay.

The facilities at *TTYC* in Bayshore, and *TTSA* in *Carenage Bay* will be discussed in upcoming sections so if you wish to leave *Chaguaramas Bay* for those locations, turn to their appropriate section for more information and approach directions.

We'll now explore each marina and haul-out yard and what marine services are available. Check the appendix in the back for phone numbers and email addresses. Bear in mind time changes all and by the time this publication reaches your hands, several of these businesses may have changed, moved, or closed. The *Chaguaramas Bay Facilities Directory*

map will give you a general idea of where some of these services are located around the periphery of *Chaguaramas Bay*. Another good source of information is the free *Trinidad and Tobago Boater's Directory*, available for free at all marinas, chandlers, the *Boca* office, and *YSATT*. Now let's see what marinas and haul-out yards are available. We'll begin by the *Customs* dock and work our way counterclockwise around the periphery of *Chaguaramas Bay*.

CrewsInn Marina

Located by the *Customs* dock is *CrewsInn Marina*, actually it's the *CrewsInn Hotel and Yachting Center*, a great place to stay, and definitely the most upscale of the marinas in Chaguaramas. The marina monitors VHF ch. 68 and 77 and there's usually somebody around 24/7. The docks have 70 slips with finger piers (rare in Caribbean marinas), and full electric (metered) with water, cable TV, Wi-fi, and a daily newspaper in your cockpit every morning. Marina guests also have access to the showers, laundry, and pool at the *CrewsInn Hotel* (a great place to stay while the yard is working on your boat). On the ground floor by the *Customs* dock is a *Hi-Lo* supermarket (open Monday-Saturday from 0900-2100, and Sundays from 0800-1200) with an excellent choice of foodstuffs, fresh produce, and spirits while upstairs is the *Lighthouse Restaurant*.

South of the docks is the huge shipwright's building, part of the old Navy base and the focus for the *CrewsInn* 4-acre haul-out yard. The building itself covers 2½ acres and has a vertical clearance of 80' so you won't have to pull your mast for inside painting (unless of course, your mast is too tall for this immense building). The yard can handle the largest yachts with a 200-ton lift as well as a 65-ton crane. Security is very good here, 24 hours a day, and the guards even check car's trunks upon entry into the yard. And just because you get in the yard, doesn't mean you can get into the shipwright's building where another gate and guard will stop you.

Tropical Marine

As you round the eastern end of *Chaguaramas Bay* you'll pass the small cove full of local fishing cove. There is a fishing co-op here but no facilities for yachts.

As you proceed west on the *Western Main Road* you'll immediately come to *Tropical Marine*. Here you'll find stern or bow-to berthing along the seawall for about 20 or so boats, depending on their beam The boats are very close together and fenders will be required to keep you away from your neighbor. Water and electricity are available and the slips are very economical. Call ahead for a slip as *Tropical* seems to stay full.

Fronting the road by *Tropical Marine* is a building housing several facilities including *Master's Laundry* where you can wash your clothes or have it done for you (there's also a book swap). Also on site is the *Wheelhouse Pub*.

Coral Cove Marina

Next door is *Coral Cove Marina*, a large haul-out facility with a 60-ton lift and long-term dry storage. The marina can handle about 40 boats (up to a 90' monohull and wide slips for catamarans) with full electric, water, and cable TV. The *Coral Cove Marina Hotel* can furnish a room if you need someplace to stay while you're hauled out. *Coral Cove* also boasts a Laundromat, showers, and a pool. The yard has a 60-ton hoist and room for 70 boats. You can do your own work or contract the yard to handle it for you. *Coral Cove* can arrange to have your propane tanks refilled. Leave them with the guard in the morning and they'll be ready the next day; make sure your boat's name is on your tank.

Tardieu Marine

At the eastern end of this building is the entrance to the facilities at *Tardieu Marine*. The office for the marina is on the upper floor in the last building on the left before the dock. The marina can accommodate 16 vessels but is often full of commercial fishing boats (although it's worth your while to see if they have a slip available). Slips have water and electric, and the marina has showers and ice for sale.

Sweet Water Marina

Next to *Tardieu* is the entrance to the *Sweet Water Marina* (formerly *Hummingbird*). *Sweet Water* has alongside berths as well as bow or stern-to berths in a small creek off the bay, water, electricity, showers, and a laundry. They can accommodate up to 30 boats depending on their beam and length. However, the marina tends to cater to the sportfishing crowd, but if there is room available they will accommodate the average cruiser. *The Lure Restaurant* is located on site.

Power Boats

Next door is the huge *Power Boats* complex, and no, its name does not imply that it is for power boats, 99% of *Power Boats* customers are sailboats. *Power Boats* monitors VHF ch. 72, and has the only fuel dock in the *Chaguaramas Bay* with diesel, gas, and water. The fuel dock can handle a 14' draft and is open from Monday-Friday, 0800-1800, and on the weekends it's open from 0600-1800. The marina has 30 slips with bow or stern-to berthing and full amenities including showers and rental apartments. Some of the slips are on the bay while others are in the small creek on the east side of the yard. The slips that are not in the creek are good in most conditions though they can get untenable in heavy southwesterlies.

The *Power Boats* yard itself is huge, with space for about 250 boats and it stays full; you must make arrangements well in advance to assure that there's room for your haulout. There's a 50-ton lift and the yard can also handle large catamarans. *Power Boats* is home to *Sails Restaurant*, the *Roti Hut*, and the well-stocked *Dockside Market*.

Power Boats has a large contingent of contractors to do your work for you and they guarantee their work. Feel free to use their dinghy dock just to the east of the Travel Lift, but you are asked to please register at the office to get your pass that allows access via the *Power Boats* main gate. There is a small fee for this but it is certainly worth it. You are also asked to not leave your dinghy tied to the dock in front of the market or restaurant. If you are a guest of the yard, be sure to get your *Power Boats Convenience Card* which gives you a 5% discount on all purchases at the *Boater's Shop* and the *Dockside Market*.

Peake Yacht Services

Further west is the large *Peakes* yard (monitors VHF ch. 69) with a 150-ton lift that can handle yachts with beams up to 31' and drafts to 15'. A unique trailer can pack about 350 boats in the yard. The waterfront docks can accommodate up to 17 boats with bow or stern-to berthing, less berths depending on beam, catamarans taking up more dock space than monohulls. You can work on your vessel yourself or contract the job, ask at the *Peakes* office located upstairs in the hotel. The popular *Bight Restaurant* is also located at *Peakes*.

Industrial Marine Services (IMS)

Next door is the *Industrial Marine Services*

compound, usually just called *IMS*. *IMS* monitors VHF ch. 68 and has a capacity of approximately 130 boats, a 70-ton lift. The yard's work bays come with free electricity and water; if you're using an air-conditioner there is a US$5 per day charge. *IMS* has a 120' long dinghy dock with bow and stern attachment points.

Next to *IMS* is the ferry dock where you can catch the water taxi to Gaspar Grande Island while west of *IMS* are only commercial facilities all the way to the end of the road where you find the entrance to the *Trinidad and Tobago Coast Guard* and *Naval Stations*.

At the northwestern end of the bay, just northeast of Gasparillo Island, is a huge floating drydock. The dock itself was built on the Tyne by the famous Newcastle firm of *Swan, Hunter and Wigan Richardson*, and was towed to Trinidad by Dutch tugs in 1907. The dock can accommodate a vessel 365' long and up to 64' wide, with a capacity of 4,800 tons.

Marine Services

Now let's see what marine services are available. We will begin our tour of services located around *Chaguaramas Bay* at *CrewsInn* and work our way westward, counterclockwise around the bay.

CrewsInn

Up the stairs at the end of A-dock is *Customs* and *Immigration* as mentioned earlier. If you leave *Customs* and *Immigration*, take a left and walk up some steps and you'll come to a nice courtyard (this area is called the *CrewsInn Village Square*) the location for Thursday night pot-lucks. Bring something to grill and have a good time. Take a right here and walk up a few steps and you'll find a gift shop as well as *Econo Car* car rentals (great prices). Here too you'll find *YSATT* and *Trump Tours*. Behind *Econo Car*, facing the parking lot, is a *Republic Bank* with a 24 hour *ATM*.

The *Shipwright's Building* is home to several marine services. Here you can enjoy the *Mariner's Office* where you can access the Internet, send and receive faxes, ship and receive packages, and make phone calls at good prices.

Nau-T-Kol can handle your marine refrigeration and air-conditioning problems and are reps for *Cruisair, Gruner*, and *Marine Air*.

Soca Sails can repair your sails, or build you a new one, and they're reps for *Doyle Sails, Andersen* winches, *Stamoid* fabrics, and *Frederiksen* hardware. You can reach *Soca Sails* on VHF ch. 68. *Soca Sails* can also handle your canvas needs.

Dockyard Electrics has just expanded and carries all your electrical needs from wire crimps to batteries and solar panels; they have the best selection of electrical supplies in Trinidad. They'll not only sell you the best of electrical systems (they are reps for *Standard Horizon, ACR, Sea Trek, Iridium, Globalstar, Xantrex Comnav, Inmarsat*, and *KVH*), they'll install it for you or repair your old system. They also carry a good selection of general nautical supplies such as rope, tools, and more, they can also repair your diesel, outboard, or genset (they are dealers for *John Deere, Perkins, Fischer-Panda, Northern Lights, Kubota, Westerbeke*, and *Mitsubishi*).

Goodwood Marine also has a shop here and they sell and service marine electronics as well as roller-furling systems and winches. *Goodwood* is the only representative in Trinidad for *B&G* and *Raymarine* and can handle their warranty work. They are also agents for *C-Map, Garmin*, and *Navionics*,

If you want somebody to handle every facet of your refit, visit *Caribbean Yacht Works* for complete service.

If you need an air-conditioner while in Trinidad, and who doesn't, Richard Hosam's *Coast to Coast* will rent you one along with a de-humidifier, fridge, and a DVD movie! If that's not enough, Richard can also clean your upholstery, rugs, carpeting, and your boat's interior.

Tropical Marine

Fronting the road by *Tropical Marine* is a building housing several facilities including Jesse Jame's *Member's Only Taxi* and *Master's Laundry* where you can wash your clothes or have it done for you (there's also a book swap).

Also facing the road is Ranier Dobring's *Electropics* where you get just about any electronic device on your boat repaired, including autopilots. They are an authorized *Simrad* dealer and repair center.

A local company, *KISS*, offers their own brand of high output wind-generators at a low price, check them out, you might be pleasantly surprised. Personally I believe them to be one of the best wind generators on the market.

Coastal Diving Services Ltd. can fill your SCUBA tank or handle any underwater repairs you require. And in back is *Shiloh Enterprises* where you can pick up bulk fiberglass cloth, resins, and epoxies.

Coral Cove

Next door, just to the west of *Tropical Marine*, is *Coral Cove Marine*. *Navtech Electronics* is located at *Coral Cove* and they are a *Coastal Marine Radio Service Station* for *Sailmail*. *Sailmail* is a non-profit association of yacht owners that operates and maintains an email communications system for use by its members through its world wide network of SSB-Pactor stations such as *Navtech*. You don't have to be a ham to take advantage of *Sailmail,* and *Navtech* invites you to stop by and learn more about the system. *Navtech Electronics* are also dealers for *Furuno*, *Garmin*, and *Standard*.

Also at *Coral Cove*, *Corsa Marine* are agents for *Mercury* and *Mariner* and can service most outboards. *LP Marine and Industrial Supplies* are agents for *Volvo Penta*, *Johnson Pumps* and *GM* generators. They carry a very good selection of cutlass bearings, control cables, paints, transmission parts, filters, instrumentation, electronics and more. If you need general hardware there is a branch of *William H. Scott Ltd.* located at *Coral Cove*; besides carrying your basic line of hardware, they also sell and rent power tools.

Tardieu Marine

Just to the west of *Coral Cove* is *Tardieu Marine,* which we'll discuss in just a moment, but first let's talk about the building facing *Western Main Road* that stretches between the two. Here you'll find *SGI Distributors Ltd.*, some might call the business an Internet café that sells sandwiches, tools, *Diehard* batteries, and plumbing supplies, but it is so varied it's much more than just an Internet café.

The two rows of buildings at *Tardieu* house some of the best marine services in Chaguaramas. *Marine Warehouse* is a popular chandlery though they don't have large stock, their forte is ordering what you need from wherever it originates at prices to compete with and beat the largest marine chains such as *West Marine.*

Lincoln at *Chaguaramas Metal* works can fabricate whatever you need in aluminum or stainless steel and creates some really nice arches and bimini frames. *West Coast Fabricators* is another welding and fabrication outfit that specialize in aluminum work. Adian Gittens' *Gittens Engine Service* repairs outboards, diesels, and generators.

Lennox Stewart has an excellent woodworking shop that repairs and constructs whatever you need. They made me a very nice teak wheel adapter for my *Monitor* wind vane and at a very nice price.

Both *Superb Sails and Canvas and Alpha Upholstery and Canvas* can handle sail and canvas repairs as well as upholstery. *Kaban* specializes in fiberglass work as does *Philo's Fiberglass.* *Maxwill Inflatable and Bike* (VHF ch. 68) deals in inflatable boats and bicycles. If you need a SCUBA tank refill, want to rent some dive gear, or need some underwater work on your vessel, visit *Rick's Dive World.*

Calypso Marine Services, Ltd.

At the end of the little creek next to *Sweet Water* is *Calypso Marine Services, Ltd.* The guys here build some very nice fiberglass pirogues that people come from all over Trinidad, Tobago, and the Windwards to purchase. They can help you with fiberglass and outboard repairs.

Skinners

A hundred yards to the west of *Calypso Marine* is *Skinners Yard* where you'll find the large *Budget Marine* store, a place all cruisers come to know and love. A very well stocked chandlery, this *Budget* is second in size only to their huge store in *Simpson Bay*, Sint Maarten. *Budget* also sells *Mercury* outboards and the *Budget Marine Rigging* shop has a very good selection of rigging hardware and can handle any rigging problem you might have from swaging to splicing. *Budget* also has a dingy dock on the creek for your convenience.

Ace Sails is also located at *Skinners*. A large loft, Ace handles a lot of sail repair work as well as commercial canvas work. They cannot build a new sail (they prefer canvas work), but they can order a new sail from *Lee Sails*. If you prefer to do your own canvas work, you can pick up your supplies here.

Dynamite Marine is located at *Skinners*. They are a yacht management business that can handle all the various facets involved in repairing or rebuilding your vessel. *Dynamite* also builds plastic covers for your vessel while in any yard. Immediately next door is *Celestine's Marine Fabricators* for your aluminum or stainless needs.

If your new paint job needs lettering, *Sign Lab* can design a boat name and furnish it in vinyl or they can paint it on your boat. If you're having mechanical problems visit *HMP Motors*.

Boatbuilders *Formula III* (VHF ch. 68) have been constructing fiberglass boats for over a decade and have a line of power and sailboats. For outboard repairs visit Jeff Jonathon's *D&D Outboard Repair*.

Power Boats
In the yard *Power Boats* does not do any type of boat work, it must all be contracted out and the yard has some of the best contractors in Chaguaramas, they have to be good to continue to work at *Power Boats*. Some of the contractors have shops on the premises, others don't, but you can reach them all through the *Power Boats* office.

In the long contractor's building in the NE corner of the yard (not all contractors are located here), near *Skinner's Yard*, is the *Boater's Shop* (VHF ch. 72), a small chandlery. Although they are small they carry almost anything you'll require during your haul-out, and if they don't have it, they'll get if for you. Next door, *Caribbean Marine* are AC and DC electrical, battery, starter and alternator, and diesel injector specialists.

Here too is *Fortress Woodworking*, whose name implies their field of expertise, all manner of woodworking (in basic and exotic woods) and teak decks. Next door is a small shop set up for the yachties to work on their projects. Here you'll find tables, electricity, and a vise.

Barrow Sails (VHF ch. 68) is upstairs in the contractor's building and can computer design and cut out your new sail (for vessels to 60') and a VERY good price. *Barrow Sails* also repairs sails and does all manner of canvas work. Next door is the *Upholstery Shop* (VHF ch. 72) where owner David Mahabir will replace all of your interior and exterior cushions, you can even go to Port of Spain to pick out the fabric.

Bayfront is *Ship's Carpenter*, specializing in marine woodwork and complete rebuilds. In the back of the same building is *Yacht Maintenance Services* providing hull painting and glass repairs of all types.

Over on the west side of the yard is another building where you'll find Mark de Gannes, an excellent fabricator and welder who can also repair some prop shafts. Here too is Ian Keiser, an *OMC* mechanic and the shop of Lawrence Placid, another good mechanic.

If you want somebody to handle all the details of your yard work so you can enjoy your time on the hard, visit *First Mate* between the bayfront and the office.

Peakes
Heading west on the *Western Main Road* from *Power Boats* is the *Royal Bank* with its 24-hour *ATM*. On the south side of the road is the *Caribbean Fisheries Training and Development Institute*.

Just east of the entrance to *Peakes*, on the north side of the *Western Main Road*, is SSL, a huge chandlery, *Exclusive Car Rental* (634-2915), and an internet café.

Peakes is home to a large chandlery with a tremendous selection of items as one might expect, everything from teak to stainless, and if they don't have it, rest assured they can order it for you. *Coating Specialists* are located at *Peakes* as well as GOMES (*Good Old Marine Equipment Specialists*), a used gear store, and *Fluid Hose and Coupling*, ideal for hoses and couplings (hence the name). For the best in wood repairs or remodeling, visit *John Francois Woodworking*.

Peakes has a good supply of experienced workers and services on hand to do whatever work your vessel requires. The award winning *Calypso Marine Canvas* is also here to assist you with your canvas needs. *KNJ Marine Services* is here and they almost any job you can present.

In *Peakes'* large service building is *Propeller and Marine Services* (prop repairs and replacement, prop shaft repair, and MIG and TIG welding), *Al's Machine Shop* (for welding, fabrication, hard to find stainless fasteners, and prop shaft repairs for shafts over 6" and to 40' in length), *Ammaco* are welders and fabricators and are shaft and rudder specialists.

Upstairs is *Billy's Rigging*. Owner Bill Wray can handle all the normal types of rigging repairs as well as rod rigging and the x-ray of fittings, and can provide *Lloyd's* approved surveys. Also upstairs is *T&T Marine Electrical* (VHF ch. 68) who can handle your electrical repair needs including the rebuilding of starters and alternators.

Also located at *Peakes* is Jonas Romell's *Trinidad Rigging*, a full service rigging shop with lots and lots of spare parts on hand.

Mariner's Haven

Mariner's Haven is fronted on the road by a large concrete wall topped with concertina wire. You'll find a lot of marine services located here including *Echo Marine*, the place to go for solar panels, watermakers, electronic nav instruments, anchors and chain (even stainless steel chain), dinghies, antifouling paint, *Kubota* generators, refrigeration systems, *Profurl* systems, and oodles and oodles of accessories. *Echo Marine* has a stainless steel and aluminum workshop on site and also manufactures their own line of quality watermakers, ECH2O Tec (www. watermakers.net).

On the opposite side of *Mariner's Haven*, *Marc One Marine Supplies* handles everything from fiberglass supplies to lexan, inverters, power tools, fuel filters, and they are dealers for *Nannidiesel*. Also, they deliver. On the west side of the dry dock is *Eswil*, the place to pick up hydraulic hoses, fittings, lubricants, and pumps. Also on site is *High Tech Fluid Power*.

Industrial Marine Services (IMS)

The *IMS* yard can handle the average haul-out job including paint and fiberglass repairs. Their popular *Galley Restaurant* serves up breakfast, lunch, and dinner with happy hours every Friday at 1700 and the occasional movie on Thursdays at 1900. *IMS* manufactures their own brand of paint, for more info speak to Glenn in the office.

Internet Access

Internet access in the area of *Chaguaramas Bay* is plentiful, most marinas have some sort of internet access point. At *CrewsInn* you can get online at the *Mariner's Office* in the *Shipwright's Building*. At *Tropical Marina*, the *2-M International Calling Center* is an internet café where you can also place international phone calls.

Located in the building between *Coral Cove* and *Tardieu* you'll find *SGI Distributors Ltd.*, an internet café that sells sandwiches, tools, *Diehard* batteries, and plumbing supplies. *Ankh Internet Café* has an office at *Tardieu Marine*; they also sell DVDs.

At *Power Boats*, just in from the dinghy dock by the lift area you'll see a flight of stairs above *Ship's Carpenter* that will take you up to the *Nautilus Internet Café* where you can check your email and surf the net to your heart's content.

Peakes has *Wi-fi* that covers the docks and part of the boatyard. *Internet Café* has an office here and across the street *Royal Bank* has two internet stations. In the small row of shops west of the *Royal Bank* is a small Internet café. *IMS* has an internet access station in their office.

Provisions

Whether you need groceries for the week, or if you need case lots to fill the larder for an ocean crossing, you'll find what you need at a good price in Trinidad.

Most marinas have small stores on site, the biggest and best, and my personal favorite, is *Hi-Lo* at *CrewsInn* (open daily 0900-2100 and on Sundays from 0800-1600). *Dockside Foodmart* at *Power Boats* is another well-stocked and popular market. As I mention in the section on TTYC, there is a huge *Hi-Lo* by *West Mall*, a maxi-taxi ride away from Chaguaramas.

Jesse Jame's *Members Only Maxi Taxi* makes weekly shopping outings to places like *Price Mart, Hi-Lo, Tru-Valu*, and the Saturday morning market in Port of Spain.

Dining

All of the marinas around *Chaguaramas Bay* have restaurants on site and it's fun to explore each one in turn and return to the ones you like best.

My favorite is *The Lighthouse*, upstairs at *CrewsInn* above *Hi-Lo*, probably the finest restaurant on the bay (with the best view) and one that will not disappoint. Also located at *CrewsInn* is *Café del Mare* featuring Italian cuisine.

At *Tropical Marine* you can dine at the *Wheel House Pub*, a very popular hangout that is open daily for lunch and dinner with good seafood and steaks, pool tables, and live music on occasion.

At *Coral Cove* you can enjoy *Joe's Pizza*, the best pizza parlor around, serving great pizza and Italian foods, a must for the visiting cruiser. Nearby is *Café Feel Oh*, open for lunch and dinner with a reservation.

At *Sweet Water Marina* you'll find *The Lure* restaurant, a very nice place owned by a couple of sports fishing devotees.

One of the most popular restaurants is *Sails*, located bayfront at *Power Boats*. Inside is their air-conditioned sports bar with a huge TV for a front row seat at the latest must-see sporting event. Sunday nights are for BBQ and pan music, quite the combination. *Sails* also has live music on Saturdays and a DJ on Wednesdays and Fridays. Also at *Power Boats* is the *Roti Hut*, a do-not-miss eatery serving breakfast and fantastic rotis.

Located at *Peakes*, *The Bight* restaurant is a very popular hangout for cruisers. You can dine outside and enjoy the view of the docks and bay, or you can amble inside to enjoy the air-conditioning. The menu is varied, economical, and the food excellent.

IMS has an open-air restaurant, *The Galley*, offering local cuisine for lunch and European fare for dinner.

If you want a quick lunch, there are a number of vendors located between *Peakes* and *Budget Marine* along the *Western Main Road* serving all manner of yummy local dishes.

Chaguaramas Boardwalk

In *William's Bay*, Chart TRI-9, is the new *Chaguaramas Boardwalk* chock full of vendor's huts and with free Wi-fi. Look for future renovations of Chaguarmas.

Gaspar Grande

Waypoints:

Gaspar Grande Island- .1 nm NE of marina
10º 39.80' N, 61º 38.90' W

Gaspar Grande Island, originally belonged to Don Gaspar de Percin, hence its name, it was originally called Gasparee. Governor Chacon once built forts on the island to defend the island as a last stand, in fact, you can view the remains of one of them at *Bombshell Bay*. *Fort Apodaca*, named after the Spanish commander of the fleet that was sent to protect Trinidad, sits atop the hill above Point Baleine. When the Spaniards surrendered in 1797, Gaspar Grande was the focus of a lengthy dispute over which country, Spain or England, actually owned the island. Shortly thereafter a whaling station was established on Gaspar Grande, and later cotton was grown here. There was an old guesthouse at Point Baleine at the western tip of the island where Noel Coward wrote his novel *Point Valeine*. Point Baleine was once home to a whaling station.

Today the island is home to several vacation homes and visitors can explore the *Gasparee Caves* at Point Baleine, said to have once been used by pirates. Walk up from the path from the jetty to the white and yellow house where you'll find a guide and once in the cave, steps lead down into a cavern where you'll see stalagmites, stalactites, and fruit bats. At high tide the caves fill with seawater. There are ferries to Gaspar Grande Island leaving the dock at *Mariners Haven* that run about every two hours. For special occasions you can catch a water taxi from *Power Boats* or *Crew'sInn*.

Navigational Information

On the eastern shore of Gaspar Grande Island, just south of *Bombshell Bay* (as shown on Chart TRI-7), you'll find the *Bay View Beach Resort and Marina*, once called *Fantasy Island*. A waypoint at 10º 39.80' N, 61º 39.80' W, will place you approximately 0.1 of a mile northeast of the entrance to the marina. Head into towards the beach and turn to port keeping the end of the jetty to port. The beach is fenced off and the entrance may appear narrower than it really is. Dockage is stern or bow-to and you must call ahead for a slip assignment on VHF ch. 68. The marina can accommodate approximately 12 vessels.

What You Will Find Ashore

The *Bay View Marina* has improved over the last decade. Today dockage is economical and there is RO water and electricity available at every slip along with showers, a laundry, a swimming pool, cable TV, a small grocery store, and a restaurant and bar. The ferry to the mainland is free for registered guests of the marina.

Winn's Bay

Waypoints:
Gaspar Grande Island, Winn's Bay- ¼ nm SW of 10° 39.55' N, 61° 39.65' W

Navigational Information

Heading to the southern shore of Gaspar Grande Island, you'll find *Winn's Bay*, a pleasant anchorage marked by a large fig tree situated on the small rock lying off the point. As shown on Chart TRI-8, a waypoint at 10° 39.55' N, 61° 39.65' W, will place you approximately ¼ mile southwest of the entrance. Head in towards the bay between the off-lying rock and the point of land to the west of it. The rock is very conspicuous, there is a small stand of fig trees on the rock, and on weekends there's usually a dozen or so people on the rock fishing.

The water will shallow towards the northern end of the bay so don't head too far in, keep an eye on the depthsounder. The wind can be fluky here, as in so many of the anchorages in Trinidad, especially the ones along the northern coast with their surrounding mountains. You might wish to set a second anchor or set a line ashore. The bay is surrounded by several vacation homes and there are no facilities ashore here. In moderate southeast winds it can get bit rolly in here.

South of Gaspar Grande Island are The Diego Islands (TRI-9), Carrera Island and Cronstadt Island (sometimes called Creteau or Begorrat Island), which were once known as the Long Islands, a holiday resort. Cronstadt Island is now a bayrite ore production station (bayrite ore is a product needed in the oilfields).

Bayview Marina, Gaspar Grande

The ore is brought in and crushed and stored on the island before shipping out. Carrera Island is a hard labor prison that was originally constructed in 1877. Like San Francisco's legendary Alcatraz, nobody has escaped from Carrera Island.

If you'd care to check your compass, you'll be happy to know that you can do it just off Gaspar Grande Island. Line up the light at Point Baleine on the western tip of Gaspar Grande and the light on

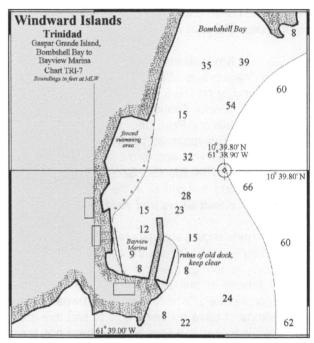

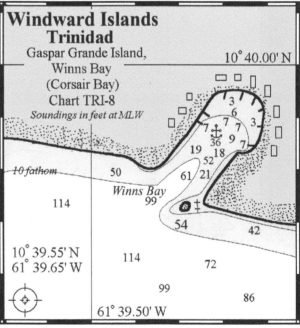

Teteron Rock off Cannings Point, and that line will be true north.

Five Islands

Waypoints:
Five Islands- ¼ nm NNW of
10° 40.00' N, 61° 36.00' W

The Five Islands, originally the Diego Martin Islands and named after the shoreside community, is a wonderful anchorage that will let you get away from all the hustle and bustle in Chaguaramas into a serene, peaceful spot without getting too far away.

Navigational Information

From *Chaguaramas Bay*, as shown on Chart TRI-6 and continuing on TRI-9, head south between Point Gourde and Gaspar Grande Island. Pass between the Diego Islands and Point Gourde (TRI-9) and make your way to a waypoint at 10° 40.00'N, 61° 36.00' W, which places you approximately ¼ mile north/northwest of the Five Islands. Simply head in toward Caledonia Island and anchor in the lee of the islands wherever your draft allows and you feel comfortable.

Most charts show a shallow area labeled *Foul* lying approximately 1½ miles southwest of Five Islands. I'm told by a former member of a marine rescue unit, of having to pull several boats off a shallow rock approximately ½ mile south/southwest of the Five Islands. I have not been able to find this rock, perhaps it is indeed that *Foul* area, perhaps not, but if you traverse the area west-south of Five Islands, use the utmost caution.

What You Will Find Ashore

Nelson Island, sometimes called Neilson's Island, is Trinidad's version of Ellis Island in New York. Between 1845 and 1917, thousands of East Indians were kept on Nelson Island before beginning their indenture on the sugar plantations of Trinidad. Nearby Pelican Island and Rock Island, the small islet just west of Nelson Island, were quarantine stations. The islands are great for exploring with small concrete buildings here and there, and steps leading into the interior of the islands.

Carenage Bay and *TTSA*

Waypoints:
Carenage Bay- ½ nm SE of *TTSA*
10° 41.40' N, 61° 36.50' W

The moorings at the *Trinidad Tobago Sailing Association* (*TTSA*) are a popular spot for cruisers, however powerboats are not permitted here. You'll be away from Chaguaramas in a small bay with little traffic, and yet you're only a short walk or bus ride away from the facilities surrounding *Chaguaramas Bay. Carenage Bay,* and the small town of the same name, were named for the fact that Spanish captains would careen their ships here so that the crews could scrape their bottoms. The settlement of Carenage almost became a ghost town after the Spanish departed in 1797. When the Americans arrived during WW II and claimed the Chaguaramas peninsula, the residents there were relocated to Carenage when the town earned a seedy reputation thanks to the servicemen that came there for rum and women.

Navigational Information

From *Chaguaramas Bay*, as shown on Chart TRI-6 and continuing on TRI-9, head south between Point Gourde and Gaspar Grande Island. Keeping

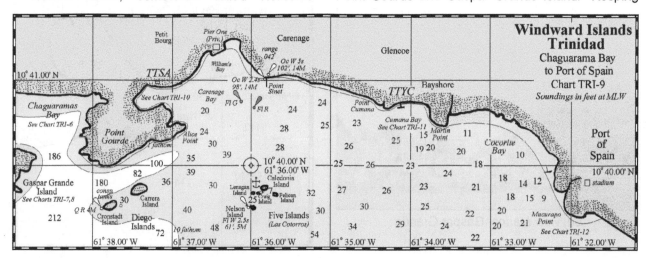

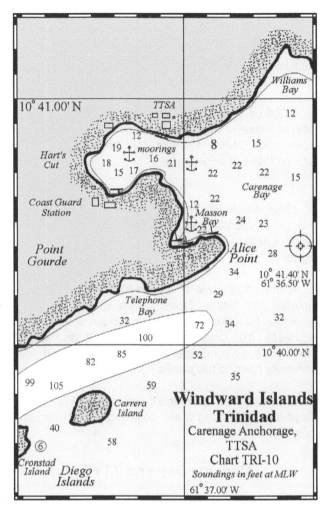

Windward Islands Trinidad
Carenage Anchorage,
TTSA
Chart TRI-10
Soundings in feet at MLW
61° 37.00' W

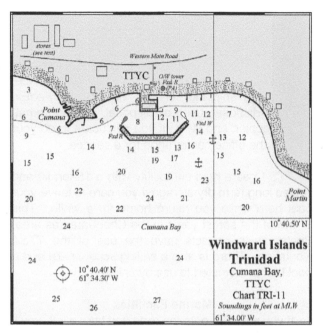

Windward Islands Trinidad
Cumana Bay,
TTYC
Chart TRI-11
Soundings in feet at MLW
61° 34.00' W

between the Diego Islands and Point Gourde (TRI-9), follow the shoreline to Alice Point to a waypoint shown on Chart TRI-10. A waypoint at 10° 41.40' N, 61° 36.50' W, places you approximately ½ mile southeast of the mooring field off *TTSA*. *TTSA* maintains moorings for visiting cruisers (sailboats only; please arrange a mooring in advance, just don't show up and pick up a mooring, you can contact *TTSA* on VHF ch. 68) and they are often full, especially during *Carnival*. If you don't care to pick up a mooring, you can anchor southeast-south of the fleet of moored boats, or behind them, between the mooring field and the beach on the mainland.

Several boats can often be seen anchored in *Masson Bay*, thought there's sometimes a barge anchored against the shore. If you anchor south of *TTSA* please don't block the *Coast Guard* docks.

If you anchor east of the moorings, it's a good idea to use two anchors and make sure they are set well as the

holding is poor to fair here. If you can pick up a mooring, please go ashore and register as soon as possible.

When the wind goes into the southeast and picks up it gets a bit choppy in the Carenage, nothing really dangerous, just uncomfortable, however if the wind were to be forecast as extremely strong, I'd certainly move to Five Islands or back to *Chaguaramas Bay*.

Hart's Cut, named after a police superintendent named Hart, was created in the 1856 to link Carenage to *Chaguaramas Bay* and was 15' wide and only 4' deep. This cut was designed for Trinidadian fisherman, saving them the long row to windward around Point Gourde

What You Will Find Ashore

On the road east of *TTSA*, and across from *Aikane*, is the *Chaguaramas Military History and Aviation Museum*, a very interesting place, where you'll learn of Trinidad's role in the wars of the 20th century. Inside you'll discover that during WW II over 80 allied ships were sunk off Trinidad by German U-boats, that Chaguaramas had a submarine net stretched across its entrance, and that there were numerous Allied bases on the island during the war years. Besides the military relics and exhibits, the museum also offers historical data on the British years on the island, the history of the Trinidad police, and even pirates are mentioned here.

TTSA

Your mooring fees allow you use of the facilities as well as water that you'll either have to jerry-jug or tie up to the dock briefly to fill up with a hose. *TTSA* offers showers, phones, a workshop, water, ice, fax sending shipping services via *UPS* or *FedEx*, garbage disposal, used oil disposal, a Laundromat, a photocopier, and *Wi-fi*. If you don't care to do your laundry the office can arrange for a service.

TTSA has a haul out facility with a 15-ton lift and limited long term dry storage if you care to leave your boat here while you return home for a while. This is one of the safest yards in the Chaguaramas area. Boaters with projects have the use of the *TTSA* workshop. There is also a sailing school here and a pool that is restricted to use by children.

Marine Facilities

If you walk out onto the road and take a left, you'll come to the *Chaguaramas Bay* area with all of its amenities. If you don't feel like walking, catch a maxi-taxi.

If you take a right on the road you'll find *La Soufriere Maritime*, a marina that focuses solely on sport fishing. If you need any sort of prop repair or replacement you'll be happy to know that *Caribbean Propellers* is located here.

A bit further east is *Aikane and Catamaran Village*, who store and repair catamarans (although they have no slips you can still live aboard while you're hauled out and being repaired).

Just a bit further east is *Bowen Marine*, a huge building, where you can have your outboard repaired or a new power boat built. In the same building you'll find *Marine Mechanix* who specialize in general marine repairs. All of these buildings that you see here are old Naval facilities dating back to World War II.

Next to *Bowen Marine* is the *Chaguaramas Hotel and Convention Center.* On the road behind the hotel you'll find *Marine Safety Equipment* where you can get your life raft serviced or purchase a new one. They are dealers for *RFD, Elliot, Zodiac,* and *Avon*.

Further down the road is *Pier 1*, with a restaurant, bar, and a pool. Once a marina, this is now more of a party palace, and believe me, if there's one thing Trinis like to do it is PARTY!

Provisions

For information on provisioning in this area, read the previous section on Chaguaramas for detailed instructions.

Internet Access

TTSA offers Wi-fi in their mooring area and office. Next to *Bowen Marine* is the *Chaguaramas Hotel and Convention Center,* a rebuilt WW II military barracks, with an Internet access site.

Dining

TTSA is home to the *Spinnaker Bar & Restaurant*, a popular yachtie hangout with Monday night pot-lucks, weekly trivia contests, and occasional movie nights.

In the small cove at the head of the bay is the *Trinidad and Tobago Coast Guard Station*. The CG dock may look like a small marina, but rest assured it is private. The long building on shore at the head of the bay is the *Anchorage*, another party palace that is generally open to the public.

To the east of *TTSA* you'll come to a *KFC* as well as several little food stalls selling good homemade local dishes

Cumana Bay and TTYC

Waypoints:
Cumana Bay- ¼ nm SW of TTYC
10° 40.40' N, 61° 34.30' W

As shown on Chart TRI-9, and in detail on Chart TRI-11, *Cumana Bay* and the *Trinidad and Tobago Yacht Club* (*TTYC*), offer a very good alternative to *Chaguaramas Bay*. In fact, before the explosion of marine facilities in *Chaguaramas Bay*, *TTYC* was the only place around for visiting yachts, it's been in existence for over 50 years.

Navigational Information
From Chaguaramas, as shown on Chart TRI-6 and continuing on TRI-9, head south between Point Gourde and Gaspar Grande Island. Then pass between Carrera Island and Point Gourde (TRI-9) and take up a heading of approximately 95° to a waypoint at 10° 40.40' N, 61° 34.30' W (TRI-11), which will place you approximately ¼ mile south/southwest of *TTYC* in Cumana Bay. From the waypoint head in towards the jetty and anchor either south or southeast of the

jetty. If you are planning to get a slip at *TTYC*, give them a call on VHF 68 for directions. If you're wishing to fill-up with fuel, the fuel dock is on the western side of the main dock by the red-roofed restaurant. Use caution entering here though as the shallows stretch out a pretty good distance from shore, but drafts of 6' and less should not have a problem. A good landmark to help you find *TTYC* is the orange and white striped tower with a fixed red light atop sitting just behind *TTYC*.

What You Will Find Ashore
TTYC

TTYC has diesel and gas, slips that include water, electricity (110 volt and 220 volt, 60 cycle), and cable TV. Although *TTYC* is a private organization, getting a slip makes you a temporary member of the yacht club and allows you to park a vehicle in their wellprotected lot. The *Yacht Club* also has showers, phones, a laundry, email service, a fuel dock with diesel and gasoline, and a lot of local flavor. S*kipper's Restaurant* is a popular hangout for yachties as well as Trinis as is the *Yacht Club Bar*.

Marine Facilities

There are a lot of shoreside facilities here for the visiting yachtsman, though if you need serious work done on your boat, you have to go to Chaguaramas. The marina can arrange for somebody to clean your boat, wax the hull, and even scrub your bottom, and they'll also assist you in acquiring any sort of help that you may need. Just speak to Joe Ramnath in the office, he's very knowledgeable and friendly, a real help to the cruising visitor at *TTYC*. And by the way, as you walk down the dock to the office, don't forget to say hello to Kaiso, the blue and gold Macaw in his huge cage by the office.

Marine Facilities

If you head west on the main road you will soon come to *Tagos Marine Limited*, a mechanical repair shop, dealers for *Cat* and *Perkins*. Nearby is *LP Marine*, a chandlery that is also a dealer for *Volvo Penta, Kohler,* and *Johnson Pumps*, they can fix just about any pump you bring them. Next door is *The Tackle Shop*, a very nice fishing supply store with top of the line rods, reels, and accessories. They also have a *Post Office* and courier service on site. Across the street is *Mohammed's Hardware* as well as *Transocean Coatings and Antifouling* and *Berger Marine Coatings*.

To the east of *TTYC*, just past the huge *West Mall* you'll find the huge *Peake Hardware* (they monitor VHF ch. 69). They are agents for *Johnson outboards, Stalok, Harken, Jabsco,* and *Crosby* as well as being an air-conditioning manufacturer.

Provisions

Within walking distance are several places to dine, pick up some groceries, ship a package, and get medical assistance. To the west on the main road are several facilities in a strip mall including a bank with an *ATM,* a nice *Hi-Lo* supermarket, the *Glencoe Pharmacie*, and a medical clinic. *Hi-Lo* will deliver your groceries to *TTYC* for you (if your purchase is large enough). There is another, larger, *Hi-Lo* to the east of *TTYC* next to *West Mall*.

Jesse James will also pick you up here for his weekly shopping trips (the best way to shop). Call Jesse's *Members Only* maxi-taxi service on VHF ch. 16 or 68.

Dining

Skippers Restaurant located at *TTYC* offers excellent seafood, steak, and burgers for lunch and dinner. The first Friday of each month is Arabic night.

If you walk out to the *Western Main Road* past the guard shack (*TTYC* has EXCELLENT security), take a left and a hundred yards away is *Linda's La Café Francais*....what can I say? Fresh bread, croissants, baguettes, all sorts of delicious baked goodies, you can spend a ton here and put on just about that much weight as well. Linda also has tables if you care to sit down and relax while munching on a *pain chocolate*.

A bit further to the west of *TTYC*, in the small strip mall, there is a nice Chinese restaurant, *Imperial Gardens* serving a daily lunch buffet with an extraordinary Wednesday night dinner buffet. Also located here are a couple of fast food take-out places (*Churchs, Captain D's, Pizza Boys, Donut Boys, Wok n' Roll*), and another French restaurant and bakery. Across from *Hi-Lo* is the *Arabian Grill*.

About a mile to the east of *TTYC*, is the three-story *West Mall* (formerly *Westmoorings Mall*), a great place to visit and shop. Here you'll find several bookstores, a gym, a dentist's office, a good fabric shop, many clothing and shoe stores, a 1-hour photo lab, and a great food court. Next door is the new huge *Hi-Lo Supermarket*. There are two machines at the *ATM* inside the *Royal Bank* facing the road, which will allow you to withdraw cash in either TT or US dollars. If you don't feel like walking here, just cross the road from *TTYC* and climb aboard a maxi-taxi. The Westmoorings area was once a swamp that was filled in during the 1940s. Just past the mall, on the north side of the road, is a hospital.

If you're staying at *TTYC* and have friends from back home visiting, there is a great little guesthouse not far from *TTYC*. *Tammy's Bed & Breakfast* is in Glencoe, the neighborhood across the Western Main Road about 1 block from *TTYC* (29 *Strathavan Rd.*, Glencoe). Tammy offers daily and weekly rates, free transportation for your guests, and she even monitors VHF ch. 68. You can phone Tammy at 637-3707.

Port of Spain

Waypoints:
Port of Spain- ¼ nm SW of Grier Channel
10° 38.10' N, 61° 33.40' W

Sprawled out between the *Gulf of Paria* and the mountain range to the north, Port of Spain, the capital of Trinidad since 1757, is the very heart of Trinidad, the cultural, economic, and social center of the island. The majestic twin *Central Bank* towers, that are landmarks along the waterfront also grace the back of TT dollar bills. At night the view is dazzling, twinkling lights dot the hills above the city from Carenage in the northwest to Arima in the east. Port of Spain is quite cosmopolitan, with over 1.2 million inhabitants living in a melange of different cultures spread about the surrounding suburbs.

Navigational Information
There is one anchorage in Port of Spain, just off the St. Vincent Jetty. The wreck-strewn shallows just south of it offer a fair degree of protection in southeast winds and the holding is good in mud. The main problem here is theft. Be sure to lock your dingy up here at night. Many cruisers use this anchorage as a base for *Carnival*, it's convenient of course, but the security at Chaguaramas, lacking as it may be at times, is better than in Port of Spain. You'll feel far more vulnerable here, but don't let that dissuade you, taking good security measures, locking your dinghy and your hatches, will usually suffice. Don't leave anything on deck or in the cockpit that you don't want to lose. And a better idea would be not to leave

the boat unattended at night, this means somebody's going to have to miss J'Ouvert.

Heading for Port of Spain from Chaguaramas or *TTYC*, you can parallel the shore, but you'll have to stay a good two miles or more offshore; the inshore waters are shoal and littered with wrecks that nobody has charted with any degree of accuracy. The waypoint I give is for the seaward end of *Grier Channel*, but you can just as easily pick up the channel between green buoys "3" and "7" if visibility is good and you don't mind a bit of shallow water, anywhere from 9'-15'.

As shown on Chart TRI-12, a waypoint 10° 38.10' N, 61° 33.40 W, will place you approximately ¼ mile west/southwest of the entrance to *Grier Channel*, just outside the first buoys. When approaching the port remember that it is a commercial facility and give the large ships and tugs the right of way. Proceed down the channel towards *King's Wharf* and turn to starboard once past R "8." Work your way to the southeastern tip of the wharf where you'll see the St. Vincent Jetty off your bow. Anchor off the jetty in about 12'-30' of water. A lot of freighters and other commercial vessels anchor here, the holding is good, but it can be crowded with larger vessels at times. As you enter the *Grier Channel*, bear in mind that you might encounter a southeasterly current, an eddy of the northward flowing current in the *Gulf of Paria*. This eddy may be as strong as ½ knot on the flood and up to 1½ knots on the ebb.

Just south of the *Grier Channel* is the *Sea Lots Channel*, which is used primarily by commercial fishing vessels. The small harbor at the end of the channel offers good protection if needed, but it will be crowded if a major storm threatens (better to go to Puerto La Cruz or *Laguna Grande* in Venezuela). As you enter the harbour as shown on the chart, R "10" is missing, but the concrete piling remains. You can anchor in the southern portion of the bay, between the large ships that lie wrecked on the shore and the mangroves. Security is important here as in Port of Spain.

What You Will Find Ashore
There is a lot to see and do in Port of Spain, and I suggest that the best way to see it is to stay at *TTYC* or Chaguaramas and catch a maxi-taxi into town.

So where do we begin? An entire guide could be written on Port of Spain itself and I can in no way show

Distinctive twin towers, Port of Spain waterfront

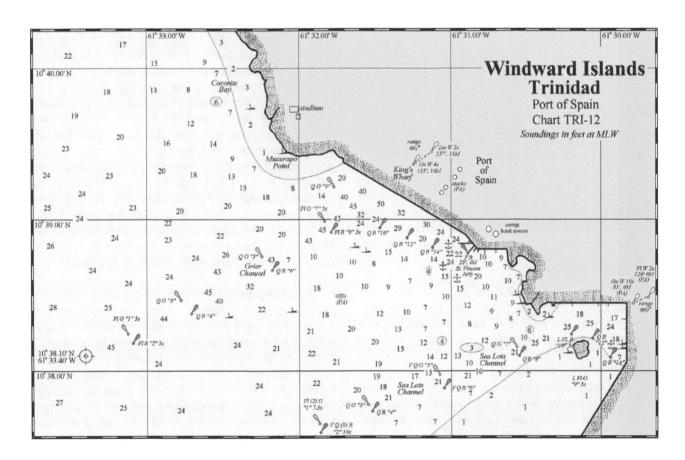

you everything here so I'll just touch on the highlights, anyway, exploring and discovery are some of the biggest joys of cruising, right? Go out and explore, keep your wallet in your front pocket gentleman, and ladies keep your money on you, leave nothing in your purse that you don't wish to lose. This is not a warning folks, think of it as precautions that you should take as you would in any large city, this is certainly not an indictment of the people of Port of Spain.

Customs and Immigration

Port of Spain is primarily a commercial port, visited daily by freighters, tankers, and ferries. Few yachts anchor here for any length of time except during *Carnival* when they are rafted together on the waterfront. Yachts are advised to clear in at Chaguaramas, it is far easier on you and on the *Customs* officials. If you are having an *Immigration* problem, their main office is located on *Frederick Street* in Port of Spain.

Marine Facilities

Located on *Charles St.* in Port of Spain, *Marine Consultants* sells all manner of nautical guides, charts, and other publications. But they are not limited to being a nautical bookstore, they also sell and service life rafts and inflatables and are dealers for *Viking, Avon, Switlik, Tideland*, and *Beaufort*. They also carry synthetic and wire rope and accessories, do safety inspections, and sell and service emergency gear such as flares, life jackets, EPIRBS, GPS, and other electronics. They also provide a compass adjusting service, hard to find in the Eastern Caribbean.

If you need a hardware store *William H. Scott* is located east of the city on *Independence Square* and is very well stocked. A bit further out of town to the east is the huge *Bagwansingh's*. Do not try to walk here-you will need to take a taxi as the road goes through some less-than-safe sections of Port of Spain; a taxi fare will cost you about US$40 each way from Port of Spain.

Provisions

Downtown Port of Spain is not rife with supermarkets, the best tend to lie outside the city such as the *Hi-Lo* at *West Mall*.

Dining

Small food vendors can be found all over town, especially in the St. James area, where you can pick up all manner of Trini treats such as rotis or doubles.

For more traditional dining atop the *Kapok Hotel* is the *Tiki Village* with the best view of Port of Spain. Located near *Queen's Park Savannah* on *Saddle Road*, the restaurant features a delicious mix Chinese/Polynesian fare. Not to be outdone, the *Hilton Hotel,* northeast of the *Queen's Park Savannah*, is home to a delightful restaurant with a great view of the bay.

A favorite American restaurant, *TGIF,* is located on the southern side of *Queen's Park Savannah* and is exactly like their American cousins in layout, ambiance, and menu items.

If you crave French fare, visit *A la Bastilee*, on *Ariapita Avenue* at *De Verteuil Street*. For Italian, find your way to *Il Colosseo* on *Rust Street* in St. Claire. *Jenny's Chinese Restaurant and Steak House* **on** *Cipriani Boulevard* is one of the more elegant eateries in Port of Spain, this is not the place to wear shorts and T-shirts.

Discovering Port of Spain

If you take a maxi taxi downtown, you can get off anywhere you like or at the main station, *Citygate*, across from the *Port Authority* at *Kings Wharf*. This is also where you can take the ferry to Tobago if you'd like. If you are driving a rental car, your best bet is to park in a pay-lot, there's one on the left just past the twin *Central Bank* towers. If you park on the streets, you can get towed away very quickly. Heading into Port of Spain you'll pass *West Mall*, and just about a mile further on the road will split, you need to take the left hand branch, the *Winston Road* turnoff, that circles back under the right hand branch which goes straight into St. James. The left-hand road (*Winston Road*) takes you along the shoreline by the stadium and into Port of Spain and the palm tree lined promenade in front of the *Port Authority*. If you continue on this road you will eventually come to the *Uriah Butler Highway* which is the road south to the *Caroni Swamp*, Chaguanas, and San Fernando.

If you decide to head into St. James, you'll enter the "city that never sleeps." There the street vendors are open 24 hours and people stroll the street all night. A lot of local men come here to meet local women and party all night long. St. James was originally a sugar plantation and the flavor today definitely is East Indian. As the *Western Main Road* passes through here, you'll find the sidewalks are wall to wall fast food establishments, bars, lottery houses, and music stores. There are numerous small stalls selling everything from East Indian foodstuffs to shoes, ice cream, colorful t-shirts, leather goods, and locally made crafts. Visitors should pay a visit to *Smokey and Bunty's*, the local bar named for the nicknames of the owners. To the east of St. James is Laventille, a poorer section of town, that is known for being the place where Spanish astronomer Don Cosmos Damien Churruca set up an observatory, the first in the New World.

The harbor at Port of Spain was dredged to handle deep draft ships in 1935. Prior to that the ships lay at anchor and passengers and cargo were ferried ashore. Directly across the street from the port is *Independence Square*, built on reclaimed swampland in 1816 by Baron Shack, who imported trees from Venezuela to line the road. Named *Independence Square* in 1962 when Trinidad and Tobago gained their independence, it was formerly called Marine Square, and during WW II, gained notoriety as the Gaza Strip. At that time dozens of night clubs lined Wrightson Road, complete with booze and strippers, and U.S. servicemen would party here all night long, even though nightly raids were common.

Nearby *Frederick Street* is the heart of Port of Spain shopping. Many Trinis have their clothes hand made and buy their fabric here. Lining the streets in this area are dozens of fabric shops, as well as clothing and shoe shops, a lot of shoe shops. Sherry, owner of *Sherry's Laundry* at *Tardieu Marine* in Chaguaramas, is a good seamstress and can make a shirt, dress, shorts, or pair of pants for you. Come here to buy our fabric and then take it to Sherry, you will not be dissatisfied. *Jimmy Aboud's* is probably the most popular fabric store in the area although even the smaller ones deserve a look.

Just off *Frederick St.*, by the Arthur Cipriani statue, is the *Drag Brothers Mall*, a dozen or so small leather shops where if you don't find what you want, they'll make it for you. A bit further east is the *Cathedral of the Immaculate Conception,* built in 1836 (started in 1820 and completed in 1836). At the corner of Frederick St. and Keate St. is the *National Museum and Art Gallery*. Built in 1892, the museum houses an extensive collection of exhibits as well as a special section on Carnival and Pan Music.

Port of Spain has its share of forts for you to visit. In Laventille, across from the Catholic church, sits

Fort Chacon, built by Spanish Governor Chacon in 1770. High above Laventille sits *Fort Picton*, another one of the oldest forts on the island. Named after British Governor Picton, it was built in 1797, when the British took over, and has the best view from atop the hills above Port of Spain.

Fort George was built by British Governor Sir Thomas Hislop in 1805 to further expand the protection Port of Spain. The British were fearful that the Spanish would yet retaliate for the British takeover in 1797 or that the French, whose fleet was nearby, might be planning their own invasion. Today you can still see the original cannon, dungeon, cannon balls and other items that the soldiers used. On *South Quay*, east of *King's Wharf*, is *Fort St. Andres,* a wooden fort built in 1787. Behind the large Victorian building on South Quay stands the old Port of Spain lighthouse, it looks out of place inland in the middle of a traffic island. The lighthouse is the Trini version of the *Leaning Tower Pisa* as it leans 5° due to the thundering traffic that passes by 24 hours a day.

Downtown you'll find the *Queen's Park Savannah*, the heart of Port of Spain, the center of its culture, and the focus of *Carnival*. Once part of a sugar estate owned by the Peschier family, the area was sold to the city in 1817 with the exception of the small family cemetery that still lies in the middle of the *Savannah* and which is still used by family members. Attempts were made to convert the area into a housing area in 1890, but vigorous opposition quashed those plans. But for decades after many more attempts were made to use parts of the *Savannah* for this reason or that, but the city planners would not give in.

Today Trinis flock to the park during all seasons. In February for *Carnival*, in the summer for kite-flying, and on weekends for family outings. The streets lining the Savannah are home to seven of the most beautiful architectural masterpieces on the island. You'll gaze in awe at what is known as the *Magnificent Seven*, seven buildings of Scottish, Moorish, Spanish, French, and Victorian roots.

Next to the Savannah is the *Botanical Gardens* and the *Emperor Valley Zoo*. The *Botanical Gardens* house the official residences of the President and the Prime Minister. The gardens were laid out in 1820 by Governor Woodford and David Lockhart, the first curator of the gardens and who is buried in the small cemetery on the grounds (along with many former governors of the island), *God's Acre* as it's known.

The collection of native and non-native trees is impressive, and in a grove of palm trees, an Australian wallaby is buried. The wallaby was a pet of the Prince of Wales and died while the Prince was on a trip to Trinidad.

The *Emperor Valley Zoo* was built in 1952 and is probably the best zoo in the Caribbean. The birds, reptiles, fish, and mammals all live in habitats that closely resemble their own natural habitat. Just off the *Savannah* is an American dining institution, *TGI Friday's*.

South of Chaguaramas, just off the *Butler Highway*, is a popular spot for tourists, the *Caroni Swamp*. Here you can take guided tours to see the elusive Scarlet Ibis. These birds come in to nest in the evening hours so tours usually don't begin until 1500 or later. As you drive down the *Uriah Butler Highway* you'll soon see the exit for the *Caroni Bird Sanctuary*. Get off and the tour operations are right at the end of the exit to the south. *Nanan's Tours*, 645-1305, leaves at 1600, *Kalpoos*, 645-8452, leaves at 1500, and *James Madoo Tours*, 622-7356, who can also set up fishing trips for you. Their boats have no motors, and you'd better bring a hat, sunglasses, and a good supply of bug spray. I got lucky one day as I was riding down the *Butler Highway* past the *Caroni Swamp*. I happened to look to the west over the swamp and saw two beautiful Scarlet Ibis casually flying along a quarter-mile off the highway.

South of the *Caroni Swamp* on the *Uriah Butler Highway* is Chaguanas, the third most important community on Trinidad, one of Trinidad's oldest settlements, a center of East Indian culture, and a shopper's delight. Chaguanas is also the location of the *Lion House*, the former home of V.S. Naipaul, the Trini novelist who now lives in London. In his 1961 novel, *A House of Mr. Biswas*, Naipaul describes his early years growing up in the house.

The name is derived from the name of an Amerindian tribe that lived here at one time, the *Chaguanes*. The town prospered during the mid-1800s when thousands of East Indians arrived to work at the surrounding plantations. By the latter 19th century Chaguanas became the most important market towns in Trinidad. After the decline of the sugar industry, the inhabitants turned to other more white-collar professions creating the intelligentsia

that spawned V.S. Naipaul. With the blossoming oil-industry, Chaguanas became a center for southern Trinis who didn't wish to travel all the way to Port of Spain shopping.

In town there are two large malls, as well as a *Price Smart* on the *Uriah Butler Highway*, but the place most visitor wish to see, and shop, is the market on the southern side of Main Road. Here you can stroll through acres of small stalls and sheds selling everything from fresh produce to crafts, clothing, jewelry, and shoes.

Just north of Chaguanas on the *Uriah Butler Highway*, you'll spy a 36' tall statue of Swami Vivekananda, the Calcutta born 19th century force for Indian education. The *Uriah Butler Highway* was originally the *Princess Margaret Highway* when it opened in 1955. It was soon renamed for Uriah "Buzz" Butler, an oilfield worker who organized labor strikes in 1937.

About four miles south of Chaguanas on the *Southern Main Road* you'll find a row of pottery stalls. The earth in this area has a high clay content, not suitable for farming, but perfect for pottery. Every year, potters make thousands of small earthen pots (deyas) for the annual *Diwali* festival. But there is more than small clay pots to be found here, a complete range of pottery is available, and if you have something particular in mind, some of the potters will make it for you.

A bit further down the Southern *Main Road* you'll come to *Friendship Hall*, a fascinating old estate house with a turret, complex balconies, and wrought iron trimmings. Built in 1864 by Scotsman Hugh MacLeod, the house is still occupied by his family.

Point-a-Pierre

Waypoints:
Point-a-Pierre- ½ nm NW of entrance channel
10° 20.30' N, 61° 29.40' W

The big draw to this area, the *Point-a-Pierre Yacht Club* (*PPYC*), is now closed to non-members. Normally, this would not be a big detriment for cruisers, but their dinghy dock was the only means to shoreside amenities and access to the main road and the beautiful *Point-a-Pierre Wildfowl Trust* that should not be missed. Visitors are not permitted here now and I have no idea when that will change, if ever.

The problem is not something as simple as dealing with foreign vessels, even the *TTSA* has cancelled their annual race to Point-a-Pierre. The reason given to the general public was that the closure was due to port security concerns in regards to US flagged vessels.

The situation may change at any time so I will still give entry instructions in the following paragraphs. For more information I suggest phoning Commodore Val Bradsham at 778-6191 or *PPYC* member Jimmy Harris at 678-3969 for the latest on this problem. I suggest that you do not venture to Point-a-Pierre without phoning in advance.

Navigational Information

Heading south from Port of Spain, the only reasonable anchorage is at Point-a-Pierre, lying just south of Cangrejos Point and the heavy industrial complexes and marked channels at Point Lisas (TRI-1). If heading south you can parallel the shore, but stay off at least three miles as shoals stretch out a good distance from shore between Port of Spain and San Fernando and wrecks litter the inshore areas. A good landmark is the oddly shaped hill at San Fernando.

Point-a-Pierre is home to a huge refinery, formerly a Texaco refinery, it was acquired by the Government of Trinidad and Tobago in 1984. During WW II, Point-a-Pierre was under heavy security because of its industrial areas. Make no doubt about it, Point-a-Pierre is still a heavy industrial area and your senses will pick that up. First, when approaching, you will see the smoke that is inherent in heavily industrialized areas, second, your nose will likely pick up the smells of industry, however the anchorage and the *Point-a-Pierre Yacht Club* (*PPYC*) are in a decent area.

Navigational Information

As shown on Chart TRI-13, a waypoint at 10° 20.30' N, 61° 29.40' W, will place you approximately 1 mile northwest of the anchorage area. Just to the south of this waypoint you'll see an offshore bunker that tankers use. Further south is a mile-long dock that works out from the point. From the waypoint,

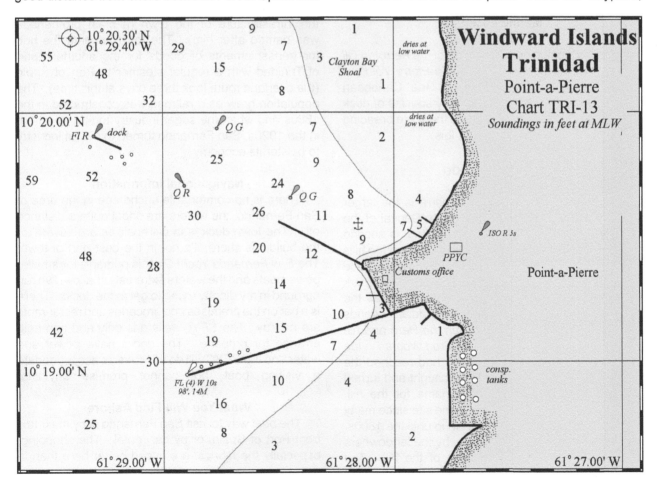

head in between the lit buoys as shown on the chart and work your way in to anchor north of the smaller dock or to anchor off the *Yacht Club* docks in 10'-20' of water. The anchorage is in the lee of the land and quite comfortable. To the northeast is a nice beach and town is reached by taxi from the yacht club or by taking a long walk over the hill.

What You Will Find Ashore

Just north of Point-a-Pierre at Point Lisas, a migration takes place every year between December and June. Across from the industrial complexes lies a large swamp, and every year thousands of blue crabs make the dangerous trek across a busy road to lay their eggs in the sea. At this time the road is littered with crushed blue crabs.

Customs and *Immigration*

Since the *PPYC* has closed for now, there is no point in attempting to clear *Customs* here as shore access is not permitted. I cannot say whether or not yachts will be able to clear here again if the *PPYC* reopens.

Marine Facilities
PPYC

PPYC is located on the grounds of the *Petrotrin Oil Refinery*, at the edge of the *Point-a-Pierre Wildfowl Trust*, the only nature reserve in the Caribbean maintained by the oil industry. Many species of duck and birdlife call the area home and there are breeding programs in place for the Scarlet Ibis.

San Fernando

A few miles south of Point-a-Pierre is the larger town of San Fernando, known as the "Capital of the South." *Sando*, as it's sometimes called, is second only in size to Port of Spain; the city is built on the hills on shore and life moves along here at a slower pace than in Port of Spain. The most notable landmark in San Fernando is a huge hill that dominates the area. The hill is prominent in Amerindian legends as the final resting place of *Haburi the Hero* and his mother who were fleeing from the *Frog Woman* in the Orinoco delta in Venezuela. They had reached the safety of *Ieri* (Trinidad), only to be caught and turned into *Anaparima*, the Amerindian name for the hill. Amerindians made pilgrimages to the site since many centuries before the birth of Christ up until the 1800s. At one time the hill was controlled by the landowners who owned the land at the base of the hill. The

landowners discovered that the hill produced fine gravel and began to quarry the rock until stopped by the government. The hill was designated a National Park in 1980 and today the hill has been enhanced with plantings and benches and offers a scenic view of the city of San Fernando.

The first European visitor was Sir Walter Raleigh who was not impressed by the area and bypassed it. Capuchin monks established a mission here in 1642, but it wasn't until the latter 1700s when the area would flourish. In 1784, French plantation owners were granted lands in the surrounding lands and established huge estates. In 1786, the Spanish Governor, Jose Maria Chacon, renamed the settlement San Fernando de Naparima in honor of King Carlos III's new son (the surrounding areas are known as the *Naparimas*).

By the time the British took over in 1797, San Fernando had over a thousand settlers, 20 mills, and 8 rum distilleries. By 1811, the population had tripled and in 1846, San Fernando was officially designated a town when British Governor Lord Harris improved the infrastructure of the town (a main promenade was named after him). The town became the hub for transshipments of goods for the southern part of Trinidad with a regular steamer to Port of Spain (the overland route took three days at this time). The population grew as a railroad was constructed in the 1880s and when the sugar industry took a downturn in the 1920s, San Fernando turned to the oil industry to bolster its economy.

Navigational Information

There is no comfortable anchorage in the area of San Fernando, the waters are shoal quite a distance off. The town dock is in disrepair as are several of the buildings shore, it's not in the best part of town. The *San Fernando Yacht Club*, is primarily for smaller powerboats and the waters extremely shallow, I've run aground in my dinghy trying to get to the docks. There is a bar on the premises and groceries and restaurants are nearby. The *SFYC* sells gas only and can help arrange for propane. The docks have power and water and the *SFYC* will do their best to accommodate a visiting boat, but cannot promise anything.

What You Will Find Ashore

The best way to visit San Fernando is by maxi-taxi from Port of Spain, or by car rental. The shopping, especially the fabrics, are priced better here than in

Port of Spain. There area lots of small shops and street vendor's stalls, the streets are alive with people. *The Chancery Lane Market* at the end of *High Street* is a good stop for fresh produce and local crafts. A popular meeting spot in Sando is "the corner," the corner of *High Street* and *Harris Promenade*, *Library Corner*, with its non-functioning clock. *Coffee Street* dates back to the 1700s and is known as a hotbed of Pan music.

The nearby panyard is decorated with colorful frescoes painted in 1995 by local artist Glen Steel. Known as the *Dancing Walls,* the paintings trace the history of pan over the last half-century. Just outside of town is a huge three story mall called *Gulf City*, with its huge *Hi-Lo* supermarket.

On the highway outside San Fernando, at the *Claxton Bay* turn-off, is a statue of a headless woman. Legend has it that the statue was erected by a local plantation overseer whose daughter had been having an affair with a laborer on his estate. The father, in an effort to keep his daughter away from the man, tried lock his daughter in the home while he placed a snake at the location where she was to meet her lover in order to scare the young man away. The girl escaped and fled to meet her boyfriend where the snake ended her life. There have been a high number of accidents in the area that have been contributed to drivers seeing the ghost of the young girl who suddenly appears in front of their cars.

Marine Facilities
The San Fernando area is home to several businesses that, although they could not be described as "nautical," offer items that every cruiser may one day want or need. However, you'll need a maxi-taxi or car rental to avail yourself of these facilities.

There are a couple of very nice and well-stocked hardware stores in the area. In Marabella you'll find *Southern Wholesale Stores* on *Union Road*. Nearby is *Samlalsingh's* while on S*utton Street* in San Fernando you can visit *Southern Supplies* with their excellent stock of stainless steel and aluminum. *TOSL* on *Maharaj Avenue* (Marabella) has a large inventory of metal stock.

For bearings and seals try *United Bearings* on *Gomez Street*, and if you need fasteners, screws, bolts, nuts, rivets, you can find them in steel and stainless at *Maska* on *South Trunk Road*.

On *Coffee Street*, *Lenny Sumadh* is a dealer for the industrial versions of *Perkins, Leyland, Ford, GM,* and *Mercedes* engines, marine specific parts are not going to be found here.

If you have any welding or fabrication needs, *Tropical Engineering* in Port Lisas can handle your job. Another good fabricator is *Trojan Engineering* and the *Superior Machine Shop*.

The Northern Coast

The northern coast of Trinidad is thick with forest, mountains, and sleepy fishing villages. Lying just a few miles inland, *Mount El Tucuche*, the second highest peak in Trinidad, is easily seen from offshore. In the 1800s, cocoa was a huge source of income for Trinidadians and many cocoa plantations sprang up in the valleys along the northern coast. Even though a small trail stretched from Blanchisseuse all the way to the *Gulf of Paria*, the principal mode of transport along the coast was the pirogue, the sturdy, wooden, high-bowed boat that ferried people and freight in the waters of Trinidad for centuries.

Trinidad's northern coast is not the place to be if northerly swells are running of if the wind moves north of east, but it certainly is pleasant enough in prevailing conditions and is fun to explore while working your way to Tobago. Don't forget, when you are checking out of Chaguaramas *Customs* bound for Tobago, to inform the *Customs* officials of your plans to stop along the northern coast.

CAUTION:
A last word on safety concerning the northern coast of Trinidad. The last decade has seen an increase in drug activity along this shore. I've heard rumors that officials are thinking of closing down anchorages along this coast to battle the problem. For now, be advised that activity has increased, and if you plan to anchor on the northern coast I would suggest going with a buddy boat.

The Northern Main Road

If you wish to access this coast by land, go to *Queens Park Savannah* in Port of Spain and take *Saddle Road* northward (originally the *Macqueripe Mail Road*, from the days when the mail was offloaded at *Macqueripe Bay* and transported overland to Port of Spain). You'll make your way past *St. Andrew's*

The picturesque northern coast of Trinidad

Macqueripe Bay

The *Pitch Lake*

Sunday at *Maracas Bay*

Moruga River bridge, Moruga

Jesse James, *Member's Only Taxi*

The southern entrance to the *Cocal*

Golf Course and Maravel, and soon you'll come upon two 10' tall stone columns that mark the junction with the *Northern Main Road*. If you take a left you'll head northward along the coast, and if you take a right, continuing along the *Saddle Road,* you'll work your way through a narrow mountain pass and arrive at the beautiful *Santa Cruz Valley*. Keeping on the *Saddle Road* you'll pass Cantaro and wind up in San Juan, a suburb of Port of Spain. However, if you continue up the *Northern Main Road* you will pass through some of the most breathtaking scenery on the island of Trinidad.

At the golf course you can pick up the hiking trail to 600' high *Edith Falls* which only exists during the height of the rainy season. You can also pick up the hiking trail to *Macqueripe Bay* here, although the bay itself is accessible by road.

The *Northern Main Road* is one of the most scenic roads in the entire Caribbean. At certain spots on the road you'll see a bamboo pipe jutting out of the rock or underbrush. Stop here to sample some cool, fresh, spring water, or bring a few empty jerry-jugs to take some back with you. The road itself was built by the U.S. Army as an expression of gratitude by the military for use of the Chaguaramas peninsula. The American military occupation of this area effectively closed off the beaches at Macqueripe and the folks from Carenage and Port of Spain had to go further, to *Maracas Beach*, for the weekend retreat. This is why the road is sometimes called the *American Road*.

A final note on an interesting stop on the *Northern Main Road*. Just outside Maracas is the *Magnetic Road* between *La Vache Bay* and *Maracas Bay*. If approaching *Maracas Bay* from *La Vache Bay*, stop just before the *North Coast Road* begins its descent to *Maracas Bay*. Stop where the cliffs to the right recede and the road appears to begin a slight incline. Keeping your foot on the brakes, put the car in neutral. Taking your foot off the brake you would think that the car would roll backward down the incline, instead the car begins to inch slowly forward, apparently defying gravity. Nobody knows for sure what causes this, most think it's just an optical illusion, but it's something to try. I am from the Atlanta, Georgia area, and just outside Atlanta, in Cumming, Georgia, we have a similar attraction, *Booger Road*, but, that's another tale for another guide.

Macqueripe Bay

Northeast of *Boca de Monos* and Chaguaramas lies *Macqueripe Bay* (see Chart TR-1), not a good anchorage for cruisers, but in the days of indentured labor, ships ferrying the laborers to Trinidad would anchor here. Soon, a medical officer and other officials would board the ships before proceeding to the quarantine stations at Nelson Island in the Five Islands area. The U.S. acquired the land around the bay in the Lend-Lease arrangement with Great Britain. Near *Macqueripe Bay* stands a great navigational landmark shown as "structure" on some charts. It's actually the remains of an old OMEGA station that is used as a beacon for local navigators (it's a great hike to the station). Today *Macqueripe Bay* is a popular beach hang-out that was a favorite of Errol Flynn in years past.

La Vache Bay

Waypoints:
La Vache Point- ¼ nm N of
10° 47.00' N, 61° 28.40' W

Saut d'Eau Island- ½ nm N of
10° 46.80' N, 61° 30.80' W

La Vache Bay- ½ nm NW of
10° 46.20' N, 61° 29.20' W

La Vache Bay is known for its fresh water spring and Venezuelan fishing boats that have been coming here for years to fill up their tanks. Saut d'Eau Island is a breeding area for brown pelicans and other seabirds.

Navigational Information
If approaching from the Bocas, keep at least ½ mile offshore to make your way to a waypoint at 10° 46.80' N, 61° 30.80' W, which will place you ½ north of Saut d'Eau Island as shown on Chart TRI-14. If approaching from Grenada or Tobago, you can also make your way to this waypoint. Vessels can also pass between Saut d'Eau Island and the mainland, but I won't give you a waypoint for this, you will have to pilot your way through by eye, but keep an eye out for the shoals south of Saut d'Eau Island.

There is a little known channel between the island called Medine Point and the mainland where deep water reaches close to shore. This is not a

Mal d'Estomac Bay

La Vache Bay

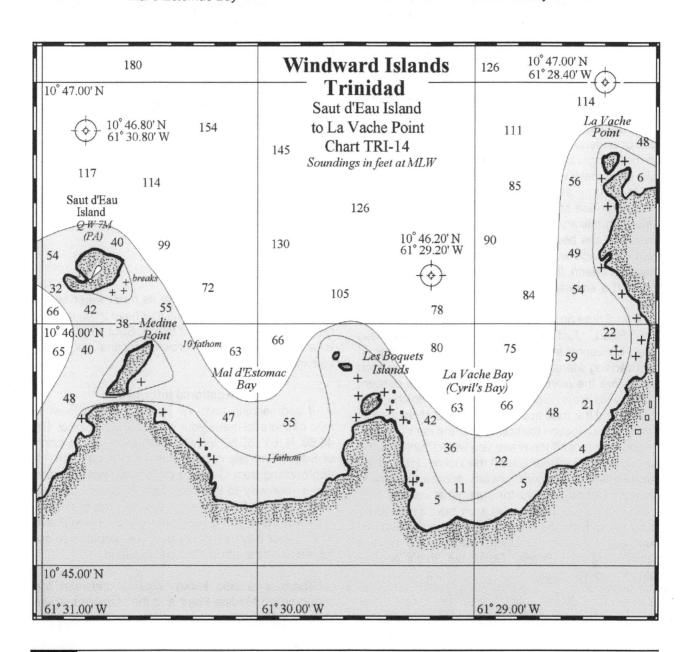

Windward Islands Trinidad
Saut d'Eau Island
to La Vache Point
Chart TRI-14
Soundings in feet at MLW

recommended route, but just a bit of local knowledge for you. Another tidbit is that the Saut d'Eau area is a good spot for kingfish.

From the waypoint north of Saut d'Eau head generally southeast toward a waypoint at 10° 46.20' N, 61° 29.20' W, which places you ½ mile northwest of the anchorage in *La Vache Bay* sometimes called *Cyril's Bay*. Give Les Boguets Islands a wide berth. *Mal d'Estomac* is not a good choice for anchoring, it's deeper than *La Vache Bay* and does not offer the protection that *La Vache Bay* does, and its bottom is rocky. Anchor about halfway down the eastern side of the bay off the northernmost of two small beaches.

What You Will Find Ashore

At the southern end of the anchorage you'll find a stone house, the home of Frank McCume, a guide to the best diving, waterfalls, and caves in the area. You'll be welcomed by Frank's menagerie of dogs, ducks, and geese, and Frank can show you how to get to a 10' waterfall that he built to supply his drinking water. Please don't ask to swim there.

Dining

Ashore is the *Timberline Resort*, now closed and not due to reopen.

On the road heading north out of *La Vache Bay,* stop at the *Hot Bamboo Hut* for a cold drink and to view the Toucans. Between 1600 and 1800, you can often get the owner to call the flock of Toucans that live in the forest above the bar. Proceeding onwards you'll come to one of the most scenic spots on the coast, the La Vache Lookout. Here you'll find a large parking lot and lookout point with vendors selling various crafts and candies from glass jugs called *safes*. On the weekends you'll probably be serenaded by a *busker*, one who improvises calypso for money. He'll expect a few dollars from you if he makes you laugh, and chances are, he will make you laugh.

Maracas Bay

Waypoints:
Morro Point- ½ nm N of
10° 47.00' N, 61° 26.50' W

One of the most popular stops along the northern coast of Trinidad is *Maracas Bay*, a good spot to overnight before heading on to Tobago. *Ash Wednesday* finds the beach packed as Carnival merry-makers come here to relax after the energy draining Carnival. Weekends, especially Sundays, also finds crowds of Trinis swimming and dining on the local favorite, *Shark n' Bake*, a sweet pastry dough, similar to a doughnut, filled with shark and with a huge choice of condiments to adorn it. If you don't like shark, some of the food stalls will serve you kingfish instead.

Navigational Information

If approaching from *La Vache Bay*, pass well to seaward of La Vache Point and make your way to a waypoint at 10° 47.00' N, 61° 26.50' W, this will place you approximately 1 mile northwest of *Maracas Bay* as shown on Chart TRI-15. Head in toward the beach and anchor in the southeastern corner to get out of any surge that may work its way in. Don't even try to anchor in *Balata Bay* as it is deeper, has more surge, and has a rocky bottom.

What You Will Find Ashore
Dining

Richard's and *Natalie's* serve up some of the best *Shark n' Bake* and are located in the car park. The *Bay View Restaurant*, just west of the beach area, has a great view and good food, though not to match *Natalie's*. At the eastern end of the beach is *Uncle Sam's*, THE spot for loud music and cold drinks. At the western end of the beach is the town of Maracas where most of the residents can claim mixed Spanish and Amerindian descent.

Las Cuevas Bay

Waypoints:
Las Cuevas Bay- ½ nm NW of
10° 47.30' N, 61° 24.00' W

Navigational Information

The next bay is called *Las Cuevas Bay*, Spanish for *caves*, where the Curagate River flows into the bay creating sandy hollows in the banks. As shown on Chart TRI-16, a waypoint at 10° 47.30' N, 61° 24.00' W, will place you approximately ½ nautical mile NW of *Las Cuevas Bay*. If approaching from *Maracas Bay*, give Point Parasol a bit of a berth, you can stay ¼ mile off and be safe of dangers here. As you enter *Las Cuevas Bay*, head in towards the fishing fleet anchoring just outside them in 15'-30' of water. Bear in mind that a bit of swell works its way in here in normal conditions, and during periods of northerly swells the anchorage is untenable.

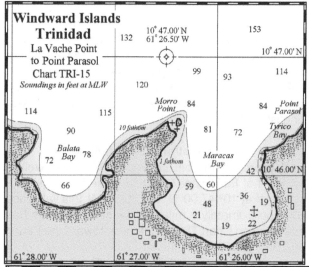

Windward Islands
Trinidad
La Vache Point
to Point Parasol
Chart TRI-15
Soundings in feet at MLW

132   10° 47.00' N
61° 26.50' W   153

                                         10° 47.00' N

99   93   114

120

Morro
Point   84   84   *Point
                               Parasol*

114   115   *10 fathom*   *Tyrico
                                           Bay*
90   81   72

Balata   78   42   10° 46.00' N
Bay
72   *Maracas
                     Bay*
66   60
            59
                   36   19
       48
   21   19   22

61° 28.00' W   61° 27.00' W   61° 26.00' W

Maracas Bay

Windward Islands
Trinidad
Point Parasol to
Chupara Point
Chart TRI-16
Soundings in feet at MLW

61° 24.00' W   61° 23.00' W   61° 22.00' W

300   180
                    196
                               10° 49.00' N
                               61° 23.85' W   121   10° 49.00' N
220   146
                               10 fathom
                                         59
242   55   *Filette
                                                Point*
                    118 49   ‡+ *rock awash*   *Chupara
                                                         Point*
350   light
              124   11   *Fl (2) W, 10s
                                   45   30   22   325', 12M*
      200   ‡   white house
                                                          old bldg.
                               85   24
225   154   119   30   11
              10° 48.00' N   40   ‡+
120   +
              150   99   78   39
                                              +
119   98   66   44   +
                               61   44
95   101
                                   42   +
59   66   50   48
Point   +   +
Parasol 28   45   1 fathom + +   +
      45   60   42   Abercromby
                             Point
10° 47.00' N   30
              Las Cuevas   Trinidad
39   Bay   18   Las Cuevas
              25
              ‡   12
              20

290

There are many caves on the western shore of the bay and actually in the seabed as well. The bottom is rocky and the holding ranges from poor to good here, and then there's the vicious sandfly population.

What You Will Find Ashore

Ashore there is a very nice public beach with shower facilities and *McLean's Bar* at the car park. The *Las Cuevas Rec Club* is a highly informal place to get a cold drink. East of *Las Cuevas Beach* is *Thousand Steps Beach*, named after the numerous concrete steps leading down the cliff to the sand below. The path leading to the beach begins about ¼ mile east of *Las Cuevas Bay*.

Across the *Northern Main Road* from Las Cuevas is a small road named *Rincon Trace* that will lead you to *Rincon Falls*, after a 2½ uphill hike of course. You'll need a guide for this one, call Laurence Pierre at 632-4204, and ask Laurence to take you to *Angel Falls* as well.

Inland from Las Cuevas you'll find *Mount el Tucuche*, and south of this peak you'll find the 300' high *Maracas Waterfall*. Although one could hike to the falls from *Maracas Bay,* a difficult 8-hour hike at best, the easiest way to view the falls starts with a rental car. Drive east on the *Eastern Main Road* from Port of Spain to the town of St. Joseph, the first capital of Trinidad, and go north on the *Maracas Royal Road* until you come to *Waterfall Road*, about 8km from the *Eastern Main Road*. A few minutes down this road you'll come to your guide's house, Trevor Raymond. It's best to take a guide through here, and Trevor will usually come out to meet any car that approaches.

After you park you'll take a wide rocky path for about 15 minutes until you arrive at a smaller trail to the right. This takes you to the first cascade, three tiers of small falls with very cold pools at the bottom suitable for taking a dip. The main cascade is still another 20-30 minutes away. As you approach you'll begin to see signs that say "No Candles" and won't have a clue as to what they mean until you near the falls and see numerous old candles and pools of wax on the surrounding rocks and colorful prayer flags blowing in the breeze. The falls are a special place for Hindus, Baptists, and others who come here for private rituals that only lend an eerie air to the beautiful falls. The falls are almost 300' and Trevor can lead you the top and the *Three Pools*, three small pools where Trevor has built a grill and camping spot.

Chupara Point

Waypoints:
Chupara Point- ½ nm NW of rock awash
10° 49.00' N, 61° 23.85' W

Navigational Information
Proceeding along the northern coast the only other protection is in the lee of Chupara Point in *La Fillete Bay* (the point is marked by a light), but it is often rough there as well. This is a good spot to anchor overnight before continuing on to Tobago. As shown on Chart TRI-16, a waypoint at 10° 49.00' N, 61° 23.85' W, will place you approximately ½ mile northwest of the rocks that are awash west of Chupara Point (when approaching from either direction, give this area a wide berth). If approaching from Tobago, head well west of Chupara Point before turning south to enter the anchorage in *La Fillete Bay*. If approaching from Las Cuevas, round Abercromby Point and its offlying rock, and head for *La Fillete Bay* staying ½ mile offshore to avoid submerged rocks just inshore. You can anchor in *Fillete Bay* just west of the white house and the older estate house that sits behind it (as shown on the chart). Try to anchor in as close to shore as your draft allows, this anchorage does get some swell at times, and during periods of northerly swells is untenable. Ashore you'll find a small beach with a path that leads up to the road. Another path, leading off to the north just before the road, leads you to Chupara Point Light.

What You Will Find Ashore
As the *Northern Main Road* proceeds along the northern coast from Las Cuevas, the road twists and turns, rising and descending, hardly wide enough for two vehicles at times with the narrow wooden bridges over the *Yarra River* being only wide enough for one car. Just offshore is a rock that bears the painted slogan "Yarradise Bay." Inland you have an excellent view of *Mount El Tucuche*, Trinidad's second highest mountain. Further east is another offshore rock labeled "Hollyweed," presumably after the baled product that is said to move through this area.

From the *Yarra River*, the next settlement to the east is Blanchisseuse, the last before the road fades out and you must turn south towards the *Asa Wright Nature Center* on the *Arima-Blanchisseuse Road*. Blanchisseuse is home to some 3,000 people and the homes indicate that this is not a sleepy fishing village, this is a favorite holiday spot with lots of accommodations. The town is actually made up of two communities, Lower Blanchisseuse lies to the west with several small homes, a few bars, a fisherman's co-op, a *Post Office*, and a church. To the east you'll find Upper Blanchisseuse, the main residential settlement and home to the *Police Station* and several stores such as *Fattah's Foods*, *Lloyd's Leather Crafts*, and the *Cocos Hut Restaurant*. Opposite the *Surf's Country Inn* are some concrete steps leading down to a beach that's popular with surfers. It's called, of course, *Surfer's Beach*, but its real name is *L'Anse Martin*.

You cannot proceed eastward from Blanchisseuse by car, but the trek to and from *Paria Bay* and its inland waterfall is a popular hike. The hardiest of trekkers continue on toward Matelot. Past Matelot is Toco, a picturesque fishing village at the northeastern tip of Trinidad. Isolated for so many years, it was finally connected to Port of Spain and other ports on Trinidad by steamer in the days of British rule.

Heading south of Blanchisseuse on the *Arima-Blanchisseuse Road* is a trip you won't forget. You'll begin a marvelous drive down a narrow, pot-holed, twisting, turning road with so many switchbacks that they'll soon begin to all look alike. This is one of the most stunning roads in the Caribbean. Make sure you have plenty of gas for the trip as the next gas stop won't be until you reach Arima.

The tropical forest infringes upon the road so completely that at times you might wonder if you are indeed on the right road. At times you'll feel like you need to turn your lights on, so heavy is the canopy. The road at times will look as if within a week's time, the huge grasses and stands of bamboo will completely reclaim the road. Keep your window down to listen for car horns at curves, and honk yours as you approach every bend to warn oncoming vehicles. Just before the 20¼ marker you'll find a small group of houses with a trail leading past them to *Avocat Falls*. A 10 minute hike will take you to a river where you can turn left and follow the bank for 20 minutes until you reach a junction with another stream. Wade across the stream and climb the steep bank and voilá, 36' *Avocat Falls*. Take a well-deserved dip in the pool at the base.

Proceeding down the road to Arima you'll come to Morne la Croix, where most of the folks still speak French Creole as well as Trini English. All along this road you'll have sweeping views of mountains and valleys, absolutely breathtaking, a don't miss drive. Past Brasso Seco you'll soon come to the *Asa Wright Nature Center,* a nature-lover's paradise. The center was originally a coffee and cocoa plantation. In 1947, the land was purchased by Dr. Newcome Wright. With his wife Asa, both naturalists and bird-watchers, soon accommodated visiting researchers at the neighboring *New York Zoological Society's Simla Tropical Research Station*. When Dr. Wright died, Asa sold the land on the condition it be used as a conservation area and a non-profit Trust was created in 1967 to maintain the Wright's 200 acres as a nature center. *Simla* closed in 1970 and donated their land to the *Asa Wright Center*, which today hosts numerous researchers and tourists on their beautiful grounds.

The heart of the center is the 90 year-old great house with its polished mahogany floors and balcony that overlooks the surrounding valleys. The restaurant serves a daily buffet, sandwiches, and of course, cold drinks.

Jesse Jame's *Members Only* maxi-taxi service makes regular trips to the center, call Jesse on VHF ch. 68 for more information. There is a lovely lodge at the center and you will really enjoy your visit here, but bring bug spray, the mosquitoes aren't that bad, but the chiggers are world class.

From *Asa Wright* the rainforest wanes and the road widens a bit as you approach Arima. From there you can head back to Port of Spain, or head down the eastern shore via Sangre Grande.

Grande Riviere Bay

Waypoints:
Grande Riviere Bay- ½ nm NNW of
10° 50.75' N, 61° 03.10' W

About twenty miles east of Chupara Point is the last usable anchorage on Trinidad's northern shore, *Grand Riviere Bay*. The bay is popular with surfers as well as turtles and those that come there to watch the turtles when they lay their eggs on the beach during the March-August nesting season. *Grand Riviere Bay* is the largest nesting site for the endangered Giant Leatherback turtles in the Western Hemisphere.

In 1992, the *Grand Riviere Environmental Awareness Trust* (*GREAT*) was established with the aim of protecting nesting Leatherback turtles on *Grande Riviere Beach*.

Navigational Information

A waypoint at 10° 50.75' N, 61° 03.10' W, will place you approximately ½ nm NNW of the entrance as shown on Chart TRI-17. From the waypoint work your way into the bay (give the shoal off the rock a wide berth using a dogleg route) and tuck up under the eastern shore to anchor in 20'-30' of water. Finding a calm spot might be difficult at times, this can be a very rolly anchorage (there is a reason surfers like this bay). There is a large rock with some trees on it and anchoring is good just north of it.

What You Will Find Ashore

The hardest part is finding a place to land the dinghy as the beach always seems to have a swell running on it. The *Mt. Plasir Estate Hotel* can arrange guides for hikes through the surrounding countryside and there's a small waterfall just a short trek from the hotel (the *Grand Riviere Waterfall*). There are several more falls up the *Matelot River* that are more than worth the hike. The hotel can arrange for local boaters to take you to popular spots such as *Paria Waterfall Beach* and *Madamas River Bay*.

The *Grande Riviere Nature Guide Association* and the *Tourism Development Organization* have built an impressive information center on the beachfront where visitors may come for advice and to sign up for daily guide services for the region. Here you may watch educational videos about the local fauna, browse the gift shop, and enjoy fresh baked snacks and drinks on the verandah.

In town there is a *Post Office* and a health centre with a nurse on duty. A doctor makes weekly visits to the health centre.

Dining

At the southwestern end of the bay is a beach and the *Mt. Plasir Estate Hotel*. In 1993, Italian photographer Piero Guerrini turned what was once a cocoa estate main house into this 12-room hotel. The dining here is superb and focuses on fresh seafood and organic vegetables grown on the estate's grounds. They even serve a great pizza baked in their brick oven.

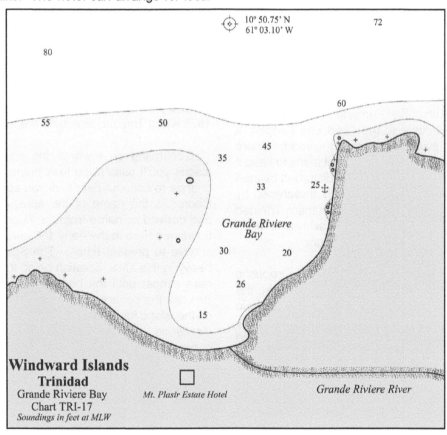

Windward Islands
Trinidad
Grande Riviere Bay
Chart TRI-17
Soundings in feet at MLW

Nearby is the *Acajou Hotel*, an eco-friendly resort with a restaurant serving fresh local produce and Trinidadian/Swedish fusion cuisine created by a Swedish chef.

The Southern and Eastern Coasts

While the southern and eastern coasts can in no way be described as cruising grounds, there are no anchorages that I know of, the area is still quite beautiful and is best visited by an arranged tour or by rental car. I'm going to assume that you have a rental car, and will describe what you can find on these coasts and in the interior of Trinidad. Many of these places are shown on Chart TRI-1, but you can pick up a road-map at most marinas and car rentals.

Driving Around
Southern and Eastern Trinidad

The southwestern peninsula of Trinidad is often called the most beautiful part of the island and is sometimes referred to as the "deep south." The land is fertile and has been home to many sugar plantations over the years. The area also lays claim to being the first area that Europeans landed. Columbus is said to have stopped at Icacos to search for water and Sir Walter Raleigh is said to have caulked his ships at La Brea (home of the *Pitch Lake*) in 1595. Raleigh, who came in search of *El Dorado*, the mythical city of gold, is also said to have traded with native Amerindians for water and provisions.

Five miles south of San Fernando on the *Southern Main Road* you'll come to the *Oropuche Lagoon,* a huge mangrove swamp alongside the road. There are no tours here and the government plans to keep it that way, maintaining the area as undisturbed by man as possible. However the swamp is threatened by old oil pumps that are all over the southern Trinidad area, over 1600, that were left to rust away and which often leak oil into the surrounding waters.

As the *Southern Main Road* crosses the *Oropuche River*, you'll notice a crematorium on your right, the *Shore of Peace*. Here you'll see piles of lumber and logs stacked up for the next cremation when family members place their loved one atop the pyre and send them into eternity. The pyre areas are numbered and have a nice view of the *Gulf of Paria*. The nearby *Godineau River* was the scene of a famous Trini murder. Here, a Dr. Singh, killed his wife and dumped her body into the river. Unfortunately for him, the tide turned and brought the body back upstream. The crime was discovered and the doctor arrested.

The *Pitch Lake* at La Brea, about 10 miles southeast of San Fernando, is a popular tourist destination. As you get closer and closer to La Brea, especially the last couple of miles or so, you will notice pitch showing up everywhere, it will appear that everybody's yard has been paved with asphalt. This is merely the pitch that has risen to the surface over the years. Residents of the area must keep a constant watch over their abodes as the ground slowly undulates over the years and can cause shifting of building foundations. The 89-acre lake is still being used as source of pitch (some of the finest quality asphalt in the world originates here-approximately 300 tons per day) with a factory on the shore and a railway of small cars that take loads of pitch up the hill for processing. There are uniformed guides that can give you a tour, but there are also unofficial guides seeking to make a dollar or two off you. Make sure that you avail yourself of a legitimate guide. Don't wear high heels (obviously) if you plan to walk on the lake (you can walk on it in places, your guide will explain).

Legend has it that Carib Indians killed and ate the *Sacred Humming Bird*, which angered the *Great Spirit* who punished them by trapping them forever under the *Pitch Lake*. Sir Walter Raleigh stopped here in 1595 to apply pitch to his ships, but the lake was not used commercially until the time of the American Civil War in the 1860s. At this time the British began to remove pitch and continue to do so for a century until 1978 when Trinidad took over the operation.

Continuing on towards the southwestern tip at Icacos you'll pass huge teak plantations which soon change to coconut palms as you approach the point. Cedros is the name of the area, not a settlement, and derived its name from the huge cedar trees that flourished here in the early 18th century, though none survive to present times. The Spanish influence is heavy in this area, Spanish being the primary tongue here almost until the beginning of the 20th century. Besides the cedars, Cedros was known far and wide on the island for its rum, the town once boasted seven distilleries. The area can claim almost the same number of lovely, and usually deserted, beaches.

The *Boca del Serpiente*, the *Serpent's Mouth*, is the southern gateway to the *Gulf of Paria* at the extreme southwestern end of Trinidad. The *boca* was named by Columbus and has a strong current running through it although the *Gulf of Paria* is relatively calm itself. The point at Icacos lies only a few miles from Venezuela and is a popular spot for modern-day smugglers bringing drugs into the island.

Well inland from Icacos lies Siparia, known for its feast of *La Divina Pastora*, the *Divine Shepherdess*. On the second Sunday after Easter, locals carry the statue of the Black Virgin through the streets while people, dressed in their best clothes, make offerings and make merry all day and most of the night. The statue, which has had many miracles attributed to it, serves dual religious duty. Some locals say that the statue was once the prow of a ship that was wrecked on *Quinam Bay*. Others claim the stature was brought to Siparia from Venezuela by a priest whose life it had saved while fleeing from an Amerindian revolt. In the 1890s, Hindu indentured servants decided that the stature was the goddess *Kali*, the destroyer of sorrow, and they renamed the statue *Soparee Kay Mai*. If the statue answers their prayers, Hindu women offer it locks of hair cut from their children's first haircut. The Catholic Church tried to dissuade the fervent Hindus in 1920, but to no avail as many still worship the statue.

The southern shore is dotted with small fishing villages and few amenities. The south-central region of Trinidad consists of rolling hills that stretch from Princes Town in the north, to Icacos in the southwest, and Mayaro in the east. Oil wells dot the landscape, as well as the waters offshore (f you're planning to transit this area, get a good government chart of the area and keep your eyes open-the wells are well lit, but there are a lot of them). Road maps can be inaccurate here, the road you're looking for will likely be unmarked, and sometimes little more than a dirt path.

Heading east from San Fernando your fist stop will be Princes Town, and it will be a stop, especially on the weekend when crowds throng through the street shopping and liming. I've driven through here before and have sat for over 30 minutes on the one-mile stretch through downtown. Just outside of town you'll pass several small stalls offering "Fresh Goat." The goats tied up outside the stalls will testify that goat doesn't come any fresher.

Princes Town was originally a mission named Savanna Grande, when in 1880 Prince Albert and

Prince George (who was later to become King), visited the mission to plant two *poui* trees at the old Anglican Church. The town was renamed Princes Town in their honor. Today it has become Princes Town.

On the outside of Princes Town are the small communities of First, Third, Fourth, and Fifth Company, named after companies of black American soldiers. The former slaves fought for the British in exchange for land and were granted parcels in Trinidad. You'll notice that there is no Second Company, this unit was lost at sea on its way to Trinidad.

Heading east from Princes Town you pass the Devil's Woodyard with its mud volcanoes. These "volcanoes" are mud mounds about 3' tall that spew gray, sulfuric mud that is supposed to be good for the skin. These volcanoes can be found all over Trinidad, *TIDCO* even marks them on some of their tourist publications. They can be dangerous as they have a tendency to explode every few years. A recent explosion in Piparo destroyed a road in 1997. The Amerindians believed the volcanoes were links between this world and the world below and that the explosions were blamed on the Devil.

Moruga celebrates the fact that Columbus anchored here in 1498, but locally, the area is known more for Obeah. Papa Neiza was an African herbal doctor who was immortalized in Calypso songs and today's locals tell tales of the Obeah woman Madame Cornstick, a very powerful woman, who still lives there but is rarely seen. They'll speak in hushed tones of her, obviously in awe and in fear of her powers (see photo of the *Moruga River* bridge).

Rio Claro is the hub of southeastern Trinidad, both commercially and socially. Southeast of *Rio Claro* is Guayaguayare, a popular vacation spot for Trinis. Gazing out to see you'll see several oil rigs on the horizon while the shoreline is studded with oil tanks. Oil was first discovered here in 1819, but recent years brought a wave of fortune to local residents literally on the tide. A smuggler's boat was being chased by the *Trinidad Coast Guard* offshore and dumped their load of cocaine overboard. The majority of the drug parcels washed up on the beach where happy locals gathered the packages before the authorities arrived. A vessel can anchor in the lee of the point, but be advised that there is a large shoal that works its way south of the point a good distance. The waters of the southern coast are thick with oil wells so use caution if you transit this area. Also be aware of the westerly current through here, 3-5 knots most of the time, but local mariners have told me they've seen the current as strong as 7 knots.

Aside the *Rio Claro-Guayaguayare Road* is the *Trinity Hills Wildlife Sanctuary*. The 65-square kilometer evergreen forest houses a watershed vital to Trinidad's water supply. The area was declared a reserve in 1900, and designated a wildlife sanctuary in 1934.

Starting at Guayaguayare, the eastern shoreline of Trinidad is one of the most beautiful areas of the island. North of Guayaguayare lies the town of Mayaro. Once home to a vast coconut plantation, Mayaro became well known as a farm from 1914 to 1965 when the railroad was closed down. The tourism industry had a brief resurgence in the 1970s only to die again in the mid-1980s. Mayaro is comprised of two smaller communities, Pierreville and Plaisance. Pierreville is the business center of town while Plaisance is the seaside resort area. Here you'll find a nice fresh seafood shop right on the highway heading north.

Heading north from Mayaro, you will enter a gorgeous area called the *Cocal,* an uninterrupted coconut plantation stretching northward as far as Manzanilla. Here you'll drive through the mile after mile of graceful, leaning coconut palms and the occasional royal palm. These trees, not in commercial use today, are said to be the descendants of coconuts washed ashore from a ship that foundered in a hurricane. The long windward beach, backed by miles of palm trees, is a popular spot with locals on weekends and holidays. You'll sometimes see huge leatherback turtles laying their eggs on the beaches here in early summer. There are many tours that will take you to the eastern beaches from Chaguaramas; try *Jesse James' "Members Only" Maxi-Taxi* in Chaguaramas.

Heading north from Mayaro (on the coast road, you pass straight through the middle of the *Cocal* and the edge of the *Nariva Swamp* where you'll find a lovely river that you can explore by kayak. The swamp is home to 58 species of mammal including the maniteel, a cousin to the Florida manatee. The swamp is also home to large water snakes (anacondas from Venezuela), caimans, various parrots, ducks, howler monkeys, and many species of fish and birdlife (171 species of birds). On the down side, it is also home to 92 different species of mosquito. It's been said

that large crocodiles have even turned up here after crossing the *Gulf of Paria* after being washed down the *Rio Orinoco* in a flood. In the middle of the swamp is an island called the *Bush Bush Sanctuary*. Bordered by palm trees and covered in hardwoods and silk cotton trees, the island is not easy to get to and is unexploited by tour guides.

At the northern end of the *Cocal* is Manzanilla, actually Upper and Lower Manzanilla. On the eastern coast you'll find the *Brigand Hill Lighthouse*, built in 1958. You can't climb to the top, but you can scale the iron stairs on the outside of the lighthouse for a good view of the eastern coast including the Cocal, the *Nariva Swamp*, and the mountains to the north. From Manzanilla you can head to Sangre Grande on your way back to Port of Spain or Chaguaramas. A bit further west is Arima which has a special place in the culture of Trinidad.

Arima is home to the descendants of the original Carib Indians who occupied Trinidad when Columbus arrived. The local descendants prefer to be known as the *Kalina Nation*, saying that the term *Carib* is a European corruption of their name. The *Santa Rosa Carib Community Association* was formed in 1974 to preserve the interests of the shrinking tribe. Their office on *Paul Mitchell Street* sells traditional handicrafts and offers information about the tribe whose intermarriages are slowly eroding the physical attributes of these people.

Tobago

Port of Entry: Charlotteville, Scarborough
Haul-Out: None
Diesel Repairs: Carnbee, *Store Bay*
Outboard Repairs: *Store Bay*
Propane: *Store Bay*
Provisions: Scarborough, Charlotteville, Crown Point
Important Lights: See *Appendix A*

Unlike her neighbor, Trinidad, with its plethora of marine services, Tobago lies at the other end of the spectrum. Tobago has no marine services to even come close to what Trinidad offers, there are no marinas, nowhere to haul out, but this island offers quality cruising grounds and excellent diving and snorkeling opportunities. Not only that, the island has only the lightest touches of the tourism industry upon it. Where Trinidad is getting more and more cosmopolitan, Tobago remains laid back, the place to be on *Ash Wednesday* after giving your all during Carnival.

Tobago is approximately 21 miles long and about 7 miles wide at its widest, Tobago has a wide low-lying coastal plain along the southwestern shore rising to a central ridge of volcanic hills reaching almost 1900' in height. The central ridge of rain forest was set aside as a nature preserve in the 1780s making it the oldest such preserve in the New World. The rain forest was

Customs office, Charlotteville
photo courtesy Katy Stickland, *SBMS*

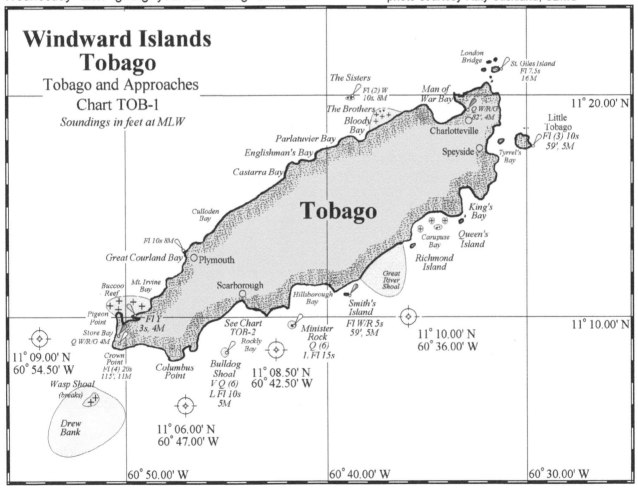

Windward Islands
Tobago
Tobago and Approaches
Chart TOB-1
Soundings in feet at MLW

Tobago

London Bridge
St. Giles Island
Fl 7.5s 16M

The Sisters
Fl (2) W 10s, 8M
Man of War Bay
Q W/R/G 82', 4M

The Brothers
Bloody Bay
Charlotteville
Little Tobago
Fl (3) 10s 59', 5M

Parlatuvier Bay
Englishman's Bay
Speyside
Tyrrel's Bay

Castarra Bay

Culloden Bay
King's Bay
Carupse Bay
Queen's Island

Fl 10s 8M
Great Courland Bay
Plymouth
Richmond Island
Great River Shoal

Buccoo Reef
Mt. Irvine Bay
Scarborough
Hillsborough Bay
Smith's Island

Pigeon Point
Fl Y 3s, 4M
Minister Rock
Q (6) L Fl 15s
Fl W/R 5s 59', 5M

11° 20.00' N

11° 10.00' N

Store Bay
Q W/R/G 4M
11° 09.00' N
60° 54.50' W

Crown Point
Fl (4) 20s 115', 11M
Columbus Point
Rockly Bay
Bulldog Shoal
V Q (6) L Fl 10s 5M

11° 08.50' N
60° 42.50' W

11° 10.00' N
60° 36.00' W

Wasp Shoal
(breaks)

Drew Bank

11° 06.00' N
60° 47.00' W

See Chart TOB-2

60° 50.00' W

60° 40.00' W

60° 30.00' W

protected to maintain the purity of the water flowing through the network of streams, rivers, and waterfalls that lead from the mountains to the sea. It is said that water nymphs inhabit the cool mountain pools.

The Spaniards named the island after the y-shaped pipe that the native Amerindians used for smoking *kohiba* (sometimes shown as *cohiba*). The pipe, called *tobacco*, was inserted into the nostrils and the smoke inhaled until the smoker fell into a stupor. The Spaniards picked up this habit, but did not inhale to the point of intoxication. Tobago is often said to be the model for the island in Robinson Crusoe, in fact, there is a cave on the southwestern tip of Tobago called *Robinson Crusoe's Cave*.

In 2010, Tobago banned jet skis in the waters from *Store Bay* to Plymouth. The law is now in place and enforcement will soon follow.

Cooking gas refills are available island wide for local bottles with a push-on regulator. All other bottles, with the exception of the new fiberglass type, can be filled in *Store Bay* at *SBMS* regardless of certification, which can be an issue in Trinidad. Drop off your bottles at *SBMS* Monday-Friday for a same day refill.

Customs and Immigration

Ports of Entry
Trinidad- Port of Spain, Chaguaramas
Tobago- Charlotteville, Scarborough

While the procedures required by *Customs* and *Immigration* on Tobago initially appear cumbersome they are relatively straight forward. These procedures were developed with commercial shipping in mind and have not been fully adapted to meet the needs of yachtsmen. Furthermore it is necessary because of the close proximity of South America for Trinidad and Tobago to have stringent rules to combat the smuggling of both drugs and people.

Entering the Country's Waters
All vessels upon entering the territorial waters of Tobago (12nm), should proceed to a Port of Entry. At present the only ports of entry in Tobago are Scarborough and Charlotteville. Once the vessel has been secured the Master of the vessel and all crew should proceed "as soon as is practically possible" to the *Immigration* office. When clearing anywhere, appropriate attire should go without saying.

Visiting *Immigration*
The *Immigration* office in Scarborough is located on the first floor of the Port building. The office is open Monday-Friday from 0800-1600. Outside of these hours, and on weekends and holidays, the ship's master should phone the telephone number posted on the door of the *Immigration* office or alternatively ask *Customs*, which is open 24 hours a day, to contact an *Immigration* officer on your behalf.

In Charlotteville, the *Immigration* office is located next to the *Police Station*. The *Immigration* office is open Monday-Friday from 0800-1600 and is unattended outside these hours. If you arrive outside normal working hours you can seek assistance from the *Customs* officer located in the same building. New regulations permit arriving outside of these hours without paying overtime fees as long as you clear in first thing in the morning during regular office hours, otherwise overtime fees are TT$100. Overtime fees are payable if you require the services of an *Immigration* officer outside of office hours or on weekends and holidays. The fee of TT$100 is payable for each service only if you present yourself at the office outside of office hours.

In the *Immigration* office the master of the vessel will be required to complete the following forms:
1: Form 10 - *Arrival Report* (4 copies)
2: Form 11 - *Crew List* (4 copies)
3. *Tobago House of Assembly Environmental Health Services Dept. Declaration* (1 copy)

These completed forms, together with the clearance forms from your last port of call, along with passports for all crew are presented to the *Immigration* officer who will sign you and your crew into the country.

As anywhere, ask for the maximum amount of time that you can stay, just in case. So many people come to Trinidad planning only to stay a week, perhaps two, or even a month, and wind up staying three months and then getting another extension for even longer. The length of your stay is completely in the hands of the *Immigration* officer on duty. Ask for three months starting out, which is the standard length of stay granted to visitors. You will pay TT$50 for every thirty days that you stay in Trinidad/Tobago.

Immigration Extensions
Extensions are available for three months to one year and cost a minimum of TT$150. Staying for

hurricane season or having work done on your vessel are valid reasons for extensions.

All extensions of *Entry Certificates* are handled by the *Immigration* office in Scarborough and you must apply for an extension before your current *Entry Certificate* expires. One week before expiration you should present yourself to *Immigration* in Scarborough and complete the *Application for Extension of Landing/ Change of Status* form.

Upon completion of this form you will be given an appointment for an interview with an *Immigration* officer. Your reasons for requesting an extension can be as simple as the fact you enjoy the island, wish to stay during hurricane season, or are having work done on your vessel (this is common in Trinidad).

Extensions can be granted for up to 90 days for a fee of TT$150. You can apply for a further extension beyond 180 days but this is granted solely at the discretion of the *Immigration* officer and there needs to be a valid reason.

Visiting *Customs*

After you have cleared *Immigration*, proceed to the *Customs* office where you must fill out additional paperwork in duplicate. The form will ask you about your ship's inventory including how many engines you have (outboard or inboard). Be truthful in your answers. If your boat is to remain in the water there is a harbor fee depending upon tonnage and length of stay.

Firearms and Pets

At *Customs* you will be required to hand over all firearms for the duration of your stay and you will have to show current vaccination records for all dogs and cats (and they will be quarantined aboard your vessel for the duration of your stay). You may not walk your pet ashore under any circumstances. If you wish to leave by plane and take your pet with you, you will need a transit permit from the veterinary services.

Transiting the Coast of Tobago

When you clear in with *Immigration*, you must inform the officer of your plans on which anchorages you plan to visit on Tobago and receive your *Temporary Certificate* for coastwise navigation. This certificate needs to be presented to the *Immigration* officer at the next Port of Entry. In other words, if you clear in at Scarborough, you will get a *Temporary Certificate* that you present to the *Immigration* officer in Charlotteville.

Transferring Crew to Another Vessel

Crewmembers wishing to transfer from one vessel to another may do so provided the crewmember signs off the vessel he arrived on and signs on to the vessel he is leaving aboard. Crew cannot sign on to a vessel that is staying longer than the vessel he or her arrived on. Arriving crew members need to have two copies of an "invitation letter" from the captain stating that he or she is part of the crew.

Crew Leaving and Rejoining a Vessel

Crew leaving and rejoining a vessel will be required to undergo the same procedure as outlined above for signing off a vessel and for signing on to a vessel and a letter of invitation will need to be prepared by the master of the vessel. If the master of the vessel is leaving then they should prepare a letter indicating who will be acting as master in their absence; especially if the vessel needs to leave Trinidad/Tobago waters.

If the entire crew (including the master) are departing then a further letter (2 copies) detailing who will be in charge of the vessel in your absence will be required and endorsed by *Immigration*. A copy of this letter should be presented to *Immigration* upon return to the country.

Removal of Crew Members from Crew List

If you have a member of your crew departing and leaving the country, the master of the vessel and the crew member should present themselves to *Immigration* 48 hours before their flight leaves in order to avoid departure tax. The departing crew member will need to provide proof of repatriation to the issuing country of their passport (i.e. a plane ticket); upon receipt of proof the crew member will be removed from the *Crew List*.

Signing on Additional Crew Members

If you plan to take on additional crew, prior to the arrival of the crew members you need to inform *Immigration* in either Scarborough or Charlotteville. The master of the vessel will need to present to the *Immigration* officer two copies of a letter of invitation which includes details such as the name of the joining crew member, their passport number, where they plan to stay in Tobago, when they plan to leave, together with an undertaking by the master of the vessel to repatriate the crew member to the issuing country of the crew member's passport.

This letter will then be endorsed by *Immigration* and a copy should be forwarded to the crew member that is joining the vessel so that it may be presented to *Immigration* upon arrival at the airport. Crew joining a vessel will be given a two day *Entry Certificate*. Prior to the expiration of this certificate the master of the vessel and the joining crew member should present themselves to *Immigration* at a Port of Entry to be added to the vessel's crew list.

Departing Tobago for Trinidad

This next part is VERY IMPORTANT! If you have cleared into Tobago and expect to visit Trinidad you must go to *Customs* and *Immigration* at your Port of Entry and present your papers, your *Temporary Certificate* from the *Immigration* office at your Port of Entry. When you visit Trinidad you will need to report to *Customs* and *Immigration* at *CrewsInn* for another stamp on your *Temporary Certificate* "as soon as practically possible." If you are on Tobago and plan to go Trinidad and leave Trinidad/Tobago from there, you must report to *Customs* and *Immigration* at your Port of Entry on Tobago to collect your papers to take to Chaguaramas on Trinidad.

Clearing Out

When you clear out the captain and all crew must report to the *Immigration* office in either Scarborough or Charlotteville to clear out. You will be required to fill out the following forms.

1: Form 5 - General Declaration (4 copies)
2: Form 16 - Notice of Approximate Time of Departure (4 copies)
3: Form 27 - Grant of Clearance (4 copies)

There is a new regulation in effect in Trinidad and Tobago that gives you 24 hours to depart after you have cleared out. If you cannot depart within 24 hours, you must return to your Port of Entry and clear in again.

Diving In Tobago

Diving in the waters off Tobago is nothing less than fantastic and should really be done with the aid of a local dive guide as the currents can be tricky, especially around Speyside. It is recommended that divers only dive with members of the *Association of Tobago Dive Operators* (*ATDO*). Details of the members of this organization can be found online at www.tobagoscubadiving.com. If you need more

proof, the first six months of 2011 saw three diving fatalities occurring without a guide as well as six missing divers, two of whom were only rescued by chance. All six missing divers were from yachts and were diving without guides.

Heading to Tobago

Navigational Information

Vessels headed to Tobago from the north, from Grenada or Carriacou, must deal with the fluky northwest set of the *Guyana Current* that flows between Tobago and Grenada. Here you'll find the current pushing you westward at 2 knots at times, at other times you would have to look hard to find any current at all. Although cruisers often head for Tobago from the southern coast of Grenada, *Prickly Bay* or Hog Island, it is not recommended unless you have a good engine or simply like tacking. A better idea would be to head northward to Carriacou and then sail to Tobago from the northeastern tip of Carriacou or Petite St. Vincent.

Another option is to sail to Tobago from Barbados to lay the island on one tack although if you have the right wind, it's easy enough to make Tobago on one tack from Grenada. Of course, those of us that don't like to go to weather might suggest that you head to the Azores and then down to the Canaries and back across the Atlantic to avoid headwinds. The choice is yours.

Vessels heading to Tobago from Trinidad have no other choice than to go against wind and current. Most cruisers make this trip in small hops, leaving from *Scotland Bay* and making *Maracas Bay* the first day by staying close inshore. Leaving *Maracas Bay* around midnight and hugging the coast at least 1½ miles off until between Chupara Point and Galera Point (see Chart TRI-1, both have lights), then changing course to account for the current and steering for the waypoint off Scarborough. The further east you go along the northern coast of Trinidad, the less you'll have to deal with the current between Tobago and Trinidad. If you wish to follow this route, then I suggest going east as far as *Grande Riviere Bay*.

Today there is a new way of transiting this route, and that is to stay close to the northern shore of Trinidad without making any stops, some even preferring to motorsail overnight in the lighter winds. Another option if voyaging during the day is to motorsail along the coast in the early morning and then sail towards Tobago when the trades fill in later in the day. The reasoning behind this non-stop sailing is due to the increased drug smuggling activity along Trinidad's northern shore which may soon make those bays off limits to anchored vessels.

When plotting your course from Trinidad to Scarborough, you must deal with a current that will be flowing westward at 2 knots and more at times (Remember your high school geometry?). If you have crossed the *Gulf Stream* off Florida on your voyage to the Caribbean, you'll be familiar with the math involved and the same principle applies here. The only difference is that the body of water that you are crossing, the *Galleon Passage*, is only about 20 miles wide instead of 50 and Tobago is easily seen in good visibility. Try to time your passage so that you will arrive in Scarborough before the trades pick up in the morning, usually by 0800-0900.

Let's begin our tour of Tobago at Scarborough and work our way clockwise around the island, which is the best way for a vessel to circumnavigate the island. The northern coast in most conditions is a bit out of the current and the roughest part is often at the northeastern tip around the St. Giles Islands. Bear in mind that you won't want to be anchored anywhere along the northern coast during the winter months when the northeasterly swells begin to roll in (and the occasional and rare northerly swell). At this time Scarborough or *King's Bay* are the best anchorages although both *Store Bay* and Charlotteville are viable anchorages. Conversely, when a southeast wind is blowing Scarborough gets a bit rolly.

Rockly Bay, Scarborough

Waypoints:
Rockly Bay, Scarborough- ¼ nm SE of
11° 10.35' N, 60° 44.05' W

Rockly Bay, Scarborough- 2 nm SE of
11° 08.50' N, 60° 42.50' W

Columbus Point- 2 nm S of
11° 06.00' N, 60° 47.00' W

Home to 18,000 of the island's 54,000+ people, Scarborough retains a certain rustic charm much unlike her sister city of Port of Spain, Trinidad. Scarborough became the capital of Tobago in 1779

and is divided into two sections, Upper and Lower Scarborough, the latter located around the dock area, a port since the Dutch constructed a fort and dock here in 1654 and named the area Lampsinburgh. At the same time Latvians were setting up across the island at Plymouth.

The 1658 the Dutch captured Plymouth and in 1666, an English fleet, in retaliation, destroyed Lampsinburgh. But the English failed to maintain a presence and the Dutch returned a few years later and rebuilt the town as well as constructing a fort for its defense. The French attacked the settlement in 1677 and a French cannonball hit the ammunition dump that destroyed the fort and killed 250 Dutch settlers and soldiers. Nothing is left of the fort today but it is remembered by the name, *Dutch Fort Road*. The British regained control of Tobago in 1762, and immediately named the settlement Scarborough.

When the French took over again in 1781, Scarborough became Port Louis, while *Fort King George* became *Fort Castries*. The town bounced back and forth like a tennis ball until the British took control in 1814 and it remained under British rule until Trinidad and Tobago became one nation in 1976. *Rockly Bay* was named by ship's captains that cursed the sharp-edged rocks around the bay.

Navigational Information
Vessels heading for Scarborough from the north, from Grenada or Carriacou, can head for a waypoint at 11° 09.00' N, 60° 54.50' W (as shown on Chart TOB-1), which will place you approximately 3 miles west of Crown Point and 3 miles northwest of *Wasp Shoal*. From this position pass between *Wasp Shoal* and the southwestern tip of Tobago and if you'd like, you can head straight for a waypoint at 11° 06.00' N, 60° 47.00' W which places you approximately 2 miles south of Columbus Point (bear in mind that once through the cut between *Wasp Shoal* and Crown Point, you will again be battling a westward setting current all the way to Scarborough).

From this position, you can make your turn towards *Rockly Bay* and Scarborough giving *Bulldog Shoal* a wide berth to arrive at a waypoint 11° 08.50' N, 60° 43.00' W, which will place you approximately 2 miles southeast of the harbor in *Rockly Bay* and well clear of *Bulldog Shoal*. From this waypoint you can head for a waypoint a 11° 10.35' N, 60° 44.05' W, which places you just outside the lit buoys that mark the entrance

The anchorage in Scarborough, Tobago

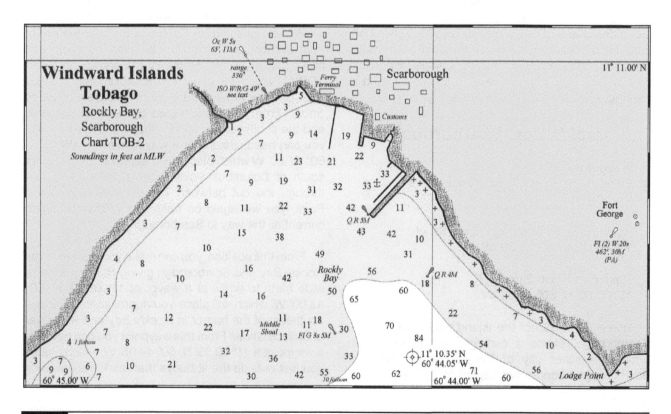

channel to the harbor at Scarborough as shown on Chart TOB-2.

As you enter the harbor you might notice an eastward flowing current, actually an eddy of the westward setting current that flows between Trinidad and Tobago. Pass between the buoys and round the tip of the jetty to starboard to anchor well out of the channel to the ferry dock as the ferry uses it daily arriving around 1900-2000. Be sure to show an anchor light here. Vessels heading from Scarborough to Crown Point and onward can follow the above directions and waypoints in reverse.

What You Will Find Ashore
Customs and *Immigration*

When you arrive, you must first present yourself at the *Immigration* office located on the first floor in the Port building at the head of the cruise ship dock and are open Monday-Friday from 0800-1600 and on Saturday mornings from 0800-1200 (overtime charges apply on Saturday). If no *Immigration* official can be found, report to *Customs* and they will help you find one.

Customs is located just to the right of the ferry terminal (east of the terminal) on the ground floor of the red-roofed building across from the pizza parlor. *Customs* is open Monday-Friday from 0800-1600 and on weekends and holidays from 0800-1800. Weekend clearance requires an overtime charge.

If you are arriving from Trinidad you will need your clearance documents from Chaguaramas. You will pay your first thirty day fee of TT$50 when you arrive and when you clear out you will pay TT$50 for each month you stayed in Tobago's waters.

Marine Facilities

There are no marine facilities in Scarborough, You can no longer fill up your water along side the town dock, but there is water available at the ice plant close to the dinghy dock, just bring your jerry jugs.

Fuel anywhere in Tobago will have to be jerry-jugged. However, mega-yachts can dock alongside next to the ferry terminal if there are no ships in the harbor and refuel, but his needs to be pre-arranged with both the *Port Authority* and the fuel supplier. The *Super Yacht Services* part of *Store Bay Marine Services, SBMS*, can coordinate this for you.

Internet Access

Core Computers is located in the *TLC* building on *Milford Rd.* and offers Internet access daily from 0900-1600.

For more Internet access try *Jupiter Tech*, located in the *Phillips Building* on *Burnett Street* or the *Rhand Credit Union Co-operative Society* on *Bacolet Street*.

At the *NIB Mall*, sometimes called the *Scarborough Mall*, just across from the ferry dock, you'll find *MG Photo Studios* which specializes in *Macs*. *Pro Computer*, located at the *TLH Building* on *Milford Road*, handles computer repairs and rentals.

Getting Around

The road in front of the ferry terminal, *Carrington Street*, is where you'll want to go to catch a taxi to anywhere on the island. The *Tobago Taxi Owners and Drivers Association* (639-2692) has an office next door to the *Customs* office.

There is a temporary bus station at *eTec Mall* off *Sangster Hill Road*. As of 2011, it's been open for 2 years already and there is no indication from the authorities as to when a new station will be built. If you plan to ride a bus to anywhere on the island, you must buy the ticket at the station before boarding your bus. Do not forget that if you are waiting at a designated bus stop, the bus will not stop for you unless you hold out your hand.

Provisions

Behind the *NIB Mall* is the *Scarborough Market*, a great place to find fresh fruits, vegetables, fish, and other local foods on Friday and Saturday mornings. Do not miss this market, it is a real treat.

Just across from *Customs* is *Food Town*, they're convenient and they have a good selection as well. Just down the road is the *View Port Supermarket* and they too have a good selection to choose from. On *Wilson Street* you'll find *Penny Savers*, while on *Main Street* you might find a few items at the small *Tobago Supermarket*.

Dining

A very popular eatery is *Ciao Café* and the next door *Ciao Pizza* on *Burnett Street*. Here you can enjoy gelato, pizza, pasta, sandwiches, home-made ice cream, wine, and Italian coffee. On *Pump Mill Road* is the *Salsa Kitchen*, a Tapas restaurant open from 1800-late.

East on *Bacolet Street* is the *Old Donkey Cart House,* home to exquisite Creole food and imported German wines, but I warn you, it might not fit well on some folk's budget. The restaurant, located in a house over a century old, is owned by Gloria Jones Schoen, a former German model who suggests reservations.

In town, and with a great view of the harbor from their *Robinson Street* location, the *Blue Crab* is open Monday-Friday for lunch and Wednesday-Friday for dinner.

Take a sharp right on *Castries Street* and you'll find a steep road, *Burnett Street,* the center of knick-knack shopping in Scarborough. On the other side of town, a good walk west of the ferry docks, is the *Ocean* View restaurant and *Bar Code*, a sports bar and grill open daily. On *Milford Road* you'll find *Jatt's Harbour Grill*.

At *NIB Mall,* just opposite the ferry dock, you'll find banks, a *Post Office*, pharmacies, and a food court. Scarborough has a new walkway called *The Scarborough Esplanade* on *Milford Road* which has a collection of food huts and craft shops where you can get a nice view of Scarborough and enjoy a cool breeze.

A note about pharmacies. There are no pharmacies along Tobago's northern shore so if you need medications you will need to visit a pharmacy in Crown Point or Scarborough.

Adjoining the *NIB Mall* is the *Botanical Gardens*, a great place to stop for a breather amid all the hustle and bustle of the street vendors and shoppers. Here on the 18-acre grounds of an old sugar estate, you can walk amid many species of flora that are indigenous to Tobago, but that are hard to find in the wild. The plants and trees are labeled and there's even a small fish pond graced by a statue created by Luise Kimme, a well-known German sculptor who resides nearby. Kimme has a museum in Mt. Irvine that is open Sunday mornings and you can view her work at http://www.luisekimme.com/.

High above the eastern side of the bay sits *Fort King George*, built by the British in 1779 and later captured by the French. The fort offers a magnificent view of Scarborough and *Rockly Bay*, and if you look to the east, you can see as far as Bacolet on the Windward Coast (what you might be inclined to call

the "southern" coast). Visitors to the fort can view the old chapel, what's left of a prison, a cemetery, and can visit a craft shop. The *Museum of Tobago History* is located in the *Barrack Guard House* at Fort George and offers several nice exhibits showcasing Tobago's history ranging from pre-Columbian Amerindian artifacts to tableware once used by Pirates and Colonial settlers as well as some African drums and other period pieces.

Just beyond is Bacolet, where The Beatles enjoyed a stay in the 1960s. Here too you'll find *The Cotton House*, a studio set in an old colonial house where you can view beautiful batiks and if you're so inclined, can create your own to take with you, they'll show you how. If lovely *Bacolet Bay Beach* looks familiar let me remind you that it was used in the Disney film *Swiss Family Robinson*.

Folks wishing to tour a bit inland should visit nearby Mason Hall to view the beautiful 50' high *Mason Falls*.

Crown Point to Pigeon Point, *Store Bay*

Waypoints:
Store Bay- ½ nm W of anchorage
11° 09.50' N, 60° 51.10' W

Crown Point-3 nm W of
11° 09.00' N, 60° 54.50' W

Pigeon Point- ½ nm W of anchorage off point
11° 10.20' N, 60° 51.20' W

Crown Point is the hub of tourism in Tobago. The airport is located here as well as several very nice hotels and quite a few car rental agencies. Many tourists that fly in to Tobago never make it past this area as so much of what they desire is here.

Store Bay, named after an early Dutch settler named Jan Stoer, has one of the most popular beaches on the island. The coconut palms that you see are remnants of the days when the land around *Store Bay* was a coconut plantation. *Store Bay* hosts several kite surfing, wind surfing, and dinghy sailing events known as the *Tobago Carnival Regatta, Festival of Wind*, usually held in February. *Store Bay* also hosts the annual *Marlin Madness Game Fishing Tournament* held every year at Pigeon Point, usually in March.

Store Bay Marine Services,
photo courtesy Katy Stickland, *SBMS*

Store Bay anchorage,
photo courtesy Katy Stickland, *SBMS*

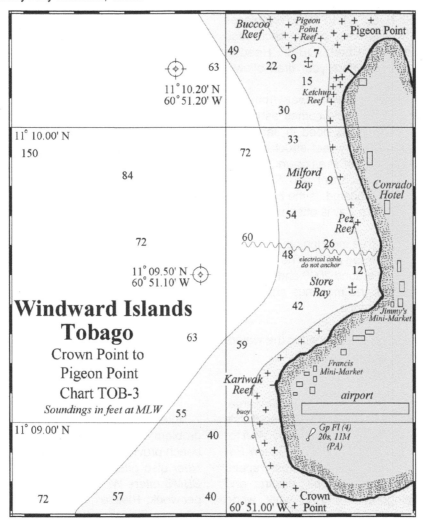

There are several anchorages here, just north of Crown Point at *Store Bay* and in *Milford Bay* off Pigeon Point (see the next section, *Pigeon Point, Buccoo Reef and Buccoo Bay*). Anchorages in the area between Crown Point and Pigeon Point can be rolly at times during the winter months during periods of northeasterly swells.

The areas around Crown Point, Pigeon Point, Buccoo, Bon Accord, Mt. Pleasant, and almost all the way to Mt. Irvine, is known as the Lowlands situated as it is on the low lying coastal plain at the southwestern tip of Tobago.

Navigational Information
Approaching Crown Point from Scarborough, follow the instructions in reverse (given in the last section, *Rockly Bay, Scarborough*) to work your way between the southwestern tip of Tobago and the shallow, and dangerous, *Wasp Shoal* as shown on Chart TOB-1. Round Crown Point a half-mile off and head for a waypoint at 11° 09.50' N, 60° 51.10' W, which places you approximately ½ mile west of the anchorage in *Store Bay* as shown on Chart TOB-3. Head in towards shore and anchor where your draft allows.

Be sure that you anchor well away from the electrical cable. Where the cable comes ashore is called *Cable Beach*. Holding is good in sand, but try not to drop the hook on any reef structure. On the beach, between *Coco Reef Breakwater* and the cable, where the *Bagos Beach Bar* and *Store Bay Marine Services* (*SBMS*) is located, is the best place to leave your dinghy as *Store Bay* is often rolly.

There are a number of free moorings that prevent any contact with the submerged cable. The moorings were poorly installed back around 2009 and have not been properly maintained: the moorings should not be used under any circumstance.

A final note: jet skis are now banned in the waters of Tobago from *Store Bay* to Plymouth.

Marine Facilities
The primary marine facility in the *Store Bay* area, and in fact on the island of Tobago, is John and Katy's *Store Bay Marine Services* (who also provide *Wi-fi* for the anchorage). Located next to *Bago's Beach Bar* on *Cable Beach*, *SBMS* can handle most repairs such as diesel and outboard repair, electric and electronic repairs, refrigeration and AC work, wood

or metalworking and fabrication, fiberglass repair and fabrication, sail and canvas repair, and marine plumbing. These services are available island-wide.

SBMS can arrange to have your much needed parts imported from either the USA or Trinidad. Cruisers can also get their propane tanks filled here (see next paragraph), as well as top off their diesel, water, gasoline, and paraffin/kerosene jerry jugs. You'll be delighted to know that you can also share the book swap that is dedicated to Tobagonian charities. You can leave your dinghy on the beach to visit *SMBS* as they have a security guard to watch over your dinghy. *SMBS* can even refuel and provision the largest mega-yacht. *SBMS* also has a launderette on site. *SBMS* can be hailed on VHF ch. 06 or 16.

Cooking gas refills are available island wide for local bottles with a push-on regulator. All other bottles, with the exception of the new fiberglass type, can be filled in *Store Bay* at *SBMS* regardless of certification, which can be an issue in Trinidad. Drop off your bottles at *SBMS* Monday-Friday for a same day refill.

If you head east on *Milford Road*, the principal highway between Scarborough and Crown Point, you'll find *Mariner's Outboards*. *Mariner's Outboards* caters primarily to the local fishermen and their stock of parts is limited to the larger outboards, 75hp and up. They do carry a limited selection of some very basic marine supplies and can get *Mercury* parts from Trinidad but do not offer service.

On *Milford Road*, just up from View Port, is *Stumpy's Hardware* offering a fair range of standard household type fixtures and fittings. *Carnbee Autos* has a good selection of tools and electrical parts and can arrange service for your diesel.

If you'd like to charter a boat in the area, *Sand Dollar Charters* has both cats and monohulls; give them a call at 620 4750.

What You Will Find Ashore
Internet Access
Internet access in the Crown Point area is not a problem, *Wi-fi* is available in the anchorage off the beach provided by *Store Bay Marine Services*. *Coco Reef* also offers *Wi-fi* at a rate of TT$60 per hour; *SBMS* offers *Wi-fi* for TT$75 for 3 days and TT$150 per week. Please note that these prices are subject to

change with time. SBMS also has an internet access station on site as well as their *Wi-fi*.

There are also three Internet access points that are only a short walk from the anchorage in *Store Bay*. Just across from the airport is the *RCS Cyber Café* with several new computers. A rather unique place is the *Clothes Wash Café* just down *Milford Road* a short distance from the airport toward Scarborough. Here you can do your laundry as you surf the net. I found the rates pricey, three times the rates in Chaguaramas. When I mentioned this to the lady in charge she offered me a discount since I was paying in cash.

Provisions
In the immediate area of Crown Point you can get groceries at *Jimmy's MiniMart* or at the *Francis Supermarket* located in the *Crown Point Beach Hotel*. About a mile east of Crown Point, on *Milford Road*, is the *Penny Saver Supermarket*, and in View Port, the *View Port Market* is just a few hundred yards up the road from *Penny Saver*.

Getting Around
If you need transportation to some of the places mentioned here, the best bet is a street car, similar to a maxi-taxi but a car instead. Crown Point to *Penny Savers* will cost TT$3 per person each way (prices given are subject to change with time). To Scarborough from Crown Point will cost you TT$6 per person each way. You get these taxi's by sticking your hand out. As with anywhere, don't forget to settle on a fare before you get in.

Dining
The Crown Point area is rife with food stalls, restaurants, and enough bars with happy hours to entertain all visitors. Local cuisine is well represented in the rotis, crab and dumplin', macaroni pie with callaloo, and curry goat and vegetable that you'll find in any one of several eateries in the area. Just take a stroll ashore and chose from *Miss Jean's, Miss Trim's, Alma's, Silvia's, Miss Esmee's*, and *Joicy's* for the best in local style eating. The dining is much the same from stall to stall and you won't be unhappy with any particular choice. They will open for lunch but you'll have to opt for an early dinner as most stalls close by 1900.

On *Cable Beach, Bagos Beach Bar* now serves food and is under new management. The *Original Pancake House* on *Milford Road* has excellent food.

The *Columbus Snackette*, known as *Uncle C's*, just across from the airport is a great spot for flying-fish sandwiches, beer, and just liming, especially on the weekends. *WYSIWYG* sits off the *Store Bay* road and boasts exceptional Mexican and Cajun flavored fare.

Nearly all of the hotels in the area have excellent restaurants located in their establishment. The *Tropikist Hotel* has a superb bar and restaurant right on the edge of *Store Bay*. Their pool features a private waterfall and swim-up bar. The *Coco Reef Resort* has two restaurants and several bars. You are not welcome to leave your dinghy on their beach unless you are dining at the resort.

You can also dine at the *Crown Point Hotel* (the *Bay Restaurant*) and the *Kariwak Village*.

If you head east on *Milford Road* you'll find *Dillon's Restaurant*, and the *Backyard Café* serving lunch and light early evening fare. Next door to the *Clothes Wash Café* is *La Cantina*, a popular pizzeria which bakes their pizzas in a clay oven and is available on weekends and holidays with advance notice. There is a selection of takeaway outlets on the corner of *Milford Road* and *Pigeon Point Road* where you can get pizza, burgers, gyros, jerk chicken and a variety of local dishes. Nearby is the *Fortune City Chinese Restaurant*.

Located at *Stumpy's Hardware* is *Boss Ah Soup* where you can dine on reasonably priced local soups such as Cow Heal, Pig Tail and Corn Soup.

Discovering Crown Point

A good snorkel is *Kariwak Reef*, just off the beach west of the airport. The beach at the resort is as pretty as any beach to be found in the Caribbean and is often the subject of photographers, from the aquamarine waters of the Caribbean to the wooden pier and thatch-roofed huts backed by graceful palm trees.

A wealth of local information can be found in the person of Allan Clovis, the owner of *Kariwak Village* (an eco-resort designated Tobago's *Top Tourism Award* winner in 1999-don't miss their Saturday night buffet). Allan knows all the best spots around and is happy to help with directions and suggestions. Ask Allan for directions to *Robinson Crusoe's Cave* off the *Bon Accord Road* past the airport at the southern extremity of Crown Point. And when you head off to the cave, take a minute or two and view the remains of *Fort Milford*. The fort was preceded by a Latvian settlement and later, a Dutch redoubt called *Belleviste*. What you see today is all that remains of the fort the British built here in 1777. Six cannon here point out to sea; five of them are British, and one is French, deposited here when the French had possession of Tobago between 1781-1793. Past the fort the road curves left and when you are past the airport runway you'll shortly come to a hand-painted sign marking the turn to the cave. Head to the last house and see Mrs. Crooks whose family owns the land which leads to the cave. She'll collect the TT$5 admission and direct you to the cave. The cave itself, once reaching all the way back to *Store Bay*, is now quite small, having been damaged over time by earthquakes.

It is said that Mr. Crooks came about the idea for the cave after reading the novel *Robinson Crusoe* to coincide with the local rumor that Tobago was actually Crusoe's island. Although the author, Daniel Defoe, is said to have based his novel on the trials and tribulations of Alexander Selkirk on the island of Juan Fernandez off the coast of Chile, the introduction to the first edition places the hero in a different area entirely. Defoe's description describes the island of Robinson Cruise as lying off the Americas near the mouth of the river "Oroonoque." It is suggested that Defoe read a pamphlet that was commissioned by the Duke of Courland describing the natural wonders of Tobago designed to entice developers to invest in Tobago. Some say that the descriptions in the pamphlet gave Defoe a basis for his novel. Whatever the case may be, it's still a pretty spot.

Pigeon Point and *Buccoo Reef,*

Waypoints:
Buccoo Reef- ½ nm WNW Bon Accord Lagoon
11° 11.30' N, 60° 50.70' W

Pigeon Point- ½ nm W of anchorage off point
11° 10.20' N, 60° 51.20' W

Buccoo Reef was established as a restricted area in 1973 and the removal or harming of corals, shells, or sea life is prohibited as is anchoring except in the designated areas. Vessels wishing to access *Buccoo Reef* for diving or snorkeling purposes, such as tenders and dinghies, are required to have a permit.

This means that if you do not have this permit, you'll have to swim out from the shore to enjoy the reef.

Please note on Chart TOB-4, the approximate boundaries of the *Buccoo Reef Marine Park* (the dashed line). Unless you have permission from the Minister you may not anchor inside these lines, dinghies are prohibited as well. For now, there is no clearly defined regulation as to when access to the lagoon is legal, but it is safe to say that it would be when a Tropical Depression/Tropical Storm/Hurricane Warning is in effect for the area.

Also take note that you are not permitted to remove any fish, bird, corals, crabs, lobsters, shrimp, turtles, turtle eggs, and any species of marine fauna or mangrove without the permission of the Minister. If you are found guilty of going afoul of these regulations the fine is $1,000 and $50 per each occurrence thereafter.

It has taken over 10,000 years to create this masterpiece which is home to over 40 species of hard and soft corals. As shown on Chart TOB-4, the *Buccoo Reef* system is actually made up of several smaller reefs, of which the outer reefs dry at low water in places. The reefs are separated by three channels, *False Channel*, *Blind Passage*, and *Gibson Channell* (the only one viable for cruising boats of any draft). *Gibson Channel* is sometimes shown as *Deep Channel* on some charts, but everybody knows it as *Gibson Channel*. It's named after Ralph Gibson, probably the most experienced and knowledgeable mariner in all of Trinidad and Tobago.

Although a lot of the *Buccoo Reef* system seems to be dying, there is still a lot of coral and marine life for you to view while snorkeling from your dinghy.

Ketchup Reef lies just southwest of Pigeon Point and stretches about 200 yards south. The reef received its name from a large cargo of ketchup that was dumped on the reef when a cargo ship ran aground there.

Navigational Information
North of *Store Bay* is an anchorage off Pigeon Point. As shown on Chart TOB-3 and TOB-4, a waypoint at 11° 10.20' N, 60° 51.20' W, will place you approximately ½ mile west of this anchorage. The anchorage itself lies between *Pigeon Point Reef,* part of the *Buccoo Reef* system, and *Ketchup Reef*, and

Pigeon Point,
photo courtesy Katy Stickland, *SBMS*

The Nylon Pool

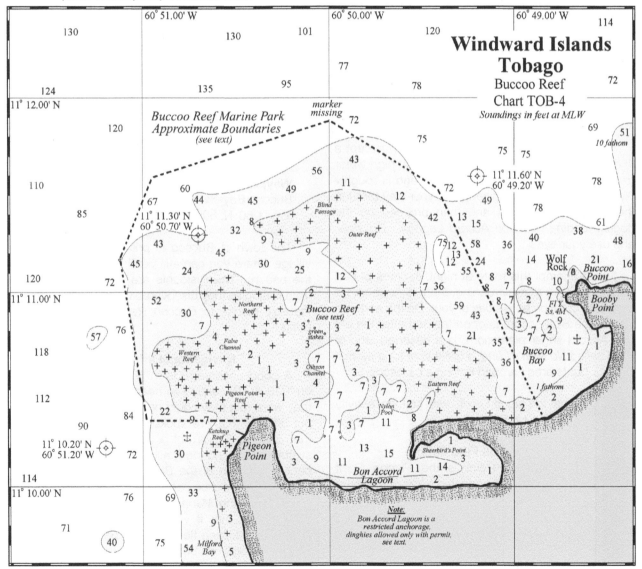

Windward Islands
Tobago
Buccoo Reef
Chart TOB-4
Soundings in feet at MLW

Buccoo Reef Marine Park
Approximate Boundaries
(see text)

Note:
Bon Accord Lagoon is a
restricted anchorage,
dinghies allowed only with permit,
see text.

lies generally west of the *Pigeon Point Resort* and is generally considered part of the exclusion area. If you plan to anchor here make sure you anchor well south of the park boundaries (see Chart TOB-4).

The best anchorage, a spot to be considered only as a hurricane hole, is in *Bon Accord Lagoon*. The anchorage here IS part of the national park and anchoring is prohibited except in the event of a hurricane. This mangrove-lined cove has good holding in 10' and offers great protection from all directions. Entrance directions will be given here with the understanding that the anchorage is only to be used for shelter from a hurricane.

As shown on TOB-4, a waypoint at 11° 11.30' N, 60° 50.70' W, will place you approximately ½ mile northwest of *Gibson Channel*, the entrance channel to *Bon Accord Lagoon*. You'll have to use your eyes to pilot through here, no waypoints can be given. If approaching from Pigeon Point, keep an eye out for *False Channel*, easily recognized, that dead ends quickly in the reef system. If you require assistance entering the lagoon, contact *SBMS* and they can help.

Gibson Channel on the other hand can accept a 4' draft a bit above low water, and 6'-7' at high water (remember that the tidal range in Tobago is roughly 3'). From the waypoint given, pilot your way through the deep water pocket and then proceed on the dogleg leading into *Bon Accord Lagoon*. Go slow, and use your eyes.

Never attempt this route at night, in times of bad visibility, or with a swell running, there is no room for error with coral on both sides of you. On the northern side of the *Bon Accord Lagoon* (named after the old Bon Accord sugar plantation), is a deserted strip of sand called *No Man's Land*, a great spot for a swim if the tour boats aren't around having a barbecue.

I'm told that the lagoon is rife with criminal activity these days so use caution.

What You Will Find Ashore
Located at Pigeon Point is the *Pigeon Point Heritage Park* whose 125 protected acres offers three restaurants and several craft shops. The park's entry fee is TT$18 per person, half that for children with kids under 6 entering free.

The park also has a parking lot for cars (just in case you're thinking of renting a car and parking it here as you are anchored out). Ask at the office for the fee for this and remember that the gates close at 1800 so make arrangements if you need to arrive or leave after that time.

Diving
Some of the best snorkeling in Tobago can be found on the many reefs that comprise the *Buccoo Reef* system. A popular spot is the *Nylon Pool*, a shallow spot only about 3' deep that lies atop a sandbar in the middle of the bay. The *Nylon Pool* is said to have been named by Princess Margaret in the 1950s when she remarked that the water was as clear as her nylon stockings. A lot of *Buccoo Reef* is dead and more still dying thanks to carelessly placed anchors, misguided fishing spears, and unscrupulous coral collectors. Today's glass-bottom-boat operators are helping out with the care and preservation of the reef by only anchoring on dead coral and reminding their charges not to touch the reef or remove any corals. A three-hour tour on one of these boats only costs about TT$60 and takes three hours including a dip in the *Nylon Pool*.

Buccoo Bay

Waypoints:
Buccoo Bay- ¾ nm N of
11° 11.60' N, 60° 49.20' W

The town of Buccoo is primarily a small fishing village where you can still purchase fresh fish along the beach. The residents are slowly getting away from fishing as they discovered the burgeoning tourist industry thanks to *Buccoo Reef* and glass bottom boats.

Navigational Information
A good anchorage is in *Buccoo Bay* as shown on TOB-4. Recently I've heard cruisers tell me that they were told they could not anchor in *Buccoo Bay*, but officials that I've spoken to have reassured me that *Buccoo Bay* is not a part of the *Buccoo Park* system and anchoring is allowed. If *Buccoo Bay* ever becomes a part of the *Buccoo Reef National Park*, anchoring will not be permitted. For more information you can call the *Marine Park Manager* at 639-4446. Please note that if you anchor in a manner that restricts the fishing fleet you will be asked to move. The anchorage can be very noise on Sundays due to

Sunday School (see the next section, *What You Will Find Ashore*).

As shown on TOB-4, a waypoint at 11° 11.60' N, 60° 49.20' W, will place you approximately ½ mile north of the entrance to *Buccoo Bay* between Booby Point and *Buccoo Reef*. If approaching from the anchorages in the *Store Bay* area, give *Buccoo Reef* a wide berth. From the waypoint, steer generally SSE into the bay, heading generally for the rocky patch in the middle of the beach, and favoring the *Buccoo Bay* side to avoid the shoals off Booby Point. The deeper water lies on the western part of the bay as shown on the chart.

Once past the shoals off Booby Point turn to port and anchor off the beach wherever your draft allows. The beach, though pretty, is not a good spot for swimming, especially the day after *Sunday School* (you will learn about *Sunday School* in a moment) when it is used as a huge urinal by the hordes of partygoers. You can tie your dinghy up to the small dock, but you'll need a stern anchor.

What You Will Find Ashore
Buccoo is known for several things, the most famous of which is *Sunday School,* a massive party packed with Tobagans and tourists. The festivities begin each Sunday evening around 8pm with live Pan music for a couple of hours. The crowd thickens by 2200-2300 as the sound systems from the beach stalls compete with each other to see who can achieve the highest decibel level as merrymakers sing and dance into the wee morning hours. A good spot to view the festivities is at *ClubBoss*, especially during Easter when the biggest *Sunday School* of the year occurs with parked cars seemingly backed up as far as Mr. Irvine.

The other event for which Buccoo is noted, are the Easter Tuesday goat races that were introduced by Barbadian Samuel Callender in 1825 as a poor man's substitute for horse racing. Racing goats, like horses, are a breed apart from their fellow goats and are never intended for the pot. They are sleek and graceful and bettors study them as their counterparts at the *Kentucky Derby* would a thoroughbred filly. The jockeys, who must be good sprinters, are tethered to their charges and attired in colorful vests and white shorts. The crowd feels the tension as the goats reach the manually operated starting gate. As the race begins the jockey's spur on their steeds with the help of a long stick, but unfortunately, and quite to the

delight of the crowd, some goats take off on a tangent tripping up other goats and jockeys. The betting is heavy on this event as well as the accompanying crab races and everybody has fun. The scoreboard for the goat race is left up for the rest of the year to inspire the next year's contestants. Buccoo has just built a new stadium for the goat races.

Provisions
As I mentioned earlier, it is still possible to buy fresh fish from the local fishermen on the beach, and you can also find local produce courtesy of vendors on the main road.

Just up from the goat stadium is *Aunty Flo's*, a basic mini-mart. Further up the road is one of the best places for provisions, *Welcome to Buccoo*, which stocks a wide variety of food stuffs and household goods. On the road leading to Buccoo from the junction is the newly opened *Buccoo Supermarket* which stocks foodstuffs and frozen meat.

Esse's is a small grocery store just down the road, and if you would like some great cold cuts, deli meats, canned goods, and English foods, try *R.T. Morshead* on the *Buccoo Road* in nearby Mt. Pleasant.

Dining
In town you can dine in any of several nice restaurants such as La *Tartaruga*, a fine Italian restaurant (serving fine Italian wines) offering terrace dining and a café bar, but only for dinner. *Papillon*, at the *Old Grange Inn*, is now a Chinese restaurant, while at the *Miller Guest House* across from the dock you'll find the *El Pescador* specializes in local fare, serving breakfast, lunch, and dinner. Around the corner, on the road to Buccoo, is *Shirl's Finger Licking* which is popular with the local crowd.

Vernon at *Zan's Bar* can cook up a good dinner with a few hours notice. For a more local flavor, visit *ClubBoss* or the *Mot Mot Restaurant* between Buccoo Junction and Carnbee. *Mot Mot* is one of the best restaurants in the area and worth a visit. Next door to *ClubBoss* is *Batik Point*, a batik studio and craft shop open Monday-Friday during the day and from 2100-late on Sunday. If you just want an air-conditioned place to enjoy a drink, try the *Polo Bar* on *Post Office Street*.

A nice side trip is a visit to *Signal Hill*, a great vantage point from which you can view the lowlands from Crown Point to *Grafton Bay*. *Signal Hill* was once used as a lookout location where observers could signal the nearby forts of approaching vessels. Today the area is home to a school and the Trinidad and Tobago Regiment whose marching band can sometimes be heard practicing. Nearby *Orange Hill Road* will take you up to *Patience Hill* where you'll find a great view of the lowlands at *Patience Hill Back Bottom Road*.

Mt. Irvine Bay

Waypoints:
Mt. Irvine Bay- ½ nm W of anchorage
11° 11.80' N, 60° 48.60' W

Lying just northeast of *Buccoo Bay* are two good anchorages at *Mt. Irvine Bay* and *Grafton Bay*.

Navigational Information
If headed for *Mt. Irvine Bay* from *Buccoo Bay*, round Wolf Rock (TOB-4) giving it a berth of at least ¼ mile and head for the northeastern tip of *Mt. Irvine Bay* to anchor in the lee of Rocky Point as shown on Chart TOB-5. If approaching from offshore head for a waypoint at 11° 11.80' N, 60° 48.60' W, which will place you approximately ½ mile west/northwest of the anchorage area. Head in towards the anchorage giving Rocky Point and its off-lying reef a wide berth.

What You Will Find Ashore
Ashore in the center of the bay is the *Mt. Irvine Bay Hotel* built on the site of a sugar plantation owned by Charles Irvine in the latter 1700s. The resort boasts the island's oldest golf course and cruisers are welcome to come ashore, pay a fee, and enjoy 18 holes or a game on the tennis court with the necessary equipment available for rent (after all, how many cruising boats carry golf clubs aboard?). The championship golf course opened in 1968 and has been rated as one of the top fifty courses in the world. You are welcome to use the beach at the hotel and take a shower if you buy a drink at the bar.

In the hills across the road from the beach, overlooking the *Mt. Irvine Golf Course*, is the *Kimme Museum, The Castle* as it's known locally. The museum is the private gallery of German-born sculptress Luise Kimme, who moved to Tobago in 1979 and set up a studio with local sculptor and fisherman Albert Prince. Her 12' tall wooden carvings, fashioned from tree trunks, depict Tobagan dancing and various creatures

of folklore such as the *Soucouyant* and *La Diablesse*. The museum is only open on Sundays from 11-2 and is free. If you wish to visit at other times call 639-0257 for an appointment.

If you need to rent a car in the area, *Frankie's Tours and Rentals* is located at the car park at Mt. Irvine.

Internet Access
The *Mt. Irvine Bay Hotel* has an Internet café on site. Most of the larger hotels on Tobago offer internet access to their guests.

Provisions
On the road leading to Plymouth is *Marie's Place* with a small market on the ground floor and a restaurant on the upper level. In Mount Irvine you can purchase fresh fish directly from the fishermen at the *Mount Irvine Fish Market*.

Dining
The *Mt. Irvine Bay Hotel* boasts three fine restaurants. The *Sugar Mill* is located next to the luxurious oval pool and a 200 year old sugar mill. the equally elegant *La Jacaranda Restaurant*, and *Le Beau Rivage*, a bit more upscale featuring the finest in gourmet French and Nouvelle Creole cuisine.

Mt. Irvine Beach is a favorite stop for tourists and locals alike. Ashore you'll find gazebos, palm trees, and beach facilities (showers!) that charge TT$1. Surfers flock here in the winter months when northerly swells create good surfing opportunities. This is why you'll spy *Surfer's Restaurant and Bar* on the shore. You'll also find a series of food huts on the road by the beach serving rotis and pies. A half mile to the northeast is an *ATM* machine.

On the road leading to Plymouth is the *Ocean View Bar* perched atop a hill with a commanding view of the local waters. Just across the road is *Marie's Place* with a restaurant on the upper floor, above the small market.

Diving
At the northern tip of *Mt. Irvine Bay* is Rocky Point, and off the point you'll find great snorkeling on *Mt. Irvine Reef*, sometimes called *Mt. Irvine Wall*, and that should give you an idea of what you'll find on that dive. Further out from the point is the wreck of the *Maverick*, another interesting dive site. On the

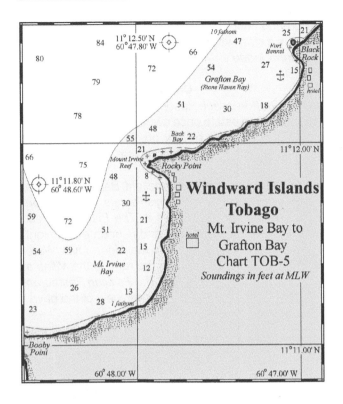

Windward Islands Tobago
Mt. Irvine Bay to
Grafton Bay
Chart TOB-5
Soundings in feet at MLW

Ft. James, Great Courland Bay

Rafael Anslim Davis, a busker, *Great Courland Bay*

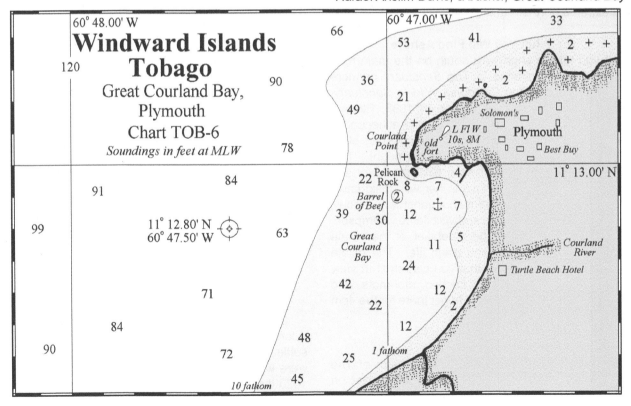

Windward Islands Tobago
Great Courland Bay,
Plymouth
Chart TOB-6
Soundings in feet at MLW

northern side of Rocky Point is a small beach known as *Back Bay*, a popular nude beach.

Grafton Bay

Waypoints:
Grafton Bay- ½ nm WNW of anchorage
11° 12.50' N, 60° 47.80' W

The next anchorage to the northeast is *Grafton Bay*, sometimes shown as *Stone Haven Bay*. The bay can get rolly so you might have to use a stern anchor or bridle setup to get a bit of comfort at night.

Navigational Information
Approaching from *Mt. Irvine Bay* is easy, it's just around the corner so to speak. As shown on Chart TOB-5, give Rocky Point a wide berth and head toward the anchorage area off the beach just inside the point at Black Rock. If approaching from offshore a waypoint at 11° 12.50' N, 60° 47.80' W, will place you approximately ¾ mile WNW of the anchorage area.

From the waypoint, head in towards the beach giving a wide berth to the point at Black Rock and round up to anchor off the posh *Grafton Beach Hotel and Resort*. Adjoining the *Grafton Beach Hotel* is *Le Grand Courlan Spa Resort*. Dinghies should land at the extreme northern end of the beach.

What You Will Find Ashore
If you take a short walk south on the main road you'll find the entrance to *The Sanctuary* or more precisely, the *Grafton Caledonia Wildlife Sanctuary*. After *Hurricane Flora* hit Tobago in 1963, Eleanor Alefounder began a bird feeding program at her cocoa estate since the animals had found themselves short of food after the damage that *Flora* wrought. This daily feeding snowballed into a bird sanctuary and Mrs. Alefounder left a clause in her will designating this part of her estate to remain a sanctuary. Today, you can enter the grounds and visit James Sampson, the "Bird Man," who is the caretaker of the estate and an authority on Tobago avian life. The estate has several marked trails that you can stroll to view birds such as bananaquits, cocrico, mot-mots, and blue tanagers (blue jays). Try to get there for the 4pm feeding at the *Copra House*.

Provisions
On the road leading to Mt. Irvine, south of *The Sanctuary*, is *Marie's Place* with a small market on

the ground floor and a restaurant on the upper level. There is a small vegetable and fruit stall just down the road from *Marie's*.

Dining
The *Grafton Beach Resort* stands on the grounds of the old Grafton estate once owned by the Smith family, a family with a long history on Tobago. Don't miss the Friday night barbecue complete with live music.

Above *Marie's* is the *Limelight Bar and Lounge*, while next door is *Pizza Boys/Rituals Coffee Shop*. On the other side of *Marie's* is *The Fish Pot* which specializes in local seafood and is open every night. A bit further down the road is the *Moon Over Water Bar*. Just a short walk down the road is the *Villas at Stone Haven* where you'll find *The Pavilion Restaurant* serving elaborate food with a great view of the bay.

Just off the beach at Stone Haven is *The Seahorse*, serving some of Tobago's best cuisine and fine wines. Just down the road is the *Buccaneers Bar* serving lunch, a perfect spot to stop and enjoy a good bite to eat, a cool place to sit, and enjoy the breeze and waves. When the sun goes down you'll have to go elsewhere as the bar closes early.

Heading north on the main road you'll find the settlement of Black Rock with several nice run shops (bars). In town you'll find the *Mon Cheri Cafe*, *Michael's*, and *Food Town*, a medium-sized supermarket that is good for basic provisions.

To seaward of Black Rock are the remains of *Fort Bennet*, built by British Lt. Robert Bennet in 1680. The British expanded *Fort Bennet* during the plantation era in 1778 to protect against American privateers during the American Revolution. Today the fort offers great views of the surrounding waters as well as particularly nice sunsets.

Great Courland Bay, Plymouth

Waypoints:
Great Courland Bay- ½ nm W of anchorage
11° 12.80' N, 60° 47.50' W

Great Courland Bay and the town of Plymouth have a long and confusing history. The British originally settled Tobago in 1625 when the first group of settlers were wiped out by the indigenous Amerindians. In 1628 the Dutch arrived at Plymouth, but a combined force of Indians and Spaniards from Trinidad arrived in canoes and killed off the Dutch settlers, the only time that Trinidad and Tobago ever went to war with each other. In 1639 the British arrived again, only to be run off once more by the Amerindians. Tiring of this, Charles I gave the island to his godson, Duke James Jekabs of Courland (Latvia), and another settlement was established at Plymouth in 1642 by the Courlanders. Again, the settlers made like a ping-pong ball being chased off by the Indians, returning in 1650, and again in 1654. In 1658 the Dutch returned and claimed dominion of the island and renamed the settlement *Nieuw Vissingen*. Twenty years later the remaining Courlanders left, but some of their Latvian descendants still make an annual pilgrimage to Plymouth. In Plymouth you can view *The Courland Monument*, a striking sculpture unveiled in 1976 that commemorates the 17th century settlers from Latvia.

The Dutch were finally driven off by the British who maintained a military presence at Plymouth, which was now the Capital of Tobago, by building a fort atop Courland Point. With an excellent view of the *Great Courland Bay*, *Fort James* sits atop Courland Point, its cannon still pointing to sea. The fort was built by the British in 1768 during the plantation era as a barracks for the troops sent to protect the settlement at Plymouth (the British were also constructing several other forts on Tobago at this time as well). Named after the Duke of Courland, James Jekabs, the fort has an interesting history. Once again the ping-pong ball was to bounce as the French arrived. A nighttime insertion of two dozen French soldiers was the key to French victory at Plymouth. The soldiers made such a ruckus the next morning that the confused British thought they were outnumbered. The French commander notified his British counterpart there were a thousand Frenchmen waiting to attack on his signal which terrified the British leader to surrender immediately with no shots fired. The conquering French destroyed the settlements and quickly abandoned the island. Luckily for us this was not the end of the story and so today you'll find a friendly residential community sitting atop the ridge overlooking the bay.

Navigational Information

If you're leaving *Grafton Bay*, simply give the point at Black Rock and its off-lying rock a wide berth, at least ¼ mile off, and head straight for the northeastern pocket of *Great Courland Bay*. Vessels arriving from offshore can head for a waypoint at 11° 12.80' N, 60° 47.50' W, which will place you approximately ½ mile west of the anchorage area as shown on Chart TOB-6. From the waypoint head a bit south of east giving the shoal off Courland Point a wide berth to round up and drop the hook just southeast of the fort atop Courland Point. Don't try to pass between the submerged rock known as *Barrel of Beef* and Pelican Rock. The bottom is rocky here and only 8'-11' deep in spots, it's best to avoid it and *Barrel of Beef,* you really don't gain anything by passing inside the submerged rock, and you put a lot at risk. Do not anchor off the *Turtle Beach Hotel*.

What You Will Find Ashore

The curving beach that you see is known as *Turtle Beach*. During the months from March to August huge leatherback turtles come ashore to lay their eggs. In just a little over thirty minutes they will dig a hole straight down 3' deep and deposit their eggs, two or three at a time, and when they cover the nest and leave, you'll hardly know they were ever there so well do they recover the spot. Within six weeks, the hatchlings begin making their way to sea to someday return to lay their eggs on the beach. For further information visit www.sos-tobago.org.

Opposite the beach is a *YMCA* with a public swimming pool.

Provisions

In Plymouth you'll find several small grocery stores with the usual basic provisions as well as a gas station if you don't mind jerry-jugging your fuel. Next door to the gas station is *TJ's Mini Mart* which stocks a good supply of groceries and has a bar attached.

You can pick up some basic groceries at *Best Buy Supermarket* (formerly *Price Right*-see the chart). Just up the road is *CP Hardware and Tackling Shop* which has a Post Office and an *ATM* on site.

Dining

You can get a bite to eat at the *Cocorite Inn* on the *Arnos Vale Road*, or the more laid back, *Fad's Homestyle* on *Shelbourne St.*, where a scrumptious local buffet awaits you. A few doors down is the Hollywood Chinese Restaurant where you can enjoy their buffet or grab some take out. One of the finest restaurants in Plymouth is on *North Street*, *Peter's Restaurant and Bar*, where owner Eddy is the former chef at the *Arnos Vale Hotel* (in Arnos Vale, the restaurant at the *Arnos Vale Hotel* is pricey and more on the elegant side, but *Peter's* is more down home).

Midway down the beach you'll find the *Turtle Beach Hotel* whose facilities are for their guests only, however feel free to visit the *Kiskadee Restaurant* with its unbeatable and unique nightly live entertainment and ever changing schedule of buffets and barbecues.

Discovering Plymouth

Taking a hike up to Courland Point to visit the fort you'll likely meet Rafael Davis. Rafael Anslim Davis is a *busker*, a *Calypso Poet*, someone who improvises Calypso for money. A *busker* must be able to improvise, to think quickly on his feet, and make up humorous verses for you that will entice you to part with a blue one (a TT$100 note), and Rafael is very good at it. Give him a listen, you can't help that, he'll sing for you whether you want him to or not, and decide if you think he's worth a blue one.

Just a bit northeast of the fort you'll find the *Mystery Tombstone*. The tombstone, dated 1783, marks the double grave of 23-year old Betty Stiven and her child. The mystery is the tombstone's inscription which states: "What was remarkable of her, she was a mother without knowing it, and a wife without letting her husband know it, except by her kind indulgencies to him." Betty is said to have been the African maid and lover of wealthy Dutch planter Alex Stiven. Local experts will give you two stories concerning the inscription. One theory is that Betty gave birth to Alex's mixed-blood child and he took charge of the infant raising it as his own and not acknowledging Betty as the mother, leaving her free to remain as his lover, making her a mother without knowing it. The other theory suggests that the affair between Betty and Alex was highly secret as Alex could not be seen as having a slave as a lover. When Betty died at childbirth Alex is said to have created the inscription as a testament of his love for her. Take your pick, I personally believe the latter...but who knows? That's why it's a mystery.

Just north of Plymouth is *Culloden Bay*, shallow and reef strewn, I only mention if for the fantastic diving available there. Here you'll find a tremendous amount of coral structure and waters rich in diverse marine life that is virtually untouched by man. It has been recommended that *Culloden Bay* be designated a marine reserve, a good idea to protect this beautiful area. *Culloden Bay* is home to *Footprints*, an eco-friendly resort whose focus is the preservation and protection of the environment. The rooms are perched on stilts and have solar heated Jacuzzis built of teak and recycled hardwoods. Another mile or so northeastward is *Arnos Vale Bay*, also shallow with access only for small fishing boats via a narrow, shallow channel. *Arnos Vale Bay* is another one of the great snorkeling sites located on the northern coast of Tobago.

If you're driving through the area you'll find that the roads through here are quite pleasant as you proceed north of Plymouth. They are well paved with few potholes, narrow and steep in places, in others the sharp curves are lined with large concrete walls and curbs. You'll pass lots of sheer drop-offs with breathtaking views of the Caribbean, the mountains and valleys of the rainforest, and several hilltop settlements. In places you'll drive through huge bamboo canopies and both sides of the roads are thick with jungle-like vegetation as you run alongside a fresh-water stream.

On the road outside Plymouth you find pineapple shaped signs that read "Follow the pineapple to the *Arnos Vale Waterwheel*." If you follow the signs you'll soon find the waterwheel, but first you'll need to make a stop at the *Adventure Farm and Nature Reserve* for some bird watching and guided tours of its 12 acres.

Following the pineapples you'll continue along amid all sorts of tropical vegetation and soon come to the *Arnos Vale Waterwheel Park*, what was once an absolutely gorgeous place but has fallen into a bit of disrepair of late. This entire area was once the Arnos Vale sugar plantation and today little is left save the beach resort at *Arnold Vale Beach* and the *Waterwheel Park*. At the park you can stroll along a wooden walkway and view the restored remains of the old waterwheel that powered the old mill, and the steam train that moved sugar cane around the estate. The restaurant and gift shop are now closed, but you can still visit the small museum and theater with exhibits of Amerindian and colonial artifacts. Take a walk through the grounds and view the sweet scented tropical plants and colorful flowers that the former British owners of this estate planted on the grounds.

If you continue past *Waterwheel Park* you'll come to a crossroads at Les Couteaux. Taking a left will allow you to continue along the northern coast with its stunning vistas. Taking a right will take you into Scarborough, and if you continue straight ahead you'll come to the *Hillsborough Dam* where there's a good chance you might spy a caiman as they like to lime in the still waters above the dams on Tobago and Trinidad. The town of Les Couteaux itself is known locally for the fact that *Obeah* is said to still be practiced here, *Obeah* being a form of magic that originated in Africa. During the *Heritage Week Festival* every July the town hosts scary storytelling sessions for those interested.

Castara Bay

Waypoints:
Castara Bay- ½ nm WNW of anchorage area
11° 17.00' N, 60° 42.70' W

Castara is a small fishing village whose 500 or so inhabitants fish and farm, though a few work for the government in a series of seemingly never-ending road improvement projects. The popular public beach has some very nice changing facilities with showers along with the *Cascreole Restaurant and Bar*. Along the working section of the beach you'll find fishermen liming away, mending their nets and waiting for the tide to change. The *Fisherman's Co-Op* (the building where the fishermen clean their catch) is a good place to buy some fresh fish and the small restaurant directly behind it a great spot for a really satisfying and economical meal.

Castara Bay is a good spot to see fisherman seine netting. Seine netting, or *pulling seine*, is the Tobagan communal fishing method and you're likely to see it anywhere in the anchorages of the island. Fishermen drop nets in a circle from the shore by small boat and anybody and everybody is welcome to haul in the net and payment is made in fish. In August the town celebrates the *Castara Fisherman's Fete* with party-goers eating, drinking, and dancing from noon until late into the night.

Navigational Information
Your next stop on your Tobago circumnavigation can be *Castara Bay* as shown on Chart TOB-1. If headed there from *Great Courland Bay*, keep at least a half-mile offshore to avoid any off-lying dangers. Yes, I know, other guides say you can keep in as close as ¼ mile, but I suggest a more conservative approach just to be on the safe side, the choice is up to you. Head for a waypoint at 11° 17.00' N, 60° 42.70' W, which places you approximately ½ mile west/northwest of the anchorage area off the public beach as shown on TOB-7.

What You Will Find Ashore
Provisions
Everything here is built on the hillsides overlooking beautiful *Castara Bay*. If you need groceries there are several small stalls set up along the roadside selling basic supplies, but your best bet is *L&H* right on the beachfront next to the fishing coop. Owners Loris and Hazel have a nice little store with a restaurant (*L&H Sunset Restaurant*) upstairs. You can also try *Jackson's Grocery*, or the *Vegetable Shop* (see chart). Just before *Cascreole Restaurant* is *Sunkiss Supermarket*, a new supermarket on the beach that is good for provisioning.

Dining
Just down from *L&H*, right on the beach, is the *Cascreole Restaurant*, the perfect spot for seafood on the waterfront. For the absolute best in local cuisine visit Rebecca at *Clay's Kitchen*. If you just want breakfast, THE spot is *Cheno's Coffee Bar* on *Main Road*.

Leading down to the *Castara Beach* facilities is *D Lime Bar* and *D'Almond Tree Restaurant*. There is an ATM and a phone located on the *Main Road*.

On the *Main Road* next to the school is *Marguarite's*, a pleasant local eatery that allows you to bring your own beer and wine (no liquor). The fare includes fish and chips and some great home made pizza. Just across from *Marguarite's* is a great lunch spot, *Riverside Cottage*.

Located on a hillside off *Main Road* is *Sandcastles*, a small and intimate restaurant that offers free shuttle service from town. Reservations are required so you'll have to call them at 732-4882 to arrange pickup in town.

Just outside of town heading north is the *Naturalist Beach Resort*. Do you think the name implies what you'll find here? You're wrong! It is for those who are into nature and a *No Nudity* sign was put up when people began getting the wrong idea about the place.

At the eastern edge of *Castara Bay* is a bridge over the *Castara River*. If you follow the river upstream for about 15 minutes you'll find a small waterfall with a deep pool at the bottom for swimming. There's another waterfall about an hour's walk away and the best way to find it is to hire a local guide such as Hilly Williams (639-6485).

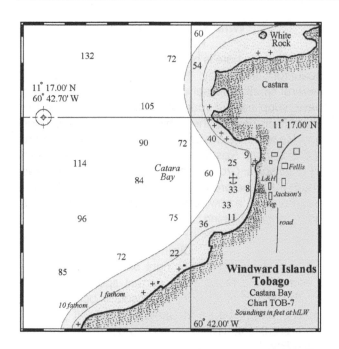

Windward Islands
Tobago
Castara Bay
Chart TOB-7
Soundings in feet at MLW

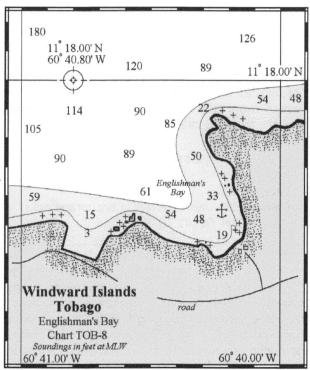

Windward Islands
Tobago
Englishman's Bay
Chart TOB-8
Soundings in feet at MLW

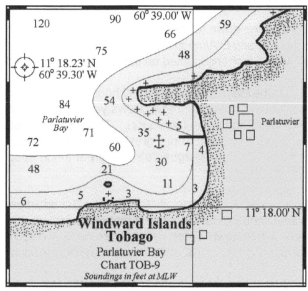

Windward Islands
Tobago
Parlatuvier Bay
Chart TOB-9
Soundings in feet at MLW

Castara Bay,
photo courtesy Katy Stickland, SBMS

Parlatuvier Bay

Englishman's Bay

Englishman's Bay

Waypoints:
Englishman's Bay- ½ nm NW of anchorage area
11° 18.00' N, 60° 40.80' W

A little further along the northern coast is one of my favorite spots, serene and secluded *Englishman's Bay*. *Englishman's Bay* is part of the *Englishman's Bay Estate Nature Reserve*.

Navigational Information
From Castarra keep ½ mile offshore and head for a waypoint at 11° 18.00' N, 60° 40.80' W, which places you approximately ½ mile northwest of the anchorage area as shown on Chart TOB-8. Head in toward the beach and anchor on the eastern side of the bay. If you see some fishermen seine netting from a small boat, don't get in their way, better to anchor elsewhere until they're finished.

An option is to anchor in the southern part of the bay until the fisherman have beached their catch, but if it's too uncomfortable there move on, either back to *Castarra Bay* or northward to *Parlatuvier Bay*. Either way, the anchorage along the eastern shore can be rolly at times also.

What You Will Find Ashore
Ashore, *Eula's One Stop Shop* offers hot meals (rotis on Sundays), cold drinks, and hand-made crafts at the small stall with outside tables. Eula is open every day except in bad weather. There are basic toilet facilities now. The *Parrot Man* comes by daily to sell his home-made ice cream (he's also available for bird-watching tours).

Parlatuvier Bay

Waypoints:
Parlatuvier Bay- 0.1 nm NW of
11° 18.23' N, 60° 39.30' W

Parlatuvier is another one of those quaint northern-shore fishing villages as is evident by the fleet colorful pirogues moored off the beach. As you gaze at your surroundings you'll notice the entire settlement is carefully placed and terraced on the hillsides surrounding this lovely bay.

Navigational Information
Parlatuvier Bay, snug and small, offers very good protection and a large dock to access the shore (and also pick up some fresh water). As shown on Chart TOB-9, a waypoint at 11° 18.23' N, 60° 39.30' W, which places you approximately ½ mile northwest of the anchorage area. From the waypoint head into the bay giving the point and its adjacent reef a wide berth and anchoring off the pier so as not to interfere with the local fishing craft. Keep an eye out for seine netting in the southern part of *Parlatuvier Bay*. The beach is sometimes used by leatherback turtles when nesting.

What You Will Find Ashore
Provisions
Duran Chance has a small grocery store where you can pick up a few supplies, refill your rum locker, or access a card phone. Duran has also opened a bar next to his grocery store and there's a phone just across the street. Located by the jetty and toilets is *Imbie's Variety Mart*, a good place to pick up a few basic provisions.

Dining
Ashore you'll find *Gloria's Riverside Restaurant* on the *Northside Road*. Here you can dine on healthy portions of the freshest locally caught fish.

At the southern end of *Parlatuvier Bay*, just up the hill, is *Glasgow's Bar* with a great view of the anchorage. A short walk up the road from the dock will bring you to a small waterfall.

Discovering Parlatuvier
If you're traveling by car through here, you'll have to take the turnoff here that leads through the rainforest to Roxborough as the road along the northern shore ends abruptly just past Parlatuvier. Only the best of four-wheel drive vehicles and drivers can make it further east along the coast to Charlotteville. So few attempt this that the sight of a tourist in the tiny settlement of L'Anse Fourmi is a rarity for the locals.

Parlatuvier is a good base for trips to the rain forest. Heading for Roxborough you'll pass through the *Tobago Forest Reserve*, a tropical rainforest high in the central mountains of Tobago. The oldest protected forest reserve in the New World, the forest was designated a reserve in 1776. One of the best spots to view the forest is at Gilpin Trace, marked by a huge rock slab on the road in front of the *Forestry* hut where you'll find a toilet and water tank. On weekends you can get snacks and drinks here from local vendors. Hikers can follow a trail into the rainforest from here, but it is recommended that they hire a guide, and only a card-carrying licensed guide. One of the best is Renson Jack (660-5175). Renson is a *Forest Ranger* who moonlights as a guide and he is highly knowledgeable about the local fauna and flora. Other guides worthy of a recommendation are David Brooks (660-5175), and Harris McMillan (639-6575).

A few miles down the road to Roxborough you'll come to another *Forestry* hut where local guides hang out looking for someone to guide. Here you can hire Fitzroy Quanima of *Bloody Bay* (660-7836) or a guide known simply as the *Parrot Man* (639-1305) who also rents rubber boots for the long and often muddy hikes.

Nearby *Bloody Bay* was named after a battle between British soldiers and African slaves in 1771 that was so horrible it turned the bay red with blood. *Dead Bay River*, which runs into the bay, was named for the same reason.

Man of War Bay, Charlotteville

Waypoints:
Man Of War Bay- 1 nm NW of anchorage
11° 20.40' N, 60° 34.50' W

The most popular stop on the northern coast, and the preferred landfall for many cruisers heading south from Carriacou and Barbados, is Charlotteville in *Man of War Bay*. Please note that all businesses are open during the winter season, but that many close down or are open shorter hours during hurricane season.

Charlotteville is a lovely town, probably the most picturesque town on the island of Tobago, where houses are perched on steep hillsides with narrow streets running here and there and winding paths heading up into the hills. The bay area was first settled by Carib Indians and later by the Dutch who, in 1633, named the bay *Jan De Moor Bay* after one of the residents. During the plantation years the area was divided into two estates, Charlotteville and Pirates Bay. In 1865 both estates were purchased by the Turpin family who still own much of the surrounding land.

For several years cruisers could anchor here and take a bus to Scarborough to clear in. This changed as of August 1, 2001, when Charlotteville became a

Port of Entry with their own *Customs* officer working out of the *Police Station* just up the road from the dock.

Today, the government of Tobago is waffling over plans for a cruise ship facility here. On one hand it will boost the local economy, on the other hand it may destroy the ambiance that is Charlotteville. Only time will tell. For now, no cruise ships docks in Charlotteville.

Navigational Information
As shown on Chart TOB-10, a waypoint at 11° 20.40' N, 60° 34.50' W, will place you approximately 1 mile northwest of the anchorage area in *Man of War Bay* off the town of Charlotteville. A caution must be made here for boats heading to *Man of War Bay* from *Parlatuvier Bay*.

As shown on Chart TOB-1, you must pass either outside the small rocks called the Sisters or inside, between the Sisters and a pair of submerged rocks lying off the Tobago shore called the Brothers. Passage between the two is deep and easy if the Brothers are breaking making their position quite conspicuous. If they're not breaking, favor the Sisters side of the channel and keep your eyes open. For your information, although I do not recommend the inside passage at night, the Sisters are lit (Fl (2) W 10s, 8M).

From the waypoint at *Man of War Bay* proceed into the bay heading toward the dock in Charlotteville at the southeastern corner of the bay. As shown on TOB-10 you can anchor in 30'-70' of water off the town dock southwest of *Pirates Reef* (keep clear of the moored fishing fleet). The eastern side of the bay, east of a line between the town dock and the point shown on the chart, is off limits to cruising vessels, it is solely for the use of the fishing fleet; these areas are used for seine netting. It is possible to anchor in *Cambleton Bay*, to the west of Charlotteville, but the holding is poor, rocky, and the area uncomfortable except in the calmest of conditions

What You Will Find Ashore
There is an *ATM* machine near *Customs* and a *Tourist Information Centre* behind *Eastman's Restaurant*.

Customs and *Immigration*
Charlotteville is a Port of Entry and the *Customs* and *Immigration* offices are located in the *Police*

Man of War Bay, Charlotteville

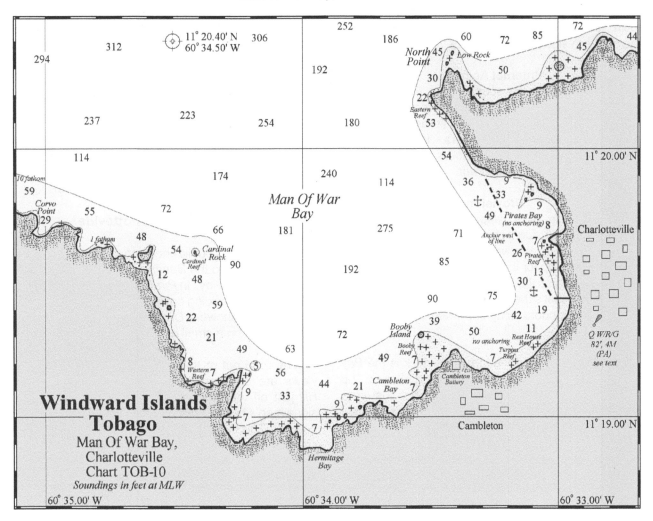

Windward Islands
Tobago
Man Of War Bay,
Charlotteville
Chart TOB-10
Soundings in feet at MLW

Station in town. Just follow the road up from the dock and you'll find the offices under the large antenna tower. Customs is supposed to be open 24 hours, but officers are not always there. Ask at the Police Station and the folks there will find a Customs officer for you.

If you plan to clear out you are not required to clear out of the port where you cleared in. You may clear out from anywhere and not exclusively from a Port of Entry. For instance, you can clear in at Charlotteville, clear to move down the coast to Store Bay, and then clear out in Scarborough via car and leave Store Bay for either Trinidad or elsewhere.

Getting Around
Route taxis run into Roxborough and Scarborough for those needing better shopping than that offered in Charlotteville.

Marine Facilities
Fuel and water will have to be jerry jugged from town. You can tie up your dinghy on the low dock on the northern side of the town dock.

Internet Access
Located just to the south of the Police Station is the public library which offers a free half-hour of Internet access. If you join the library you'll have greater access to their computers. Internet access is also available at Workshop Tours just across from Sharon and Phebe's Restaurant.

Provisions
Charlotteville is a fisherman's village, in fact, 60% of the fish brought into Tobago come in through Charlotteville. To the west of the town dock is the fishermen's co-op for those who want to pick up some fresh fish. If you hear the sound of a conch shell being blown, that's the signal for fresh fish. For fresh produce the vendors along the waterfront might have what you require.

Directly across the road from the dock is the Bay View Shopping Mart, a good stop for groceries; up the hill from Bayview is Front Page which just sells alcohol. Behind the gas station is Tanty's Kitchen Grocery and Bar.

Dining
Ashore you'll find lots of amenities to please almost any cruiser. All around the dockside area are several small shacks where you can get a bite to eat. At the head of the dock is Eastman's Restaurant. On the other side of town Sharon and Phebe's Restaurant serves lunch and dinner on their balcony, and can also arrange to take care of your laundry needs. They are the nicest restaurant in town and have an excellent flying fish sandwich. Across from Sharon and Phebe's is Marilyn Gray's G's Restaurant, tiny, but the food is good. Nearby, Jane at Jane's Quality Kitchen can whip up some great baked goods and superb rotis for you.

If you head north from the town dock, close to Pirate's Bay you'll find the very popular Gail's restaurant. Open for dinner and closed Sundays, Gail's has the best Creole cuisine in town.

If you want ice cream you're in luck; Nick's Ice Cream just a short walk from Bay View on the seafront

In town you'll find the Cappuccino Bar, which should hopefully be open again by the time this guide is published. The restaurant is open during the winter but only by request during the summer months. Open from 0830 till sunset, you can get some of the best cappuccino on the island here as well as taking one of the chef's cooking courses.

On the road behind the Man of War Bay Cottages you'll find the Golden Dove Restaurant where you can choose from several local dishes. Behind the gas station is Tanty's Kitchen Grocery and Bar.

Discovering Charlotteville

The beach has public changing areas and showers (TT$1). You'll find the Banana Boat bar located next to the beach facilities. In Pirate's Bay you will discover a small stream trickling down into the bay and offering a fresh water shower. Climb the 150 concrete steps and you'll be on a small dirt road leading into town.

The road out of town is long and steep, but the views are stunning from the crest atop Flagstaff Hill just off the main road. Here you'll find an old signalman's hut and pylon topped with a navigational beacon. This outpost was used by British and French soldiers who used mirrors to signal the approach of a ship to their comrades at the Cambleton Battery below. Cambleton Battery was built by the British in 1777 to defend against American privateers working the waters of the Caribbean during the American Revolution.

Good snorkeling abounds in *Man of War Bay*. *Pirates Reef* is shallow and offers some excellent coral structures, but watch out for the fire coral. At the southern end of the bay, lying just southeast of the extensive *Booby Reef* and just off the shoreline, lie *Turpins Reef* and *Rest House Reef*. *Booby Reef* is gorgeous, lots of elkhorn coral and a steep slope to deeper water. Another nice spot is *Cardinal Reef* with its almost vertical drop to over 10 fathoms.

The Northeastern Tip, The Melville Islands

Waypoints:

London Bridge inside passage western waypoint
11° 21.00' N, 60° 32.25' W

London Bridge inside passage eastern waypoint
11° 21.00' N, 60° 31.00' W

Tyrrel's Bay- 3/4 nm NE of
11° 18.90' N, 60° 30.40' W

On Chart TOB-11, you'll notice the Melville Islands, comprised of several small islands such as St. Giles Island and London Bridge. On some charts these are shown as the St. Giles Islands, while on others they are simply called the Melvilles. In 1968, Charles Turpin, the proprietor of the *Charlotteville Estate* in northeastern Tobago, presented the Melville Islands to the Government of Tobago to be used as a bird sanctuary. Due to the lack of predators, and the lack of man, the islands are able to support a large population of nesting seabirds, terns, boobies, frigate birds, and the uncommon tropic-bird.

The hairiest part of your circumnavigation of Tobago will be rounding the northeastern tip of Tobago. You have two choices here, either passing inside the Melville Islands, or passing outside the Melville Islands. I recommend the outside passage, but be advised that you will find yourself in a strong current of over two knots as you head north around Marble Island. This is generally not a problem and, you won't have to worry about submerged rocks like the one lying south of St. Giles Island.

The outside route is just a little longer, it certainly won't delay you more than an hour or two when heading for *Anse Bateau* and Speyside, so I suggest you take a few more tacks and enjoy the sailing. If

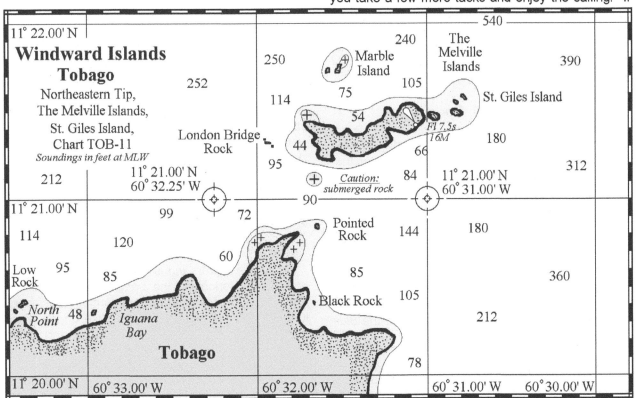

you're not convinced, or if you have a good motor and the wind and seas are down, you can pass south of St. Giles Island.

Navigational Information

As shown on TOB-11 a waypoint at 11° 21.00' N, 60° 32.25' W, will place you ½ mile west of the channel between St. Giles Island and Pointed Rock. Head eastward favoring the Pointed Rock side of the channel to avoid the submerged rock south of St. Giles Island. If there are any seas the rock will be breaking and easily seen, if not, use caution and keep your eyes open, watch for water turbulence to help you locate the rock. Never attempt this route at night, go north, around the Melville Islands instead. Once past Pointed Rock you can begin to work your way down the eastern side of the island, the Windward shore keeping ½ mile offshore as you approach Tyrrel's Bay. Watch out for strong and erratic currents when passing south of St. Giles Island.

What You Will Find Ashore

London Bridge, lying just a bit west of St. Giles Island, is a naturally formed arch atop a pinnacle that rises from a depth of over 100'. You can snorkel through the arch, but caution must be exercised. Never try this with any sort of swell if possible. You can swim right through the arch and if using SCUBA, you can drop down to 80' and more to ride the current around the canyons and crevasses at the base of the pinnacle. Use caution, the local dive shops warn that you are putting yourself at risk due to the strength of the currents here.

Anse Bateau, Speyside

Tyrrel's Bay undoubtedly has very good snorkeling and a fairly nice anchorage at *Anse Bateau* that doesn't look as good on paper as it really is.

Navigational Information

Vessels heading for the *Anse Bateau* from the Melville Islands area can head for a waypoint at 11° 18.90' N, 60° 30.40' W, which places you ½ mile north/northeast of the entrance to *Tyrrel's Bay* between Long Rock and Little Tobago Island as shown on Chart TOB-12. From this waypoint take Long Rock to starboard to anchor in *Anse Bateau* just off the *Blue Waters Inn*.

Use caution when approaching this anchorage, never attempt to enter during periods of poor visibility.

You can enter the anchorage by lining up your stern on the conspicuous house on Goat Island (see photo), and your bow on the *Blue Waters Inn*, and then just follow your bow to the inn over coral patches 15' deep, passing between *Bateau Reef* and Weather Rocks. If you have any concerns about entering the small anchorage area you give hail the *Aquamarine Dive Shop* on VHF ch. 05 for guidance on the best place to anchor so you do not damage the fragile coral ecosystem.

On paper it looks like this bay is open to the southeast, and it is to an extent, but Little Tobago Island, Goat Island, and Weather Rocks combine to diminish most seas.

There is also a small anchorage in the lee of Little Tobago Island, but it is difficult to get into, but if you can gain access, you'll likely be alone and the waters quite calm. Approach Little Tobago Island's western shore and head towards the northern end of the conspicuous green water which delineates the reef that lies west of Little Tobago Island. There is a narrow passage at the northern end of the reef that leads to a small pocket behind the reef. Unfortunately the passage is directly over reef structure and only carries 5'-6' at high water. This anchorage is not recommended unless you have a very shallow draft and can sound your way in by dinghy first.

What You Will Find Ashore

The *Blue Waters Inn* at *Anse Bateau* is a hub of activity in the Speyside area. An eco-friendly resort, the inn offers 38 rooms set amid 46 lush acres. Their dinghy dock makes shore access a breeze; you might even be able to bring in the big boat to take on water (8' at the end of the dock), just ask at the dive shop. The inn requests that you use your holding tank while anchored here since the onshore breeze pushes everything onto the beach. If you do not have a holding tank you are welcome to use the toilets on the shore. There is a *Post Office* in Speyside.

Dining

The *Blue Waters Inn* is home to the *Lobster Pot* restaurant overlooking the beach at *Anse Bateau*. The *Lobster Pot* is open for an informal breakfast or lunch, or for a dinner that's a bit more on the fancy side (advance notice is requested for dinner). Also on site is the *Shipwreck Bar* if you care for drinks or light fare.

On the main road in Speyside are several nice restaurants ranging from the *Speyside Inn's* international menu, to the *Bird Watcher's Restaurant* serving good Creole food. A restaurant that is an institution here is *Jemma's* Seaview Kitchen (see chart), open Sunday through Thursday for lunch, tea, and dinner. This is a very popular spot, all the tour buses stop here to show their customers the restaurant that is built around a tree.

At the *Speyside Inn* you'll find *Extra Divers*, a German based dive company, and the *Manta Dive Lodge/Tobago Dive Experience* which also has a bar that is open daily.

Conspicuous house on Goat Island,
photo courtesy Katy Stickland, *SBMS*

Anse Bateau
photo courtesy Katy Stickland, *SBMS*

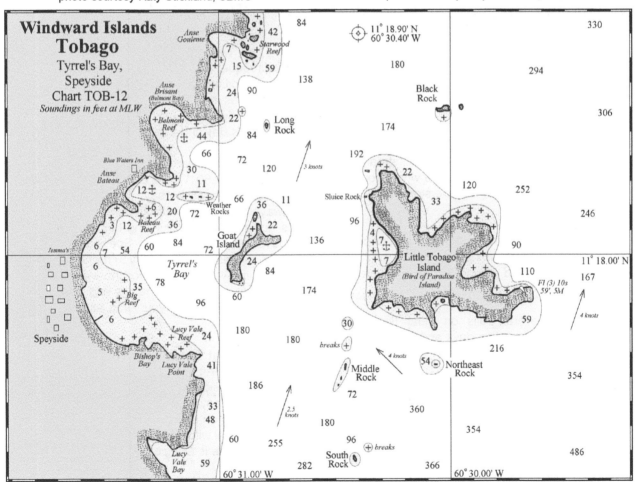

Diving

The *Aquamarine Dive Shop* is a great spot to begin a diving adventure in the surrounding waters. *Tyrrel's Bay* offers some of the best reef diving and snorkeling in the Trinidad/Tobago area and there are several dive shops and glass bottom boat tours for those so inclined.

The best reefs in the area are shown on Chart TOB-13 and can be used as guide to give you the general location of the best dive areas. Divers must be aware that there is a prevailing northerly current in *Tyrrel's Bay* and makes open water dives drift dives. Some of the best snorkeling is just off the beach at the *Blue Waters Inn*, Goat Island, Weather Rocks, and Little Tobago Reef that lies west and south of Little Tobago Island. For more specific information, please see one of the local dive shops.

Discovering Speyside

Until a little over a decade ago, Speyside had just one road and no tourism industry. Today the *Windward Highway* passes directly though the town connecting Charlotteville and Scarborough, and there are several inns and dive shops to accommodate tourists and dive aficionados. The public beach, like so many others on the island, has public changing and shower facilities and the nearby sports field is a focal point for the community.

Northeast of the *Blue Waters Inn* you'll find the ruins of an old water wheel and a small stream that leads into the bay. In years past the wheel powered a mill and furnished water, and the stream was used as a fresh water bath.

Goat Island's conspicuous house was once the holiday home of Ian Fleming, the creator of James Bond. The house and grounds are now private and visits ashore must be by invitation only.

There are several trails on Goat Island that date back to the plantation days and guides can be found in Speyside to give you the grand tour of the island. Landing on the small beach on the western side of the island you'll find a small hut with a toilet and a list of do's and don'ts for visitors. Concrete steps lead up the hillside past the old caretaker's house and several trails branch off leading through the surround landscape. You could not find a more knowledgeable guide than David Rooks (639-4276),

who once persuaded David Attenborough to include Little Tobago Island in his famous BBC documentary *Trials Of Life*.

Little Tobago Island, sometimes called Bird of Paradise Island, is the easternmost point of Trinidad and Tobago. The island was once a cotton plantation and then, in the early 1900s, the island was purchased by ornithologist Sir William Ingram. In 1909, Ingram imported several dozen Greater Birds of Paradise from Aru Island in New Guinea. Over the years the bird population was decimated by hurricanes and poachers. After the death of Sir William in 1924, his heirs gave the island to the Government of Tobago with the proviso that the island be a protected area. It has remained a seabird colony ever since although you won't find any Birds of Paradise anywhere around.

King's Bay

Waypoints:
King's Bay- ½ nm SE of
11° 14.90' N, 60° 32.60' W

Navigational Information

Picturesque *King's Bay* is a fair enough anchorage in most conditions save a strong southeasterly, but the bay comes in to its own during the winter months when northerly swells make all Tobago anchorages except *King's Bay* and Scarborough untenable.

As shown on Chart TOB-13, a waypoint at 11° 14.90' N, 60° 32.60' W, will place you approximately ½ mile southeast of the bay. Don't head directly to this waypoint unless well offshore as the waypoint does not allow for surrounding land. For instance, if you're approaching from Speyside, keep well offshore, at least ½ mile, until you round Pedro Point at which time you can head for the waypoint. From the waypoint head up into the bay and anchor off the eastern shore wherever your draft allows as shown on TOB-13.

What You Will Find Ashore

Once a large Amerindian settlement, the folks that live here now reside in houses set high up on the hills well above the bay. Just south of the central part of the bay well up on the road is the *King's Bay Cafe* if you'd like a meal with a spectacular view. Next to the *Kings's Bay Cafe* is *Dougie's Bar and Restaurant*.

Kings Bay,
photo courtesy of Katy Stickland, *SBMS*

Waterwheel ruins at *Arnos Vale Waterwheel Park*,
photo courtesy of Katy Stickland, *SBMS*

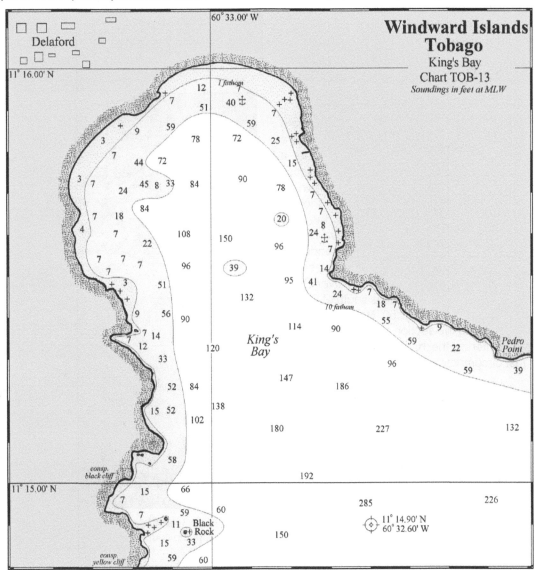

At the northeastern corner of the bay is a public beach facility with showers. At the end of the beach is a small restaurant that is sometimes open, sometimes not. If you hike up to the main road and take a left you'll come to a trail opposite the northern end of the bay where a 20 minute walk will take you to the 100' high *King's Bay Waterfall*. Unfortunately, if there has been little rain the falls are little more than a trickle, but if the water is flowing you can take a dip in the pool at the base of the falls. The *Tourism Office*, *TIDCO*, provides changing rooms for those inclined to take a dip in the pool.

Southwest of *King's Bay* is the large town of Roxborough with all the amenities. Just outside town is the multi-tiered *Argyle Falls*, Tobago's highest waterfall. The falls are actually in the town of Delaford on the old *Rosenwald Estate*. Official guides will meet you and take you on the twenty minute hike to the falls, but be sure to ask to see their badge.

Bacolet,
photo courtesy Katy Stickland, *SBMS*

King's Bay to Scarborough

Navigational Information

From *King's Bay* to Scarborough, pass well offshore Queen's Island and Richmond Island to avoid inshore shoals in the vicinity of *Carapuse Bay*. Head for a waypoint at 11° 10.00' N, 60° 36.00' W, which places you 2 miles south of *Great River Shoal* as shown on Chart TOB-1. Although the better part of the shoal is quite deep, deep enough for cruising boats, the area is susceptible to rough seas and parts of it even break at times...it's best to avoid this area unless conditions and visibility permit you to venture safely closer to shore. From the waypoint south of *Great River Shoal* you can head for the waypoint 2 miles south of *Rockly Bay* and Scarborough at 11° 08.50' N, 60° 42.50' W. At this position turn to the section on Scarborough for directions on entering the harbor. Congratulations, you have just circumnavigated Tobago!

Giant brain coral, Speyside,
photo courtesy Katy Stickland, *SBMS*

Where to Go for Hurricane Season

When hurricane season arrives most boaters in the Caribbean begin to move to safer waters although some take their chances and remain close to a hurricane hole for the season. Some head south to Trinidad, a popular destination at the bottom of the Windward Island chain. Others make their way to Venezuela and the ABC's where hurricanes don't threaten.

The Southwest Caribbean offers excellent protection in places like Columbia and Boca del Toros, Panama, both popular stops and out of the path of tropical storm systems.

The Northwest Caribbean, particularly Guatemala, has come into its own as a very popular destination for cruisers wishing to spend hurricane season with other like-minded crews. Both the SW and NW Caribbean are downwind from the Eastern Caribbean and that makes for some very good sailing.

As far as actual protection from hurricanes for cruisers in the Northwest Caribbean, the finest protection is on the *Río Dulce* in Guatemala. In fact, the *Río Dulce* is probably the finest hole in the entire Caribbean offering excellent protection, economical prices, and an eclectic group of gregarious cruisers. The marinas are well upstream, miles from the coast and the worst of any hurricane surge, and the surrounding hills go a long way in lessening the strength of the wind. Arguably this may be the best hurricane hole in the entire Caribbean because its location makes it very difficult for a hurricane to make a direct hit on the river without crossing a good bit of mountainous land that would only weaken the storm.

Whatever choice you make, whether to stay in the Eastern Caribbean, the Virgins, Puerto Rico, the DR, or head for better protection for the season, know where the best protection lies, how long it takes to get there, and be prepared to move early and quickly.

References
and
Suggested Reading

A Cruising Guide to the Caribbean and the Bahamas; Jerrems C. Hart and William T. Stone, Dodd, Mead and Company, New York
A History of Modern Trinidad, 1783-1962; B. Bereton, Heinnemann Pub., U.S./U.K.
American Practical Navigator; Nathaniel Bowditch, LL.D., DMA Hydrographic Center
Another Look at Trinidad and Tobago; Noel Norton, Maclean, 1999
A Preliminary Study of the Buccoo Reef/Bon Accord Complex; J.S. Kenny, UWI, TT, 1976
A Short History of the West Indies; J.P. Parry, P. Sherlock & A. Maingot, Caribbean Pub, UK
A Visitor's Guide to St. Lucian Patois; Mary W. Toynbee, Lithographic Press, St. Lucia
Best Dives Of The Caribbean; Joyce and Jon Huber, Hunter Publishing, Edison, New Jersey, USA
Coastal And Offshore Weather, The Essential Handbook, Chris Parker, Christopher Parker Jr., Green Cove Springs, Fla. 2003.
Concise Guide To Caribbean Weather; David Jones, Carib.Weather, Road Town, Tortola, BVI
Cote ce Cote la, Trinidad and Tobago Dictionary; John Mendes, College Press, Trinidad 1986
David Frost Introduces Trinidad and Tobago; Andre Deutsch Ltd. 1975
HF Radio E-Mail For Idi-Yachts, Captain Marti Brown, Cruising Companion Publications, Marathon, Fla. 2003.
Insight Guides, Trinidad and Tobago; APA Productions Ltd. 1987
Isles Of The Caribbees; Laddie McIntyre, National Geographic Soc., Washington DC, USA
On And Off The Beaten Path; Stephen J. Pavlidis, Seaworthy Pub., Cocoa Beach, FL, USA
Passages South; Bruce Van Sant, Cruising Guide Publications, Dunedin, Fla. USA
Sailing Directions For The Caribbean Sea; Pub. #147, Defense Mapping Agency, #SDPUB147
Spanish Trinidad; C.R. Ottley, Longman Pub., U.K.
St. Vincent and The Grenadines; Jill Bobrow and Dana Wilkins, Concepts Pub., Vermont, USA
St. Vincent and The Grenadines; Lesley Sutty, MacMillan Education, Ltd. London, UK
Street's Cruising Guide to the Eastern Caribbean; Donald M. Street Jr., W.W. Norton, NY, USA
Tales Of The Caribbean; Fritz Seyfarth, Spanish Main Press, St. Thomas, USVI
The Abaco Guide; Stephen J. Pavlidis, Seaworthy Pub., Cocoa Beach, FL, USA
The Concise Guide To Caribbean Weather; David Jones, 1996
The Cruising Guide to Martinique; Jérôme Nouel, ARDTM, Schoelcher, Martinique
The Exuma Guide; Stephen J. Pavlidis, Seaworthy Pub., Cocoa Beach, FL, USA
The Ocean Almanac; Robert Hendrickson, Doubleday, New York, USA
The Puerto Rico Guide; Stephen J. Pavlidis, Seaworthy Pub., Cocoa Beach, FL, USA
The Story of Tobago; C.R. Ottley, Longman Pub., U.K.
The Tainos; Irving Rouse, Yale University Press, New Haven and London, UK
The Trinidad and Tobago Guide; Stephen J. Pavlidis, Seaworthy Pub. Cocoa Beach, FL, USA
The Turks and Caicos Guide; Stephen J. Pavlidis, Seaworthy Pub., Cocoa Beach, FL, USA
This Is Grenada; Francis Key, Carenage Press, St. George's, Grenada
Two Years in the West Indies; Lafcadio Hearn

Appendices

Appendix A: Lights

Navigational light characteristics may differ from those published here and are subject to change without notice. It is not unusual for a light to be out of commission for long periods of time. Lights are broken down into each Island and also by area.

LIGHT	CHARACTERISTICS	HT.	RNG.
Martinique-West Coast			
Pointe Precheur	Fl R 5s	72'	18 M
Pointe des Nègres	Fl W 5s	118'	25 M
Fort St. Louis	Fl (4) W/R/G 15s*	102'	*
Bai du Carenage Range-Front	Iso G 4s	135'	14 M
Bai du Carenage Range-Rear	Iso G 4s	164'	14 M
Quai Quest-SW Corner	Oc R 4s	3'	6 M
Quai Quest-SE Corner	Oc G 4s	3'	6 M
Quai Aux Huiles	Oc (2) G 6s	3'	6 M
Quai des Annexes	Oc R 4s	3'	6 M
Quai des Tourelles	Oc G 4s	3'	6 M
Container Wharf	Oc (2) R 6s	7'	6 M
#7	Fl (2) R 6s		
#3	Fl R 2.5s		
Pointe du Bout-East Jetty	Fl G 2.5s	13'	2 M
Pointe du Bout-West Jetty	Fl R 2.5s	13'	2 M
Martinique-South Coast			
Pointe du Marin	Q W/R/G **	23'	**
North Head Light	Fl (3) R 12s	20'	2 M
Banc Major #6	Fl (4) G 15s	7'	2 M
Banc du Milieu #5	Fl (4) R 15s	7'	2 M
Banc de la Douane #8	Fl G 2.5s	7'	2 M
Banc de la Douane #10	Fl (2) G 6s	7'	2 M
Martinique-East Coast			
Baie Trinite Range-Front	Iso W 4s	20'	8 M
Baie Trinite Range-Rear	Iso W 4s	23'	8 M
La Caravalle	Fl (3) W 15s	423'	20 M
Bai du François	Q W/R/G***	108'	***
Port Vauclin	Q W/R/G****	46'	****
Digue Est	Fl G 2.5s	13'	2 M
Epi Quest	Fl R 2.5s	10'	2 M
Pointe à Pommes	Q W/R/G*****	30'	*****
Ilet Cabrit	Fl (4) W 15s	141'	20 M
St. Lucia-North, West and South Coasts			
Foureur Rock	Fl (2) W 5s	23'	2 M
Rodney Bay Marina-N entrance	Q G	3'	2 M
Rodney Bay Marina-S entrance	Q R	3'	2 M
Rodney Bay Marina Range-Front	Fl W	15'	2 M
Rodney Bay Marina Range-Rear	Fl W	31'	2 M
Barrel O' Beef	Fl (2) W 8s	22'	2 M
Vigie	Fl (2) W 10s	320'	22 M
Tapion Rock	Q W	50'	8 M
Port Castries Entrance	Q G		
Port Castries Entrance	Q R		

LIGHT	CHARACTERISTICS	HT.	RNG.
Castries Airfield Extension	Q G	14'	2 M
Castries West Wharf Range-F	F R	56'	5 M
Castries West Wharf Range-R	F R	110'	5 M
Castries North Wharf	F Y		1 M
Cul de Sac Bay Range-Front	Fl G 6s	39'	7 M
Cul de Sac Bay Range-Rear	F G	66'	7 M
Range-Front	F G	167'	7 M
Range-Rear	F G	203'	7 M
Bananes Point	Fl R 4s	85'	7 M
Mathurin Point Light	V Q (2) W 5s	16'	2 M
Vieux Fort Range-Front	Q R	26'	8 M
Vieux Fort Range-Rear	Iso R 6s	65'	9 M
North Entrance Channel	Q G	13'	5 M
South Entrance Channel	Q R	13'	5 M
Battery Point-North	Fl Y 2.5s	13'	5 M
Battery Point-South	Fl Y 2.5s	13'	5 M
Cape Moule à Chique	Fl W 5s	745'	22 M
St. Lucia-East Coast			
Mt. Tourney Aviation	Iso R	485'	
Mt. Bellevue Aviation	Fl W G 5s	351'	
Cape Marquis	Fl (2) W 20s	197'	
Barbados-West Coast			
Harrison Point	Fl (2) W 15s	193'	22 M
Maycock's Bay Jetty-North End	Q R		3 M
Maycock's Bay Jetty-South End	Q G		3 M
Port St. Charles Marina	Fl G		
Tom Snooch Reef S	Fl R		
Tom Snooch Reef N	Fl R		
Port St. Charles Breakwater N.	Fl W		
Port St. Charles Breakwater S.	Fl W		
Bridgetown Bulk Facility	Fl G 5s	29'	5 M
Shallow Draft Jetty-North	F R		18 M
Shallow Draft Jetty-South	F R		18 M
Container Berth	Q G	26'	6 M
Bridgetown Breakwater	Q (3) R 10s	49'	12 M
Oil Pier-SE end	Q R	16'	5 M
Oil Pier-Center	F R	39'	5 M
Oil Pier-NW end	Q R	16'	5 M
Fishing Harbor Entrance-S side	F G		
Fishing Harbor Entrance-N side	F R		
Bridgetown Carenage	Fl (3) G 10s	26'	2 M
Needham Point	Fl W/R 8s*	43'	*
Oistins Fishing Jetty	F R	20'	5 M
Barbados-East Coast			
Ragged Point	Fl W 15s	213'	21 M
Seawall Aviation	Fl W/G 4s	210'	
South Point	Fl (3) W 30s	145'	17 M
St. Vincent and the Grenadines			
Owia (Cows and Calves)	Fl W 10s	118'	10 M
Dark Head	Fl W 5s 338'		12 M
Fort Charlotte	Fl (3) W 20s	640'	16 M

LIGHT	CHARACTERISTICS	HT.	RNG.
Kingstown Wharf NW	F R		
Kingstown Wharf SE	F R		
Young Island Carenage	Fl G 4s		
Rookes Point Shoal	V Q (6) + L Fl W 10s		
Durvernette Island	V Q (2) W 2s	229'	6 M
Brighton Light (Gunn Point)	Fl W 4s	118'	8 M
Bequia to Canouan			
Devil's Table	V Q (9) W 10s		
Admiralty Bay	Fl W/R/G*	19'	5 M
West Cay	Fl W 10s	42'	8 M
Battowia Island	Fl (2) W 20s	708'	8 M
Mustique-Montezuma Shoal	Fl (2) W		
Petit Canouan Island	Fl (4) W 40s	252'	8 M
Charlestown Bay Range-Front	F W	18'	
Charlestown Bay Range-Rear	F W	165'	
Range-Front	Iso W 4s	46'	5 M
Range-Rear	Fl W 5s	91'	5 M
Charlestown Bay Pier Head	F W 5s		
Grand Bay	Fl G 4s		
Grand Bay South	Fl R 4s		
Catholic Island to Union Island			
Catholic Island	Fl (2) W 20s	144'	8 M
Mayreau	VQ W (9) 10s		
Jondell	VQ (3) 5s		
Clifton Harbor Range-Front	F W	13'	
Clifton Harbor Range-Rear	F W	125'	
Thompson Reef-SE edge	Fl R		
Thompson Reef-SW edge	Fl R		
Roundabout Reef-SW edge	Fl R		
Westward	Fl G		
Grand de Coi	V Q (9) W 10s		
Miss Irene Point	Fl (2) W 20s	410'	8 M
Carriacou			
Jack A Dan	Fl G 5s	14'	3 M
Sandy Island	Q R		
Sisters Rocks	Fl W (9) 15s		
Grenada			
St. George's Harbor	F R	188'	15 M
St. George's Range-Front	F R	46'	
St. George's Range-Rear	F R	92'	
Range-Front	F R	102'	
Range-Rear	F R		
Petite Cabrits	Fl (2+1) W 20s	354'	18 M
Point Saline	Q (9) W 15s		7 M
Glover Island	Q (6) + L Fl W 15s		7 M
Grenville	Q R		
Grenville	Q G		
Trinidad-North Coast			
Galera Point	Oc W 10s	141'	16 M
Petite Matelot Point	Fl (3) W 15s		7 M
Chupara Point	Fl (2) W 10s	325'	12 M

LIGHT	CHARACTERISTICS	HT.	RNG.
Saut d'Eau Island	Q W		7 M
North Post, Point a Diable	Fl W 5s	747'	14 M
Trinidad-Northwestern Tip Including Chaguaramas Bay			
Chacachacare	Fl W 10s	825'	26 M
Chacachacare Beacon	Fl W 2s	502'	11 M
Point de Cabras	V Q (6) + L Fl W	40'	5 M
Le Chapeau Rock	Fl (3) W 10s		
Teteron Rock	Fl G 4s	24'	4 M
La Retraite Coast Guard Station	2 F R		
Gasparillo Island	Q W	36'	
Espolon Point	Fl W 4s	42'	12 M
Cronstadt Island	Q R		4 M
Reyna Point	Q G	33'	4 M
Escondida Cove	Q R	17'	
Furness-Smith Floating Dock2	F R		
Nelson Island	Fl W 2.5s	61'	5 M
Point Sinet Range-Front	Oc W 2.5s	98'	14 M
Point Sinet Range-Rear	Oc W 5s	102'	14 M
Trinidad-Port of Spain			
Grier Channel Range-Front 061°	Oc W 4S	135'	10 M
Grier Channel Range-Rear 061°	Iso W 2s	157'	11 M
Grier Channel #1	Fl G 3s		
Grier Channel #2	Fl R 3s		
Grier Channel #3	Q G		
Grier Channel #4	Q R		
Grier Channel #5	Q G		
Grier Channel #6	Q R		
Grier Channel #7	Fl G 5s		
Grier Channel #8	Fl R 5s		
Grier Channel #9	Q G		
Grier Channel #10	Q R		
Grier Channel #12	Q R		
Grier Channel #14	Q R		
Head of St. Vincent Jetty	F R	3'	4 M
Sea Lots Channel #1	Fl (2) G 7.5s		
Sea Lots Channel #2V	Q (9) R 10s		
Sea Lots Channel #3	Q G		
Sea Lots Channel #4	Q R		
Sea Lots Channel #5V	Q G		
Sea Lots Channel #6V	Q R		
Sea Lots Channel #7	Q G		
Sea Lots Channel #8	Q R		
Sea Lots Channel #10	L Fl R 5s		
Sea Lots Channel #12	Q R		
Sea Lots Channel #14	Q R		
Sea Lots Channel Range-Front	Oc W 10s	85'	6 M
Sea Lots Channel Range-Rear	Fl W 2s	128'	6 M
Trinidad-Point Lisas			
Range #13-Front	Q W	30'	8 M
Range #14-Rear	Oc W 5s	52'	8 M
Marine Terminal Range-Front	Q Y	69'	10 M

LIGHT	CHARACTERISTICS	HT.	RNG.
Marine Terminal Range-Rear	Oc Y 3s82'	10'	
Channel Entrance #1	Fl (2) G 5s	26'	8 M
Channel Entrance #2	Fl W 3s	26'	8 M
Savonneta Range-Front	Fl W 2s	98'	8 M
Savonneta Range-Rear	Fl W 2s	135'	8 M
Trinidad-Pointe a Pierre			
La Carriere	Fl W 2.5s	233'	23 M
Head of Pipeline Viaduct	Fl (4) W 10s	98'	14 M
Turning Basin	Fl R		
Oropuche Bank Beacon	V Q W		4 M
Brighton-Pier Front	Fl (3) W 10s	52'	5 M
Brighton-Pier Rear	Fl W 5s	100'	8 M
La Brea	Iso W 2s	26'	10 M
Trinidad-Point Fortin			
Head of Pipeline Pier	Fl (2) W 10s	98'	14 M
North Breakwater	Fl G 3s		
South Breakwater	Fl R 3s		
Trinidad-South Coast			
Soldado Rock	Fl W 10s		8 M
Wolf Rock	Q (6) L Fl W 15s	13'	5 M
Punta del Arenal	Fl W 7.5s	72'	16 M
Chatham Jetty	F R		3 M
Taparo Point	Fl (3) W 15s	226'	14 M
La Lune Point	Fl (4) W 20s	148'	14 M
Galeota Point	Fl W 5s	285'	16 M
Trinidad-East Coast			
Brigand Hill	Fl (2 + 1) W 30s	712'	20 M
Tobago-North Coast			
St. Giles Island	Fl W 7.5s		16 M
Man of War Bay	Q W/R/G*	82'**	
The Sisters	Fl (2) W 10s		8 M
Courland Point	L Fl W 10s		8 M
Booby Point	Fl Y 3s		4 M
Milford Bay	Q W/R/G***		****
Crown Point	Fl (4) W 20s	115'	11 M
Tobago-South Coast			
Little Tobago	Fl (3) W 10s	59'	5 M
Smiths Island	Fl W/R 5s*		**
Scarborough-Ft. George	Fl (2) W 20s	462'	30 M
Scarborough-Range Front	ISO W/R/G***	49'	****
Scarborough-Range Rear	Oc W 5s	66'	11 M
Bulldog Shoal	VQ (6) + L Fl 10s	16'	
Scarborough "1"	Fl G 3s	13'	4 M
Scarborough "2"	Fl R 3s	16'	5 M
Scarborough Channel East	Q R	13'	4 M
Scarborough Channel West	Fl G 3s	16'	5 M
Scarborough Breakwater	Q R	13'	5 M

Martinique

* White is visible 057°-087°, 14M; Red is visible 320°-057°, 11M; Green is visible 087°-140°, 11M
** White is visible 071°-075°, 10M; Red is visible 015°-071°, 7M; Green is visible 075°-080°, 7M
*** White is visible 245°-248°, 8M; Red is visible 200°-245°, 6M; Green is visible 248°-280°, 6M

**** White is visible 230º-232º, 11M; Red is visible 220º-230º, 9M; Green is visible 232º-250º, 9M
***** White is visible 304º-306º, 10M; Red is visible 291º-304º, 7M; Green is visible 306º-319º, 7M

The Grenadines-Bequia
* White is visible 048º-058º; Red is visible shore-048º; Green is visible 058º-shore

Tobago-North Coast
* White is visible 108º-131º; Red is visible 098º-108º; Green is visible 131º-141º
** White-5 M; Red-4 M; Green-4 M
*** White is visible 083º-128º; Red is visible 073º-083º; Green is visible 128º-138º
**** White-5 M; Red-4 M; Green-4 M

Tobago-South Coast
* White is visible 276º; Red is visible 068º-276º
** White-7 M; Red-5 M
*** White is visible 323.5º-335.5º; Red is visible 315.5º-323.5º; Green is visible 335.5º-345.5º
**** White-7M; Red-5 M; Green-5 M

Appendix B: Marinas

Some of the marinas listed below may be untenable in certain winds and dockside depths listed may not reflect entrance channel depths at low water. Always check with the Dockmaster prior to arrival. All the marinas can handle your garbage disposal problems however some may levy a charge per bag for those who are not guests at their docks. For cruisers seeking services *Nearby* may mean either a walk or short taxi ride away.

MARINA	LOCATION	FUEL	DEPTH	GROC.	DINING	EMAIL
MARTINIQUE						
Caren Antilles	Baie Tourelles	D & G	10'	Nearby	Yes	carenfdf@sasi.fr
Club Nautique Fran.	Le François	D & G	6'	Nearby	Nearby	
La Mar. de Robert	Le Robert	D & G	4'	Nearby	Nearby	
Marina de Pt. Cohé	Cohé Lamentin	No	5½'	Nearby	No	
Marina La Neptune	Cohé Lamentin	No	6'	Nearby	No	
Port de Plaisance	Le Marin	D & G	10'	Yes	Yes	
Somatras Marina	Pointe du Bout	No	10'	Yes	Yes	
ST. LUCIA						
Chateau Mygo	Marigot Bay	No	7'	Nearby	Yes	info@chateaumygo.com
Marigot Bay Marina	Marigot Bay	D & G	16'	Yes	Nearby	manager@marigotbaymarina.com
Rodney Bay Marina	Rodney Bay	D & G	12'	Yes	Yes	rbm@igymarinas.com
Waterside Landings	Rodney Bay	No	7'	Nearby	Nearby	waterside@beachcombers.com
BARBADOS						
Port St. Charles	Six Man's Bay	D & G	13.5'	Nearby	Yes	dockmaster@portstcharles.com.bb
ST. VINCENT						
Barefoot Yacht	Calliaqua	No	6'	Nearby	Yes	VHF ch. 68
Lagoon Marina	Blue Lagoon	D & G	10'	Limited	Yes	sunsailsvg@spiceisle.com (VHF 68)
Ottley Hall Marina	Ottley Hall Bay	D & G	30'	Yes	Yes	ottleyhall@spiceisle.com (VHF 68)
BEQUIA						
Bequia Marina	Admiralty Bay	D & G	9'	Nearby	Nearby	
UNION ISLAND						
Anchorage YC	Clifton	No	7'	Nearby	Yes	aycunion@spiceisle.com
Bougainvilla	Clifton	D & G	7'	Nearby	Yes	bougainvilla@spiceisle.com
GRENADA						
Clarke's Court Bay	Clarke's Court	No	10'	Nearby	Nearby	office@clarkescourtbaymarina.com
Grenada Marine	St. David's	D & G	10'	Nearby	Nearby	info@grenadamarine.com
Grenada Yacht Club	St. George's	D & G	7'-14'	Nearby	Nearby	gyc@spiceisle.com
Le Phare Bleu	Phare Bleu Bay	D & G		Yes	Yes	contact@lepherebleu.com
Martin's Marina	Mt. Hartman	D & G	10'	Ltd.	Yes	martinsmarina@spiceisle.com

MARINA	LOCATION	FUEL	DEPTH	GROC.	DINING	EMAIL
Port Louis Marina	St. George's	D & G	20'	Yes	Yes	info@cnportlouismarina.com
Prickly Bay Marina	Prickly Bay	D & G	17'	Yes	Yes	pricklybaymarina@spiceisle.com
True Blue Marina	True Blue	D	7'	Nearby	Yes	mail@truebluebay.com
Whisper Cove Mar.	Clarke's Court	None		Limited	Yes	
Trinidad						
Bay View	Gaspar Grande	No	7'	No	Yes	
Coral Cove	Chaguaramas	No	7'	Nearby	Yes	coralcove@trinidad.net
CrewsInn	Chaguaramas	No	15'-25'	Yes	Yes	crewsinn@trinidad.net
Hummingbird	Chaguaramas	No	7'	Nearby	Yes	
Peake's	Chaguaramas	No	9'	Nearby	Yes	pys@cablenett.net
Power Boats	Chaguaramas	D & G	12'	Yes	Yes	pbmfl@powerboats.co.tt
PPYC	Point-a-Pierre	Gas	6'	Nearby	Yes	
SFYC*	San Fernando	Gas	4'-6'	Nearby	Nearby	
Sweet Water Marina	Chaguaramas			Nearby	Nearby	sweetwatermarina@tstt.net.tt
Tardieu Marine	Chaguaramas	No	7'	Nearby	Yes	
TTYC	Bayshore	D & G	7'	Nearby	Yes	

* *The San Fernando Yacht Club* is geared primarily to shallow-draft powerboats; the waters at the dock are less than 6' at MLW, usually ranging from 6' on the outside to less than 4' further in.

Appendix C: Service Facilities

As with any place, businesses come and go, sometimes seemingly overnight. Certain entries on this list may no longer exist by the time this is published. If you plan to rent a car and you don't have an *International Driver's License*, you will need to purchase a temporary license in St. Lucia. In Martinique you must drive on the right, on all the other islands you will drive on the left. The area code for Martinique telephones is 0596 except for cell phones which are 0696.

Appendix C-1: Service Facilities on Martinique

FACILITY	LOCATION	TELEPHONE	EMAIL ADDRESS
AUTO RENTALS			
Avis	Fort-de-France	0596-73 73 20	
Avis	Sainte Anne	0596-76 70 74	
Avis	Trois Ilets	0596-66 04 27	
Budget	Fort-de-France	0596-63 69 00	
Budget	La Diamant	0596-66 04 29	
Budget	Pointe du Bout	0596-66 00 45	
Budget	Schoelcher	0596-61 66 60	
Budget	St. Pierre	0596-78 28 38	
Caravelle	Tartane	0596-58 68 95	
CBS	Fort-de-France	0596-71 73 91	CBS@sasi.fr
CBS	Le Marin	0596-74 70 30	CBS@sasi.fr
Discount	La Trinité	0596-58 51 63	
Discount	Pointe du Bout	0596-66 05 34	
Dom Car	Pointe du Bout	0596-66 11 63	
Domaine de Belfond	Sainte Anne	0596-76 81 83	
Eugene Garage	Martinique	0596-78 13 21	
Europcar	Fort-de-France	0596-73 33 13	
Europcar	Pointe du Bout	0596-05 96 66	
Europcar	Sainte Marie	0596-69 21 09	
Europcar	Schoelcher	0596-61 28 18	
Europcar	Ste. Anne	0596-76 93 34	

FACILITY	LOCATION	TELEPHONE	EMAIL ADDRESS
Europcar	Trois Îlets	0596-66 04 29	
Hertz	Fort-de-France	0596-05 96 60	hertz@candw.lc
Hertz	Pointe du Bout	0596-60 06 59	hertz@candw.lc
Jumbo Car Rentals	Le Marin	0596-74 71 77	
Jumbo Cars	Le Marin	0596-42 22 22	resamar@jumbocar.com
Madicar	Anse à l'Âne	0596-68 31 65	
Nad in Car	Case Pilote	0596-61 14 00	
Ozier Lafontaine	Basse Pointe	0596-78 53 92	
Ozier Lafontaine	Le Marin	0596-74 82 49	
Pop's Car Rental	Aeroport	0596-42 16 84	
Pop's Car Rental	Carbet	0596-78 40 40	
Pop's Car Rental	Ducos	0596-56 06 22	
Pop's Car Rental	Fort-de-France	0596-70 00 70	
Pop's Car Rental	La Diamant	0596-76 29 11	
Pop's Car Rental	Le Carbet	0596-78 40 40	
Pop's Car Rental	Le François	0596-54 59 91	
Pop's Car Rental	Le Marin	0596-74 82 82	
Pop's Car Rental	Ste. Anne	0596-76 88 88	
Pop's Car Rental	St. Pierre	0596-78 28 78	
Pop's Car Rental	Trois Îlets	0596-66 16 16	
Rent Eco	Le Marin	0596-74 89 90	
Rent Eco	Sainte-Anne	0596-76 76 65	
Rent Eco	Sainte-Luce	0596-62 46 94	
Thrifty	Baie du Galion	0596-58 02 22	
Thrifty	Le Carbet	0596-78 08 08	
Thrifty	Le Marin	0596-74 71 77	
Thrifty	Pointe de la Chéry	0596-76 15 96	
Thrifty	Pointe du Bout	0596-66 09 59	
Thrifty	Sainte-Anne	0596-76 80 82	
Tropicar	Le Robert	0596-65 39 65	
Tropicar	La Trinité	0596-58 26 81	
Véro Locations	Le Lorrain	0596-53 74 01	

CANVAS WORK

FACILITY	LOCATION	TELEPHONE	EMAIL ADDRESS
Captio-Land	Fort-de-France	0596-70 26 32	
Helenon	Fort-de-France	0596-60 22 05	
La Voilerie du Marin	Le Marin	0596-74 73 10	
Madinina Confection	Fort-de-France	0596-73 09 73	LYRO@wanadoo.fr
Voilerie Caraibe	Anse Mitan	0596-66 07 24	

DIESEL/GENERATOR REPAIRS

FACILITY	LOCATION	TELEPHONE	EMAIL ADDRESS
Antilles Marine Services	Le Marin	0596-74 70 78	antillesmarine@wanadoo.fr
Chantier Naval	Le Marin	0596-76 79 39	
Croquet	Dillon	0596-71 91 50	
Crosier	Anse Mitan	0596-66 17 82	
C.S. Services	Le Marin	0596-74 91 13	cs.services@wanadoo.fr
IBB	Le Marin	0596-76 56 51	ibb@nonstop-services.com
Inboard Diesel	Case Pilote	0596-78 71 96	Beatrice.ids@wannadoo.fr
Madia (Yave) Nautic	Baie des Tourelles	0596-63 10 61	
Martinique Diesel	Fort-de-France	0596-51 16 13	
Mécanique Assistance	Le Marin	0596-45 40 48	
Mécanique Plaisance	Trois Îlets	0596-66 05 40	mecaplai@sasi.fr
Mécanique Plaisance	Le Marin	0596-74 68 74	mecaplai@sasi.fr

FACILITY	LOCATION	TELEPHONE	EMAIL ADDRESS
Multicap Caraibes	Fort-de-France	0596-71 41 81	multicapcaraibes@cgit.com
Proto Meca	St. Pierre	0596-78 34 49	
Speedy Jet Services	Baie des Tourelles	0596-63 56 20	
Volvo Penta	Fort-de-France	0596-71 35 28	

ELECTRONICS & ELECTRICAL

Cadet-Petit	Baie des Tourelles	0596-63 79 18	
Carib Electronic Eng.	Baie des Tourelles	0596-60 07 00	
Chantier Naval	Le Marin	0596-76 79 39	
Coopemar	Baie des Tourelles	0596-73 37 54	coopemar@sasi.fr
Crosier	Anse Mitan	0596-66 17 82	
C.S. Services	Le Marin	0596-74 91 13	cs.services@wanadoo.fr
Diginav	Le Marin	0596-74 76 62	diginav@wanadoo.fr
IBB	Rivière Salée	0596-76 56 51	ibb@nonstop-services.com
Inboard Diesel	Case Pilote	0596-78 71 96	Beatrice.ids@wannadoo.fr
Plus Nautique	Fort-de-France	0596-60 58 48	plus-nauti@sasi.fr
Plus Nautique	Le Marin	0596-74 62 12	plus-nauti@sasi.fr
Sud Marine Electronique	Le Marin	0596-74 65 56	sudme@wanadoo.fr
Tilikum	Le Marin	0596-49 53 30	tilikumfred@minitel.net

FABRICATION/WELDING

Altec Marine	Le Marin	0596-28 44 78	
Chalmessin	Baie des Tourelles	0596-60 03 75	
ETPI	Rivière Salée	0596-68 11 21	
Jean-Michel Rolland	Baie des Tourelles	0596-71 49 28	
Mécanique Plaisance	Fort-de-France	0596-66 05 40	pc.mecaplai@wanadoo.fr
Multicap Caraibes	Fort-de-France	0596-71 41 81	multicapcaraibes@cgit.com
PBS	St. Pierre	0596-78 17 00	
Phillipe Lafont	Le Marin	0596-74 66 60	
Proto Meca	St. Pierre	0596-78 34 49	
Renovboats	Case Pilote	0596-25 01 92	
Tony Crater	Le Marin	0596-74 66 60	
Tour de Fraise	Le Marin	0596-74 85 65	

FIBERGLASS REPAIR/PAINTING

Caren Antilles	Fort-de-France	0596-63 76 74	carenfdf@sasi.fr
Caren Antilles	Le Marin	0596-74 77 70	carenfdf@sasi.fr
Chantier Naval	Le Marin	0596-76 79 39	
Latitude 14° 28'	Le Marin	0596-74 78 58	
Multicap Caraibes	Fort-de-France	0596-71 41 81	multicapcaraibes@cgit.com
Nautic Services	Le Marin	0596-74 70 45	
Plastic Services	Le Marin	0596-74 70 37	
Polymar	Baie des Tourelles	0596-70 62 88	polymar@wanadoo.fr
Polymat et Composites	Rivière Salée	0596-77 81 03	
Renovboats	Case Pilote	0596-25 01 92	
Servi Marine	Le Marin	0596-45 35 37	
Ship Shop	Le Marin	0596-74 78 22	

HAUL OUT

Caren Antilles	Fort-de-France	0596-63 76 74	carenfdf@sasi.fr
Caren Antilles	Le Marin	0596-74 77 70	carenfdf@sasi.fr
Chantier Naval	Le Marin	0596-76 79 39	
Martinique Dry Dock	Quai Quest	0596-72 69 40	
Multicap Caraibes	Quai Quest	0596-71 41 81	multicapcaraibes@cgit.com
Ship Shop	Le Marin	0596-74 78 22	

FACILITY	LOCATION	TELEPHONE	EMAIL ADDRESS
INFLATABLES/LIFE RAFTS			
Eurosurvie	Petit Bourg	0596-32 24 51	eurosurvie@wanado.fr
La Survy	Fort-de-France	0596-74 63 63	la.survy@wanadoo.fr
La Survy	Le Marin	0596-74 63 63	la.survy@wanadoo.fr
Le Ship	Le Marin	0596-74 87 55	le-ship-martinique@wanadoo.fr
Multicap Caraibes	Fort-de-France	0596-71 41 81	multicapcaraibes@cgit.com
Plus Nautique	Fort-de-France	0596-60 58 48	plus-nauti@sasi.fr
Plus Nautique	Le Marin	0596-74 62 12	plus-nauti@sasi.fr
INTERNET ACCESS			
Alphatext	Troi Ilets		
Balade de Mer	Le Marin		
Croque Pain	Ste. Anne		
Cyber Base	Ste. Anne		
Cyber Caren	Le Marin		
Cyber Marin	Le Marin	0596-74 77 95	psc@business.ool.fr
Definitel Micro	Fort-de-France		
Fish Bo Kai	St. Pierre	0596-78 32 42	valeregilles@yahoo.fr
Kay Zaza	Grande Anse d'Arlet	0596-68 74 22	kayza@ool.fr
Laverie Prolavnet	Anse Mitan	0596-66 07 79	
Le Marine	Anse Mitan		
Le P'ti Bateau	Grande Anse d'Arlet	0596-65 50 19	
Leading Boutique	Anse Mitan		
L'Escapade	St. Pierre	0596-69 64 26	
Mango Bay	Le Marin		
Marin Yacht Harbour	Le Marin	0596-74 83 83	
Pizza Place	Anse Mitan		
Quai 13	Le Marin		
Sud Bureautique	Le Marin		
SAEPP	Le Marin	0596-74 83 83	
Snack Boubou	Ste. Anne		
Web Café	Fort-de-France		
MARINE SUPPLIES			
Accastilleur	Le Marin	0596-74 80 33	
Barnett Marine	Martinique	0596-70 26 69	
Captain's Shop	Martinique	0596-74 70 08	
Caraibe Greemont	Le Marin	0596-74 80 33	cgmar@wanadoo.fr
Carene Shop	Le Marin	0596-74 74 80	carene.shop@wanadoo.fr
Coopemar	Baie des Tourelles	0596-73 37 54	coopemar@sasi.fr
Le Marin Pecheur	Le Marin	0596-74 67 54	marin.pecheur@wanadoo.fr
Le Ship	Le Marin	0596-74 87 55	le-ship-martinique@wanadoo.fr
Littoral	Fort-de-France	0596-70 28 70	
Multicap Caraibes	Fort-de-France	0596-71 41 81	multicapcaraibes@cgit.com
Plus Nautique	Baie des Tourelles	0596-63 75 49	plus-nautique@mer-et-sport.com
SCIM	Fort-de-France	0596-63 39 89	
Sea Services	Fort-de-France	0596-70 26 69	
Ship Shop	Le Marin	0596-74 78 22	
W.I.N.D.	Rivière Salée	0596-68 21 28	wind@wind-flag.com
OUTBOARD REPAIR			
Alain Tissier	Le Marin	0596-74 68 52	
CBS	Baie des Tourelles	0596-71 73 91	CBS@sasi.fr
CBS	Le Marin	0596-74 70 30	CBS@sasi.fr

FACILITY	LOCATION	TELEPHONE	EMAIL ADDRESS
Global Impex	Baie des Tourelles	0596-72 83 92	
Madia (Yave) Nautic	Baie des Tourelles	0596-74 72 30	
Multicap Caraibes	Fort-de-France	0596-71 41 81	multicapcaraibes@cgit.com
Roby Mechanic	Grande Anse d'Arlet	0696-98 59 37	
S.A.V. des Moteurs	Baie des Tourelles		
SCIM-*OMC*	Fort-de-France	0596-63 39 89	
Yave Marine (*Mercury*)	Fort-de-France	0596-45 68 55	Yave-marine@wanadoo.fr

PROPANE

Antilles Gas	Fort-de-France	0596-50 33 30	

PROPELLERS

PBS	St. Pierre	0596-78 17 00	pbsfrancehelice@wanadoo.fr

REFRIGERATION/AC REPAIR

Fraicheur Service	Grande Anse d'Arlet	0696-82 24 04	
Mécanique Plaisance	Fort-de-France	0596-66 05 40	
Mécanique Plaisance	Le Marin	0596-74 68 74	
Tilikum	Le Marin	0596-49 53 30	tilikum@wanadoo.fr

RIGGING

Caraibe Greement	Le Marin	0596-74 80 33	cgmar@wanadoo.fr
Multicap Caraibes	Fort-de-France	0596-71 41 81	multicapcaraibes@cgit.com
Sea Services	Fort-de-France	0596-70 26 69	
Servi Marine	Le Marin	0596-45 35 37	

SAIL REPAIR

Caraibe Greemont	Le Marin	0596-74 80 33	cgmar@wanadoo.fr
Helenon	Fort-de-France	0596-60 22 05	
La Voilerie du Marin	Le Marin	0596-74 73 10	
North Sails	Le Marin	0596-48 55 77	e.baray@free.fr
Tech Sails (North)	Rivière Salée	0596-68 03 34	
Voilerie Assistance	Le Marin	0596-74 88 32	didier-et-maria@wanadoo.fr
Voilerie Caraibe	Anse Mitan	0596-66 07 24	incidences.caraibes@wanadoo.fr
Voilerie Caraibe	Le Marin	0596-74 77 47	incidences.caraibes@wanadoo.fr
Voilerie du Marin	Le Marin	0596-25 94 01	dan.karner@wanadoo.fr

WOODWORKING

IBB	Le Marin	0596-76 56 51	ibb@nonstop-services.com
Latitude 14° 28'	Le Marin	0596-74 78 58	
Les As Tek	Le Marin	0596-74 72 85	
Nautic-Bois	Baie des Tourelles	0596-71 95 74	
Proto Meca	St. Pierre	0596-78 34 49	

Appendix C-2: Service Facilities on St. Lucia
AUTO RENTALS

Avis	Castries	758-452-2700
Avis	St. Lucia	758-452-2202
Budget	Castries	758-452-0233
Budget	Halcyon	758-459-0304
Budget	Hewanorra	758-454-5311
Budget	Latoc	758-452-6124
Budget	Marigot	800-263-4202
Budget	Morgan Bay	758-450-4071
Car and Truck Leasing	Rodney Bay	758-452-0732
Charley's Car Rental	Vieux Fort	758-454-6448
Cool Breeze Rental	Gros Islet	758-458-0824

FACILITY	LOCATION	TELEPHONE	EMAIL ADDRESS
Cool Breeze Rental	Soufrière	758-459-7729	
Cost Less	Gros Islet	758-450-3416	mathurinc@candw.lc
Courtesy Car Rental	Gros Islet	758-452-8140	
CTL Rent-a-Car	Castries	758-452-9404	ctlslu@candw.lc
CTL Rent-a-Car	Rodney Bay	758-452-0732	ctlslu@candw.lc
Drive-A-Matic	Reduit Park	758-452-0544	
Economy Car Rental	Gros Islet	758-450-7997	
Gibin Rent-A-Car	Gros Islet	758-452-9528	
Guy's Car Rental	Castries	758-451-7147	
H & B	Gros Islet	758-452-0872	hbrentals@candw.lc
Hertz	Airport (Vigie)	758-451-7351	hertz@candw.lc
Hertz	Castries	758-452-0680	hertz@candw.lc
Hertz	Gros Islet	758-452-0679	hertz@candw.lc
Hertz	Rodney Bay	758-458-4043	hertz@candw.lc
Holiday & Business	Castries	758-452-0872	
Moncherry Car & Jeep	Vieux Fort	758-454-9591	
National	Gros Islet	758-450-8721	carrental@candw.lc
New Frontier	Vieux Fort	758-454-6133	
SLYS	St. Lucia	758-452-5057	
Strategic Car Rental	Castries	758-451-4388	
TJ's Car Rentals	Rodney Bay	758-452-0116	
Toucan Travel	Rodney Bay	758-452-0896	

CANVAS WORK

FACILITY	LOCATION	TELEPHONE	EMAIL ADDRESS
B&L Upholstery Clinic	Rodney Bay	758-452-7644	
Broco Sail Repair	Rodney Bay	758-450-8864	
MC	Rodney Bay	758-450-0300	
Rodney Bay Marina	Rodney Bay	758-452-0324	rbm@igymarinas.com
The Sail Loft	Rodney Bay	758-452-8648	syachts@candw.lc

DIESEL/GENERATOR REPAIRS

FACILITY	LOCATION	TELEPHONE	EMAIL ADDRESS
Beachcomber Ltd.	Castries	758-452-5241	
Destination St. Lucia	Rodney Bay	758-452-8531	deststl@candw.lc
Int. Diesel & Marine	Castries	758-453-2287	idams@candw.lc
Marigot Bay Marina	Marigot Bay	758-451-4275	marina@marigotbay.com
Quick & Reliable	Rodney Bay	758-452-9094	alwinagustin@engineer.com
Rodney Bay Marina	Rodney Bay	758-452-0324	rbm@igymarinas.com
Ryte Welding	Rodney Bay	758-450-8019	
Tony's Engineering	Rodney Bay	758-715-8719	
Vergel Joseph	Rodney Bay	758-450-4741	

ELECTRONICS & ELECTRICAL

FACILITY	LOCATION	TELEPHONE	EMAIL ADDRESS
Amtek Electronics	Rodney Bay	758-452-0550	sinsolution@yahoo.com
Cay Electronics	Rodney Bay	758-452-9922	ayslu@candw.lc
Island Water World	Rodney Bay	758-452-1222	
Regis Electronics	Rodney Bay	758-452-0205	stlucia@regiselectronics.com
Rodney Bay Marina	Rodney Bay	758-452-0324	rbm@igymarinas.com

FABRICATION/WELDING

FACILITY	LOCATION	TELEPHONE	EMAIL ADDRESS
Arc Dynamics	Rodney Bay	758-450-0065	
Caribbean Metals	Castries	758-450-2249	
Chinaman	Rodney Bay	758-518-1234	
Rodney Bay Marina	Rodney Bay	758-452-0324	rbm@igymarinas.com
Ryte Weld Enterprises	Rodney Bay	758-450-8019	

FACILITY	LOCATION	TELEPHONE	EMAIL ADDRESS
FIBERGLASS REPAIR/PAINTING			
Cox Enterprises	Rodney Bay	758-384-2269	
Destination St. Lucia	Rodney Bay	758-452-8531	
Marigot Bay Marina	Marigot Bay	758-451-4275	marina@marigotbay.com
Mermaid Marine	Rodney Bay	758-488-5291	
Rodney Bay Marina	Rodney Bay	758-452-0324	rbm@igymarinas.com
HAUL OUT			
Rodney Bay Marina	Rodney Bay	758-452-0324	rbm@igymarinas.com
INFLATABLES/LIFE RAFTS			
Island Water World	Rodney Bay	758-452-1222	
Liferaft & Inflatable Ctr.	Rodney Bay	758-452-8306	francis@liferaft&inflatable.com
INTERNET ACCESS			
The Bistro	Castries	758-452-9494	bistro@candw.lc
Cable & Wireless	Castries		
Cafe Ole	Rodney Bay	758-452-8726	
Chateau Mygo	Marigot Bay	758-451-4772	info@chateaumygo.com
Doolittles	Marigot Bay	758-451-4974	
H2O	Rodney Bay	758-452-0351	
Harmony Beach	Malgretout	758-459-5050	harmonyiii@hotmail.com
Hummingbird	Soufrière	758-459-7232	hbr@candw.lc
Jambe de Bois	Pigeon Island	758-452-0321	btipson@candw.lc
Lime	Rodney Bay	758-453-9055	
Marigot Bay Marina	Marigot Bay	758-451-4275	marina@themarinavillage.com
Pizza Pizza	Rodney Bay	758-452-8282	
Red Snapper	Rodney Bay	758-456-8377	
Rent A Ride	Rodney Bay	758-452-9404	reservations@vcrentals.com
SMMA	Soufrière	758-459-5500	smma@candw.lc
MARINE SUPPLIES			
Captain Bravo	Rodney Bay	758-452-5155	
Island Water World	Rodney Bay	758-452-1222	iwwsljan@candw.lc
Johnson' Marine Hardware	Rodney Bay	758-452-0299	
Marigot Bay Marina	Marigot Bay	758-451-4275	marina@marigotbay.com
NAPA	Rodney Bay	758-452-5034	
Rodney Bay Marina	Rodney Bay	758-452-0324	rbm@igymarinas.com
Rod. Bay Mar. Hardware	Rodney Bay	758-452-9973	
OUTBOARD REPAIR			
Island Water World	Rodney Bay	758-452-1222	
Mac's Marine	Rodney Bay	758-485-1530	
Marigot Bay Marina	Marigot Bay	758-451-4275	marina@marigotbay.com
Marin Tek	Rodney Bay	758-484-6031	marintek@gmail.com
Mystic Man	Soufrière	758-459-7783	aimblec@candw.lc
NAPA-*OMC*	Vigie	758-452-5034	
Rodney Bay Marina	Rodney Bay	758-452-0324	rbm@igymarinas.com
Valmont & Co.	Castries	758-452-3817	
PROPANE			
Julien's Supermarket	Gros Islet		
Shell Station	Gros Islet		
REFRIGERATION/AC REPAIR			
Cay Electronics	Rodney Bay	758-452-9922	cayslu@candw.lc
Destination St. Lucia	Rodney Bay	758-452-8531	
Ray's Refrigeration	Castries		

FACILITY	LOCATION	TELEPHONE	EMAIL ADDRESS
Rodney Bay Marina	Rodney Bay	758-452-0324	rbm@igymarinas.com
RIGGING			
Island Water World	Rodney Bay	758-452-1222	
Rodney Bay Marina	Rodney Bay	758-452-0324	rbm@igymarinas.com
The Sail Loft	Rodney Bay	758-452-8648	syachts@candw.lc
SAIL REPAIR			
B & L Upholstery Clinic	Rodney Bay	758-452-7644	
Broco Sail Repair	Rodney Bay	758-450-8864	
Marigot Bay Marina	Marigot Bay	758-451-4275	marina@marigotbay.com
MC	Rodney Bay	758-450-0300	
Rodney Bay Sails	Rodney Bay	758-452-8648	
Sunsail	Rodney Bay	758-452-8848	
The Sail Loft	Rodney Bay	758-452-8648	syachts@candw.lc
WOODWORKING			
Andrew Tyson	Rodney Bay	758-452-5794	
Rodney Bay Marina	Rodney Bay	758-452-0324	rbm@igymarinas.com
UNDERWATER REPAIRS			
Complete Marine Services	Marigot Bay	758-458-3188	info@cms.sl.com

Appendix C-3: Service Facilities on Barbados

FACILITY	LOCATION	TELEPHONE	EMAIL ADDRESS
AUTO RENTALS			
Auto Rentals Ltd.	Christ Church	246-228-1520	
Coconut Car Rentals	St. Michael	246-437-0297	coconut@spiceisle.com
Corbins Car Rentals	Bridgetown	246-427-9531	corbins@ndl.net
Courtesy Rent.A.Car	Christ Church	246-431-4160	
Direct Car Rentals	St. Michael	246-228-2491	
Drive-A-Matic	St. James	246-422-4000	
National	Bridgetown	246-426-0603	
P & S Car Rentals	Bridgetown	246-424-2052	
Stoutes Car Rental	St. Philip	246-435-4456	
Sunny Isle Motors	St. Philip	246-435-7979	
CANVAS WORK			
Roger Edgehill	Bridgetown	246-429-5800	
DIESEL/GENERATOR REPAIRS			
DI Manufacturing	Guinea	246-423-3866	
McEnearney's	Bridgetown	246-467-2400	
Plantrac	Bridgetown	246-430-3600	plantrac@spiceisle.com
FIBERGLASS REPAIR/PAINTING			
Andrew Burke	Bridgetown	246-228-1864	
Pelican Marine	Bridgetown	246-430-6664	
Willie's Mar. Serv.	Bridgetown	246-424-1808	mikie@spiceisle.com
HAUL OUT			
Willie's Mar. Serv.	Bridgetown	246-424-1808	mikie@spiceisle.com
INFLATABLES/LIFE RAFTS			
McEnearney's	Bridgetown	246-467-2400	
INTERNET ACCESS			
A&R Computer Services	Hastings	246-435-8608	arcomputers@sunbeach.net
Axses Systems Carib.	Bridgetown	246-431-8950	contactus@axses.net
Broad St. Mall	Bridgetown	246-431-0756	
Computer Internet Ser.	Bridgetown	246-431-0756	cis1@sunbeach.net

FACILITY	LOCATION	TELEPHONE	EMAIL ADDRESS
Connect	Bridgetown	246-228-8648	info@connectbarbados.com
Global Business Center	Bridgetown	246-432-6508	global@globalbizcentre.com
Internet Access	Bridgetown	246-431-0756	
Nationlogic, Inc.	Bridgetown	246-436-3212	info@nationlogic.com
Netsurf Internet Café	Bridgetown	246-420-8079	
Port St. Charles	Heywoods	246-419-1000	
MARINE SUPPLIES			
Fisherman's Corner	Bridgetown	246-436-6049	VHF Ch. 06
Harris Paints	St. Michael	246-429-6500	
OUTBOARD REPAIR			
DI Manufacturing	Guinea	246-423-3866	
McEnearney's	Bridgetown	246-467-2400	
Star Products- *Yamaha*	Bridgetown	246-426-3066	
RIGGING			
Marine Mgt. Serv.	Bridgetown	246-234-4733	
SAIL REPAIR			
Doyle Offshore Sails	Six Cross Roads	246-423-4600	doyle@caribnet.net
Edge Hill Sails	Hastings	246-429-5800	
Undercover	Bridgetown	246-226-6937	

Appendix C-4: Service Facilities on St. Vincent

FACILITY	LOCATION	TELEPHONE	EMAIL ADDRESS
AUTO RENTALS			
Abbott & Sons	Kingstown	784-456-1511	
Avis	Kingstown	784-456-4389	humps@spiceisle.com
Ben's Auto Rental	Arnos Vale	784-456-2907	
DAC	Kingstown	784-456-9739	dac@spiceisle.com
Kim's Car Rentals	Arnos Vale	784-456-1084	mail@kimsrentals.com
Reggie Rentals	Kingstown	784-456-9331	reggierents@spiceisle.com
Star Garage	Kingstown	784-456-1743	
Unico Auto Rentals	Kingstown	784-456-5744	
DIESEL/GENERATOR REPAIRS			
Barefoot	Blue Lagoon	784-456-9526	
Howard's Marine	Calliaqua	784-457-4328	VHF ch. 68
Ottley Hall Marina	Kingstown	784-456-1302	ottleyhall@spiceisle.com
Rannie & Redman	Kingstown	784-458-4270	
ELECTRONICS & ELECTRICAL			
Barefoot	Blue Lagoon	784-456-9526	
Nichol's Marine	Calliaqua	784-456-4118	VHF ch. 68
Ottley Hall Marina	Kingstown	784-456-1302	ottleyhall@spiceisle.com
FABRICATION/WELDING			
Carlton King	Kingstown	784-457-9311	
Nichol's Marine	Calliaqua	784-456-4118	
Oscar's Machine Shop	Calliaqua	784-456-4118	
Ottley Hall Marina	Kingstown	784-456-1302	ottleyhall@spiceisle.com
FIBERGLASS REPAIR/PAINTING			
Barefoot	Blue Lagoon	784-456-9526	
Howard's Marine	Kingstown	784-457-4328	
Ottley Hall Marina	Kingstown	784-456-1302	ottleyhall@spiceisle.com
HAUL OUT			
Howard's Marine	Kingstown	784-457-4328	

FACILITY	LOCATION	TELEPHONE	EMAIL ADDRESS
Ottley Hall Marina	Kingstown	784-456-1302	ottleyhall@spiceisle.com
INFLATABLES/LIFE RAFTS			
KP Marine	Calliaqua	784-457-1806	kpmarine@spiceisle.com
INTERNET ACCESS			
Barefoot Yacht Charters	Blue Lagoon	784-456-9526	
Computec	Kingstown		
Lagoon Hotel	Blue Lagoon	784-458-4308	sunsailsvg@spiceisle.com
Ottley Hall Marina	Kingstown	784-456-1302	ottleyhall@spiceisle.com
Port Authority Int. Café	Kingstown		
Rock Side Café	Kearton Bay	784-456-0815	rosimorgan@vincysurf.com
Sam's Taxi (*Wifi*)	Young Island cut	784-456-4338	*Sam's Taxi*, VHF ch.16 or 68
Wallilabou Anch. Rest.	Wallilabou	784-458-7270	wallanch@spiceisle.com
MARINE SUPPLIES			
Barefoot	Blue Lagoon	784-456-9526	
Howard's Marine	Calliaqua	784-457-4328	
KP Marine	Calliaqua	784-457-1806	kpmarine@spiceisle.com
Nichol's Marine	Calliaqua	784-456-4118	
Lagoon Marina & Hotel	Blue Lagoon	784-458-4308	
Ottley Hall Marina	Kingstown	784-456-1302	ottleyhall@spiceisle.com
St. Vincent Sales & Serv.	Kingstown	784-457-1820	
OUTBOARD REPAIR			
Ace- *Yamaha*	Kingstown		
Barefoot	Blue Lagoon	784-456-9526	
Howard's Marine	Calliaqua	784-457-4328	
KP Marine- *Yamaha*	Calliaqua	784-457-1806	kpmarine@spiceisle.com
Ottley Hall Marina	Kingstown	784-456-1302	ottleyhall@spiceisle.com
PROPANE			
Texaco (airport)	Arnos Vale		
PROPELLERS			
Ottley Hall Marina	Kingstown	784-456-1302	ottleyhall@spiceisle.com
REFRIGERATION/AC REPAIR			
Ottley Hall Marina	Kingstown	784-456-1302	ottleyhall@spiceisle.com
RIGGING			
Barefoot	Blue Lagoon	784-456-9526	
SAIL AND CANVAS REPAIRS			
Barefoot	Blue Lagoon	784-456-9526	
Ottley Hall Marina	Kingstown	784-456-1302	ottleyhall@spiceisle.com
WOODWORKING			
Ottley Hall Marina	Kingstown	784-456-1302	ottleyhall@spiceisle.com

Appendix C-5: Service Facilities in The Grenadines

FACILITY	LOCATION	TELEPHONE	EMAIL ADDRESS
AUTO RENTALS			
Challenger Taxi	Belmont, Bequia	784-458-3811	challengertaxi@yahoo.com
Francis Car Rental	Clifton, Union Island	784-458-8245	
Handy Andy	Bequia	784-452-3722	
Lubin Ollivierre	Bequia	784-458-3349	
Mustique Mechanical	Mustique	784-458-4621	
CANVAS WORK			
Bequia Canvas	Admiralty Bay, Bequia	784-457-3291	

FACILITY	LOCATION	TELEPHONE	EMAIL ADDRESS
DIESEL/GENERATOR REPAIRS			
Arthur Roach	Saline Bay, Mayreau		
Caribbean Diesel	Admiralty Bay, Bequia	784-457-3114	VHF ch. 68
Gizmo Marine	Charlestown, Canouan	784-491-1177	
Fixman Engineering	Admiralty Bay, Bequia	784-457-3406	
Island Marine	Clifton, Union Island	784-458-8039	VHF ch. 16
KMS Marine Services	Admiralty Bay, Bequia	784-530-8123	
Mustique Mech. Serv.	Britannia Bay, Mustique	784-458-4621	
Simpson Engineering	Admiralty Bay, Bequia	784-457-3692	dee.williams@hotmail.com (VHF 68)
Unitech Marine Services	Clifton, Union Island	784-458-8913	unitech@vincysurf.com
ELECTRONICS & ELECTRICAL			
Gizmo Marine	Charlestown, Canouan	784-491-1177	
Grenadines Engineering	Clifton, Union Island	784-458-8778	
GYE	Admiralty Bay, Bequia	784-458-3347	gye-bequia@vincysurf.com
Fixman Engineering	Admiralty Bay, Bequia	784-457-3406	
KMS Marine Services	Admiralty Bay, Bequia	784-530-8123	
Unitech Marine Services	Clifton, Union Island	784-458-8913	unitech@vincysurf.com
FABRICATION/WELDING			
Caribbean Diesel Repair	Admiralty Bay, Bequia	784-457-3114	
Castello Steel Works	Clifton, Union Island	784-458-8755	
Clement Brothers	Petite Martinique	473-443-9110	
Fixman Engineering	Admiralty Bay, Bequia	784-457-3406	
KMS Marine Services	Admiralty Bay, Bequia	784-530-8123	
Unitech Marine Services	Clifton, Union Island	784-458-8913	unitech@vincysurf.com
FIBERGLASS REPAIR/PAINTING			
Bequia Slip	Admiralty Bay, Bequia	784-458-3272	
Castello Steel Works	Clifton, Union Island	784-458-8755	
East Coast Yacht Refin.	Admiralty Bay, Bequia	784-458-3722	
Grenadines Yacht Ref.	Admiralty Bay, Bequia	784-458-3722	
Lighthouse	Admiralty Bay, Bequia	784-458-3084	
Unitech Marine Services	Clifton, Union Island	784-458-8913	unitech@vincysurf.com
INTERNET ACCESS			
Anchorage Yacht Club	Clifton, Union Island	784-458-8221	aycunion@vincysurf.com
Bequia Technology Center	Admiralty Bay, Bequia	784-458-3045	info@bequiatech.com
Captain Gourmet	Clifton, Union Island	784-458-8918	capgourmet@vincysurf.com
Cyber City	Port Elizabeth, Bequia	784-457-3161	
Cyber Net	Charlestown, Canouan	784-430-4045	
Erika's Marine Services	Clifton, Union Island	784-485-8335	info@erikamarine.com
Frangipani Yacht Serv.	Admiralty Bay, Bequia	784-458-3255	frangi@vincysurf.com
Gingerbread Café	Admiralty Bay, Bequia	784-458-3800	ginger@vincysurf.com
Iconet	Admiralty Bay, Bequia		iconet@vincysurf.com
Internet Café	Clifton, Union Island	784-485-8326	
L' Aquarium	Clifton, Union Island	784-458-8311	
Lenroc Internet Café	Admiralty Bay, Bequia	784-456-3439	info@lenroc.net
Millennium Connection	Petite Martinique		
Mustique Comm. Library	Mustique	784-456-3556	mustiquelibrary@vincysurf.com
Palm Beach Restaurant	Petite Martinique		
RMS	Admiralty Bay, Bequia	784-458-4556	rms@vincysurf.com
Sailor's Cyber Café	Admiralty Bay, Bequia	784-457-3105	vinsea@vincysurf.com
Tamarind Beach Hotel	Charlestown, Canouan	784-458-8044	
Tradewinds Yacht Chart.	Admiralty Bay, Bequia		

FACILITY	LOCATION	TELEPHONE	EMAIL ADDRESS
MARINE SUPPLIES			
Bequia Marine Supply	Admiralty Bay, Bequia	478-457-3157	
Bequia Venture	Admiralty Bay, Bequia	478-458-3319	
Bo'sun's Locker (Budget)	Admiralty Bay, Bequia	784-458-3634	budmarbequia@vincysurf.com
Caribbean Diesel	Admiralty Bay, Bequia	784-457-3114	
Clement Bros.	Petite Martinique	473-443-9022	windwardmarine@hotmail.com
GYE	Admiralty Bay, Bequia	784-458-3347	gye-bequia@vincysurf.com
Lulley's Tackle Shop	Admiralty Bay, Bequia	784-458-3420	
Piper Marine	Admiralty Bay, Bequia	784-457-3856	
Wallace & Co.	Admiralty Bay, Bequia	784-458-3360	wallco@vincysurf.com
OUTBOARD REPAIR			
Arthur Roach	Saline Bay, Mayreau		
Bequia Marine Supply	Admiralty Bay, Bequia	784-457-3157	
Gizmo Marine	Charlestown, Canouan	784-491-1177	
GYE- *OMC*	Admiralty Bay, Bequia	784-458-3347	gye-bequia@vincysurf.com
Island Marine Special	Clifton, Union Island	784-458-8039	
KMS Marine Services	Admiralty Bay, Bequia	784-530-8123	
Simpson Engineering	Admiralty Bay, Bequia	784-457-3692	dee.williams@hotmail.com (VHF 68)
Unitech Marine Services	Clifton, Union Island	784-458-8913	unitech@vincysurf.com
Vilton's Marine Services	Admiralty Bay, Bequia	784-457-3792	viltonsmarine@hotmail.com
PROPANE			
GYE	Admiralty Bay, Bequia	784-458-3347	gye-bequia@vincysurf.com
Unitech Marine Services	Clifton, Union Island	784-458-8913	unitech@vincysurf.com
REFRIGERATION/AC REPAIR			
KMS Marine Services	Admiralty Bay, Bequia	784-530-8123	
Knock Refrigeration	Admiralty Bay, Bequia	784-529-1682	
RIGGING			
GYE	Admiralty Bay, Bequia	784-458-3347	gye-bequia@vincysurf.com
Piper Marine	Admiralty Bay, Bequia	784-457-3856	VHF ch. 68
SAIL REPAIR			
Allick Sails	Admiralty Bay, Bequia	784-458-3992	VHF ch. 68
Bequia Canvas	Admiralty Bay, Bequia	784-457-3291	beqcan@vincysurf.com
Grenadines Sails	Admiralty Bay, Bequia	784-457-3507	gsails@vincysurf.com

Appendix C-6: Service Facilities on Carriacou

FACILITY	LOCATION	TELEPHONE	EMAIL ADDRESS
AUTO RENTALS			
Barba's Auto Rentals	Hillsborough	473-443-7454	
John Gabriel	Carriacou	473-443-7454	
Linky Jeep Rental	Carriacou	473-406-2457	linkytaxiservice@hotmail.com
Martine Bullen	Carriacou	473-443-7204	
Silver Beach Resort	Carriacou	473-443-7337	
CANVAS WORK			
Dominique Wer	Tyrrel Bay	473-407-1151	
DIESEL/GENERATOR REPAIRS			
Danson Refrigeration	Tyrrel Bay	473-443-8625	
Tool Meister	Tyrrel Bay	473-445-8178	tmmachine@spiceisle.com
ELECTRONICS & ELECTRICAL			
Mike Forshaw	Tyrrel Bay	7473-443-7128	
FABRICATION/WELDING			
Cleandro	Tyrrel Bay		

FACILITY	LOCATION	TELEPHONE	EMAIL ADDRESS
Dominique Wer	Tyrrel Bay	473-407-1151	
Tool Meister	Tyrrel Bay	473-445-8178	tmmachine@spiceisle.com
FIBERGLASS REPAIR/PAINTING			
Dominique Wer	Tyrrel Bay	473-407-1151	
George Schmitt	Tyrrel Bay	473-443-6906	
Tyrrel Bay Yacht Haulout	Tyrrel Bay	473-443-8878	Asmelt@gmail.com
HAUL OUT			
Tyrrel Bay Yacht Haulout	Tyrrel Bay	473-443-8878	Asmelt@gmail.com
INTERNET ACCESS			
Carriacou Childrens Ed.	Tyrrel Bay	Check at TBYH	
Digi-Soft	Hillsborough	473-443-8955	digisoft@gmail.com
Services Unlimited	Hillsborough	473-443-8451	servicesunlimited@spiceisle.com
MARINE SUPPLIES			
Tyrrel Bay Yacht Haulout	Tyrrel Bay	473-443-8878	Asmelt@gmail.com
OUTBOARD REPAIR			
Cleandro	Tyrrel Bay		
Tyrrel Bay Yacht Haulout	Tyrrel Bay	473-443-8878	Asmelt@gmail.com
REFRIGERATION/AC REPAIR			
Danson Refrigeration	Tyrrel Bay	473-443-8625	
Hezron Wilson Refrigeration	Tyrrel Bay	473-443-6212	
RIGGING			
Tool Meister	Tyrrel Bay	473-445-8178	tmmachine@spiceisle.com
Tyrrel Bay Yacht Haulout	Tyrrel Bay	473-443-8878	Asmelt@gmail.com
SAIL REPAIR			
Dominique Wer	Tyrrel Bay	473-407-1151	
Geniveve	Tyrrel Bay	473-443-8175	
In Stitches (at *TBYH*)	Tyrrel Bay	473-443-8878	

Appendix C-7: Service Facilities on Grenada

FACILITY	LOCATION	TELEPHONE	EMAIL ADDRESS
AUTO RENTALS			
Archie Auto Rentals	St. George's	473-444-2535	archie@spiceisle.com
Avis	St. George's	473-440-3936	
Blue Diamond	Prickly Bay	473-444-1703	
Budget	St. George's	473-444-2277	
C. Thomas & Sons	True Blue	473-444-4384	
D' Keys Car Rental	Sauteurs	473-442-9294	
Dab's	St. George's	473-444-4116	wavecrest@spiceisle.com
David's Car Rental	St. George's	473-444-3399	cdavid@spiceisle.com
Dollar Rent A Car	Airport	473-444-4786	
EZE Car Rentals	Grand Anse	473-444-3263	
Funseeker Tours	St. George's	473-444-1342	
General Rent-A-Car	St. George's	473-440-2894	
Grenada Car Rental	True Blue	473-443-0600	
Grencab	Grand Anse	473-444-4444	
Hestel	Morne Rouge	473-444-4247	
Indigo Car Rentals	True Blue	473-439-3300	indigocars@spiceisle.com
Island Rentals	St. George's	473-443-5624	
Jeep Rentals	St. George's	473-440-2441	
Jerry's Rentals	St. George's	473-440-1730	
Maitland's Car Rentals	Grand Anse	473-444-4022	

FACILITY	LOCATION	TELEPHONE	EMAIL ADDRESS
McIntyre Bros.	St. George's	473-440-3944	macford@spiceisle.com
MCR Car Rentals	St. George's	473-440-5398	
New Image	St. George's	473-439-0423	nicecars@spiceisle.com
Outfitter's International	St. George's	473-440-7949	footloos@spiceisle.com
Quality Rentals	St. George's	473-440-9789	
Sanvics Car Rental	Grand Anse	473-444-4753	
Sunsation Rentals	Grand Anse	473-444-1594	qkspice@spiceisle.com
Sunshine Tours	St. George's	473-444-2831	
Thomas & Sons	St. George's	473-444-4384	
Thrift Car Rentals	Morne Rouge	473-444-4984	
Tropicana	St. George's	473-444-8849	
Y&R Car Rentals	St. George's	473-444-4448	y&r@carbsurf.com

CANVAS WORK

Canvas Shop	St. George's	473-443-2960	thecanvasshop@spiceisle.com
Clarke's Upholstery	St. George's	473-4147827	v-clark-upholstery@hotmail.com
Johnny Sails & Canvas	St. George's	473-444-1108	jsails@spiceisle.com
Spice Island Marine Serv.	Prickly Bay	473-444-4257	simsco@spiceisle.com

DIESEL/GENERATOR REPAIRS

Anro Agencies	St. George's	473-444-2220	
Ben	St. George's	473-440-5360	
Enza Marine	St. George's	473-407-3692	enzamarine@spiceisle.com
Grenada Boat Services	St. George's	473-415-2092	
McIntyre Bros.	St. George's	473-440-3944	macford@spiceisle.com
Palm Tree Marine	Le Phare Bleu	473-407-2783	Lucy@palmtreemarine.com
Spice Island Marine	Prickly Bay	473-444-4257	simsco@spiceisle.com

ELECTRONICS & ELECTRICAL

Grenada Boat Services	St. George's	473-415-2092	
Grenada Marine	St. David's	473-443-1667	info@grenadamarine.com
Island Water World	St. David's	473-443-1028	sales@islandwaterworld.com
Island Water World	St. George's	473-435-2150	sales@islandwaterworld.com
Palm Tree Marine	Le Phare Bleu	473-407-2783	Lucy@palmtreemarine.com
Ricardo Moultrie (ACR tech)	St. George's	473-407-4989	
Turbulence Sails	St. George's	473-439-4495	sail@spiceisle.com

FABRICATION/WELDING

Albert Lucas	St. George's	473-440-1281	
Enza Marine	St. George's	473-407-3692	enzamarine@spiceisle.com
Grenada Marine	St. David's	473-443-1667	info@grenadamarine.com
Tech Metal Works	St. George's	473-440-2895	

FIBERGLASS REPAIR/PAINTING

Cottle Boatworks	Prickly Bay	473-444-1070	
Grenada Boat Services	St. George's	473-415-2092	
Grenada Marine	St. David's	473-443-1667	info@grenadamarine.com
Shipwrights Ltd.	St. David's	473-440-1062	shipwrights@spiceisle.com
Spice Island Marine	Prickly Bay	473-444-4257	simsco@spiceisle.com
Tan Tan	Grenada	473-440-1870	

FUEL FILTERING

Palm Tree Marine	Le Phar Bleu	473-407-2783	Lucy@palmtreemarine.com
Ricardo Moultrie	Grenada	473-407-4989	

HAUL OUT

Grenada Marine	St. David's	473-443-1667	info@grenadamarine.com
Spice Island Marine	Prickly Bay	473-444-4257	simsco@spiceisle.com

FACILITY	LOCATION	TELEPHONE	EMAIL ADDRESS
INFLATABLES			
Grenada Boat Services	St. George's	473-415-2092	
INTERNET ACCESS			
Boats and Harbours,	Prickly Bay	473-435-8888	
Boatyard Restaurant	Prickly Bay	473-444-4662	boatyard@spiceisle.com
Grenada Marine	St. David's,	473-443-1667	info@grenadamarine.com
Grenada Yacht Club	St. George's	473-440-3050	gyc@spiceisle.com
Hankey's Computers	St. George's	473-443-0505	hanks@spiceisle.com
Nimrod's	Lower Woburn	473-443-3683	bernadettenimrod@hotmail.com
Onsite Software	Marquis Mall	473-444-3653	
Rendezvous Beach Resort	Prickly Bay	473-444-3040	info@rendezvousresort.com
True Blue Marina	True Blue	473-443-8783	mail@trueblue.com
MARINE SUPPLIES			
Ace Hardware/NAPA	St. George's	473-440-5090	
Anro Agencies	St. George's	473-444-2220	
Grenada Marine	St. David's	473-443-1667	info@grenadamarine.com
Island Water World	St. David's	473-443-1028	sales@islandwaterworld.com
Island Water World	St. George's	473-435-2150	sales@islandwaterworld.com
Land & Sea Marine	Gouyave	473-444-9696	
Palm Tree Marine	Le Phare Bleu	473-407-2783	Lucy@palmtreemarine.com
Spice Island Marine	Prickly Bay	473-444-4257	simsco@spiceisle.com
MARINE SURVEYOR			
Bob Goodchild	St. George's	473-407-4388	surveyor@flyingfishventures.com
Alan Hooper	St. George's	473-440-3693	
OUTBOARD REPAIR			
Anro Agencies	St. George's	473-444-2220	
Grenada Boat Services	St. George's	473-415-2092	
McIntyre Bros.	St. George's	473-440-3944	macford@spiceisle.com
Palm Tree Marine	Le Phare Bleu	473-407-2783	Lucy@palmtreemarine.com
Ricardo Moultrie	St. George's	473-407-4989	
PROPANE			
Dave's Gas Service	Prickly Bay	473-444-5571	
George	Mt. Hartman	*Survival Anchorage* on VHF ch. 16	
Grenada Yacht Club	St. George's	473-440-3050	gyc@spiceisle.com
Henry Safari Tours	Prickly Bay	473-444-5313	*Henry's Safari Tours* VHF ch. 16
Spice Island Marine	Prickly Bay	473-444-4257	simsco@spiceisle.com
True Blue Marina	True Blue	Call Henry's Safari Tours: 473-444-5313	
Texgas	St. George's		
REFRIGERATION/AC REPAIR			
Enza Marine	St. George's	473-407-3692	enzamarine@spiceisle.com
Clyn Henry	Woburn	473-420-1100	
Lagoon Marine Ref.	St. George's	473-440-3381	
Subzero Air Control	St. George's	473-440-4072	
RIGGING			
Grenada Marine	St. David's	473-443-1667	
Johnny Sails & Canvas	St. George's	473-444-1108	jsails@spiceisle.com
Spice Island Marine	Prickly Bay	473-444-4257	simsco@spiceisle.com
Turbulence Sails	St. George's	473-439-4495	sail@spiceisle.com
SAIL REPAIR			
Johnny Sails & Canvas	St. George's	473-444-1108	jsails@spiceisle.com
Neil Pryde	St. George's	473-440-2556	fisher@spiceisle.com

FACILITY	LOCATION	TELEPHONE	EMAIL ADDRESS
Spice Island Marine	Prickly Bay	473-444-4257	simsco@spiceisle.com
Turbulence Sails	St. George's	473-439-4495	sail@spiceisle.com
UNDERWATER REPAIRS			
Underwater Solutions	Le Phare Blue	473-456-3927	www.underwatersolutions.com
WOODWORKING			
Cottle Boat Works	St. George's	473-443-1070	
Grenada Marine	St. David's	473-443-1667	info@grenadamarine.com
Shipwright's Ltd.	St. David's	473-443-1062	shipwrights@spiceisle.com
Spice Island Marine	Prickly Bay	473-444-4257	simsco@spiceisle.com

Appendix C-8: Service Facilities on Trinidad and Tobago

FACILITY	LOCATION	TELEPHONE	EMAIL ADDRESS
AUTO RENTAL			
Alfred's Rentals	Crown Point, Tobago	868-639-7448	
Amar Rentals Ltd.	San Fernando, Trinidad	868-657-6089	
AR	Crown Point, Tobago	868-639-0644	
AR	Morvant, Trinidad	868-675-7368	
AR	Piarco Airport, Trinidad	868-669-2277	
AR	Point Fortin, Trinidad	868-648-7368	
AR	San Fernando, Trinidad	868-657-7368	
Autocenter	Crown Point, Tobago	868-639-4400	autocenter@wow.net
Autocenter	Port of Spain, Trinidad	868-628-8800	autocenter@wow.net
Avis	Trinidad	868-628-8996	
Baird's	Crown Point, Tobago	868-639-2528	
Carlton James Rentals	Crown Point, Tobago	868-639-8084	jameshol@tstt.net.tt
Carnetta's Inn Ltd.	Maraval, Trinidad	868-622-5165	carnetta@trinidad.net
Cat 4	Chaguaramas, Trinidad	868-634-1479	cat4@tstt.net.tt
Convenient (Tropical)	Chaguaramas, Trinidad	868-634-4017	crl@carib-link.net
Discount Auto Rentals	St. James, Trinidad	868-622-6596	BrettPillac@hotmail.com
Econo-Car	Crown Point, Tobago	868-660-8728	
Econo-Car (CrewsInn)	Chaguaramas, Trinidad	868-634-2154	
Econo-Car	Port Of Spain, Trinidad	868-622-8072	
Econo-Car	Piarco Airport, Trinidad	868-669-2342	
Exclusive Car Rental	Chaguaramas, Trinidad	868-634-2915	
Executive Limo Rental	Port of Spain, Trinidad	868-625-1170	clbattoo@trinidad.net
Furness Car Rentals	Port Of Spain, Trinidad	868-627-4959	furness@wow.net
George's Rentals	Charlotteville, Tobago	868-639-8295	
Greene's (motorcycles)	Arouca, Trinidad	868-646-2453	
Hill Crest Car Rental	Scarborough, Tobago	868-639-5208	
Island Bikes	Crown Point, Tobago	868-639-8587	
Kalloo's	Caroni, Trinidad	868-645-5182	kallocan@tstt.net.tt
Kalloo's (CrewsInn)	Chaguaramas, Trinidad	868-634-4041	kallocan@tstt.net.tt
Kalloo's	Piarco Airport, Trinidad	868-669-5673	kallocan@tstt.net.tt
Kalloo's	Port of Spain, Trinidad	868-622-9073	kallocan@tstt.net.tt
Manta Car Rentals	Crown Point, Tobago	868-639-9209	mantaray@tstt.net.tt
Monique's Guest House	Maraval, Trinidad	868-628-3334	moniques@carib-link.net
Peter Gremli Car Rental	Crown Point, Tobago	868-639-8400	carman@tstt.net.tt
Paradise Car Rentals	Speyside, Tobago	868-660-4341	
Quashie's Car Rentals	Crown Point, Tobago	868-639-8397	
Rattan's Car Rentals	Crown Point, Tobago	868-639-8271	
Reesal's Auto Rentals	Piarco Airport, Trinidad	868-669-3330	

FACILITY	LOCATION	TELEPHONE	EMAIL ADDRESS
Rodriquez	Crown Point, Tobago	868-639-8507	eontab@tstt.net.tt
Rollock's	Crown Point, Tobago	868-639-0328	
Sherman's Rentals	Lambeau, Tobago	868-639-2292	shermans@trinidad.net
Singh's Auto Rentals	Crown Point, Tobago	868-639-0191	
Singh's Auto Rentals	Piarco Airport, Trinidad	868-669-5417	
Singh's Auto Rentals	Port of Spain, Trinidad	868-623-0150	
Southern Sales Car Rentals	Chaguaramas, Trinidad	868-634-4777	ssrental@tstt.net.tt
Southern Sales Car Rentals	Piarco, Trinidad	868-669-2226	ssrental@tstt.net.tt
Southern Sales Car Rentals	Point Galeota, Trinidad	868-630-4777	ssrental@tstt.net.tt
Southern Sales Car Rentals	Point Lisas, Trinidad	868-679-2424	ssrental@tstt.net.tt
Southern Sales Car Rentals	Port of Spain, Trinidad	868-675-2424	ssrental@tstt.net.tt
Southern Sales Car Rentals	San Fernando, Trinidad	868-653-2424	ssrental@tstt.net.tt
Southern Sales Car Rentals	Tobago	868-639-0328	ssrental@tstt.net.tt
Speedy Car Rentals	Crown Point, Tobago	868-639-7038	
Spence Car Rentals	Crown Point, Tobago	868-639-8082	
Sue's Auto Rentals	Chaguanas, Trinidad	868-665-4713	contact@tstt.net.tt
Sue's Auto Rentals	Piarco Airport, Trinidad	868-669-1635	contact@tstt.net.tt
Ted's Sunshine Ent.	Crown Point, Tobago	868-639-0547	sunshine@trinidad.net
Tewar's	Crown Point, Tobago	868-651-5120	
Thrifty	Crown Point, Tobago	868-639-8507	
Thrifty	Trinidad	868-669-0602	
Tobago Car Rental	Crown Point, Tobago	868-639-0350	
Tobago United Rentals	Crown Point, Tobago	868-639-4973	
Tropical (*Peake's*)	Chaguaramas, Trinidad	868-634-4017	
Waukie's Car Rentals	Mt. Pleasant, Tobago	868-639-9072	

DIESEL/GENERATOR REPAIRS

FACILITY	LOCATION	TELEPHONE	EMAIL ADDRESS
Alle Wright (*Tardieu*)	Chaguaramas, Trinidad	868-634-2553	allewright@tstt.net.tt
Budget Marine	Chaguaramas, Trinidad	868-634-2006	sales@budmar.co.tt
Carnbee Auto & General	Carnbee, Tobago	868-639-9304	
Dockyard Elt. (*CrewsInn*)	Chaguaramas, Trinidad	868-634-4272	dockelec@trinida.net
General Diesel	La Romain, Trinidad	868-652-5441	
General Diesel	San Fernando, Trinidad	868-657-6351	
Gitten's Engine (*Tardieu*)	Chaguaramas, Trinidad	868-634-2304	adian@tstt.net.tt
LP Marine Supplies	Chaguaramas, Trinidad	868-634-2094	lmarine@opus.co.tt
LP Marine Supplies	Pt. Cumana, Trinidad	868-633-3395	lmarine@opus.co.tt
L & W Marine Engines	Laventille, Trinidad	868-624-5618	
Store Bay Marine Services	Store Bay, Tobago	868-390-5408	john@sbms.co.tt
Tropical Power	Chaguaramas, Trinidad	868-665-8833	

ELECTRONICS/ELECTRICAL

FACILITY	LOCATION	TELEPHONE	EMAIL ADDRESS
Boyce Electronics	Marabella, Trinidad	868-658-2943	
Budget Marine	Chaguaramas, Trinidad	868-634-2006	sales@budmar.co.tt
Carib. Marine Electrical	Chaguaramas, Trinidad	868-634-2359	electromarine@tstt.net.tt
Dockyard Electrics	Chaguaramas, Trinidad	868-634-4272	info@dockyardelectrics.com
Echo Marine	Chaguaramas, Trinidad	868-634-2027	sailfly@trinidad.net
Electropics Marine Serv.	Chaguaramas, Trinidad	868-634-2322	info@electropics.com
Goodwood Mar. (*CrewsInn*)	Chaguaramas, Trinidad	868-634-2203	goodwood@tstt.net.tt
LP Marine Supplies	Chaguaramas, Trinidad	868-634-2094	lmarine@opus.co.tt
LP Marine Supplies	Pt. Cumana, Trinidad	868-633-3395	lmarine@opus.co.tt
Navtech (*Coral Cove*)	Chaguaramas, Trinidad	868-634-1231	navigationalelectron@hotmail.com
Peake Chandlery	Chaguaramas, Trinidad	868-634-4006	
Peake Thomas & Co.	Cocorite, Trinidad	868-622-8816	

FACILITY	LOCATION	TELEPHONE	EMAIL ADDRESS
Serge Electrical (*Peakes*)	Chaguaramas, Trinidad	868-634-4420	
Solar Power Systems	Laventille, Trinidad	868-624-2665	climate@tstt.net.tt
Store Bay Marine Services	Store Bay, Tobago	868-390-5408	john@sbms.co.tt
Stuart Electronics	Chaguaramas, Trinidad	868-634-1164	stutron@tstt.net.tt
Tagos Marine Ltd.	Cumana Bay, Trinidad	868-694-0722	tagosmarine@tstt.net.tt
T&T Marine Elec. (*Peakes*)	Chaguaramas, Trinidad	868-634-1042	

FABRICATION/WELDING

AK Engineering	Tunapuna, Trinidad	868-663-9776	
Ali's Mach. (*Power Boats*)	Chaguaramas, Trinidad	868-634-4420	
Alle Wright (*Tardieu*)	Chaguaramas, Trinidad	868-634-2553	allewright@tstt.net.tt
AMMSCO	Chaguaramas, Trinidad	868-634-2168	ammsco@tstt.net.tt
Caribbean Welders (*IMS*)	Chaguaramas, Trinidad	868-634-1074	
Celestine Marine	Chaguaramas, Trinidad	868-634-2844	
Chag. Metal (*Tardieu*)	Chaguaramas, Trinidad	868-631-1164	
Degannes (*Power Boats*)	Chaguaramas, Trinidad	868-634-4025	
Sean Duprey's	Chaguaramas, Trinidad	868-620-5484	sduprey@wow.net
Superior Machine Shop	San Fernando, Trinidad	868-653-1874	
Store Bay Marine Services	Store Bay, Tobago	868-390-5408	john@sbms.co.tt

HAUL OUT

Coral Cove Marina	Chaguaramas, Trinidad	868-634-2040	coralcove@trinidad.net
CrewsInn Marina	Chaguaramas, Trinidad	868-634-4828	crewsinn@tstt.net.tt
IMS Yacht Services	Chaguaramas, Trinidad	868-625-2104	ims@imsyacht.com
Peake Yacht Services	Chaguaramas, Trinidad	868-634-4423	pys@cablenett.net
Power Boats	Chaguaramas, Trinidad	868-634-4303	bmfl@powerboats.co.tt
TTSA	Carenage, Trinidad	868-634-4519	

HOSPITALS

Arima District Hospital	Arima, Trinidad	868-667-3503	
Community Hospital	Port of Spain, Trinidad	868-622-1191	
Mount Hope	St. Augustine, Trinidad	868-662-3552	
Port of Spain General	Port of Spain, Trinidad	868-623-2951	
San Fernando General	San Fernando, Trinidad	868-658-3581	
St. Clair Medical Center	Port of Spain, Trinidad	868-628-1451	
Tobago County Hospital	Scarborough, Tobago	868-639-2551	

HULL REPAIR/PAINT

Coral Cove Marina	Chaguaramas, Trinidad	868-634-2040	coralcove@trinidad.net
CrewsInn Marina	Chaguaramas, Trinidad	868-634-4828	crewsinn@tstt.net.tt
IMS Yacht Services	Chaguaramas, Trinidad	868-625-2104	ims@imsyacht.com
KNJ Marine (*Peakes*)	Chaguaramas, Trinidad	868-634-1021	knjm@cablenett.net
Peake Yacht Services	Chaguaramas, Trinidad	868-634-4423	pys@cablenett.net
Power Boats	Chaguaramas, Trinidad	868-634-4303	bmfl@powerboats.co.tt
Rainbow (*Power Boats*)	Chaguaramas, Trinidad	868-646-5020	
Store Bay Marine Services	Store Bay, Tobago	868-390-5408	john@sbms.co.tt

INFLATABLES/LIFE RAFTS

Budget Marine	Chaguaramas, Trinidad	868-634-2006	sales@budmar.co.tt
Echo Marine	Chaguaramas, Trinidad	868-634-2027	sailfly@trinidad.net
Marine Safety Equipment	Chaguaramas, Trinidad	868-634-4410	msafe@tstt.net.tt
Power Boats	Chaguaramas, Trinidad	868-634-4303	bmfl@powerboats.co.tt

INTERNET ACCESS

2-M Int'l. Center (*Tropical*)	Chaguaramas, Trinidad	868-634-2748	
Ankh Internet Club (*Tardieu*)	Chaguaramas, Trinidad	868-634-1360	
Blue Waters Inn	Anse Bateau, Tobago	868-660-2583	bwi@bluwatersinn.com

FACILITY	LOCATION	TELEPHONE	EMAIL ADDRESS
Clothes Wash Café	Crown Point, Tobago	868-639-0007	
Core Computers	Scarborough, Tobago	868-639-1100	
Internet Cafe (*Peake's*)	Chaguaramas, Trinidad	868-634-1206	
Island Surf Cafe (*IMS*)	Chaguaramas, Trinidad	868-634-2407	islandsurfcafe@chaguaramas.com
Mariners Off. (*CrewsInn*)	Chaguaramas, Trinidad	868-634-4183	mariner@tstt.net.tt
Master's Laundry (*Tropical*)	Chaguaramas, Trinidad	868-634-1294	
Nautilus (*Power Boats*)	Chaguaramas, Trinidad	868-634-1034	
Public Library (free)	Charlotteville, Tobago		
SameS@me	Chaguaramas, Trinidad	868-634-1360	samesame@whoever.com
Shenda's Email	Charlotteville, Tobago		

MARINE SUPPLIES

Boater's Shop	Chaguaramas, Trinidad	868-634-4148	
Budget Marine	Chaguaramas, Trinidad	868-634-2006	Trinidad@budgetmarine.com
Caribbean Marine	Chaguaramas, Trinidad	868-634-4561	
Coatings Specialist (*Peakes*)	Chaguaramas, Trinidad	868-634-2261	coatings@tstt.net.tt
Corsa Marine (*Tropical*)	Chaguaramas, Trinidad	868-634-1054	
CrewsInn Boatyard	Chaguaramas, Trinidad	868-634-4384	
Dockyard Elect. (*CrewsInn*)	Chaguaramas, Trinidad	868-634-4272	dockelec@trinida.net
Echo Marine (*Mariner's*)	Chaguaramas, Trinidad	868-634-2027	info@echomarine.com
GOMES (*Peakes*)	Chaguaramas, Trinidad	868-680-3525	
Goodwood Marine	Goodwood Park, Trnd.	868-632-4612	
LP Marine Supplies	Chaguaramas, Trinidad	868-634-2094	lmarine@opus.co.tt
LP Marine Supplies	Pt. Cumana, Trinidad	868-633-3395	lmarine@opus.co.tt
Marine Warehouse (*Tardieu*)	Chaguaramas, Trinidad	868-634-4150	tiems@tstt.net.tt
Peake Chandlery	Chaguaramas, Trinidad	868-634-4388	peakechn@carib-link.net
Power Boats	Chaguaramas, Trinidad	868-634-4303	pbmfl@powerboats.co.tt
Shiloh (*Tropical*)	Chaguaramas, Trinidad	868-634-4735	
Store Bay Marine Services	Store Bay, Tobago	868-390-5408	john@sbms.co.tt

OUTBOARD REPAIR

Boat Yard (*Power Boats*)	Chaguaramas, Trinidad	868-634-4536	
Bowen Marine	Chaguaramas, Trinidad	868-634-4543	
Budget Marine	Chaguaramas, Trinidad	868-634-2006	sales@budmar.co.tt
Corsa Marine (*Tardieu*)	Chaguaramas, Trinidad	868-634-1054	
Corsa Marine	San Fernando, Trinidad	868-657-4880	
D&D Outboard (*Skinners*)	Chaguaramas, Trinidad	868-634-1744	
Gitten's Engine (*Tardieu*)	Chaguaramas, Trinidad	868-634-2304	
LP Marine Supplies	Chaguaramas, Trinidad	868-634-2094	lmarine@opus.co.tt
LP Marine Supplies	Pt. Cumana, Trinidad	868-633-3395	lmarine@opus.co.tt
Peake Chandlery	Chaguaramas, Trinidad	868-634-4006	peakechn@carib-link.net
Peake Chandlery	Cocorite, Trinidad	868-622-8816	peakechn@carib-link.net
Store Bay Marine Services	Store Bay, Tobago	868-390-5408	john@sbms.co.tt

PROPANE

Coral Cove Marina	Chaguaramas, Trinidad	868-634-2040	coralcove@trinidad.net
Ian's Taxi	Chaguaramas, Trinidad	868-637-8719	
Ramco	Port of Spain, Trinidad	868-640-2626	
Store Bay Marine Services	Store Bay, Tobago	868-390-5408	john@sbms.co.tt

PROPELLERS

Caribbean Propellers	Chaguaramas, Trinidad	868-634-3376	props@caribprops.com
LP Marine Supplies	Pt. Cumana, Trinidad	868-633-3395	lmarine@opus.co.tt
LP Marine Supplies	Chaguaramas, Trinidad	868-634-2094	lmarine@opus.co.tt

FACILITY	LOCATION	TELEPHONE	EMAIL ADDRESS
REFRIGERATION/AIR CONDITIONING			
Cosmos/Betty	Glencoe, Trinidad	868-637-9761	
Daco Engineering	Glencoe, Trinidad	868-637-3528	
KNJ Marine (Peake's)	Chaguaramas, Trinidad	868-634-1021	knjm@cablenett.net
Nau-T-Kol	Chaguaramas, Trinidad	868-634-2174	
Store Bay Marine Services	Store Bay, Tobago	868-390-5408	john@sbms.co.tt
Ultra Cool	Port of Spain, Trinidad	868-627-7700	
RIGGING			
Billy's Rigging (Peake's)	Chaguaramas, Trinidad	868-634-4161	surveys@tstt.net.tt
Budget Marine	Chaguaramas, Trinidad	868-634-2006	rigging.trinidad@budgetmarine.com
Echo Marine	Chaguaramas, Trinidad	868-634-2027	sailfly@trinidad.net
Goodwood Mar. (CrewsInn)	Chaguaramas, Trinidad	868-634-2203	goodwood@tstt.net.tt
Peake Yacht Services	Chaguaramas, Trinidad	868-634-4423	pys@cablenett.net
Store Bay Marine Services	Store Bay, Tobago	868-390-5408	john@sbms.co.tt
Trinidad Rigging (Peakes)	Chaguaramas, Trinidad	868-634-2227	trinidadrigging@yahoo.com
SAIL/CANVAS REPAIR			
Ace Sails (Skinner's)	Chaguaramas, Trinidad	868-634-1521	info@drawtheace.com
Barrow Sails (Power Boars)	Chaguaramas, Trinidad	868-634-4137	barrow@tstt.net.tt
Frankie's Upholstery	San Fernando, Trinidad	868-679-3925	
KNJ Marine (Peake's)	Chaguaramas, Trinidad	868-634-1021	knjm@cablenett.net
Soca Sails (CrewsInn)	Chaguaramas, Trinidad	868-634-4178	info@socasails.com
Store Bay Marine Services	Store Bay, Tobago	868-390-5408	john@sbms.co.tt
Superb Sails (Tardieu)	Chaguaramas, Trinidad	868-754-7531	superbcanvas@hotmail.com
Upholstery Shop (PB)	Chaguaramas, Trinidad	868-634-4134	davidmahabir@wow.net

Appendix D: GPS Waypoints

Caution: GPS Waypoints are not to be used for navigational purposes. GPS waypoints are intended to place you in the general area of the described position. All routes, cuts, and anchorages must be negotiated by eyeball navigation. Waypoints do not take into account reefs and rocks between other waypoints, it is the navigator's responsibility to clear these either by heading offshore, or by passing inshore of the hazards. The author and publisher take no responsibility for the misuse of GPS waypoints. Waypoints along any tight passage offer a false sense of security and any navigator who uses waypoints to negotiate a tricky passage instead of piloting by eye is, to be blunt, a fool and deserving of whatever fate befalls him or her. Waypoints are listed from north to south. Latitude is "North" and longitude is "West." Datum used is WGS84.

DESCRIPTION	N Latitude	W Long.
MARTINIQUE- WESTERN COAST		
St. Pierre- ¼ nm W of anchorage	14° 44.50'	61° 11.00'
Case Pilote- ¼ nm W of anchorage	14° 38.50'	61° 08.70'
Schoelcher- ¼ nm W of anchorage	14° 36.90'	61° 06.50'
Marina de Port Cohé- ¼ nm WNW of entrance channel	14° 35.75'	61° 01.30'
Baie des Flamands, Fort-de-France- ½ nm SSW of anchorage	14° 35.50'	61° 04.50'
Baie de Fort-de-France- ¾ nm WNW of marked entrance channel	14° 35.00'	61° 05.40'
Anse Mitan- ½ nm NNW of	14° 33.80'	61° 03.50'
Trou Etienne- ¼ mile NNE of the entrance	14° 33.65'	61° 02.80'
Trois Îlets- 1 nm NNW of	14° 33.60'	61° 01.95'
Anse à l'Âne- ½ nm NW of anchorage	14° 33.20'	61° 04.50'
Anse Noire- ¼ nm NW of anchorage	14° 31.80'	61° 05.50'
Grand Anse d'Arlet- 1 nm W of anchorage	14° 30.02'	61° 06.50'
Petite Anse d'Arlet- ½ nm W of anchorage	14° 29.30'	61° 05.50'
Anse Chaudière- ½ nm W of anchorage	14° 28.85'	61° 05.50'

DESCRIPTION	N Latitude	W Long.
MARTINIQUE- SOUTHERN COAST		
Pointe Giroud anchorage- ½ nm S of entrance channel	14° 27.45'	60° 59.25'
Anse du Céron- ½ nm S of entrance channel	14° 27.45'	60° 58.75'
Anse de Trois Rivières- ¼ nm S of entrance channel	14° 27.45'	60° 58.30'
Baie du Marigot- ¾ nm S of entrance	14° 27.40'	61° 00.25'
Ste. Luce- ¾ nm S of anchorage	14° 27.00'	60° 55.00'
Cul de Sac du Marin- ¾ nm SSW of entrance, 1 nm SW of Ste. Anne	14° 26.00'	60° 54.10'
MARTINIQUE- EASTERN COAST		
Hâvre de la Trinité- 2 nm NNW of	14° 46.50'	60° 57.00'
Baie du Galion- ½ nm ENE of Passe de Loup Bordelais	14° 44.90'	60° 51.00'
Hâvre du Robert- ½ nm E of Passe de Loup Garou	14° 40.45'	60° 50.10'
Passe de l'Est, Hâvre du François- ½ nm NE of	14° 38.40'	60° 50.60'
Passe de Caye Pinsonelle- 2 nm E of	14° 36.20'	60° 47.50'
Îlet Petite Grande- ¼ nm NNE of entrance	14° 34.80'	60° 49.65'
Îlet Chevalier- ¼ nm SE of entrance channel	14° 25.80'	60° 49.20'
Baie des Anglais- ½ nm SE of entrance	14° 24.60'	60° 49.30'
ST. LUCIA		
Rodney Bay- ¼ nm NW of	14° 05.20'	60° 58.50'
Castries- ¼ nm NW of entrance to harbor	14° 01.30'	61° 00.60'
Marigot Bay- ¼ nm W of	13° 58.10'	61° 02.10'
L'Anse Pilori- ¼ nm W of anchorage	13° 57.00'	61° 02.90'
Trou l'Orange- ¼ nm WNW of anchorage	13° 56.70'	61° 03.20'
L'Anse la Raye- ½ nm W of	13° 56.50'	61° 03.50'
Anse Cochon- ½ nm W of	13° 55.75'	61° 04.20'
Soufrière- 1½ nm W of	13° 51.25'	61° 05.25'
Malgretout- ¼ nm W of moorings	13° 50.60'	61° 04.40'
Jalousie, between the Pitons- 1½ nm W of	13° 49.50'	61° 05.25'
Laborie- ½ nm S of entrance to bay	13° 44.52'	61° 00.00'
Vieux Fort Bay- ½ nm W of anchorage	13° 43.10'	61° 58.10'
BARBADOS		
Port St. Charles- ½ nm W of entrance	13° 15.75'	59° 39.25'
Speightstown- ½ nm W of anchorage	13° 14.90'	59° 39.25'
Payne's Bay- ½ nm W of anchorage	13° 09.80'	59° 39.00'
Bridgetown Harbour- ½ nm W of entrance	13° 06.55'	59° 38.60'
Carlisle Bay- 1 nm W of anchorage	13° 05.40'	59° 37.60'
ST. VINCENT		
Chateaubelair Bay- 1 nm NW of anchorage	13° 18.50'	61° 14.90'
Troumakar Bay- ¼ nm W of anchorage	13° 16.75'	61° 16.95'
Cumberland Bay- ¼ nm NW of entrance to bay	13° 16.10'	61° 16.00'
Wallilabou Bay- ¼ nm NW of anchorage	13° 15.00'	61° 16.60'
Princess Bay- ½ nm WSW of anchorage	13° 14.20'	61° 16.90'
Buccament Bay- ¼ nm WSW of anchorage	13° 11.30'	61° 16.40'
Petit Byahaut- ¼ nm WSW of	13° 10.85'	61° 16.30'
Ottley Hall Bay- ¼ nm SW of entrance to marina	13° 09.45'	61° 15.10'
Kingstown Bay- ¼ nm W of docks	13° 09.00'	61° 14.00'
Young Island- ½ nm WSW of anchorage in Carenage	13° 07.90'	61° 12.50'
Calliaqua Bay- ½ nm SW of entrance	13° 07.30'	61° 12.30'
GRENADINES		
Bequia, Admiralty Bay- ½ nm W of	13° 00.50'	61° 15.20'
Bequia, West Cay, ½ nm W of	12° 59.40'	61° 18.10'
Bequia, Friendship Bay- ½ nm S of entrance	12° 58.70'	61° 14.10'

DESCRIPTION	N Latitude	W Long.
Mustique, Britannia Bay- ¾ nm W of Montezuma Shoal	12° 52.60'	61° 12.30'
Canouan, Jupiter Head - ½ nm NW of	12° 44.60'	61° 20.40'
Canouan, Charlestown Bay - ½ nm NW of entrance	12° 42.90'	61° 20.60'
Mayreau- Northern Channel, between Baleine Rocks and Jondell	12° 39.60'	61° 23.00'
Mayreau, Saltwhistle Bay - ¼ nm NW of anchorage	12° 39.10'	61° 23.75'
Tobago Cays - Southern Approach, 1nm SW of Jamesby	12° 37.25'	61° 22.70'
Union Island - 1 nm N of channel between Thompson's R. & Palm I.	12° 36.80'	61° 24.20'
Union Island, Chatham Bay- ¾ nm west of anchorage	12° 36.00'	61° 27.75'
Union Island, Clifton – ½ nm S of and ¼ nm W of Grand de Coi Reef	12° 35.00'	61° 25.00'
Punaise and Mopion - ½ nm NNW of passage between them	12° 33.00'	61° 24.20'
Petit St. Vincent - ½ nm W of anchorage	12° 32.00'	61° 23.50'
Petite Martinique - ½ nm ESE of Petite Dominique	12° 30.30'	61° 23.40'
CARRIACOU		
Windward- ½ nm N of windward reef	12° 31.75'	61° 25.00'
Hillsborough Bay - ¾ nm NW of	12° 29.90'	61° 28.60'
Tyrrel Bay- ¾ nm W of anchorage	12° 27.50'	61° 30.10'
Île de Ronde- 1½ nm W of	12° 19.00'	61° 37.00'
GRENADA		
Grenada Bay- ½ nm NNW of passage between Sugar Loaf & Green I.	12° 14.20'	61° 36.20'
Grenada Bay- ½ nm S of shoal off Sandy Island	12° 12.60'	61° 35.20'
Grenville- ¼ nm SE of entrance channel	12° 06.90'	61° 36.40'
Halifax Harbour- ¼ nm WNW of entrance	12° 06.70'	61° 45.25'
Flamand Bay (Flamingo Bay), Happy Hill- ½ nm NW of anchorage	12° 05.80'	61° 45.80'
Dragon Bay- ½ nm NW of anchorage	12° 05.40'	61° 46.00'
Grand Mal Bay- ½ nm W of anchorage	12° 04.50'	61° 45.90'
St. George's Harbour- ¼ nm WSW of entrance to harbor	12° 02.70'	61° 45.55'
Westerhall Bay- ¼ nm SSE of entrance	12° 00.45'	61° 41.50'
St. David's Harbour- ½ nm S of entrance channel	12° 00.40'	61° 40.60'
Point Salines- ½ nm W of	12° 00.10'	61° 48.60'
Chemin Bay- ¼ nm SSE of entrance	12° 00.00'	61° 42.00'
True Blue Bay- ¼ nm W of True Blue Point	11° 59.60'	61° 46.27'
Prickly Bay- ½ nm W of Prickly Point	11° 59.10'	61° 46.15'
Egmont Harbour- ½ nm S of entrance	11° 59.10'	61° 42.80'
Hog Island- ½ nm SSE of entrance to anchorage	11° 58.95'	61° 44.25'
Clarke's Court Bay- ½ nm S of entrance channel	11° 58.95'	61° 43.80'
Mt. Hartman Bay- ¼ nm SSW of entrance channel	11° 58.90'	61° 45.05'
TRINIDAD		
Grand Riviere Bay- ½ nm NNW of entrance to bay	10° 50.75'	61° 03.10'
Chupara Point- ½ nm NW of rock awash	10° 49.00'	61° 23.85'
Las Cuevas Bay- ½ nm NW of	10° 47.30'	61° 24.00'
Morro Point- ½ nm N of	10° 47.00'	61° 26.50'
La Vache Point- ¼ nm N of	10° 47.00'	61° 28.40'
Saut d'Eau Island- ½ nm N of	10° 46.80'	61° 30.80'
La Vache Bay- ½ nm NW of	10° 46.20'	61° 29.20'
Bocas del Dragon, Boca Grande- 1 nm N of	10° 43.00'	61° 46.25'
Bocas del Dragon, Boca de Navios- 1 nm N of	10° 43.00'	61° 44.35'
Bocas del Dragon, Boca del Huevos- 1 nm N of	10° 43.00'	61° 42.25'
Bocas del Dragon, Boca del Monos- ½ nm N of	10° 43.00'	61° 40.50'
Scotland Bay- ¼ nm SW of entrance	10° 41.75'	61° 40.20'
Carenage Bay- ¼ nm E of Alice Point and ½ nm SE of *TTSA*	10° 41.40'	61° 36.50'
Monos Island, Morris Bay- ½ nm SSE of	10° 41.40'	61° 40.20'

DESCRIPTION	N Latitude	W Long.
Monos Island, Grand Fond Bay- ½ nm SE of	10° 40.60'	61° 40.40'
Chaguaramas Bay- 1 ½ nm W of anchorage area	10° 40.50'	61° 40.00'
Chacachacare Island- ¼ nm SE of entrance to Chacachacare Bay	10° 40.40'	61° 44.00'
Cumana Bay- ¼ nm SW of TTYC	10° 40.40'	61° 34.30'
Five Islands- ¼ nm NNW of	10° 40.00'	61° 36.00'
Gaspar Grande Island- .1 nm NE of marina entrance	10° 39.80'	61° 38.90'
Gaspar Grande Island, Winn's Bay- ¼ nm SW of	10° 39.55'	61° 39.65'
Port of Spain- ¼ nm SW of entrance to Grier Channel	10° 38.10'	61° 33.40'
Point-a-Pierre- ½ nm NW of entrance channel to dock	10° 20.30'	61° 29.40'
TOBAGO		
London Bridge inside passage western waypoint	11° 21.00'	60° 32.25'
London Bridge inside passage eastern waypoint	11° 21.00'	60° 31.00'
Man Of War Bay- 1 nm NW of anchorage off Charlotteville	11° 20.40'	60° 34.50'
Tyrrel's Bay- 3/4 nm NE of and ½ nm N of Little Tobago Island	11° 18.90'	60° 30.40'
Parlatuvier Bay- .1 nm NW of	11° 18.23'	60° 39.30'
Englishman's Bay- ½ nm NW of anchorage area	11° 18.00'	60° 40.80'
Castara Bay- ½ nm WNW of anchorage area	11° 17.00'	60° 42.70'
King's Bay- ½ nm SE of	11° 14.90'	60° 32.60'
Great Courland Bay- ½ nm W of anchorage area	11° 12.80'	60° 47.50'
Grafton Bay (Stone Haven Bay)- ½ nm WNW of anchorage	11° 12.50'	60° 47.80'
Mt. Irvine Bay- ½ nm W of anchorage	11° 11.80'	60° 48.60'
Buccoo Bay- ¾ nm N of	11° 11.60'	60° 49.20'
Buccoo Reef- ½ nm WNW of entrance to Bon Accord Lagoon	11° 11.30'	60° 50.70'
Rockly Bay, Scarborough- ¼ nm SE of entrance channel	11° 10.35'	60° 44.05'
Pigeon Point- ½ nm W of anchorage off point	11° 10.20'	60° 51.20'
Great River Shoal- 2 miles SW of	11° 10.00'	60° 36.00'
Store Bay- ½ nm W of anchorage	11° 09.50'	60° 51.10'
Crown Point-3 nm W of	11° 09.00'	60° 54.50'
Rockly Bay, Scarborough- 2 nm SE of and clear of Bulldog Shoal	11° 08.50'	60° 42.50'
Columbus Point- 2 nm S of	11° 06.00'	60° 47.00'

Appendix E: Metric Conversion Table

Visitors to The Bahamas, Turks and Caicos Islands, and the Dominican Republic, will find the metric system in use and many grocery items and fuel measured in liters and kilograms. As a rule of thumb, a meter is just a little longer than a yard and a liter is very close to a quart. If in doubt use the following table.

1 centimeter (cm) = 0.4 inch	1 inch = 2.54 centimeters
1 meter (m) = 3.28 feet	1 foot = 30.48 centimeters
1 meter = 0.55 fathoms	1 fathom = 1.83 meters
1 kilometer (km) = 0.62 miles	1 yard = 0.92 meters
1 kilometer = 0.54 nautical miles	1 nautical mile = 1.852 kilometers
1 liter (l) = 0.26 gallons	1 gallon = 3.79 liters
1 gram (g) = .035 ounces	1 ounce = 28.4 grams
1 metric ton = 1.1 tons	1 pound = 454 grams

Appendix F: Quick French for Cruisers

The bilingual sailing terms and chandlery items listed below will probably be of use to you. Some of the terms will appear on charts in this guide as well as other publications. As far as the foodstuffs and other items are concerned I've included a few simple French phrases that will be of help. For the sake of expediency, I am listing *le*, *la*, or *les* to denote gender or quantity in the following listing. These are known in French as the definite article(s), as in a specific number required. For instance, you probably would not order one banana, *une banane*, rather you would order a bunch of bananas, or *les bananes*. A special thanks to Malcolm Moritz and Danielle Courteau for their help with this appendix.

le - **the**; for singular masculine nouns
la – **the**; for singular feminine nouns
les – **the**; for both masculine and feminine plural nouns
un – **a** or one; for masculine singular nouns
une – **a** or one; for feminine singular nouns
des – **some**; for both masculine and feminine plural nouns

ENGLISH	FRENCH	ENGLISH	FRENCH
Sailing Terminology	*Terminologie de Voile*	*Menu Terminology*	*Terminologie deMenu*
Anchor	L'ancre	Apple	La pomme, les pommes
Anchorage	Le mouillage	Bacon	Lard fumé
Backstay	Le pataras	Banana	La banane, les bananes
Bank	Banc	Beans	Les haricots
Battens	Les lattes de voile	Beef	Le bifstek
Bay	Une baie	Beer	Bière
Bay, with a beach	Une anse	Boiled	À la coque, bouilli
Bay, deep	Cul de Sac	Braised	À l'étouffée
Bay, large	Hâvre	Bread	Le pain
Bay, small	Marigot	Breakfast	Le petit déjeuner
Beach	La plage	Butter	Le beurre
Beacon	La balise	Cheese	Fromage
ENGLISH	**FRENCH**	**ENGLISH**	**FRENCH**
Sailing Terminology	*Terminologie de Voile*	*Menu Terminology*	*Terminologie deMenu*
Beacon with a light	Le phare	Chicken	le poulet
Boom	Le bôme	Chocolate	le chocolat
Buoy	La bouée	Coffee	café
Channel	Passe, Le chenal	Conch	Lambi
Clew	Le point d'écoute	Duck	Le canard
Cliff	La falaise	Eggs	Les œufs
Coast	La côte, le littoral	Fish	Les poissons
Compass	Le compas	Fried	Sur le plat, frit*
Coral reef	Caye	Frog's legs	Cuisses de grenouille
Customs	Douanes, La Douane	Ham	Le jambon
Fish trap	Le piège aux poissons	Ice cream	La glace
Fishing net	Senne	Juice	Le jus
Foot (of a sail)	La bordure de la voile	Lamb	L'agneau**
Forestay	L'étai	Lemon	Le citron
Full Battens	Entièrement lattée	Lettuce	La laitue
Genoa	Gênes	Lobster	La langouste
Gooseneck	Le ferrure de bome	Lunch	Le déjeuner
Halyard	La drisse	Mashed	En purée
Head (of a sail)	Le Point de Drisse	Milk	Du lait
Inflatable dinghy	Le canot pneumatique	Medium	À point***

English	French
Jib	Le foc
Keel	La quille
Leech	Le chute de la voile
Leeward	Sous le vent***
Leeway	La dérive
Life raft	Le canot de sauvetage
Luff	Le guindant de la voile
Main sheet	L`écoute de Grand Voile
Mainsail	La Grand Voile
Mast	Le mât
Notice To Mariners	AVURNAV
Outboard motor	Moteur hors-bord
Quick Flashing	Scintillant
Rigging	Le gréement
Roller furler	Enrouleur
Rudder	Le gouvernail
Rudder blade	Le safran
Rudder stock	La mèche du gouvernail
Sails	Les voiles
Sandy bottomed shoal	Le fond blanc
Sextant	Le sextant
Sheet	Écoute
Shoal	Loup
Shroud	Le hauban
Spinnaker	Le spinnaker
Spinnaker pole	Le tangon
Stern	La poupe
The tack	Le point d'amure

ENGLISH	**FRENCH**
Sailing Terminology	*Terminologie de Voile*
Tiller	Le stick, la barre
To tack	Tirer des bords
Transom	Le tableau arriére
Windward	Au-vent
Wreck	Épave
Yawl	Yole

ENGLISH	**FRENCH**
Black	Noir
Blue	Bleu
Dear	Chéri
Do you speak English?	Parlez vous anglais?
Excuse me	Excusez-moi
Good Afternoon	Bon après-midi
Good Night	Bonne nuit
Green	Vert
Hello	Bonjour
Hill	Morne, colline
House, small traditional	Case
How much is that?	C'est combien?

Mushrooms	Les champignons
Omelet	L'omelette**
Onions	Les oignons
Orange	Les oranges
Oysters	Les huitres
Pastry	La pâtisserie
Pepper	poivre
Pork	Le porc
Pork chop	Une côtelette de porc
Potato	La pomme de terre
Provisions	Les provisions
Pumpkin	Giraumon
Rare	Saignant
Rice	Le riz
Roast Beef	Le rosbif, le rôti
Rum	Rhum
Salad	Salade
Salt	Sel
Sausage	Saucisse
Shark	Requin
Snails	Escargots
Soup	Consommé
Steak	Le bifsteck
Sugar	Le sucre
Sweet potato	Patate douce
Tea	Thé
Tomatoes	Tomates
Water	Eau

ENGLISH	**FRENCH**
Menu Terminology	*Terminologie deMenu*
Well done	Bien cuit
Whiskey	Whiskey
Wine	Vin
Wine, red	Vin rouge
Wine, white	Vin blanc
Yam	Igname

ENGLISH	**FRENCH**
I don't speak French	Je ne parle pas Français
I don't understand.	Je ne comprends pas.
I want to buy…	Je veux acheter…
No	Non
Red	Rouge
Telephone me, call me	Téléphonez-moi
Thank you	Merci
Where is the market?	Où se trouve le marché?
Where is the toilet?	Où se trouve le cabinet?
White	Blanc
Yellow	Jaune
Yes	Oui

* denotes adjective
** le and la are elided before a noun beginning with a vowel, i.e. l'
*** denotes adverb

Appendix G: Flags of the Windward Islands
Listing of flags is from north to south

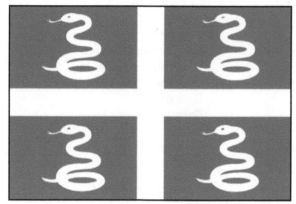

Martinique (Snake Flag)

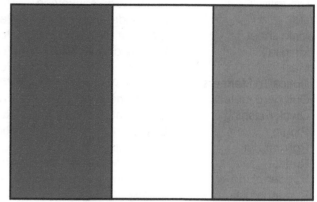

Martinque (French Flag)

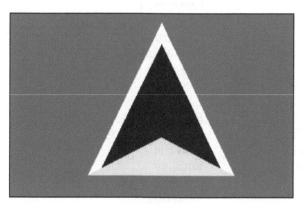

Saint Lucia

Barbados

St. Vincent and The Grenadines

Bequia

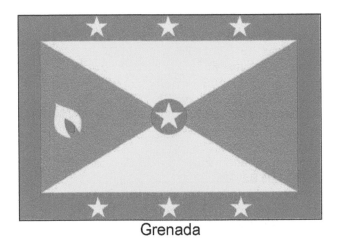
Grenada

Trinidad and Tobago

Appendix H: Distances Between Ports - Martinique to Grenada

You'll need to double check the distances given with what your GPS tells you.

Ports	S. Pier.	F.D.F.	S. A.	R. Bay	Cast.	Mar. B.	Souf.	Wall.	Kings.	Young	Bequia	Must.	Clift.	Tyr. B.	S.G.
St. Pierre		12	31	42	45	47	57	91	97	99	105	116	130	139	166
F. de France	12		22	33	37	39	48	84	90	93	99	109	123	133	160
St. Anne	31	22		21	26	31	41	76	84	85	91	101	115	126	157
Rodney Bay	42	33	21		5	8	17	55	63	65	71	80	95	106	136
Castries	45	37	26	5		5	13	50	57	59	66	75	90	100	130
Marigot Bay	47	39	31	8	5		10	45	53	56	61	71	86	96	127
Soufrière	57	48	41	17	13	10		37	44	46	52	62	77	87	117
Wallilabou	91	84	76	55	50	45	37		7	10	15	25	40	50	80
Kingstown	97	90	84	63	57	53	44	7		3	9	16	35	45	75
Young Isl.	99	93	85	65	59	56	46	10	3		9	15	35	45	75
Bequia	105	99	91	71	66	61	52	15	9	9		12	29	38	68
Mustique	116	109	101	80	75	71	62	25	16	12	12		25	31	61
Clifton	130	123	115	95	90	86	77	40	35	35	29	25		9	39
Tyrrel Bay	139	133	126	106	100	96	87	50	45	45	38	31	9		30
St. George's	166	160	157	136	130	127	117	80	75	75	68	61	39	30	

Appendix I: Distances Between Ports - Grenada to Trinidad and Tobago

Ports	P. Bay	Bocas	Chag.	PoS	S. Bay	Scar.	Ply.	Cas. B.	Eng. B.	Char.
Prickly Bay		78	82	90	74	84	75	77	78	82
The Bocas	78		4	10	56	63	63	66	70	80
Chaguaramas	82	4		8	60	67	68	70	73	83
Port of Spain	90	10	8		66	73	74	76	80	90
Store Bay	74	56	60	66		10	7	10	13	22
Scarborough	84	63	67	73	10		17	20	23	25
Plymouth	75	63	68	74	7	17		5	7	17
Castara Bay	77	66	70	76	10	20	5		3	13
Englishman's Bay	78	70	73	80	13	23	7	3		10
Charloteville	82	80	83	90	22	25	17	13	10	

Index

About the Author

Photo Courtesy of Danielle Courteau

Stephen J. Pavlidis has been cruising and living aboard his 40' cutter-rigged sloop, *IV Play,* since the winter of 1989.

Starting in the Exuma Cays, 20 years ago, Steve began his writing career with guides to the many fascinating destinations he visited. Many of his books stand alone to this day as the quintessential guides to the areas he covers.

His books are different than most other cruising guides in some very significant ways. All of the charts in Steve's books were created using data personally collected while visiting each area using a computerized system that interfaces GPS and depth soundings.

You can find out more about this exceptional author by visiting his Web site, www.Seaworthy.com where there is current news and information about Steve's latest projects, as well as contact information.

Other books by Stephen J. Pavlidis:
Life at Sea Level, ISBN 978-1-892399-33-5
The Exuma Guide, 3rd Edition, ISBN 978-1-892399-31-1
A Cruising Guide to the Leeward Islands, 2nd Edition, ISBN 978-1-892399-36-6
The Northern Bahamas Guide, ISBN 978-1-892399-28-1
The Northwest Caribbean Guide, ISBN 978-1-892399-24-3
The Puerto Rico Guide, 2nd Edition, ISBN 978-1-892399-32-8
The Southern Bahamas Guide, ISBN 978-1-892399-29-8
A Cruising Guide to the Virgin Islands, 2nd Edition, ISBN 978-1-892399-35-9